ANALECTA
BIBLICA
197

I0817248

Andrés García Serrano

The Presentation in the Temple

The Narrative Function of Lk 2:22-39 in Luke-Acts

ROMA 2016

Vidimus et approbamus ad normam Statutorum Pontificii Instituti Biblici de Urbe
Romae, die 14 mensis iulii anni 2011
Prof. Dean Béchard
Prof. François Bovon

Cover: Serena Aureli

Layout: Lisanti srl - Roma

Gregorian & Biblical Press
Piazza della Pilotta, 35 - 00187 Roma, Italy
www.gbpress.net - books@biblicum.com

ISBN: 978-88-7653-**197**-2

To my family
and friends

ACKNOWLEDGMENTS

This book, which Fr. P. Bovati has been so kind as to include in the *Analecta Biblica* series, is a revised version of my dissertation defended at the *Pontifical Biblical Institute* of Rome in June 2011. I wish to acknowledge those who have guided and sustained me in the work of this project. First of all, I would like to thank God, who called me to follow him closely as his minister, and entrusted me to preach his Word. I also would like to thank the Church, where I have received and learned everything that I am and know. I will always be thankful to my bishop, Cardinal D. Antonio María Rouco Varela, who commended me to study God's word and accompanied me throughout the years of study.

I would like to thank the director of my thesis, Fr. Dean Béchard, and the main reader, Prof. François Bovon. They are, for me, a continuous example of patient study, rigorous investigation and exquisite humanity. They not only taught me about Luke-Acts, but something more important: how to do scholarship, how to teach, and how to treat my students. Dante described St. Luke as the "scribe of the gentleness of Christ who has given Jesus to the world to love." These professors have helped me to love Jesus present in the Lukan writings and to study with passion.

I also thank the third and fourth reader, Fr. Scott Brodeur and Fr. Pino di Luccio, for their interest, encouragement, and suggestions to improve the thesis. In the person of the Rector, Fr. José María Ábrego, I thank the whole *Pontifical Biblical Institute*, all the professors, the General Secretary, Mr. Carlo Valentino, and all the personnel, especially the library staff, for all the good they did for me during my time in Rome.

Finally, I would like to thank all my friends who have helped me with the English redaction and corrections of this publication, and those who have been so supportive of me and my work, in Rome: in the *Pontifical Biblical Institute*, in the *Colegio Español San José* - especially its directors - and in the Parish *Santa Paola Romana*; and in

Boston: in the *Harvard Divinity School*, especially in its library, and in the parishes where I served, *Saint Mary of the Nativity* (Scituate), *Saint Catherine of Genoa* (Somerville), *Saint Ann* (Somerville), and *Saint Mary* (Waltham). A thesis is an individual work, but also, at the same time, a collective one. This dissertation is, first of all, done with God's help, but also with theirs.

To the elderly Simeon, who had the joy of embracing the Word of God, I ask him, that I and all the readers of this book may know how to welcome and contemplate with his very same veneration and spiritual intuition, Jesus Christ, who is always present in God's Word and his Church.

Thanks to the companionship of my family and friends I could dare to face this work, which I dedicate as a tribute to them.

The author
Madrid, Spain
February 2, 2012
Feast of the Presentation of our Lord

PREFACE

Andrés García is a Roman Catholic priest anchored in the faith of his Church and at the same time open to the unfolding of contemporary developments. He is trained as a biblical scholar and is eager to build bridges between the biblical heritage and the life of today's parishioners.

I met him first in Rome when I was teaching at the Facoltà Valdese di Teologia some years ago. Later while enrolled as a doctoral student at the Pontificio Istituto Biblico, he—with the agreement of his superiors and advisors—decided to spend more than a year at Harvard Divinity School to work with me on Lukan studies and, more particularly, on his dissertation: "The Presentation in the Temple." He earned a Master of Theology degree from Harvard Divinity School while during that same period I enjoyed his presence, his intellectual awareness, and his kindnesses.

As far as methodology is concerned Andrés García prefers a multi-faceted approach rather than a uni-dimensional process. He is well trained in composition-criticism and narratology methods of his generation and is equally at home with the form-critical and redaction-critical methods of my generation. The co-ordination of these two ways of reading biblical texts, of course, cannot be achieved without tensions, but the benefits of these additional complexities is greater than a single methodological approach. I would like to add that Andrés's applications of these types of interpretations provide a theological dimension: the main thesis of his monograph is highly christological. Luke's main purpose in his presentation of Jesus in the Temple is to offer the readers a vivid picture of who Jesus Christ is. It is Andrés's conviction that Luke 2: 22-39 is the only text of Jesus's infancy narrative revealing so many theological insights. To be more precise: according to him the infancy narrative develops a unified plot revealing progressively the main features of Jesus' identity and mission.

After an insightful *status quaestionis* on the Lukan infancy gospel (Luke 1-2), the author of this dissertation presents a chapter on the infancy narratives in Greek, Roman and Jewish ancient literature. Common in all of these texts is the forward-looking aspect: as a child, the hero anticipates his future remarkable acts.

The story of Jesus in the Temple does not serve primarily to describe the purification of the mother or the redemption of the son. This narrative reveals and makes clear the identity of the newborn and his relationship to the divine, as well as to humanity. It serves also to embed Jesus's life in the story of the elect people of God. He connects Jesus Christ's being with his human story. It underscores also the dimension of suffering as a result of the sinful attitude of his opponents. It shows that Jesus's ministry will divide Israel. Finally, it reveals how the boundaries of Israel have to be crossed, how universalism fits God's final intention, how—at the local level—there is a shift from the Jerusalem Jewish Temple to the Christian house churches. To say it in other words: the Presentation in the Temple announces the division of Israel following Jesus' teaching and universalism as God's final intention. These features are fulfilled throughout Luke-Acts in Jesus' life and his disciples's ministry, particularly Paul's mission. They become an essential part of the Lukan composition.

It is my pleasure to write these opening statements to what, in my opinion, is an important contribution—not only to Lukan studies, but also to biblical criticism and more generally to Christian theology.

François Bovon
Frothingham Research Professor
of the History of Religion
The Divinity School
Harvard University
Cambridge, Massachusetts
March 2, 2012

TABLE OF CONTENTS

ACKNOWLEDGMENTS 7

PREFACE 9

TABLE OF CONTENTS 11

ABREVIATIONS 19

1. Biblical Abreviations 19
2. Primary Sources 19
3. Other Abreviations 19
4. Journals, Series, Dictionaries and Lexicons 20

INTRODUCTION 21

1. The Goal and Novelty of the Research 21
2. Methodology: Narrative Analysis Aided by Redaction Criticism 23
3. Outline of the Dissertation 26

CHAPTER I. *STATUS QUAESTIONIS* 29

1. *Status Quaestionis* on Luke 1–2, Especially in Connection with Jesus' Presentation in the Temple 30
   - 1.1. Historical Tradition Criticism 30
     - 1.1.1. Joseph and Mary 32
     - 1.1.2. Mary Through John, the Apostle 33
     - 1.1.3. Mary Through Joanna, the Wife of Chuza, Herod's Steward 33
     - 1.1.4. James, the Lord's Brother 34
   - 1.2. Source Criticism 35
     - 1.2.1. The "Hymns" 36
     - 1.2.2. Other Possible Sources of Luke 1 39
     - 1.2.3. Other Possible Sources of Luke 2 41

1.2.4. Is there a Single Source throughout Luke 1–2? 42
1.2.5. Written Sources or Oral Information? 43
1.3. Form Criticism 44
1.3.1. Plurality of Literary Forms in Luke 1–2 44
1.3.2. OT Background in Luke 1–2 45
1.3.3. A Literary Genre for Luke 1–2 47
a) Legend as a Possible Literary Genre? 48
b) Midrash as a Possible Literary Genre? 48
c) The Infancy of the Hero as a Literary Genre? 50
d) The Infancy of the Main Character of the Gospel 51
1.4. Redaction Criticism 53
1.4.1. Redaction Criticism within the Lukan Infancy Narrative 53
a) The Possible Insertions 53
b) Luke, not Only Compilator, but Author 55
1.4.2. Redaction Criticism within the Entire Lukan Work 58
a) Lack of References to the Infancy of Jesus in the First Preaching 58
b) The Beginning of Mark's Gospel and the Solemn Beginning of Luke 3 58
c) Were there Different Beginnings of Luke's Gospel? 60
1.5. Narrative Analysis 63
1.5.1. The Infancy Narrative: the Overture to Luke-Acts 64
1.5.2. The Importance of Places, Times, and Characterization 71
1.6. Rhetorical and Semiotic Analysis 72
1.7. Sociological and Feminist Approaches 73

2. *Status Quaestionis* of Lk 2:22-39 75
2.1. Source Criticism 75
2.2. Form Criticism 77
2.3. OT Background 79
2.4. Redaction Criticism 82
2.5. Narrative Analysis 83
2.6. Rhetorical and Semiotic Analysis 83

3. Contributions and Lacunae 84

CHAPTER II. INFANCY NARRATIVES AS PROLEPTIC PRESENTATION 87

1. The Greco-Roman Biographies 91
   1.1. Introducing the Biographies Studied 94
      1.1.1. Alexander's Romances: Pseudo Callisthenes' *The Life and Deeds of Alexander of Macedon* (Greek) and Quintus Curtius Rufus' *The History of Alexander* (Latin) 94
      1.1.2. Plutarch's *Parallel Lives* (Greek) 95
      1.1.3. Suetonius' *The Lives of the Twelve Caesars* (Latin) 97
   1.2. The Greco-Roman Infancy Narratives 99
      1.2.1. Types of Signs in the Infancy Narratives 99
      1.2.2. Actors of the Signs 103
      1.2.3. Contents of the Signs 105
      1.2.4. Location of the Signs 106
   1.3. Divine Orientation and Character Development 107

2. The Jewish Literature 109
   2.1. Introducing the Literary Works Studied 111
      2.1.1. Philo's *The Life of Moses* (Greek) 111
      2.1.2. Pseudo-Philo's *Biblical Antiquities* (Hebrew) 112
      2.1.3. Josephus' *The Jewish Antiquities* (Greek) 114
   2.2. The Jewish Infancy Narratives 115
      2.2.1. Solving Exegetical Problems 115
      2.2.2. Types of Signs in the Infancy Narratives 118
      2.2.3. Actors of the Signs 120
      2.2.4. Contents of the Signs 123
      2.2.5. Location of the Signs 124

3. Intended Literary Function of the Infancy Narratives 124
   3.1. The Position of the Infancy Narratives' Signs within the Whole Work 125
   3.2. Harmony between Infancy Narrative and Public Life: a Characterization 126
   3.3. Infancy Narratives within Biographies 131

4. Comparative Synthesis 133

CHAPTER III. NARRATIVE STUDY OF LK 2:22-39 147

1. Delimitation of the Passage 148
   1.1. Delimitation of the Beginning of the Passage 148
      1.1.1. Time 148
      1.1.2. Place 149
      1.1.3. Characters 150
      1.1.4. Theme 150
      1.1.5. Parallel Structure 151
   1.2. Delimitation of the End of the Passage 151
      1.2.1. Time 151
      1.2.2. Place 151
      1.2.3. Characters 152
      1.2.4. Theme 152

2. Textual Criticism 154
   2.1. Verse 22 155
   2.2. Verse 27 158
   2.3. Verse 33 159

3. Structure of the Passage and Function of its Scenes 160
   3.1. Introduction: vv. 22-24 162
   3.2. The Account of Simeon: vv. 25-35 170
      3.2.1. The Description of Simeon: vv. 25-26 171
      3.2.2. The Reaction of Simeon to Jesus: vv. 27-35 173
         a) Introduction to the Hymn (vv. 27-28) and Hymn (vv. 29-32) 176
         b) Introduction to the Prophecy (vv. 33-34a) and the Prophecy (vv. 34b-35) 181
   3.3. The Account of Anna: vv. 36-38 192
      3.3.1. The Description of Anna: vv. 36-37 193
      3.3.2. The Reaction of Anna to Jesus: v. 38 196
   3.4. Conclusion: v. 39 200

4. The Plot of the Passage: The Meaning of the Entire Pericope 202

5. Synthesis of the Passage 207

CHAPTER IV. THE NARRATIVE FUNCTION OF LK 2:22-39 IN ITS IMMEDIATE CONTEXT 211

1. Characterization of Jesus in Luke 1–2 220
   1.1. General Structure of Luke 1–2: the Breakdown of the John-Jesus Parallelism 220
   1.2. The Unified Plot of the Sequence Luke 1–2 227
   1.3. The Different Passages in the Unified Plot of Luke 1–2 233
      1.3.1. The Plots and Commission Statements throughout Luke 1–2 233
      1.3.2. Jesus' Characterization throughout Luke 1–2 238
      1.3.3. Reliable Characters throughout Luke 1–2 248
      1.3.4. Locations throughout Luke 1–2 251
      1.3.5 Scriptural Quotations in Luke 1–2 255

2. Conclusion 256
Table I. Comparison Table between Lk 2:22-39 and Luke 1–2 262

Appendix: Four Other Possible Presentations 263
   1. The First Preaching of John (Lk 3:1-18) 264
   2. The Baptism of Jesus (Lk 3:21-22) 265
   3. The Temptation of Jesus (Lk 4:1-13) 266
   4. The First Preaching of Jesus (Lk 4:16-30) 268
   5. Conclusion of Appendix 269
   Table II. Comparison Table between Lk 2:22-39 and Luke 3–4 271

CHAPTER V. THE NARRATIVE FUNCTION OF LK 2:22-39 IN LUKE-ACTS 273

1. Jesus in the Temple 276
   1.1. Presentation/Commission by Simeon through the Holy Spirit 276
   1.2. Fulfillment in His Public Life 278
      1.2.1. At the Beginning: Jesus in Nazareth 278
         a) Incipient Universalism 279
         b) Incipient Division in Israel 280
      1.2.2. Travel Narrative to Jerusalem 281
         a) To the Temple of Jerusalem 281

b) Incipient Universalism 282
c) Incipient Division in Israel 286
1.2.3. At the End: Jesus in Jerusalem 287
a) Presentation of Jesus in the Temple 287
b) Division in Israel 288

2. Christians in Jerusalem 293
2.1. Presentation/Commission by Jesus 293
2.1.1. An Incipient Commission: The Mission of the 70 (72) 293
2.1.2. Commission by Jesus before His Passion: Rejection by Everyone 297
2.1.3. Commission by Jesus after His Resurrection: Universalism 301
a) From the Temple... 302
b) ...To the Gentiles 304
2.2. Fulfillment in the Public Lives of Jesus' Disciples 307
2.2.1. At the Beginning: Christians in Jerusalem 307
a) Presentation of the Infant Church in the Temple 308
b) Incipient Universalism in Peter's First Speech 309
c) Division in Israel 311
2.2.2. Dispersion Narrative: A Progressive Universalism 315
2.2.3. At the End: the Council at Jerusalem 318
a) Division among Jewish-Christians and Gentile-Christians 318
b) The Universalism of Peter's Speech in Acts 15 319
c) James' Speech: The Gentiles' Inclusion from ἔθνη to λαοί 320

3. Paul in the Diaspora 322
3.1. Presentation/Commission by Jesus 322
3.1.1. Universalism 324
3.1.2. Rejection 325
3.2. Fulfillment in Paul's Public Life 326
3.2.1. At the Beginning: Paul in Antioch of Pisidia 326
a) Rejection by Jews 326
b) Paul as Jesus: God's Salvation and Light for the Gentiles 328
3.2.2. Travel Narrative to Jerusalem and Rome 330
a) A Geographical Universalism 330

b) The Increased General Rejection by the Jews (Ἰουδαῖοι) 338
3.2.3. At the End: Paul in Rome 342
a) The *Inclusio* in Luke-Acts: Universal Salvation through Rejection 343
b) Rejection Everywhere: by Jews, Pagans, and Christians 345

4. Conclusion 348

FINAL CONCLUSIONS AND FURTHER IMPLICATIONS 359

1. Final Conclusions 359
2. Further Implications 366

WORKS CITED 369

1. Primary Sources 369
2. Secondary Sources 372

INDICES 405

I. INDICES OF ANCIENT LITERARY SOURCES 405

a. Index of Classical Texts 405
b. Index of Old Testament Texts 408
c. Index of Pseudoepigrapha 413
d. Index of Dead Sea Scrolls 413
e. Index of Hellenistic Jewish Texts 414
f. Index of New Testament Texts 416
g. Index of Early Christian Apocryphal Texts 439
h. Index of Early Christian Texts 440

II. INDEX OF MODERN AUTHORS 440

ABREVIATIONS

1. Biblical Abreviations

For the biblical books the abbreviations of *The New Jerusalem Bible* (London 2002) are used.

2. Primary Sources

I follow the abbreviations proposed in ALEXANDER, P. H. – KUTSKO, J. F. – ERNEST, J. D. – DECKER-LUCKE, S. A. (ed.), *The SBL Handbook of Style*. For Ancient Near Eastern, Biblical, and Early Christian Studies (Peabody, MA 2007), for the OT Pseudepigrapha (pp. 74-75), for the Nag Hammadi codices (pp. 82-83), for the NT Apocrypha (pp. 83-84), and for the classical Greek and Latin books (pp. 238-264).

3. Other Abreviations

acc.	accusative case
AD	The year of our Lord
BC	Before Christ
cf.	confront
Ch./Chs.	Chapter
dif.	different
Dt-Is	Deutero-Isaiah (Is 40–55)
ed.	editor(s)
et al.	and others
LXX	Septuagint
MT	Masoretic Text
n./nn.	note/notes
NT	New Testament
OT	Old Testament
OxyP	Oxyrhynchus Papyri
par.	parallels
p./pp.	page/pages
s. l.	without any location
§	subsection
v./vv.	verse/verses
x	occurrences

4. Journals, Series, Dictionaries and Lexicons

I have followed the abbreviations of secondary sources proposed by Schwertner,[1] and Bazyliński[2] for abbreviations not contained in Schwertner. I have used the following abbreviations which are not listed in either volume:[3]

AncBRL	The Anchor Bible Reference Library
BECNT	Baker Exegetical Commentary on the New Testament
BellS	Bellarmine Series
DV	Dei Verbum
EncRel	Encyclopedia of Religion
EtB.NS	Études bibliques. Nouvelle série
F&F.LF	Foundations & Facets. Literary Facets
F&F.NT	Foundations & Facets. New Testament
GBS.NTS	Guides to Biblical Scholarship. New Testament Series
GNT[4]	The Greek New Testament (Stuttgart [4]2000)
HKNT	Handkommentar zum Neuen Testament
Int.BCTP	Interpretation, a Bible Commentary for Teaching and Preaching
JSJ.S	Journal for the Study of Judaism. Supplements
KNTS	*Korean New Testament Studies*
LIntI	Luke Interpreter of Israel
LitCBI	Literary Currents in Biblical Interpretation
MVI	Miscellanea Vangeli dell'infanzia
NA[27]	Novum Testamentum graece (Stuttgart [27]2004)
NSBTh	New Studies in Biblical Theology
Rahlfs[9]	Septuagint (Stuttgart [9]1984) I-II
SSNT	Studia Semitica Novi Testamenti
StudBL	Studies in Biblical Literature

---

[1] See SCHWERTNER, *Internationales Abkürzungsverzeichnis.*

[2] See BAZYLIŃSKI, *A Guide to Biblical Research*, 222-232.

[3] The journal is presented in *italics.*

INTRODUCTION

1. The Goal and Novelty of the Research

The research of this thesis studies the passage of Jesus' Presentation in the Temple (Lk 2:22-39).[1] It is striking that there are no other lengthy studies which analyze this pericope. Thus, this thesis represents the first scientific study to address all significant aspects of Lk 2:22-39.[2] In addition, although the text says that Joseph and Mary went to the Temple for purification and redemption through the presentation of Jesus to the Lord, these cultic rites are controversial and the narrator does not narrate them in detail. The episode frequently named "Presentation in the Temple" does not develop this presentation to the Lord, neither as purification nor as redemption. Does that name fit the meaning of the passage? In what sense can we call it *presentation*?

The Presentation passage is part of the Lukan infancy narrative. As we will see in Ch. I, Luke composes Luke 1–2 without allowing his sources to appear clearly: it is truly a Lukan compo-

[1] I use the word *presentation* with two different meanings. When I refer to the passage of Lk 2:22-39, I capitalize the first letter, *Presentation*. When I refer to a narrative presentation as a characterization of the identity and mission of a protagonist, even inside of the Presentation passage, I use the lower case, *presentation*. I follow the abbreviations of the books of the Bible according to *The New Jerusalem Bible*, whose translation I use when citing biblical texts, except when I employ my own translation to refer to Lk 2:22-39.

[2] See section I.3, subsequently refered to as § I.3, on the lack of a full study of the passage of the Presentation in the Temple.

sition.[3] Furthermore, Luke 1–2 is likely to be a later addition by Luke himself, perhaps after he had written his Gospel, and possibly even after the composition of Acts, thereby serving to introduce the main topics of Luke-Acts. In addition, the beginnings of the different Gospels have been studied at length as keys that present their respective Gospels. Finally, the generally accepted structure of Luke 1–2 emphasizes the passage of the Presentation in the Temple because it breaks the parallelism between the announcements, births, circumcisions, and namings of John and Jesus respectively.[4]

These findings bring us to the exegetical question that this thesis addresses in depth. Boyce has claimed that "shepherds, Elizabeth and Zechariah, Mary and Joseph do not appear again in Luke's narrative, but their witness is important for understanding the themes that continue to resonate throughout the Gospel."[5] Keeping in mind Boyce's comment, what can we say about Simeon and Anna? If the evangelist underlines Jesus' appearances in the Temple in the structure of Luke 1–2, and if the Lukan infancy narrative is an introduction, what role does the Presenta-

---

[3] I will refer to the author as Luke and to his work as Luke-Acts or the Lukan composition. Following the majority of the scholars, of whom the first was CADBURY, *Luke-Acts*, 8-11, I consider Luke-Acts as two parts of a single account, the Lukan work. PARSONS – PERVO, *Rethinking*, have challenged scholars to examine what was in danger of becoming an unquestioned and unexamined assumption and have called attention to differences in genre and style between the Gospel and Acts. Nevertheless, their challenge has led to a stronger and more defensible case for the unity of Luke-Acts. As MARSHALL, "Israel", 340-357, has showed, it seems apparent that Luke intended Acts to be a essential part of the Gospel (Acts 1:1; cf. Lk 1:1-4), with significant narrative connections between the two books. In order to avoid repetitions in the different chapters and unnecessarily long footnotes, I will always cite an abbreviated reference to each work. The reader will find the full citation in the bibliography of works cited. The translation into English of the few direct quotations from other original languages come from the respective published translation whose page number is indicated in square brackets in the respective footnote. In the bibliography of works cited, in the same entry as the original book, the reader will find the published translation used. When there is no published translation into English, the translations are my own and there is no page number indicated in square brackets.

[4] See § IV.1.1.

[5] BOYCE, "For You Today a Savior", 380.

tion passage in Lk 2:22-39 play within the general introduction of Luke-Acts? Is the Presentation in the Temple only a presentation of the Gospel, as Boyce claimed? Is it only a presentation of Jesus? What is the narrative function of this passage in the whole Lukan work?[6]

2. Methodology: Narrative Analysis Aided by Redaction Criticism

On the one hand, Luke 1–2 is called an infancy *narrative*. These chapters, especially the Presentation in the Temple, are a narrative. This is the reason why a study of this passage requires a narrative analysis.[7] On the other hand, this dissertation provides possible answers to the exegetical questions which deal with Luke's literary developments throughout his entire work. In trying to answer these exegetical questions, I will use both literary methodologies: narrative analysis, aided by redaction criticism, when it is possible and useful.[8]

---

[6] A similar question has been considered in another dissertation. BERLINGIERI, *Il lieto annuncio*, studies the function of the announcement of the birth of John the Baptist (Lk 1:5-25) within the entire Lukan work. According to BERLINGIERI, the announcement of John's birth and his conception anticipate the Lukan topic of promise-fulfillment, which is vital to the understanding of Lukan theology. However, I think that the structure of Luke 1–2 does not highlight the passage of the announcement of John's conception and his birth. In addition, I think that the topic of promise-fulfillment is also present in Lk 2:26.29.

[7] I follow the nomenclature proposed by THE PONTIFICAL BIBLICAL COMMISSION document, *The Interpretation of the Bible in the Church*, which makes a distinction between methods, analysis and approaches (See *The Scripture Documents*, 249-272, edited by D. P. Béchard).

[8] When I refer to these literary methodologies I do not intend them as a replacement for an interest in theology. On the contrary, I understand a literary approach to be a good way of exploring the religious significance of biblical texts, which can exercise religious influence as stories. They can do so in complex and subtle ways through the details of the text, which can be only recognized through literary methodologies. The Incarnation of the Divine Word makes access to divine revelation possible where the human word is communicated (*Dei Verbum* § 13). Because of the mystery of the Incarnation, a rigorous literary study is a good way to access divine revelation.

I will primarily use narrative analysis to study the passage itself, its newness in comparison with the rest of Luke 1–2, and the development of its distinctive topics throughout Luke-Acts.[9] The study of NT narrative, at least from a narrative critical point of view, cannot match the range of the study of OT narrative which has produced interpretations of such high quality.[10] But this analysis is also valuable for the NT. I am convinced that a different emphasis will be placed on Lk 2:22-39 by approaching Luke-Acts as a unified narrative with the help of narrative analysis.[11] I intend to carry the discussion a step further in the narrative analysis of the Lukan work.[12]

I will also use redaction criticism to compare the Lukan text and structure with its parallels in the other synoptic gospels in order to better grasp Luke's specific perspective.[13] Brief comparisons of Luke's Gospel with its sources, especially Mark and Q, are useful,

---

[9] The dissertation will be concentrated on Luke-Acts in its finished form. I follow the NA[27] text of Acts, which mainly presents the Alexandrian version. The longer Western text of Acts raises issues that I do not discuss. Although such a study would be very interesting, it would lead me away from my goal. For discussion of the issues involved in the text of Acts, see HEAD, "Acts in Its Texts", 415-444. The textual criticism of Lk 2:22-39 is studied in § III.2.

[10] Good examples are ALTER, *The Art of Biblical Narrative*; STERNBERG, *The Poetics of Biblical Narrative*; and BAR-EFRAT, *Narrative Art*. For a good introduction to narrative analysis see, for instance, POWELL, *What is Narrative Criticism?* and MARGUERAT – BOURQUIN, *Récits bibliques*.

[11] In addition, as we will see in § I.2.5, there are no narrative studies of this pericope. Despite the massive historical critical attention it has attracted, it remains all but unexplored territory for narrative analysis.

[12] Objections to narrative analysis usually focus on what the method is not able to do. Scholars of the historical-critical school sometimes complain that it treats texts as mere stories rather than as records of significant moments in history. And as BÉCHARD says, "historical data, usually eschewed by most modern literary critics, can successfully advance our understanding of a Lukan text" (BÉCHARD, *Paul Outside the Walls*, 79). In an attempt to advance our understanding of the text, I will use such historical data when they are useful to better understand the text.

[13] I use redaction criticism to discern the structural and the redactional decisions. The structural decisions show the author's order to form a coherent macro-narrative, while the redactional decisions present the author's reformulation of received sources of the different micro-narratives.

since these comparisons help us to recognize the distinctiveness of the Lukan composition.[14] But detailed analysis of the changes and additions introduced in Luke's Gospel would lead me away from my main task. I do not intend to explore pre-Lukan tradition, or the possible sources of Acts, either. Furthermore, I do not engage in elaborate arguments to distinguish tradition from Lukan redaction of that tradition. All material in Luke-Acts, whether it originated as tradition or redaction, is potentially important for my task because the decision by the author to include it in the work is a choice which affects the structure of the entire work.[15]

I will not be a slave to theory, but will use methodology and theory clearly at the service of the interpretation of the text, that is, using the terminology and methodology only to understand the text better.[16] What stands at the heart of this dissertation is an attention to the way in which the narrative works as a process of communication, from the author to the reader[17]

[14] The modified two-source hypothesis theory is presupposed in this thesis. To ignore known sources is actually to forfeit insight into Luke's narrative. I will note Luke's use of Mark where it does in fact help to draw out the significance of Luke. Although Luke likely did not know of Matthew's Gospel, I compare Luke and Matthew when the juxtaposition of these texts, especially the double tradition of Q, helps to illuminate distinctive features of Luke.

[15] Even if the wording of the traditional unit is unchanged, it has been redacted by inclusion in a new writing. "The literary shaping of the total work highlights this unit in some way, giving it an important function within the whole or linking it with other material and thereby suggesting that it reveals something of continuing importance," according to TANNEHILL, *Narrative Unity* I, 6.

[16] The study by ALETTI, *L'art*, is a model of solid narrative analysis, simultaneously useful and unobtrusive. I will leave the majority of the theoretical reflection in the background because I agree with Frei, who holds that in an exegetical dissertation "there should be enough (theory) to elucidate what is actually being done in exegesis, and no more" (FREI, *The Identity of Jesus Christ*, 61).

[17] Knowing the narrative nomenclature and definitions purposed by MARGUERAT – BOURQUIN, *Récits bibliques*, 18-22, and SKA, *Our Fathers*, 40-43, about *real reader, implied reader, real author*, and *implied author*, when I speak about reader or author, I refer to the *implied* one because I usually stay in the literary sphere. The few times in which I consider the role played by the real reader, I will explicitely refer to him as *real reader*. As DARR, "Narrator as Character", 44-46, affirms, contrary to DAWSEY, *The*

via the text.[18] I do not want an excess of terminology to prevent my text from engaging my reader.[19]

3. Outline of the Dissertation

The order of the chapters is determined by the goals of the study: to explain the narrative function of the Presentation passage in Luke-Acts.

The dissertation begins with a study on the *status quaestionis* on the Lukan infancy narrative in general and the pericope of the Presentation in the Temple in particular (Ch. I). It surveys the most important recent approaches, affirming what is more generally accepted by scholarship, and it relates the present study on Lk 2:22-39 to the different approaches and their results while taking it one step further.

Luke 1–2, although it is part of the Gospel, is linked to other infancy narratives of other important personages. Literary genre is a crucial tool for the interpretation of a text since it provides the initial clue to understand what an author actually means by what he has written. Ch. II undertakes the study of the features of other

Lukan Voice, 143-147, I identify *author* and *narrator* because I do not think that the narrator of the different passages of Luke-Acts expresses characteristics distinct from those that the story as a whole wishes to affirm, the characteristics of the author.

[18] This research is interested in how the text may engage readers and change their way of thinking. Telling a story involves an intentional rhetoric, because the narrator constructs the narrative, characters, settings, and actions, with a persuasive power in order to transmit certain values and beliefs. TANNEHILL, "Zacchaeus as Rhetoric", 73-83, names it *narrative rhetoric*.

[19] The first audience of Luke was made up of *hearers* and *readers*, perhaps more hearers than readers because in ancient times many literary works would be read in public. However, I have chosen to simplify the nomenclature and instead of always saying readers/hearers, I will only speak of readers. In addition, if I refer to the word *reader* (or narrator or author) by the pronouns *he* or *his*, it is because these narrative categories are abstractions, distinct from the *real reader*, who is a real man or woman. This is the reason why I will not use the so-called *inclusive language*. It seems that, in these cases, the pronoun *he* or *his* is not obtrusive and does not have discriminatory connotations.

infancy narratives in Greco-Roman and Jewish literature during the approximate time of Luke's composition, since linguistic problems are resolved by comparison with other texts of a similar epoch.[20] This chapter will seek to develop a better understanding of this broad *topos*, which shares narrative patterns across different texts. The similarities and differences between Luke 1–2 and other infancy narratives will give us clues to illuminate the literary function of these chapters and the Presentation in the Temple in the entire Lukan work.

Ch. III analyzes the passage of the Presentation in the Temple in depth. It pays special attention to the structure and narrative plot of the passage, as these help the reader to understand the presentation of Jesus that Luke is making through Simeon and Anna. The expressions used about Jesus, which thereby present him, are also studied. All of these factors show that this passage does not describe a purification or a redemption, but rather the presentation of Jesus.

The function of the Presentation is better appreciated in connection with its immediate literary context, the sequence of the Lukan infancy narrative. Having studied all of the expressions used to describe Jesus in the previous chapter, Ch. IV then analyzes the progressive characterization of Jesus. Especially useful is a comparison with the expectations concerning him implied in earlier passages, which allows us to discern the distinctive function of Lk 2:22-39 within the Lukan infancy narrative. In an appendix I also examine other possible presentations of Jesus immediately after the infancy narrative. Using different narrative criteria, the main innovations of the characterization of Jesus in the Presentation passage and its broader portrayal are proposed.

---

[20] The text of Luke-Acts and its internal articulation are the main data for this research. However, it is necessary to study the passage in its entire context, historical and literary, in order to better understand its value and meaning. It is therefore necessary to analyze the historical use of infancy narratives in the time of Luke. As the infancy narratives literary genre existed prior to Luke 1–2 and is fundamental to its interpretation, I begin by treating this subject. In addition, the three chapters that deal directly with the text of Luke-Acts, Ch. III (Lk 2:22-39), Ch. IV (Luke 1–2), and Ch.V (Luke-Acts) are directly connected, each depending upon the previous chapter for its logical development, and must be consecutively presented to the reader.

However, the function of the Presentation passage can be comprehended only through its wider literary context, the complete Lukan composition. While the previous chapter studied the novel features of Jesus' characterization in Luke 1–2, Ch. V studies the narrative function in Luke-Acts of these features. The significance of the pericope expands as we are able to relate it to more and more of the entire Lukan narrative. When a narrative element like Lk 2:22-39 is isolated from the story as a whole, it loses power and significance. The relation of the narrative element to the complete story may also lead to a discovery of a meaning that was previously unrecognized, a narrative surprise. In an attempt to show how that characterization introduces important features of the literary work, the distinctive *prolepsis* in Luke-Acts of this characterization of Jesus will be studied.[21]

Finally, I will propose the conclusions of my research. The implications of these conclusions will open to two broader and more theological prospectives: the unity of Luke-Acts and the identification of Jesus' disciples with Jesus. Luke develops the passage of the Presentation in the Temple not only through Jesus but, surprisingly, also through his disciples; both in Luke's Gospel, and in Acts. The usefulness of this research is not only its narrative study of Lk 2:22-39 in connection with Luke-Acts as a whole, but also its consequences for Luke's christology and ecclesiology.

[21] This prolepsis is an *internal* or *homodiegetic* one because it refers to events that are about to be told inside the Lukan work. On these terms, see ALETTI, *et al.*, *Vocabulaire raisonné*, 71; MARGUERAT – BOURQUIN, *Récits bibliques*, 115-116; SKA, *Our Fathers*, 8; DE JONG, "Homer and Narratology", 324.

CHAPTER I

STATUS QUAESTIONIS

This sketch of contemporary Lukan studies is intended to accomplish two purposes: to survey the most important recent approaches in connection with this research; and to relate the present study to these different approaches and their results. I will summarize the textual evidence that has given rise to certain questions, identify the main theories proposed by scholars to answer these questions, and state the position that will be adopted in my thesis. I will organize my study by means of the different methodologies used by the scholars, as well as their results. Within the different methodologies I will expound the ideas of scholars according to the logic of the exposition, rather than to the chronology of the publications.

As understanding the wider sequence of Luke 1–2[1] is important to better understand Lk 2:22-39, first I will study the *status quaestionis* on Luke 1–2, especially in connection with the Presentation passage. Then, I will explore the *status quaestionis* of Lk 2:22-39. Finally I will summarize the main contributions achieved by the majority of scholars and the main lacunae in connection with my topic; thus this research can be taken one step further in the interpretation of the passage.

---

[1] I do not include the dedication to Theophilus (Lk 1:1-4) in the Lukan infancy narrative (Luke 1:5–2:52), which I refer to simply as Luke 1–2. Lk 1:1-4 is a unique Greek periodic sentence, an elegantly phrased prologue, whose language, style, and content are very different from the following verses. In addition, Lk 1:1-4 is external to the narrative, addressing the reader directly, and Lk 1:5 clearly presents the chronological and geographical setting of the following passage.

1. *Status Quaestionis* on Luke 1-2, Especially in Connection with Jesus' Presentation in the Temple

The literature on the Lukan infancy narrative is so vast that any attempt to engage the entire corpus is doomed before it starts. For this reason I will focus on that part of the scholarship which is in direct relationship with the Presentation passage. The various works engaged here represent only a fraction of the entire corpus.[2]

1.1 Historical Tradition Criticism

The question of historicity was the first question raised by scholars. On the one hand, the reader notices the many differences between the two infancy narratives that we find in the Gospels: Matthew 1–2 and Luke 1–2. The problems that both infancy narratives create with regard to historicity are the following: (1) The striking structural difference of the two accounts; they cannot be put in parallel columns in a synopsis.[3] (2) The angelic announcement of Jesus' birth comes to Mary in the Lukan Gospel (Lk 1:26-38) and to Joseph in the Matthean (Mt 1:20-25). (3) Matthew's narrative has a genealogy (Mt 1:2-16), but Luke's does not, and how different the Lukan one in Lk 3:23-38 is! (4) More crucial still, Matthew knows nothing of the census of Quirinius (Lk 2:1-3), the reason Luke gives for Jesus' being born in Bethlehem. However, Matthew gives a picture wherein Mary and Joseph live at

[2] Although there are many scholars who defend the same thesis, I have cited only the main scholars of each proposal. Otherwise, this *status quaestionis* would be still longer.

[3] Luke knows nothing of the Magi (Mt 2:1-12), the flight to Egypt (Mt 2:13-15), the massacre of the innocents (Mt 2:16-18), and the return from Egypt (Mt 2:19-23), just as Matthew knows nothing of the Presentation (Lk 2:22-24), the *Magnificat* (Lk 1:46-56), the *Benedictus* (Lk 1:67-79), or the finding of Jesus in the Temple (Lk 2:40-52). According to Luke, after Jesus' Presentation, when Jesus was 40 days old, Jesus' family went to Nazareth (Lk 2:39) for twelve years (Lk 2:42). Yet according to Matthew, after the visit of the wise men, Jesus' family stayed in Bethlehem for approximately two years (Mt 2:16), then fled to Egypt, and afterwords went to Nazareth (Mt 2:23).

Bethlehem where they have a house. Nazareth is a point of departure for Luke, and a point of arrival for Matthew.[4]

On the other hand, there are difficulties in reconciling the historical dates with some parts of the Lukan infancy narrative. For example, the census of Quirinius affecting Galileans during the reign of Herod the Great is a historical difficulty; it is an inaccuracy because Quirinius was never governor of Syria during Herod's lifetime (Lk 2:1-3);[5] Quirinius became governor of Syria in the year 6,[6] at which point in time Herod the Great was already dead.[7]

In an attempt to resolve these historical difficulties, scholars have looked for historical traditions that could guarantee the historical value of the infancy narrative.[8] Just as the apostles and disciples would have served as the witnesses of events reported in Luke 3–24, so scholars looked for corroborating witnesses, who could warrant the historicity of the events of Luke 1–2.[9] The ex-

---

[4] According to Matthew, the fact that Herod's son, Archelaus, rules in Judea makes Joseph afraid to return from Egypt to Bethlehem, and so he takes the child and his mother to Galilee to the town of Nazareth, obviously for the first time (Mt 2:19-23). In contrast, Luke tells us that Mary received the Annunciation at Nazareth (Lk 1:26), that Mary and Joseph lived at Nazareth (Lk 2:39), and that they went to Bethlehem only temporarily because they had to register there during a Roman census (Lk 2:4-5). The statement that Mary gave birth to her child and laid him in a manger because there was no place for them in the inn implies that they had no house of their own in Bethlehem. On this matter see BENOÎT, "Non erat", 174-177; CUNNINGHAM, "A Tale of Two Creches", 378-381; BROWN, *A Coming Christ*, 8-10; ORSATTI, "Storicità e Vangeli dell'infanzia", 613.

[5] On the historicity of a Census under Quirinius see SCHÜRER – VERMÉS – MILLAR, Jewish People, 399-427; OGG, "The Quirinius Question Today", 231-236; BENOÎT, "Quirinius", column 713-715.

[6] Unless otherwise indicated, dates refer to the time after Christ, AD. When dates refer to before Christ, BC will be written.

[7] For the argument that Luke's chronology would place the birth of Jesus in or after the year 6 see DERRETT, "Further Light", 82.

[8] By historical tradition, I mean the origin of the memory of the infancies of Jesus and John which was first orally transmitted and then put in writing.

[9] KUHN, "Beginning the Witness", 237, argues that numerous parallels between the characters in the infancy narrative and the disciples as portrayed in Luke 24 and Acts signal the evangelist's intent to present the faithful heralds of John's and Jesus' births in Luke 1–2 as among those who are "eyewitnesses and ministers of the word"

egetical question was: Who communicated the information contained in Luke 1–2 to Luke?

1.1.1 Joseph and Mary

A common supposition has been that the tradition about Jesus' infancy came from Joseph or Mary. Joseph could be a corroborating witness of the Matthean infancy narrative, where he appears very often; and Mary of the Lukan infancy narrative, where she appears very often. Plummer first supported this thesis.[10] Years later, Laurentin,[11] Daniélou,[12] and Serra[13] echoed this thesis. However, Brown is opposed to this possibility and denies that Mary could be a Lukan witness, and Joseph a Matthean witness.[14] According to Brown, Joseph never appears during the ministry of Jesus and seems almost certainly to have been dead by that time, so that it is really pure speculation to posit him as a witness. His absence in Mk 6:3, where the list of Jesus' family at Nazareth is being invoked, would otherwise be inexplicable. Although Joseph as a witness is unlikely, the possibility of Mary is still open; neither her witness nor her non-witness has been proved.

(Lk 1:2). Kuhn says: "The fact that the prologue is directly followed by the birth stories makes it hard to believe that Luke did not consider this part of this part of the narrative as presenting an eyewitness report" (KUHN, "Beginning the Witness", 252).

[10] According to PLUMMER, *St. Luke*, xxiii, it is probable that the witness for Luke 1–2 is one and the same, perhaps some member of the holy family, and probably Mary herself.

[11] LAURENTIN, *Structure*, 96-99, believes that everything is clarified if Mary is the source.

[12] DANIÉLOU, *Les Évangiles de l'enfance*, 7-10, has studied the role of Jesus' family in the early Christian community, and contends that Mary could be a trustworthy witness for Luke 1–2.

[13] SERRA, "Maria conservava", 423-438, affirms that since the end of the second century, Church fathers and ecclesiastic writers have identified Mary as the source for information about Jesus' human genesis and early years. Serra argues as well referring to the custom in the Bible of "keeping, remembering, and proclaiming," and gives examples of this attitude either in the OT or in the NT. In fact, the memory-commemoration of the "great things of God" implies their transmission from one generation to the next. According to Serra, Mary could be another person who "kept, remembered and proclaimed" the infancy of her son (Lk 2:19.51b).

[14] BROWN, *Birth*, 33. MEIER, *A Marginal Jew*, 209-211, agrees with Brown and points out that there is no convincing evidence that either Mary or Joseph ever spoke of Jesus' birth.

1.1.2 Mary Through John, the Apostle

The Johannine tradition has been suggested as a source of information for the Lukan infancy narrative.[15] Burrows went a step further, affirming that the original author of the first two chapters of Luke's Gospel was John, the apostle.[16] In addition, it is a *priori* likely that Mary gave some account of the infancy of Jesus to the first disciples, especially to that disciple about whom Jesus had said to Mary: "This is your son" (Jn 19:25-27). John would be the most natural recipient of the memories of Mary. However, according to Schnackenburg and Bailey, none of the standard discussions about contacts between the Johannine and Lukan gospels includes details in Luke 1–2.[17] Moreover, as Brown points out, the Johannine Gospel shows no awareness of the birth and childhood stories of Jesus.[18]

1.1.3 Mary Through Joanna, the Wife of Chuza, Herod's Steward

According to W. J. Brown, on the one hand, a careful reading of the Lukan infancy narrative makes it clear that it was a woman who communicated the information to Luke. Thus the dating of events in connection with the pregnancy (Lk 1:24.26.57; 2:6),

---

[15] So McHugh, *The Mother of Jesus*, 8-10; 147-149; Sánchez Mielgo, "¿Historia?", 140.

[16] Burrows, "The Gospel of the Infancy", 34-57. The reasons are the following: (1) Parallels between the story of John in Luke 1 and the Johannine prologue. (2) The affinity between the Lukan and Johannine Gospels is nowhere more marked than in Luke's own source, especially in the infancy narrative. (3) The Johannine Gospel cannot be wholly detached from John, the son of Zebedee, and Luke must include him among "the eyewitnesses from the beginning" (Lk 1:2). However, the editor of Burrows' book, E. F. Sutcliffer, affirms that the author's notes suggest that he afterwards abandoned this idea ("The Gospel of the Infancy", 39).

[17] Schnackenburg, *Das Johannesevangelium* I, 20-23; Bailey, *Common to Luke and John*, 103-116, claims that the traditions common to Luke and John come from Jesus' activity in Samaria, and Jerusalem for the passion accounts (Lk 19:37-40/Jn 12:12-19; Lk 22:3/Jn 13:2.27; Lk 22:14-38/Jn 13:1-17; Lk 22:39-53a/Jn 18:1-12; Lk 22:53b-71/Jn 18:13-28; Lk 23:1-25/Jn 18:29–19:16; Lk 23:25-56/Jn 19:17-42).

[18] Brown, *Birth*, 238.

the predominance of women in the narration (Elizabeth, Mary, and Anna the prophetess), the chief character of Mary, all point to a female source.[19] The hypothesis is that Mary supplied the information to Luke through a female intermediary.

On the other hand, still according to W. J. Brown, there are indications in Luke's Gospel, as well as in Acts of the Apostles, that Luke possessed a special source of information connected with the court of Herod. To this information Luke was indebted for facts not given by the other evangelists (Lk 8:3; Acts 12:20; 13:1). In addition, Joanna, the wife of Chuza, Herod's steward, is mentioned four times throughout Luke-Acts (Lk 8:3; 23:49; 24:10; and Acts 1:14). For these reasons, W. J. Brown suggests that since Luke had special information connected with the court of Herod, it was to Joanna that Mary communicated her story.[20] The very same W. J. Brown recognizes that this is only conjecture. In this I agree with him.

1.1.4 James, the Lord's Brother

In the second century, James, the "brother of the Lord," was thought to be a plausible source for information about Jesus' infancy.[21] However, according to Brown, the resultant *Protoevangelium Iacobi* is highly legendary, makes elementary mistakes about the Temple procedure, and is more obviously folkloric than the canonical infancy narrative.[22] Bovon, however, thinks that Luke

---

[19] Dornish affirms that "the complexity of the interweavings of the infancy narrative makes a new case for hypothesizing a 'women's source'" (DORNISCH, "Introduction and Luke 1", 7).

[20] W. J. BROWN, *The Gospel of the Infancy*, 23.

[21] On the historical value of the witness of James, the brother of the Lord, see CULLMANN, "Infancy Gospels", 370-374. On the three main characters who bear the name "James" in the NT, James the son of Zebedee, the brother of John (Lk 5:10; 6:14 and par.; 8:51; 9:28.54; Acts 1:13; 12:2; Mt 4:21; 10:2; 17:1; Mk 10:35; 13:3; 14:33; Jn 21:1-2), James son of Alphaeus, who also belongs to the Twelve (Lk 6:15 and par.; Acts 1:13; Mk 3:18), and James of Nazareth, the brother of Jesus (Acts 12:17; 15:13; 21:18; Mt 13:55; 27:56; Mk 6:3; 15:40; 16:1; 1 Co 15:7; Ga 1:19; 2:9.12), see MONTES PERAL, "A la búsqueda de identidades", 113-118.

[22] BROWN, *Birth*, 238.

may have taken the traditions from the Jewish Christian circle of James, the Lord's brother.[23]

The plethora of opinions means that we have no real knowledge whether any or all of the Lukan infancy material came from a tradition for which there was a corroborating witness. There is still no agreement among the scholars. However, the possibility of Mary as eyewitness is still open. Luke could have received some information about Jesus' infancy from family traditions in the early Jewish Christian community in Jerusalem.

1.2 Source Criticism

In searching for eyewitnesses whose information would be reliable, scholars have looked for different sources within the Lukan infancy narrative. The existence of two different sources throughout Luke's Gospel is accepted by the majority of scholars: Mark's Gospel and the Q source. Neither of these sources is present in Luke 1–2,[24] where it is likely that Luke used other sources, as he did elsewhere in the rest of his Gospel.[25] Therefore we are forced to look elsewhere, to a source peculiar to Luke himself, for the possible sources of the infancy narrative.

---

[23] See BOVON, *Lukas* I, 48; and QUARLES, "Protevangelium of James", 139-149. Schaberg thinks that it is likely that the basis of the tradition, especially the illegitimate conception, does stem from the family of Jesus, probably from Mary or from the brothers or sisters of Jesus, for example, from James (SCHABERG, *The Illegitimacy*, 153-156).

[24] The only author who believes Luke got the germ of the idea for the organization of his first two chapters from Mark, and that his birth stories were not written independently of Mark, but based on his Gospel, is GOULDER, *Luke* I, 205-207. Schuler does not see the connection with Mark, but contends that Luke knew Matthew and his infancy narrative (SHULER, "Rhetorical Character", 174). I think that the parallels between Matthew 1–2 and Luke 1–2 are very remote, and I agree with the majority of scholars who support the independence of both infancy narratives.

[25] The existence of these sources is suggested by the relatively high frequency of divine intervention through angelic messengers (15x in Luke 1–2 and just 11x in Luke 3–24), the prominent role of the Holy Spirit in the Lukan infancy narrative in comparison with the rest of the Gospel, and the hightly semitized style of Luke 1–2.

1.2.1 The "Hymns"

On the one hand, it is striking that in Luke 1–2, almost all of the characters who speak do so through speeches, which often exhibit poetic diction and structure. The speeches by Mary (Lk 1:46-55), Zechariah (Lk 1:68-70), the angels (Lk 2:14), and Simeon (Lk 2:29-32) bear a particular resemblance to Hebrew poetic forms, Hebrew "hymns."[26] It is still more striking that in the rest of Luke's Gospel this literary phenomenon appears only in Jesus' triumphal entry into Jerusalem (Lk 19:38).[27]

On the other hand, numerous studies have called attention to the importance of OT precedents for understanding both the form and the content of these hymns.[28] Especially relevant are parallel instances in the OT where poetic material is inserted into a prose narrative.[29]

---

[26] I prefer to speak of four "hymns" in Luke 1–2 and put the word in quotation marks because of the difficulty of defining in the NT what a "hymn" is (see OSBORNE, "Un état de la question", 77-80). The number of "hymns" in Luke 1–2 has been debated. SCHILLE, *Frühchristliche Hymnen*, 136-138, thinks that Lk 2:8-20 is a fifth hymn. And GRYGLEWICZ, "Die Herkunft", 265-273, adds the oracle by Simeon, Lk 2:34-35, as the fifth "hymn." AYTOUN, "The Ten Lucan Hymns", 274-288, proposed ten different "hymns." According to MUÑOZ IGLESIAS, *Los Evangelios de la Infancia* I, 297, only the *Magnificat*, *Benedictus*, *Gloria*, and *Nunc Dimittis* are addressed to God, only these show evidence of Hebrew poetic composition, and only these have been considered "hymns" from the first centuries in the Christian liturgy. These four infancy "hymns" receive their titles from their first Latin words. Among these four hymns, the *Gloria* has not been discussed as much as the other three because of its brevity. In the context of Luke 1–2, I will often refer to them by these Latin titles. In the context of Lk 2:22-39, I sometimes refer to the *Nunc Dimittis* as Simeon's "hymn," *canticle*, *prayer*, or *first speech* (Lk 2:29-32), in opposition to his *second speech* or *prophecy* (Lk 2:34b-35).

[27] This fact is still more striking when we compare Luke 1–2 with Matthew 1–2 where there are many quotations of the OT (Mt 1:23; 2:6; 2:15; 2:18; 2:19), but there is no hymn.

[28] See, for example, MUÑOZ IGLESIAS, *Los Evangelios de la Infancia* I, 2-8.

[29] LOHFINK, "Das Alte Testament", 223-236, has studied several hymns of the OT, especially Exodus 15, 1 Samuel 2, Jonah 2, and Judges 5. He argues that we find the same procedure of interruption in the four hymns of Luke 1–2 (LOHFINK, "Psalmen im Neuen Testament", 105-125). Muñoz Iglesias also affirms that there was a literary convention among the Jewish writers that consisted of inserting poetic speeches into the mouths of characters of the narrative (MUÑOZ IGLESIAS, *Los Evangelios de la Infancia* I, 55-60). On the hymns in the OT and the difficulty of distinguishing between prose and poem see WEITZMAN, *Song and Story*, 1-14.

The content of these hymns in Lk 1–2 incorporates many different OT texts with few explicitly Christian references. These hymns also seem to be appendages and could be easily excised so that the reader would never miss them. Indeed, the narrative would read more smoothly without them.

There are four different theories that have been proposed about the composition of these hymns: (1) They were actually composed by those reported as their speakers, for example, the *Benedictus* by Zechariah. This theory originated before the era of critical scholarship, when the importance of the author and the community in the redaction procedure was not yet well known. (2) Luke composed the canticles when he wrote the rest of his narratives. However, if they were not there, we would never miss them. It is important to note that sometimes the hymns do not fit well with the surrounding narratives. (3) The canticles were composed by Luke and added subsequently to an already existing narrative. (4) The canticles were pre-Lukan or non-Lukan and were added by Luke to an already existing Lukan narrative. Theories (3) and (4) have much support among modern scholars.[30]

Although there is no agreement among scholars, the evidence, in my view, favors the last theory. The strong presence of distinctively Jewish expressions that occur in the hymns suggests the possibility of a Jewish Christian source, which would argue against their composition by a Gentile Christian. According to this theory, Luke inserted the hymns in his narrative, altering them where necessary.

We can go a step further. Are all of the hymns inserted by Luke from a non-Lukan source? The two first hymns, the *Magnificat* and the *Benedictus*, are more closely connected to each other than either is to the *Nunc Dimittis*.[31] According to Gryglewicz, the main terms

---

[30] For example, theory (3) is defended by FREED, *The Stories of Jesus' Birth*, 157; ALETTI, "Passages néotestamentaires en prose rythmée", 243-244; and OSBORNE, "La fonction des hymnes de Lc 1-2", 293-294. Theory (4) is defended, for example, by BROWN, *Birth*, 350-353; FITZMYER, *Luke I-IX*, 309.

[31] Already Harnack in 1900 affirmed that the *Magnificat* and the *Benedictus* came from the same pen (HARNACK, "Das Magnificat der Elisabeth", 538-556). They are similar in length and tone, diction and structure.

employed in the *Magnificat* and in the *Benedictus* are 46 and 58, respectively. Among them, there are fifteen common terms. As many of them appear more than one time, there are seventeen common terms in the *Magnificat* and 24 in the *Benedictus*. That means that more than one third are common to both hymns.[32] However, between the *Nunc Dimittis* and the *Magnificat*, there are only three common terms (νῦν: 1:48; 2:29; δοῦλος/δούλη: 1:48; 2:29; and Ἰσραήλ: 1:54; 2:32), and between the *Nunc Dimittis* and the *Benedictus* there are six (εἰρήνη: 1:79; 2:29; ἑτοιμάζω: 1:76; 2:31; Ἰσραήλ: 1:80; 2:32; λαός: 1:68.77; 2:31.32; πᾶς: 1:71; 2:31; σωτηρία/σωτήριον: 1:71.77; 2:30).[33] In addition, George has proved that the *Magnificat* and *Benedictus* are inspired by the Psalms, while the *Nunc Dimittis* is inspired by Isaiah 40–55.[34]

On the one hand, the vocabulary of the *Nunc Dimittis*, in contrast with the other hymns, is notably Lukan.[35] As George establishes, the following words are used more often by Luke than the other evangelists, and they all appear in the *Nunc Dimittis*: νῦν, δοῦλος, ῥῆμα, εἰρήνη, and σωτήριον.[36]

On the other hand, the *Nunc Dimittis* is very well connected to the surrounding narrative. According to Lohfink, it is linked to its context not only by the opening thought about death (2:26b.29), but also by the key word ὁράω (2:26c.30). However, Benoit has proved that Luke has made redactional changes in the *Magnificat*

---

[32] GRYGLEWICZ, "Die Herkunft", 267.

[33] VALENTINI, "I cantici in Lc 1–2", 105-107, adds that the *Nunc Dimittis* differs from the *Magnificat* and *Benedictus* because of its theological insight. According to him, the *Nunc Dimittis* presents a more developed conception of salvation.

[34] GEORGE, "Le parallèle", 153-154; 167-168.

[35] As we will see in § 1.2.4, MUÑOZ IGLESIAS, *Los Evangelios de la Infancia* I, 316-318, defends a Hebrew source for the whole of Luke 1–2, including the hymns. Yet among the many examples he gives of Hebraisms in the hymns, he does not give any examples from the *Nunc Dimittis*.

[36] GEORGE, "Le parallèle", 168: νῦν (Mt: 4x; Mk: 3x; Lk: 14x; Jn: 28x; and Acts: 25x); δοῦλος (Mt: 0x; Mk: 0x; Lk: 3x; Jn: 0x; and Acts: 4x); ῥῆμα (Mt: 5x; Mk: 2x; Lk: 19x; Jn: 12x; and Acts: 14x); εἰρήνη (Mt: 4x; Mk: 1x; Lk: 13x; Jn: 6x; and Acts: 7x); and σωτήριον (Mt: 0x; Mk: 0x; Lk: 2x; Jn: 0x; and Acts: 1x).

(see v. 48b) and *Benedictus* (see v. 76-77) to readjust both hymns to their context.[37]

Fitzmyer has affirmed that "the *Magnificat* and *Benedictus* come from a Jewish-Christian source, possibly the *Nunc Dimittis*."[38] Because of the independent vocabulary of the *Nunc Dimittis* with respect to the *Magnificat* and *Benedictus*, because of the Lukan vocabulary of the *Nunc Dimittis*, and because of the good insertion of the *Nunc Dimittis* within its narrative context, I agree with Grelot, Rossé, and Brown, in defending the Lukan origin of the *Nunc Dimittis*.[39]

1.2.2 Other Possible Sources of Luke 1

Bultmann, following Dibelius,[40] posits a Baptist source in the announcement of John's birth (vv. 5-25), his birth (vv. 57-58), and circumcision (vv. 59-63).[41] Sometimes Christian origins are argued for this source, but more often a composition by followers of John the Baptist.[42] It is argued that the tradition about Jesus

---

[37] BENOÎT, "L'enfance de Jean-Baptiste", 167-191. See SPITTA, "Chronologischen Notizen", 281-317, and SPITTA, "Das Magnificat", 63-94, who agrees with Benoît and claims that neither the *Magnificat* nor the *Benedictus* belong to the original prose redaction.

[38] FITZMYER, *Luke I-IX*, 309.

[39] See GRELOT, "Le Cantique de Siméon", 481-509; ROSSÉ, "Approcci esegetici", 21; and BROWN, *Birth*, 622, who, in his second version in 1993, admits: "I am more open to this view than I was when I wrote the first edition because it explains better not only the differences from the *Magnificat* and *Benedictus*, which are community productions, but also the likelihood that it lays out the program for the spread of the Christian message described in Acts."

[40] See DIBELIUS, *Die urchristliche Überlieferung*, 67-77.

[41] According to BULTMANN, *Die Geschichte der synoptischen Tradition*, 320-321, the reasons for this Baptist literary source are the following: (1) The Baptist and his parents have no further part to play in Luke 2. (2) The relationship of the Baptist with Jesus in Luke 1 is only secondary because the Annunciation to Mary plays a small part in Luke 1. And (3) the Baptist originally had no relation to a coming Messiah, but was to prepare a way for God himself (Lk 1:14-17).

[42] BROWN, *Birth*, 245, cites Wilkinson's theory which claims that the Baptist source once contained not only the material in Luke 1 that now refers to John the Baptist, but also other material which has been readapted to Jesus, for example Lk 1:26-38,

was added to this Baptist source to make a double infancy narrative.[43] Fitzmyer and Bovon speak of a "Baptist source;"[44] Brown of "Baptist information" shaped by Luke.[45] Following Brown and Benoît,[46] Berlingieri, in his doctoral dissertation on Lk 1:5-25, does not admit a Baptist source. He affirms that it is a Lukan composition which uses some previously existing information, but without any other single source.[47] It is likely that Luke used some set of traditions about John's origins which he supplemented with reports about John's adult life and ministry.

According to Manicardi, the narrative of John the Baptist has been interrupted by the presence of Mary. Manicardi defends Luke's reliance on a source for the Annunciation.[48] Indeed, the virginal conception of Jesus is not present at all in Luke 2. This discordance between the Annunciation and Luke 2 suggests the existence of a separate source.

---

originally addressed to Elizabeth as a parallel to the announcement to Zechariah, and even the *Magnificat* originally spoke by Elizabeth as a parallel to the *Benedictus* by Zechariah. Brown does not agree with this theory (see WILKINSON, *A Johannine Document*, 7-35). Even earlier, in 1911, Völter had affirmed that all of Lk 1:5-80 come from a baptist source, a non-Christian document (VÖLTER, *Die Erzählungen*).

[43] According to SILBERMAN, "A Model", 491-492, Luke took the model of two different infancy narratives, John and Jesus, from the rabbinic literature. Two lessons were read in the synagogue on *Rosh Hashanah*. The first one was a prophetic lesson from 1 Samuel 1–2. The second one was from the pentateuchal lesson of the day, Gn 21:1-34. Both readings give two visitations and two births. Samuel and Isaac respectively prefigured John and Jesus. I find this hypothesis too complicated. Did Luke know this synagogal liturgy?

[44] See FITZMYER, *Luke I-IX*, 309, and BOVON, *Lukas* I, 50-51.

[45] See BROWN, *Birth*, 622.661. The difference between *source* and *information* seems to be that the *source* is written, more stable and precise, while the *information* is oral, a bit less stable and imprecise.

[46] See BENOÎT, "L'enfance de Jean-Baptiste", 194.

[47] BERLINGIERI, *Il lieto annuncio*, 41-49, demonstrates that the reasons argued by Bultmann (see n. 41) are not convincing enough to accept a Baptist source.

[48] See MANICARDI, "Redazione e tradizione", 47-48.

1.2.3 Other Possible Sources of Luke 2

The differences between Luke 2 and Luke 1 have been clearly underlined. Luke 2 has its own introduction (2:1-3) and curiosly ignores some details and unnecessarily repeats other details of Luke 1. Luke 2 presupposes nothing from Luke 1, neither the virginal conception nor the identity of the parents.[49] Although prominent in Luke 1, John the Baptist, Zechariah, and Elizabeth have completely disappeared from the scene. Mary is again introduced as Joseph's betrothed (2:5), even though she was already so described in 1:27; the origin of Joseph from the house of David is repeated (1:27; 2:4); Mary has been informed at length about her son (1:31-35; 1:43-44), but in Luke 2 she appears surprised and ignorant of everything (2:19.33.51); finally, through the decree of Caesar Augustus the frame of the narrative is the Roman Empire (2:1-3), while Luke 1 was located only in a Jewish setting. This is why Bultmann claims that Luke 2 is not only fully intelligible on its own without Luke 1, but that also every single passage of Luke 2 comes from individual stories.[50] And Manicardi sees a source in the passage of the shepherds (2:8-20).[51]

Finally, the story in 2:41-52 is easily distinguished from the rest. As Brown states, not only does it deal with a different phase of Jesus' life, closer to his public life, but its emphasis on the parents' lack of understanding (2:48-50) seems to clash with the revelations given to them in what has gone before. In addition, one could argue that 2:40 was the original conclusion, noting the growing up of Jesus, and a story of different provenance was added, requiring a second and duplicate conclusion in 2:52.[52]

---

[49] ORTENSIO DA SPINETOLI, "I problemi", 29-34, highlights that in Luke 2 there is no reference to the virginal conception, Joseph is presented as "Jesus' father" (2:48), and Mary and Joseph as his "parents" (2:16.22.27.33.39.40.43.47.48).

[50] See BULTMANN, *Die Geschichte der synoptischen Tradition*, 320.

[51] See MANICARDI, "Redazione e tradizione", 47. I do not see enough textual reasons to suppose the existence of that source.

[52] BROWN, *Birth*, 244, believes it stemmed from a popular tradition of pre-ministry marvels, seemingly attested in Jn 2:1-11 and clearly attested in the apocryphal gospels.

These reasons could be enough to suppose a source that has been added in a subsequent redaction.

However plausible these reasons, there is no agreement among scholars in this matter. I believe that there are connections between Luke 1 and Luke 2, and throughout Luke 2 that unify these chapters, even if some sources might exist.[53]

1.2.4 Is there a Single Source throughout Luke 1–2?

Boismard has reconstructed the text of Luke 1–2 as it was read in an anterior redaction that he names "Proto-Luke."[54] In my opinion, Boismard's thesis is too hypothetical and complicated, reducing its credibility.

Muñoz Iglesias argues that the hymns (1:46-55; 1:68-79; 2:14; 2:29-32) and the announcements (1:13-20; 1:30-38; 1:42-45) fit perfectly in the narrative context where they are found. According to him, nothing prevents us from attributing the hymns, announcements, and narrative to the same author. Luke received a written Semitic document of the entire Luke 1–2, translated this unique source, slightly retouched it, and incorporated it into his entire literary work.[55] The strong presence of Lukan vocabulary throughout Luke 1–2 would be the result of this Lukan translation and adaptation.[56]

---

[53] The prophecies of Jesus' birth in 1:30-35 are fulfilled in 2:6-7; the parallelism John-Jesus keeps through the birth, circumcision and naming of Jesus; God comunicates through an angel; the news still provokes astonishment; those who receive the announcement transmit the good new. On these connections within Luke 1–2 see COLERIDGE, *The Birth*, 129.

[54] BOISMARD, *L'évangile de l'enfance*, and BOISMARD, *En quête du Proto-Luc*, uses a medieval evangelical harmony of the forteenth century, written in English, to establish the reconstruction of "Proto-Luke." This English document is the translation of a French document, now lost. That French document would be the translation from a Latin harmony that we likewise no longer posses, and would translate an original Greek harmony.

[55] See MUÑOZ IGLESIAS, *Los Evangelios de la Infancia* I, 315-318. This very same hypothesis had been formulated years earlier, in 1940, by Burrows, who defended the theory of a single author for both parts, the prose and the poetry (see BURROWS, "The Gospel of the Infancy", 34-57). WINTER, "Some Observations", 111-121, followed Burrows. DÍEZ MERINO, "Trasfondo semítico", 70, and PÉREZ RODRÍGUEZ, *La infancia de Jesús*, 55-57, follow Muñoz Iglesias.

[56] On the Lukanism throughout his infancy narrative see § 1.4.1.b.

However, there are disjunctions and differing structures throughout Luke 1–2, which suggest that the Lukan infancy narrative is not a slightly adapted translation of a preexistent single account. In addition, there is a question over the connection between the infancy narrative and the entire Lukan work. Did Luke adapt his entire work to the written source he inherited?[57] I do not agree with Muñoz's hypothesis.

1.2.5 Written Sources or Oral Information?

I have just stated that a unique written source for Luke 1–2 is unlikely. Were there any short written sources in the composition of Luke 1–2? The question is very hypothetical and difficult. There are many opinions among scholars, and there is no agreement among them. However, we can extract two results from the position of current scholarship.

First, the existence of some written sources is most likely.[58] The extent of these written sources is difficult to determine. I would accept as written sources only the *Magnificat*, the *Benedictus*, and, perhaps, the presence of Jesus in the Temple when he was twelve. I agree with Brown, who affirms that "most of the infancy narrative was freely composed by Luke on the basis of pre-Lukan information, but there was a Jewish Christian written source for the hymns *Magnificat* and *Benedictus*."[59]

Second, Luke could have used some oral information. The information about John and Jesus' announcements, births, and circumcisions, and the presentation of Jesus in the Temple, could come from oral traditions closer to the events related by Luke.[60]

---

[57] In § 1.4.2 we will note that Luke probably redacted the infancy narrative after having written the rest of his work. It is hard to accept that the single source that he received would fit so well with his entire work (see § 1.5.1) if he had not written it.

[58] The language, style, and terminology of these chapters differ from Luke's ordinary manner of writing that it is hard to envision common authorship without the utilization of dissimilar sources. The frequent presence of hymns, announcements of births, and OT expressions suggest that part of these sources existed in literary form and were not merely transmitted orally. On these hypothesises see SALAZAR, "St Luke's Sources", 316; TURNER, "Relation", 100-109.

[59] BROWN, *Birth*, 661.

[60] See ROUILLER, *Il vous*, 15; RADL, *Der Ursprung Jesu*; and BROWN, "Gospel Infancy Narrative Research (Luke)", 661, who defend this hypothesis.

Luke could have had at his disposal few written sources, and more oral information to freely redact and compose his infancy narrative according to the written and oral tradition he received.

1.3 Form Criticism

According to form criticism it is necessary first to study the literary form of each pericope, especially in those sources discovered by source criticism (§ 1.3.1) and then the literary genre of the entire unity of Luke 1–2 (§ 1.3.3). The literary genre is defined by the composite form of the different pericopes.[61]

1.3.1 Plurality of Literary Forms in Luke 1–2

The literary forms of the pericopes of the Lukan infancy narrative are different from those of the rest of the Gospel. There is no miracle story, or speech, or dispute. They do not fit into any of the usual categories of form criticism, since those categories were mainly worked out in the analysis of the accounts of Jesus' public ministry. In fact, form criticism separated the infancy narrative from the rest of the Gospel, and did not pay too much attention to it.[62] The passages of Luke 1–2 exhibit different literary forms. According to Laurentin, we find three announcements (Lk 1:5-22; 1:26-38; 2:10-14), four hymns (1:46-56; 1:68-79; 2:14; and 2:29-32), one visitation (1:39-45), two birth stories (1:57-58; 2:1-7), two circumcisions (1:59-66; 2:21), and two infancy stories (2:22-39;

---

[61] ZIMMERMANN, *Neutestamentliche Methodenlehre*, 135-169, differentiates between literary form for the pericope and literary genre for the larger unity composed of several pericopes. Among the literary forms of the NT, he speaks of prophetic sayings, wisdom sayings, comparisons, paradigms, miracle stories, disputes, historical narratives, faith confessions, doxologies, etc. Among the literary genres of the NT, he speaks of Gospels, Acts of the Apostles, Letters, and Revelations. According to him, Gospels and Acts of the Apostles are Christian creations, while Letters and Revelations existed already and were adopted by the first Christians.

[62] Form criticism started with Gunkel in the OT (GUNKEL, *Genesis*) and went forward with Dibelius and Bultmann in the NT (DIBELIUS, *Die Formgeschichte*; BULTMANN, *Die Geschichte der synoptischen Tradition*), who did not pay too much attention to Luke 1–2.

2:40-52).[63] From these forms, only the first two, the announcement[64] and the hymn,[65] are generally accepted by the scholarship as literary forms and are likely pre-existent forms.

1.3.2 OT Background in Luke 1–2

Lukan scholarship has become increasingly conscious of the influence of the OT Scriptures on the composition of the Lukan Gospel, especially in the infancy narrative.[66] It is now clear that such influence extends far beyond direct quotations and obvious parallels, to rather subtle verbal reminiscences and allusions. This influence could be subdivided into a formal influence and a content influence.

As we have seen above, at least two forms of Luke 1–2, the announcements and the hymns, have been strongly influenced by the OT. The scholarship generally accepts the background of the OT in the form of these compositions.[67] For example, the child-

---

[63] See LAURENTIN, *Les Évangiles de l'enfance*, 114-121. The second story, that of the twelve-year-old Jesus in the Temple, is not actually an infancy story due to the fact that Jesus was already twelve years old.

[64] According to ORTENSIO DA SPINETOLI, *Introduzione*, 13, and MASINI, "Vangeli dell'Infanzia", 453, the form of announcement is used in the OT for the announcement of a future birth or mission: of the birth of Ishmael (Gn 16:7-16); of the birth of Isaac (Genesis 17–19); of the vocation of Moses (Exodus 3–4); of the vocation of Gideon (Judges 6); of the birth of Samson (Judges 13); of the birth of Samuel (1 Samuel 1–3); and of the vision by Daniel (Daniel 7–10). On the traditional elements of the announcement, the appearance of an angel, the fear of the announcement's addressee, and the reassurance through words and signs, see FITZMYER, *Luke I-IX*, 396.

[65] Hymns are part of the history of salvation told in the Scripture. VALENTINI, "I cantici in Lc 1–2", 81, presents more than 70 minor hymns and more than 50 hymns of a considerable extension in the OT. For example, he underlines the hymn of Lamech (Gn 4:23-24); of Miriam (Exodus 15); of Balaam (Numbers 23–24); of Moses (Dt 32:1-43); of Deborah (Judges 5); of Hannah (1 S 2:1-10); of David (2 S 22:2-51); and of Hezekiah (Is 38:10-20).

[66] According to LAURENTIN, *Les Évangiles de l'enfance*, 57, this influence of the OT is due to the very same Jesus who himself made wide use of it (Lk 24:7.26.27.32.46.47).

[67] On the announcements see MUÑOZ IGLESIAS, *Los Evangelios de la Infancia* II, 49-67. On the hymns see MUÑOZ IGLESIAS, *Los Evangelios de la Infancia* I, 25-60.

less couple promised children by angelic visitation revive the tales of Elkanah and Hannah (1 Samuel 1–3).[68]

But the influence of the OT is not only in the form but also in the content. Fitzmyer, following Laurentin,[69] believes that the dawning of messianic times, the coming of the great and awesome day of the Lord, and the coming of the Lord to his Temple, are the OT themes present in the story of John and Jesus. These themes are made present by allusions to Dn 7:9; 9:20-26; 10:7; 12:16-17 and to Ml 2:6; 3:1.23-24. Thus "the angel of the Lord" (Lk 1:11) is identified as "Gabriel" (Lk 1:19), who in Daniel announces the prophecy of 70 weeks and the coming of an Anointed One (Dn 9:25). This messianic era is associated with "the great and awesome day of the Lord" (Ml 3:23) as the conclusion of John's preparation of the people in the spirit and power of Elijah (Lk 1:17). Moreover, Jesus is identified as "Lord" (Lk 2:11) and made to come to the Temple (Lk 2:22-39) in the spirit of Ml 3:1.[70]

This influence of Daniel was used by Neirynck to affirm that it is not possible to understand Luke 1–2 while forgetting its contacts with the book of Daniel and apocalyptic themes.[71] Finally, Ruddick introduces the influences of the birth narratives of Genesis as a model for the evangelist. According to Ruddick, the language and events of Genesis 27–43, from the birth of Jacob's children through their migration to Egypt, are remarkably paralleled by Luke 1–2, even in the same order in both documents.[72]

---

[68] The influence of Elkanah and Hannah has been studied in a special way. BURROWS, "The Gospel of the Infancy", 1-12, believes that the author of Luke 1–2 composed a narrative using as his principal model the story of the child Samuel.

[69] See LAURENTIN, *Les Évangiles de Noël*, 74-87, and LAURINI, "Lc 1-2", 127-144.

[70] FITZMYER, *Luke I-IX*, 316, contends that Lk 1:12-13 depends on Dn 10:7.12; Lk 1:16 on Ml 2:6; Lk 1:17 on Ml 3:1.23-24 (cf. Si 48:1.3.10); Lk 1:19 on Dn 9:20-21; Lk 1:26-29 on Dn 9:21-24; Lk 1:64-65 on Dn 10:16-17; Lk 1:76 on Ml 3:1.23.

[71] Neirynck's opinion is based on the coming of the new apocalyptic era, by the angelic appearance, by the name of "Gabriel," by the silence of Zechariah, by Mary's difficulty in understanding (NEIRYNCK, *L'Evangile de Noël*, 13-14). Legrand proposes that the Annunciation (Lk 1:26-38) presents an apocalypse (LEGRAND, "L'Arrière-Plan", 161-192; LEGRAND, *L'Annonce à Marie*).

[72] See RUDDICK, "Birth Narratives", 343, where he shows some 30 verbal parallels,

We may be surprised to find that Luke has only two direct quotations from the OT (Lk 2:23.24), in his first two chapters, although there are many more in the later chapters of his Gospel and in Acts. Although there are no actual quotations, these two chapters are full of OT allusions, and are written in a style very reminiscent of the OT. Judging from the work of Drury, OT references, in both form and content, can be found in Luke 1–2 in such quantity that there can be no doubt that the OT, handled with skill and conservative reverence, is a source for Luke 1–2. "To turn," he says, "from Luke 1–2 to OT narrative is to cross no boundaries but to remain in the same country, to hear the same language in the same forms describing similar events."[73] The OT is the thread that interweaves the whole of Luke 1–2.[74]

1.3.3 A Literary Genre for Luke 1-2

Ortensio da Spinetoli has claimed that the main question regarding Luke 1–2 is not the question of the sources, or forms, but is rather the question of the literary genre. In other words, the main question is the question of the mode of expression as well as the kind of composition that the author has written. As Ortensio da Spinetoli says, "the literary genre is the fundamental key

---

some of them very weak, between Luke and the Greek of the Septuagint. For example, the first example that Ruddick proposes parallels "Mary is visited by the angel Gabriel, who is sent by God" (Lk 1:26: ὁ ἄγγελος Γαβριὴλ ἀπὸ τοῦ θεοῦ) with "Jacob in a dream sees a ladder with the angels of God" (Gn 28:12: οἱ ἄγγελοι τοῦ θεοῦ).

[73] DRURY, *Tradition and Design*, 8. Similar affirmations are found in GREEN, "Beginning", 61-86; and MARTINS TERRA, "O Evangelho da infância", 41-59.

[74] ORSATTI, "Storicità e Vangeli dell'infanzia", 621, contends that the Lukan and Matthean infancy narratives are full of Biblical threads which recall and gather the Old Covenant. Matthew 1–2 points back to the OT, beginning with a genealogy which goes back to Abraham (Mt 1:1-16), and with a whole series of OT quotations which are the conclusion of each passage of his infancy narrative (Mt 1:23 which concludes Jesus' birth's announcement; Mt 2:6 which concludes the visit of the wise men; Mt 2:15 which concludes the escape to Egypt; Mt 2:18 which concludes the massacre of the infants; and Mt 2:23 which concludes the return from Egypt). However, the influence of the OT in Luke 1–2 is implicit, through different forms and images.

for the understanding of Luke 1–2."[75] However, it is not easy to classify its literary genre. Because of this, I will review the different literary genres that the scholarship has proposed for the Lukan infancy narrative so far, and then give my own opinion.

a) Legend as a Possible Literary Genre?

Klostermann and Gressmann, Dibelius, and Bultmann considered Luke 1–2 to be a *legend*.[76] They believe these narratives are religious and edifying texts that should be read. This legend builds up what is called *theologoumenon*, which designates the author's theological conception of Jesus, expressed in a narrative. However, legend is not the literary genre accepted by the majority of the scholars.[77]

b) Midrash as a Possible Literary Genre?

Because the Lukan infancy narrative has this strong OT influence that we have just studied, many scholars, following, first, Wellhausen, and then Bloch,[78] classify Luke 1–2 in the literary genre of *midrash*. The term comes from the ancient Jewish interpretations of the OT which popularized and expanded the biblical ac-

---

[75] ORTENSIO DA SPINETOLI, "I problemi", 34. The literary genre is the point about which the scholarship should achieve a more uniform conclusion in order to better understand Luke 1–2.

[76] See KLOSTERMANN – GRESSMANN, *Die Synoptiker Evangelien*, 151-167; DIBELIUS, *Die Formgeschichte*, 121-124; and BULTMANN, *Die Geschichte der synoptischen Tradition*, 316-328. According to Dibelius, the clearest example is the account of the twelve-year-old Jesus in the Temple (Lk 2:41-50), but the entire unity of Luke 1–2 was considered a legend.

[77] On this rejection and the related bibliography see SCHNEIDER, *Lukas*, 77.

[78] WELLHAUSEN, *Das Evangelium Lucae*, writes in 1904 and BLOCH, "Écriture et tradition", in 1954. The main scholars who follow Bloch are: LAURENTIN, *Structure*, 116-119; and MUÑOZ IGLESIAS, "Midrás y Evangelios de la Infancia", 331-359. On the *midrashic* methodology and the study of the NT see MANNS, *Le Midrash*; MUÑOZ IGLESIAS, "Derás y Nuevo Testamento", 303-314; DÍEZ MACHO, "Derás y exégesis del Nuevo Testamento", 37-89; DEL AGUA PÉREZ, *El método midrásico*; DEL AGUA PÉREZ, "Aproximación al relato", 257-284; DEL AGUA PÉREZ, "El papel de la 'escuela midrásica'", 333-349; and GERTNER, "Midrashim in the New Testament", 267-292.

counts.[79] It is a commentary on older OT texts, trying to bring forth new teachings for the present time.[80]

However, some major scholars have found difficulties considering Luke 1–2 a *midrash*. According to Brown, the purpose of *midrash* was to make the OT account intelligible, and that is not the purpose of the infancy narrative, which was written to make Jesus' origins intelligible.[81] Bovon claims that it is essential to *midrash* to apply an earlier revelation to the present situation. He argues that the Lukan infancy narrative wants to enrich the previously written revelations with information about more recent events. That is why Bovon affirms that Luke 1–2 can be described as a *midrash*, but only with great restrictions.[82] Fitzmyer thinks that the term is better avoided and is, in any case, quite unsuitable for the Lukan infancy narrative.[83]

---

[79] On the different types of *midrashim*, *haggadah midrash* (narrative texts), *halakah midrash* (legislative texts), *pesher midrash* (prophetic texts), *homiletic midrash* (synagogal cult), and *exegetical midrash* (Jewish school), see CAVALLETTI, "Il metodo derashico", 5-7. The infancy narrative would be an implicit *haggadah midrash*. Muñoz León improved our knowledge of *midrash* by studying the *midrash* methodology in intertestamental Judaism (MUÑOZ LEÓN, *Derás*). Today scholars prefer to speak of *derash* to express a particular way to interpret the OT text in Christianity, reserving the term *midrash* for the interpretative works of the Jewish tradition.

[80] Wellhausen began his commentary on Luke's Gospel at Luke 3, arguing that Luke 1–2 was a *midrash*, and gave a pejorative meaning to *midrash* as a synonym for legend and fable (WELLHAUSEN, *Das Evangelium Lucae*, 3). However, those scholars who claim *midrash* as the literary genre of Luke 1–2 affirm that *midrash* does not contradict historicity. According to them, *midrash* is a way to express the historical facts through biblical models. On *midrash* as a way to recount history see MUÑOZ LEÓN, "Acontecimiento-base y artificio literario", 148; DEL AGUA PÉREZ, "Los evangelios de la infancia", 283.

[81] See BROWN, *Birth*, 584. Harrington insists that the "Gospel infancy narratives are stories about Jesus, not explications of biblical texts" (HARRINGTON, "Birth Narratives", 324). See further WRIGHT, "Genre Midrash", 105-138; 417-457, specially 454-456.

[82] See BOVON, *Lukas* I, 45.

[83] See FITZMYER, *Luke I-IX*, 309. While the starting point of the *midrash* was a scriptural text, the starting point of Luke 1–2 is a historical event, Jesus. While the finishing point of the *midrash* was a current event, the actual situation, the finishing point of Luke 1–2 is a past text, which at the same time illuminates and is being illuminated by the present event.

The problem may be purely terminological, pertaining only to nomenclature. What do we gain by calling the infancy narrative *midrash*? I affirm the strong influence of the OT, and do not classify Luke 1–2 in the literary genre of *midrash*.

c) The Infancy of the Hero as a Literary Genre?

Thanks to different Jewish documents of the first century, we know several *midrashim* about the lives of important personages, for example Moses, Samson, and David. Some of these *midrashim* include the infancy of these characters.[84] Does this literary phenomenon happen in Hellenistic literature?

The important study of the development of Greek "biography"[85] by Momigliano has proved that in the first century interest in biography increased, including in infancy narratives.[86] In Greco-Roman literature the infancy of the hero is sometimes told in order to praise the life of the hero since his childhood.[87] According to Shuler, Hellenistic βίος narratives incorporate the events that precede the birth, the events of the birth, and the events following the birth into the entire biography of the hero.[88] It is what is called by Brenner the genre of the *infancy of the hero* which describes the stories of birth and youth shaped in retrospect after the subjects had become famous.[89] Brown names this literary phenomenon *infancy narratives of famous*

---

[84] See PHILO, *De vita Moysis*, 6; JOSEPHUS, *The Jewish Antiquities*, 2,9; 5,8; 5,10; PSEUDO-PHILO, *The Biblical Antiquities*, 9; 42; 49; 50; 51; 53. On these examples see § II.2.1.

[85] I write "biography" with quotation marks because ancient biographies must not be understood in terms of modern historical biographies. However, as the term "biography" appears very often, especially in Ch. II, from now on I will not keep writing the quotation marks.

[86] Momigliano thinks it is not mere chance that so much biographical material, both Greek and Roman, has come down to us from the time of the Roman Empire. It reflects the importance of biography in that epoch (MOMIGLIANO, *The Development of Greek Biography*, 104).

[87] See *The Lives of the Twelve Caesars*, by SUETONIUS; *The Life and Deeds of Alexander of Macedon*, by PSEUDO CALLISTHENES; *The History of Alexander*, by QUINTUS CURTIUS RUFUS. This praise is a sort of *enkomio* or eulogy. On these examples see § II.1.1.

[88] SHULER, "Rhetorical Character", 188.

[89] BRENNER, "Female Social Behaviour", 257-273.

men. He recognizes a common tendency to shape stories about the infancy and boyhood of those who have become famous, in order to show a unity in the pattern of the whole career.[90] That is why Talbert argues for a greater role of the Greco-Roman milieu, not simply by way of background, but in terms of basic literary genre.[91]

Knowing these Jewish and Greco-Roman backgrounds, Luke 1–2 may be viewed as a popular story about the infancy of the main character. Luke could have composed his infancy narrative in a fashion that incorporates both Jewish and non-Jewish literary traditions. Luke could have presented Jesus' infancy in this narrative fashion in order to introduce a persuasive narrative biography of Jesus. That is why Fitzmyer used Burrows' term of *imitative historiography*,[92] which means that whatever historical matter has been preserved by Luke has been assimilated by him into other literary accounts, either biblical or extra-biblical.[93]

d) The Infancy of the Main Character of the Gospel

So far, we have seen that the genre of *midrash* does not fit very well as the literary genre of Luke 1–2. The strong influence of the OT is evident, but this unique event of Jesus complicates their denomination as *midrash*. We have seen as well that some Jewish and Greco-Roman authors commonly included the infancies of famous people as part of their biographies. As those biographies began with the infancy of the main character, the Lukan composition begins with the infancy narrative. However, Luke 1–2 falls within a wider literary work, the Gospel, whose literary genre is difficult to catalog. Normally, the Gospel is understood as a new literary genre, close to Greco-Roman biography, created by the early Christian community to explain the event of Christ.[94] This new event is expressed in a

---

[90] BROWN, *Birth*, 579-580.

[91] TALBERT, *Literary Patterns*, 68-74.

[92] See BURROWS, "The Gospel of the Infancy", 1-58. Bovon calls it "OT historiography" (BOVON, *Lukas* I, 45 [28]).

[93] See FITZMYER, *Luke I-IX*, 309, and SILBERMAN, "A Model", 492, who agrees with Fitzmyer.

[94] BURRIDGE, *What Are the Gospels?*, 243-247, claims that the Gospels share with ancient

new way.[95] This is the main reason why it is so difficult to classify the infancy narrative's literary genre,[96] and it cannot be classified in any previous literary genre.[97]

Fitzmyer thinks that, like the passion narrative or the resurrection narrative, the infancy narrative is a sub-genre in the genre of Gospel in Christian literature.[98] I believe that the Lukan infancy

---

biography some general similarities of content, form, and function. In content, they focus on the life of one person, especially that person's public career. In form, they fit, to various degrees, the pattern of ancient biographies that frame a person's public career with narratives of his origin and youth, at the beginning, and of his death, at the end. In function, many ancient biographies were concerned with praising their subject as an exemplar of the virtues to be honored and emulated in the community. The Gospels have a similar function for the Christian community, while serving other functions as well. The readers of the Gospels would have understood them with some of the same expectations with which they heard biographies. On the connection of Luke-Acts with classical biography see AUNE, *The New Testament*, 17-67; and BARR – WENTLING, "Classical Biography", 76. Acts, however, is usually classified in the genre of historiography. Sterling argues that Luke-Acts should be considered within the sub-genre of apologetic historiography, which is "the story of a subgroup of people in an extended prose narrative written by a member of the group who follows the group's own traditions but Hellenizes them in an effort to establish the identity of the group within the setting of the larger world" (STERLING, *Historiography and Self-definition*, 17). Ó FEARGHAIL, *Introduction to Luke-Acts*, 179, classifies the Gospels as *kerygmatic history*. The term *kerygmatic* expresses the uniqueness of the biography with respect both to the purpose of its narration and to the nature of the events it recounts. The qualification *kerygmatic* also indicates the active role of the evangelist who, while respecting the faithfully transmitted tradition that has come down to him, is nontheless intent on strengthening faith in the message of salvation. Finally, I believe that Acts is a salvation historiography which describes the very ancient history of God's salvation.

[95] I believe that Luke-Acts does not fit perfectly with any known literary genre, but does share certain affinities with different genres; it nearly resembles the literary genre of biography, especially Luke's Gospel, and the literary genre of historiography, especially Acts of the Apostles. On the flexibility of both literary genres, biography and historiography, in the first century see § II.1, especially n. 17.

[96] Other reasons are: its strong OT background, and its wide variety of forms. Schürmann contends that the literary genre of the infancy narratives cannot be classified in any of the literary genres known in the first century. On a good *status quaestionis* of this exegetical question see SCHÜRMANN, *Das Lukasevangelium* I, 21-24.

[97] BERLINGIERI, *Il lieto annuncio*, 50-54, maintains that the literary genre of Luke 1–2 is the Gospel. I believe that the differences between Luke 3–24 and Luke 1–2 suggest a slightly different literary genre.

[98] FITZMYER, *Luke I-IX*, 305.

narrative could be classified as a sub-genre of the literary genre of Gospel, a sub-genre in connection with other infancy narratives of its milieu, and with a strong OT background.

1.4 Redaction Criticism

Redaction criticism studies how, why, and when the different pre-existent sources or traditions were combined by the author in the structure of his final redaction. From the discoveries of the form critics who posed the question of the theological and literary creativitity of the early Church, we pass on to the discoveries of the redaction critics who pose the question of the theological and literary creativitity of the final author. I will first review redaction-critical studies of Luke 1–2, and then I will consider the redaction criticism of Luke 1–2 within the whole Lukan work.

1.4.1 Redaction Criticism within the Lukan Infancy Narrative

First I will summarize the main proposals concerning the possible insertions made by the final author. Then I will study the importance of the editorial work of Luke in his first two chapters.

a) The Possible Insertions

Muñoz Iglesias posits that the whole infancy narrative came to Luke from an early unique Jewish-Christian source written in Hebrew and composed of prose sections and hymns. According to Muñoz Iglesias, the editorial work by Luke is limited to the translation into Greek and a few adjustments.[99]

Those scholars who propose a plurality of sources have proposed many different theories of consecutive additions by the different sources or by Luke. Schweizer posits a Baptist source, with two hymns from the Jerusalem priestly tradition, the *Benedictus* and the *Magnificat*, and a Jesus source, which were joined before Luke's editing.[100] Neirynck suggests that Luke received the Bap-

---

[99] MUÑOZ IGLESIAS, *Los Evangelios de la Infancia* I, 315-318.
[100] SCHWEIZER, "Zum Aufbau", 309-335.

tist source and added traditions about Jesus so as to Christianize it.[101] Brown's claim is that the story in Lk 2:41-52 seems to have been appended late in the process of composing the infancy narrative.[102] Sánchez Mielgo, concurring with Brown, holds that the first redaction finished with the conclusion of v. 40. When Luke added a pre-existent source regarding the twelve-year-old Jesus in the Temple, he had to add a second conclusion (v. 52).[103]

There are many scholars who claim the opinion that only the hymns have been added to a pre-existent narrative. Brown and Fitzmyer agree, affirming that most of the infancy narrative was freely composed by Luke on the basis of pre-Lukan information, but there was a Jewish-Christian source for the hymns. The absence of a tight connection between the *Magnificat* and its context, and the *Benedictus* and its context, might suggest that at least these passages were added at a later date than the rest. These hymns would have been the longest "prefabricated" elements Luke added to increase the Jewish background.[104]

The situation of the *Nunc Dimittis* is a little different. Like the other hymns, Simeon's hymn has been interpreted as a later insertion. Luke would have added it in his last redaction, when he had already written the rest of the passage.[105] However, the *Nunc Dimittis* has been interpreted as a Lukan composition by Grelot, who maintains that it was a later Lukan composition skillfully introduced into the passage of the Presentation in the Temple. Luke inserted it into the infancy chapters during the last editorial stage, to announce the program of Luke's double work.[106]

---

[101] NEIRYNCK, *L'Evangile de Noël*, 10-11, contends that Luke added the hymns after he added the Jesus tradition to the Baptist source.

[102] See BROWN, *Birth*, 247.

[103] SÁNCHEZ MIELGO, "¿Historia?", 138.

[104] See BROWN, *Birth*, 622; and FITZMYER, *Luke I-IX*, 309.

[105] Brown's first edition claims that Luke added the *Nunc Dimittis* later, when he added the other hymns that came from a specific source: the *Magnificat*, the *Benedictus* and the *Gloria* (BROWN, *Birth*, 426-427; 434-436). However, Brown slightly modified his opininion in his second edition, where he is more open to the Lukan authorship of the *Nunc Dimittis* (BROWN, *Birth*, 622).

[106] See GRELOT, "Le Cantique de Siméon", 481.505-506.VALENTINI, "I cantici in

There is no agreement among the scholars on the possible insertions throughout Luke 1–2. It is not possible for us to be certain about the insertions of pre-Lukan material and the reasons why they were added. On the one hand, scholars, following Brown, in his first edition, and Fitzmyer, defend the thesis that the hymns were added from an independent source in a second Lukan redaction. However, following Grelot, and Brown in his last edition, I think that only the *Magnificat* and *Benedictus* come from a different source to increase the Jewish background. On the other hand, it is likely that the passage about the twelve-year-old Jesus in the Temple (Lk 2:41-52) was added later to fill the lack of passages on Jesus' adolescence, according to the Hellenistic biographical genre.

b) Luke, not Only Compilator, but Author

The infancy narrative, even though dependent on a few prior sources, has become an integral part of the Lukan Gospel, and the scholars affirm that Luke was its author.[107] However, because of the Semitic character of the language and the use of OT models in the composition of Luke 1–2, a number of scholars at the end of the 19th century called into question the Lukan authorship of these two chapters.[108] Plummer reacted in the year 1908, dedicating 30 dense pages in the introduction to his commentary to the coincidence of vocabulary, grammatical constructions, and stylistic mannerisms between Luke 1–2 and the rest of the Lukan work. At the end of these pages he concludes: "The vocabulary, Luke's style and diction run

---

Lc 1–2", 81-108, follows Grelot. If the prose narration and the hymn of *Nunc Dimittis* are Lukan compositions, I believe it is very difficult to distinguish a later insertion by the same author, especially when the possible insertion fits well with its context.

[107] "It is most likely," says Fitzmyer, "to be ascribed to Lukan composition, based at times on some information that may have been available. To admit such sources, however, does not mean that Luke has not reworked them in his own style" (FITZMYER, *Luke I-IX*, 309). BERLINGIERI, *Il lieto annuncio*, 42-44, and FREED, *The Stories of Jesus' Birth*, 155-159, follow Fitzmyer.

[108] For example, WELLHAUSEN, *Das Evangelium Lucae*, began his commentary on Luke's Gospel by Lk 3:1. Other examples of this rejection of the Lukan authorship of Luke 1–2 are HILLMANN, "Die Kindheitsgeschichte Jesu", 192-261, and UNSNER, "Geburt und Kindheit Christi", 1-21.

through our Gospel from end to end. In the first two chapters they are perhaps somewhat more frequent than elsewhere."[109] A bit later, in 1954, Conzelmann reopened the debate over the authenticity of Luke 1–2 stressing that the authenticity of these first two chapters is questionable; according to him Luke 1–2 is an alien body of disparate traditions which contradicts the Evangelist's conception of redemption history.[110] However, the reaction to Conzelmann was swift in affirming that in Luke 1–2 we find the Lukan features of his entire literary work in his vocabulary and his style.

The vocabulary of Luke 1–2 is Lukan vocabulary. The detailed examination of the vocabulary by Morgenthaler clearly demonstrates that the author of Luke 1–2 is consistent with the vocabulary of the rest of the Gospel (Luke 3–24), and Acts. According to Morgenthaler, in Luke 1–2 we find 46 out of the 62 favorite words of Luke.[111] Minear raised the number of Lukanisms in Luke 1–2 to 55.[112]

The Lukan authorship and his important editorial work result in the unity of style and composition techniques within the entire literary work. The style of Luke 1–2 is consistent with the style of the rest of the Lukan work.[113] Scholars have given two main examples.

The first example is the composition of the narrative through pairs of characters, one male and one female. In Luke 1–2 we find Zechariah and Elizabeth (1:5-25), Joseph and Mary (2:1-20), and

---

[109] PLUMMER, *St. Luke*, xli-lxx.

[110] CONZELMANN, *Die Mitte der Zeit*, 160. On a synthesis of the arguments against the unity of Luke 1–2 with the rest of the Lukan work see MATHER, "The Search", 132-134.

[111] See MORGENTHALER, *Statistik des neutestamentlichen Wortschatzes*, 52.

[112] See MINEAR, "Birth Stories", 113; and BENOÎT, "Les récits évangéliques", 63-94, who affirms the "numerous Lukanisms" within Luke 1–2.

[113] MORGENTHALER, *Geschichtsschreibung* I, 16-133, highlights that the birth stories reflect the same stylistic phenomena as the entire corpus: doubling of words, sentences and sections (the cognate words for emphasis, the matching of sounds and forms of alliteration, the tautologies, the antitheses, the chiastic structures, the parallel sentences, the double citation formulas, and the parallel sections). MINEAR, "Birth Stories", 115-118, finds homogeneity in the use of speeches, and citations, common ecclesiological conceptions, and the reliance upon epiphany and angels.

Simeon and Anna (2:22-39). In the rest of the Lukan work we find the healing of a Centurion's slave and a widow whose son was cured (7:1-17), the Pharisee Simeon and the anonymous sinner (7:36-50), the healing of the Gerasene demoniac and the resurrection of the dead girl (8:26-56), the woman bent over and the leader of the synagogue (13:10-17), the man planting mustard seeds and the woman leavening dough (13:18-21), the parable of the lost sheep, which deals with traditionally masculine activity, and the lost coin parable, which highlights a woman and her world (15:4-10), the wicked judge and the importunate widow (18:1-8).[114]

The second example is the composition of the narration through the parallelism between two characters. The parallelism between the conception, birth, circumcision, and naming of John the Baptist and Jesus, a Lukan parallelism, evokes other parallelisms in the rest of the Lukan work.[115] Mather stresses the John the Baptist-Jesus parallelism by detecting it throughout the entire Gospel (3:1-20.23-25; 4:16-30; 7:31-35).[116] And Berlingieri emphasizes the parallelism Peter-Paul in Acts.[117]

There is consensus among the scholars that the vocabulary and style show that Luke is the redactor and author of Luke 1–2. It is a Lukan composition based on different authoritative sources; however, his editorial work is much more important than the source he could have received, which becomes almost unrecognizable and unrecoverable. Legrand and Mount affirm that this is one of the few points in which the scholarship arrives at a certain convergence.[118]

---

[114] Six of these nine examples are present only in Luke's Gospels (1:5-25; 2:1-20; 7:36-50; 13:10-17; 15:4-10; 18:1-8). FLANAGAN, "The Position of Women", 292-293, finds not only nine, but thirteen man-woman parallel stories in Luke's Gospel. In Acts we can add the examples of Ananias and Sapphira (Acts 5,1-11), and of Peter's healing of a paralytic and a woman (Acts 9:32-43). On the man-woman passages in Luke-Acts see FLENDER, *Heil und Geschichte*, 15-16.

[115] On the John-Jesus parallelism throughout Luke 1–2 see § IV.1.1.

[116] See MATHER, "The Search", 123-140.

[117] BERLINGIERI, *Il lieto annuncio*, 71-72. On the parallelism Jesus-Paul see § V.3.2.2.a.

[118] See LEGRAND, *L'Annonce à Marie*, 29; and MOUNT, "Jesus in Luke 1-2", 41-46.

1.4.2 Redaction Criticism within the Entire Lukan Work

The redaction history of the whole Lukan work has been discussed by the scholars who also achieve a general agreement in the following ideas.

a) Lack of References to the Infancy of Jesus in the First Preaching

According to Brown and Fitzmyer, fragments of the early kerygma have been preserved in 1 Co 15:3-4; Rm 1:3-4; 1 Th 1:9-10, and possibly also in Acts 2:23-24.32.36; 3:14-15; 4:10; 10:39-40. The infancy narrative materials were never part of the early kerygma or teaching itself.[119] In a pre-Gospel period, as attested by Paul and the sermons in Acts, the resurrection was the chief moment associated with the divine proclamation of the identity of Jesus, and his infancy was not part of this proclamation. Also, in the summary of Jesus' life (Acts 10:37-43) and when Peter demands that they appoint as the twelfth apostle one "out of the men who have been with us [...] from the time when John was baptizing until the day when he was taken up from us" (Acts 1:21-22), there is no mention to Jesus' childhood. In addition, Mk 3:21 and 6:1-6 insinuate that there have not been major revelations about Jesus' infancy and family.

b) The Beginning of Mark's Gospel and the Solemn Beginning of Luke 3

The Markan Gospel has no sequence about the birth and childhood of Jesus. Mark begins his Gospel with the declarative statement, "The beginning of the good news of Jesus Christ, the

---

[119] See BROWN, *Birth*, 26; and FITZMYER, *Luke I-IX*, 305-306. The only exception might involve the indirect relation to Jesus being the Son of God, descended from David, and related to the Holy Spirit in Rm 1:3 (see LEGRAND, *L'Annonce à Marie*). According to Fitzmyer, this identification of Jesus in Romans is made *a propos* of the resurrection. Fitzmyer stresses that the infancy narrative materials were not really part of the "Gospel" in the theological sense, as Paul would have meant when he spoke of "my Gospel" (Rm 2:16) or "the Gospel of God" (Rm 1:1; 15:16). The only mention of the actual birth of Jesus is Ga 4:4, which says only that Jesus was "born of a woman, born a subject of the Law."

Son of God" (Mk 1:1), and immediately starts his account with the ministry of John the Baptist. Mark tells the reader nothing about Jesus' birth or youth, not even the name of Joseph.[120]

The solemn beginning of Luke 3 has captured the attention of scholars. Brown tells us that historiographical parallels in other Greek writing suggest that Lk 3:1-2 could well have served as the original opening of the Lukan Gospel.[121] The placing of the genealogy in the third chapter of Luke makes more sense if that had been done before an infancy narrative had been written. As Fitzmyer suggests, it seems that Lk 3:1-2 was at one time a formal introduction to the work. In fact, Lk 3:1-2 resembles the prologue (Lk 1:1-4), even though it is not as perfectly composed in a periodic sentence. In introducing the ministry of John the Baptist, it seems that the Lukan Gospel once began at the point at which the Markan Gospel now begins. Moreover, the position of John the Baptist in Luke 3 explains the peculiar Lukan emphasis on a *beginning* associated with the baptism-preaching of John. In fact, all the main characters of Luke-Acts, Jesus (Lk 7:26-27), Peter (Acts 1:22; 10:37), and Paul (Acts 13:24-25), in crucial moments of the narrative and with formulations from the early stage of the tradition, refer to the preaching of John the Baptist as the formal beginning of the story.[122] Lk 3:1 likely began the Gospel according to the first Christian preaching and with the Baptist's proclamation in the traditional sense of the beginning of Mark.[123]

---

[120] John's Gospel prefixes a hymnic prologue to the story of the Baptist's ministry (Jn 1:1-18), and begins the story with John the Baptist's testimony about Jesus (Jn 1:19-34). John the evangelist also does not tell the reader anything about Jesus' birth, not even the name of his mother, Mary.

[121] See BROWN, *Birth*, 240.

[122] On this beginning associated with John's preaching see FITZMYER, *Luke I-IX*, 305-307.311. The fact that Luke did not follow the traditional beginning of the story with John's preaching (Mk 1:1-8; see also Acts 1:21; 10:38; 13:25) represents a deliberate departure which suggests that Luke did not compose his infancy narrative solely on the basis of the kerigmatic preaching, but he had reliance on other traditions whose authority would explain Luke's decision to tolerate this dissonance of the new beginning.

[123] See BOVON, *Lukas* I, 45.

c) Were there Different Beginnings of Luke's Gospel?

Scholarship, recognizing these findings, has asked whether or not Luke 1–2 is a later addition to the Lukan work.[124] Did Luke begin writing with the birth stories, or with the account of the ministry, or with the passion narrative? According to Brown and Fitzmyer, the first stage in development would have been a passion narrative, the kerygma, to which an account of Jesus' ministry, constructed out of early Christian teaching and based on recollections of what Jesus did and taught, was eventually prefixed. Jesus' deeds and words were particularly useful as further teaching for those who had come to faith through the proclamation of Jesus' death and resurrection. Collections of sayings, parables, and miracles grew, and the evangelists drew upon these in composing accounts of the ministry of Jesus.[125] Then, at a still later stage, the resurrection appearance and infancy narrative were added.[126]

---

[124] We have two textual witnesses that could make us suspicious about a possible beginning of Luke's Gospel without the infancy narrative: the "Gospel" of Marcion and the commentary of Ephraem of Syria on Tatian's *Diatessaron*. On the one hand, Tertullian says that the "Gospel" of Marcion began with the descent of Jesus from Nazareth into Capharnaum, Lk 4:30-32, (TERTULLIAN, *Contre Marcion IV*, 7,1). Did Marcion delete the infancy narrative because of its "objectionable" OT language or did he receive a Gospel that had no Luke 1–2? (see KNOX, *Marcion and the New Testament*, 77-113, which is the chapter on Marcion's "Gospel" and the Gospel of Luke, especially pp. 84-86). On the other hand, the Armenian translation of the commentary of Ephraem of Syria on Tatian's *Diatessaron* (§ 2-6), also regards Luke 1:5–2:52 as a later insert into the Lukan Gospel (see CONYBEARE, "Fehlen von c. 1 und 2", 192-197). According to Ephraem Luke begins his Gospel with John's preaching (Luke 3) in contrast with another Gospel, perhaps Matthew's Gospel, which begins with Abraham. Because of these textual witnesses, scholars of the 19th century already had thought of an earlier form of Luke's Gospel without Luke 1–2 (see ZELLER, "Die Überlieferung", 528-572). If Luke 1–2 was indeed added later, it was quickly added because there are no known manuscripts of Luke's Gospel without the birth narrative, and because the Muratorian fragment affirms in line 8: "Luke began his story from the birth of John."

[125] It is noteworthy that the first written Gospel, Mark, contains a smaller body of teaching than do Matthew and Luke.

[126] If one prescinds from its appendix (Mk 16:9-20), not found in the best Greek manuscripts, Mark, the earliest Gospel to attain shape, lacked both an infancy narrative and resurrection appearances; it is similar, in fact, in structure to the

According to Cullmann, the reader, in picking up the Lukan Gospel, is first confronted with the infancy narrative and might not be aware that this maybe represents the latest part of the Gospel tradition to take shape.[127] None of the Lukan infancy narrative has had a major influence on the body of the Gospel, so that, if the first two chapters had been lost, we could not have suspected their existence.[128] And Brown not only affirms that "the stories of the ministry were shaped in Christian tradition without a knowledge of the infancy material,"[129] but also demonstrates the dependence of the infancy narrative on Acts.[130] All of these data suggest that Luke composed the infancy narrative after having already composed the rest of his Gospel and Acts. Even if the infancy narrative was pre-

---

summary of Jesus' career in Acts 10:36-41. See BROWN, *Birth*, 26; FITZMYER, *Luke I-IX*, I, 306. The understanding of Jesus' identity goes back to Jesus' baptism in Mark, to Jesus' conception and birth in Matthew and Luke, and to Jesus' preexistence in Jn.

[127] CULLMANN, "Infancy Gospels", 363.

[128] Only Jesus is important in the rest of the Lukan work. Neither Gabriel, nor Zechariah, nor Elizabeth, nor Simeon, nor Anna appear again. Joseph appears only in Lk 3:23, and Lk 4:22 as a reference to Jesus' father. Only in Lk 8:19-21, and Acts 1:14 does Mary appear as a reference to Jesus' Mother. John the Baptist appears more often (Lk 3:2.15-20; 5:33; 7:18-33; 9:7-9.19; 11:1; 16:16; 20:4-6; Acts 1:5.22; 10:37; 11:16; 13:24-25; 18:25; 19:3-4) but we cannot say that he is an important character of the narrative because his references depend on the beginning of Jesus' preaching.

[129] BROWN, *Birth*, 27. The evangelists, claims Brown, never really smoothed out all the narrative rough spots left by the joining of two bodies of once-independent material, even though in their own minds they presumably would have reconciled the different theologies therein contained.

[130] According to BROWN, *Birth*, 242-243, there is a foreshadowing in the infancy narrative of things to come in the rest of Luke-Acts, but it is there because the infancy narrative has been composed with hindsight. BOVON, *Lukas* I, 46, highlights the similar structure of Lk 1:5-80 and Cornelius' story (Acts 10–11): a) a non-Christian just man receives a divine message (Lk 1:5-25; Acts 10:1-8); b) a Christian person receives another divine message somewhat later (Lk 1:26-38; Acts 10:9-23); c) the meeting between both characters and the Christian kerygma (Lk 1:39-56; Acts 10:24-43); and d) fulfillment of the previously announced happening and its consequences (Lk 1:57-80; Acts 10:44–11:18). The dependence of the infancy narrative on Acts is defended as well by HOOKER, *Beginnings*, 43-48; MINEAR, "Birth Stories", 111-130; BUSSE, "Das 'Evangelium' des Lukas", 161-177; and RESENHÖFFT, *Die Apostelgeschichte*, 28-46. See § 1.5.1 as well.

fixed after the Gospel and Acts had been completed, this reverse order of composition raises no doubt that it was Luke himself who prefixed it. There is consensus therefore regarding the Lukan authorship.[131]

Finally, four main reasons for this possible later insertion have been conjectured by scholars:[132] (1) Christological motives: the interest in the earlier stages of Jesus' life could be provoked by the question: Did Jesus only become God's Son or Christ at his resurrection? The Christological motives were operative in the retrojection of the identity of Jesus as the Son of God, Lord, and Messiah from the time of his resurrection to his very birth and conception (Lk 1:32-35; 2:11), or even to his pre-existence (Jn 1:1-3).[133] (2) Missionary motives: the increase of Gentile converts brought with it the likelihood of misunderstanding. The early Christians interacted creatively with the wider culture in an attempt to proclaim Christ in his own terms by means of the infancy of the main character of the literary work. By composing the birth narrative of Jesus, Luke has thus completed the adaptation of the Jesus tradition to the requirements of the Hellenistic biographical genre.[134] (3) Chronological motives: Luke could have later had at his disposal information about Jesus' infancy that he wanted to add to his

---

[131] It is true that a belief in the Lukan authorship of Luke 1–2 rejects a much later composition of these first two chapters. I believe that Luke himself could have written his infancy narrative as an introduction shortly after he had written the rest of his literary work. In fact, many authors write their introduction when they already know what they want to introduce, their full composition. This likely later addition does not mean that the form and content of Luke 1–2 were derived only from the model of apostolic preaching of Acts, nor that Luke did not use sources for his infancy narrative.

[132] See BOXALL, "Christ in the Gospels", 455-459.

[133] Fitzmyer affirms: "The moments at which the christological affirmations were made were gradually pushed further and further back in Jesus' existence, as reflection on him and his relation to *Yhwh* continued to develop" (FITZMYER, *Luke I-IX*, 447).

[134] Gerber thinks that Luke's infancy narrative gives a soteriological value to Jesus' infancy, thereby trying to avoid the "scandal" or "madness" that a crucified Messiah could represent for the Gentiles. According to Gerber, Luke preferred to present to the pagans the light of Bethlehem, rather than the darkness of Golgotha (GERBER, *"Il vous est né un Sauveur"*, 27).

Gospel. And (4) motives of curiosity: the second and third generation of Christians, who had not known Jesus, became curious about the personal life of Jesus, even about his infancy.[135] I believe that these reasons do not oppose each other, and taken together could be responsible for this later insertion.

1.5 Narrative Analysis

With the remarks about redaction criticism we have moved into the present stage of scholarly research: the quest for the purpose of the passage and the evangelist's intent.[136] In recent years attention has shifted away from the pre-Gospel history of narratives, to the role of those narratives in the final form of the Gospel. Scholarship has moved from historical criticism into literary criticism.[137] Lukan studies were largely absorbed with the

---

[135] As time progressed, interest grew in the earlier stages of Jesus' life. Natural curiosity wished to learn something of that part of the life of Jesus and to fill that gap of his life. The last step of this desire for knowledge is the apocryphal gospels. On the *Protoevangelium Iacobi*, the *Evangelium Pseudo-Thomae de infantia Salvatoris*, and extracts from *Evangelium infantiae salvatoris arabicum*, which were written to satisfy this popular curiosity about the missing years of Jesus' life, see CULLMANN, "Infancy Gospels", 364-369. I believe that Christological motivations, Jesus' affinity with God's will and with the OT, were more important in the canoncial infancy narratives than in the apocryphal infancy narratives, where curiosity became predominant, although theological interests are still present. For the NT Apocryphal literature I use the bilingual edition by A. Santos Otero.

[136] The development of narrative criticism is one aspect of a larger movement involving application of modern literary theory to Biblical studies. For a survey of this movement see POWELL, *The Bible*. The narrative studies of Luke-Acts have been influenced by work done on the other gospels. On Mark's Gospel see KERMODE, *The Genesis of Secrecy*; and RHOADS, *Mark as Story*. On Matthew's Gospel see KINGSBURY, *Matthew as Story*. On John's Gospel see CULPEPPER, *Anatomy of the Fourth Gospel*. The main narrative studies on Luke's literary work are: ALETTI, *L'art*; TANNEHILL, *Narrative Unity*; KURZ, *Reading Luke-Acts*, and specifically in the infancy narrativies GUEURET, *L'engendrement*; and COLERIDGE, *The Birth*. Finally, GROS LOUIS and RYAN have written several articles on the Lukan infancy narrative (GROS LOUIS, "Different Ways", 33-40; GROS LOUIS, "The Jesus Birth Stories", 273-284; and RYAN, "Luke's Infancy Narrative", 340-344).

[137] Redaction criticism, being part of historical criticism, considers the text through time, the history of the formation of the current text, its sources (diachronic methodology). Narrative analysis, being part of literary criticism, examines the text

question of Luke as historian and the closely related question of sources. With the rise of redaction criticism and narrative criticism, the focus has shifted more to questions about the theological thrust and temper of Luke.

The question of the passage's function and the evangelist's intent has been tackled using two slightly different perspectives, namely redaction criticism and narrative criticism. In the way that narrative criticism seeks to trace the creative work of the evangelist (understood as more than the arranger of received materials), narrative criticism aligns itself with redaction criticism. But where redaction criticism seeks to trace the work of the evangelist primarily as theologian, narrative criticism is more concerned with the disposition of the whole literary work and the value of the evangelist as an artist.[138] This is not to say that it ignores the theological question. It simply approaches it differently.[139] In addition, narrative criticism does not examine the pericopes in isolation, but in relation to the whole of Luke-Acts. Events, characters, and themes of one part of the literary work shed light on another part. Therefore the text is not regarded as an isolated element but as an operative member of the total narrative.[140]

1.5.1 The Infancy Narrative: the Overture to Luke-Acts

The most famous modern analyst of Lukan theology, Hans Conzelmann, never spoke about narrative criticism. He does, however, study the theology of Luke throughout the entire narrative of

---

looking for the unity, relationship, and simultaneity of its parts (synchronic methodology). Once concerned with the situation that gave birth to a certain text, scholars are now more interested in the response which a narrative elicits from a reader who has to understand the text's guidelines.

[138] On the artistic value of the relationship between poetic hymns and prose in Luke 1–2 see FLICHY, "Quand le récit se fait poésie", 389-406.

[139] In his commentary on the Acts of the Apostles, Ernst Haenchen suggests that if Lukan scholarship has in recent times been concerned with studying Luke first as historian and then as theologian, then perhaps the time is ripe for the study of Luke as writer (HAENCHEN, *Die Apostelgeschichte*, 102).

[140] See DAWSEY, "The Literary Unity", 49; TANNEHILL, *Narrative Unity* I, 3.

Luke's Gospel. In presenting the theology of Luke, Conzelmann does not draw upon the infancy narrative. To him, Luke 1–2 is not Lukan, and preserves a theology different from and contrary to the rest of Luke-Acts. Therefore, according to Conzelmann, Luke 1–2 is not relevant for the reconstruction of the characteristically Lukan theology.[141]

However, Plato is right in stating that the beginning is the chief thing in any process.[142] According to Aristotle, a preamble or introduction should give the readers an indication of what the literary work will be about so that they do not remain ignorant and become confused. One who "puts the beginning in their hands makes it possible for them to follow the literary work."[143] In more recent times and with specific reference to narrative, Perry has described in detail what he calls *the primary effect* in literary texts, which suggests that that material placed early in the narrative takes on special importance.[144] The exceptional and enduring importance of the narrative's opening establishes the ground rules of the rhetorical transaction between the author and the reader.[145] Readers need to orient at the beginning of a narrative. The perspective established there will continue to influence their understanding of characters until they are told something that indicates a change or requires them to change their opinion of them. This suggests that the question of which elements a narrator chooses to introduce in the opening scene of a narrative is neither trivial nor preliminary. This is the reason why scholars pay special attention to the way in which every single evangelist goes straight into his subject. Moloney, Hooker, and Kilgallen have written three different books on the beginnings of the four gospels as

---

[141] See CONZELMANN, *Die Mitte der Zeit*, 160-161.

[142] PLATO, *Resp.*, 2.377b.

[143] ARISTOTLE, *Rhet.*, 3.14.5-6 (1415a).

[144] PERRY, "Literary Dynamics", 35-63; 311-361.

[145] DRURY, *Tradition and Design*, 46, claims that the beginning of a book is a good index of its character because the author makes his initial, and therefore crucial, bid for attention, contriving to hook his audience. On Luke using his first two chapters to present his principal theme and capture the attention of his public see DANKER, "St. Luke for a New Millennium", 6.

keys that open each respective Gospel; in particular, the way in which beginnings can help the reader to make sense of what follows.[146] Hooker affirms: "Luke, the literary man, surely knew the importance of beginnings, and he made the most of them."[147]

Introducing his book *The Birth of the Messiah*, Brown affirms: "It is the central contention of this volume that the infancy narratives are worthy vehicles of the Gospel message; indeed, each is the essential Gospel story in miniature."[148] This direct connection between Luke 1–2 and the whole Lukan work has been proved by Brown through the parallelism between the two transitional sections (Luke 1–2 and Acts 1–2) of the two parts of his work, Luke's Gospel and Acts of the Apostles.[149] Brown demonstrates that the infancy narrative is closer in spirit to the stories in Acts than to the Gospel material which Luke took from Mark and Q.[150]

---

[146] MOLONEY, *Beginning the Good News*; HOOKER, *Beginnings*; and KILGALLEN, *Wealth of Revelation*. Although the article by LÉTOURNEAU, "Commencer un Évangile", 326-339, deals especially with the prologue (Lk 1:1-4), it deals as well with the Lukan infancy narrative as starting point of the Lukan literary work.

[147] HOOKER, *Beginnings*, xiii.

[148] BROWN, *Birth*, 7. He contends that to give to the infancy narratives less value than other parts of the gospels is to misread the minds of the evangelists, for whom the infancy narratives were fitting vehicles for a message they wanted to convey. Radl asserts that "Luke 1:5–2:52 is the Gospel before the Gospel" (RADL, "Die Beziehungen", 302-308).

[149] BROWN, "Luke's Method", 138, believes that Luke 1–2 and Acts 1–2 play the same bridging function. Luke 1–2 unites the OT with the rest of the story of Jesus, just as Acts 1–2 unites Jesus' life with his followers' lives.

[150] BROWN, *Birth*, 243, gives his reasons (the numbering is mine):

> (1) The outpouring of the prophetic spirit which moves people to act and speak (Lk 1:15.41.67.80; 2:25-27) is not well attested in the ministry, but very closely resembles the pentecostal outpouring of the prophetic spirit in Acts 2:17. (2) The speeches of Acts and the hymns of the infancy narrative are both compositions reflecting older material, but compositions which convey the tonality of the character to whom they are attributed. (3) The angelic appearances which are frequent in the infancy narrative (Lk 1:11.26; 2:9) have little parallel in the ministry of Jesus, but close parallels in Acts (5:19; 8:26; 10:3; 12:7; 27:23). (4) The title "Messiah Lord" (χριστὸς κύριος), given by the angels to the infant Jesus in Lk 2:11, echoes the christology of the post-resurrectional speeches in Acts (2:36: κύριος χριστός).

Moreover, Borg and Crossan claim that three important themes surface in Luke's infancy narrative as microcosm to his literary work as macrocosm: his emphasis on women, the marginalized, and the Holy Spirit.[151] Hooker states that the Holy Spirit, present in the majority of the passages of Luke 1–2, is the key for understanding the Lukan work because Luke wants to stress, above all, that the Holy Spirit is at work in Jesus and in the mission of his followers.[152] Schubert insists that the nativity story presents the *proof-from-prophecy theology* which dominates Luke-Acts.[153] Busse argues that the long development of John the Baptist's character in Luke 1–2 corresponds to the emphasis in Acts 1:22; 10:37; 13:24 that Jesus' proclamation of the good news has begun with the baptizing by John.[154]

Furthermore, Coleridge thinks that the first two chapters of the third Gospel set the Lukan narrative in motion and lay the ground for all that follows by articulating in narrative form a vision of the *divine visitation*. Coleridge believes that the concept of visitation which appears in Lk 1:68.78, the visitation by God of his people, appears again and again in Luke's Gospel (Lk 7:16; 19:44) and is its key term.[155] Gerber thinks that the four hymns of Luke 1–2 are a perfect introduction to the entire Lukan work.[156] Cavalletti believes that the infancy narrative announces the main topic of Luke's work,

---

[151] These scholars compare these themes, on one hand in Matthew 1–2 and in Luke 1–2, and in the other hand in the rest of the Matthean and Lukan work. After this comparison they prove that these emphases in Luke 1–2 introduce the same emphasis in Luke-Acts (BORG – CROSSAN, *The First Christmas*, 46-52).

[152] HOOKER, *Beginnings*, 43-48.

[153] In these stories SCHUBERT, "Structure and Significance", 178-179, observes that no fewer than eight prophets speak successively concerning the redemption of Jerusalem, which is fulfilled in the Lukan work.

[154] BUSSE, "Das 'Evangelium' des Lukas", 161-177, points out too that the heavy OT echoes (Abraham, David, Sarah, Hanna, and Samuel) in Luke 1–2 correspond to the program laid out by Jesus for himself and the Christian preachers in Lk 24:27.

[155] COLERIDGE, *The Birth*, 22-27, claims that the notion of *divine visitation* is the general rubric of which other notions such as salvation or peace are specifications.

[156] GERBER, "Quatre hymnes", 353-367; GERBER, "Ton salut que tu as préparé", 93-97.

the resurrection.[157] And Shuler and Segalia contend that Luke has structured the first two chapters in order to prepare his reader for the portrait of the adult Jesus, especially his death.[158]

The literary importance of beginnings and these connections between Luke 1–2 and the rest of Luke's work, show us that there are not only vocabulary and stylistic connections between these chapters and Luke-Acts, but there are also significant themes that introduce the Lukan work. According to Lane, Luke deliberately wrote Luke 1–2 in such a way as to prepare for the rest of the Lukan work. Luke 1–2 not only lays the groundwork for the rest of the Lukan work, but does so consciously.[159] Responding to Conzelmann's exclusion of the infancy narrative in his theological study of Luke, I say that the scholarship agrees in affirming that Luke 1–2 is a prologue to the Lukan work because it presents the entire literary work.[160] Oliver,[161] Thomas,[162] Busse,[163] and Tatum,[164] working indepently, argue that the infancy narrative, presenting the main topics of the en-

---

[157] C. CAVALLETTI, "Il metodo derashico", 12-14, emphasizes that, just as a woman, Mary, receives the announcement of the Incarnation, other women receive the announcement of the resurrection (Lk 24:1-22). As the shepherds go to Bethlehem looking for Jesus, so the women go to the tomb looking for Jesus (Lk 24:3). As the shepherds receive the announcement of the angel, the women receive the announcement of the angel (Lk 24:5.23). As the shepherds are amazed because of what the shepherds say, so Peter is amazed because of what the women say (Lk 24:12). Finally, both announcements need to be transmitted (Lk 2:17; 24:9).

[158] SHULER, "Rhetorical Character", 173-185; SEGALIA, "L'Ombra della Croce", 39-45.

[159] LANE, *Gentile Mission*, 19.

[160] Coleridge claims that the Lukan narrative confirms the truth of the affirmation: "the child is the father of the man" (COLERIDGE, *The Birth*, 234). Luke 1–2 is the child who is going to develop into a man throughout the whole Lukan narrative; at the same time this passage is father to the rest of Luke-Acts because it is the origin from which everything is developed. Lk 1:1-4 and Lk 1:5-2:52 differ in style but share one aim, namely, that of preparing the reader for the narrative that follows.

[161] OLIVER, "The Lucan Birth Stories", 202-226.

[162] THOMAS, "The Infancy Narrative", 295.

[163] BUSSE, "Das 'Evangelium' des Lukas", 161-177, argues not only by means of the topics, but with the syntax and vocabulary as well.

[164] See TATUM, "Epoch of Israel", 184-185.

tire work, is important for Luke's literary project, and it allows the reader to better understand the theology of Luke-Acts. I contend that the two first chapters of Luke affect the way we read the text and, even more, that the non-use of these two chapters has led to a misinterpretation of the whole Lukan composition.[165]

Although the importance of Luke 1–2 as the key for reading his work is accepted by present-day scholars, there are discrepancies in the nomenclature. What is the correct way to designate the relationship between Luke 1–2 and the rest of the Lukan work? Hooker affirms that Luke 1–2 is a *prologue*, which in a sense stands apart from what follows,[166] and yet is an essential part of the book.[167] However, Sánchez Mielgo rejects calling it a prologue because it is much more closely linked to the Gospel than the Johannine hymn to John's Gospel, while that hymn is called *prologue* by scholars (Jn 1:1-18).[168] Rodger, noting the theological character of the infancy narrative, affirms that the infancy stories of Jesus become "more than simply prologue" to the accounts of Jesus' words and deeds.[169]

Tyson thinks rather of a *prologue to the Greek drama*, where there is action and often an introduction of the characters that will be featured.[170] Along the same lines we find the recent book by D'Agostino,[171] who proposes that the articulation of the dialogues,

---

[165] MINEAR, "Birth Stories", 111, says: "Conzelmann bases his analysis of Luke's theology not on the whole corpus, but on the chapters of the Gospel beginning with Luke 3. If he had taken full account of the nativity stories, I believe his position would have been changed at several major points." See as well SCOTT, "The Birth of the Reader", 83.

[166] HOOKER, *Beginnings*, xiii. The same idea is shared by LANE, *Gentile Mission*, 29. Indeed, sometimes there is a disjunction between the prologue and the body of the play because the prologue deals with what happened before the time of the play.

[167] MARGUERAT – BOURQUIN, *Récits bibliques*, 159, claim that Luke 1–2 is a *prologue* which orientates the reading through guiding the reader. It is an instrument at the disposition of the narrator to indicate *why and how* one must read the text with the intention of the one who conceived it.

[168] SÁNCHEZ MIELGO, "¿Historia?", 106.

[169] RODGER, "Child as a Metaphor", 58-59.

[170] TYSON, "Birth Narratives", 114-120.

[171] D'AGOSTINO, *L'annuncio come rappresentazione*.

the economy of the spaces, the division of the narrative into episodes divided into scenes, and the dialectics between the individual and choral groups, connect Luke 1–2 with the Greek theater mechanism, functioning like a prologue to the Greek drama.

Finally, Boxall claims that Luke 1–2 are like a *trailer* of a movie in which key scenes and characters from the forthcoming feature are flashed before our eyes.[172] In connection with Boxall's consideration, Schürmann affirms that the infancy narrative is like a pure lake which reflects the entire mountain standing over the lake.[173] All of the different voices yet somehow agree on the proleptic value of the infancy narrative and its importance for understanding Luke-Acts.

If I had to name Luke 1–2, I would follow Fitmyer's nomenclature. According to him, Luke's infancy narrative functions as a sort of *overture* to the Gospel, striking the chords that will be heard again and again in the coming narratives.[174] Tiede agrees with Fitmyer and affirms that "the birth narratives function like an overture to the Gospel, sounding the crucial themes in visions, oracles, and songs, alerting the reader to watch and listen for what is coming."[175] Brown disagrees with this nomenclature, but he does not propose an alternative term.[176] I think that *overture* is the term which best fits

[172] BOXALL, "Christ in the Gospels", 457.

[173] SCHÜRMANN, *Das Lukasevangelium* I, 21.

[174] FITZMYER, *Luke I-IX*, 306; also see BUSSE, "Das 'Evangelium' des Lukas", 161-177.

[175] TIEDE, *Luke*, 39. It would be like the famous repetition of Beethoven's Fifth Symphony, which not only opens the piece in a dramatic fashion but also can be heard clearly, with variation, in all four movements, directing our listening. Borg and Crossan follow Fitzmyer and claim that Luke 1–2 are *parabolic* overtures, a miniature version of the succeeding Lukan work, an opening part that serves as summary, synthesis, metaphor, or symbol of the whole (BORG – CROSSAN, *The First Christmas*, 38-39). LÓPEZ MAULEÓN, "τὸ πνεῦμα", 281.313, and RYAN, "Luke's Infancy Narrative", 340-344, follow Fitzmyer as well.

[176] Brown thinks that overture is not a satisfactory term, for although there are melodies in the overture that are picked up in the body of an opera, there is no action in the overture and most often it is played without presenting the characters of the opera (BROWN, *Birth*, 620).

with the relationship between Luke 1–2 and the rest of the Lukan work. It is part of the entire work, closely linked to the rest, and it is its first meeting with the reader, who is being helped to come into the work through the right clues. The infancy narrative, overture of Luke-Acts, is the focusing agent whose audition introduces and orientates the whole literary work.

1.5.2 The Importance of Places, Times, and Characterization

Gros Louis offers a popular but very perceptive overview of what narrative criticism can contribute to understanding Luke 1–2. Studying the narrative differences between Matthew 1–2 and Luke 1–2, he underlines the different choices of the two narrative styles, offering us two different interpretations of the same reality. Gros Louis highlights the importance of place because characters move from place to place with narrative logic. According to him, the announcement of the conception of John the Baptist is in a public setting, while that of the conception of Jesus is more private. Gros Louis believes Luke's narrative gives much greater attention than Matthew 1–2 to character development and characterization. The greater prominence of women moves it away from male domination. If not female-dominated, Luke's infancy account is at least more balanced in presenting us with the responses and emotions of Elizabeth, Mary, and Anna, as well as those of Zechariah and Simeon. The Lukan characters exclaim, rejoice, marvel, ponder; they are troubled, perplexed, filled with fear.[177]

Coleridge does not compare the two infancy narratives, but studies the Lukan one in depth. He insists on the difference between the sacred sphere (the Temple) and the secular sphere (the house), between the main city (Jerusalem) and the province (Bethlehem), between heaven and earth. Coleridge underlines the omniscience of the narrator, and the fact that the knowledge of the reader is always greater than the knowledge of the characters.[178]

---

[177] See GROS LOUIS, "Different Ways", 37-40; GROS LOUIS, "The Jesus Birth Stories", 273-284.

[178] COLERIDGE, *The Birth*, 214-217.

Moloney analyzes the protagonist, in the first two chapters of Luke's Gospel. Although present from the story of his birth (2:1-21), Jesus is not active until the final episode (2:41-52), where he responds to the action of God (2:49). The study of Moloney shows that the narrative concentrates its attention upon the initiative of God, through his agents, and the response of those whom God visits. In obedience to the command of the angel (1:31), the name *Jesus* is given in 2:21 and used after that moment (2:27.43.52), but all other references to the child born of Mary look to the future. Moloney concludes that God is the prime mover and protagonist throughout the infancy narrative, even though God never appears or speaks. God's ways are made known to human beings through a series of agents and events.[179]

1.6 Rhetorical and Semiotic Analysis

Shuler claims that the parallel structure between John the Baptist and Jesus in Luke 1–2 is the rhetorical technique of comparison; it is a *syncrisis*. Shuler notes that *Parallel Lives* by Plutarch provides numerous examples of the rhetorical use of comparison in Hellenistic biographical introductions.[180]

R. Meynet applies rhetorical analysis to Luke's Gospel.[181] He understands rhetoric only in terms of the *dispositio* or composition of the speech.[182] W. Kurz, however, uses Greek rhetoric to better explain the whole of Luke-Acts. He argues that the art of rhetoric is particularly helpful for understanding the peculiarly Lukan form of christological proof or argument from Scripture that Jesus is the prophesied Christ. According to him, only Luke-Acts follows the commonly known rules of the Hellenistic art of rhetoric in

---

[179] See MOLONEY, *Beginning the Good News*, 101-128. However, I contend that God is presenting Jesus to the reader through the different agents and events.

[180] SHULER, "Rhetorical Character", 177-188, gives numerous examples from ARISTOTLE, *Rhet.*, 1.9.20-25 (1366b), and especially from *Parallel Lives* by PLUTARCH.

[181] MEYNET, *L'Évangile de Luc*.

[182] See MEYNET – MOUNIN, *Quelle est donc cette parole?*, 14-15.

order to prove, from premise to conclusion, that the Christ must suffer and rise and that, therefore, Jesus is the Christ.[183]

Testa puts the semiotic charts, proposed by Greimas' semiotic analysis,[184] into practice for Luke 1–2.[185] I, however, agree with Brown, who thinks that "semiotic hermeneutics are so complex and filled with created jargon that I cannot understand them; sometimes I can understand but do not see that they have added much to what had already been perceived by other methods."[186] This is what happens with some of the semiotic analysis by Laurentin, Gueuret, or Panier.[187]

1.7 Sociological and Feminist Approaches

A sociological approach tries to illuminate the ancient text through an examination of the social context. Prema argues that the infancy narrative is populated by *lowly* and *common* people who have no standing in society, and so are oppressed and marginalized. Who could be lower than shepherds on day-and-night duty in open fields, or an elderly widow praying in the Temple? Prema also believes that Luke's theological strategy in the infancy narrative is to link the event of the birth of Christ to the little and lowly in the

---

[183] See KURZ, "Hellenistic Rhetoric", 171-195; KURZ, "Narrative Approaches", 195-220; and KURZ, *Reading Luke-Acts*. The usefulness of a methodology depends on the text to which it is applied. Rhetorical analysis can be very useful for some texts, especially long speeches. Because of the narrative character of Luke 1–2, I do not find it very useful to apply rhetorical analysis to it.

[184] See GREIMAS, *Sémantique structurale*.

[185] TESTA, *Maria Terra Vergine*, 254-278, affirms that semiotic methodology shows that the child Jesus is the *to be* which is in opposition to the *to show off*. He is the king, and not the one who pretends to be a king. He is the one who is *true*, and *life*, who defeats the *falseness*, and *death*.

[186] BROWN, *Birth*, 581, believes that the semiotic technicalities of the interpretive analysis can become almost an end in themselves, so that those who are searching for worthwhile exegetical gain from the application of a method run up against a barrier of jargon and hermeneutical philosophy.

[187] See LAURENTIN, *Les Évangiles de l'enfance*; GUEURET, "Luc I-II", 35-42 ; and PANIER, *La naissance du Fils de Dieu*, 123-270.

stark reality of subjugation and oppression. According to him, the liberation that these lowly and common people were expecting (Lk 2:38) has both political (tension in the days of King Herod because of the oppressive Roman rule revealed by the census) and social aspects (stratification measured by complex phenomena such as religious purity, family heritage, land ownership, gender, ethnicity, and age). Liberation would mean the coming of God to bring an end to political and social oppression.[188]

Horsley's distinctive approach is indicated in the subtitle: "The infancy narratives in Social Context." He agrees with Prema in affirming that Luke 1–2 is a story of liberation of all the Jewish people from socioeconomic, political, and religious oppression. Horsley adds a modern analogy to Prema's work: the United States and its client-regimes in Central America.[189]

Finally, Dornisch focuses on women in society. She reads Luke 1–2 from a woman's perspective, trying to bring fresh insights for today. According to her, other approaches, whether they are called feminist, womanist, or liberationist, are raising new questions; for example, hypothesizing a women's source in Luke 1–2.[190] Yet, while acknowledging these contributions to our understanding of the text and that religion is always embedded in the social context, I believe that the religious aspects of Luke 1–2 are more important than these social aspects (see 1:16.77; 2:11.30.49).[191]

---

[188] See PREMA, "The Shepherds and the Widow", 451-463.

[189] HORSLEY, *The Liberation of Christmas*, 127-143.

[190] DORNISCH, "Introduction and Luke 1", 7. Her book, *A Woman Reads the Gospel of Luke*, follows the feminist interpretation started by SCHÜSSLER FIORENZA, *In Memory of Her*. On this feminist perspective see O'DAY, "Singing Woman's Song", 203-210.

[191] TALBERT, "Jesus' Birth", 89-90, has critized these sociological approaches arguing that a religious language should be present in a commentary to a religious text.

2. *Status Quaestionis* of Lk 2:22-39

I will now examine the specific questions of the *status quaestionis* of the Presentation in the Temple passage. Being part of Luke 1–2, I will put it in connection with the *status quaestionis* that we have just studied.

2.1 Source Criticism

The entire passage has been proposed as pre-Lukan material. Schürmann claims that this passage in its origin was an independent individual story, coming from a single source from around fifteen years after the destruction of the Temple.[192] Wilkinson thinks that a source for the entire passage of Lk 2:22-39 is the source for John the Baptist. It is posited that the Baptist source once contained not only the material in Luke 1 that now refers to John the Baptist, but also other material which has been reapplied to Jesus; for example, Lk 2:22-39, which is a continuation of the Samuel motif evident in the image of John the Baptist as a Nazirite.[193]

Bultmann thinks that both of Simeon's speeches and the descriptions of both Simeon and Anna come from one individual source (2:25-38). As a matter of fact, v. 33 tells of the parents' astonishment, which has a proper motive only if nothing had previously been said to them about their child.[194] Nolland thinks that the description of Anna (2:36-38) is traditional and was transmitted separately from the Simeon tradition, which was tra-

---

[192] SCHÜRMANN, "Aufbau", 110-111. Evans affirms that the strong Semitic influence suggests that Luke used a written source for this passage (EVANS, *Saint Luke*, 211).

[193] See WILKINSON, *A Johannine Document*, 7-35; and GEYSER, "The Youth of John", 70-75. Völter suggests that Simeon and Anna in the later narrative of Jesus correspond to Zechariah and Elizabeth in the earlier narrative of John (VÖLTER, *Die Erzählungen*, 58-59). Muñoz Iglesias rejects this John the Baptist source (MUÑOZ IGLESIAS, *Los Evangelios de la Infancia* I, 199-201).

[194] BULTMANN, *Die Geschichte der synoptischen Tradition*, 326-327, also believes that it was originally in a different order: first Simeon's prophecy (vv. 33-35), and then Simeon's hymn (vv. 29-32). In addition, according to Bultmann, there is an artificial motivation for bringing the child Jesus into the Temple, to underline the scene of the prophecy.

ditional too. "They lack," he says, "strong links with vv. 22-24 and probably came to Luke as a separate source."[195]

Aside from the entire passage (2:22-39), or almost the whole pericope (2:25-38), it has been argued that some specific parts of the pericope come from different sources. Specifically, both of Simeon's speeches have been discussed as coming from different sources.[196] The most frequent argument is for a special source for the *Nunc Dimittis* (2:29-32).[197] However, George defends Simeon's hymn as a Lukan composition.[198] Grelot analyzes in detail the text of Luke 2:29-32, framed by verses 27b-28 and 33, to try to discover its origin and the manner of its composition. According to him, the linguistic examination of the hymn of Simeon shows that its text contains Hellenisms irreducible to a Semitic (Hebrew or Aramaic) original. It is a Lukan composition.[199] As we have seen in § 1.2.1, I agree with George and Grelot and believe that the *Nunc Dimittis* is not a pre-Lukan source.

George believes that Simeon's prophecy (2:34-35) comes from another source, a Palestinian one. This scholar points out that the prophecy is very different from the rest of the passage: its vocabulary is a Semitic vocabulary and not a Lukan vocabulary; its structure is not homogenous, and it refers exclusively to Israel, and not to the Gentiles.[200] Bovon agrees with George and affirms that the only source that Luke received in the Presentation passage was Simeon's prophecy and the noting of the admiration of the parents (2:33-35).[201] However, Manicardi postulates that both of Simeon's speeches are Lukan compositions. He believes

---

[195] According to Nolland, the use of two different names to designate the same city (v. 22: Ἱεροσόλυμα, and v. 25: Ἰερουσαλὴμ) denotes two different sources (NOLLAND, *Luke 1-9:20*, 115).

[196] According to DANIÉLOU, *Les Évangiles de l'enfance*, 102-124, Simeon's hymn and prophecy come from different pre-Lukan sources.

[197] For example, KELLERMANN, "Jesus", 10-15.

[198] GEORGE, "La présentation", 29-35.

[199] GRELOT, "Le Cantique de Siméon", 481-509.

[200] See GEORGE, "La présentation", 33-39.

[201] BOVON, *Lukas* I, 145-146.

that only the introduction (2:22-24) and Anna's portrait come from a pre-Lukan source.[202]

The thorough stylistic analysis of Miyoshi recognizes Luke's formative hand throughout the entire unit, and thus presupposes no written exemplar, but rather a fixed *oral information* of Jewish Christian origin.[203] Rossé accepts that Luke could have used some memory from the circles of the community of Jerusalem, but he believes that the redactional work of Luke is predominant. He thinks that the different parts of the passage do not seem to stem from a pre-existing source, but appear to be an original composition adapted to fit within its context.[204] And Fitzmyer argues that the Presentation in the Temple has signs of pre-Lukan *oral information*.[205] I agree with these scholars and consider the editorial redaction by Luke to be more important than the possible oral information that he received.

2.2 Form Criticism

Dibelius defines the form of the Presentation in the Temple as a *legend*. He tells us that the legend of Simeon bears witness to the greatness and announces the future significance of the child during his childhood.[206] Bultmann, following Dibelius, considers that the

---

[202] According to MANICARDI, "Redazione e tradizione", 38-40, although there are Lukanisms like the expressions ὅτε ἐπλήσθησαν αἱ ἡμέραι, ἀνήγαγον αὐτὸν εἰς, or κατὰ τὸν νόμον, the use of νόμος Μωϋσέως (v. 22) and the Greek form εἰς Ἱεροσόλυμα reveal this pre-Lukan source in the introduction of the passage. The precise description of Anna, including father's name, tribe's name, the years of marriage and widowhood, and the fact that there are no words spoken by her, show its source in her portrait. However, this tradition has been modified by Luke with some Lukanisms like ἐπιστᾶσα and προσδεχομένοι λύτρωσιν Ἰερουσαλήμ. MINEAR, "Birth Stories", 113, agrees with Manicardi, affirming that Simeon's prophecy is a Lukan composition because of its Lukanisms.

[203] MIYOSHI, "Jesu Darstellung", 92-111.

[204] See ROSSÉ, "Approcci esegetici", 21.

[205] According to FITZMYER, *Luke I-IX*, 419-423, these signs of pre-Lukan oral traditions are: the Semitisms, the tension (especially in v. 33), the stylistic inconsistency in vv. 27-29.36-37a, and the repeated expression of "his parents" (vv. 27.33).

[206] DIBELIUS, *Die Formgeschichte*, 122-129; 268, maintains that many lives of characters are composed in a similar manner: an important man, while still a child, is recognized by an aged seer.

double prophecy of Simeon and Anna is reminiscent of the form of a first prophecy after the birth of an important character.[207]

Schürmann acknowledges that it is difficult to know the form of the Presentation. He claims that it is neither a legend nor a *midrash*, but rather it is a Hebraic *haggada*, whose *Sitz im Leben* was the sermon in the Synagogue. Later it was used in early Palestinian Jewish Christian circles to proclaim the kerygma about who Jesus was. This kerygma was reflected in Jesus' beginnings, even right after his birth.[208]

"From a form-critical perspective," says Bovon about Lk 2:22-39, "this is a *meeting directed by God*, as in 1:39-56. There, and here, mother and child are received by a believing member of the expectant people of God."[209] According to Bovon, the motif of this believer as an old man who, late in life, still experiences something remarkable, has roots in both Greek and Jewish literature.[210]

Laurentin believes that Lk 2:22-39 belongs to the form of a *presentation in a Temple*. But the only previous text that he proposes is 1 Samuel 1–2, the presentation of Samuel, and Laurentin recognizes that Samuel's presentation is very different: Samuel's mother asked for her son (1 S 1:10-11), while Mary does not; Samuel's mother lay with her husband (1 S 1:19), while nothing is said about Mary; Samuel was presented in the Temple when his mother had weaned him (1 S 1:24), while Jesus is presented when he was 40 days (Lk 2:22); Samuel stayed in the Temple for ever (1 S 1:28; 2:11), while Jesus returned immediately to his house in Nazareth (Lk 2:39); finally, Samuel's presentation is not linked to any rite of the Law, while Jesus' presentation is directely connected to the Law (Lk 2:22.23.24.39).[211]

---

[207] BULTMANN, *Die Geschichte der synoptischen Tradition*, 326-327. Both Dibelius and Bultmann give the example of Buddha. On the connection between the Lukan infancy narrative and Buddha's infancy see KATTENBUSCH, *Einflüsse*. Bultmann also adds the oracle of Ammon that reveals Alexander's divine origin.

[208] See SCHÜRMANN, *Ursprung*, 222-226; and SCHÜRMANN, *Untersuchungen*, 198-208.

[209] BOVON, *Lukas* I, 137 [97]. The *italics* are mine.

[210] Bovon quotes the examples of Eumaios and Eurykleia (two old servants of Odysseus); Joseph, Tobit, and Moses (in the Hebrew Bible); and Buddha.

[211] LAURENTIN, *Les Évangiles de l'enfance*, 114.

Berger has studied Simeon's hymn at length.[212] He classifies it as belonging to the form of *thanksgiving uttered before death*. He cites some good examples from the Greco-Roman world and from Hellenistic Judaism as well (testamentary literature, but especially *Jubilees* 22:7-9). Laurentin notes that the place of the thanksgiving is the Temple.[213] And Daniélou adds that it is a liturgical action: the gesture of taking the child in Simeon's arms, the vocabulary of the hymn, especially εὐλογέω (v. 28), and the opposition of the nouns δέσποτα-δοῦλος (v. 29).[214] These authors believe that Simeon's first speech is a liturgical prayer of thanksgiving.

2.3 OT Background

Throughout the passage, we find the only two explicit quotations of the OT in Luke 1–2: "Every first-born male must be consecrated to the Lord" (2:23) and "to offer in sacrifice (...) a pair of turtledoves or two young pigeons" (2:24).

The OT tradition that is most commonly referenced by the scholars as greatly influencing Luke 1–2 is the Samuel tradition.[215] Many of them believe that Jesus' Presentation in the Temple depends on Samuel's presentation in the Temple (1 Samuel 1–2).[216] The Simeon account certainly owes something to the OT account of the bringing of the child Samuel to Eli at the Temple (1 S 1:24-28; 2:20.21.26).[217]

---

[212] BERGER, "Das Canticum Simeonis (Lk 2,29-32)", 27-39.

[213] LAURENTIN, *Les Évangiles de l'enfance*, 114.

[214] DANIÉLOU, *Les Évangiles de l'enfance*, 117-124.

[215] I understand by biblical tradition the interpretation and application of a biblical text to someone else, to a different character. The author of the final text elaborates an implicit interpretation and adaptation with the aid of the Scriptures, understood in a *midrashic* manner (see BOVON, *Luc le théologien*, 170). For example, WINANDY, "La prophétie du Syméon", 321-351, speaks of many different traditions in Simeon's prophecy: Ho 6:2; Is 26:19; Ezk 14:17; 37:1-14.

[216] BURROWS, "The Gospel of the Infancy", 1-12, thinks that the Presentation passage, following the order of 1 Samuel 1–3, employs 1 S 2:18-21: the visit of Samuel's parents to the Temple, the meeting with the aged Eli, who blessed them, and their return "to their own place."

[217] Nolland affirms that "the story of the bringing of Jesus to the Temple is told

Kilgallen, looking for the meaning of Simeon's hymn, especially the expressions "Jesus savior" (2:30) and "glory of your people, Israel" (2:32), has investigated the diverse meanings with which the term "glory" is used in the Scriptures, above all in the major prophets and Psalms. In his conclusions he affirms the existence of Ezekiel, Jeremiah, and Psalm traditions, and emphasizes that Jesus as savior and as the glory of Israel is intimately associated with the humiliation, suffering, and death of the Messiah in obedience to the divine will formulated in the Scriptures.[218]

Figueras posits that Simeon and Anna respectively depend on a tradition concerning the Law (Moses) and the Prophets (Elijah).[219] Nevertheless, Nolland opposes this interpretation, believing that Simeon and Anna represent the best of OT faith witnessing to Jesus, and that Luke intends nothing more precise; Simeon and Anna are neither directly nor exclusively related to the Law and to the prophecy.[220]

Visser, following the path of Figueras, has examined the interrelation of Simeon and Anna with essential characters and important events from the history of Israel. On the one hand, from Deuteronomy 31–34 he presents the relation between Moses and Joshua as a figure of the encounter between Simeon and Jesus: from this perspective, it makes sense that Luke would have attributed to Jesus the place that, in that decisive moment of the history of salvation, is occupied by Joshua. Jesus, in the Lukan story of his Presentation in the Temple, would be characterized as a new

---

somewhat under the influence of 1 Samuel 1–2 where Samuel is brought to the Temple. [...] Jesus will be dedicated to the service of the Lord as was Samuel" (NOLLAND, *Luke 1-9:20*, 124). Many scholars defend the presence of this tradition in Lk 2:22-39. Among them see MUÑOZ IGLESIAS, *Los Evangelios de la Infancia* III, 169-170; BROWN, *Birth*, 446-447; MANICARDI, "Il racconto", 262-266.

[218] KILGALLEN, "Jesus, Savior, Glory", 305-328.

[219] FIGUERAS, "Syméon et Anne", 84-99, compares Simeon's actions with Moses' coming into the promised land (Dt 34:1-12), and Anna's description, her prophetic vocation, her age and widowhood, and her family ancestry, with different prophetic figures of the OT, especially Elijah.

[220] See NOLLAND, *Luke 1-9:20*, 125.

Joshua entering in the Promised Land.[221] On the other hand, Anna has been interpreted in function of other traditions and personages of the OT. Elliot makes Anna depend on Judith (Jdt 16:23) because they were both prophetesses and were the same age.[222] Figueras underlines the importance of the Miryam (Ex 15:20-21; Nb 12:2; Mi 6:4), Deborah (Jg 4:4), and Hulda (2 K 22:12-20) traditions to better understand the figure of Anna.[223]

Finally, the hypothesis accepted by the majority of the scholars is the following. A series of echoes of Isaiah are to be noted, especially in the *Nunc Dimittis* and vv. 25 and 38.[224] On the one hand, there is a consensus among the scholars that the theology of the hymn reflects diverse elements derived from the Deutero-Isaiah prophecy. According to George, Lk 2:30 refers to Is 40:5; 2:31 refers to Is 52:8-12; 2:32a to Is 42:6 and Is 49:6; 2:32b to Is 45:25 and Is 46:13.[225] It is supposed that Luke used these texts to emphasize the universal character of the salvific action of the Messiah Jesus.[226] For Ballhorn, Simeon becomes the Isaiah of the NT by means of Simeon's hymn.[227] On the other hand, the expressions of vv. 25 (προσδεχόμενος παράκλησιν τοῦ Ἰσραήλ) and 38 (προσδεχομένοι λύτρωσιν Ἰερουσαλήμ) are interpreted as depending on the Deutero-Isaiah prophecy by the majority of scholars (see Is 40:1; 52:9). In addition, Simeon's prophecy of Jesus' rejection (2:34) has been interpreted by Muñoz Iglesias as a tradition which comes from the servant canticles of Isaiah.[228]

---

221 VISSER, "Meer dan Jozua", 139-154, emphasizes the Hebrew connection between Jesus' name and Joshua's name, and the 40 days after Jesus' birth and the 40 years after Israel's liberation.

222 See ELLIOTT, "Anna's Age (Luke 2:36-37)", 100-102.

223 FIGUERAS, "Syméon et Anne", 96-97.

224 See REICKE, "Jesus, Simeon, and Anna", 103-104; NOLLAND, *Luke 1-9:20*, 116.

225 GEORGE, "Le parallèle", 153-168. On the Dt-Is background of the *Nunc Dimittis* see BROWN, *Birth*, 458-460; TANNEHILL, *Narrative Unity* I, 40; DEL AGUA PÉREZ, *El método midrásico*, 128-130; VALENTINI, "I cantici in Lc 1–2", 95-106; GEORGE, *Études sur l'oeuvre de Luc*, 63-65.

226 On the relationship between the universalism in Luke-Acts and in Dt-Is see HANFORD, "Straightforward Universalism?", 141-152.

227 See BALLHORN, "Simeon: Der Jesaja des Neuen Testaments (Lk 2,21-40)", 75-77.

228 MUÑOZ IGLESIAS, *Los Evangelios de la Infancia* III, 188-189.

Concurring with the majority of the scholars, I believe that the Deutero-Isaiah tradition is the most important background of the passage.

2.4 Redaction Criticism

Nolland suggests that vv. 25-38 were added to Luke's infancy narrative to increase the Jewish background at the later stage of editing when Luke also added the *Magnificat* (1:46-55) and the *Benedictus* (1:67-79). This later addition would affect both Simeon's speeches and the description of Anna.[229] Erdmann believes that Anna had a place in the original redaction and that Simeon was later added; both of Simeon's speeches are an insertion (2:25-35) to present the character of Jesus.[230]

Nolland's position is more detailed and he believes that it is best not to treat the *Nunc Dimittis* (2:28-33) as a later insertion. He also states it is at least possible that the focus on Mary in v. 34, along with the words addressed specifically to her in v. 35a, is a secondary expansion, perhaps by Luke (2:33-35).[231] In other words, Nolland maintains that Simeon's first speech is not an interpolation, but that his second speech is indeed an interpolation designed to introduce the topic of rejection.

Finally, Rossé has proposed that the entire passage comes from the very same redaction by Luke and that there are no later insertions.[232] I agree with Rossé. As we have seen in § 2.1, Luke could use some traditional information, as the presence and characterization of Anna, but he redacts the entire pericope.

---

[229] NOLLAND, *Luke 1-9:20*, 115, believes that previously these additions, vv. 22-24.39, completed the section 2:1-21 expanding on the legal interest of v. 21.

[230] ERDMANN, *Die Vorgeschichten*.

[231] NOLLAND, *Luke 1-9:20*, 116.119.

[232] ROSSÉ, "Approcci esegetici", 20.

2.5 Narrative Analysis

Using narrative analysis, Coleridge studies the different passages of the Lukan infancy narrative. Commenting on the passage of Lk 2:22-39, the author underlines that the text makes an explicit reference to Jesus only once (2:27). This means that the narrative does not focus on Jesus and his coming into the Temple. Coleridge suggests that the passage underlines the way in which the characters, Simeon and Anna, interpret Jesus' presence.[233] I agree with Coleridge in this last idea. The narrative emphasizes the reaction of these characters to Jesus. However, this reaction itself becomes a literary presentation of Jesus through these characters. Although there is only one explicit reference to Jesus, there are many other implicit references to Jesus through the words spoken about him. These reactions and words by the narrator and Simeon (2:25.26.27.30.31.32.38) do indeed focus on Jesus.[234]

2.6 Rhetorical and Semiotic Analysis

Meynet has studied the Presentation in the Temple using rhetorical analysis.[235] He uses a structuralist perspective to study the passage, and in his study includes v. 21 (ἐκλήθη τὸ ὄνομα αὐτοῦ Ἰησοῦς, τὸ κληθὲν ὑπὸ τοῦ ἀγγέλου πρὸ τοῦ συλλημφθῆναι αὐτὸν ἐν τῇ κοιλίᾳ) and the addition of manuscript D after v. 39: καθὼς ἐρρέθη διὰ τοῦ προγετοῦ ὅτι Ναζωραῖος κληθήσεται. Meynet notes that the entire passage is bracketed by the names assigned to the newborn child: Jesus (2:21) and Nazorean (2:39: D). After the first name and before the last name, the figures of Simeon (2:25-28a) and Anna (2:36-38) appear. After the description of Simeon and before the description of Anna, we find Simeon blessing and making his two speeches (vv. 28b-32 and vv. 34.35). Right in the center of this rhetorical structure, the narrator places

---

[233] COLERIDGE, *The Birth*, 157.

[234] See § III.4.

[235] See MEYNET, *L'Évangile de Luc*, 127-139; and MEYNET, "Dieu donne son Nom", 39-72.

the reaction of Jesus' parents, wondering at the things that were being said about Jesus (2:33). Therefore, according to Meynet's analysis, the passage is built upon a solid structure around the things said about Jesus. Contrary to Coleridge, Meynet believes that Jesus is the focus of the passage.

Close to Meynet's analysis is the semiotic analysis of Gueuret. She argues that the pericope is made up of two meetings in the Temple between two displacements: from Bethlehem to Jerusalem (2:21)[236] and from Jerusalem to Nazareth (v. 40). Gueuret does not consider the variant of D of v. 39. Nevertheless, she claims that the play on words of the verb καλέω (vv. 21 and 23) to name the child Jesus structures the passage.[237] In v. 21 they named him Jesus, which etymologically means *Yhwh saves*, and in v. 23 Jesus is named "Holy for the Lord." This presentation of Jesus is accepted and admitted by two characters, Simeon and Anna. That is why Jesus is recognized as the salvation of God by Simeon (2:30) and as the redemption by Anna (2:38). The first proper name, *Jesus* (2:21), announces and prepares the presentation of Jesus. Once again Jesus is at the center of the passage for Gueuret.

3. Contributions and Lacunae

This *status quaestionis* brings forth different conclusions. Throughout the studies, the so-called diachronic methodologies have been clearly predominant in the study of Luke 1–2. The majority of the articles try to discern the different sources employed by Luke, the different phases of his redaction, and the possible historicity of the narrative. Different sources, forms, and redactions have been claimed, but there is no common agreement among scholars. It is likely that only the *Magnificat* and the *Benedictus* come from a written source; perhaps the passage about the twelve-year-old Jesus. Throughout the entire infancy narrative we can see the

[236] This movement is not explicitly present in the Greek text. However, the previous passage takes place in Bethlehem, and this one in Jerusalem.

[237] See GUEURET, *L'engendrement*, 119-127; 196-202; and GUEURET, "Luc I-II", 35-42, which is a summary of her monograph.

editorial work by Luke. He is the real author of Luke 1–2, and he does not allow his sources to appear clearly.

Many different forms, often different from the forms of the rest of the Gospel, make up the infancy narrative. Some of them, like the hymns, could come from the early Jewish-Christian liturgy. The *Nunc Dimittis* presents the form of a liturgical *thanksgiving prayer*. The literary genre of Luke 1–2 is difficult to define. Acknowledging that Luke 1–2 is part of Luke's Gospel, being an infancy narrative in connection with other infancies of important characters, it could be a sub-genre of the literary genre of Gospel, a sub-genre in connection with other infancy narratives of its milieu, and with a strong OT background.

It is likely, as well, that Luke composed Luke 1–2 after he had already written the rest of his literary work. This is why the Lukan infancy narrative was composed with the hindsight not only of the Gospel tradition prior to Luke, but also of the Lukan Gospel proper and Acts of the Apostles. This knowledge of the rest of his literary work allowed Luke to build a real overture in which the main topics of his work are placed before the reader. The general importance of the beginnings is clear in the way that Luke 1–2 helps the reader to enter into the literary work with the right clues.

Only one monograph exists, as far as I know, concerning the passage of the Presentation in the Temple, and this monograph does not study the narrative about Anna (2:36-38), the setting of the passage (2:22-24), or Simeon's characterization (2:25-28). It concerns only vv. 29-35, or in other words, both of Simeon's speeches.[238] The passage as a whole has only been studied in the brief descriptions of the different commentaries to the third Gospel. The majority of the studies are partial articles, mainly focused on Simeon and his speeches. The introduction of the passage (2:22-24) and particularly the character of Anna (2:36-38) have not been studied as closely as the verses focused on Simeon.[239] The passage, taken as a

---

[238] See SIMÓN MUÑOZ, *El Mesías y la hija de Sión*.

[239] Anna has been largely forgotten by scholars. Although it is true that she does not speak at all, it is also true that her characterization is very extensive. Her presence and full characterization clearly add something to the meaning of the passage. Simeon's characterization has not been sufficiently studied either (2:25-28).

whole with a so-called synchronic methodology, with all of its different parts, has not yet been studied in the depth that it deserves. Similarly, there have not been conclusive studies on the relationship of the passage, and its communicative function, to the rest of the Lukan infancy narrative and Luke's entire work.

It is important to recognize that each stage in the developing history of interpretation has depended upon the work already done. There would have been no form criticism without the research by source criticism that proposed the possibility of different sources of the current text. Form criticism, by seeing a Gospel as a string of sources, proceeds to reveal the historically original sociological situation. There would have been no redaction criticism without the discoveries of the form critics who posed the question of the theological and literary creativity of the early Church. Redaction criticism stands on form criticism's shoulders. Where the latter saw Luke exercising the limited freedom of choosing his sources and ordering them, redaction criticism sees Luke exercising a decisive freedom in the enterprise of writing. There would have been no narrative criticism without the work of redaction critics who turned narrative criticism's attention from the individual pericope to the theological perspective of the complete work. Thus, while today we strive to understand the entire passage as we have received it, looking for the communicative intention of the final author, we are unable to do this without first seeing where the text came from.[240] Acknowledging all of this background of the history of interpretation, this dissertation serves as another link in this chain, seeking to go one step further. Building upon the works of previous scholars, it studies the role that the Presentation passage plays within the general overture to Luke-Acts and its narrative function in the whole Lukan work.

[240] On this mutual dependence between different methodolgoies see MOLONEY, *Beginning the Good News*, 39-40.

CHAPTER II

INFANCY NARRATIVES AS PROLEPTIC PRESENTATION

The genre of a literary work is fundamental to its interpretation. Genre provides the initial context to understand what an author actually means by what he has written.[1] Genre establishes a sort of contract between author and reader,[2] giving a set of expectations for interpretation.[3] In this chapter I examine different infancy narratives looking for their common features and the main differences between them. The essential characteristics will be determined by a process of induction from particular works linked by certain shared affinities, such as shared content, form, or function.

Infancy narratives of heroic figures are very well known in ancient literature. They participate in a broad *topos* in which different texts share narrative patterns. They include announcements before the hero's birth, descriptions of how a hero is born, and, despite many hardships, how he spends his early formative years. The

---

[1] For example, a politely distant tone would have one meaning if employed in a business letter, but quite a different meaning in correspondence exchanged between lovers. On the importance of literary genre see BONZ, *The Past as Legacy*, 182-185.

[2] LEJEUNE, *Le pacte autobiographique*, 13-46, speaking about autobiography, underlines the importance of what he calls the *contract* between author and reader. According to him, this contract at the beginning of the literary work determines the way in which the reader reacts to the text and reads it. I contend that this contract might be understood as the agreement of the reader to accept the dynamics of the world internal to the story. Powell tells an illustrative example: "If a story features talking animals, we are expected to suspend our disbelief and to accept that, in this story, that is the way things are" (POWELL, "Narrative Criticism", 243).

[3] BURRIDGE, *What Are the Gospels?*, 55-56, remarks that genre is a set of expectations.

study of selected infancy narratives aids in helping one to better understand this broad *topos* and its common features. Therefore, by studying different authors, this chapter will seek to explain some nuances found in the infancy narrative of Luke's Gospel, especially the Presentation in the Temple, and the significance of its similarities and differences with Greco-Roman and Jewish literature.

I will not endeavor to prove the dependency of some texts on others, nor the historical reality of the narrated stories. My investigation will be focused on the literary level, namely, on the narrative function of the infancy story in connection with the whole life of the respective hero. What was the purpose of such material dealing with the hero's life prior to his public career? How would this material have been understood by an ancient reader? How does the narrative function give authority to the main character? In order to answer these questions, I will closely examine the ways in which the ancient author guided the reader towards a proper understanding of the hero, whose birth is therein described.

Studying this common *topos*, I argue that the events of infancy narratives often have a proleptic function. Words and deeds in the infancy narratives, at the beginning of the literary work, raise expectations about the main character, which play an important role in the reader's understanding of the work, particularly the public career of the hero. Luke's infancy narrative has this proleptic function and adds further new features.

As I want to study different texts across time and geographical space, only prominent biographies from the ancient Mediterranean region dating to around the first century are the primary source of reference for this chapter.[4] The criteria to choose the

[4] There are also infancy narratives in the life of Buddha, where we can also find a royal genealogy, an extraordinary conception, his birth during a journey by his mother, the great joy because of his birth, his presentation in the temple and a prophecy of his future life by an old person (see MÜLLER, *The Dhammapada*, § 679-698). In the Mediterranean area, years before the second century, there are other infancy narratives. For example, there is also an infancy narrative of Plato told by his nephew and successor, Speusippus. It is a speech given in the year following Plato's death and reports, among other things, Plato's supernatural generation by Apollo. This very same infancy

authors to be studied will be the selection of the "well-known" stories, which can show us the context in which both author and reader would have written, read, or interpreted the infancy narratives. I will divide the chapter into three sections.

The first section explores Greco-Roman texts, both Greek and Latin: Pseudo-Callisthenes' *The Life and Deeds of Alexander of Macedon*, Quintus Curtius Rufus' *The History of Alexander*, Plutarch's *Parallel Lives*, and Suetonius' *The Lives of the Twelve Caesars.*[5] The second section attempts to answer the following questions: Do we find similar examples in Jewish literature, or was it only a Greco-Roman phenomenon? Do Jewish works show that the Hellenistic biographical tradition had an impact on Judaism? Do Jewish infancy narratives share features with Greco-Roman infancy narratives? I will study Jewish texts, which comment on and explain infancy narratives of the OT. Comparing them to the biblical text, I will be able to highlight the specific features of the infancy narratives of the following Jewish biographies: Philo's *The Life of Moses*, Pseudo-Philo's *Biblical Antiquities* and Josephus' *The Jewish Antiquities.*[6] Having previously studied the Greco-

narrative was told as well by Clearchus in his *Encomium on Plato*, and Anaxilaïdes in his second book *On Philosophers* (see DIOGENES LAERTIUS, *Vitae Philosophorum*, 3,2). However, I will focus my study in the Mediterranean area around the first century which is the natural context of Luke-Acts.

[5] Henceforward I will refer to these primary works in this way: AUTHOR, *name of the character*, number of the section, number of the paragraph. For all this Greco-Roman literature I have quoted from the English translation of the bilingual collection of the *Loeb Classical Library*. Before Suetonius' *The Lives of the Twelve Caesars*, Suetonius also wrote *The Lives of Illustrious Men* (*De viris illustribus*), which is the title given to a series of biographies written by Suetonius about men of distinction who rose to an elevated status in the Roman literary culture: poets, historians, philosophers, orators, and professors of rhetoric. Unfortunately, only a small portion of these works has reached us. Since they are very brief descriptions, I did not find a single appropriate text that was useful for my purpose.

[6] Henceforward I will refer to these primary works in this way: AUTHOR, *name of the literary work*, number of the section, number of the paragraph. For Philo and Josephus I have quoted from the English translation of the bilingual collection of the *Loeb Classical Library*. For Pseudo-Philo I have followed the bilingual collection of *Source chrétiennes*. I have also examined *The Lives of the Prophets*, a work which concerns the

Roman and the Jewish texts,[7] the third section studies how the infancy narratives operate as an intended literary tool. I will study the *position* of the infancy events within the whole literary work (looking for the narrative purpose in the structure of the entire work);[8] and the harmony between the events narrated and the rest of the person's life (looking for the narrative function that lets the reader know, from the beginning, what the reader can expect of the main character throughout the entire literary work). In the final synthesis, I will compare the related and different features of the different kinds of texts, Greco-Roman and Jewish, with each other and with Luke's infancy narrative.

How are the passages to be studied chosen? According to McGaughy,[9] the fully developed structure of the infancy narratives often consisted of the following elements: a) Genealogy; b) Miraculous conception; c) Angelic annunciation or parental vision; d) Birth accompanied by supernatural signs; and e) Human responses to the hero's birth.[10] As I am studying the Presentation in the Temple, I will primarily focus on the events between the hero's birth and the beginning of his public life. However, I will also deal

---

names of the prophets, their origins, deaths and places of burial. However there are no infancy narratives in those short descriptions of the lives of the Prophets. I have also included the Book of *Jubilees*, which is a rewriting of the Hebrew Bible, but without any infancy narrative. Nor in the *Life of Adam and Eve* is there a single text of interest for my purpose.

[7] I begin with Greco-Roman literature because MOMIGLIANO, *The Development of Greek Biography*, 101-104, has proved that the infancy narratives are linked with the biographies and that the first Greco-Roman genealogies, political histories, autobiographical travel books, and encomiums, were the first "biographies" in the history of literature (see the introduction to § 1).

[8] By *position* I understand the specific place within the entire literary work in which a passage has been placed by the author.

[9] MCGAUGHY, "Infancy Narratives", 30.

[10] To McGaughy's general structure, I would add the information about the character's physical appearance, formation and development. Each particular instance may contain all the elements that make up a complete literary structure or only some of those pertinent to the message. There could be variations in every instance. Every author has his own liberty to adapt these literary elements to his own purpose. See BRENNER, "Female Social Behaviour", 257.

with events which occur before the hero's birth to try to better understand the overall patterns of the infancy narratives.

My *modus operandi* in the first two sections of the chapter will be as follows. First, I will briefly introduce the context in which each literary work appears: the date and provenance of a text, as far as it is known. Second, I will extract the common features of the selected infancy narratives according to topics. In the chosen passages, I will examine various simple topics such as the *types of events* before, during and after the birth of the hero; the *actors*, the kind of persons who are involved in the events; the reaction of the witnesses of the event as a clue for the readers (looking for the pragmatic function in the audience of the literary work); the presence of titles for the hero (looking for the characterization of the hero and key descriptive terms for him); and the *location* where the event takes place (looking for the religious reason for that kind of event).

1. The Greco-Roman Biographies

Infancy narratives occur within biographical literature.[11] Momigliano, in his four lectures on the development of Greek biography, affirms that the inventors of biography were the ancient Greeks.[12] Though our evidence for the fifth century BC is admittedly poor, the first biographies seem to belong to the period between 500 and 480 BC and to be contemporary with the first works on genealogy. Greeks had funeral orations and songs in honor of the dead, all of which are potential biographies. But biography began in close connection with history, especially political history.[13] The study of local history, institutions, and customs

[11] The nomenclature of the biographical literature used from the Hellenistic age onwards was simply *Lives*, βίοι, or *vitae*. I will use both terms: biography and βίος.

[12] See MOMIGLIANO, *The Development of Greek Biography*, which work I follow, especially pp. 101-104. The titles of his four lectures are: *Modern Theories on Ancient Biography; Fifth-Century Biographies and Autobiographies?; The fourth Century;* and *From Aristotle to the Romans*.

[13] Biography presents a person's deed and words as illustrations of character, while history is interested in a person's achievements in so far as they had consequences for society.

existed in the fifth century but was less influential than the study of political and military history. The history of the individual, particularly the significant politicians and warriors, developed into the first biographies, biographies which remained close to political history. Herodotus and Thucydides are the principal names associated with this development.[14] According to Momigliano, this fifth century saw the beginning of autobiographical travel books, which became the first "autobiographies."[15]

The philosophic and rhetorical schools of the fourth century BC developed the art of discussing individuals. Philosophers developed the idealized biography of the politician and of the philosopher. The exploration of individual lives developed greatly in the fourth century BC through the writings of Plato, Isocrates and Xenophon.[16] The characterization of different individuals, the art of portrayal, and the study of human motives became more subtle.[17] Aristotle realized that careful collection of authentic facts about individual lives could contribute positively to the construction of his own philosophy, and more particularly of his poetics, morals, and politics. Thus, describing individual lives, the biography

---

[14] Homeyer contends that the first actual βιοί may have been written during the fifth century BC, but are no longer preserved today (HOMEYER, "Zu den Anfängen", 75-85).

[15] The accounts of geographical explorations and travels, beginning with the *Odyssey*, were inevitably a kind of partial autobiography. However, Josephus' autobiography, *The Life of Flavius Josephus*, is the first to come down to us from the ancient world.

[16] According to BURRIDGE, *What Are the Gospels?*, 71, there are three main factors which explain why βίοι were especially written in the fourth century BC: a new political mood in which the individual is more prominent than the collective; philosophical concerns and interest in the individual philosophers; and rhetorical interest through the use of encomiastic speeches.

[17] Barr and Wentling say: "Some biographers were encyclopedists, others were objective while others were more subjective and sought to involve their readers with the hero. [...] It should be clear that biography was not a static or homogeneous kind of literature in antiquity. There were numerous kinds of biographies and a spectrum of ways of presenting them. There were diversity and fluidity of the genre, the great variety of techniques indicating the vitality and range of the genre. Yet in each case there is little doubt that one is reading the same sort of literature" (BARR – WENTLING, "Classical Biography", 67-68). The genre is capable of flexibility, adaptation and growth.

occupied the intermediate zone between history and *encomium*. Biography takes from *encomium* the interest in the individual character and from history the importance of his achievements, especially in the political, social, and cultural arenas.[18]

The biographers of Alexander the Great developed enormously the biographical genre. A general fascination in his career and life spread immediately. The existence of eighty versions of Alexander's biographies in twenty-four languages, the length of time it has appealed to readers,[19] and the number of literary works it inspired testify to a popularity and diffusion exceeded only by the Bible. Due to the success and fame of the life of Alexander the Great, the important phenomenon of biography was clearly developed. What we call *Hellenistic biography* with its distinctive features of erudition, scholarly zeal, realism of details, and gossip, seems to come from the importance and success of Alexander the Great.[20]

Interest in biography quickly spread among Greeks and reached Rome a little later, in the first century BC. It is not mere chance that so much biographical material, both Greek and Latin, has come down to us from the time of the Roman Empire. The wise man, the poet, the artist, the writer, and the saint became central subjects of biography, in addition to the king and the philosopher.

---

[18] "The genre of βίος," says BURRIDGE, *What Are the Gospels?*, 80, "was a flexible genre found between history, *encomium*, rhetoric and moral philosophy, with overlaps and relationships in all directions." According to the introduction by Aurelio Pérez to PLUTARCH, *Vidas paralelas*, 73-78, Plutarch himself differentiates his biographies from other histories: "It is not *Histories* that I am writing, but *Lives*" (PLUTARCH, *Alexander*, 1,2). The italics are mine.

[19] There are Alexander romances from their first composition in antiquity well into today, as a hero in Greece and as an enemy in Persia.

[20] Only in Alexander's biography, Plutarch speaks of the huge fame of the character: "I am writing in this book the life of Alexander, and the multitude of the deeds to be treated is so great that I shall make no other preface than to entreat my readers, in case I do not tell of all the famous actions of this man, nor even speak exhaustively at all in each particular case, but in epitome for the most part, not to complain" (PLUTARCH, *Alexander*, 1,1).

1.1 Introducing the Biographies Studied

1.1.1 *Alexander's Romances: Pseudo Callisthenes'* The Life and Deeds of Alexander of Macedon *(Greek) and Quintus Curtius Rufus'* The History of Alexander *(Latin)*

As we have just seen, the unique figure of Alexander the Great was very important for the development of biography. The *Alexander Romance* is one of the most successful novels in antiquity. Its author and its date are unknown. Although the original is lost, written sometime in the fourth century BC, many redactions of it survive in great variety, forming a complex network of interrelated texts. In a sense there is no *Alexander Romance*, only Alexander romances.

The author of the first complete recension, represented in Greek by a single manuscript, Pseudo-Callisthenes,[21] was more a compiler than a creative artist. A Greek speaker, living in Alexandria at some time between 140 and 210, he seems to have primarily used two books, merging them to form *The Life and Deeds of Alexander of Macedon*. The first of the two books was a varied collection of fictional accounts concerning Alexander. It included a sort of epistolary novel dating from about 100 BC, which consisted chiefly of the correspondence of Alexander with his adversaries. The other main source for *The Life and Deeds of Alexander of Macedon* was a history deriving from Kleitarchos (*circa* 300 BC), who is said by Cicero to have written it "rhetorically and dramatically." Although we do not know the precise date of this first recension by Pseudo-Callisthenes, we can affirm the antiquity and the well known character of its two sources.[22]

Although the brilliant career and complex character of Alexander the Great received frequent mention from Latin writers, in particular the rhetoricians and the historians, only one work in

---

[21] We call him Pseudo-Callisthenes because the manuscripts falsely attribute the work to Callisthenes, Alexander's court historian. See *Collected Ancient Greek Novels*, 654-735, edited by Reardon, whose numbering and translation I follow; and PFISTER, *Der Alexanderroman*, 82-92, where the author comments on the texts of Alexander's childhood.

[22] On the sources of *The Life and Deeds of Alexander of Macedon* and its redaction, see *Leben und Taten Alexanders*, xiii-xl, edited by van Thiel; CURTIUS RUFUS, *The History of Alexander*, 4-9; HAMILTON, *Alexander the Great*, 11-22.

Latin devoted exclusively to his life has come down to us,[23] and in an incomplete form.[24] Its author's identity and the date of composition of *The History of Alexander* have been vigorously debated. In the past century, Quintus' time of writing has been assigned to the reigns of more than a dozen emperors from Augustus to Constantine. Nevertheless, the date commonly accepted is *circa* 40.[25]

I will use the infancy narratives of Alexander by Pseudo-Callisthenes and by Quintus Curtius Rufus for my study. Both infancy narratives are found at the beginning of the respective literary works, Pseudo-Callisthenes, *Alexander*, 1,1-25, and Quintus Curtius Rufus, *Alexander*, 1,1-11, and describe the family of Alexander, the events before and during his birth, his training with different teachers, and his childhood until he succeeded to the kingdom of Philip.

1.1.2 Plutarch's Parallel Lives *(Greek)*

Plutarch was born *circa* 45 at Chaeroneia, a small town on the northern confines of Boetia (Greece). He belonged to a family of ample means and high culture, and was liberally educated. He studied at Athens, the most attractive university town in his day. Returning to his native town, he was soon called upon to represent it as deputy to the Roman governor of the province of Greece. Then, after an Athenian education, generous travels, diplomatic missions,

---

[23] On Quintus Curtius Rufus' *The History of Alexander* see QUINTUS CURTIUS, *Historiae Alexandri Magni Macedonis* I, ix-xxxiv, edited by Warmington, whose numbering and translation I follow; CURTIUS RUFUS, *The History of Alexander*, 1-15; KORZENIEWSKI, *Die Zeit des Quintus*, 51-86; MCQUEEN, "Quintus Curtius Rufus", 17-43.

[24] The first and second of its ten books are wholly lost, and there are extensive gaps at the end of Book Five and at the beginning of Books Six and Ten, as well as some lesser lacunae. Reconstructions of the two lost first books and of the lacunae in the existing books were published by J. Freinshem in his editions, basing them upon material furnished by Arrian, Diodorus Siculus, Justin, Plutarch, and others. Therefore, these supplements are based upon old material and show us the high diffusion of biographies of Alexander and what was expected in a biography of Alexander.

[25] In CURTIUS RUFUS, *The History of Alexander*, 1-3, Yardley and Heckel date it through the internal references of the work (QUINTUS CURTIUS RUFUS, *Alexander*, 4,4,21; 10,9,3-6).

modest literary celebrity, and a considerable period of residence in Rome, he seems to have retired to his little country home, with his books, notes, lectures, essays, and philosophy, and there wrote *Morals* in Greek, and composed the work on which his fame chiefly rests, *Parallel Lives of Greeks and Romans*.[26] He died about 120.

He was among the most prolific of ancient writers, authoring works of philosophy, moral, rhetoric, biography and antiquarian history. About half of his work still survives. For the most part *Morals* was composed before *Parallel Lives*, and is an invaluable prelude to them. Plutarch's *Parallel Lives* probably belongs to the period around 96, writing individual biographies, of which four survive, and others in parallel pairs, comparing Greeks with Romans.[27] *Parallel Lives* exemplifies the flexible nature of this genre, nestling between history, rhetoric and moral philosophy, with a variety of artistic purposes. Among these *Parallel Lives*, Plutarch occasionally speaks about the infancy of the character. For my study I will employ the infancy narratives concentrating on the figures of: *Theseus*, 3-7, *Romulus*, 1-9, *Numa*, 3-7, *Themistocles*, 1-2, *Cato*, 1-2, *Lucullus*, 1-2, *Pericles*, 3-6, *Crassus*, 1-2, *Coriolanus*, 1-3, *Alcibiades*, 1-7, *Sulla*, 1-2, *Brutus*, 1-2, *Pompey*, 1-2, *Demosthenes*, 4-5, *Cicero*, 1-5, *Alexander*, 1-10, *Demetrius*, 2-4, *Philopoemen*, 1-4, *Pyrrhus*, 1-4, *Antony*, 1-2, *Caius Marius*, 1-4, *Artaxerxes*, 1-2, and *Agis*, 4.[28]

---

[26] For a deeper knowledge of these data see PLUTARCH, *Plutarchi vitae parallelae* I, xi-ixx, edited by Goold and Warmington, whose numbering and translation I follow; WARDMAN, *Plutarch's Lives*, 2-10; JONES, *Plutarch and Rome*, 3-64.

[27] I do not deal with the comparisons that Plutarch makes between different characters. They would not be useful for my purpose of examining the biographies and their infancy narratives.

[28] These infancy narratives appear at the beginning of the literary work. When it is not immediately at the beginning, it is because Plutarch starts with a short comparison between both lives that he is comparing. For the text on the infants presented by Plutarch see FACQ, "Les enfants", 305-309.

1.1.3 Suetonius' The Lives of the Twelve Caesars *(Latin)*

We have very few sources of information about Gaius Tranquillus Suetonius.[29] In fact, they are limited to five brief references that Suetonius writes about himself and his ancestors,[30] to four citations by other writers,[31] to some inscriptions,[32] and to six letters from Pliny the Younger.[33]

Consequently, we move in the terrain of conjecture with regard to the personal details of Suetonius' life. His date of birth is a question that is often discussed. Scholars place the birth circa the year 65. Independent of the location of his place of birth, all agree that Suetonius came from a sufficiently prosperous family. He received an excellent education in language, both grammatical and rhetorical. At least part of this academic education was received in Rome, where he was educated in the main Roman school of the epoch to become a Latin grammarian. He was established in the imperial administration at a young age, and this facilitated his ability to gather anecdotes from the court. As a grammarian and literary scholar, his work was meticulous. He was interested in lively stories, often to the point of being seen as a scandal-monger. This fact, together with his simple, easy-to-read style, ensured him lasting popularity. Some scholars date his death to the middle of the second century.

The Lives of the Twelve Caesars is the only work of Suetonius that has been preserved almost intact.[34] As indicated already in his title,

---

[29] On these few pieces of information see SUETONIUS, *Lives of the Caesars* I, 1-31, edited by Henderson, whose numbering and translation I follow; SUETONIUS, *Vida de los doce Césares*, ix-xxxii; WALLACE-HADRILL, *Suetonius*, 50-72; STEIDLE, *Sueton und die antike Biographie*, 1-12.

[30] See SUETONIUS, *Caligula*, 19,3; *Otho*, 10,1; *Domitian*, 12,2; *Nero*, 57,2; *Ep. 94*.

[31] See SPARTIANUS, *Vita Hadriani*, 11,3; LYDUS, *De magistratibus populi romani*, 2,6; FRONTO, *Ad Verum*, 14 and FRONTO, *Ad Amicos*, 1,13. This last one is discussed elsewhere by scholars.

[32] GROSSO, "L'epigrafe", 263-296; MAREC – PFLAHM, *Nouvelle inscription*, 76-85.

[33] See PLINY THE YOUNGER, *Ep.*, 1:18; 1:24; 3:8; 5:10; 9:34; 10:94-95, which correspond to a very limited period, between 97 and 112. Naturally, they refer only to the cited interval of time and do not provide the dates of his birth and death.

[34] Apart from some small gaps, we need solely to lament the loss of the first small

it contains the biographies of the first twelve Roman emperors from Julius Caesar to Domitian. We do not possess any precise testimony about the date on which these biographies were published. According to the testimony of Lydus, Suetonius had dedicated them to Septicio Claro, when he was still praetorian prefect (from 119 to 122); therefore, the work was published during that time.[35]

I will employ for my study what Suetonius says about the infancy narratives of the following emperors: *Tiberius*, 1-7, *Gaius Caligula*, 1-9, *Claudius*, 1-6, *Nero*, 1-7, *Galba*, 2-5, *Vespasian*, 2-5, *Titus*, 1-5, *Domitian*, 1-2.14, and *Octavian Augustus*, 94.[36]

The following table helps to locate the texts to be studied in their place and time.

Author	Literary work	Language	Place	Date
Ps-Callisthenes	*The Life and Deeds of Alexander of Macedon*	Greek	Alexandria	140-210[37]
Curtius Rufus	*The History of Alexander*	Latin	?	40?[38]
Plutarch	*The Parallel Lives*	Greek	Greece	45-120
Suetonius	*The Lives of the Twelve Caesars*	Latin	Rome	65-140

part of the First Book. The testimony of Lydus in the VI century, in which he alludes to its dedication, demonstrates the loss of the cited book (LYDUS, *De Magistratibus populi romani*, 2,7). That part of the book contained the title of the work, a dedication to Septicio Claro, probably a diagram or genealogical family tree of Augustus and a story of the birth of Julius Caesar, his infancy and childhood until 16 years of age. From this point the narration continues with the life of the dictator. In addition, the fact that the narration in the other biographies begins with the birth and the first years of the emperor underlines the abrupt form of Julius Caesar's biography, starting when he was already 16 years old.

[35] See LYDUS, *De Magistratibus populi romani*, 2,7-8.

[36] These two last biographies present an infancy narrative at the end of the literary work.

[37] This is a later recension of the original the *Alexander Romance*, written sometime around the fourth century BC. This recension is made up of two different sources written around 100 BC and 300 BC.

[38] As Curtius Rufus' dates of birth and death are unknown, I include here the likely date of composition of his literary work.

1.2 The Greco-Roman Infancy Narratives

1.2.1 Types of Signs in the Infancy Narratives

The main events of the infancy narratives are often expressed through different *signs*:[39] prodigies (or portents), prophecies (or omens, oracles, predictions, or auguries) and dreams.[40] This terminology is widely employed by these authors. On the night when Alexander was born, Plutarch relates the first *prodigy*: "The temple of the Ephesian Diana was destroyed by fire, since the goddess was busy bringing Alexander into the world. The Magi interpreted it as meaning that a firebrand had that day been born somewhere, by which the whole Orient would be destroyed."[41] When Alexander was less than seven years old we find a *prophecy*. Several kings and generals took refuge at his house. Afterwards, they felt such admiration for Alexander that one of them could not keep from exclaiming: "This boy will be a great king; ours is a rich prince!"[42] Finally, Augustus' father *dreamt* of his son's greatness: "He dreamt that his son appeared to him in a guise more majestic than that of mortal man, with the thunderbolt, scepter, and insignia of Jupiter Optimus Maximus, wearing a crown begirt with rays and mounted upon a laurel-wreathed chariot drawn by twelve horses of surpassing whiteness."[43]

These signs happen before, during and after the birth of the protagonist of the literary work. *Before* Alexander's birth, according to Pseudo-Callisthenes, we find many prophecies, dreams and

[39] We are able to embrace all this terminology under the word *sign* (Lat: *signum*), a word that the Latin writers utilize with frequency. For example, see PSEUDO-CALLISTHENES, *Alexander*, 1,4.

[40] The importance of dreams in Greek, Roman, Jewish and Christian antiquity has been sufficiently studied by BOVON, "The Christians Who Dream", 144-162.

[41] PLUTARCH, *Alexander*, 3,5-6. We can find other prodigies in PSEUDO-CALLISTHENES, *Alexander*, 1,14; 1,17; QUINTUS CURTIUS RUFUS, *Alexander*, 11,1; 4; PLUTARCH, *Cato*, 1,2; SUETONIUS, *Augustus*, 94,2; 94,5-7; *Galba*, 4,3; *Vespasian*, 5,2.

[42] QUINTUS CURTIUS RUFUS, *Alexander*, 5,7. We can find other prophecies in PSEUDO-CALLISTHENES, *Alexander*, 1,16; SUETONIUS, *Tiberius*, 14,2; *Galba*, 4,2; *Vespasian*, 5,2; *Titus*, 5,1-2.

[43] SUETONIUS, *Augustus*, 94,6. We can find other dreams in SUETONIUS, *Augustus*, 94,4.8; *Galba*, 4,3.

prodigies that speak about Alexander. The Egyptian king Nektanebos had intercourse with the Macedonian queen Olympias, Alexander's mother. When Olympias knew that she was pregnant and was afraid of her husband, the Macedonian king Philip, Nektanebos announced to Olympias: "Have strength, woman! You have in your womb a male child to be your avenger and king and sovereign of the whole world. [...] Have no fear, mistress, the god Ammon will help you with this by appearing to Philip in his dreams and letting him know what has happened." And the very same Philip recognizes his dream: "Wife, why are you upset at what has happened? It is someone else's fault -that has been shown to me in a dream- so you cannot be blamed. We kings have power over all, but we do not have power over the gods. Your affair was not with one of the people, but with one of the most magnificent beings." A prodigy also happened. In order to prove the divine origin of Alexander, during a great banquet in the palace, "Nektanebos turned himself into a serpent [...] and came into the middle of the dining hall [...] and stirred himself to rest his head in Olympias' hand and coiled down to Olympias' knees and, putting out his forked tongue, kissed her."[44]

The description of the birth is usually told through references to the place and the political situation in which the character was born. Suetonius describes the birth of Vespasian as follows: "Vespasian was born in the Sabine country in a small village beyond Reate, called Falacrina, in the consulate of Quintus Sulpicius Camerinus and Gaius Poppaeus Sabinus, five years before the death of Augustus."[45]

Pseudo-Callisthenes describes a prodigy which occurred even *during labor*. When Alexander was about to be born, the astrologer

---

[44] PSEUDO-CALLISTHENES, *Alexander*, 1,7-11. A very similar portent is told in PLUTARCH, *Alexander*, 2,6. The reader finds other prodigies (QUINTUS CURTIUS RUFUS, *Alexander*, 1,4,1; SUETONIUS, *Augustus,* 94,3.4), dreams (PLUTARCH, *Alexander*, 2,3-5; *Pericles*, 3,2), and prophecies (PLUTARCH, *Romulus*, 2,4; SUETONIUS, *Tiberius,* 14,2) before birth.

[45] SUETONIUS, *Vespasian,* 2,1. And SUETONIUS, *Titus,* 1, describes Titus' birth as follows: "He was born in the year memorable for the death of Gaius in a mean house near the Septizonium and in a very small dark room besides." For other examples see SUETONIUS, *Domitian,* 1,1; *Augustus*, 5; *Caligula*, 8,1; *Claudius*, 2,1; *Nero*, 6,1; *Galba*, 4,1; *Otho*, 2,1; PLUTARCH, *Alexander*, 3,5; *Cicero*, 2,1-2; *Numa*, 3,6.

stood beside his mother, Olympias, and calculating the courses of the heavenly bodies, discouraged her from delivering too quickly, saying: "Woman, hold yourself back and defeat the situation nature presents. If you give birth now, you will produce a servile prisoner or a monster." And a bit later: "Persevere a little longer, woman. If you give birth now your offspring will be a eunuch and a failure." When the astrologer realized that the whole cosmos was at its zenith, and he saw a brilliance shining from heaven, he said to Olympias: "Now give out the birth cry! You are on the point of bearing a king who will rule the world." And the narrator himself says: "Olympias, bellowing louder than a cow, gave birth with good fortune."[46]

The years *after* the hero's birth are narrated as well. During boyhood of the hero, references to the education of the main character predominate.[47] The literary works give quite a thorough treatment of the various instructors and the honors paid them. Plutarch says that in Alexander's childhood, his father, feeling that it was a matter of great importance, directed all his thoughts to his education and care, and he entrusted the training of the boy to special teachers. He asked Aristotle, the most famous and learned among philosophers, to teach his son.[48] This training could last many years because Suetonius affirms of Claudius that, "for a long

---

[46] PSEUDO-CALLISTHENES, *Alexander*, 1,12. See also PLUTARCH, *Alexander*, 3,5-6; 3,9, where, right after Alexander's birth, Philip receives three messages at the same time of three different victories. These things delight Philip, and the seers raise their spirits still higher by declaring that the son whose birth coincided with three victories would be always victorious. For other examples of signs during labor see PLUTARCH, *Cicero*, 2,1; *Theseus*, 7,2-4; *Cato*, 1,2-3.

[47] Pseudo-Callisthenes tells that "when Alexander was twelve, he started accompanying his father on troop maneuvers: he armed himself, swept along with the armies, and leapt on the horses. As a result, Philip, seeing him, said, 'Alexander, my boy, I like your character and your bravery.'" (PSEUDO-CALLISTHENES, *Alexander*, 1,14). See as well PLUTARCH, *Cato*, 2,1-4.

[48] See PLUTARCH, *Alexander*, 5,7-8; 7,1; 8,1; SUETONIUS, *Nero*, 7,1, where Nero was confided to the training of Annaeus Seneca, who on the following night dreamed that he was teaching Caesar. Or PLUTARCH, *Pericles*, 4-6, where his different teachers are described. We can find other examples of the importance of education in PSEUDO-CALLISTHENES, *Alexander*, 1,13; 1,16; QUINTUS CURTIUS RUFUS, *Alexander*, 4,1; 5,7; 11,1; PLUTARCH, *Demosthenes*, 4,1-5; 5,5-6; *Cicero*, 2,2-3; 3-4; *Theseus*, 4; *Numa*, 3,7; *Themistocles*, 2,1-3.

time, even after he reached the age of independence, he was in a state of tutelage and under an educator."[49] This education shows the progressive development of the character. In fact, Suetonius affirms that "even in boyhood his (Titus') mental gifts were conspicuous and they became more and more so as he advanced in years. He had a handsome person, in which there was no less dignity than grace."[50]

There are as well several general descriptions of the outward appearance of the protagonist. I have chosen one example from Pompey's biography to illustrate this:

> At the outset, too, he had a countenance which helped him in no small degree to win the favour of the people, and which pleaded for him before he spoke. For even his boyish loveliness had a gentle dignity about it, and in the prime and flower of his youthful beauty there was at once manifest the majesty and kingliness of his nature. His hair was inclined to lift itself slightly from his forehead, and this, with a graceful contour of face about the eyes, produced a resemblance, more talked about than actually apparent, to the portrait statues of King Alexander.[51]

Finally, often before the hero's birth, the author informs the reader about the hero's family. It is information which, like a genealogy, is always at the beginning of the literary work.[52] This information is more a description of the whole family, brothers, sisters, parents, and grandparents, and the most important things

---

[49] SUETONIUS, *Claudius,* 2,2-3,1.

[50] SUETONIUS, *Titus,* 2,1; 3,1.

[51] PLUTARCH, *Pompey*, 2,1-3. For other examples see PLUTARCH, *Alexander*, 4,2; *Cato*, 1,3-5; *Sulla*, 2,1; *Alcibiades,* 1,3-5; *Caius Marius*, 2,1; *Pyrrhus*, 3,4; *Fabius Maximus*, 1,4-6; *Coriolanus*, 2,1-2; *Philopoemen*, 2,1-6; *Demetrius*, 2,2.

[52] SUETONIUS, *Galba,* 4, says: "It would be a long story to give in detail his illustrious ancestors and the honorary inscriptions of the entire race, but I shall give a brief account of his immediate family." For other ancestors' descriptions, see PSEUDO-CALLISTHENES, *Alexander*, 1,1-3; QUINTUS CURTIUS RUFUS, *Alexander*, 1,4,1; PLUTARCH, *Caius Marius*, 3,1; *Theseus*, 3,1-2; *Themistocles*, 1,1-4; *Coriolanus*, 1,1-2; *Alcibiades*, 1,1-3; *Cato*, 1,1-3; *Pryrhus*, 1; *Lucullus*, 1,1; *Antony*, 1,1-2; *Brutus*, 1-2; *Artaxerxes*, 1,1-4; *Demosthenes*, 4,1-3; SUETONIUS, *Otho,* 1; *Vitellius,* 1-2; *Augustus,* 1-4; *Tiberius,* 1-4; *Caligula,* 7; *Nero,* 1-5.

that they have done, rather than a genealogy with the ancestor's names only.[53]

1.2.2 Actors of the Signs

By *actors* of the infancy narratives, I am referring to the people who are present and carry out the signs. They may be those who perform the signs or are eyewitnesses to the signs. The protagonists of these proleptic signs were as likely to be most directly familiar with the infant main character (father,[54] mother,[55] grandfather,[56] or grandmother[57]), as to be different authorities (priests,[58] prophets,[59], teachers,[60] astrologers,[61] magi,[62] fortune tellers,[63] or the Caesar that is reigning at the moment).[64] It is also possible that the protagonist of the sign is the infant himself.[65]

---

[53] I refer to the description of the hero's family, the information about the physical hero's appearance, and the normal training of the hero at the end of the section because they do not enter into the category of *signs*.

[54] See PSEUDO-CALLISTHENES, *Alexander*, 1,17; SUETONIUS, *Augustus*, 94,6; *Nero*, 6,1; *Domitian*, 14,1.

[55] See SUETONIUS, *Vespasian*, 5,2.

[56] See SUETONIUS, *Galba*, 4,2-3.

[57] See SUETONIUS, *Vespasian*, 5,2.

[58] See SUETONIUS, *Augustus,* 94,5-7.

[59] See PSEUDO-CALLISTHENES, *Alexander*, 1,18.

[60] See PSEUDO-CALLISTHENES, *Alexander*, 1,16; PLUTARCH, *Themistocles*, 2,1-3.

[61] See PSEUDO-CALLISTHENES, *Alexander*, 1,12; SUETONIUS, *Tiberius*, 14,2; *Domitian*, 14,1. Only in the case of Tiberius do we know the name of the astrologer, Escribonio.

[62] See QUINTUS CURTIUS RUFUS, *Alexander*, 4,1.

[63] See PSEUDO-CALLISTHENES, *Alexander,* 1,12; PLUTARCH, *Alexander*, 2,3-5; SUETONIUS, *Augustus,* 94,2; *Vespasian*, 5,2.

[64] See SUETONIUS, *Nero,* 6,2; *Galba*, 4,2. It is interesting to note the number of religious (priests, prophets, magi, fortune tellers) and civil protagonists (the emperor and his family) who are protagonists of the infancy narratives' signs. There was an interrelationship of religious and political power in these societies which tended to promote the religious integration of the empire (BEARD – NORTH, *Pagan Priests*, 47-48; RIVES, *Religion in the Roman Empire*, 155-157). The emperor's political leadership was announced in religious practice during his infancy. Suetonius especially conveys images of emperors performing traditional ritual acts with personal piety as the embodiment of Roman piety (SUETONIUS, *Nero*, 56; *Galba,* 4).

[65] See SUETONIUS, *Augustus*, 94,5-7; *Galba*, 4,3.

The signs are often related and described by the narrator, and thus the narrator makes known to the reader, but not to the actors within the narrative, the new information; it implies that the reader has always more information than the actors within the narrative. The narrator, sharing his information with the reader, is building the implied reader so that he is more informed than the actors themselves.[66] Speaking actors who present the signs in direct speech are rarely found.[67] But when they do occur, the narrator allows these speaking actors to impose their point of view, and the author makes the information known to the actors within the narration and, through these, to the reader. These signs, in which there is a direct speech, acquire more prominence because this fact emphasized the information in the mind of the reader.

In the examples in which there is a speaking actor, the narrator usually tells the reaction of those present. This reaction, especially of the parents, is always surprise, admiration, and confidence in the veracity of the sign.[68] This reaction implicitly invites the reader to react in the same way. I believe that the reaction to these signs are used by the author to influence the behavior of others, the readers. They are means of generating confidence, supporting and guiding the interpretation of the readers.[69] I suggest that the confidence that actors, *intradiegetically*, had in the sign is the confidence that the reader, *extradiegetically*, is invited to have, being able to confidently approach the text knowing in advance the main traits of the protagonist.[70]

---

[66] See DE JONG, "Homer and Narratology", 324.

[67] The only phrases that are found in direct speech are always brief and summarize the prophecy: "You are on the point of bearing a king who will rule the world" (PSEUDO-CALLISTHENES, *Alexander*, 1,12); "This boy will be a great king" (QUINTUS CURTIUS RUFUS, *Alexander*, 5,7); "My boy, thou will be nothing insignificant, but something great, of a surety" (PLUTARCH, *Themistocles*, 2,1-3); "You too, child, will enjoy our power" (SUETONIUS, *Galba,* 4,2).

[68] However, the grandparents do not always believe the authenticity of the sign. In fact, Galba's grandfather and Vespasian's grandmother laughed at signs (SUETONIUS, Galba, 4,2-3; Vespasian, 5,2).

[69] On this pragmatic function of the signs see LIEBESCHUETZ, *Continuity and Change*, 2-29.

[70] I use the term *intradiegetic* to express the internal elements of the text: charac-

1.2.3 Contents of the Signs

When speaking of the *contents* of the signs, I refer to the character which is affirmed of the child through the signs associated with his infancy. If the sign is a prophecy, the content would be what is prophesied, or rather the titles which are foretold of the character. Nevertheless, what we mostly find in the signs are generalizations about youthful promise, or a routine collection of prodigies, dreams, or prophecies of greatness that one could call *routine generalization*.[71] For example:

> It is said that Cicero was born, without travail or pain on the part of his mother, on the third day of the new Calends, the day on which at the present time the magistrates offer sacrifices and prayers for the health of the emperor. It would seem also that a phantom appeared to his nurse and foretold that her charge would be a great blessing to all the Romans. And although these presages were thought to be mere dreams and idle fancies, he soon showed them to be true prophecy; for when he was of an age for taking lessons, his natural talent shone out clear and he won name and fame among the boys.[72]

There are not much content foretold of the main character. The contents usually speak about his future social role: "world ruler"[73] and "king."[74]

---

ters, actions, plots, etc; and the term *extradiegetic* to express the external elements of the text: narrator, author, reader, etc. On these terms see ALETTI, *et al.*, *Vocabulaire raisonné*, 70. On the relationship between the character's belief and the readers' belief see PERROT, "Les recits d'enfance", 495-497.

[71] I borrow this expression from PELLING, "Childhood and Personality", 216.

[72] PLUTARCH, *Cicero*, 2,1. The biography of Augustus affirms that the "signs occurred on the very day of his birth, and afterwards, from which it was possible to anticipate and perceive his future greatness and uninterrupted good fortune" (SUETONIUS, *Augustus*, 94,1). For other examples of generalizations see PLUTARCH, *Cicero*, 2,1; *Cato*, 1,2; and *Lucullus*, 1,2-5.

[73] Pseudo-Callisthenes speaks of "world ruler" and "sovereign of the whole world" (PSEUDO-CALLISTHENES, *Alexander*, 1,12.16.17).

[74] PSEUDO-CALLISTHENES, *Alexander*, 1,12; QUINTUS CURTIUS RUFUS, *Alexander*, 5,7; SUETONIUS, *Augustus*, 94,3.

1.2.4 Location of the Signs

The majority of the infancy narrative scenes happen in unspecified places. However, there are two examples where the narrator gives the location of the scene: the temple. First, when Suetonius describes the days immediately following the birth of Nero, the narrator affirms that an unequivocal sign of his ill-fated destiny manifested itself on his *lustration* (Lat: *lustrico*).[75] This word refers to the familiar religious ceremony that took place in the temple on the ninth day after the birth of a boy and eight days after the birth of a girl. In the course of this ceremony, the family purified themselves through a propitiatory offering to the temple and found out the name of the newly born child.[76] When Caligula was allowed to give the child whatever name he wished, he "looked at his uncle Claudius, and said that he gave him his name. This he did, not seriously, but in jest, and Agrippina scorned the proposal, because at that time Claudius was one of the laughingstocks of the court."[77] The ceremony of imposition of the name is seen by Suetonius as a prediction, in this case ill-fated, of the destiny of the protagonist. In this way, from the beginning of Nero's biography, the author presents Nero's character, which was considered inauspicious.[78]

Second, when Alexander was still a child, he wanted to take part in a horse race. The narrator describes the race and Alexander's victory at length. After his victory, Alexander was crowned

---

[75] SUETONIUS, *Nero,* 6, 2.

[76] See ANDREWS, *et al.*, *A Latin Dictionary*, 1087.

[77] The connection is made clear in this text between the imposition of a name and the future fate of the personage, who is characterized also by his name. If Nero had taken the name of a laughingstock, it would have had bad consequences in his future life. Moreover, they also considered the words of Nero's father, Domitian, as an ill-fated omen: "Nothing that was not abominable and a public bane could be born of Agrippina and himself" (SUETONIUS, *Nero,* 6,1).

[78] All of the examples of characterization through the infancy narratives proposed so far are positive ones. The good features and virtues of the protagonist are presented in his childhood. However, in this example we also find a negative characterization. Another example of ill-fated characterization is PLUTARCH, *Crassus*, 1,1-2,2, where his sole vice of avarice goes back to the fact that he was reared in a very small house with many siblings and siblings-in-law living together.

and, wearing his victory crown of wild olive, went up to the temple of Olympian Zeus, where the prophet of Zeus prophesized about Alexander's future life.[79]

1.3 Divine Orientation and Character Development

These Greco-Roman texts show some kind of belief in fate or divine indications. The importance ascribed to the infancy narratives' signs presupposes an understanding of *character traits* as a fixed qualification of a person's identity. Those who achieve a noble death, and thus become heroes, are oriented to their roles from birth. The infancy narratives' signs indicate the divine intention in connection with the character.[80] Unusual births are thus prodigies, prophecies, and dreams that signal to the perceptive interpreter that the infant is destined for greatness. The function of infancy narratives within the Greco-Roman biography is to announce that, by divine ordination, a hero had been born, though this heroism would not be widely recognized until after the hero's career was completed.

Throughout the infancy narratives, however, after the divine intention was manifested through different signs, we find the development of the character through his education. The primary divine intention is not enough. It should be confirmed by human free choice through the intellectual and physical training of the character. The references to *training* and *education* imply that such *divine talents* or *abilities* that are given needed to be carefully nurtured and developed.[81]

The divine intention is first affirmed usually before, during, or right after the hero's birth through different prodigies, prophecies

---

[79] PSEUDO-CALLISTHENES, *Alexander*, 1,18-19.

[80] See GILL, "The Character-Personality Distinction", 1-31; WARDMAN, *Plutarch's Lives*, 132.

[81] JAEGER, *Paideia* I, xiv-xxvi, defends the opinion that education is the transversal topic of the entire Greek culture. Jaeger contends that, for Greeks, education in the early years of life was the *beginning* (ἀρχή), not only temporally, but also spiritually, of every individual person. For the value of education in the Greco-Roman culture see FACQ, "Les enfants", 247-257.

and dreams. There was a special connection between the divinity and the infancy.[82] Later, during childhood, in the early formative years, the free human cooperation appears in the infancy narratives.[83] Divine intention and human freedom join strength to achieve the success of the public life of the hero. Thus, during Alexander's childhood, "Philip (Alexander's father), having the highest hopes of his son because of so many omens, directed all his thoughts to his education and care."[84] And Plutarch, speaking about Cicero, unites again both dimensions, the divine intention, through his natural talents, and the human response, through his studies:

> When he (Cicero) was of an age for taking lessons, his natural talent shone out clear and he won name and fame among the boys [...] And although he showed himself, as Plato thought a nature should do which was fond of learning and fond of wisdom, capable of welcoming all knowledge and incapable of slighting any kind of literature or training, he lent himself with somewhat greater ardor to his formation.[85]

This feature of the infancy narratives could have its origin in Stoicism. Spanneut has proved the presence and influence of Stoicism on the Greco-Roman world. According to him, the Latin and Greek literature around the first century BC had been especially strongly influenced by Stoicism.[86] In the Stoic system, the

---

[82] After a careful research with many examples of children in the Greco-Roman, canonical and apocryphal literature, Bovon affirms that the "Greeks and Romans had the wisdom to detect in children a special relation to the gods" (BOVON, "The Child and the Beast", 19).

[83] MCGAUGHY, "Infancy Narratives", 27, thinks that Hellenistic biographies inserted between the account of the miraculous birth and the summary of the hero's adult career one incident from the hero's childhood to telescope precisely how the hero responds and begins to pursue his task.

[84] PLUTARCH, *Alexander*, 8,1; see as well QUINTUS CURTIUS RUFUS, *Alexander*, 1,5,2.

[85] PLUTARCH, *Cicero*, 2,2-3.

[86] See SPANNEUT, *Permanence du Stoïcisme*, 107-110. For example, Luke, in the speech of Paul in Athens, seems to know Stoic philosophy (Acts 17:22-34, particularly Acts 17:18). Some scholars have suggested that Luke's portrayal of the prayer on the Mount of Olives (Lk 22:39-46) mirrors a Stoic philosopher who conquers the irrational passions of sorrow and is able to face his inminent death with serenity.

rational principle operating inside reality receives its primarily name of *reason* (λόγος). All things of the world are brought about and linked in the most rational way through *reason*, or active principle, which determines the causes of existing things. The causes manifest the *Logos'* divine intention through different prodigies and dreams. These signs contain statements about the future, and are given by the gods to enable human beings to acquire information about the future. This information about the future could be predicted by something like divination.[87] However Stoic determinism is distinct from ancient theories of necessitarianism.[88] There are things which depend upon the human agents who perform the action. Stoic determinism was not opposed to freedom. The human person can choose to conform his life to the *Logos* or not. This is the reason why Stoic morality is designed to let the person be drawn along, without any resistance, by the causes of the universe.[89] Among these things that happen because of human action, Stoics included formation and training during childhood. Thus the character is involved in causal determinism through formation.[90]

2. The Jewish Literature

Throughout the OT we find several narratives about important characters which could be classified as "biographies." Within these "biographies" there are a few occasions in which we have stories concerning the birth and infancy of those important per-

---

However, Jesus expresses his revulsion at his suffering and death (Lk 22:42), and he considers the life of this world as a gift from God (Lk 22:46). I believe that this passage depends more on the suffering servant figure in Deutero-Isaiah.

[87] On divination and prediction see GOODENOUGH, *An Introduction to Philo*, 87-88.

[88] MAGRIS, "Stoicism", 8741-8742, claims that fate does not have to be identified with a necessity that compels a person to do something. The environment lays down certain necessary conditions, but consent to action comes from the person's own nature. Fate does not fulfill its plan automatically, but coordinates the freely chosen actions of humans with the circumstances.

[89] On Stoic determinism see MAGRIS, *L'idea di destino nel pensiero antico* II, 514-547.

[90] On human fulfillment in willing conformity to a pre-ordained plan see BOBZIEN, *Determinism and Freedom*, 400-402; and SEDLEY, "Stoicism", 157-158.

sons. The most extensive infancy narratives in the OT are: Isaac (Genesis 17:15–18:15; 21–22); Esau and Jacob (Gn 25:19-28); Moses (Ex 2:1-10); Samson (Judges 13); and Samuel (1 Samuel 1–3). Jewish writers have commented on the OT, especially on those different "biographies" and infancy narratives of the OT. The life of Moses, in particular, has been commented on by many Jewish writers. I believe that the role that Alexander the Great played in the development of Greco-Roman literature was played by Moses in Jewish literature. There is abundant evidence that since the second century BC, oral traditions have created a new framework for the OT birth narratives, which were retold by way of additions and small changes, making them more attractive.[91] Jewish infancy narratives display a marked tendency to embellish the details that they find in the Scriptures with elements from Jewish traditions or their own imaginations. Biographies, however, were not written about the great rabbinic teachers, even teachers like Hillel and Shammai.[92]

Because of their importance, length, and close similarity to Luke's infancy narrative, I have selected the passages of Moses, Samson, and Samuel to examine examples of developments of biblical

[91] PHILO, *The Life of Moses*, 1,4, affirms that he tells the story as he has learned it from some of the elders and from the sacred books: "For I always interwove what I was told with what I read."

[92] Jewish literature described the teaching of important rabbis, but not their lives. Probably because the center of rabbinic Judaism was the Torah, biographies of the important rabbis are absent, while their teachings on the Torah were included. The *Qumran* community produced nothing biographical about the *Teacher of Righteousness* or any other members of the community. According to the Jewish tradition, we could have received Jesus' teaching without a narrative about his life. The very existence of the Gospel, as Jesus' "biography," however, bears witness to the importance attached not only to his preaching and teaching, but even to his person by the early Church. This is the reason why GEORGI, "The Records of Jesus", 527-542, holds that Gospel's authors were claiming that the center of Christianity was the person of Jesus and contends that the main difference between the Gospels and the accounts of Hillel and other rabbinic traditions is that for the Gospel the person and life of Jesus is everything which is necessary. On this topic see as well HILTON – MARSHALL, *The Gospels and Rabbinic Judaism*, 13.

birth narratives in Jewish biographies.[93] How do these developments expand the infancy narratives? Did the Jewish narratives mirror the features of the Greco-Roman narratives? Starting from the biblical text, I will explore how different authors "improved" the biblical narratives by explaining some mysterious elements and adding new motifs. We will be able to notice the devices used by one Jewish writer in the first century in recounting the birth of biblical heroes. This will illustrate some patterns that Luke may have used in writing about the birth of Jesus.

2.1 Introducing the Literary Works Studied

2.1.1 Philo's The Life of Moses *(Greek)*

Philo's home and birthplace have been faithfully reflected in his writings.[94] It will suffice to say that he came from a rich Jewish family and that he was trained in Greek as well as Jewish learning. The one public event in his life was his participation in an embassy sent by the Jews of Alexandria to Caligula to complain about the persecutions which they had been suffering. This is dated 39-40, and since Philo when writing his account of this mission some time later speaks of himself as an old man, it has been generally held that he was born about 30-20 BC. The date of his death is uncertain, but his lifetime covers the lifetimes of Jesus Christ and John the Baptist, and much of that of Paul.[95]

Philo is a citizen of the place that was at once the center of the Jewish Diaspora and Hellenistic culture: Alexandria. He owes his position in history mainly to that remarkable fusion of Hellenism

[93] The infancy narrative of Isaac is focused on the covenant, his circumcision, and his numerous descendants. The infancy narrative of both Esau and Jacob tells of the relationship between them. In addition, these infancy narratives have not been commented upon by Jewish writers as often as the infancy narratives of Moses, Samson and Samuel.

[94] See PHILO, *De vita Moysis*, 274-595, edited by Colson, whose numbering and translation I follow.

[95] There is no intimation that he knew anything of their life or work.

and Judaism which is evident in his voluminous writings. It is very likely that he was influenced by Greek literature, even by their biographies and infancy narratives. Most of his work clearly intends to re-interpret Jewish beliefs via Greek philosophy, often using allegorical methods. He manages this so successfully that many commentators see him as more Greek than Jewish.

The Life of Moses is a little different, and uses less allegory than his other works. Philo seeks to make Moses known to a wider Gentile audience.[96] With this mixture of Greek and Jewish background, *The Life of Moses* offers an interesting comparison with Luke's infancy narrative. I will focus my study on the texts which addresses Moses' infancy, particularly *The Life of Moses*, 1, 1-31.

2.1.2 Pseudo-Philo's Biblical Antiquities *(Hebrew)*

Biblical Antiquities tells the story of Israel from Adam to David.[97] It uses the framework of biblical books from Genesis to 2 Samuel and selectively expands and contracts certain episodes. It now exists in a Latin version whose idiom and style represent the vulgar Latin in which the old Latin versions of the Bible were written. However, the Latin text is a translation from the Greek, and underlying the Greek there must have been a Hebrew original.[98]

Attempts to date the composition of the original Hebrew version have paid attention to the presence of what may be called a *Palestinian* biblical text, rather than a *Babylonian* or an *Egyptian*

---

[96] See BORGEN, *Philo of Alexandria*, 46-62, where Borgen speaks about how Philo reviewed and rewrote biblical material. On Philo's writings, especially *The Life of Moses*, see GOODENOUGH, *An Introduction to Philo*, 30-51.

[97] See PSEUDO-PHILO, *Liber antiquitatum biblicarum*, 60-387, edited by Harrington and Cazeaux, whose numbering and translation I follow.

[98] See HARRINGTON, "The Original Language", 505-508, about the Greek stage; 508-512, about the Hebrew stage; and 512-514, about the original text as Hebrew and not Aramaic. According to Harrington there are several texts that are best explained if we presume a Greek stage in the transmission (3,10; 9,2.15; 45,6). There are also examples of mistranslation implying a Hebrew original (15,6; 53,6). Lastly, some biblical texts are best explained as translations from Hebrew into Greek and then into Latin (3,4).

text.[99] As the *Palestinian* biblical text was probably suppressed around 100, it makes the latest possible date around 100. Some other considerations lead us to suspect that *Biblical Antiquities* was composed before 70.[100] Therefore, a date before the destruction of the Temple seems most likely.

The Latin text of Pseudo-Philo was transmitted along with the Latin translations of Philo's works, but the attribution of this work to Philo cannot be sustained.[101] In addition, if Pseudo-Philo's work had really been composed by Philo the Jew, Alexandria would have been its obvious place of origin. Many factors point to Palestine as the place in which Pseudo-Philo's writing originated.[102] Pseudo-Philo seems to reflect the milieu of Palestine at the turn of the Common Era. I will concentrate my study on the infancy narratives of Moses (*Biblical Antiquities* 9), Samson (*Biblical Antiquities* 42), and Samuel (*Biblical Antiquities* 49-53).

---

[99] For these classification of archaic texts types and early recensions see CROSS, *The Ancient Library of Qumran*, 121-142; 163-194; and HARRINGTON, "The Biblical Text", 16-17.

[100] The reasons are the following: the attitude toward the Temple and sacrifice (32,3) is what we would expect before 70; the expression "unto this day" in 22,8 suggests that the Temple still stands; the negative attitude toward Jewish rulers not chosen by God (possibly an anti-Herodian polemic) would have been a dead issue after 70; the silence about the destruction of the Temple would be strange if indeed the Temple had been already destroyed; and the free attitude toward the biblical text fits the period before 70 better than after it.

[101] The manner of dealing with the biblical text is very different from Philo's allegorizing. Moreover, there are several points at which Pseudo-Philo explicitly contradicts the views of Philo. Among these examples are the 1,652 years from Adam to the Flood (3,6) against Philo's 2,242; the favorable or at least neutral portrayal of Balaam (18) against Philo's negative description; Moses' burial by God (19,16), not by the angels. Finally, Philo wrote in Greek (how much Hebrew he knew is debatable) but our author apparently wrote in Hebrew. On these differences see HARRINGTON, "Birth Narratives", 317.

[102] It was apparently composed in Hebrew since the biblical text that the author had at his disposal was a Palestinian one; there are many literary parallels with 4 Ezra and 2 Baruch, both of Palestinian origin; some of the author's theological interests (the Temple, the rules of sacrifice, the covenant and the Law, eschatology, and angelology) point toward a Palestinian provenance; and the author seems to know the geography of Palestine (55,7).

2.1.3 *Josephus'* The Jewish Antiquities *(Greek)*

Flavius Josephus was a first-century Jew who passed an eventful life as a diplomat, general, and historian. Josephus was born in a good time and place for his future career: in Jerusalem in the year 37, a few years before the Jewish war. Further details of his life derive from a brief autobiography he wrote later in life, *The Life of Flavius Josephus*, as well as from the references he makes to his own role as commander in *The Jewish War*. Josephus must have died sometime after 100.[103]

Schooled in Aramaic, Josephus wrote a massive history in Greek for a Roman audience. Many of the historical works that he used have perished, but his own have survived. The writings of Josephus, then, provide a vital political, topographical, social, literary, and religious supplement to our biblical information. They are a crucial source for extending our knowledge of the times. In chronological order, he wrote *The Jewish War, The Jewish Antiquities, The Life of Flavius Josephus* and *Against Apion. The Jewish Antiquities*, Josephus' major work, appeared late in the reign of Domitian (93-94)[104] and provides a massive "introduction" to *The Jewish War* by presenting the whole panorama of Jewish history from creation and the patriarchs up to 62. It finishes with the gathering war clouds of the Jewish revolt. For *The Jewish Antiquities*, Josephus had three audiences in mind: Roman, Greek, and Jewish. In this study I will use the infancy narratives of Moses (*The Jewish Antiquities,* 2,9), Samson (*The Jewish Antiquities,* 5,8), and Samuel (*The Jewish Antiquities,* 5,10), and his own infancy narrative that he wrote in his autobiography (*The Life of Flavius Josephus*, 1-2).

The next table helps to locate the studied texts in space and time.

---

[103] See JOSEPHUS, *The New Complete Works of Josephus*, 47-661, edited by Wishton and Maier, whose numbering and translations I follow. On the historical origin of *The Jewish Antiquities* see TROIANI, "La genèse historique des antiquités juives", 21-28.

[104] Josephus provides the date of the thirteenth year of the reign of Domitian (93-94) in the last paragraph of the work (JOSEPHUS, *The Jewish Antiquities*, 20,12,1).

Author	Literary work	Language	Place	Date
Philo	*The Life of Moses*	Greek	Alexandria	30 BC-40
Ps-Philo	*Biblical Antiquities*	(Hebrew)	Palestine	60?[105]
Josephus	*Jewish Antiquities*	Greek	Rome	30-100

2.2 The Jewish Infancy Narratives

I will first introduce the biblical infancy narratives to show how the Jewish authors commonly clear up problems in the biblical texts on Moses, Samson and Samuel. Then, having presented the biblical text, I will be able to underscore, with the same procedure as in § 1.2, the additions that the Jewish authors introduce.

2.2.1 Solving Exegetical Problems

Moses' birth and childhood are described in Ex 2:1-10. It is a brief passage introduced by the description of the oppression of the Israelite people because they were becoming more numerous and powerful than the Egyptians (Exodus 1). After that we find the early life of Moses; his parents cast him into the river and he was taken by the pharaoh's daughter as her son (Ex 2:1-10). One example of clearing up exegetical problems in the biblical text is shown when Philo solves the problem of why the pharaoh's daughter adopted Moses:

> The king of the country had but one cherished daughter, who, we are told, had been married for a considerable time but had never conceived a child, though she naturally desired one, particularly of the male sex, to succeed to the magnificent inheritance of her father's kingdom, which threatened to go to strangers if this daughter gave him no grandson.[106]

---

[105] As Pseudo-Philo's dates are unknown I write here the likely date of composition.

[106] PHILO, *The Life of Moses*, 1,13. For other examples of Moses see PSEUDO-PHILO, *Biblical Antiquities,* 9,14-15, where Pseudo-Philo explains why Pharaoh's daughter, according to Ex 2:6, could have recognized Moses as "one of the Hebrews' chil-

Samson's birth announcement and birth are described in Judges 13. After affirming that the Israelites were in the hands of the Philistines, the narrator refers to two different prodigies: the announcements of Samson's birth by the angel of the Lord. The difference among them is that in the first one only Samson's mother takes part (Jg 13:2-7), but in the second one both Samson's mother and his father, Manoah, take part (Jg 13:8-25). The second one repeats the first, adding the presence of Manoah (Jg 13:22). Pseudo-Philo tries to solve the problem of this duplicate appearance by prefacing the angel's first appearance to Manoah's wife, named Eluma, by the report of daily quarrels between Manoah and Eluma about which of them is sterile. The first appearance answers this question: "You are the sterile one who does not bring forth, and you are the womb that is forbidden to bear fruit."[107] Manoah does not consider himself worthy to receive the angel and voices the following worry: The second appearance answers this consideration: "Run and announce to your husband that God has accounted him worthy to hear my voice."[108]

The infancy narrative of Samuel (1 Samuel 1–3) starts with the genealogy of Elkanah, Samuel's father. After Elkanah's genealogy, his wife Hannah is introduced as a sterile woman who begs for a son (1 S 1:9-16), and makes this vow: "O Lord, if only you [...] give to your servant a male child, then I will set him before you as a nazirite until the day of his death" (1 S 1:11). With simplicity the priest Eli says to her: "Go in peace; may the God of Israel grant the petition you have made to him" (1 S 1:17). The woman went to her quar-

---

dren": Moses was "in the covenant of the flesh" having been circumcised; and JOSEPHUS, *The Jewish Antiquities*, 2,9,5, where Josephus solved the problem of why Pharaoh's daughter gave Moses to a Hebrew mother to be fed by her (Ex 2:9); Moses would not admit of any other woman's breast who was not a Hebrew woman.

[107] PSEUDO-PHILO, *Biblical Antiquities*, 42,3.

[108] PSEUDO-PHILO, *Biblical Antiquities,* 42,6. Josephus gives another reason for this second appearance. After hearing from his wife, Manoah was immeasurably jealous of her because the apparition seen by her was an angel of God, and resembled a young man, beautiful and tall. Knowing his jealousy, Manoah's wife asked for a second apparition in order that her husband could see the angel of God and not be jealous (JOSEPHUS, *The Jewish Antiquities*, 5,8,3).

ters and her countenance was no longer sad. When she had weaned the child, she took him up with her to the house of the Lord at Shiloh to offer him to God as she had promised (1 S 1:19-28). Having offered him to God, Hannah prays without making any reference to her son's future life (1 S 2:1-11). Then, Eli's wicked sons are presented and because of their evil a prophecy by an anonymous man against Eli's household is made (1 S 2:12-36). Finally, Samuel receives his calling and his first prophetic activity (1 Samuel 3). Adopting the framework of 1 Sam 1–3, Pseudo-Philo and Josephus try to resolve a difficulty in the biblical passage by explaining the reason why the God of Israel raised Samuel to become a prophet. Pseudo-Philo's narration begins with an entire chapter that is added to the biblical narrative.[109] In this chapter, the author describes the search of the sons of Israel for a new leader chosen by God: Samuel. Josephus' narration starts with the sons of Eli who were guilty of injustice towards men and impiety towards God. Samuel, and not an anonymous man, prophecies the condemnation of Eli's household, and he replaces Eli's household.[110]

The Hebrew authors clear up problems in the biblical text, but that is not all. They interpret the biblical infancy narratives in their own way, expanding passages and even adding new topics. For example, the next table on Moses' infancy narrative shows the elements in these Jewish versions of the biblical infancy narrative that are not directly derived from the biblical text.[111] These elements, not present in the biblical text, will be examined in the next sections.

---

[109] PSEUDO-PHILO, *Biblical Antiquities*, 49.

[110] JOSEPHUS, *The Jewish Antiquities*, 5,10,1.

[111] This table shows how Philo is the Jewish author most influenced by Greco-Roman literature. The genealogy, training, and physical appearance of the child, which were all common features of Greco-Roman literature, are added by Philo to the biblical narrative. Pseudo-Philo, writing in Palestine, adds more Jewish contents through several prophecies and dreams. Finally, Josephus adds both Jewish contents through prodigies, prophecies and dreams, and Greco-Roman features such as training and physical appearance. Being a Jew, he writes in Greek specially for a Roman audience.

	Ex 2:1-10	Philo	Ps-Philo	Josephus
Prodigy	–	–	–	2,9,4
Prophecy	–	–	9,3.6.7	2,9,2
Dream	–	–	9,9.10	2,9,3
Genealogy	–	1,5-7	–	2,9,6
Training	–	1,21-23	–	2,9,6.7
Physical appearance	–	1,9	–	2,9,6

2.2.2 Types of Signs in the Infancy Narratives

In the Jewish literature are found the same kind of *signs* to describe the infancy narratives that we found in the Greco-Roman literature:[112] prodigies (or portents), prophecies (or omens, oracles, predictions, or auguries) and dreams. A *prodigy* is recounted in relation to Moses' birth. His mother's labor was without pain: "The mother's labor was such as afforded a confirmation to what was foretold by God; for it was not known to those that watched her, by the easiness of her pains, and because the throes of her delivery did not fall upon her with violence."[113]

Pseudo-Philo's infancy narrative for Samuel relates a divine *prophecy*. The sons of Israel began to make a request of the Lord and said: "Let all of us cast lots to see who it is who can rule us as Kenaz did. For perhaps we will find a man who may free us from our distress, because it is not appropriate for the people to be without a ruler." God himself answers his people and prophesies as follows:

> Now know that Elkana, upon whom the lot has fallen, cannot rule among you; but rather his son who will be born from him, he will rule among you and prophesy. And from this time on, a ruler will not

---

[112] Manoah, referring to Samson's prophecy, says to the angel: "I am not worthy to hear the *signs* and *wonders* that God has done among us" (PSEUDO-PHILO, *Biblical Antiquities*, 42,5). In addition, God himself speaks of "signs and wonders" in PSEUDO-PHILO, *Biblical Antiquities*, 9,7.

[113] JOSEPHUS, *The Jewish Antiquities*, 2,9,4. For other prodigies see PSEUDO-PHILO, *Biblical Antiquities*, 42,9;. JOSEPHUS, *The Jewish Antiquities*, 5,8,3.

> be lacking from you for many years. None of the sons of Peninnah can rule the people, but the one who is born from the sterile woman whom I have given to him as a wife will be a prophet before me.[114]

Amram, Moses' father, had a *dream* before Moses' birth. God stood by him in his sleep and exhorted him not to despair of his future favors. He added that he did not forget their piety towards him and would always reward them for it. God said to Amram in his dream: "Know, therefore, that I shall provide for you all in common what is for your good; for that child, out of dread of whose birth the Egyptians have doomed the Israelite children to destruction, shall be this child of yours, and shall be concealed from those who watch to destroy him."[115] After the dream, Amram awakened and told it to his wife Jochebed.[116]

Like the Greco-Roman writers, the Jewish writers add information about the training of the child, physical appearance, and genealogy. The *education* of Moses is clearly told by Philo:

> With a modest and serious bearing he applied himself to hearing and seeing what was sure to profit the soul. Teachers at once arrived from different parts, some unbidden from the neighbouring countries and the provinces of Egypt, others summoned from Greece under promise of high reward. [...] Arithmetic, geometry, the lore of metre, rhythm and harmony, and the whole subject of music as shown by the use of instruments were imparted to him by learned teachers. [...] But in a short time he advanced beyond their capacities; his gifted nature forestalled their instruction, so that he himself devised and propounded problems which they could not easily solve.[117]

---

[114] PSEUDO-PHILO, *Biblical Antiquities,* 49,7-8. For other prophecies see PSEUDO-PHILO, *Biblical Antiquities,* 9,3-6; 9,7; 50,8; 51,2; 53,12; JOSEPHUS, *The Jewish Antiquities*, 2,9,2.

[115] JOSEPHUS, *The Jewish Antiquities*, 2,9,3.

[116] In JOSEPHUS, *The Jewish Antiquities*, 2,9,3-4, either an Egyptian sacred scribe, or a Jewish father prophesies his birth. For other dreams see PSEUDO-PHILO, *Biblical Antiquities,* 9,10; 9,15.

[117] PHILO, *The Life of Moses*, 1,21-23. For other texts about training see JOSEPHUS, *The Jewish Antiquities*, 2,9,6; and JOSEPHUS, *The Life of Flavius Josephus*, 1,2.

Josephus affirms that everybody was greatly in love with the child Moses, on account of his *outward appearance* and beauty:

> God did also give him that height as was wonderful. And as for his beauty, there was nobody so impolite as, when they saw Moses, they were not greatly surprised at the beauty of his countenance. In fact, it happened frequently, that those that met him as he was carried along the road, were obliged to turn again upon seeing the child; that they left what they were about, and stood still a great while to look on him; for the beauty of the child was so remarkable and natural to him on many accounts, that it detained the spectators, and made them stay longer to look upon him.[118]

And Pseudo-Philo starts Samson's infancy narrative with a *genealogy* that does not appear in the biblical text: "There was a man from the tribe of Dan, whose name was Manoah, son of Edoc, son of Odon, son of Eriden, son of Fadesur, son of Dema, son of Susi, son of Dan. And he had a wife whose name was Eluma."[119]

2.2.3 Actors of the Signs

Again, as in Greco-Roman literature, the family of the child (father,[120] mother,[121] sister,[122] and Pharaoh's daughter[123]), the religious authorities (an Egyptian sacred scribe[124] and the prophet Eli, see 1 S 1:9) are the protagonists of the infancy narratives' signs. And to these the

---

[118] JOSEPHUS, *The Jewish Antiquities*, 2,9,6. For other physical descriptions see PHILO, *The Life of Moses*, 1,9; and PSEUDO-PHILO, *Biblical Antiquities,* 51,1.

[119] PSEUDO-PHILO, *Biblical Antiquities,* 42,1. In fact, Pseudo-Philo's *Biblical Antiquities* starts with three genealogies, in a form very similar to Samson's genealogy: from Adam to Noah, from Cain to Lamech, and the genealogies of the sons of Noah (PSEUDO-PHILO, *Biblical Antiquities,* 1.2.4). For other genealogies see PHILO, *The Life of Moses*, 1,5-7; JOSEPHUS, *The Jewish Antiquities*, 2,9,6; JOSEPHUS, *The Life of Flavius Josephus*, 1,1.

[120] See PSEUDO-PHILO, *Biblical Antiquities,* 9,3.6; JOSEPHUS, *The Jewish Antiquities*, 2,9,3; 5,10,1.

[121] See PSEUDO-PHILO, *Biblical Antiquities,* 50,3.7.8; 51,3-4.

[122] See PSEUDO-PHILO, *Biblical Antiquities,* 9,9-10;

[123] See PSEUDO-PHILO, *Biblical Antiquities,* 9,15.

[124] See JOSEPHUS, *The Jewish Antiquities*, 2,9,2.

Jewish tradition adds two important actors, the angel of the Lord, and *Yhwh* himself. The angel of the Lord appears to the child's parents and announces his birth (Jg 13:3.9).[125] And *Yhwh* himself speaks to the child's father,[126] and to the child himself (1 S 3:4.8.10-14).[127]

The majority of the information told in the Jewish infancy narratives comes from these speaking actors who speak in direct speech.[128] Thus the narrator makes known the information not only to the characters within the narration, but also to the reader. This direct speech gives it more importance and vivacity.

When the information is shared by the narrator with the actors within the narration, often the narrator underlines their reaction. Josephus justifies the action of Moses' parents casting him into the river because God himself had told Amram in a dream that Moses was going to be brought up in a surprising way and that he would be cast forth into the water. They believed that God would in some way procure the safety of the child, in order to secure the truth of his own predictions. Moses' parents trusted in God's word through Amram's dream. This is why they cast Moses into the river.[129]

However, not only the child's parents trust in the signs, but also the whole people. After the divine prophecy that promises the birth of Moses as the savior of Israel, Josephus says to the reader through the narrator that

> so the Hebrews depended on him, and were of good hopes that great things would be done by him; but the Egyptians were suspicious of what would follow. Yet because, if Moses had been killed, there was no

---

[125] PSEUDO-PHILO, *Biblical Antiquities,* 9,10; 42,3.5; JOSEPHUS, *The Jewish Antiquities*, 5,8,2.3

[126] See JOSEPHUS, *The Jewish Antiquities*, 2,9,3; PSEUDO-PHILO, *Biblical Antiquities,* 49,7-8.

[127] See PSEUDO-PHILO, *Biblical Antiquities*, 53; JOSEPHUS, *The Jewish Antiquities*, 5,10,4.

[128] See PSEUDO-PHILO, *Biblical Antiquities,* 9,16; JOSEPHUS, *The Jewish Antiquities*, 2,9,2; 5,10,1.2.3.4.

[129] See JOSEPHUS, *The Jewish Antiquities*, 2,9,3-4. Pseudo-Philo adds the parents' response to the Samson infancy narrative signs: "See to it, Lord, that your word be accomplished regarding your servant." And the angel said: "It will be accomplished" (PSEUDO-PHILO, *Biblical Antiquities,* 42,7).

> one, either akin or adopted, that had any oracle on his side for pretending to the crown of Egypt.[130]

The Israelite hopes and the Egyptians' fears depend on this event in Moses' childhood. Both Hebrews and Egyptians trusted the sign and its future fulfillment.[131]

The main difference between the version of Pseudo-Philo and biblical account of Samuel's infancy falls on those who look forward to Samuel's birth. While in the biblical text there is a stress on Hannah's personal need for a child, in Pseudo-Philo's text there is a stress on the people's need for a prophet. In the biblical narration, only Hannah knew that a boy was going to be born to her, and she did not know anything more. In the *Biblical Antiquities,* the entire people of Israel asked for a new prophet and trusted in God's prophecy that a new prophet was going to be born: "'God has remembered us so as to free us from the hand of those who hate us.' And on that day they made peace offerings and feasted according to their customs."[132] In addition, when Hannah was going to present her child to Eli, the

> entire people came down to Shiloh together with timbrels and dances, lutes and harps, and they came to Eli the priest and brought to him Samuel. And they placed Samuel before the Lord, anointed him, and said, "Let the prophet live among the people, and may he be a light to this nation for a long time!"[133]

The promise of a new prophet has been publicly made to Israel. The entire people, and not only the mother, heard, trusted, and collaborated with God's promise. The reader is also questioned about this. The reader is invited to join the people of Israel in believing the sign and accepting Samuel as the new prophet for the rest of the literary work.

---

[130] JOSEPHUS, *The Jewish Antiquities*, 2,9,7.
[131] See PSEUDO-PHILO, *Biblical Antiquities,* 9,16.
[132] PSEUDO-PHILO, *Biblical Antiquities*, 49,8.
[133] PSEUDO-PHILO, *Biblical Antiquities*, 51,7.

2.2.4 Contents of the Signs

The Jewish writers' characterization through the contents of the signs is much more concrete than the Greco-Roman routine generalizations. In Miriam's dream, Moses is called by the spirit of God "savior," and "heir of the kingdom."[134] Even the narrator names Moses "savior."[135] Samson is characterized not only by his strength, but also as a "prophet"[136] and "savior."[137]

While in the biblical text Hannah presents her boy and prays without any reference to Samuel's life (see 1 S 2:1-10), in *Biblical Antiquities* Hannah refers her prayer to Samuel's vocation, and her song becomes a programmatic introduction to Samuel's prophetic life: "For he who is nursed will be raised up, and the people will be enlightened by his words, and he will show to the nations the statutes and his horn will be exalted very high [...] because from me will arise the ordinance of the Lord, and all men will find the truth."[138] The contents of the infancy narratives' signs also are clearer and more precise: "prophet,"[139] "ruler,"[140] "light to this nation,"[141] "light for the nations,"[142] "anointed one and king,"[143] and "advantage for the peoples and fountain for the twelve tribes."[144]

---

[134] JOSEPHUS, *The Jewish Antiquities*, 2,9,7.

[135] PSEUDO-PHILO, *Biblical Antiquities,* 9,10.16; and JOSEPHUS, *The Jewish Antiquities*, 2,9,3.7.

[136] JOSEPHUS, *The Jewish Antiquities*, 5,8,4.

[137] JOSEPHUS, *The Jewish Antiquities*, 5,8,2; PSEUDO-PHILO, *Biblical Antiquities*, 42,3.

[138] PSEUDO-PHILO, *Biblical Antiquities,* 51,3-4.

[139] See PSEUDO-PHILO, *Biblical Antiquities,* 49,8; 50,8; 51,6.7; and JOSEPHUS, *The Jewish Antiquities*, 5,10,1.2.3.4.

[140] PSEUDO-PHILO, *Biblical Antiquities*, 49,7.

[141] PSEUDO-PHILO, *Biblical Antiquities,* 51,3.6.7.

[142] PSEUDO-PHILO, *Biblical Antiquities*, 51,6.

[143] PSEUDO-PHILO, *Biblical Antiquities*, 51,6.

[144] PSEUDO-PHILO, *Biblical Antiquities,* 51,2. Both Josephus and Pseudo-Philo clearly characterize Samuel in his infancy as a prophet. While the announcement of Eli in the biblical text only says that Hannah will have a child, Pseudo-Philo adds the twofold nature of Samuel's ministry: he will be both a prophet for Israel and a light for the nations. On the relationship between this text and Lk 2:22-39 see KOET, "Holy Place", 123.

2.2.5 Location of the Signs

Moses' infancy narrative takes place around the river where Moses was deposited. The biblical narration of Samson does not say exactly where it takes place. It speaks of the field and the house (Jg 13:9), and, at the end of the narration, of the altar (Jg 13:20), which is reintroduced by the Jewish writers.[145] However, Pseudo-Philo locates all of the prayers asking for a miraculous birth in the "upper chamber." Samson's mother[146] and father[147] went up to the "upper chamber" and prayed. And while they were speaking the angel of the Lord came and spoke. In this way, Pseudo-Philo underlines the "upper chamber" as a special place for revelations. Finally, Samuel's infancy narrative takes place in the Temple (1 S 1:9.24; 3:3). The house of the Lord is a perfect place to make such a disclosure about Samuel's future life.[148] The Jewish writers usually do not name the place where the sign happens. However, when they give this information, it is in the Temple or in a special place for prayer.

3. Intended Literary Function of the Infancy Narratives

The infancy narratives' signs are often accompanied by an interpretation in an effort to understand their real significance. *Divination* is a central element in traditional religious systems, providing access to the divine will or knowledge of future events through the interpretation of all kinds of signs, whether prodigies, prophecies, or dreams.[149] In antiquity divination was perceived not only as due to a person's relationship with the gods, but also as a "science."[150] Divination was accepted as one of a range of methods to

---

[145] See PSEUDO-PHILO, *Biblical Antiquities,* 42,9; JOSEPHUS, *The Jewish Antiquities*, 5,8,3.

[146] See PSEUDO-PHILO, *Biblical Antiquities,* 42,2.

[147] See PSEUDO-PHILO, *Biblical Antiquities,* 42,5.

[148] PSEUDO-PHILO, *Biblical Antiquities*, 53,5.

[149] In Greco-Roman literature, the prodigies were regularly interpreted by divination. In Jewish literature, the special role of the prophet is to interpret both dreams and prophecies.

[150] The early Stoics considered divination as an art or expertise (τέχνη) or as a sci-

understand the world. The same or similar signs are taken to announce the same or similar future events. In other words, divination was a form of knowledge and understanding. This latter aspect of divination is especially important for our goal. For example, Alexander's birth had been interpreted by the Magi as the birth of a firebrand who was going to destroy the entire Orient. As, *intradiegetically*, the actor could better know and understand through this sign and its interpretation, so, *extradiegetically*, the reader also does. The reader also knew that the prophecy had been interpreted by the narrator: "The young prince early gave indications of a lofty man who would undertake great deeds."[151] Thus, this sign is an event full of significance and meaning inside the narrative, and also outside the narrative.[152] Through the literary representation of divination and the knowledge it imparts, the reader could know some aspects of the literary work that follows.

3.1 The Position of the Infancy Narratives' Signs within the Whole Work

All of the infancy narratives studied, except two,[153] are located at the beginning of their respective literary works, as an intro-

---

ence (ἐπιστήμη). "Chrysippus defined divination as 'science which contemplates and interprets the signs which are given to human beings by the gods.'" (BOBZIEN, *Determinism and Freedom*, 87).

[151] PLUTARCH, *Alexander*, 3,5-6.

[152] I believe that Plutarch refers to this meaning of the infancy narratives' signs when he says: "Each of these signs has been made, through some causal adaptation, to have some other meaning" (PLUTARCH, *Pericles*, 6,1-3). The author gives those signs "some other meaning." The infancy narratives' signs are a valuable literary tool to introduce the main features which are later developed. This is their additional meaning and significance.

[153] There are only two exceptions in the Greco-Roman literature, SUETONIUS, *Augustus*, 94; *Domitian*, 14, where they are situated at the end of the biographies. At the end of his work Suetonius returns to speaking of the emperor's infancy. The pretext was the omens that announce the day and mode of the death of the emperor. While addressing these death predictions Suetonius reminds us of other predictions and happenings in the emperor's infancy. They show the reader the nobility of the emperor, which was already developing when he was a child. In addition, they show

duction.[154] I attest that they serve to present the protagonist of the biography, anticipate the main topics, and prepare the reader for a better understanding of the accounts that will subsequently be narrated. There is a rhetorical purpose, a proleptic function, in the structure of the entire work. At the beginning of the literary work infancy narratives make known to the reader, through the narrator or a speaking character, information that is important for the rest of the work.

3.2 Harmony between Infancy Narrative and Public Life: a Characterization

The ancient methods of characterization were much more indirect than their modern counterparts. Although modern literature, especially modern biography, is greatly interested in the psychological dimension of character and personality, such ideas cannot be transferred wholesale into ancient literature.[155] Detailed character analysis and psychological descriptions are lacking in ancient biography. Instead, character is revealed by words and deeds.[156] The words and deeds, especially in the hero's infancy, become the literary tools to describe the main character

---

the fulfillment of the premonitory signs as well as lay the foundation for the veracity of the auguries referring to the death of Caesar. They are analepsis or *flash back*, in which the narrator goes back to previous events that took place earlier than the point in the story where we are at that given moment.

[154] There are two very old Greek texts of the book of Esther which display several amplifications in comparison with the Hebrew version. Both Greek texts, the LXX or the so-called B-text, and the so-called A-Text, present a dream of Mordecai at the beginning of the book (Esther B, 1-17; Esther A, 1-11; CLINES, *The Esther Scroll*, 69-92, introduces Esther B and Esther A; and in pp. 215-216, Clines gives the Greek A-text, 1-11). According to MARGUERAT – BOURQUIN, *Récits bibliques*, 118-119, the dream is a premonition. Put at the beginning of the book, it is an important introduction for understanding the events to come: overthrow, oppression, battle, victory, fall, rise, liberation and joy, which are developed at length in the rest of the narrative of the book of Esther.

[155] On this difference between ancient and modern characterization see MOMIGLIANO, *The Development of Greek Biography*, 84.

[156] ARISTOTLE, *Rhet.*, 59.33 (1367b) states, "actions are signs of character."

that emerges from the stories about the protagonist. These stories can be initiated by the character or can be words said about the character and deeds done in relationship to the character. The ancient indirect method of characterization uses infancy narratives' words and deeds to present the protagonist with a proleptic characterization.[157] Sometimes, with these presentations and characterizations, the author is simply projecting back aspects of the person's later career, inferring what sort of youth grew up into the person he describes in the rest of his writing.[158]

In my opinion this characterization through infancy implies a harmony between the infancy narrative's signs and their fulfillment in the public life.[159] I have chosen examples of characterization from the main examples of Greco-Roman and Jewish literature, Alexander's and Moses' infancies respectively. The characterization of Alexander's adult strength is presented in the infancy through his words and deeds. Alexander, being still a boy, wanted to enter the chariot race. His father told him that he was too young, and that he had to train more seriously. Alexander insisted and Philip, his father, astounded at his determination, said to him: "Boy, this is what you want; so go with my blessing." When Alexander arrived at the chariot race, King Nikolaos asked Alexander why he was there: "Did you come here as a spectator or a competitor?" "I may be young," Alexander replied, "but I am here to compete with you in the horse-racing." The narrator describes the race and Alexander's victory at length. Alexander was crowned and, as he was wearing his victory crown of wild olive, the prophet of the temple of Zeus said to him: "Alexander, Olympian Zeus makes this prediction for you: 'Be of good cheer! As you have defeated Nikolaos, so shall you de-

[157] When these signs, words and deeds, have to be interpreted by divination, the presentation of the character is yet more solemn because the deity gives witness to that presentation; even more so when the prophecy or dream has God as its main agent.

[158] In PLUTARCH, *Alcibiades*, 2,1-3; *Agis*, 4,1-2; 7,2-4.19-20; 14,3-4, the narrator explains the protagonist's character in later life through his character in boyhood.

[159] The relationship between the infancy narratives' sign and the future life is clear in PLUTARCH, *Themistocles*, 2,1-3, where after a sign, the narrator affirms "Thus it came about that, in after life...," and he explains the connections between the sign and its fulfillment in Themistocles' future life.

feat many in your wars.'"[160] Alexander's strength in defeating kings in a horse race when he was a boy is interpreted by the prophet as a prediction of Alexander's strength in defeating kings in wars as a man. Alexander is characterized through his victories.[161]

Furthermore, an interpreter of dreams announces to the Greek king Philip, "This child who is going to be born will reach the rising sun, waging war with all and capturing cities by force. King, you will have a son who will go round the whole world, bringing everyone under his sway. But, turning back towards his own kingdom, he will die young."[162]

The interpretation of Philip's dream, which occurred prior to Alexander's birth, foretells not only Alexander's victories throughout the world, but also his early death.

---

[160] PSEUDO-CALLISTHENES, *Alexander*, 1,18-19. For other examples of Alexander's characterization see PSEUDO-CALLISTHENES, *Alexander*, 1,17; 1,13-14; and PLUTARCH, *Alexander*, 6,2-8.

[161] QUINTUS CURTIUS RUFUS, *Alexander,* 5,7, says: "Alexander already gave promise of being the king which he afterwards became." For other examples of harmony between infancy and adult life see PSEUDO-CALLISTHENES, *Alexander*, 1,13; PLUTARCH, *Alexander*, 4,8-11; 8,1.

[162] PSEUDO-CALLISTHENES, *Alexander*, 1,8. Another example outside of Alexander's infancy narratives is that after Romulus and Remus were born, carried to the riverside, and laid down there, a she-wolf visited the babes and suckled them while all sorts of birds brought morsels of food and put them into their mouths (PLUTARCH, *Romulus*, 2,3-6). Years later, they resolved to dwell by themselves and to found a city in the region where, at first, they were nourished and sustained; this surely seems a most fitting reason for their course (PLUTARCH, *Romulus*, 9,1). The author, presenting the place where they were nourished after being born, thereby presents the place where they will be fed later in the city founded by them. On the other hand, Numa was born, moreover, by a divine gift, on the very day when Rome was founded by Romulus, that is, the twenty-first day of April (PLUTARCH, *Numa*, 3,4-5). This fact determined him to become that man who had to re-found and re-unify Rome (PLUTARCH, *Numa*, 5,1-7,1). Pindar's biography offers us another clear example. "When he was a boy, he went hunting and fell asleep from exhaustion. As he slept a bee landed on his mouth and built a honeycomb there. Others say that he had a dream in which his mouth was full of honey. That is why Pindar decided to write poetry." (quoted in LEFKOWITZ, *The Lives of the Greek Poets*, 59). For other examples of characterization through childhood see PLUTARCH, *Alexander*, 3,7-9; *Caius Marius*, 3,1; *Demosthenes*, 5,1-4; *Cicero*, 2,4-5.

The biblical Moses' infancy narrative does not say anything about Moses' future life. However, Moses' public life, even more clearly than Alexander's, has been characterized by his infancy narrative's signs in the later Jewish commentaries. God himself says to Amram, Moses' father, that his son

> will serve me (God) forever, and I (God) will do marvelous things in the house of Jacob through him and I will work through him signs and wonders for my people that I have not done for anyone else; and I will act gloriously among (the Egyptians) and proclaim to them my ways [...] I will show him my covenant that no one has seen. And I will reveal to him my Law and statues and judgments.[163]

It is difficult to be more precise about the future life of Moses. The plagues, wrought by God through Moses, are anticipated by Moses' "signs and wonders." In addition, the reference to the fact that God will reveal to Moses his Law, statues and judgments, is a forecast of the future handing over of the Law in the desert.

Moreover, Miriam, Moses' sister, had a dream: "Behold he who was born from your parents will be cast forth into the water; likewise through him the water will be dried up. And I will work signs through him and save my people, and he will exercise leadership always.'"[164] As Moses was cast forth into the river when he was a child, likewise he will dry up the water when he is an adult. As he was saved from the Egyptians from the water when he was a child, likewise he will save the Israelite people from the Egyptians from the water when he is an adult.[165] Again the expression

---

[163] PSEUDO-PHILO, *Biblical Antiquities*, 9,7-8.

[164] PSEUDO-PHILO, *Biblical Antiquities*, 9,10

[165] The mission of Moses as an adult takes its starting point from the fanciful etymology based on the Hebrew root משה. In Ex 2:10 it is said that Pharaoh's daughter named him Moses, "because," she said, "I drew him out of the water." It is stated in great detail by PHILO, *The Life of Moses*, 1,17, and JOSEPHUS, *The Jewish Antiquities*, 2,9,6. In the Pseudo-Philo narration, the name imposed on Moses and its explanation present him as the one saved from the waters who will become the savior through the waters: "she called him by the name Moses [...] because through him God freed the sons of Israel from the water" (PSEUDO-PHILO, *Biblical Antiquities*, 9,16).

"I will work signs through him" seems a reference to the plagues; "He will save my people" foresees the liberation from Egypt;[166] and "he will exercise leadership always" foreshadows Moses' leadership through the desert to the Promised Land and his future importance in the history of Israel. The different stages of Moses' adult life are already present in Miriam's dream.

Furthermore, according to Josephus, one of the sacred scribes told the pharaoh that about that time there would be a child born to the Israelites, who, if he were reared, would bring the Egyptian dominion low, and would raise the Israelites; that he would surpass all men in virtue, and obtain a glory that would be remembered through all ages.[167] After Pharaoh's daughter had saved Moses from the water, she carried Moses to her father. She showed Moses to Pharaoh, and said to her father that she had adopted him for her son, and the heir of his kingdom. And when she had said this, she put the infant into her father's hands; so he took him, and hugged him to his breast, and on his daughter's account, in a pleasant way, put her father's diadem upon Moses' head. But Moses threw it to the ground, and, in a puerile mood, he kicked it around, and trod upon it with his feet, which action seemed to bring along with it an evil omen concerning the kingdom of Egypt. When the sacred scribe, the person who foretold that his birth would bring the dominion of that kingdom low, saw this, he made a violent attempt to kill him; and crying out in a frightful manner, he said: "This, O king, this child is he of whom God foretold, that if we kill him we shall be in no danger; he himself affords an attestation to the prediction of the same thing, by his trampling upon your government,

---

As SKA, *Our Fathers*, 59, notices, "the name should be *māšûy* ('drawn out,' passive participle) and not *mōšeh* ('drawing,' active participle). The unconscious mistake of Pharaoh's daughter foretells Moses' future action of drawing Israel out of Egypt and out of the waters of the sea." For other names with a proleptic function in the stories where they appear see Esau and Jacob (Gn 25:25; 27:22.36).

[166] A similar prophecy appears in Josephus: "He shall deliver the Hebrew nation from the distress they are under from the Egyptians" (JOSEPHUS, *The Jewish Antiquities*, 2,9,3).

[167] See JOSEPHUS, *The Jewish Antiquities*, 2,9,2.

and treading upon your diadem."[168] Moses, the greatest opponent of Pharaoh's power, who will be strongly persecuted by Pharaoh, is already twice persecuted in his childhood: in the slaughter of the Hebrew children and in this attempt to kill him. His persecution during his childhood foreshadows his persecution in his adult life. This event, in which Moses, being still a child, threw to the ground the diadem of the Egyptian power, kicked it around, and trod upon it with his feet is a clear proleptic sign of his defeating the Egyptian power as an adult, destroying Egyptian dominion and raising the Israelites.[169]

3.3 Infancy Narratives within Biographies

Biography normally focuses on the public career of the subject. Everybody notices when a great man dies; it is more difficult to notice when one is born or when one is growing up. It is not surprising that ancient biographers often faced a dearth of material on their protagonist's childhood. However, in some biographies we find infancy narratives that tell of the first years of the character.[170] Why did biographers add an account of the birth, infancy, and early experiences of the protagonist? I suggest that the reason was the understanding of human life as an integrated one. According to Pelling,

> most or all ancient writers have an extremely integrated conception of character. The differing elements of a character are regularly brought into some sort of relationship with one another and rec-

---

[168] JOSEPHUS, *The Jewish Antiquities*, 2,9,7.

[169] Samson is also characterized in his infancy. Josephus, unlike the biblical text, attributes Samson's name to the angelic announcement, and adds the connection of Samson's name with his future strength, as long as his hair is not cut, and ability to afflict the Philistines (JOSEPHUS, *The Jewish Antiquities*, 5,8,2). On midrash as a symbolic revelation for the future see CAVALLETTI, "Il metodo derashico", 5-11.

[170] According to BARR – WENTLING, "Classical Biography", 69, antiquity was dominated by oral traditions; many of these stories figured in the tradition which the biographers were using.

onciled. This understanding of human life is presupposed by these biographies. One element at least goes closely with another, and each element predicts the next.[171]

This understanding of human life as an integrated one provides three different reasons to include an infancy narrative in a biography. *One* such reason is retroversion of important features of adult life into earlier life. Those who achieve a noble death, and thus become heroes, were destined for their roles from birth. Unusual births are thus omens that signal to the perceptive interpreter that the infant is destined to become a hero.[172] In other words, biographies that told the deeds of the hero during his public life and death added the infancy narratives to show the heroic dimension of the character even in his childhood. The author explains what made that hero the sort of politician, philosopher, or religious leader he was in order that the reader can understand him.[173] *Second*, the infancy narratives are a literary tool of proleptic characterization, the infancy narratives' signs explaining and introducing the adult life. The *third* reason is curiosity with regard to the private life, even during childhood. The biographical interest in the public life of a hero began to be extended to an interest in the private life of the character. These could be the reasons why the infancy narratives start to appear in the biographies.[174]

If the infancy narratives introduce the main features of the literary work, do we already know everything about the literary work from the infancy narratives? The answer must be that we do not. *First*, the way in which the announcements are fulfilled is al-

---

[171] PELLING, "Childhood and Personality", 235.

[172] It was only after an individual had become a hero that a birth narrative was added to match the hero's adult accomplishments (MCGAUGHY, "Infancy Narratives", 29). BOVON, "The Child and the Beast", 20, affirms: "After an initial period of reflection on the cross and resurrection, the first Christians, influenced more by the Greek philosophy of the *beginnings*, developed the story of Jesus' beginning."

[173] These narrated features increase as the information about the public life increases. With so much more to understand in the adult figures, there is therefore more to prefigure.

[174] See a similar procedure on the Lukan infancy narrative in § I.1.4.2.c.

ways unknown. In the terms of modern narrative criticism, the infancy narrative shows the *who* and *what*, but not the *how*.[175] The author, giving the *who* the protagonist is, and the *what* he will perform, creates a suspense or narrative tension about *how* he will fulfill it. *Second*, the rest of the literary work can fulfill, change, reverse or reorient the proleptic characterization given at the beginning. There could be surprises or mismatches between announcement and fulfillment.[176] *Third*, the proleptic characterization introduces some aspects of the literary work, but not the entire work. The technique of gradual redefinition means that ancient writers often hold back important information until a point later than a modern reader would expect. Ancient writers can give a telling anecdote or generalization prefiguring the main topics with which the literary work is going to deal. Those traits that we know from the beginning can develop, while also permitting new traits to appear throughout the entire work. The infancy narrative introduces the main traits, but there can be additions which did not exist in the infancy narrative.

4. Comparative Synthesis

The analysis of the texts allows us to affirm that the Jewish infancy narratives share many similarities with the Greco-Roman. Both make use of the same broad *topos* with similar motifs. The recurrent appearance of this type of story, albeit with modifications, is indicative of its popularity in both Greco-Roman and Hebrew traditions. This *topos* contained some diversity and also points of correlation.[177] Although there are several differences, I have encountered numerous similarities between the Greco-Roman and

[175] CHATMAN, *Story and Discourse*, 19, contends that the *who* and *what* provide the content of a narrative, while the discourse is the *how*, the particular way in which the story is developed. On this understanding of the narrative *how* see COLERIDGE, *The Birth*, 224.

[176] Scholars often saw it as a characteristic mistake or correction attributed to multiple authorship. Today the concept of *misdirection* offers the possibility to see it as an effective narrative technique.

[177] The biography genre had already a great diversity (see p. 92, n. 17).

the Jewish infancy narratives. I will summarize, first, the major similarities and then the major differences.

First, the form of both traditions is very similar. A life of a character should include something about the hero's family lineage, signs of his future greatness, and examples of the child's education as part of his pre-public career. However, the simple narratives concerning genealogy,[178] and especially physical appearance,[179] are less common in the Jewish tradition. The infancy narratives' signs, before, during and after the hero's birth, are prodigies, prophecies, and dreams, which are widely used for the period of a hero's life before he enters upon his public career. Yet, in the Jewish tradition, while the number of prodigies diminishes, the number of prophecies increases.[180] The divine dimension of the Greco-Roman literature, expressed by signs around the birth and interpreted by divination, appears in the Jewish literature by means of an increased emphasis on divinely inspired prophecy. The free cooperation through the

---

[178] Only in PHILO, *The Life of Moses*, 1,5-7; PSEUDO-PHILO, *Biblical Antiquities*, 42,1; JOSEPHUS, *The Jewish Antiquities*, 2,9,6; and 1 S 1:1-2. In addition, while the Greco-Roman biography records the ancestors of the hero and what they had done (PSEUDO-CALLISTHENES, *Alexander*, 1,1-3; QUINTUS CURTIUS RUFUS, *Alexander*, 1,4,1; PLUTARCH, *Caius Marius*, 3,1; *Theseus*, 3,1-2; *Themistocles*, 1,1-4; *Coriolanus*, 1,1-2; *Alcibiades*, 1,1-3; *Cato*, 1,1-3; *Pryrhus*, 1; *Lucullus*, 1,1; *Antony*, 1,1-2; *Brutus*, 1-2; *Artaxerxes*, 1,1-4; *Demosthenes*, 4,1-3; SUETONIUS, *Otho*, 1; *Vitellius*, 1-2; *Augustus*, 1-4; *Tiberius*, 1-4; *Caligula*, 7; *Nero*, 1-5; *Galba*, 4), the Jewish biographies, especially Pseudo-Philo (PSEUDO-PHILO, *Biblical Antiquities*, 1.2.4; 42,1), simply repeat the names of the ancestors.

[179] Only in PHILO, *The Life of Moses*, 1,9; JOSEPHUS, *The Jewish Antiquities*, 2,9,6. Pseudo-Philo does not present any physical and educational information.

[180] Four different prophecies are found in the Moses infancy narratives: prophecies by God himself (PSEUDO-PHILO, *Biblical Antiquities*, 9,7-8; JOSEPHUS, *The Jewish Antiquities*, 2,9,3); by an angel (PSEUDO-PHILO, *Biblical Antiquities*, 9,10); and by a very wise sacred seer (JOSEPHUS, *The Jewish Antiquities*, 2,9,2). An angel prophesies that Samson will rescue Israel from the power of the Philistines and Samson's great strength (Jg 13:6; PSEUDO-PHILO, *Biblical Antiquities*, 42,3; JOSEPHUS, *The Jewish Antiquities*, 5,8,2). Five different prophecies are found in the Samuel infancy narratives, announced by God himself (PSEUDO-PHILO, *Biblical Antiquities*, 47,7-8), by the priest Eli (1 S 1:17), by Hannah, Samuel's mother (PSEUDO-PHILO, *Biblical Antiquities*, 51,3-6), by Samuel himself about Eli's sons' future (1 S 3:12-13) and their death (JOSEPHUS, *The Jewish Antiquities*, 5,10,3-4), and by the narrator himself (JOSEPHUS, *The Jewish Antiquities*, 5,10,3.4).

child's education, which develops the character, appears in both literatures, but it is less prominent in the Jewish literature.[181] The affirmation of the growth of the character appears only discretely at the end of the infancy narratives of the Jewish literature, occupying only one verse (Jg 13:24; 1 S 3:19; Ex 2:11). Both aspects of a complete infancy narrative, signs which reveal the divine intention and development thanks to human cooperation, appear repeatedly.

Second, in Greco-Roman and Jewish literature the infancy narratives are almost always situated at the beginning of the entire literary work.[182] This use at the start of a literary work is intended as a clear general *introduction*. I contend that they serve to present the principal character of the biography and to prepare the reader for a better understanding of the accounts that will be narrated afterwards. This *proleptic* presentation is always done through words and deeds, and it is almost always a positive characterization.[183] The later Jewish comments never annul the proleptic signs of the biblical texts. Rather, they augment the proleptic signs present in the biblical text, adding new prophecies. Even the name of the main character becomes a literary tool to introduce the character's main features. Moses', Samson's and Samuel's names are used to present them.[184] I believe, therefore, that infancy narratives were a wonderful literary tool to characterize the literary work.[185]

---

[181] In the Greco-Roman literature see PLUTARCH, *Cato*, 1,3-5; *Alcibiades,* 1,4-5; *Sulla*, 2,1; *Pompey,* 2,1-3; *Alexander*, 4,1-7; *Caius Marius*, 2,1; *Pyrrhus*, 3,4; *Fabius Maximus*, 1,4-6; *Coriolanus*, 2,1-2; *Philopoemen*, 2,1-6; *Demetrius*, 2,2. In the Jewish literature see only PHILO, *The Life of Moses,* 1,21-24; JOSEPHUS, *The Jewish Antiquities,* 2,9,6.

[182] The only exceptions are in the Greco-Roman literature, in the Life of Augustus and Domitian, where we find the infancy narrative at the end (SUETONIUS, *Augustus*, 94; *Domitian*, 14).

[183] The only negative characterization is that of Nero, where the narrator affirms an unequivocal sign of his ill-fated destiny (SUETONIUS, *Nero*, 6,1-2).

[184] On Moses' name see Ex 2:10; PHILO, *The Life of Moses,* 1,17; PSEUDO-PHILO, *Biblical Antiquities,* 9,10.16. On Samson's name see JOSEPHUS, *The Jewish Antiquities,* 5,8,4; PSEUDO-PHILO, *Biblical Antiquities,* 42,3. On Samuel's name see 1 S 1:20; JOSEPHUS, *The Jewish Antiquities,* 5,10,3; PSEUDO-PHILO, *Biblical Antiquities,* 51,1. Nevertheless, in the Greco-Roman literature, only Nero's name is used to characterize him (SUETONIUS, *Nero,* 6,1).

[185] See TALBERT, "Prophecies of Future Greatness", 134. The use of this literary

Third, the actors of the infancy narratives' signs come from the politico-religious (priests, prophets, emperor, pharaoh) and family area (especially the child and the parents of the infant). The Jewish tradition adds two important religious protagonists: God himself,[186] and the angel of God.[187] The proximity of God is greater in the Jewish literature than in the Greco-Roman literature. Moreover, there are two cases in which the entire Israelite people receive the prophecy.[188] They are instances which show us how these signs try to involve all the people, especially the reader. Furthermore, the reaction of those present for the sign is trust.[189] This intradiegetic

---

tool continues after Luke's Gospel. The apocryphal literature presents several examples. *The Protoevangelium Iacobi*, 1–16, especially 4,1–9,3 and 16,1-3, narrates the birth and education of Mary in the Temple as a prediction of her virginity (see as well The *Evangelium Pseudo-Matthaei*, 1–5; 14). The *Evangelium Pseudo-Matthaei*, 18,1-2; 23, narrates how Jesus performed miracles during his childhood. Some of these miracles, such as profaning the precept of Sabbath (The *Evangelium Pseudo-Thomae de infantia Salvatoris*, 2,2-5) or raising the dead (The *Evangelium Pseudo-Thomae de infantia Salvatoris*, 9,1-3; 17,1-2; 18,1-2) clearly anticipate his deeds in adult life. The hagiographic literature presents the infancy of Saint Athanasius where one day Alexander, the bishop of Alexandria, saw a group of boys amusing themselves on the seashore, playing bishop and imitating Church services. Alexander interrogated the children, asking them about the game and the acts they were performing. They admitted that they had picked the boy Athanasius as their bishop (see *PG* 873,3084-3085 [*sic*], quoted in DUFFY, "Playing at Ritual", 201). On this hagiographic literature which attests that the infancy narratives often foretell the future infant's greatness see DUFFY, "Playing at Ritual", 199-209.

[186] PSEUDO-PHILO, *Biblical Antiquities,* 53; 9,16; JOSEPHUS, *The Jewish Antiquities*, 2,9,2; 5,10,1.2.3.4.

[187] Moses' (PSEUDO-PHILO, *Biblical Antiquities,* 9,10) and Samson's (Jg 13:2-7; 8-25; JOSEPHUS, *The Jewish Antiquities,* 5,8,1-2; PSEUDO-PHILO, *Biblical Antiquities,* 42,3) infancy narratives present an angel. Josephus and, especially, Pseudo-Philo add the divine prophecies.

[188] See PSEUDO-PHILO, *Biblical Antiquities,* 49; JOSEPHUS, *The Jewish Antiquities*, 2,9,4.7.

[189] The entire Jewish people trusted Moses as their liberator, and hoped that good things would be done by him (JOSEPHUS, *The Jewish Antiquities*, 2,9,4.7). And the entire people of Israel dance and sing, showing their confidence in Samuel's prophecy (PSEUDO-PHILO, *Biblical Antiquities,* 51,7). Moses' parents throw their child into the river because they trust the sign that they have received (JOSEPHUS, *The Jewish Antiquities*, 2,9,4; PSEUDO-PHILO, *Biblical Antiquities,* 9,6). And Samson's parents trusted their son's prophecy (PSEUDO-PHILO, *Biblical Antiquities,* 42,7).

positive reaction influences the behavior of the reader, who extradiegetically can then more willingly accept the protagonist, trusting his characterization during his infancy.

Fourth, the information is often given to the reader by the narrator, and some times also by a speaking character. However, through the prophecies, hymns, songs, and prayers, the presence of direct speeches considerably increases in the Jewish tradition.[190] This fact gives more importance and vivacity to this kind of sign because they provide information not only to the reader, but also to the characters within the narration, thus allowing the information to effortlessly remain in the memory of the reader.

The final similarity between the Greco-Roman and Jewish infancy narratives is that, when there is mention of the location of the signs, it is often in the Temple, especially in the Jewish tradition, which becomes an appropriate place to present the main character.[191]

The main difference is encapsulated in the contents of the infancy narratives' signs, on the words that are prophesied about the main character. While the Greco-Roman infancy narratives were often generalizations about portents, dreams, and prophecies,[192] the

[190] Almost all of the prophecies are direct speeches (see JOSEPHUS, *The Jewish Antiquities,* 2,9,2; 2,9,3; 5,8,2; 5,10,3-4; PSEUDO-PHILO, *Biblical Antiquities,* 9,7-8; 9,10; 42,3; 51,3-6; 47,7-8).

[191] Eli's prophecy concerning Samuel (1 S 1:17), Hannah's song which in Pseudo-Philo's narration becomes a characterization of Samuel (PSEUDO-PHILO, *Biblical Antiquities,* 51,3-5), the people's prophecy concerning Samuel (PSEUDO-PHILO, *Biblical Antiquities,* 51,7) and Samuel's prophecy concerning Eli's sons (1 S 3:11-13; PSEUDO-PHILO, *Biblical Antiquities,* 53,9-11) take place in the Temple. It is true that there is no Temple in the Moses and Samson narratives. Nevertheless, after the second appearance, Samson's father prepared a burnt offering on an altar (Jg 13:16.19). In addition, both appearances are preceded by a prayer in the upper room (PSEUDO-PHILO, *Biblical Antiquities,* 42,2.5), which is considered a "holy" place. In the Greco-Roman literature the location often is not mentioned. However, when it is described, it is the temple (PSEUDO-CALLISTHENES, *Alexander,* 1,18-19; SUETONIUS, *Nero,* 6,1).

[192] The only titles that I have found in Greco-Roman infancy narratives are "world ruler" and "king" (PSEUDO-CALLISTHENES, *Alexander,* 1,12.16.17; QUINTUS CURTIUS RUFUS, *Alexander,* 5,7; SUETONIUS, *Augustus,* 94,3).

Jewish infancy narratives are more concrete; they have a marked presence of titles that characterize the infant. First, Moses is characterized as "savior"[193] and "heir of the kingdom."[194] Second, Samson is also characterized as "prophet"[195] and "savior."[196] Third, Samuel is characterized as: "prophet,"[197] "ruler,"[198] "light to this nation,"[199] "light for the nations,"[200] "anointed one and king,"[201] and "advantage for the peoples and fountain for the twelve tribes."[202] These titles give a specifically Jewish content which responds to the expectations of the prophecies. The Jewish infancy narratives take the form and purpose from the Greco-Roman infancy narratives but fill it with their own specific contents.

Why is this study significant with regard to Luke's infancy narrative (Luke 1–2), especially Jesus' Presentation in the Temple (Lk 2:22-39)? Does Luke 1–2 contain the same kind of signs and descriptions that the contemporary Greco-Roman and Jewish infancy narratives contain? Luke's infancy narrative shares similar features with other infancy narratives, particularly in its form. At the same time, the content of Luke's infancy narrative still has its own defining characteristics. Generally speaking, the Lukan infancy narrative more closely mirrors features of the Jewish literature, but shares features with both Greco-Roman and Jewish literature alike.[203]

---

[193] JOSEPHUS, *The Jewish Antiquities*, 2,9,3.7; PSEUDO-PHILO, *Biblical Antiquities,* 9,10.

[194] JOSEPHUS, *The Jewish Antiquities*, 2,9,7.

[195] JOSEPHUS, *The Jewish Antiquities*, 5,8,4.

[196] JOSEPHUS, *The Jewish Antiquities*, 5,8,2; PSEUDO-PHILO, *Biblical Antiquities*, 42,3.

[197] JOSEPHUS, *The Jewish Antiquities*, 5,10,1.2.3.4; PSEUDO-PHILO, *Biblical Antiquities,* 49,7; 50,8; 51,6.7.

[198] PSEUDO-PHILO, *Biblical Antiquities*, 49,7.

[199] PSEUDO-PHILO, *Biblical Antiquities,* 51,3.6.7.

[200] PSEUDO-PHILO, *Biblical Antiquities*, 51,6.

[201] PSEUDO-PHILO, *Biblical Antiquities*, 51,6.

[202] PSEUDO-PHILO, *Biblical Antiquities,* 51,2. The presence of these titles is still clearer in Pseudo-Philo.

[203] Among the Jewish writers, Philo, writing in Alexandria, is closer to the Greco-Roman literature, Josephus, between Jerusalem and Rome, is an intermediate example, and Pseudo-Philo, writing in Palestine, is the closest to the Lukan infancy narrative.

I will begin with the similarities. First, throughout Luke's infancy narrative we also find the same form of *prodigies* and *prophecies* before and after Jesus' birth.[204] Luke begins episodes with unusual events or prodigies that are taken to be supernatural signs pointing to the special status of Jesus.[205] Those who are able to interpret the signs then make prophecies about the future.[206] The extraordinary sign of Elizabeth's child leaping in her womb (Lk 1:41), for example, is interpreted by Elizabeth herself (Lk 1:42-45). Luke likewise follows the ancient method of characterization.[207] Like the other infancy narratives, the Lukan one is found at the beginning of the literary work as an introduction (Luke 1–2). Luke displays Jesus' character through deeds and words.[208]

Second, the signs around Jesus' birth introduce the divine intention concerning Jesus, while the wisdom and prowess of the boy dominate the scene of the twelve-year-old Jesus in the Temple. Jesus' growth is twice affirmed, through two different verses (Lk 2:40.52).[209] Both stages which are characteristic of the infancy narrative, first the divine intention and later the human cooperation through the boy

[204] Dreams are found in the other infancy narrative of the Gospels: see Mt 1:20-24; 2:12; 2:13-15; 2:19-20. The Matthean infancy narrative, however, lacks important episodes of the ancient biographies. Nothing is said about the birth of Jesus itself or of childhood stories characteristic of him. Finally, there is no report of the course of Jesus' education, unless one is to regard the meetings with John the Baptist and the devil as such (see LUZ, *Matthew 1-7*, 72). Matthew's Gospel presents, right at its beginning, a genealogy (Mt 1:2-16). However, Luke's Gospel presents it a little later (Lk 3:23-38). They both contain lists of names, which have a closer connection to Pseudo-Philo's genealogies than with Josephus and the Greco-Roman authors who provide broader information about the ancestors of the protagonist.

[205] Three prodigies are the three angelophanies of Lk 1:11-20; 1:26-38; and 2:8-20.

[206] Three prophecies are Lk 1:67-79; 2:29-32; and 2:34-35.

[207] Like Samuel's mother's song (PSEUDO-PHILO, *Biblical Antiquities,* 51,3-6), Simeon's song could be a programmatic introduction to Jesus' life (Lk 2:29-32).

[208] Luke himself describes this twofold method clearly when he says that his gospel deals with "all that Jesus did and taught" (Acts 1:1). This twofold method of Jesus' characterization is applicable not only to Jesus' deeds and sayings, but also to deeds and sayings about Jesus.

[209] KRÜCKEMEIER, "Der zwölfjährige Jesus", 307-319, and HENK, "Sonship, Wisdom, Infancy", 317-354, show how Lk 2:40-52 has a lot of parallels in the Hellenistic biog-

Jesus' growth, appear in the Lukan infancy narrative.[210] Moreover, some of the information of both stages is told in the Temple. The Presentation in the Temple and Simeon's prophecy present part of the divine intention while the account of the twelve-year-old Jesus in the Temple presents part of the typical human collaboration through the mention of his progressive growth (Lk 2:40.52). The gradual characterization of Jesus throughout the infancy narrative achieves its critical point in the Temple.

Third, the actors of the infancy narrative's signs, as in the Greco-Roman and Jewish infancy narratives, are religious people (the priest Zechariah, 1:67; the righteous and devout Simeon, 2:25; the prophetess Anna, 2:36) and Jesus' parents, who are also religious people doing what the Law required concerning him (2:27; see 1:26-38; 2:22-24.39; 2:41-42). As the Jewish commentators, Luke adds the angel as an actor of the signs (1:11-20; 1:26-38; 2:8-20). There are no politicians, emperors, or pharaohs. Furthermore, all the personages, also the simple shepherds (2:15), trust the words and deeds which present Jesus. The reader is persuaded to trust in the signs concerning the main character as the witnesses of the signs did. The author, with the persuasive power of the narrative, endeavors to persuade the reader to view the character from a certain perspective.

---

raphies, which show the wisdom and growth of the protagonist. As in the Greco-Roman literature, this episode occurs during the boyhood of Jesus, and underlines Jesus' collaboration with the divine intention. The affirmations that the child Jesus "grew to maturity, he was filled with wisdom; and God's grace was with him"(2:40) and that he "increased in wisdom, in stature" (2:52) are similar to the one that we find in SUETONIUS, *Titus,* 3,1: "Being a child, all of his gifts and graces, corporal and spiritual, were growing progressively in order to be used in his public career. His bodily and mental gifts were conspicuous and they became more and more so as he advanced in years. He had a handsome person, in which there was no less dignity than grace." However, although Lk 2:40.52 speaks of Jesus' growing up, it is a more spiritual description about his wisdom and God's favor than a comment on his physical appearance (see FREED, *The Stories of Jesus' Birth*, 148-149). In addition, in the episode of the twelve-year-old Jesus in the Temple nothing is said of his training and teachers.

[210] While the structure of signs that show the divine intention and human cooperation appears, the presence of this training and growth is nevertheless very discrete in comparison with the Greco-Roman literature.

Fourth, when the location is told, the Lukan infancy narrative's signs often take place in the Temple, which appears as a special place of characterization.[211]

I will now draw attention to the differences. First, the contents of the Jewish infancy narratives' signs were richer than in the Greco-Roman literature. The Lukan infancy narrative's contents, however, are even more, so that the characterization of Jesus is still more precise. Throughout the Lukan infancy narrative Jesus is described as "Son of the Most High" (Lk 1:32), "Holy and Son of God" (Lk 1:35), "Horn of salvation" (Lk 1:69), "Savior," "Christ the Lord" (Lk 2:11), "salvation,"[212] "Messiah of the Lord" (Lk 2:26), "glory for your people Israel," "light of revelation for the Gentiles" (Lk 2:29-32) and "sign contradicted" (Lk 2:34c). In addition, the prophetess Anna spoke of Jesus "to all who looked forward to the redemption of Jerusalem" (Lk 2:38). In the episode of the twelve-year-old Jesus in the Temple, Jesus introduces himself as God's Son who must be in his Father's house (Lk 2:49). These specific contents are in connection with the Jewish tradition, but they occur more often. The variety and number of these descriptions show Luke's attempt to describe the uniqueness of the child.

Second, in the Greco-Roman and Jewish biographies, the characterization of the hero normally included the promise of future greatness. Only in the case of Nero have we found a promise of an ill-fated future.[213] In any case, the infancy narrative of a main character foretells his future greatness or his ill-fated future. Jesus' infancy narrative speaks both about his future greatness

[211] The last two passages in Luke's infancy narrative both take place in the Temple (Lk 2:22-39; 2:40-52). The prophecy of John's birth also takes place in the Temple (Lk 1:5-25). Nero's presentation in the temple, with the imposition of his name and the purification rite (SUETONIUS, *Nero,* 6,1-2), is very similar to Jesus' Presentation in the Temple.

[212] Even Jesus' name is a literary tool to characterize him: "for he will save his people from their sins" (Mt 1:21; cf. Lk 2:21). On all of this characterization of Jesus see § IV.1.3.2.

[213] SUETONIUS, *Nero,* 6,1-2.

("Savior," 1:29; 2:11; "Lord," 1:43; 2:11; "will be holy and will be called Son of God," 1:34; "will be great and will be called the Son of the Most High," 1:32; "of his kingdom there will be no end," 1:33; "glory for your people Israel," 2:32) and about his ill-fated future ("this child is been appointed as a sign that is contradicted," 2:34).[214] Jesus' paradoxical mystery is presented by both positive and negative predictions.

Third, Luke tells us nothing about Jesus' physical appearance. This kind of description decreases in the Jewish commentaries, and it is absent in Luke's Gospel. Jesus' characterization lies at a deeper level.

Fourth, while the Greco-Roman infancy narratives spoke about important characters, such as an emperor, politician, philosopher, orator, or poet, Luke's hero does not already have a status in the culture as a superior or noble person. By class, he is a commoner, and commoners usually were not thought worthy of literary attention.[215] Moreover, Luke narrates this common character with great simplicity and sobriety.[216] His sobriety and the fact that both greatness and an ill-fated future are prophesied show us Luke's wish to be faithful to historicity.

Finally, the actors of Jesus' proleptic presentations are speaking characters: Zechariah, the angel Gabriel, Elizabeth, Mary, the angels and Simeon. In Lk 2:49, the protagonist is the same child, who speaks as well. Whereas the Greco-Roman infancy narratives rarely give us the name of the actors, who make the proleptic sign, Luke's infancy narrative, following the Jewish tradition, frequently gives us their names. In addition, the prophecies themselves are presented in long direct speeches (Lk 1:13-17; 1:30-37; 1:46-56; 1:68-79; 2:10-12; 2:29-32). These features lend credence to their prophecies

---

[214] It is also prophesied about his mother that "a sword will pierce your own soul" (Lk 2:35).

[215] The infancy narratives of the common people had already begun in the Jewish literature with Isaac, Esau, Jacob, Samson and Samuel.

[216] The descriptions of Jesus' birth and where it took place are very simple and sober (Lk 2:1-7). The witnesses of the signs are not emperors, nor pharaohs; they are simple shepherds (Lk 2:8-20).

and help to affix the information more securely in the memory of the reader.

These differences show us that Luke uses the infancy narrative in his own way. Luke respects the common pattern, yet exercises his own originality and liberty. Luke uses a Greco-Roman literary tool, which had been already adopted by Jewish writers, with Jewish-Christian content.[217] In the biographical beginning of Jesus the readers are led into a different world than that of the ancient Greco-Roman biography: the world of the Bible and Israel's background. The significance ascribed to the names and titles given to the infant Jesus allows the author to elicit from the reader certain expectations precisely because they are loaded with meanings that are recognizable to readers familiar with the history and literature of Israel. The great number of expressions about Jesus and their contents declares the uniqueness of the character that Luke is presenting. The uniqueness of Luke's infancy narrative depends on the uniqueness of the infant. Luke wrote his first two chapters not only so as to respect the typical rules for beginning a "biography," but also in order to begin the narrative with a revealed Christology that would be a model for the rest of the work. This distinctive feature of Luke is very significant because it shows the Lukan adaptation of the common model.

Despite these differences, having seen the main features shared by Lukan, Greco-Roman and Jewish infancy narratives, one can say with confidence that Luke 1–2 contains the same kind of signs that are in the contemporary infancy narratives. I do not argue that Luke directly knew the texts which we have studied, so that they served as models for him. Nevertheless, one can assuredly argue that Luke's infancy narrative exhibits a common compositional pattern: an account of the main character's career before he embarked on his public activity which included material on his family background,

---

[217] As TALBERT, *Literary Patterns*, 125, believes, the evangelist used the conventional *topos* of the infancy narratives to provide the framework for the independent units of tradition regarding Jesus that he received from various oral and written Jewish-Christian sources. See also STERLING, *Historiography and Self-definition*, 371-374; MEYER, *Ursprung und Anfänge des Christentums*, 65; VAN BIEMA, "Behind the First Noel", 50.

reference to his conception, prodigies, prophecies and some information of his development.[218] Luke has made use of the pattern of infancy narratives which was widespread in the Greco-Roman and the Jewish literature of his time. The fact that Luke made use of this common topos has further implications.

First, by composing the birth narrative of Jesus, Luke adapts the Jesus tradition to the requirements of the Hellenistic usage which were already well known in the Jewish tradition. The use of known Hellenistic techniques by the Jewish writers and by Luke is deliberate.[219] Luke realized that Christianity, moving out into the world, needed to present its historical beginnings in accordance with standard conventions. Luke inserts Jewish-Christian contents into a structure that was familiar not only to Jewish ears, but to pagan ears as well, in an attempt to appeal even to a Hellenistic audience. Writing in a form which was very well known in his literary milieu, Luke gives a broader interpretative context to his literary work. Luke writes for Gentile-Christian and for Jewish-Christian readers proclaiming the uniqueness of Jesus.

Second, according to this common *topos*, Luke 1–2 could be understood as a disclosure which is an eye-opener for the reader. In this common category of thinking, it is expected that the infancy narrative introduces the main character. The narrative form was the most frequent and persuasive form used to disclose the main topics of the literary work. The stories of the infancy narrative serve Luke's purpose and are included for this reason. The narrative may assist readers by providing a set of expectations to guide their understanding. It may function as a kind of implicit contract between author and reader to guide the interpretation of the text.

We can indeed expect that the signs in Luke's infancy narrative are proleptic signs. We shall only be sure of this after studying the connection with the entire work; and at this time we shall know whether or not Luke's infancy story, found at the begin-

---

[218] On this resemblance among different infancy narratives see DRURY, *Tradition and Design*, 47; NOCK, *Conversion*, 240; Ó FEARGHAIL, *Introduction to Luke-Acts*, 153; and DENAUX, "Divine Visits", 265.278.

[219] The hellenization of Jewish writers such as Philo is well known.

ning of his literary work, presents Jesus' character, destiny and role and whether or not they are an anticipation of the entire Lukan literary work. Due to these uncertainties, in the next chapter I will study the passage of the Presentation in the Temple and its characterization of Jesus (Lk 2:22-39) in greater depth. And in Chs. IV and V I will study the relationship between the Presentation in the Temple and Luke's complete work, in order to determine its proleptic significance.

CHAPTER III

NARRATIVE STUDY OF LK 2:22-39

Having studied the pericope Lk 2:22-39, it is my claim that the structure of the passage, the expressions which refer to Jesus, and the plot of the narrative show us that this passage does not describe the *purification* of the mother or the *redemption* of the son but rather the *presentation* of Jesus in the Temple. In this passage, Luke presents Jesus in multiple dimensions, especially his identity and his mission. Jesus is presented as the Holy One and the awaited Messiah who fulfills prophecies. His mission is to accomplish a universal salvation, although fulfilling this mission means that he is going to be rejected by many in Israel. To better demonstrate this, I will first delimit the passage. Then, while paying special attention to the textual variants, I will select from them the Greek text that I think is the earliest attainable text. Third, studying its structure, I will divide the pericope into its different scenes and study their function in the passage.[1] Fourth, I will study the text in its unity, looking for the plot which is developed in the different scenes and the meaning of the whole text. I will conclude by summarizing my claims in a

---

[1] Concerning the different divisions of a text, I will consistently use the terms *macro-narrative*, *sequence*, *micro-narrative*, and *scene*. *Macro-narrative* is the maximal narrative unit conceived of as a whole by the narrator. The macro-narrative sometimes will be called the *whole Lukan work*, the *whole narrative*, or simply *Luke-Acts*. *Micro-narrative* is the minimal narrative unit presenting a narrative episode, the unity of which can be identified by the indicators of closure. I will also call it a *passage*, *pericope*, or *episode*. A series of micro-narratives linked by a unifying theme or common character can be called *sequence-narrative*, or simply *sequence*. Finally, a single micro-narrative can be divided into *scenes*, which are the sub-units of a micro-narrative. This nomenclature and definitions are borrowed from SKA, *Our Fathers*, 33.

synthesis of the passage, paying attention to the expressions which characterize Jesus.

Since Lk 2:22-39 is a narrative,[2] I will explain the pericope through narrative criteria. I will appeal to other texts only when my text cannot be explained by itself clarifying the text through the text itself, looking to its own self-intelligibility.

1. Delimitation of the Passage

The first task is to define the narrative unit which can be distinguished from what precedes and what follows. I suggest that the narrative unity of the Presentation in the Temple is delimited by Lk 2:22-39.

1.1 Delimitation of the Beginning of the Passage

1.1.1 Time

The preceding episodes take place the night of the birth of the baby Jesus (2:8) and eight days after his birth (2:21). The pericope of the Presentation occurs "when the days of their purification were over according to the Law of Moses" (2:22). According to vv. 23-24, it has the purpose of redeeming the first born male who can be redeemed a month after his birth (Ex 13:2.12.15; Nm 18:15.16), and of purifying the mother. According to Lv 12:1-4, the Law of Moses states that when a woman has a male child, she remains impure for seven days; the eighth day, the child will be circumcised, as the text states (2:21), but she will spend 33 more days purifying

[2] According to MARGUERAT – BOURQUIN, *Récits bibliques*, 24 [16], for it to be a narrative there is a need for: "(1) A temporal succession of actions/events; (2) The presence of an agent-hero inspired by an intention which draws the story towards its close; (3) A plot which overhangs the chain of events and integrates them into the unity of a single action; (4) A relationship of causality and consecutiveness which structures the plot by an interplay of causes and effects". I believe that these four features are present in Lk 2:22-39.

herself of her blood.[3] This fact permits us to affirm that the passage of the purification of Mary in the Temple takes place at a minimum of 40 days after Jesus' birth.[4]

These facts chronologically separate the pericope of the circumcision (Lk 2:21) from Jesus' birth which precedes it (Lk 2:1-20), and from the scene which follows it (Lk 2:22-39), distinguishing the previous passages from that of the Presentation.

Birth	Lk 2:1-20	The birth
Circumcision	Lk 2:21	8 days after the birth
Redemption of the firstborn	Lk 2:23	At least 30 days after the birth
Purification of the mother	Lk 2:22.24	At least 40 days after the birth

1.1.2 Place

The last geographic reference before Jesus' Presentation in the Temple is in v. 15: "Let us go now to Bethlehem" where Jesus' birth took place. Even though the scene of the circumcision does not give any geographic reference, we know that the circumcision did not usually take place in the Temple.[5] However, the episode of the Presentation is carried out in Jerusalem (vv. 22.25), more specifically in the Temple (vv. 27.37). This location differentiates our passage from those that precede it.

---

[3] The presence of Mary in the Temple is affirmed explicitly in v. 34 and implicitly in vv. 27 and 33. If she was to be found in the Temple it is because she was already purified.

[4] On these dates see GANE, "The Function", 9-17; KLAWANS, *Purity*, 17-20.

[5] The circumcision was carried out by the father, Gn 21:4, by the mother in the exceedingly particular case of Ex 4:25, and, later, by a doctor or a specialist, 1 M 1:61. "There was no ruling about the place where it was to be performed, but it was never done in the Temple or by a priest" (DE VAUX, *Les institutions de L'Ancien Testament* I, 79 [46]). Moreover, the absence of any geographical reference maintains the continuity of space in Bethlehem.

1.1.3 Characters

The principal characters that take part in the earlier pericope are Mary, Joseph, and the child, accompanied by the angels and the shepherds (2:1-20). In the verse of the circumcision (2:21) no person is mentioned, and all of the verbs are in the third person of the passive voice. Because no new characters are mentioned, it is presumed that the passage concerns the main characters from the earlier pericope: Mary, Joseph, and the child Jesus.[6] Furthermore, these main characters coincide with the Judaic customs of the time, in which normally the father and the mother surround the child during his circumcision. However, in the episode of the Presentation, the narrative speaks not only about Mary, Joseph, and the child Jesus, but also about two new characters, Simeon and Anna, who are extensively presented (Simeon in vv. 25-27 and Anna in vv. 36-37), and the pericope is intensely focused on them. As these characters were totally absent from the previous passages, they show a clear break that indicates a new passage.

Birth	Lk 2:1-20	Mary, Joseph, and child (shepherds and angels)
Circumcision	Lk 2:21	Supposedly Mary, Joseph, and child
Presentation	Lk 2:22-39	Simeon and Anna (Mary, Joseph, and child)

1.1.4 Theme

The theme of the Presentation, that Jesus is, in the words of Simeon, a "light," or "sign of contradiction" (vv. 32.34), does not appear in the episodes immediately before, which turn to past events, the birth of Jesus (2:1-20) and his circumcision (2:21); but the theme of the Presentation is centered around what it is going to happen in the future.

[6] In fact, the text notes that the other characters from the previous episode have withdrawn: the angels in 2:15 and the shepherds in 2:20.

1.1.5 Parallel Structure

I argue that a parallel structure exists between vv. 21 and 22. The two verses begin with the same expression: Καὶ ὅτε ἐπλήσθησαν (αἱ) ἡμέραι (ὀκτὼ) τοῦ... In addition, in these verses a temporal subordinate sentence precedes the main sentences in the indicative aorist form. The same structure is found in v. 6.

v. 6		**ἐπλήσθησαν** αἱ **ἡμέραι τοῦ** [...]	ἔτεκεν τὸν υἱὸν αὐτῆς
v. 21	**Καὶ ὅτε**	**ἐπλήσθησαν ἡμέραι τοῦ** [...]	ἐκλήθη τὸ ὄνομα αὐτοῦ
v. 22	**Καὶ ὅτε**	**ἐπλήσθησαν** αἱ **ἡμέραι τοῦ** [...]	ἀνήγαγον αὐτὸν

This parallel structure shows the existence of three distinct episodes that maintain a clear relation among themselves: the birth of Jesus (2:1-20), his circumcision (2:21), and his Presentation in the Temple (2:22). The three episodes are marked by the fulfillment of the time prescribed.[7]

1.2 Delimitation of the End of the Passage

1.2.1 Time

Verse 42 affirms that the passage described takes place "when Jesus was twelve years old;" that is to say, twelve years separate the two pericopes.

1.2.2 Place

Like the previous scene, the geographical setting is Jerusalem and its Temple (2:41.43.46). However, between both sojourns in the holy city v. 39 is inserted, which states that "they returned to Galilee, to their own town of Nazareth." This stay in Nazareth clearly distinguishes both episodes.

---

[7] In fact, the verb πίμπλημι only appears these three times throughout Luke 2.

1.2.3 Characters

To the customary characters in the stories of the infancy narrative, Mary, Joseph, and Jesus, v. 46 adds the teachers and v. 47 adds "all those who heard him," people that were in the Temple. The previous passage does not state anything about the teachers of the Law, and it definitely speaks of two concrete persons, Simeon and Anna; on the contrary, in the episode of the finding of Jesus in the Temple at the age of twelve, the people in the Temple remain anonymous.

1.2.4 Theme

The passage about the boy Jesus among the teachers is focused on the dialogue that Jesus has with his mother (2:48-50). In this dialogue, one senses the awareness that Jesus, at twelve years of age, had about his unique relationship with his Father. In the Presentation in the Temple, the subject matter is not Jesus' perception of himself, but rather Simeon and Anna's perception of Jesus.

These criteria show the separation which exists between the episode of the Presentation of the newborn Jesus in the Temple and the episode of the teaching that the twelve-year-old Jesus performs in the Temple. However, v. 40 states that "the child grew to maturity, he was filled with wisdom; and God's favour was with him." This verse occurs between both pericopes as a transitional verse.[8] Is it more in connection with the Presentation passage[9] or with the teaching of the twelve-year-old Jesus?[10] I suggest that v. 40 is a transitional verse more in connection with the later episode for the following reasons:

---

[8] This verse is similar to v. 21, which is a transition between vv. 1-20 and 22-39.

[9] So KELLERMANN, "Jesus", 10-25; BROWN, "The Presentation of Jesus", 2-11; STRICKERT, "The Presentation of Jesus", 33-37; GALBIATI, "La presentazione", 28-37; ROSSÉ, "Approcci esegetici", 17-30; SOARDS, "Luke 2:22-40", 400-405; STRAMARE, "Significato esegetico e teologico", 37-61; and REICKE, "Jesus, Simeon, and Anna", 96-108.

[10] So LAGRANGE, "La présentation de Jésus au Temple", 129-135; HERRANZ, "Presentación", 35-42.

(1) Throughout the infancy narrative of Luke, we find a typical way of ending the episodes with the expression "and he/they returned" as a conclusive element. A verb of movement of some of the characters in the end of the episode always appears. We find this conclusive element regarding Zechariah (1:23), the angel (1:38), Mary (1:56), the shepherds (2:20), and Joseph, Mary, and Jesus (2:51).[11] The presence of this expression in v. 39: "and they returned to Galilee" makes us think that this phrase concludes the pericope. (2) The three verbs of v. 40, as well as those of v. 41, are in the imperfect, the tense that is frequently used to describe a situation introducing a story.[12] The imperfect also shows a continuous action, the progressive and gradual growth of the child Jesus, happening progressively throughout the twelve years that elapsed in Nazareth. This fact separates it from the punctual act of the Presentation of the newborn Jesus in Jerusalem.[13] (3) The topic of v. 40 relates to the childhood and hidden life of Jesus, more than to the newborn Jesus. The statements concerning the growth of Jesus in knowledge and grace provide a much better setting in the following episode, in which "all were amazed at his understanding and his answers" (2:47). (4) The progressive and gradual

---

[11] Certainly the Greek verbs used are not the same (ἀπέρχομαι, ὑποστρέφω, ἐπιστρέφω and ἔρχομαι), but, according to LOUW – NIDA, *Greek-English*, § 15.34-15.74, all of them pertain to the same semantic field and conclude the passages by means of verbs of movement.

[12] While the verbs in v. 39 are aorist verbs, all the verbs from vv. 40-41 are in the imperfect (ηὔξανεν, ἐκραταιοῦτο ἦν, and ἐπορεύοντο) and they present the framework of the second episode, describing the situation prior to the story which is going to be narrated. The action itself, having been introduced by the verbs in the imperfect, begins with the aorist from v. 42.

[13] The emphatic position of δέ, with which v. 40 begins: Τὸ δὲ παιδίον ηὔξανεν... gives it an adversative meaning distancing v. 40 from the previous verse. Throughout the work of Luke we find seven recurrences of the sequence τὸ δέ (Lk 1:80; 2:40; 3:17; 8:14-15; 11:39; and Acts 23:6). Normally, the author uses it in order to oppose different elements: the wheat and the straw (Lk 3:17); the different terrain in which the seed falls (Lk 8:14-15); the interior and the exterior (Lk 11:39); and the Sadduces and the Pharisees (Acts 23:6). The only times in which this expression is used by itself are in the narrative of the infancy (Lk 1:80; 2:40). In these two cases, it separates action from the previous events and introduces the gradual growth of John the Baptist (1:80) and Jesus (2:40).

growth of Jesus' knowledge told in v. 40 (τὸ δὲ παιδίον ηὔξανεν ... **σοφίᾳ**, καὶ **χάρις θεοῦ**) is corroborated by v. 52 (Καὶ Ἰησοῦς προέκοπτεν ... **σοφίᾳ** ... καὶ **χάριτι** παρὰ **θεῷ**). These verses form an *inclusio* that defines the continuous growth of Jesus.

Because of these reasons I think that v. 40, although it is a transitional verse, is less connected to the previous episode (2:22-39) than to the following one (2:41-52). Together with v. 41, it describes the situation and introduces the framework of the passage that begins. Certainly both episodes unfold in the Temple and are directly related: the first is the presentation of Jesus through Simeon and Anna (2:22-39); the second makes up the presentation of Jesus through his own teaching and from his particular awareness of his divine filiation (2:40-52). Despite these connections, they concern distinct episodes.

Finally, I claim the existence of an *inclusio* between vv. 22 and 39. Both verses present a structural and a thematic parallel. Both begin with a temporal subordinate, preceded by the conjunction καί, which makes reference to the fulfillment of the Law. Then follows the main clause with a verb of motion in the aorist. Both sentences, the principal and the subordinate, present an implicit plural subject.

v.	Conj.	Temporal Sub.	Ref. to the Law	Movem.	Localization
22	Καὶ	ὅτε ἐπλήσθησαν	κατὰ τὸν νόμον	ἀνήγαγον	εἰς Ἱεροσόλυμα
39	Καὶ	ὡς ἐτέλεσαν	κατὰ τὸν νόμον	ἐπέστρεψαν	εἰς τὴν Γαλιλαίαν

2. Textual Criticism

In this section I look for the Greek text that I think is the earliest attainable form of the text with which I will be dealing in the rest of the research.[14] There are three textual problems which are important for the exegesis of the passage.

---

[14] On the problem of the "original text" in NT textual criticism see Epp, "The Multivalence", 245-281. For the study of the different variants of each verse I follow NA[27], GNT[4], and the *New Testament Greek Manuscripts*, edited by Swanson, whose

2.1. Verse 22

The verse speaks about a purification: αἱ ἡμέραι τοῦ καθαρισμοῦ αὐτῶν κατὰ τὸν νόμον Μωϋσέως. To whom does the purification refer? In other words, exegetically it is important to identify which is the genitive that follows καθαρισμοῦ. There are four different variants: (1) αὐτῶν: B*, ℵ, A, Θ^c, etc; (2) αὐτοῦ: D; (3) αὐτόν: Θ*; and (4) texts where the definite pronoun is absent: 435, pc, Bo (*bohariticus*), *Ir* (lat). The external evidence is favorable to variant 1 since it presents better and more varied witnesses, belonging to both Alexandrian and Byzantine text types.[15] Variant 2 is supported by the Western text type but only represented by a unique attestation, D. Variants 3 and 4 have a very inferior attestation.

The noun καθαρισμός appears little in the Greek Bible. In its scarce recurrences, it is concerned with the necessary purification after some sin, ἁμαρτία (Ex 29:36; 30:10; Nb 14:18; Pr 14:9; Jb 7:21); with the purification of a leper (Lv 14:32); with the purification of sexual impurities (Lv 15:13); with the purification of sacred objects (1Ch 23:28; Ne 12:45); and with the purification of the final day (Dn 12:6). In the NT it only appears on seven occasions: in our verse; in Lk 5:14 and its parallel of Mk 1:44, where the evangelist describes the purification of a leper after his cure; in Jn 2:6 in relation to the purifications prior to meals; in Jn 3:25 in a confusing text that seems to refer to the baptism of John the

---

nomenclature I use. EPP, "It's All about Variants", 275-308, and CERQUIGLINI, *Eloge de la variante*, give special attention to understanding early Christian thought by means of the array of meaningful variants.

[15] For the nomenclature and classification of the different text types see CROSS, *The Ancient Library*, 163-194 and METZGER, *A Textual Commentary*, 15*-16*. Origen quotes this verse in his fourteenth homily on the Gospel of Luke, which deals with the circumcision and purification. It discusses the difficulty that is involved in the plural αὐτῶν. If a variant had been known, certainly he would have made reference to it. This homily was written in Caesarea, after the exile of Origen from Alexandria to that city in the year 231. We can assume, therefore, that the plural αὐτῶν was in the text of Luke 2:22 both in Cesarea and in Alexandria in the first half of the third century (ORIGEN, *Homélies sur s. Luc*, 218-223 [*Hom. Luc.* 14.2-5]). For all Fathers of the Church I have followed the bilingual and critical collection of *Source chrétiennes*.

Baptist; and in Heb 1:3 and 2 P 1:9 where it refers to the purification of sins. The term has a broad meaning applicable to different circumstances. Yet we do not find any case in the Greek Bible which speaks of the purification of a newborn or firstborn,[16] nor of the husband of the mother. As the firstborn belongs to *Yhwh* (Ex 34:29), it has to be freed (λυτρόω: Ex 13:13.15; 34:20) or consecrated (ἁγιάζω: Ex 13:2.12), but not purified (καθαρίζω). Still, the woman who has just given birth has to be cleansed (καθαρίζω) of her impurities (ἀκαθαρτός: Leviticus 12).

The main characters in the episode come to carry out the Law. Since the Mosaic Law stipulated only the purification of the mother,[17] the reader could expect a feminine singular determinant, αὐτῆς. Only the Siro-Sinaitic version and several old Latin manuscripts could be interpreted as feminine because the ambiguous Latin form *eius* can be understood as masculine or as feminine.[18] But it is striking that there is no Greek manuscript with the feminine genitive that would represent the purification of the mother (αὐτῆς).[19] The absence of the pronoun in variant 4 can be explained as the elimination of the difficulty of the designation of this pronoun. Variant 3, αὐτόν, being an accusative with the verb in the passive voice (ἐπλήσθησαν), syntactically does not make any sense in the sentence. Besides, it can be explained as an error of interpretation with respect to variant 1. The scribe could have mistaken the ο for a ω. Variant 2, reading in the singular, is strange since it concerns a masculine genitive that in this context would apply to the infant Jesus,[20] not to the mother who should be purified. Variant 1, read-

---

[16] The case of Ps 88:45 speaks of "the throne of purification" of the "anointed" or servant of *Yhwh*, but nothing is said of his purification.

[17] Lv 12:4.6, speaks of the technical term κάθαρσις, rather than the term καθαρισμός.

[18] See THE AMERICAN AND BRITISH COMMITTEES OF THE INTERNATIONAL GREEK NEW TESTAMENT PROJECT, *The Gospel According to St. Luke* I, 43.

[19] As we see in *Catenae Graecorum Patrum in Novum Testamentum* II, 22, the only witness which presents a feminine pronoun (αὐτῆς) is a *catena*.

[20] It could only refer to Jesus, whose circumcision and naming are narrated in the previous verse, v. 21. As we have just seen, from the point of view of the Mosaic Law, it is improper to speak of the purification of the new born child.

ing in the plural, is also strange because the reader does not know who its antecedents are,[21] but it could not be just the mother. That is why both variant 1 and variant 2 are the *lectio difficilior.*

The sentences that follow our controversial determinant pronoun do not present textual variations and help us to clarify the two remaining possibilities. After the principal sentence, "they took him up to Jerusalem," there follow two subordinate clauses of purpose: "in order to present him to the Lord [...] and also to offer in sacrifice, in accordance with what is prescribed in the Law of the Lord." There are two events that make up the framework of the story: a) the ransom of the firstborn one month after his birth (vv. 22b and 23): "every first-born male must be called Holy for the Lord"; and b) The purification of the mother 40 days after the labor (vv.22a and 24): "A pair of turtledoves or two young pigeons." This double purpose develops and specifies the expression καθαρισμοῦ αὐτῶν. Therefore, I believe that the term καθαρισμός, which is applied to different situations in the Bible as we have just seen, is used here in a broader sense that can refer to both actions. The text does not use the technical term to refer to the purification of the mother (κάθαρσις: Lv 12:4.6). The "purification of them" (καθαρισμὸς αὐτῶν) consists principally in the purification of the mother (κάθαρσις), but it also refers to the redemption of the firstborn.[22] In addition, according to

[21] There are three possible precedents in the plural: the mother and the son; the mother and Joseph; and the mother, the son, and Joseph. I reject the possibility of Joseph and the child because it does not include the mother, who is the one who should be purified. Syntactically the plural of the pronoun (αὐτῶν = of them) seems to refer to Joseph and Mary, because they are the implicit subjects of the principal verb ἀνήγαγον (= they brought). Bock says that "it could be argued that Joseph, because he aided in the delivery, was himself made unclean, since according to the *Mishnah* contact with blood in the delivery made one unclean" (BOCK, *Proclamation*, 83-84). Nevertheless, I believe that the context speaks of Jesus and not of Joseph because the implicit direct object of the principal verb ἀνήγαγον is Jesus and not Joseph. The context suggests, therefore, that the plural refers to Mary and to Jesus; to the mother and the son. In addition, since the time of Origen, many commentators have understood that plural as a reference to Mary and Jesus (see ORIGEN, *Homélies sur s. Luc.*, 223-231 [*Hom. Luc.*, 14.5-10]).

[22] On this possibility see Bill. II, 123.

Vaccari, it is a case of *zeugma*, a grammatical phenomenon in which one word is used to modify or govern two or more other words in such a way that it makes sense only in one case and not in the other(s).[23] The ritual of the mother and the ritual of the son are unified and this is referred to through the expression καθαρισμὸς αὐτῶν.

Since variant 1 presents a superior attestation, is in agreement with the following context, and better explains the rest of the variants,[24] I believe that it is the earliest attainable text. The other variants show us the difficulty of the expression and in different ways try to explain these difficulties. Therefore, the text affirms the "purification" of two different persons: the purification of the mother and the redemption of the son.

2.2 Verse 27

The words τοὺς γονεῖς (= parents) appear in all of the manuscripts except in the minuscule manuscripts 245, 1347, 1510, and 2643 so that the external evidence is very weak for this variant. The absence of this noun, which fulfills the function of the subject of the subordinate temporal phrase ἐν τῷ εἰσαγαγεῖν, could be due to either an error of omission or a theological intention; this omission clearly circumvents calling Joseph the father of Jesus. On the other hand, if the subject remained implicit, the pronoun αὐτούς of the second part of the same verse would remain without an antecedent to replace. It is remarkable that the aforementioned pronoun is found in the minuscule manuscripts where τοὺς γονεῖς does not appear. Even though these miniscule manuscripts are the *lectio brevior*, I believe that both the external evidence (already reasonably superior) and the internal evidence (theological correction or error of omission) allow us to retain the words τοὺς γονεῖς.

---

[23] VACCARI, "ΕΔΗΣΑΝ ΑΥΤΟ ΟΘΟΝΙΟΙΣ (Joh. 19,40)", 383.

[24] The change from αὐτῶν to αὐτοῦ present in D remains to be explained. Is it a simple copyist's error? The scarce attestation of αὐτοῦ suggests this choice. On the possibility that αὐτῶν is a correction from αὐτοῦ in order to be able to include the purification of Mary and to try to explain the act see HATCH, "The Text of Luke II, 22", 377-381.

2.3 Verse 33

Firstly, we find two variants: (1) ὁ πατὴρ αὐτοῦ; and (2) Ἰωσήφ. The attestation of ὁ πατὴρ αὐτοῦ is superior in both the number and variety of witnesses. It is present in manuscripts from the Alexandrian text type (particularly represented here by B, ℵ, W, L), and the Western text type (represented here by D). The internal evidence shows us that ὁ πατὴρ αὐτοῦ was replaced by Ἰωσὴφ and is explained as a subsequent doctrinal correction in order to avoid calling Joseph "father of Jesus" with the intention of safeguarding the doctrine of the virginal conception of Jesus.[25] There may be a conscious correction from the earlier attainable text.[26] Because of all of this, I choose variant 1 as the original reading.[27]

In addition, after ἡ μήτηρ some manuscripts (ℵ*, A, L, M, ψ, θ, K, f13, etc.) add αὐτοῦ. The external attestation that does not include this genitive is much superior. We find manuscripts from the Alexandrian text type (represented here by ℵ1, B, D, W, 1, 33, etc.), the Western text type (represented here by D), and the Byzantine text type (f1). The internal evidence explains this addition as a stylistic assimilation with ὁ πατὴρ αὐτοῦ in the manuscripts that have not yet replaced it with Ἰωσήφ. In the manuscripts that have already replaced it with Ἰωσήφ, it is understood as a specification of the maternity, or as transference of the aforementioned genitive αὐτοῦ when it was no longer necessary after ὁ πατήρ because of the presence of the proper noun Ἰωσήφ. Finally, manuscript 157,[28] which presents Ἰωσήφ ὁ πατὴρ αὐτοῦ καὶ ἡ μήτηρ αὐτοῦ, is a clear combination of the oldest readings. The conflation present in minuscule manuscript 157 is clear.[29]

---

[25] VOGELS, "Die 'Eltern' Jesu", 33-43, thinks that the correction was first made by Tatian.

[26] There is a similar conscious correction in Lk 2:43: the original "his parents" was consciously amended to "Joseph and his mother." Therefore, we find a tradition that seems not to know of the virginal birth of Jesus (v. 27; see § 2.2).

[27] See METZGER, *A Textual Commentary*, 111-112.

[28] On the different minuscule manuscripts of v. 33 see ALAND – ALAND – WACHTEL, *Text und Textwert* III, 5-6.

[29] On this conflation see OMANSON – METZGER, *A Textual Guide*, 112.

3. Structure of the Passage and Function of its Scenes

Once our passage has been delimited and the earliest attainable text has been identified, we can study the internal threads which structure and link the different scenes together in the narrative chain. On one hand, its meaning can be better understood through the sum of threads between the different elements of the text. On the other hand, for our exegesis it is crucial to perform an accurate segmentation of the pericope into smaller units. The scenes of the text allow us to recognize their content in connection with the total meaning of the passage. This is why I will not limit myself to showing the division between the different parts of the passage (diversity); instead I will also show the relation between the parts and the entire narrative passage (unity).

The strong presence of the coordinating conjunction καί shows the preference for paratactic relations. In our passage, *hypotaxis* occupies a much smaller proportion than parataxis.[30] This preference for *parataxis* shows the development of the narrative plot by means of parallels structures. In fact, all the scenes begin with the coordinating conjunction καί. The introduction and the conclusion begin in a similar way: καί + temporal conjunction + aorist verb of fulfillment. The interventions of the narrator introducing the different characters that appear throughout the passage (Simeon, the parents of Jesus, and Anna) begin with the construction καί + ἦν.[31] We find a narrator's intervention at the beginning of each scene, and the intervention of the narrator presenting Mary and Joseph helps to divide the scene concerning Simeon into two speeches. I suggest the following concentric structure.[32]

---

[30] Seventeen phrases begin with a coordinating καί; scenes are simply juxtaposed. But there are only seven subordinate conjunctions which express logical and temporal connections (ὅτε: v.22; καθώς and ὅτι: v. 23; πρίν: v. 26; ὅτι: v. 30; ὅπως: v. 35; and ὡς: v. 39).

[31] The presentation of Simeon (v. 25), that of the parents of Jesus (v. 33), and that of Anna (v. 36) are accomplished with this construction. In the case of v. 25, between καί and ἦν we find the words ἰδοὺ ἄνθρωπος which emphasize the character of Simeon through the deictic ἰδού. According to MARSHALL, *The Gospel of Luke*, 117, the καὶ ἰδού of v. 25 introduces a new event, a new scene.

[32] There are different types of models: rhetorical, narrative, oral, etc. The chiasmus and lexical repetition, which I propose, belong to the oral model. Although this

Introduction (vv. 22-24):	**Καὶ ὅτε** ἐπλήσθησαν
Simeon (vv. 25-28a):	*Καὶ* ἰδοὺ ἄνθρωπος *ἦν* (…) ᾧ ὄνομα Συμεὼν
Simeon's hymn (vv. 28b-32):	καὶ εὐλόγησεν (…) καὶ εἶπεν
Mary and Joseph (v. 33):	*καὶ ἦν* ὁ πατὴρ αὐτοῦ καὶ ἡ μήτηρ
Simeon's prophecy (vv. 34-35):	καὶ εὐλόγησεν (…) καὶ εἶπεν
Anna (vv. 36-38):	*Καὶ ἦν* Ἄννα
Conclusion (v. 39):	**Καὶ ὡς** ἐτέλεσαν

I believe, therefore, that the text is well unified, with distinct parts that make reference to others, with distinct factors, both syntactic and semantic, that together give coherence to the text. The introduction gives the setting of the Temple of Jerusalem (vv. 22-24); and Simeon lives in Jerusalem and goes to the Temple (vv. 25-27). The characterization of Simeon introduces his divine promise of seeing the Messiah of the Lord (v. 26); and Simeon's hymn blesses God because he has already seen the Messiah (vv. 29-32). Jesus' parents are surprised because of what is said about Jesus (v. 33); and Simeon blesses them and speaks to Mary in his prophecy (vv. 34-35). As Simeon goes to the Temple and speaks about Jesus, Anna never leaves the Temple and speaks about Jesus (vv. 36-38). Finally, everything the Law of the Lord required is fulfilled. The center of this concentric structure is the surprise of Mary and Joseph, who "were amazed about the things said about him (Jesus)" (v. 33). In other words, the center of the passage is the admiration for the things said about Jesus. Everything in this text resolves around the things said about Jesus.[33]

---

model only shows the *signifier* of the narrative, I consider this model because, as these repetitions hold together the poem or oracle, so they do with the narrative. Moreover, these repetitions are threads between the different elements of the text, threads which help to articulate the narrative units, and thus the *signified* of the narrative. Furthermore, this articulation also comes from the narrative analysis of the pericope's verbal tenses in connection with the foreground and background (see the beginning of § 3.2 and 3.3). According to ALETTI, *L'art*, 17, the articulation of the narrative units, even more than the elegance of the sentences or the beauty of the style, gives the story its breadth. On the terminlogy introduced by Saussure of signifier and signified and their inseparable union see ABRAMS, *Literary Terms*, 215.

[33] The main functions of a chiastic structure are the following: an aesthetic motivation, a mnemotechnic function, and a conceptual motivation, in which the center or climax of the structure underscores the most important idea.

3.1 Introduction: vv. 22-24

The syntax helps to define the scenes since a change of scene cannot divide a grammatical clause; two different parts of a phrase cannot belong to two different scenes. The linguistic criteria are strong and cannot be underestimated. This first scene is made up of a unique grammatical sentence: a main clause (ἀνήγαγον αὐτὸν εἰς Ἱεροσόλυμα), preceded by a temporal subordinate (ὅτε ἐπλήσθησαν αἱ ἡμέραι τοῦ καθαρισμοῦ αὐτῶν κατὰ τὸν νόμον Μωϋσέως) and followed by two other purpose subordinates (παραστῆσαι τῷ κυρίῳ,...καὶ τοῦ δοῦναι θυσίαν...).

Temporal Subordinate	Main Clause	Purpose Subordinates
Ὅτε ἐπλήσθησαν αἱ ἡμέραι...		
	ἀνήγαγον αὐτὸν εἰς Ἱεροσόλυμα	
		παραστῆσαι τῷ κυρίῳ... καὶ τοῦ δοῦναι θυσίαν...

The introduction of a story normally presents the characters. This introduction does so through implicit subjects of a verb in the third person plural (ἀνήγαγον) and through pronouns, αὐτῶν and αὐτόν.[34] The implicit subject of the main clause can only be identified as Mary and Joseph (2:4-5.16.19). The antecedent of the pronoun αὐτόν is found in the earlier verse,[35] where the antecedent

[34] Luke presents a clear principle of economy: implicit subjects, pronouns whose antecedent the reader has to supply. This principle of economy appears throughout the passage, especially when the narrator refers to Jesus, Mary, and Joseph (see vv. 28.33.34.35.39).

[35] As we have seen in § 1.1.5, both verses begin in the same way (Καὶ ὅτε ἐπλήσθησαν ἡμέραι τοῦ + infinitive), a chronological succession exists between both verses ("at the eighth day," "when the days of the purification were fulfilled"), and there is a continuity of some characters (Jesus, Mary, and Joseph).

of the aforementioned pronoun appears. There we find the same pronoun αὐτόν in connection with the name of the child, Ἰησοῦς. The context clearly shows that the antecedent of this pronoun is the child Jesus.[36]

The introduction of the pericope presents the intention of Mary and Joseph in going to Jerusalem (vv. 22b-24). In v. 22 we find a purpose infinitive (παραστῆσαι) which is followed in v. 24 by a second purpose infinitive preceded, this time, by the article in the genitive case (τοῦ δοῦναι).[37] Both intentions are united by the conjunction καί (v. 23) leading us to consider both infinitives (παρασιτῆσαι and τοῦ δοῦναι) in parallel and to interpret them as two purpose infinitives. This interpretation shows the existence of two purposes for the trip to Jerusalem. Both purposes are explained by an explicit commentary, an *explanatory gloss* introduced by the narrator.[38] This gloss explains what the reader does not know through two Scriptural quotations. On one hand, they want to redeem the firstborn (2:7) from the Lord (v. 23: "every first-born male must be called Holy for the Lord"). On the other hand, they intend to offer a sacrifice according to what is stipulated in the Law of the Lord (v. 24: "a pair of turtledoves or two young pigeons"). Both quotes, the first scriptural quotations in Luke-Acts and the only ones in Luke 1–2, are not literal,[39] but what they refer to is clear. The first one arises out of the setting of the story of the last plague in the liberation from Egypt. Every firstborn male of

---

[36] See 2:16.17.21. Later, the presence of τὸ παιδίον Ἰησοῦν in the v. 27 will reaffirm this identification.

[37] Luke has the tendency to put a τοῦ before a second purpose infinite in order to improve the clarity of the expression. We find a similar sequence in Lk 1:76-77; 1:78-79; Acts 26:18.

[38] WINTER, "Ὅτι Recitativum", 213, proves that ὅτι introduces a direct speech, a Scripture quotation and could be translated as "for indeed, every male birth..."

[39] The first quotation, πᾶν ἄρσεν διανοῖγον μήτραν ἅγιον τῷ κυρίῳ κληθήσεται (v. 23), freely quotes ἁγίασόν μοι πᾶν πρωτότοκον πρωτογενὲς διανοῖγον πᾶσαν μήτραν (Ex 13:2). Luke adds the word ἄρσεν from Ex 13:12 and changes the imperative ἁγίασόν μοι by the expression ἅγιον τῷ κυρίῳ κληθήσεται. The second quotation, ζεῦγος τρυγόνων ἢ δύο νοσσοὺς περιστερῶν (v. 24), quotes δύο τρυγόνας ἢ δύο νεοσσοὺς περιστερῶν (Lv 12:8). Luke only changes δύο to ζεῦγος, "a pair," a variation for the sake of elegance.

Israel belongs to the Lord because they were saved from the final plague (Ex 13:1-2.11-16). The original idea was that the firstborn should dedicate his life to the service of God in a special way in order to be redeemed from death. Nevertheless, the tribe of Levi was finally charged to serve the Lord in the cult and thus to replace the firstborns. This substitution was recognized in the legal dispositions of Nb 3:12; 18:15-16 which exempted the firstborn from that service through the payment of five shekels.[40] "I have chosen the Levites from the Israelites instead (ἀντί) of all the first-born" (Nb 3:12). This is why his parents should redeem Jesus,[41] who is "Holy for the Lord." The second one refers to the purification of the mother after the delivery (Lv 5:11; 12:1-8).[42] We find two rituals according to the Law: the ransom of the firstborn and the purification of the mother.[43]

However, the purification of the mother is not recounted. And the narration does not tell anything about the five shekels of silver for the ransom of the firstborn,[44] so that the redemption of the son

[40] A first born human cannot be sacrificed, and, if he was not a Levite, he could not be consecrated to the service in the Temple. That is why the parents could redeem him.

[41] Only MIYOSHI, "Jesu Darstellung", 85-115, interprets the action regarding the son as a nazirite vow (Numbers 6); Jesus was a nazir for his entire life. Although I believe Jesus belonged to the Father for his entire life, I do not believe that he can be considered as a nazir. According to Numbers 6, the nazir "will abstain from wine and fermented liquor" (v. 3), "no razor will touch his head, he will let his hair grow freely" (v. 5) and "he will not go near a corpse" (v. 6). I do not think we can affirm these injunctions in Jesus' case.

[42] This purification is in connection with the blood of the delivery; it is not in connection with the conception. That is why Mary, though she is a virgin (Lk 1:26-38), should be purified (Lv 12:1-8).

[43] This double purpose could justify the existence of the plural genitive αὐτῶν of v. 22 that, as I have said in § 2.1, I believe is the earliest attainable text. The author could have the precise intention of uniting both purposes in the genitive αὐτῶν. Thus, he sets the actions regarding the son in the center of religious Judaism, in the Temple, where the purification of the mother had to take place.

[44] The silence regarding the paying of the ransom makes a great impression on any reader who would have known this prescription of the Law. As we will see later, Jesus is presented as the "salvation" of God (v. 30). Perhaps in the mind of the author the one who was characterized as redeemer should not be redeemed. Perhaps Luke is thinking of other ways of being offered and paying his ransom. Is he thinking of Jesus' passion and death? This silence gives the impression that Jesus still belongs to God, that he is still consecrated, and that he is going to be truly consecrated for his

is not described either.[45] Because of this, Power defended the thesis that Joseph and Mary did not redeem Jesus and that Mary was not purified.[46] Herranz responded to Power's article affirming that they did pay the five shekels because "although Saint Luke does not say it specifically, they maintained their privileges and behaved as all good Israelites."[47] I believe that Luke does say it specifically. The only prescription of the Law was the redemption of the first born, and the purification of the mother. And Luke says that Joseph and Mary fulfilled "what the Law required concerning him (Jesus)" (v. 27), and did "everything according to the Law of the Lord" (v. 39). I suggest that these affirmations allow us to believe that they paid the five shekels and that the mother was purified. Luke does affirm it, while not describing how it was performed.[48]

Does Luke want to accentuate one of these purposes (vv. 23-24)? Are both equally important for the author? I believe that the main purpose of the narrative by Luke is the redemption of the first born, παραστῆσαι τῷ κυρίῳ, for the following reasons. (1) The fact that both quotations are subordinated to the principle sentence, bringing *him* up to Jerusalem, underlines that the main purpose is in connection with the child because the main clause speaks of ἀνήγαγον αὐτόν. (2) The term *Law* shows an evolution as the pericope progresses. At the beginning (vv. 22-24), the Law refers to the

---

entire life (2:49). The adjective ἅγιον, Holy, applied to Jesus (v. 23), expresses this special consecration to God. Lk 1:35, in saying that Jesus is "Holy for the Lord," could be seen as a hint in this direction. In fact, Luke's point lies in the description of Jesus as Holy because Luke modifies the text of Ex 13:2, "consecrate all the first-born to me, the first birth from every womb" into the expression of Lk 2:23, "Every first-born must be called Holy for the Lord." Thus, Luke is presenting Jesus as Holy in the biblical meaning, entirely dedicated to God.

[45] On this absence see GARCÍA VIEYRA, "Purficación de María", 7-36.

[46] POWER, "In festo Purificationis", 34-41.

[47] HERRANZ, "Presentación", 35.

[48] We find the same Lukan procedure in other passages of the Lukan infancy narrative where the prescriptions are mentioned but not narrated. In 1:5-25 the incense-burning and priestly rites are not narrated; in 1:57-80 and 2:21 there is no narration of the circumcision; in 2:40-52, the Passover festival is not narrated. Luke provides the starting point and the context of the action which the episode recounts, but the focus is never on the performance of the Jewish rites.

καθαρισμὸς αὐτῶν (v. 22), that is to say, to the "purification" understood in a wider sense, meaning both of the son (v. 23) and of the mother (v. 24). Later (v. 27) the Law exclusively concerns Jesus (περὶ αὐτοῦ). (3) The description of the offering for the purification of the mother (v. 24) is placed after the prescription regarding the first born (v. 23). And, furthermore, (4) in the purification of the mother the presence of the child was not necessary and the child is in the center of this narrative.

What is, therefore, the point of the expression παρίστημι, which Luke underlines as the main purpose of the passage? In non-biblical Greek the verb παρίστημι has two main semantic fields. When it is an intransitive verb it usually means "to stand by," "to approach," "to be present," "to assist." When it is a transitive verb it general means "to present," "to place," "to place at disposal," "to provide."[49] This diversification of meaning in secular Greek is carried over into Luke-Acts.[50] Throughout the Lukan work παρίστημι functions as both an intransitive and transitive verb. When it is an intransitive verb, it usually means "to be present," "to stand by."[51] When it is a transitive verb, it usually means "to present."[52] Lk 2:22 uses the verb παρίστημι preceded by the pronoun αὐτόν and followed by the expression τῷ κυρίῳ. It is a transitive verb with a double object, one direct and another indirect.[53] All the occurrences of παρίστημι in Luke-Acts with a double object add a nu-

[49] REICKE – BERTRAM, "παρίστημι, παριστάνω", 836, give numerous examples.

[50] See SAND, "παρίστημι, παριστάνω", 96.

[51] Lk 1:19; 19:24; Acts 1:10; 4:10.26; 9:39; 23:2.4; 24:13; 27:23. The only exception is Acts 4:26 where the presence implies a hostile approach.

[52] Acts 1:3; 9:41; 23:24.33; 27:24. The only exception is Acts 23:24 where it means "to place at the disposal," "to provide."

[53] The pronoun αὐτόν is the direct object of both verbs, ἀνάγω and παρίστημι. It would be an example of what YULE, *Pragmatics*, 23, calls *zero anaphora*. According to him, the use of zero anaphora as a means of maintaining reference clearly creates an expectation that the listener will be able to infer who or what the author intends to identify. This is the reason why the author does not write the explicit anaphoric pronoun. CRESPO, *Sintaxis del Griego Clásico*, 355-364, applies this *zero anaphora* linguistic concept to classical Greek.

ance of solemnity, or special importance:[54] Acts 1:3: οἷς καὶ παρέστησεν ἑαυτὸν ζῶντα, where Jesus presents himself, alive, to the apostles;[55] Acts 9:41: τοὺς ἁγίους καὶ τὰς χήρας παρέστησεν αὐτὴν ζῶσαν,[56] where Peter presents Tabitha, alive, to the saints and widows; Acts 23:33: τῷ ἡγεμόνι παρέστησαν καὶ τὸν Παῦλον, where the Jews present Paul to the governor; and Acts 27:24: Καίσαρί σε δεῖ παραστῆναι, where the angel of God clearly commands Paul to present himself to Caesar.[57] In Lk 2:22-39 the indirect object τῷ κυρίῳ adds a religious context to this solemn presentation: Jesus is solemnly presented to the Lord.[58] The expression παρίστημι τῷ κυρίῳ does not afterward appear in Luke's work, but in the non-Lukan literature of the NT and in the OT, it means "to consecrate" or "to redeem."[59] This means that this ex-

---

[54] The only recurrence with a single object is Acts 23:24 where the tribune orders his subjects to "provide a mount for Paul" (κτήνη τε παραστῆσαι).

[55] This example is like a summary of his presentation after his resurrection, for 40 days before the ascension. As Jesus was solemnly presented 40 days after his birth at the beginning of his earthly life, Jesus solemnly presents himself before his ascension at the beginning of his risen life.

[56] This example has a double object, but both in the accusative. Its reason might be that the indirect object, "to the saints and widows," is also a direct object of the previous verb, "to call:" Peter called the saints and widows and presented Tabitha alive to them. It would be another example of *zero anaphora*.

[57] I think that the personal pronoun σέ plays the function of subject and direct object of the verb παρίστημι; it is necessary that Paul present *himself* to Ceasar. Trying to avoid the redundancy, one of the pronouns could be implicit because of the referential identity. These two last examples are used along with forensic expressions. They present Paul before the governor, or before Caesar, for trial. These sayings within a judicial setting are useful to better understand the expression παραστῆσαι τῷ κυρίῳ of Lk 2:22 as an official presentation to his Lord.

[58] As REICKE – BERTRAM, "παρίστημι, παριστάνω", 838, claim, the verb παρίστημι is sometimes used along with various concepts of religious service: "to assist," "to serve." Thus the angel in Lk 1:19 says: "I am Gabriel who serves (ὁ παρεστηκώς) in the presence of God."

[59] In the NT, with the object of Θεός insted of κύριος it means to offer or consecrate oneself to God (Rm 6:13.19; 12:1; 2 Tm 2:15). In the OT the expression means to minister or to serve the Lord (see Dt 10:8; 17:12; 18:5; 1 K 12:32; 18:15; 2 K 3:4; 5:16). See REICKE-BERTRAM, "παρίστημι, παριστάνω", 837.

pression in Lk 2:22 has the meaning of an official presentation, which, being to the Lord, becomes a consecration, a redemption.[60]

Since, however, the child was brought to the Temple, which was not necessary for the act of redemption,[61] we should probably find a third element in the narrative. According to Maggioni, Joseph and Mary made the most of their travel to the Temple for her purification to redeem their first born and to solemnly present him to God.[62] This third element in the narrative is the pious and devotional presentation of the son in the Temple.[63] This act was not mandatory, but none would reproach it.

Through the verb παρίστημι, with its main transitive meaning of "to present," the author prepares the subsequent development of the passage, the presentation of Jesus through Simeon and Anna.[64]

---

[60] This interpretation of consecration/redemption finds confirmation in the following verse, in which the narrator adds the quotation of the Law of the Lord: "Every first-born male must be called Holy for the Lord" (v. 23), which refers to the redemption of the first born (Ex 13:2).

[61] It appears that Luke does not understand the Jewish ritual ceremonies very well. The reader does not know them well either because Luke has to explain them through quotations of the OT (vv. 23b.24b). The mother's purification in the Temple after her child's birth (Lv 12:2-8) did not require the presence of the infant; and the redemption of the firstborn (Ex 13:1-2.11-16; Nb 18:15-16) did not involve a ritual in the Temple (see DIBELIUS, *Die Formgeschichte*, 122-123; BULTMANN, *Die Geschichte der synoptischen Tradition*, 326). I am not studying the historicity of the event, which would require another methodology. On the historicity of these rites see LAURENTIN, "Vérité", 691-710; and GRELOT, "Le Cantique de Siméon", 481-509.

[62] MAGGIONI, "The Ordinary Made Extraordinary", 13, claims that three ceremonies are performed in the Temple. See as well MUÑOZ IGLESIAS, *Los Evangelios de la Infancia* III, 161-164.

[63] MARSHALL, *The Gospel of Luke*, 117, suggests a presentation of Jesus as Samuel, who was presented to God in 1 S 1:11.22.28. Ne 10:33-37 mentions the bringing the new-born to the Temple as a particular devotion: "Let us bring to the Temple of our God the first-fruits of our sons" (v. 37). In addition, *The Protoevangelium Iacobi*, 6,2 describes the pious and devotional presentation of Mary in the Temple.

[64] The verb παρίστημι would be a case of plurality of meaning. With *polysemy* narratology puts its finger on an original effect: deliberate imprecision. The author would be aware of this polysemy and did not want to reduce it. I think that the ambiguity is removed later in the course of the narrative because the only presentation told by Luke is the presentation of Jesus by Simeon and Anna. According to MARGUERAT – BOURQUIN,

There is, therefore, a double movement, a double presentation. First, Joseph and Mary, making the most of the mother's purification and the son's redemption, took Jesus to Jerusalem to present him to the Lord (plural subject of vv. 22-24). These events are fulfilled according to the Law (νόμος occurs 3x in vv. 22-24), but they are not described. The intention of this "OT" presentation introduces the result of the "NT" presentation, which is narratively described and developed.[65] This second unforeseen presentation is performed by Simeon, vv. 25-35, and Anna, vv. 36-38 (singular subject), and it is fulfilled according to the Spirit (πνεῦμα occurs 3x in vv. 25-27). The first one is the act of the intradiegetical presentation of Jesus to God. The second one presents Jesus to those who were present in the Temple and, *extradiegetically*, to the text's readers through Simeon's and Anna's response to Jesus' presence.

The introduction also gives us the setting of the passage. Through its main clause it shows us the geographic location, Jerusalem, in which the narrated event takes place (v. 22). And both dependent clauses present an OT citation that explains the Law that the characters come to fulfill. In fact, the term νόμος structures this section; it is present in all the dependent clauses.[66] I believe that the three occurrences are in parallel and, from the beginning, place all of the passage in relation to the fulfillment of the requirements of the Law.[67] The fulfillment of the Law in Jerusalem becomes the setting of the pericope and the first engine which

---

Récits bibliques, 148-149, the author of Luke-Acts is a specialist in this type of deliberate indecision (see Lk 2:49; 23:47; Acts 17:22; 27:20-44).

[65] The terms OT, NT, Christian, Jewish-Christian, Pagan-Christian, are anachronisms. However, I use them for the sake of convenience.

[66] Notice the strong presence of the noun νόμος in vv. 22-24 (3x). The νόμος Μωϋσέως (v. 22) or νόμος κυρίου (vv. 23.24) is concretized by two quotes from the Law of the Lord taken from the Pentateuch or Torah (Ex 13:1-2 and Lv 5:11; 12:1-8), in other words, from the Law of Moses. In addition, five of the nine occurrences of the noun νόμος in Luke's Gospel occur in these verses (2:22.23.24.27.39; 10:26; 16:16.17; 24:44).

[67] The characters from the episode, Joseph, Mary, and Jesus, are bound, from the beginning, to the perfect fulfillment of the Law. Jesus' circumcision (v. 21) and Jesus' redemption (v. 22-23) incorporate Jesus into the Israelite community and guarantee the continuation between Judaism and Christianity.

drives the narration forward. The narrator could not have better emphasized the total integration of Jesus in the tradition of his people and his total observance of its rites and laws. This point is significant because of Jesus' later conflict with the Jewish religious leadership. Does he challenge them because he was raised in a home that did not honor the Law? Jesus came from a family that sought to honor God and the Jewish traditions.[68]

3.2 The Account of Simeon: vv. 25-35

The principal verb of vv. 22-24 (ἀνήγαγον) is in the plural. But from v. 25, all of the principal verbs are in the singular. The implicit subject of the plural verb is Mary and Joseph; while the subject of the singular verbs is Simeon first (vv. 25-35, explicitly vv. 25-28.34) and then Anna (vv. 36-38). This change of the subject of the phrases shows the change of the character and emphasizes the change of scenes. Still concerning different scenes, the introduction is connected with Simeon's scene through the link-word "Jerusalem." Precisely the same place in which they present Jesus (v. 22), Jerusalem, is where Simeon lives (v. 25).[69] There is also a continuity between

---

[68] On this topic see BOCK, *Luke*, 92.

[69] In the introduction it is affirmed that the holy family is headed "toward Jerusalem" (εἰς Ἱεροσόλυμα) while Simeon is "in Jerusalem" (ἐν Ἰερουσαλήμ). Notice that the text presents two different roots to refer to the same city. Ἱεροσόλυμα appears four times in Luke and 25 times in Acts. Ἰερουσαλήμ appears 26 times in the Gospel and 39 times in Acts. The first one is the Greek name of the city, while the second one is practically a transcription of the Hebrew. Exegetes have seen a different motives behind both names. There it has been supposed that the Jewish term Ἰερουσαλήμ qualifies the city following a salvific-history perspective, while the Greek term Ἱεροσόλυμα represents merely a geographic concept (see DE LA POTTERIE, "Les deux noms de Jérusalem", 153-187; ELLIOTT, "Jerusalem in Acts", 462-469; DE YOUNG, "Jerusalem in the New Testament", 16-22; MORALES GÓMEZ, "Jerusalén-Jerosólima", 131-186; BOTTINO, "La missione", 337-338). Nevertheless, many manuscripts do not coincide in their use of the two denominations. Therefore, all theological interpretation from each term remains in the realm of mere hypothesis (see BACHMANN, *Jerusalem und der Tempel*, 13-66; JEREMIAS, "Miszelle: Ierousalem/Ierosolyma", 273-276; SYLVA, "Jerousalem and Hierosoluma in Luke-Acts", 207-221). Moreover, it is enough to cite the pericope of the Presentation in the Temple, in which the two different names appear (Lk 2:22.25.38), without any variants, leaving no space for these nuances of meaning. I believe that both names refer to the same city without any special difference.

both scenes through the link-word νόμος (vv. 22.23.24.27). The setting remains the fulfillment of the Law in Jerusalem.

3.2.1 The Description of Simeon: vv. 25-26

The principal verb from the introduction (v. 22) was aorist, showing the foreground of the scene.[70] Now we find all the verbs in the imperfect (ἦν: vv. 25a.25c.26), a subordinate participle (προσδεχόμενος: v. 25), and a nominal sentence (ἄνθρωπος οὗτος δίκαιος καὶ εὐλαβής: v. 25). The function of these verbs is the description, in the background of the scene, of the character of Simeon.[71] Simeon's characterization is a descriptive pause, an extreme slowing down of the narrative.[72] This descriptive pause is made up by an explicit commentary by the narrator, an inner view of Simeon. It is an observation made by the omniscient narrator who characterizes Simeon.[73]

The hendiadys, using two adjectives δίκαιος and εὐλαβής to ex-

---

[70] On the meaning of the principal verbs in connection with the foreground and background of the narrative, as the author's means to establish logical links and hierarchical importance between the different scenes, I follow NICCACCI, "Dall'aoristo all'imperfetto", 85-108.

[71] The apocryphal literature identifies Simeon as a famous man. *The Protoevangelium Iacobi*, 24,4, affirms that Simeon was the priest who replaced Zechariah. In *The Evangelium Nicodemi,* in the narration of *Christ's Descent into Hell,* 1,1-2, Simeon is called priest, and he and his two sons, Carino and Leucio, were raised from the dead by Christ when he rose from the dead. Culter identifies Simeon with the son of Hillel (CULTER, "Does the Simeon of Luke 2 Refer to Simeon the Son of Hillel?", 29-35). Riesner believes that Simeon is that Simeon referred to by James in his speech in Acts 15:13-21 (RIESNER, "Jame's Speech", 263-278). Finally, REICKE, "Jesus, Simeon, and Anna", 101, identifies Simeon with a famous Essene prophet in Jerusalem by the name of Simon. However, I suggest that the Greek expression ἰδοὺ ἄνθρωπος ἦν ἐν Ἰερουσαλήμ, ᾧ ὄνομα Συμεών, without any definite article, indicates that Simeon was an unknown character for the reader. This fact discredits all the identifications with some other famous Simeon.

[72] As MARGUERAT – BOURQUIN, *Récits bibliques*, 113 [89], affirm, in a descriptive pause "a segment of the narrative corresponds to zero duration at the level of the story." The pause is the moment when the narrator can give the readers a key which will make them gain in knowledge.

[73] The omniscient narrator going beyond time and space gives access to this inner view which is characteristic of the internal focalization (see MARGUERAT – BOURQUIN, *Récits bibliques*, 133).

press the one concept, gives emphasis to his inner just and devout character.[74] But what characterizes and unifies the description of this person is the presence in him of the Holy Spirit.[75] Simeon is empowered by the Holy Spirit which is in him (v. 25c), he had received the prophecy from the Holy Spirit (v. 26), and he has been docile to the Holy Spirit in going to the Temple (v. 27a). The Spirit reveals the child to Simeon, who then reveals him to the others present with him. Simeon is described in a continuous state of justice, devotion, and presence of the Holy Spirit (vv. 25-26). The purpose of presenting the character of Simeon as a reliable character is clear. This presentation of Simeon invites the reader to trust him.

As there was a triple reference to the Law (vv. 22-24), now there is a triple reference to the Holy Spirit (vv. 25-27). As the Law is the first engine of the first scene, now the Holy Spirit is the engine which drives this second scene forward. Jesus' family went to the Temple obeying the Law. Simeon went to the Temple obeying the Holy Spirit. The obedience to the will of God through his Law and through the Holy Spirit made that meeting possible. The presence of the Holy Spirit, leading Simeon to the Temple, means that God has wanted this meeting to happen right in the Temple. The traditional place of divine revelation is the place chosen for the presentation of Jesus.

Although the text does not say that Simeon is a prophet, there are signs which link Simeon to prophecy. (1) Luke mentions three times the connection between the Holy Spirit and Simeon (vv. 25.26.27), and through the infancy narrative there is a close connection be-

---

[74] On the concept of hendiadys applied to this verse see KOEHNE, "Jesus the Torah", 8.

[75] Even though the expression πνεῦμα ἅγιον (v. 25) appears without an article, it evidently refers to the Spirit of God, as deduced from the previous context (Lk 1:15.35.41.67). In fact, in the following references, both in v. 26 and in v. 27, it appears with a definite article. Besides, the absence of the article in proper nouns is very frequent. Finally, the Greek translations from Dn 5:12; 6:4 (LXX) and from Dn 4:8.18 (Theodotion) present the Spirit of God with the expression πνεῦμα ἅγιον without the article. Although there is no Trinitarian reflection, Luke is referring to the Holy Spirit (see BROWN, *Birth*, 124-125.138-143).

tween the Holy Spirit and the spirit of prophecy.[76] (2) The experience of the locution in which he had been told that he would not see death before he had seen the Lord's Messiah (v. 26) suggests a prophetic dynamic.[77] (3) The references to the future life of Jesus (v. 34b), and to that of Mary (v. 35a) present Simeon as a prophet who foresees the future.[78]

Simeon is presented as one who is expectant. He is expecting "the consolation of Israel" (v. 25), and he is expecting to see the "Messiah of the Lord" (v. 26) performing the "consolation of Israel."[79] The fulfillment of the Law and the prophecies converges in Jerusalem.

3.2.2 The Reaction of Simeon to Jesus: vv. 27-35

After the introduction, the narrator describes Simeon without relation to the child Jesus (vv. 25-26). In fact, until the last words of v. 26 (χριστὸν κυρίου) we do not find any direct reference to Jesus.[80] However, the narrator connects the expression χριστὸν

---

[76] John will be able to prophesy because "even from his mother's womb he will be filled with the Holy Spirit" (1:15); "Elizabeth was filled with the Holy Spirit" (1:41) to prophecy about Mary and her son; and the introduction to Zechariah's canticle says: "Zechariah was filled with the Holy Spirit and spoke this prophecy" (1:67).

[77] On this prophetic dynamic see KELLERMANN, "Jesus", 13-16.

[78] We can add to these three reasons another one. Simeon presents himself as a δοῦλος. According to PLYMALE, "The Prayer of Simeon", 28-31, it could be a conscious adoption of the designation of the prophets as δοῦλοι τοῦ Θεοῦ, and therefore the appropriation of the title of prophet to Simeon. The title δίκαιος was also assigned to prophets of the OT, for example, Jb 1:1.

[79] The expressions connected to Simeon, "he looked forward to the consolation of Israel" (v. 25) and "Messiah of the Lord" (v. 26) show that Simeon was expecting the fulfillment of the messianic hope of his people, Jesus, the promised Messiah. Bill. II, 124-126, contributes rabbinic examples which interpret the expression in this sense.

[80] According to BLASS – DEBRUNNER – REHKOPF, *Grammatik*, § 183, the expression χριστὸν κυρίου is a genitive *agentis* construction; it expresses the divine origin of the anointing. This Greek expression, χριστὸς κυρίου, is connected with the Davidic messianic theme which permeates the nativity. In the light of Luke's description of Jesus in 1:27.32-33.69 and 2:4.11, χριστὸν κυρίου must here mean the anointed king by the Lord, the Davidic messiah. The phrase would recall for Luke's readers both the "saving" power in the House of his servant David (1:69) and the child born in the town of David, "Savior," "Messiah" (2:11). See STRAUSS, *Davidic Messiah*, 117-120.

κυρίου with the expression τὸ σωτήριόν σου through the repetition of the verb ὁράω (vv.26, 2x, and v. 30). The Holy Spirit had prophesied to Simeon that "he would not *see* death until he had *seen* the Messiah of the Lord" (v. 26). Later Simeon affirms: "Now, Master, according to your word, you let your servant go in peace; for my eyes have *seen* your salvation" (v. 30).[81] There is a triple link. A link (1) exists between the promise revealed to Simeon by the Holy Spirit (v. 26) and κατὰ τὸ ῥῆμά σου (v. 29). Which word is Simeon referring to? It is the word prophesied by the Holy Spirit. Another link (2) exists between "seeing death" and "being able to go in peace." The expression "seeing death" (v. 26: ἰδεῖν θάνατον) speaks clearly of the death. The NT and LXX bears witness that the expression ἀπολύεις (...) ἐν εἰρήνῃ (v. 29) could refer to death.[82] Another link (3) exists between the direct objects of the verbs: "seeing the Messiah of the Lord" and "seeing your salvation," which personifies the divine salvation[83] in the Lord's Messiah.[84]

v. 26	ἦν αὐτῷ κεχρηματισμένον ὑπὸ τοῦ πνεύματος τοῦ ἁγίου,	μὴ ἰδεῖν θάνατον	πρὶν ἂν ἴδῃ τὸν χριστὸν κυρίου
vv. 29-30	κατὰ τὸ ῥῆμά σου	ἀπολύεις (...) ἐν εἰρήνῃ·	νῦν εἶδον οἱ ὀφθαλμοί μου τὸ σωτήριόν σου

[81] Marconi argues that Simeon's hymn reveals the beauty of what he sees in the presence of the light; vision goes throughout the entire passage (MARCONI, "Il bambino da vedere", 629-654).

[82] See Jn 8:51; Heb 11:5. Abraham in Gn 15:2; Aaron in Nb 20:29; Tobit in Tb 3:6.13; a martyr in 2 M 7:9. See as well Ps 88:49. KELLERMANN, "Jesus", 10-11, gives abundant examples in the Greek literature in which the expression is a euphemism for death.

[83] The expression τὸ σωτήριόν σου refers to God's salvation because Simeon's words are addressed to God: the vocative δέσποτα and the verb in the second person singular (ἀπολύεις) are proofs of this. In addition, the pronoun σοῦ is proleptic (v. 30), advancing the subject of the second person singular verb, ἡτοίμασας (v. 31).

[84] There is another smaller link between the fact that Simeon is not going to die until (πρὶν) he sees the Lord's Messiah and the fact that right now (νῦν) his eyes have seen the salvation. This link connects Simeon's hymn with the hour of his death. The eschatological salvation is present in the newborn child (see DILLON, "Simeon as a Lucan Spokesman", 197-199).

Simeon, after having seen Jesus and taken him in his arms, says that "now my eyes have seen your salvation." Simeon sees "your salvation" when he sees the one who has just received the name of Jesus (v. 21), which means *Yhwh* saves (see Mt 1:21). Simeon clearly identifies the child Jesus, whom in that precise moment he is seeing (νῦν),[85] with the "Messiah of the Lord" and God's salvation, and thus with the fulfillment of his expectations: it is the vision of the Lord's Messiah who brings the consolation of Israel along with the salvation of God. The identity of Jesus is seen by Simeon as the "Messiah of the Lord," as the consolation of Israel and as God's salvation.[86] Clearly, in these verses Lukan Christology (χριστὸν κυρίου) is soteriology (τὸ σωτήριόν σου).

This connection between Jesus, the "Messiah of the Lord," and God's salvation leads to two conclusions. First, the promise revealed to Simeon by the Holy Spirit, that "he would not see death until he had seen the Messiah of the Lord" (v. 26), defines the contract of the narrative program of Simeon's scene: he has received this promise. The following verses (vv. 27-35) further solidify the resolution of that contract: the fulfillment of that promise. Secondly, although vv. 25-26 presented Simeon independently of Jesus, all the sayings and actions of Simeon after the expression "Messiah of the Lord" (v. 26) are dependent on Jesus: Simeon takes Jesus in his arms and talks about Jesus. Simeon becomes a character in function of another one, Jesus, who is characterized through different images. The focus on Simeon translates into a focus on Jesus; Jesus is presented by Simeon.

---

[85] Notice the emphatic character of the temporal adverb νῦν. Its position at the beginning of the hymn (v. 29) emphasizes that in the precise moment in which he takes up the child Jesus he can rest in peace. It stresses the current reality of fulfilled promises. The adverb νῦν points out the turning point in Simeon's life. The adverb νῦν occurs four times in Matthew, three times in Mark, twelve times in Luke, and 25 times in Acts. Luke uses it frequently in order to emphasize the actuality of the moment, the fulfillment of the salvation (see Lk 12:52; 19:42; 22:69).

[86] On the topic of recognizing the Messiah see WITHERINGTON, "Mary, Simeon", 12-51.

a) *Introduction to the Hymn (vv. 27-28) and Hymn (vv. 29-32)*

With Simeon's presentation in the background, the narrator returns to the foreground distinguishing between the presentation of Simeon and the introduction to his first speech. The action of this scene begins with the aorists of the main clauses, ἦλθεν, ἐδέξατο, εὐλόγησεν and εἶπεν,[87] whose subject is always Simeon. He presses the action forward: "Simeon came to the Temple," "took the child Jesus into his arms," "blessed God,"[88] and "said." The second main sentence is preceded by its dependent clause and the last principle sentence is followed by its dependent clause.[89] The second case (vv. 29-32) concerns a subordinate of direct complement that recounts what Simeon says in direct speech. This discourse appears in the form of prayer addressed directly to the Lord (δέσποτα, vocative)[90] with the principal verb in the second person (ἀπολύεις). This is the first time in the whole of the infancy narrative that a human character addresses God directly.[91] That is why it is often called a *hymn* or *prayer*.

[87] These four verbs are preceded by the corresponding coordinate καί.

[88] Why does Simeon praise God? Simeon saw the fulfillment of the oracle that had been awarded to him (v. 26). God has fulfilled his word and has permitted him to see the Messiah of the Lord. Simeon praises God not only for his fidelity to his promises, but also for his ability to even exceed his promises. Moved by the Holy Spirit, Simeon could not only see the Lord's Messiah, but also take him into his arms, and interpret what he sees. According to ESTRADA, "Praise for Promises Fulfilled", 5-16, throughout the infancy narrative Luke has a pattern of promise-fulfillment-praise, instead of just Matthew's promise-fulfillment. The praise is attested by the verb εὐλογέω and the hymns of Luke's infancy narrative (1:46-56; 68-79; 2:29-32).

[89] The first case (v. 27bc) concerns a temporal subordinate which also has a purpose subordinate. The temporal subordinate expresses the very moment in which Joseph and Mary brought the child Jesus into the Temple, the moment in which Simeon took the child Jesus into his arms.

[90] The vocative δέσποτα intends simply to identify and glorify God as God. In the NT δέσποτα is applied to God primarily in liturgical language such as Acts 4:24 or Rv 6:10. It recurs in later Christian prayers as well (see WILCOX, *The Semitisms of Acts*, 73). It also serves in cooperation with Simeon's use of the self-designation δοῦλός σου to establish his relationship toward God. By the juxtaposition of the words δέσποτα and δοῦλος Simeon acknowledges his utter subjection to God.

[91] Gabriel in his oracles, Elizabeth in her prophecy, Mary in her hymn, Zechariah in his prophecy, and the angels, have spoken about God in the third person singular, but now Simeon addresses God directly in the second person singular.

v.	Main sentence	Dependent clause
27a	καὶ ἦλθεν...εἰς τὸ ἱερόν·	
27b 27c	(temporal) (purpose)	ἐν τῷ εἰσαγαγεῖν τοὺς γονεῖς τὸ παιδίον τοῦ ποιῆσαι αὐτοὺς (...) περὶ αὐτοῦ
28a	καὶ αὐτὸς ἐδέξατο αὐτο	
28b	καὶ εὐλόγησεν τὸν θεὸν	
28c	καὶ εἶπεν	
29	(direct object)	νῦν ἀπολύεις τὸν δοῦλόν σου, δέσποτα...

Simeon's hymn consists of three "lines."[92] The first line (v. 29) expresses Simeon's disposition to die when God provides. The second line (v. 30) affirms the reason for that disposition: Simeon's expectations have been fulfilled in seeing the salvation (σωτήριον). In the third line (vv. 31-32) Simeon explains the meaning of that salvation. The first two lines deal only with Simeon, and the third line deals with what Simeon has seen, the salvation for all the peoples.[93]

The expression εἶδον οἱ ὀφθαλμοί μου shows that Simeon is eyewitness of that salvation. This is why he can die in peace. The term σωτήριον, which Simeon applies to Jesus, is equivalent neither to σωτήρ nor to σωτηρία. This word, the neuter of the adjective σωτήριος, "saving," denotes an apparatus fitted to save.[94] Simeon sees in this little child the means of deliverance which God is giving to the world. Jesus' *mission* will be to become this instrument of salvation.

---

[92] I use the term "line" because each "line" does not correspond to each verse of the Bible.

[93] IRIGOIN, "Composition rythmique", 23-25, claims a bipartite structure of the hymn of Simeon. Lines one and two would be the first part (vv. 29-30) and line three would be the second part (vv. 31-32). Irigoin contends that the expression σωτήριόν σου, at the end of v. 30, divides both parts and is the center of the hymn. The reasons that he presents refer to the Greek rhythm and accentuation: the counting of the number of syllables and words, and the fact that σωτήριον is the only word with two accents, its own accent and the enclitic accent. I prefer the division into three lines since I find these reasons a bit weak, referring as they do only to the signifier without any reference to the signified.

[94] On Jesus described as σωτήριον, as the means used by God to perform His salvation, see DANKER, "St. Luke for a New Millennium", 12.

The term σωτήριον is specified through the defining relative clause: ὃ ἡτοίμασας κατὰ πρόσωπον πάντων τῶν λαῶν. The idea of the preparation for salvation is unique, and it means the providential preparation of this means of salvation through Israel's history until the time of fulfillment, which is now recognized as having come.[95] The prepositional construction κατὰ πρόσωπον, with its Semitic background, could mean "in the presence of," but also "at someone's disposal."[96] The expression πάντων τῶν λαῶν refers to all the peoples, from either pagan nations or the Jewish nation. The term λαός in the singular, in the NT, usually designates Israel.[97] In the plural it unites Israel with other nations to refer to all the peoples.[98] It is striking that in Simeon's hymn it appears in

[95] The verb ἑτοιμάζω could refer to the divine initiative described throughout Luke 1–2 (Lk 1:55.70.73). In addition, Simeon is speaking under the influence of the Holy Spirit and speaks about the preparation of the divine plan (v. 31). In fact, the emphatic position of the adverb νῦν, first word of the *Nunc Dimittis*, highlights that Jesus' coming starts a *now* prepared for at length by the past. According to GERBER, "Ton salut que tu as préparé", 94-95, Acts 13:16b-41, especially vv. 17.23, are the best narrative commentary to the verb ἑτοιμάζω in Lk 2:31 showing its relationship with the eternal divine plan in Jesus. See as well ZIPPERT, "Des alten Simeon Lobgesang", 33-38.

[96] The expression κατὰ πρόσωπον corresponds to the Hebrew expression לפני. It is usually understood in its primary meaning as "before," but it can also be understood in its secondary meaning as "at someone's disposal." See Gn 13:9; 24:51; Ps 23:5; JOÜON, "Notes philologiques", 352. This salvation is not just to be put before all the peoples, and all the peoples are not going to be mere spectators or observers of the salvation. They are, rather, going to take part in this salvation and embrace it; it is at all the peoples' disposal. The one who was presented to the Lord, put at his disposal, is now put at the disposal of all people (v. 31).

[97] See Lk 2:10; 21:23; Acts 12:11; 13:17; 28:26.27; Mt 13:15; 15:8; 1 Co 14:21. In the OT see Ps 47:9-10; 77:15; 87:6.

[98] See Rm 15:11; Rv 7:9; 10:11; 11:9; 17:15; 21:3. In the OT see Ps 9:9; 67:3; 97:6; 98:9; 99:1-2; 148:11. Nevertheless, there is a text in the NT in which λαοί refers to Israel (Acts 4:25.27). Kilpatrick interpreted πάντων τῶν λαῶν in Lk 2:31 as "peoples of Israel" because of the meaning of λαοί in Acts 4:25.27 (KILPATRICK, "Laos (*sic*) at Luke 2:31 and Acts 4:25, 27", 127). However, the meaning of Acts 4:25-27 cannot be extended to Lk 2:31. In Acts 4:27 λαοί is followed by Ἰσραήλ, and the recurrence of Acts 4:25 is clearly influenced by Acts 4:27. In addition, Acts 4:25-27 is a forced adaptation of Ps 2:2 trying to identify "Kings" and "rulers" with Herod and Pilate. As Ps 2:1-2 parallels on the one hand ἔθνη and λαοί, and on the other hand

the plural (v. 31) and in the singular (v. 32). The first occurrence includes all the peoples, Israel and all the nations; it includes both these groups also in the following v. 32: ἔθνη and λαός σοῦ Ἰσραήλ, which are in parallel, specifying the expression that precedes, κατὰ πρόσωπον πάντων τῶν λαῶν.

The order of this specification is contrary to what would be expected, first Israel and later the Gentiles.[99] The order found in the hymn highlights even more the universalism of the expression, the salvation made ready by God "in the sight of the peoples."[100] Luke's use of the plural παντῶν τῶν λαῶν and the listing of the two groups, Gentiles and Jews, can only mean that Simeon is announcing a universal salvation, one available to all people.[101]

J.M. Creed raises the question of the syntactical function of δόξα (v. 32b).[102] Does one have to understand δόξαν as parallel to φῶς (v. 32a), so that the two terms are in apposition to τὸ σωτήριόν σου (your salvation: v. 30)? Or rather, would one have to consider

---

βασιλεῖς and ἄρχοντες, so Acts 4:25-27 parallels these same terms. Being influenced by the language of Psalm 2 cannot be used as a criterion for determining Luke's usage of the word. Finally, Acts 4:25-27 is the only case throughout the NT in which λαοί refers to Israel. Trying to explain other texts by means of this odd case is not legitimate. I believe that λαοί in Lk 2:31 does not refer to the "peoples of Israel," but to the "peoples" in general. On a wider discussion on the plural expression πάντες οἱ λαοί see WASSERBERG, *Aus Israels Mitte*, 139-140.

[99] Luke, throughout his work, makes parallels between ἔθνη and λαός (Acts 4:27; 26:17.23; 28:27.28). However, while here he speaks first of the Gentiles and later of Israel, Luke usually speaks first of Israel and later of the Gentiles (Acts 26:17.23; 28:27.28).

[100] By *universalism* I mean the divine offer of salvation which includes not only Israel, but also the Gentiles. As Simeon does not speak about the reception of that salvation, or the conversion or faith of the individual, I do not focus on the subjective aspect of salvation, but on the objective nature of the divine redemption which is destined for all humanity.

[101] After Simeon's hymn the narrator expresses the surprise of Joseph and Mary (v. 33): "they were amazed at what was being said about him." The wonder and amazement are a typical motif in stories of miracles and revelations. But what was said of the child Jesus to cause such a reaction? The only new element for Joseph and Mary is the inclusion of the Gentiles in salvation. Joseph and Mary's surprise underlines this universalism. I disagree with HANFORD, "Straightforward Universalism?", 142, who interprets Lk 2:31-32 as a Lukan particularism opposed to universalism.

[102] CREED, *The Gospel According to St. Luke*, 41.

the accusative δόξαν as parallel to the accusative ἀποκάλυψιν (revelation), both depending on the preposition εἰς? In the first option, the *salvation* would be both the *light* for the pagans and the *glory* for Israel. In the second option, the *salvation* would be *light* that would be both for the *revelation* of the Gentiles, and for the *glory* of Israel.[103] Certainly the differences are not great, but, as Simeon identifies Jesus with τὸ σωτήριον, it concerns whether the text assigns only the images of *salvation* and *light* to Jesus' mission, or whether it adds the image of *glory* to his mission. Luke frequently uses the construction εἰς + acc. +...+ καί + acc.[104] But, he sometimes repeats the conjunction εἰς after the conjunction καί, reflecting the following structure: εἰς + acc. + ... + καί + εἰς + acc.[105] I believe that the syntactical arguments are not enough to interpret the text.

We have to appeal to other arguments to answer the question raised by Creed. I choose the construction in parallel of the three images. The term φῶς and the term δόξα are added in apposition to the term σωτήριον in an attempt to explain its meaning. It concerns an apposition that specifies Jesus' mission which will be a universal *salvation* which consists of *light* of revelation for the Gentiles and *glory* for Israel. (1) The words of J. Nolland seem most convincing: "while 'glory' for a 'light' is what we might expect..., a 'light' for 'glory' is less intelligible."[106] (2) In the book of Isaiah we find four texts that successively put in parallel *salvation*, *light*, and *glory*.[107] Is 49:6 puts in parallel the *salvation* and the *light*; Is 46:13 puts in parallel the *salvation* and the *glory*; finally, Is 60:1.19 put in parallel the *light* and the *glory*; All these cases concern the action of bringing about a totally new situation that is described as *salvation*, or as *light*, or as *glory*.[108]

---

[103] The apposition of *salvation* and *light* is clear; the *light* colors the nature of the *salvation*. The three terms are in the accusative singular, but the apposition between these and *glory* is not clear.

[104] So Lk 1:50; 2:34; 19:29; Acts 4:30; 6:11; 14:21; 15:30; 22:4.

[105] So Lk 22:33; Acts 14:21; 16:1.

[106] NOLLAND, *Luke 1-9:20*, 120. Other scholars as C. F. EVANS, *Saint Luke*, 217; CRADDOCK, *Luke*, 33; KILGALLEN, "Jesus, Savior, Glory", 305; SIMÓN MUÑOZ, "Cristo, luz de los gentiles", 28, agree with Nolland, and add other arguments.

[107] The term ἀποκάλυψις does not appear in parallel with δόξα in the entire OT.

[108] The strong Isaian influence of the passage supports my argument (see § I.2.3).

29 Νῦν ἀπολύεις τὸν *δοῦλόν* σου, *δέσποτα,* κατὰ τὸ ῥῆμά σου, ἐν εἰρήνῃ·
30 ὅτι εἶδον οἱ ὀφθαλμοί μου τὸ σωτήριόν σου,
31 ὃ ἡτοίμασας κατὰ πρόσωπον *πάντων τῶν λαῶν*·
32 φῶς εἰς ἀποκάλυψιν ἐθνῶν καὶ
δόξαν λαοῦ σου Ἰσραήλ.

The content of the hymn is clearly christological and soteriological. There are three images that try to describe Jesus' mission: a universal salvation prepared by the Lord, "in the sight of the peoples," as "light of revelation for the Gentiles,"[109] and as "glory for your people, Israel." Jesus' mission will be to become an instrument of salvation for all the peoples, Jews and Gentiles, and thus to bring the glory of Israel, fulfilling the Jewish expectations.

b) Introduction to the Prophecy (vv. 33-34a) and the Prophecy (vv. 34b-35)

The reaction of Joseph and Mary to Simeon's first speech indicates the change of scene. We pass from the speech in the foreground to their reaction in the imperfect ἦν (v. 33), that is to say, in the background. Their reaction is the introduction to the second intervention of Simeon.[110]

Once the parents have reacted to the first speech, the narration turns to the foreground to describe the actions of Simeon, who "blessed the parents" and "said to Mary." The narrator first

---

[109] The expression φῶς εἰς ἀποκάλυψιν is difficult to analyze but the meaning is clear. The light is for the purpose of revelation for the Gentiles. Characteristically Gentiles need light by which to find the true God, to escape from what is considered their "normal" state, darkness, blindness. Moreover, the noun ἀποκάλυψις is a hapax in Luke-Acts and the verb ἀποκαλύπτω only appears in Lk 2:35; 10:21.22; 12:2; 17:30, and often expresses the revelation of the divine plan (Lk 10:21.22; 17:30). The other two occurrences are in the passive voice and could be interpreted as a divine passive in which God reveals the secret thoughts (Lk 2:35) or everything now hidden (Lk 12:2). Thus the illumination for the Gentiles is part of the divine plan.

[110] The reaction to the speech contributes to Mary and Joseph's characterization. It is a presentation dependent upon Jesus. They were amazed at the things said about Jesus. It is a smaller presentation (v. 33) than Simeon's (vv. 25-26) and Anna's (vv. 36-37). The reason for this is that Mary and Joseph have already been presented to the reader (Lk 1:26-27).

describes the encounter that Simeon had with the child Jesus (vv. 27-32) and afterwards describes the encounter that he had with his parents (vv. 33-35). In both encounters there is a speech, and in both encounters the same sequence appears: description in the background, followed by action described in the foreground, including the speeches. The action is similar: to bless (εὐλογέω)[111] and say (λέγω).[112] In both cases the direct discourse is about Jesus' mission.[113] The parallel structure of the speeches shows the intention of Luke in presenting Jesus' mission with only one coin but with two sides.

vv.	Presentation	Simeon's action	Christological speech
25-32	Καὶ ἰδοὺ ἄνθρωπος ἦν	καὶ εὐλόγησεν (...) καὶ εἶπεν	τὸ σωτήριόν σου φῶς ἐις ἀποκάλυψιν ἐθνῶν δόζαν λαοῦ σου Ἰσραήλ
33-35	καὶ ἦν ὁ πατὴρ αὐτοῦ καὶ ἡ μήτηρ	καὶ εὐλόγησεν (...) καὶ εἶπεν	κεῖται εἰς πτῶσιν καὶ ἀνάστασιν εἰς σημεῖον ἀντιλεγόμενον

The parallelism not only permits us to connect the two scenes but also to differentiate them. *First*, there is a qualitative difference between the act of blessing God (v. 28) and the act of blessing

---

[111] Before the hymn Simeon blessed God because he had been faithful to his word and allowed him to see the Messiah of the Lord. Why does he now, in the prophecy, bless the parents of Jesus? Because it is also thanks to them that his eyes can see the salvation of God.

[112] Notice that in the first direct discourse Simeon blesses God and addresses God, Jesus' Father (Lk 2:49). In the second discourse Simeon blesses the parents (of Jesus) and addresses "Mary, his (Jesus') mother." The Greek play on words εὐλογέω-λέγω cannot be rendered in English.

[113] In the second discourse, since the text does not tell us otherwise, Simeon still has the child in his arms. In addition, the masculine pronoun οὗτος can only refer to Jesus. In the Lukan infancy narrative we often find two speeches connected. Elizabeth's words (Lk 1:42-45) precede the *Magnificat* (Lk 1:46-55), and the angel's speech to the shepherds (Lk 2:10-11) precedes the praise of a great throng of the hosts of heaven (Lk 2:14).

human beings (v. 34). *Second*, in contrast with the previous hymn, the prophecy (vv. 34b-35) is addressed in the introduction to an explicit person, Mary (εἶπεν πρὸς Μαριὰμ τὴν μητέρα αὐτοῦ).[114] *Third*, in the second discourse Jesus is presented in the perfect (κεῖται)[115] and the consequences of his presence are presented in the future indicative (διελεύσεται) or in aorist subjunctive (ἀποκαλυφθῶσιν). In other words, while the first speech describes Jesus in the past,[116] the second describes the effects that Jesus' presence provokes both in the present and in the future.[117] *Fourth*, although both speeches show the consequences of Jesus' presence for Simeon and Mary, while the presence of Jesus brings an advantage to Simeon, that he can rest in peace, the same presence brings to Mary a difficulty: "a sword will pierce your soul."

As in his first discourse, Simeon's affirmations about Jesus' mission are presented in parallel, as successive explanations of each other. The prophecy has four "lines"[118] and the four have the same topic. They are as four progressive dimensions of Jesus' mission. The repetition of the preposition εἰς preceded by the conjunction καί puts the first two affirmations about Jesus in parallel: this child "has been appointed for the fall and for the rise of many in Israel, and as a sign that is contradicted" (v. 34b). The first two dimensions will lead to the definitive one, expressed through the

---

[114] The addressee of the hymn is not explicit in the introduction, which says just εἶπεν (v. 28).

[115] The passive verb κεῖται might be understood as a divine passive: God has established Jesus as a sign of contradiction (Lk 2:34b). The rejection of Jesus is part of the divine plan for Jesus. The Messiah will be rejected, but it is still more remarkable that his rejection, far from falling outside the scope of God's plan, is part of God's plan. This idea is implied here, but stated more clearly in the prophecies of the passion (see Lk 9:22; 9:44; 18:31-33; I do not take into account Lk 13:31-33 which is a further reference to the passion of Jesus), and this point emerges with absolute clarity in Lk 24:26 or Act 2:23.

[116] What is affirmed about Jesus was in the aorist indicative (v. 30: εἶδον; and v. 31: ἡτοίμασας).

[117] This is why I consider the first as a hymn of praise for what has already happened in Jesus' birth and the second as a prophecy of what is about to happen in Jesus' life.

[118] The first "line" is v. 34b; the second "line" is v. 34c; the third "line" is v. 35a; and the fourth "line" is v. 35b.

conjunction ὅπως. Halfway through this explanation of the coming of Jesus, the prophecy concerning Mary is inserted.

34b Ἰδού, οὗτος κεῖται εἰς πτῶσιν καὶ ἀνάστασιν *πολλῶν* ἐν τῷ Ἰσραὴλ, καὶ
εἰς σημεῖον ἀντιλεγόμενον·
35 καὶ σοῦ αὐτῆς τὴν ψυχὴν διελεύσεται ῥομφαία
ὅπως ἂν ἀποκαλυφθῶσιν ἐκ *πολλῶν* καρδιῶν διαλογισμοί.

M. Black has affirmed that the prophecy of Simeon "is among the most difficult passages of the Greek Bible; it is virtually impossible to find a logical connection of thought running through the passage."[119] Let us successively analyze every line according to its structure.

The interjection ἰδού shows the change of tone of the second speech with respect to the first one.[120] The pronoun οὗτός referring to Jesus, follows the deictic ἰδού. The first affirmation of Jesus' mission (κεῖται) is that he has been destined "for the fall (πτῶσις) and rise (ἀνάστασις) of many in Israel."[121] Are these to be successive experiences of the same group, or do they express the diverging fortunes of different people? Who are those who fall and who are those who rise?[122] The image of κεῖται εἰς πτῶσιν καὶ ἀνάστασιν is connected with the imagery of building stones[123] that the NT often employs to explain the different reactions to Jesus. It can, then, be either a stumbling block (Lk 21:24; Rm 9:30-32; 1P 2:8; Is 8:14), or a cornerstone on which a house is built (Mt 21:42; Ps 118:22; Is 28:16).[124]

---

[119] BLACK, *An Aramaic Approach*, 153.

[120] WINANDY, "La prophétie du Syméon", 342, translates ἰδού as "be careful!"

[121] Although the noun ἀνάστασις usually means *resurrection*, its contrast with the previous noun πτῶσις gives it a more generic meaning of *rising* as opposed to *falling*.

[122] On a brief discussion of this problematic matter see WOLTER, "Israel Zukunft", 410-412.

[123] BOVON, *Lukas* I, 147 [104], says: "Though Is 8:14 is not cited, it remains in the background. According to Is 8:18, the prophet and his children will become signs and portents in Israel. Thus the image of falling and rising is also inspired by Isaiah 8." The figure that causes rising and falling was also used at Qumran (1QH 2.8-10; 1QM 14.10-11; passages quoted in BOCK, *Luke* I, 246).

[124] Lk 2:34 serves as a fulfillment of Is 8:14, Jesus will be a stumbling block (LAURENTIN, *Structure*, 90), and as a fulfillment of Is 28:16; Jesus will be the foundations, a cornerstone (SERRA, "E anche a te", 72).

This combination appears on Jesus' lips when he speaks about destroying those tenants and giving the vineyard to others: "The stone which the builders rejected has become the cornerstone. Anyone who *falls* on that stone will be dashed to pieces" (Lk 20:16-18). The parable of the two foundations (Lk 6:46-49) speaks about coming to Jesus, listening to his words, and acting on them. In other words, he who receives Jesus builds a house laying the foundation on a rock. He who rejects Jesus builds a house without foundation, which collapses, and is completely destroyed. According to Jesus the reason for the destruction of the house of Jerusalem is because they have rejected him (Lk 13:34-35). I believe that the meaning of the expression πτῶσις καὶ ἀνάστασις lies in the rejection or apprehension of Jesus. The salvation that Jesus offers does not assert itself by force. It is not an imperative. Every person has the choice to reject or accept it.[125] The reaction to Jesus will divide the people. Some will fall because of their rejection of Jesus; others will be raised because of their acceptance of Jesus. Jesus' presence becomes a judgment for everybody.

According to Feuillet and Ockenga, the καί which separates πτῶσις and ἀνάστασις is disjunctive; they refer to different people.[126] In contrast to them, I suggest that the persons can be both the same and different. They can be the same if they first reject Jesus and later accept him.[127] They can be different if some consistently rejecting Jesus and others consistently receive him.[128]

---

[125] The expression is followed by πολλῶν ἐν τῷ Ἰσραήλ. Jesus will affect the whole nation. The many (πολλῶν) is used to stress the wide-ranging effects (BAUER, *Greek-English Lexicon*, 694). All of the people of Israel have to choose when faced with Jesus, against him or for him (Lk 12:51).

[126] See FEUILLET, "L'épreuve prédite à Marie", 246; and OCKENGA, "Simeon and the Child Jesus", 5-6.

[127] Peter and Paul are good examples of this successive rejection and acceptance.

[128] According to SCHWEIZER, "Zum Aufbau", 320, the most important exegetical difficulty of Simeon's prophecy lies in the interpretation of the expression πτῶσις καί ἀνάστασις. Simón Muñoz proposes another suggestive interpretation of this difficult expression. Giving a great number of examples, basing his ideas on a Semitic background of the noun ἀνάστασις (the connection between the Hebrew verbs עמד and קום and their translation into Greek in the Septuagint, in Theodotion and in the

The expression εἰς πτῶσιν καὶ ἀνάστασιν is explained by the expression εἰς σημεῖον ἀντιλεγόμενον. The *second line* can act as the key to the first. Jesus' mission is to be put as a sign, σημεῖον. As Noah was a sign for the people of Nineveh, Jesus becomes an even greater sign (Lk 11:29-32).[129] The word σημεῖον expresses a manifest token, an object of sense perception, a phenomenon impossible to ignore. Every single person will have to take sides and decide. The reaction can be rejection or acceptance, but a reaction to the *sign* is expected.

This manifest sign is a σημεῖον ἀντιλεγόμενον, a sign that can be contradicted. All the Lukan occurrences of this verb show opposition.[130] The participle ἀντιλεγόμενον is a present participle,[131] expressing a continuous action, an action never finished. It is also true that in *Koine* Greek, the future participle is often substituted by the present participle with future meaning.[132] That is why also

---

quotations of the OT into the NT), and examining the comparison falling-standing in the OT and in Rm 9–11, he holds that ἀνάστασις comes from an error of translation of the root קום which should have been translated by "standing, remaining firmly upright." The opposition of the expression is not falling-rising, but falling-not falling; in other words, falling-standing, falling-remaining firmly upright (SIMÓN MUÑOZ, "La 'permanencia' de Israel", 191-223). Those who persevere in receiving Jesus are represented by this interpretation of Simón Muñoz: they are those who stand and who firmly maintain their support of Jesus.

[129] There is another occurrence in which σημεῖον is applied to Jesus (Lk 2:12). Jesus is the sign which demonstrates the truth of the message given to the shepherds.

[130] It recurs in the characterization of the Sadducees' denial of the resurrection (Lk 20:27; dif. Mk 12:18), in the opposition to the first Christians (Lk 21:15) and Peter and John (Acts 4:14), and in the Jewish opposition to Paul's mission at Pisidia (Acts 13:45) and at Jerusalem (Acts 28:19.22). In the NT the verb ἀντιλέγω also has the meaning of opposition (Jn 19:12; Rm 10:21; Tt 1:9). Apart from these four references in the rest of the NT, ἀντιλέγω is a special Lukan verb.

[131] Jesus will be a σημεῖον ἀντιλεγόμενον from his birth. The child Jesus, from the moment of his birth, becomes a *sign of contradiction* before whom many fall and rise. In fact, the acceptance of John the Baptist in the womb of his mother (Lk 1:41), Elizabeth (Lk 1:42-43), the shepherds (Lk 2:20), the Magi (Mt 2:11), and the rejection of Herod (Mt 2:16) prove it. I believe that from the very beginning of his earthly existence he is a *sign of contradiction*.

[132] See ZERWICK, *Graecitas biblica*, § 283; in the work of Luke: Lk 1:35; 14:31; 22:19-20; Acts 21:2.3; 26:17; in the rest of the NT: Mt 25:14; Jn 17:20.

in Lk 2:34, the present participle could have future meaning as a sign that is contradicted and will be contradicted. This interpretation in the future tense permits us to identify the rejection to Jesus' mission with his entire life, especially the end of his earthly life, his passion and death on the cross.[133] This interpretation as a continuous action, never finished, lasting into the future, also allows us to interpret the σημεῖον ἀντιλεγόμενον as a metaphor not only of the entire life of Jesus, but also of his disciples' life.[134] Because of Jesus' rejection even his followers will be rejected.

This radical dimension of Jesus' mission will affect even his mother. Benoît sets out very well the exegetical difficulties of v. 35a: "Why this sudden direct reference to Mary? What is the connection with the general announcement of v. 34? Finally, and this is the fundamental question, what does the sword represent?"[135] Different solutions have been offered to explain the meaning of the sword.[136] The sword has been interpreted as a crisis that Mary was scandalized and doubted (Origen); as the violent death of Mary (Epiphanius);[137] as God's word (Ambrosius);[138] as the participation of Mary in Jesus'

---

[133] On the one hand, Joseph and Mary went up (ἀνήγαγον) to Jerusalem to present Jesus in the Temple (v. 22). Of the 23 times that the verb ἀνάγειν occur in the NT, twenty are in Luke-Acts. It reflects the technical OT concept, carried over to the NT, of going up to Jerusalem or to the Temple to celebrate the Passover, which becomes Jesus' passion. On the other hand, as we have seen above, the expression παραστῆσαι τῷ κυρίῳ was employed to refer to the redemption of the firstborn who, since the Passover of Egypt, belonged to God. And Jesus is offered to his Father in his passion. Yet, that is not the only connection. The participle ἀντιλεγόμενον links the passage with Jesus' passion. In Heb 12:3 the passion of Jesus is described as an ἀντιλογία, a noun of the same root.

[134] As SCHÜRMANN, *Das Lukasevangelium* I, 129, and BETORI, "Perseguitati", 26-29, claim, the prophecy does not exclude Jesus' death, nor can it be restricted to that.

[135] BENOÎT, "Et toi-même", 251. The difficulty of v. 35a lies in the fact that Luke decided to include it in the middle of a prophecy which would be more coherent without it. Luke was willing to tolerate the destruction of the smooth argument.

[136] Although my study is on Jesus' presentation, I cannot ignore this Mariological difficulty. I will limit my comments to how my study helps to better understand the prophecy to Mary. For a fuller exposition of the history of interpretation of v. 35a see DÍEZ MERINO, "La transfixión de María", 36-69.

[137] There is no textual indication of Mary's scandal or Mary's violent death.

[138] This interpretation lies in Heb 4:12: "The word of God is something alive and

passion (Augustine, Paolino of Nola, Feuillet);[139] as the demands of the Father which go beyond the human bond and divide even Mary's family (Brown and Fitzmyer).[140] I am not convinced by any of these interpretations. As the coordinate conjunction καί and the parallel structure of the prophecy suggest that the thought goes in the same direction, I believe that the sword that will pierce Mary's soul is linked with the "sign of contradiction," the opposition that her son will suffer. The sword of Mary is the rejection of Jesus. The sudden direct reference to Mary has its reason: the connection between mother and son, which appeared at the beginning of the passage (v. 22: καθαρισμοῦ αὐτῶν) with her purification and his redemption, appears again in the prophecy. The plural αὐτῶν underlines the unity between mother and son. Verse 22 was a veiled announcement of the clearer affirmation of vv. 34c-35a.[141] Mary

---

active: it cuts more incisively than any two-edged sword: [...] it can pass judgement on thoughts of heart." Although the Greek terms do not fit, there is a semantic link because both verses affirm that a sword pierces a soul and judges secret thoughts of many hearts. However, the Lukan image of the sword cannot be interpreted as God's word by means of a non-Lukan text such as Heb 4:12. In Rv 1:16; 2:16; 19:15.21 comes a sharp sword out of Jesus' mouth.

[139] However, the Lukan image of the sword cannot be interpreted as her participation in her son's passion by means of only a non-Lukan text such as Jn 19:25-27. Mary the mother of Jesus, does not appear in the Lukan account of Jesus' passion, nor in the other synoptic Gospels.

[140] In the following passage, the twelve-year-old Jesus in the Temple, Mary asks her son: "My child, why have you done this to us? See how worried your father and I have been, looking for you" (Lk 2:48). Jesus answers by appealing to the predominence of his heavenly Father (Lk 2:49). In addition, Lk 8:19 shows how Jesus' family, his mother and brothers, tried to meet Jesus but they could not get to him because of the crowd. However, if Luke's goal had been to identify the sword with the division in Mary's family, he would have used the word *sword* when Jesus speaks about the family's division. In Lk 12:51-53 Jesus says: "Do you suppose that I am here to bring peace on earth? No, I tell you, but rather division. For from now on, a household of five will be divided: three against two and two against three; father opposed to son, son to father, mother to daughter, daughter to mother." The parallel of Mt 10:34 affirms: "Do not suppose that I have come to bring peace to the earth: it is not peace I have come to bring, but a sword."

[141] On the link between these verses see VALENTINI, "Due cruces interpretum", 169.187.

has been told not only about the opposition that her son will suffer, but also that, being his mother, that rejection will affect her as a sword that will pierce her soul.[142] The v. 35 presents the consequence of Jesus' rejection, first in his mother (v. 35a), and then in many hearts (v. 35b).[143] There is a direct link between Jesus and Mary. As an unknown woman praises the mother to honor the son: "Blessed the womb that bore you and the breasts that fed you!" (Lk 11:27), now Simeon foretells the mother's suffering because of the son's rejection and early death.

There is a double grammatical problem in the *fourth line* of the prophecy by Simeon. On the one hand, to which principle clause does the conjunction ὅπως of the end of v. 35 refer? Does v. 35b refer to v. 35a or to v. 34? In my opinion the proposition of v. 35b depends on κεῖται (v. 34), which is the principal verb of the oracle, since everything refers to that verb and consequently to Jesus. I believe that v. 35a is placed immediately after v. 34c because Jesus' rejection is the cause of Mary's sword, and v. 35b is the consequence of that rejection in many. (1) First, the fact that a sword pierces the soul of Mary does not cause the inner thoughts to be revealed. "The fall and rise of many" due to the fact that Jesus has become "a sign of contradiction" indicates why the intentions of many would be revealed. The external manifestation of the falling and rising makes evident the internal decision of how to respond to Jesus. (2) Second, the repetition of the genitive πολλῶν links v. 34b with v. 35b: the fall and rise of "many" causes the revelation of the intentions of "many" hearts. (3) Third, in contrast with the rest of the oracle, only in v. 35a does Simeon refer to Mary (second person singular: διελεύσεται). The rest of the oracle speaks of Jesus, οὗτος, and in the third person singular κεῖται. Therefore, the compo-

[142] The first feature of a piercing sword is that it hurts. Mary will be hurt by the rejection of her son. The second feature of a piercing sword is that it divides. Mary as a personification of Israel will be divided into those who accept Jesus and those who reject Jesus, which is affirmed in v. 34b and developed in Luke-Acts.

[143] On the consecutive sense of v. 35b see the following paragraphs.

sition and the emphatic position of the expression καὶ σοῦ αὐτῆς distances this sentence from its context.[144]

On the other hand, a second question emerges: the conjunction ὅπως, with which v. 35b begins,[145] is a subordinate conjunction that usually expresses a meaning of purpose.[146] In classical Greek, and particularly in its Hellenistic evolution, the fusion between purpose and consecutive aspects is not uncommon.[147] According to this, constructions that in classical Greek meant purpose can express consecutive meaning in NT Greek.[148] Only the context could ultimately decide if it denotes consequence or purpose in these similar conjunctions. The intention of the one who sent Jesus is not only to "reveal the intentions of many." Certainly this could be a consequence of his mission, but not its purpose.[149]

---

[144] In fact, the phrase of v. 35 begins with an emphatic καί followed by a personal pronoun of the second person in the genitive singular (σοῦ = of you, yours) and by a demonstrative pronoun in the genitive singular feminine (αὐτῆς), with emphatic function, "of your own."

[145] The conjunction ὅπως has, usually, lost the ἄν which is frequent in the ancient texts, with the exception of some passages from Luke and some quotes from the LXX. Our verse is a case in which Luke keeps the particle ἄν after the conjunction ὅπως. Other examples of this same phenomenon are Acts 3:20; 15:17 (which cites Am 9:12 but the LXX text does not present the particle ἄν). It is a demonstration of the stylistic quality of the author of the third Gospel and his imitation of the style of the LXX (see BLASS – DEBRUNNER – REHKOPF, *Grammatik*, § 369,5).

[146] See SMYTH – MESSING, *Greek Grammar*, § 2193; HANSEN – QUINN, *Greek*, 68-70; BERENGUER AMENÓS, *Gramática griega*, 188-189.201.

[147] In fact, the purpose conjunction shows the ending toward which an action moves due to the intent of the agent; but the consecutive conjunction shows the ending toward which an action moves by its nature or by necessity. Both meanings are, then, very close. In both cases a consequence is given; the purpose adds only the intention of the agent.

[148] Even more, the distinction begins to fade between the purpose conjunction ἵνα and the consecutive conjunction ὥστε; ὥστε is used with a clear meaning of purpose, (Lk 4:29; 9:52; 20:20; Mt 10:1; 27:1 and perhaps Mt 24:24 and Mk 13:22) and ἵνα with clear consecutive meaning (Lk 9:45; Jn 6:7; 11:37; 1 Co 5:2; 9:24; 2 Co 1:17; Ga 5:17; 1 Ts 5:4; 1 Jn 1:9; Rv 9:20; 13:13.15; 22:14).

[149] Abel interprets the conjunction ὅπως of Lk 2:35 as a consecutive subordinate conjunction (ABEL, *Grammaire du grec biblique*, § 65).

Finally, this fourth line of the stanza affirms that Jesus' mission, causing the fall and rise of many, "will reveal the thoughts (διαλογισμός) of many." Throughout Luke's work διαλογισμός always has negative connotations.[150] In our case, the proximity to σημεῖον ἀντιλεγόμενον suggests this meaning of rejection. The consequence of Jesus' mission is that the thoughts of those who reject him will be revealed by means of their rejection.[151] The external reaction towards Jesus shows where hearts really are with regard to Jesus.

The function of this second speech is to continue presenting different features of Jesus' mission by way of new images. The brief exegetical analysis of both discourses leads us to affirm that the account of Simeon (vv. 25-35), through Simeon's characterization, actions, and two discourses, has the purpose of presenting Jesus' identity, "the Messiah of the Lord" (v. 26), and mission.

Yet the Messiah's mission is a double-sided coin. His mission is to become an instrument of salvation for all the peoples, bringing light for the Gentiles and glory for Israel by fulfilling the Jewish expectations.[152] The second discourse introduces a new facet of the Messiah's mission. His universal salvation will not be unanimously received. Perhaps the consequences of the hymn are expressed in the prophecy. Besides other reasons, he will be rejected because of his universal mission. While the hymn presented universal salvation, the prophecy presents the way in which Jesus will be accepted, and also, perhaps, the way in which that salvation will happen: through rejection, opposition, suffering and death.[153] In fact, the parallel struc-

---

[150] It refers to the thoughts of the Pharisees who oppose Jesus (Lk 5:22; 6:8); it refers to the thoughts of the disciples who reject Jesus' Passion and only think of being the first (Lk 9:46-47); finally, it refers to the thoughts of the disciples who doubt and fear Jesus risen (Lk 24:38). Throughout the NT, the other eight recurrences of διαλογισμός have a pejorative meaning as an indication of hostile thoughts (Mt 15:19; Mk 7:21; Rm 1:21; 14:1; 1 Co 3:20; Ph 2:14; 1 Tm. 2:8; Jm 2:4). Ph 2:14 (διαλογισμός with γογγυσμός, which means murmuring) and 1Tm 2:8 (διαλογισμός with ὀργη, which means anger) demonstrate the juxtaposition of the negative tendencies. See PETZKE, "διαλογισμός", 741; SCHRENK, "διαλογισμός", 97.

[151] See DERRETT, "The Hidden Context", 209-213.

[152] Implicitly Luke also presents Jesus' salvation as "the consolation of Israel" (v. 25).

[153] See STOCK, "Maria nel Tempio", 117-119; RADL, "Die Beziehungen", 303.

ture of both scenes, introduction and speech, shows the intention of Luke in linking them.[154] The fact that Jesus' mission will be rejected by many in Israel and accepted by others brings a division. While the hymn united Israel with all the peoples in only one group, presenting international unity, the prophecy divides Israel, foretelling a national division.

3.3 The Account of Anna: vv. 36-38

While the principal verbs from vv. 25-35 had Simeon as their subject, the main verbs of vv. 36-38 have Anna as a subject. The change of subjects demonstrates the change of scene. In addition, the previous scene has ended with verbs of the foreground (the actions expressed in the aorist of Simeon blessing and announcing his prophecy). This new scene develops in the background in order to present Anna.[155] Moreover, the scene centered on Simeon had two speeches. The direct speeches characterize the *showing* scenes in which the narrator describes the scene with the help of dialogues. The reader hears and sees the scene presented by the author, every-

---

This connection would suggest that Luke here links salvation with Jesus' rejection and suffering, implying a redemptive salvation. However, although Luke was certainly aware of the interpretation of Jesus' death as the basis for human salvation (Lk 22:19-20; Acts 20:28), he did not choose to develop this notion as a critical element either of his understanding of the crucifixion of Jesus or of his soteriology. For example, Luke neglects to recount the saying about the Son of man as a "ransom" (Mt 20:28; Mk 10:45). I believe that Luke presents the entire life of Jesus, from his birth (Lk 2:11) until his resurrection (Acts 5:31), as salvation (Lk 2:30.38; 7:50; 17:19; 19:5.9; 24:21; Acts 13:23; 15:11; 16:31). For Luke, salvation is not an abstract word; it is a concrete person. Jesus is savior and the only one who can grant and give salvation (Acts 4:12). In Luke-Acts, Jesus offers salvation in that present moment, σήμερον, also before his passion (Lk 2:11; 4:21; 19:10; 23:43). Luke does not deny salvation through Jesus' passion and death; but he does not develop it either. Salvation in Luke-Acts is more related to the coming of Jesus than to his death.

[154] See the second paragraph of § 3.2.2.b.

[155] As in the case of Simeon, the presentation of the character from this new scene happens through principal verbs in the imperfect (v. 36: ἦν; v. 37: ἀφίστατο; v. 38: ἀνθωμολογεῖτο), nominal sentences (v. 37: αὐτὴ χήρα ἕως ἐτῶν ὀγδοήκοντα τεσσάρων), and dependent participles of the principal verbs (vv. 36: προβεβηκυῖα and ζήσασα; v. 37: λατρεύουσα; v. 38: ἐπιστᾶσα).

thing that Simeon does and says. Nevertheless, when Anna is presented, we do not find a showing scene but rather a *telling* scene with the verb in the imperfect, descriptive and repetitive actions. The narrator says what happens without describing the scene in detail. The narrator tells us about Anna and what she usually does, but not what she is saying and doing in that precise moment.[156]

The presence of the noun ἱερόν (v. 37) gives continuity to the scenes of Simeon and of Anna. Simeon goes toward the Temple ἦλθεν ... εἰς τὸ ἱερόν, and Anna does not leave the Temple (οὐκ ἀφίστατο τοῦ ἱεροῦ).[157] Even though both scenes occur in the same geographic place, the change of character implies the change of scene.

3.3.1 The Description of Anna: vv. 36-37

Neither Simeon nor Anna is described in a superficial manner. The development of the description of both indicates the importance of their characterizations. In vv. 36-37 all the references are exclusively to Anna, who is extensively described. Throughout Luke's works, no other characters receive such biographical details as Anna. As a character who never re-appears and does not say anything, her description is striking. Perhaps her extensive description compensates for the absence of any speech on her part. Pehaps the descriptive pause by the narrator gives a key to reading the story.

A very important description of Anna is the first one: she was a prophetess.[158] The feminine word προφῆτις appears only one other time in the NT (Rv 2:20), where Jezebel is a false prophet who

---

[156] *Showing* is a mode of presentation in which the narrator shows events rather than telling them. While in the *telling* the narrator uses the indirect style for spoken words, in the *showing* the narrator gives a direct transcription of spoken words (see MARGUERAT – BOURQUIN, *Récits bibliques*, 89).

[157] The expression τοῦ ἱεροῦ is a genitive of separation. As this genitive sense is denied by the verb (οὐκ ἀφίστατο) Anna does not leave the Temple but is in the Temple always, even more underlined by the imperfect tense (WALLACE, *Greek Grammar*, 107-109). Simeon goes to the Temple (v. 27) and Anna does not leave the Temple (v. 37). The entire pericope happens in the Temple.

[158] Anna is the only person besides Jesus who is called "a prophet" in the Gospel of Luke.

lures the people of God. Anna and the four unmarried daughters of Philip (Acts 21:9) are the only real prophetesses in the NT. Luke gives a full description of Anna and her prophetic lineage. She is identified in relation to her father Phanuel of the tribe of Asher. All these names bear a certain connection with prophecy.[159]

After naming Anna and her lineage, Luke affirms that Anna was very old (v. 36).[160] Anna's age is a very controversial question. Was she a widow who was 84 years old or was she a widow for 84 years? Was Anna 84 years old or was she more than 100?[161] Why does Luke insist on the numbers, even saying that she has been married for seven years? It could be that Luke here is speaking in a figurative way.[162] Both numbers, seven and 84, can have a symbolic meaning. The number seven is well-known as an expression of abundance.[163] In addition, the number twelve also expresses perfection.[164] It is therefore

---

[159] Phanuel is the Greek form of פניאל, "face of God", "for he has seen God face to face" (Gn 32:31; Jg 8:8; 1 K 12:25). Jacob (Gn 32:31), Moses (Ex 33:11; Nb 12:7-8; Dt 34:10), and Elijah (1 K 19:11-12) have seen God face to face. In other words, the name of Phanuel refers to those important prophets who could speak about their vision of God. Asher is the name of one of the Northern tribes (Dt 33:24-25 and Jos 19:24-31). It is the tribe where Elijah's preaching took place (1 Kings 17–18). See FIGUERAS, "Syméon et Anne", 94-98; THURSTON, "Who was Anna?", 49.

[160] The expression αὕτη προβεβηκυῖα ἐν ἡμέραις πολλαῖς is very similar to the expressions referring to Zechariah and Elisabeth: προβεβηκότες ἐν ταῖς ἡμέραις (Lk 1:7.18). The terms used further underline her old age through the adjective πολλαῖς.

[161] On this problematic matter see JOHN, "How Old Was Anna?", 247.

[162] By looking for the right age we may be applying a modern scientific way of thinking to a piece of literature which is not intended to be scientific, but symbolic. Bovon says: "It is my hypothesis that the early Christians used the category of 'number' as theological tools. Often they consciously interpreted numbers in a symbolic way" (BOVON, "Names and Numbers", 266).

[163] In the Christian field, "the number seven, so significant for the book of Genesis, still has a special role in the book of Revelation, as seen in the seven churches (Rv 1:4), the seven letters (Revelation 5), the seven seals (Revelation 5–8), the seven trumpets (Revelation 8–11), the seven cups and the seven angels (Revelation 15–17). The seven baskets of the second story of the feeding miracle evoke the Church of the Hellenists and its organization of seven leaders (Mk 8:20 par.)" (Bovon, "Names and Numbers", 270).

[164] The number twelve is also a favorite number in Hebrew thinking: There were twelve sons of Jacob, twelve tribes of Israel, twelve gates of Jerusalem, twelve foundations of its wall, twelve precious stones that ornament the foundations, and so on.

striking that 84 is seven times twelve.[165] If this symbolism is intended, then the text would indicate that Anna had lived a perfect married life and an even more perfect widowhood. Moreover, if twelve means Israel because of the twelve tribes of Israel, Anna is a perfect representation of Israel, seven times twelve.[166]

While Simeon was described through two qualifying adjectives (δίκαιος and εὐλαβής),[167] Anna is not described with any adjectives but rather through her activity. She does not leave the Temple, worshipping by fasting and praying, night and day (see v. 37b).[168] The Temple is her place to stay and pray.

Taking into account all the descriptions of Anna, we can answer the question about the reason for such an extensive characterization.

Among Christians, "the number twelve is used for the twelve apostles (Mk 3:13-19 par.; Mt 19:28 par.), for the twelve baskets of leftovers of bread in both feeding miracles (Mk 6:43 par.), and later by the author of the Book of the Resurrection according to Bartholomew, for their twelve thrones and their twelve garments (*Book of the Resurrection According to Bartholomew* 21,8)" (BOVON, "Names and Numbers", 269).

[165] Both AMBROSE, *Exp. Luc.*, 2,62, and BEDE, *Exp. Luc.*, 2,38, suggest this symbolic interpretation. VARELA, "Lk 2,36-37", 446, ELLIOTT, "Anna's Age (Luke 2:36-37)", 100, and CORSATO, "La Expositio", 90-113, suggest the same interpretation. Reicke goes further. He says that Anna "met Jesus in the important moment when she had completed twelve periods of seven years. Assuming that she had married at the normal age of fourteen years (2x7), she was 21 when she became a widow seven years later (3x7) and had now served in the Temple for 63 years (9x7), which corresponds to her reported age of 84 (12x7). The reader would conclude that her life had reached its culmination when she met the messianic child" (REICKE, "Jesus, Simeon, and Anna", 106). I believe Reicke goes too far. The text does not reveal Anna's age when she got married and when her husband died.

[166] The first one who interpreted, in connection with Anna, the number twelve representing the twelve tribes of Israel was ELTROP, "Simeon und Hanna", 136.

[167] The description of Simeon is also extensive, but it describes more interior aspects of his person through an internal focalization: he was just, merciful, awaiting the consolation of Israel, the Holy Spirit was upon him and had announced a prophecy to him. This gives the impression that Simeon is described more internally while Anna is described through an external focalization.

[168] The nouns νύκτα καὶ ἡμέραν are accusatives of extension, which expresses the temporal duration of the verbal action: "during night and day," in other words, she was praying always. However, the nouns νηστείαις καὶ δεήσεσιν are dative of mode which express the way in which Anna worships (see WALLACE, *Greek Grammar*, 202).

The description of Anna bears in itself the history and spiritual experience of Israel. In some way the entire OT is represented there. Anna embodies the worship in the Temple, the tribes of Israel, the prophetic ministry, the prayer and praise of Israel.[169] Anna is presented as a true prophetess who has lived a perfect life as a wife and widow. It is a perfect presentation of a reliable character.[170] Her prophecy is reliable. Anna is presented as such a figure of wisdom and maturity. The reader can trust Anna's witness because she has lived a perfect life. She is a reliable spokesperson for God.

3.3.2 The Reaction of Anna to Jesus: v. 38

What is Anna's witness? Although the description of Anna is more verbose than Simeon's, her description of Jesus is much shorter than Simeon's. Simeon's characterization of Jesus is evident through his direct discourses about Jesus, whereas in Anna's description of Jesus it is the narrator who shows us her reaction as she ponders the child Jesus. The prefix ἀντι- from the verb ἀνθωμολογεῖτο, which is present in the same verse, indicates that it is concerning an action in response to something, a reaction. The goodness of God and his benefits are manifested in the child Jesus causing Anna to praise God.[171] That is to say, Anna praises God and speaks repeatedly about Jesus in response to the presentation of Jesus in the Temple.[172]

---

[169] See LEFEBVRE, "Anne de la tribu d'Asher", 3-32.

[170] "The manner in which characters are presented in a narrative," says Powell, "is especially significant for determining the effect that the narrative is expected to have on its readers" (POWELL, "Narrative Criticism", 245). These effects are often determined by the empathy that these readers feel with particular characters in the narrative. Simeon and Anna have qualities or experiences the readers wish to emulate and thus readers feel empathy for Simeon and Anna.

[171] The ἀντι- does not refer to Simeon, meaning that "she in turn gave thanks." It refers to giving something in return, which is involved in all thanksgiving: Ps 78:13; Ezr 3:11; 3 Macc 6:33. See ROGERS – ROGERS – RIENECKER, *The New Linguistic*, 113.

[172] Unlike Simeon, these actions of Anna, her praise and speaking, are described in the imperfect. In the case of Simeon they were in aorist (vv. 28.34: εὐλόγησεν [...] καὶ εἶπεν). Perhaps it was to show the exact action of the direct discourse that was going

Both expressions, ἀνθωμολογεῖτο τῷ θεῷ and ἐλάλει περὶ αὐτοῦ are placed together and directly related. It seems that they are two sides of the same action. The way in which Anna praises God is by speaking about Jesus.[173] Anna seems to be one of the first Christian missionaries. The witness of Anna is repeatedly to recognize God's action through Jesus and speak about him "to all who looked forward to the redemption of Jerusalem." Anna repeatedly speaks to them because she recognizes that God is about to redeem Jerusalem through Jesus.

Certainly the response of Anna to Jesus is not developed by the narrator like the response of Simeon to Jesus. Nevertheless, both presentations reveal four parallel elements that allow us to put them in relation to one another.

(1) On the one hand, Simeon is presented in background (vv. 25-26), and "praises God" (v. 28) before speaking about Jesus through his discourses. On the other hand, the narrator presents Anna in background (vv. 36-37) and states that Anna "was praising God" before saying that she "was speaking of Jesus" (v. 38).[174]

(2) Simeon is presented in the Temple as probably an old man since he announces that he is now ready to die (v. 29), as a devout and faithful man (v. 25), and as a Spirit-inspired man who can prophesy (vv. 34-35). Anna also is presented in the Temple as a very old woman (v. 36), as a woman engaged in fasting, praying and worshipping (v. 37), and as a prophetess (v. 37).

(3) The narrator says of Simeon that "he looked forward to the consolation of Israel" (v. 25) while he says that Anna speaks about Jesus to all those that "looked forward to the redemption of Jerusalem"

---

to be addressed. The action of Anna expressed in the imperfect (v. 38: ἀνθωμολογεῖτο [...] καὶ ἐλάλει) is a continuous action, not restricted to a single discourse. It has a repetitive-frequent aspect.

[173] LAURENTIN, *Les Évangiles de l'enfance*, 78, affirms that Luke is presenting Jesus as God through the unity of these expressions. I believe that both actions are presented together, but it does not imply that both objects, God and Jesus, are identified.

[174] Simeon blesses God (εὐλόγησεν) while Anna praises God (ἀνθωμολογεῖτο). Both expressions pertain to the same semantic field (LOUW – NIDA, *Greek-English*, § 53.64).

(v. 38). The similarity of these expressions is striking.[175] The fact that the narrator affirms something so similar of the two different characters further highlights the links between them that the narrator builds. Both expressions act as a pair of brackets, as an *inclusio* that holds together both figures, Simeon and Anna, and marks the principal thematic context of the episode: the expectation of Israel fulfilled in Jesus. First, both expressions start with the verb προσδέχομαι, which is linked with hopes of the definitive coming of the awaited Messiah.[176] Second, the substantives παράκλησις (v. 25) and λύτρωσις (v. 38) express in different ways the Messiah's mission: his consolation and his redemption.[177] And third, these consequences are applied to Israel (v. 25) and Jerusalem (v. 38). I believe that *Jerusalem* should be understood as a synecdoche of *Israel* and, therefore, should be understood as a synonym of *Israel* in v. 25.[178] Both hopes, that of the consolation of Israel and that of the redemption of Jerusalem, could be applied to the people of Israel understood in its totality. Simeon and Anna represent the long history of an expectant people, nourished by God's promise.[179] In fact, both expressions appear together in Is 52:9 when it is said the Lord has consoled Israel, and he has redeemed Jerusalem.[180]

---

[175] Fitzmyer does not speak simply of similarity of these expressions, but he affirms that it concerns parallel and synonymous expressions (FITZMYER, *Luke I-IX*, 427).

[176] Throughout Luke-Acts the verb προσδέχομαι appears on only five other occasions (Lk 12:36; 15:2; 23:51; Acts 23:21; 24:15). It concerns people who await the coming of the Messiah in different ways. In Lk 12:36 "the men wait for their master to return from the wedding"; in Lk 23:51, "Joseph of Arimathea (…) who was waiting for the Reign of God." In Acts 24:15 Paul awaits with hope the future resurrection that God has promised. Only twice does προσδέχομαι refer to a normal expectation (Lk 15:2; Acts 23:21).

[177] According to ZERWICK, *Analysis philologica*, 135, both nouns are interpreted as expressions of the Messianic coming. Bill. I, 66, affirms that the titles *Consolator* and *Redeemer* were Messianic titles in the Rabbinic tradition.

[178] On the literary figure of synecdoche see ALETTI, *et al.*, *Vocabulaire raisonné*, 93.

[179] As Zechariah and Elizabeth, or Joseph and Mary, they represent the Jewish-Christians who accept Jesus.

[180] The expressions are not the same, παράκλησις-ἐλέεω and λύτρωσις-ῥύομαι but their meaning and semantic fields are the same (LOUW – NIDA, *Greek-English*, § 37.127-37.138). Furthermore, the preacher who announces this good news in Dt-Is is male, as Simeon (Is 41:27; 52:7) and female, as Anna (Is 40:9).

Finally, (4) there is a formal indicator which underlines the simultaneity of Simeon and Anna's reaction: καὶ αὐτῇ τῇ ὥρᾳ.[181] As the narrative is sequential two actions which could happen simultaneously have to be told consecutively. The narrator usually highlights that simultaneity through a temporal complement located at the beginning of the phrase ("at that moment," "that day," etc.).[182] This simultaneity links both actions even more among themselves. The former action (Simeon's) explains the latter one (Anna's), which is narratively less developed.

The parallelism between Simeon and Anna and their actions and sayings helps us to better understand their function. Why did Luke present both characters? Why did he also present Anna who does not say anything throughout the pericope? Anna contributes to the validity of the testimony. The inclusion of the prophetess Anna serves to augment the *authority* of what has been disclosed by Simeon. Now it is a story supported by two reliable witnesses who testify to Jesus. They respond to the Jewish requirement for two witnesses for legal testimony (Dt 19:15). The close relationship between Simeon and Anna allows us to think that Anna agrees with Simeon's words. They are complementary verification. This way of presenting both Simeon and Anna causes the reader to link immediately the fulfillment of the hopes of consolation and of redemption of the people of God with the presence of Jesus. The narrator links Jesus' mission with the consolation and redemption of God's people.

---

[181] As Simeon was emphasizing the νῦν with which his first discourse began, in order to highlight the moment in which he was holding Jesus, in the case of Anna the narrator emphasizes that same moment through the expression αὐτῇ τῇ ὥρᾳ. Concerning a temporal dative that is emphasized by the proleptic pronoun αὐτῇ, it could be translated as "in that precise moment." In the precise moment in which they see the child Jesus, their hopes have been fulfilled (see BLASS – DEBRUNNER – REHKOPF, *Grammatik*, § 200).

[182] The expression αὐτῇ τῇ ὥρᾳ is a special one to express this: Lk 10:21; 12:12; 13:1.31; 20:19; Acts 16:18; 22:13; outside of Luke see Mt 15:28. With other expressions such as ἐκεῖνος καιρός see Acts 12:1; 19:23; Mt 11:25; 12:1; 14:1, or for αὐτῷ τῷ καιρῷ see Lk 13:1. In the OT see Gn 21:22; 38:1; Dt 10:1.8; 1 K 14:1; 2 K 16:6; 18:6.

That is not all, though. It is a story comprised of a man and a woman, as is common in the work of Luke.[183] Simeon and Anna not only present Jesus, but they embody the human recognition of him and inform the reader what is the authentic human response to Jesus. They both await him with great expectations (vv. 25.38b), receive him (vv. 28.38a), speak about him (vv. 29-32.34b-35.38b), and praise God (vv. 28b.38a). The exemplary recognition and acceptance of Jesus comes not from the Jewish authorities, nor the chief priests, scribes and elders of the people, but from simple representatives of the ancient Jewish piety, the people of God. The reader is invited to react in the very same way.

3.4 Conclusion: v. 39

After the lengthy description of Anna in the imperfect aspect (vv. 36-38), a new main sentence follows with an aorist verb (ἐπέστρεψαν).[184] While the description as background has a singular subject, Anna, the narrator continues with an implicit plural subject, Mary and Joseph. The actors that carry out the action are, therefore, different. While the previous scene was centered on Anna and situated in the Temple of Jerusalem, this verse is centered on the journey of Jesus' family to Galilee. The spatial coordinates vary from Jerusalem to Nazareth.[185]

---

[183] The technique of these doublets is one of the ways that the evangelist Luke demonstrates both the inclusiveness of the Christian Gospel and the spiritual equality of men and women in the Christian community. Pairing Simeon and Anna adds another dimension to the passage's universality: all people are included, male and female. The dividing lines disappear with the advent of the Messiah. His presence actively offers a new reality. Strickert argues that the old distinctions are broken down by the new reality present in the child named Jesus: race, class, gender, and age (STRICKERT, "The Presentation of Jesus", 33-37).

[184] It is some kind of summary, an acceleration of the narrative which relates succinctly what has been done over a relatively long period of the story.

[185] Throughout the passage we find four proper nouns that refer to geographic places: Jerusalem (vv. 22.25.38); Israel (vv. 25.34); Galilee, and Nazareth (v. 39). We also find a common noun which refers to a geographical place: the Temple (v. 27.37). Some of these names form part of the prepositional locutions that show the geographic movements: εἰς Ἱεροσόλυμα (v. 22); εἰς τὸ ἱερόν (v. 27); εἰς τὴν Γαλιλαίαν (v. 39b); εἰς Ναζαρέτ (v. 39c). These prepositional locutions reflect a double move-

The conclusion returns to the subject of the fulfillment of the Law that is explicitly present throughout vv. 22.23.24.27: "When they fulfilled (τελέω) everything according to the Law of the Lord" (v. 39a). In different ways the fulfillment is implicitly present in all the different scenes of the passage.[186] In addition, the prophets are present through Simeon and Anna, who announce the fulfillment of the Jewish expectations in Jesus, and prophesy about the future Jesus' life.[187] Everything happens in the Temple of Jerusalem (vv. 22.25.27.37). The Law, the prophets and the Temple, the standard Lukan designation for the heritage of Israel,[188] bring to the passage the entire OT.[189] The story of the fulfillment of the Law has been interrupted by the reactions of Simeon and Anna to Jesus. Jesus' parents brought him into the Temple to present him to God in accordance with the Law, but the Holy Spirit took part to reveal Jesus through Simeon and Anna.[190] Thus, what the Holy Spirit had

---

ment: toward Jerusalem at the beginning of the passage (v. 22), and, at the end, towards Galilee (v. 39). These two movements distinguish the first scene (introduction) and the last scene (conclusion) from the two scenes in the middle (Simeon and Anna), which take place in the Temple of Jerusalem. Both movements are shown, at first in a more generic way and then with a more specific description later: from Jerusalem (v. 22) to the Temple (v. 27), and from Galilee (v. 39b) to Nazareth (v. 39c). Thus, the place is increasingly specified and concretized in each scene.

[186] The introduction speaks about the fulfillment of the number of days according to the Law (πίμπλημι: v. 22). Simeon's scene shows how his prophecy of seeing the Messiah of the Lord and his expectations of consolation are fulfilled (vv. 26-28). In Anna's scene, the prophetess speaks of Jesus to all who expected the redemption of Jerusalem. In doing that, she implicitly proclaims the fulfillment in Jesus of that expectation (v. 38). Finally, the conclusion affirms that they fulfilled everything the Law of the Lord required (v. 39). Regarding the fulfillment there is a chiastic structure in the four scenes (A, B, B', A'). A: fulfillment of the Law; B: fulfillment of Simeon's prophecy; B': fulfillment of Anna's prophecy; A': fulfillment of the Law.

[187] There is a fulfillment of old prophecies and a proclamation of a new prophecy.

[188] See Lk 9:30; 16:16; Acts 13:15; 24:14; 26:22; 28:23.

[189] Obedience to the Law (vv. 22-25), the notion of Israel as the people of God (v. 32), the messianic hope (vv. 25-26.29.30.38) and a reference to Moses (v. 22) are mentioned. In addition the passage takes place in the Temple, where cultic acts such as the rite of purification with the accompanying sacrifice are prominent (see TATUM, "Epoch of Israel", 194).

[190] If the introduction (in which the purpose of remaining in the Temple is described,

revealed to Simeon is fulfilled (v. 26) and the prophetic expectations of Simeon and Anna are fulfilled (vv. 25.38). The Holy Spirit leads Jewish piety as far as the recognition and revelation of the Messiah. I believe that Luke shows the revelation made by the Spirit through the prophets Simeon and Anna to be the true fulfillment of the whole OT. Recognizing the Messiah who comes, in all his aspects, including his universal salvation and rejection, becomes the fulfillment of the entire OT.[191] The prophets Simeon and Anna, with the Law and the Holy Spirit, testify to Jesus in the Temple of Jerusalem itself. The entire OT points to Jesus.

4. The Plot of the Passage: The Meaning of the Entire Pericope

The majority of the narrative episodes have a combination of two types of plots with their own coherence and their own development: a plot of resolution and a plot of revelation.[192] Both kinds of plots might appear in the very same pericope.[193] On the one

---

vv. 22-24) were consecutive with the affirmation of the fulfillment of everything according to the Law (v. 39), the scenes of Simeon and Anna would remain on the edge of the framework of the fulfillment of the Law. I do not say that the Law is already over with the coming of Jesus; nevertheless, the order of the scenes that we find introduces Simeon and Anna who present Jesus in the Temple in connection with the fulfillment of the Law and the prophecies (FIGUERAS, "Syméon et Anne", 84-99).

[191] Perhaps the strange presence of the pronoun τά in v. 39 (πάντα τὰ κατὰ τὸν νόμον κυρίου) is trying to include all the actions and prophecies accomplished in the Presentation in the Temple.

[192] I follow the terminology proposed by SKA, *Our Fathers*, 18, and MARGUERAT – BOURQUIN, *Récits bibliques*, 72 [56]. The point of the plot of resolution is the transforming action which essentially involves a doing, and thus is situated at a pragmatic level. The main question is: "What will happen?" The point of the plot of revelation is not in the order of doing but in that of knowing. The revelation plot culminates in a gain in knowledge: the doing becomes the instrument of an increase in knowledge. The reader can gain new insights from the most insignificant incidents.

[193] As paradigmatic of this combination of plots, I propose the story of the disciples of Emmaus (Lk 24:13-35), in which is developed and interwoven the plot of resolution (will they recognize him?) and the plot of revelation (the Mystery of all of the Scriptures revealed in Jesus, dead and resurrected). The composition of plots lends

hand, the first scene of the passage, its introduction, presents Joseph and Mary going up to Jerusalem with the child Jesus in order to redeem him and to purify the mother, offering the sacrifice according to what was stipulated (vv. 22-24). The reader asks immediately whether they will truly carry it out and how they will do it. There is a *plot of resolution* which lies in the act of the affirmation of the necessity of "purification." This plot of resolution starts in v. 22 but it is not developed. It leaves the way clear for other plots.[194]

On the other hand, the following scene presents Simeon referring to his expectations. As we have seen, v. 25 shows how he awaits the coming of the Messiah and the consolation he will bring. In addition, Simeon had received an earlier revelation of the Spirit promising him that he would see the Messiah before his death (v. 26). This kind of "contract" becomes dramatic because he is about to die (v. 29).[195] This tension shows a plot of resolution. Will he see the Messiah? The encounter with the child Jesus does, in fact, resolve this dramatic tension. After taking Jesus into his arms (v. 28), Simeon is transformed. He blesses God and is ready for death. The resolution of the plot of resolution introduces a *plot of revelation*, the revelation of the person who Simeon was waiting for (vv. 27-38). Both resolution plots are minor plots which are quickly resolved in similar ways. As the figure below shows, the resolution plot of Mary's purification and Jesus' redemption is resolved through their obedience to the Law, going to the Temple. The resolution plot of Simeon's expectations is resolved through his obedience to the Spirit. The obedience to the Law and the Spirit finishes the resolution plots and begin the revelation plot, which is developed through the direct witness of Simeon, his speeches, and through the indirect witness of Anna.

---

itself to numerous combinations of which the biblical narrators make use: linked, overlapping, inserted or interlaced plots.

[194] It is simply resolved when the characters enter into the Temple and in v. 39 when the narrator affirms that they did "everything according to the Law of the Lord."

[195] A similar dramatic tension and expectation are ascribed to the elderly Anna who spoke about Jesus to those who were looking forward to the redemption performed by the Messiah (vv. 36.38).

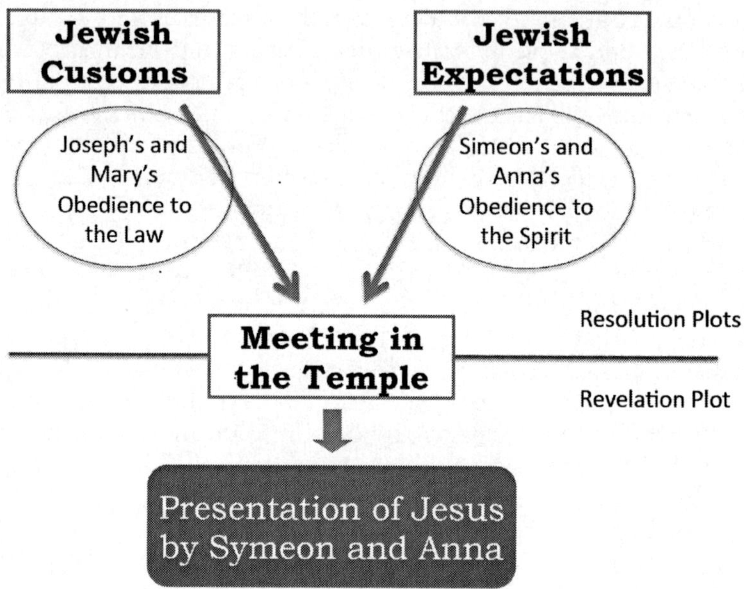

I contend that in this episode the plots of resolution decrease, which in turn allows the plot of revelation to become prominent. This claim is based on the following. (1) The typical action in the stories of resolution is the transforming action. Our story does not tell how or when they have been purified, which would be the turning point that would resolve the plot.[196] If a program is not developed, it means that it is not important. This disappearance shows that the plot of resolution is at the service of the plot of revelation which is developed. There is a tension in the expectations of Simeon but that tension is resolved in meeting Jesus in v. 28. Afterwards there is no more plot of resolution.

[196] A story may or may not have a progression. However, the plot of resolution has to progress to demonstrate the gradual resolution until the climax with the transforming action.

(2) The existence of direct discourses and the extensive visual description are indications of showing. As the showing facilitates the imparting of important information, it is a typical feature of the plot of revelation. (3) In our passage there is a strong typological presence from the OT that helps to reveal different shades of Jesus' identity.[197] This accumulated typology from the OT is indicative of the plot of revelation. (4) The characters, both Simeon and Anna, are described extensively, and make up the plot. The predominance of the actors beyond the actions emphasizes the precedence of the plot of revelation over the plot of resolution.

It seems to me, therefore, that throughout the whole passage there is a combination of plot, an overlapping. The last stage of the resolution plot forms the start of the revelation plot, which then prevails. But who is revealed, Simeon, Anna, or Jesus? Which of them is revealed through the narrative plot of the passage?

I believe Jesus is revealed for the following reasons. (1) The majority of the pronouns[198] and different images in strategic positions[199] refer to Jesus who is explicitly referred to in v. 27: τὸ παιδίον Ἰησοῦν. Once he is identified, the titles, metaphors, and allusions are very useful to present him, especially those with an OT background.[200] (2) The entire passage speaks about the "child Jesus." What is said about Jesus structures and unites the passage. The prepositional ex-

---

[197] In Lk 2:22-39 we find two quotes from the OT (vv. 23.24); the description of Anna, in explicitly Jewish terms (prophetess, daughter of Phanuel, from the tribe of Asher, very elderly, and a widow), and images of the OT used to describe Jesus (Messiah of the Lord, salvation, light, glory, consolation of Israel, and redemption of Jerusalem).

[198] Αὐτόν (v. 22), αὐτοῦ (v. 27), αὐτό (v. 28), ὃ (v. 31), αὐτοῦ (v. 33), αὐτοῦ (v. 34), οὗτος (v. 35), and αὐτοῦ (v. 38).

[199] There are references to the child Jesus in all scenes of the passage, at the beginning and at the end (vv. 22 and 38-39); but above all, the reference is strategically relevant to Jesus in all of the direct discourses of the passage that speak of him (vv. 30-32; 34b-35).

[200] While our text is built up through different images to present the identity of Jesus, in other stories (see Lk 22:47-52, the arrest of Jesus) the name of Jesus is continually repeated (4x in 5 verses). In these cases the narrator considers it more important to tell who the actor of the passage is (Jesus) than to characterize a subject that has already been sufficiently presented. In Lk 2:22-39, however, Luke does not repeat Jesus' name, but characterizes him by introducing different images of him.

pression περὶ αὐτοῦ (vv. 27.33.38), whose pronoun refers to the child Jesus, appears three times. It expresses what the Law says about the child Jesus, the things that are said by Simeon about Jesus, and what Anna says about Jesus. It becomes a type of refrain that is repeated throughout the passage. This refrain is underlined by the narrator by its placement in the center of the structure, highlighting the wonder at the things that were being said about Jesus (v. 33).[201] (3) There are few transitive verbs present in the passage, and very frequently the direct object of these verbs is the child Jesus, affirmed directly or through some image.[202] (4) The point of view of the secondary characters, Simeon and Anna, is highly developed.[203] The way in which both Simeon and Anna see and speak about Jesus orients the narrative perspective and becomes the way in which Luke reveals the child Jesus. The narrator adopts the point of view of these characters, and sees through their eyes, with their angle of vision. Through them, the principal character is disclosed and revealed to Mary and Joseph.[204] It concerns an indirect revelation, because it is not Jesus that manifests himself.[205] However, the revelation offered by Simeon and Anna is inspired by the Holy Spirit acting through the prophets. Finally, (5) the revelation of the mystery of Jesus that the reader receives

---

[201] See the beginning of § 3, p. 161, with the general structure of the passage.

[202] See vv. 22.25.26.27.28.32.

[203] On the theoretically complex and multifaceted bases of the concept *point of view*, I follow Yamasaki's definition of *point of view*: "The essence of point of view (...) is the narrator leading the audience to see the events of the story line as filtered through the consciousness of one of the characters, or simply through the consciousness of the narrator" (YAMASAKI, *Watching a Biblical Narrative*, 94-95). For further studies see USPENSKI, *A Poetics of Composition*, 8-117. On a new approach to these concepts see BOURQUIN, "Nouvelle approche", 498-500, and RABATEL, *La construction textuelle*, who contend the distinction between *focalization by* and *focalization on*.

[204] According to CULPEPPER, *Anatomy of the Fourth Gospel*, 104, intermediate characters, secondary characters, or supporting characters exist to reveal the protagonist. On how minor characters shape the main character see BAR-EFRAT, *Narrative Art*, 86-92.

[205] Although Jesus does not do or say anything, everyone, especially Simeon and Anna, speaks about him. Besides, the only time in which the child Jesus is a grammatical subject of a sentence, he is a passive subject (v. 34). This detail shows that the revealed character throughout the passage is presented not because he takes the initiative, but because everyone speaks about him.

from Luke's work is not only the one that the actors, intradiegetically, experience (Simeon, Anna, Mary and Joseph) but also, the revelation by the narrator.[206] The narrator identifies the child Jesus as "the Holy one for the Lord" (v. 23), "the Messiah of the Lord" (v. 26), and the one who will bring to fulfillment the hopes of the people of Israel, the "consolation of Israel" and the "redemption of Jerusalem" (vv. 25.38). That is why the reader may surpass the actors themselves in the knowledge of the mystery of Jesus.[207]

The plot of revelation was not previewed at the beginning of the story but, once it begins, it is developed such that everything depends on this plot of revelation. He who was going to be redeemed and presented by his parents in the Temple is presented in another distinct way. Simeon and Anna present him through their particular vision and interpretation of Jesus. Extradiegetically, Jesus is revealed to the reader who perceives the mystery of the child presented through the characters and through the narrator.

5. Synthesis of the Passage

The Presentation of Jesus in the Temple is a real presentation of this character. Although Luke introduces the legal setting of the purification of the mother and the redemption of the son, it remains clear that Luke is not interested in these customs except to affirm their fulfillment. Luke introduces a resolution plot around these Jewish customs and another resolution plot around the Jewish expectations of the Messiah. However, the obedience to the Law of Mary and Joseph and the obedience to the Spirit of Simeon soon resolve these resolution plots and Luke uses them

[206] It is what GENETTE, *Figures III*, 207-210, names *reader-elevating position* where the reader knows more than the characters.

[207] And in any case, the reader who is about to read the work of Luke already knows the end of the story, since he already knows of the preaching of the early Church of the death and resurrection of Jesus. The fact that the addressee of the Lukan work had already received some teachings (Lk 1:3-4), whose soundness he is about to learn, implies knowledge of the first apostolic preaching and, therefore, of the first *kerygma* of the early Church.

to introduce the real plot of the passage: the revelation of Jesus. The deeds and words of Simeon and Anna in relationship to Jesus clearly present the main features of Jesus to the reader. The character of Jesus is not perceived by the reader directly, but rather filtered through the narrator and the other two characters, Simeon and Anna, two reliable witnesses, a male and a female witness. The long characterization of both actors emphasizes their reliability. They embody the human recognition of Jesus and inform the reader with regard to the authentic human response to Jesus. They invite the reader to trust them, accepting Jesus as they have presented him, and making the reader see Luke's work through the clues they have given. Luke uses the pious presentation of Jesus by his parents to present Jesus in a very concrete frame. Jesus is presented by his parents to God in the Temple, and Jesus is presented by Simeon and Anna to those who were present, and to the reader. The verb παρίστημι (v. 22) contributes, intradiegetically, to Jesus' presentation to God but also, extradiegetically, to his literary presentation to the reader.

Throughout the whole passage Jesus' identity, *who* he is, his mission, *what* he will do, are all presented. He is the "Holy" one (v. 23b) and the "Messiah of the Lord" (v. 26b). His mission will be to perform God's "salvation" (v. 30), the "consolation of Israel" (v. 25), the "redemption of Jerusalem" (v. 38). This salvation will be a universal salvation illuminating the Gentiles (v. 31-32). This mission will be rejected by many in Israel who will fall down (v. 34). His mission will also be to reveal the secret thoughts of many, which he will do through the fall of many in Israel (v. 35). Through this wide presentation Jesus remains at the center of the pericope. In fact, the center of the structure of the passage is the admiration for the things said about Jesus, admiration by Mary and Joseph, who "were amazed about the things said about him (Jesus)" (v. 33).

Although Simeon addresses God and later Mary, the child Jesus remains at the center of his speeches. A single character, Simeon, presents Jesus with a single prophecy with two different sides, like a coin with two sides, two speeches which are a single diptych. Jesus is presented as a universal Messiah, prepared by God through the history of Israel to save all the nations, both Israel and the Gentiles. As the Messiah comes from Israel and fulfills the Law and prophecies, he is the Glory of Israel. As the Gentiles were in darkness, the Messiah is the light for their illumination. But this universal Messiah will be a rejected Messiah. Simeon does not only foretell universal salvation; he also foretells the way in which this salvation will happen.[208] Many in Israel will reject the Messiah of the Lord and there will be in Israel a division. This rejection of the Messiah and his followers will affect Mary who will suffer the rejection of her son and followers.

Simeon and Anna present Jesus in the Temple and under the expectation of the fulfillment of the Law and the Prophets. They both expect the consolation of Israel (v. 26), the redemption of Jerusalem (v. 38), which they both see fulfilled in Jesus. The Temple, the Law, and the Prophets come together to establish a setting for the life of Jesus. In the Temple itself, Luke presents Jesus as the fulfillment of the entire OT, which seems to be present through the characters of Simeon and Anna. In addition, Anna is described as an elderly woman and Simeon is ready to die. These old characters, who represent the expectations of the OT, recognize the fulfillment of their expectation in the child Jesus. Simeon, presented in connection with his death, takes into his arms the baby Jesus, who is presented in connection with his birth. The one who is about to die embraces that one who is just born. It might express the continuity between a new season and the old season which it fulfills.[209] The old expectations welcome a new reality. The OT, represented by these old characters, meets its fulfillment, made present in the newborn Jesus.

I hope I have made clear through this chapter that the passage of Lk 2:22-39 is first and foremost a portrayal of the presentation of Jesus in the Temple as the awaited universal Messiah who will be rejected by many in the days and years to come. The message

---

[208] While Simeon's hymn speaks about peace, salvation, light, and glory, his prophecy speaks about rejection, division, and a sword.

[209] Simeon and Anna, as John the Baptist, are on the threshold between both covenants. They are prophets of the OT, and they are part of the flowering recognition of Jesus by the NT.

of the presentation is the crux of this passage, having much greater importance and meaning than the concepts of the purification of the mother or the redemption of the son.

CHAPTER IV

THE NARRATIVE FUNCTION OF LK 2:22-39 IN ITS IMMEDIATE CONTEXT

Throughout the Lukan literature there are developments which unite pericopes or short episodes into bigger unities. These are sequences in which we find clear plot developments through a series of interrelated passages. The sequences are significantly longer than the small units and represent an intermediate level between the short episode and a complete literary work. One of these unified sequences is the Lukan infancy narrative. The single passage of the Presentation in the Temple, which we have just studied in Ch. III, is influenced by its longer context. In this chapter I explore the relationship of the Presentation in the Temple with its close context so that I may better understand its importance within the Lukan infancy narrative.

Luke's readers do not encounter a presentation of Jesus for the first time in Lk 2:22-39.[1] Readers have already formed impressions and expectations concerning him from material presented earlier in the accounts of Luke. I contend that throughout the first chapters of Luke's Gospel there is a gradual presentation of Jesus. These opening chapters of the Gospel are a gradually unfolding

---

[1] After studying the episode of the Presentation in the Temple, a number of questions arise. On the one hand, is the Presentation in the Temple a special presentation of Jesus with respect to the infancy narrative? Does it repeat what has been said about Jesus or does it say anything new? On the other hand, we can ask ourselves as well whether there is any other characterization of Jesus after Luke 1–2. Is there another passage which presents Jesus to the reader in a better and wider sense? I will answer the former questions in this chapter and the latter in the Appendix.

characterization of Jesus.[2] Lk 2:22-39 is one more part which contributes to this progressive overture. However, no other presentation of Jesus is as broad and complete as the narrative in Lk 2:22-39. I argue that the Presentation in the Temple reflects aspects of the characterization of Jesus given previously and adds important new dimensions to his character. To demonstrate this, I will study the general structure and plot of Luke 1–2, and examine the role of Lk 2:22-39 within the sequence. I will pay close attention to what is said about Jesus in the different passages, who says it, where it is said, and the way in which it is said. Finally, I will note the conclusions drawn from a comparison of these findings with the results I have just detailed in Ch. III.

The construction of the character of Jesus is developed during the reading process from textual indicators and connotations.[3] The reader infers features of the character indirectly from words and deeds, from other characters, or from the character himself.[4] These textual indicators become traits of the characters. The traits may not exist in the text as actual verbal adjectives, but we must infer these traits to understand the narrative.[5] The whole discourse is expressly designed to prompt a specific understanding of the character in the reader's consciousness.

---

[2] Although characterization refers to the process by which the reader constructs characters from the mass of diverse textual and extratextual indicators available, I will focus my study only on internal textual indicators which characterize Jesus throughout Luke 1–2. On extratextual indicators in ancient Mediterranean literature which characterize Jesus, see DARR, *Herod the Fox*, 92-136.

[3] See BACH, "Characterization in the Bible", 61-79; FOWLER, "Characterizing", 97-104.

[4] According to MALBON, *Mark's Jesus*, 16-19, there are four basic ways Jesus becomes known to the audience: (1) by what he says (deflected Christology); (2) by what he does (enacted Christology); (3) by what others, the narrator and other characters, say in relation to him (projected Christology); and (4) by what others do about or in relation to him (reflected Christology). LEE, *Luke's Stories*, 202-327, however, classifies the characterization of Jesus in the Gospel of Luke as the narrator's characterization of Jesus, the self-characterization of Jesus, and the demon's characterization of Jesus. In the whole of Luke 1–2 there is only one passage in which Jesus both speaks and acts (Lk 2:40-52). Without forgetting the importance of this passage, my study will be focused on what others, the narrator and other characters, say and do in relation to Jesus.

[5] CHATMAN, *Story and Discourse*, 125, defines *traits* in terms of narrative criticism as "a narrative adjective out of the vernacular labeling a personal quality of a character, as it persists over a part or the whole of the story."

How are these traits of Jesus' characterization given to the reader? Darr suggests that characterization is cumulative, and the manner, means and timing of its accumulation is hermeneutically significant.[6] Because the characterization is cumulative, it is essential that the critic be cognizant at all times of the degree to which a character has been constructed at particular points along the text continuum. The focus is on the degree of characterization rather than on characterization itself. There is a progression between the different degrees of characterization from *agent* to *type* to *character*.[7] It is shown via a step by step transformation that Jesus goes from being a *flat* character, to becoming a *round* character throughout the Lukan infancy narrative.[8] The character of Jesus gradually emerges more clearly.[9] Revelation and recognition are a process in which knowledge and concealment[10] of Jesus are both progressively imparted to the reader.[11]

---

[6] See DARR, *Herod the Fox*, 73-78.

[7] Berlin says: "1) the agent, about whom nothing is known except what is necessary for the plot; the agent is a function of the plot or part of the setting; 2) the type, who has a limited and stereotyped range of traits, and who represents the class of people with these traits; 3) the character, who has a broader range of traits (not all belonging to the same class of people), and about whom we know more than is necessary for the plot" (BERLIN, *Poetics and Interpretation*, 32). There is no real line separating these three types; the difference is a matter of the degree of characterization.

[8] The *flat* characters have only a single trait, and they appear only once in the story. Characters considered more complex, constructed by means of several traits, are called *round* characters (see SKA, *Our Fathers*, 84-85). According to Harvey, round characters, who usually are protagonists, are "what the novel exists for; it exists to reveal them" (HARVEY, *Character and the Novel*, 56). Jones claims that flat and round characters should be understood on a continuum rather than as mutually exclusive categories; a flat character can be transformed, even momentarily, into a round one (JONES, "Flat and Round", 120-122).

[9] Burnett claims that this better characterization of Jesus is even more striking when one realizes that ancient literature preferred indirect characterization, and personages were for the most part typical and flat (BURNETT, "Characterization", 19).

[10] According to COLERIDGE, *The Birth*, 218, there is a procedure of revelation-concealment. Being a process, the revelation will have an element of concealment until the end when all will be revealed. This interaction of revelation and concealment in the narrative provides the dynamic of the reading process ensuring that the reader continues to read.

[11] The reader knows the literary character as we know other persons, step by step. According to Burnett, observing real persons from real life and reconstructing a char-

These traits, which progressively increase the degree of characterization, can be expressed in different ways. How can we perceive these different traits? I will employ seven narrative criteria to study the narrative function of Lk 2:22-39 in its more immediate context (Ch. IV) and in Luke-Acts as a whole (Ch. V).

First, I will underline the kind of *plot*[12] developed throughout the sequence of Luke 1–2[13] and in its different passages.[14] The unifying structure which links the various happenings in the story and organizes them into a continuous account is called *plot*.[15] The plot safeguards the unity of action and gives meaning to the multiple elements in the story. It is through the plot that the reader perceives, in the series of related actions, something more than an accumulation of facts lined up in no particular sequence. The kind of plot is a very important tool to better understand the meaning of a sequence or a pericope and how it underscores traits of the characters.

Second, the different plots can develop *commission statements* which give an important trait of the character.[16] Characters are primarily represented by their commission statements revealing not only *who* the character is, but also *what* he will perform. God's

---

acter from a narrative are parallel phenomena. Indicators, acts or words, at different points in the continuum of the person's life or text, may cause the inferred pattern of traits which develops the progressive understanding of the person or character (BURNETT, "Characterization", 17). On the differences between the reader's knowledge of literary characters and our knowledge of other people see DARR, *Herod the Fox*, 78.

[12] The *italics* underline the terms that I will consistently use.

[13] The plot of a sequence or macro-narrative might be a *unified plot* or an *episodic plot*. On the difference between both kinds of plots see the beginning of § 1.2.

[14] The plot of a passage or micro-narrative might be a *revelation plot* or a *resolution plot*. On the difference between both kinds of plots see the beginning of § III.4. The plot of revelation presents a character and introduces his main features better than the plot of resolution. All of these modern categories of plots are artificial and could be discussed, but they are convenient and useful to study Jesus' characterization throughout Luke 1–2.

[15] BOURNEUF – QUELLET, *L'univers du roman*, 43, say: "The plot, as a chain of facts, is based on the presence of an internal tension between these facts which has to be created at the beginning of the story, maintained during its development and which must find its resolution in the denouement." On the notion of plot since Aristotle's Poetics see RICŒUR, *Temps et récit* I, 55-84.

[16] I will use three narrative criteria proposed by Tannehill: *commission statement*, *reliable character*, and *direct scriptural references* (TANNEHILL, *Narrative Unity* I, 21-22).

purpose is realized through persons commissioned by God to carry out some aspect of this purpose. At various points in Luke-Acts there are statements of the commission which have been received by John the Baptist, Jesus, the twelve, Paul, etc. These commission statements are also programs for action by particular characters and keys to the general plot of the macro-narrative.

The third and fourth criteria are from Genette's narrative studies. Genette, who discusses narrative criticism in terms of *order* and *frequency*,[17] proposes two ways to discern the important traits of characters. The third criteria, the *order* of events narrated in Luke-Acts, is important because readers are expected to consider each new episode in light of what has gone before. The impulse for following a sequential order derives from both ancient and contemporary sources: on the one side, from the Lukan prologue (Lk 1:1-4) in which Luke claims to have written his narrative (διήγησις)[18] in order, successively, in a sequence (καθεξῆς);[19] and, on the other, from hermeneutical work that emphasizes narrative itself as the bearer of meaning.[20] The ancient and modern directives together forcefully make the point that the *order* in which things appear in the narrative is important for the interpretation.[21] The reader receives the information, particularly the

---

[17] GENETTE, *Figures III*, 77-182.

[18] The noun διήγησις refers to the narrative that "many others" have written (Lk 1:1). However, implicitly Luke refers to it when he affirms that he, in his turn, has decided to write it (Lk 1:3).

[19] The adverb καθεξῆς has several shades of meaning depending on the particular context, but as a whole Luke uses it to mean "in order" or "in sequence" (Lk 1:3; 8:1; Acts 3:24; 11:4; 18:23). Luke's accurate investigation of his sources (Lk 1:1-2) gave rise to a particular sequence for the narrative.

[20] See RICŒUR, "Interpretative Narrative", 237-257. If one ignores the constraints of narrative order, one can create a character almost at will.

[21] One example of the importance of the ordering of events by the narrator is the preaching of John the Baptist (Lk 3:1-18), the imprisonment of John the Baptist (Lk 3:19-20), and the baptism of Jesus by John the Baptist (Lk 3:21-22). The sequence of events concludes not as we would expect. Although Jesus' baptism must have occurred before John was arrested, we are not told about it until later. According to Powell, "one effect of relating the events in this order is to create a definite break for readers between the stories of John and Jesus. The story of Jesus' ministry does not begin until that of John's is essentially complete" (POWELL, "Narrative Criticism", 248).

traits of the main character, through the *order* of the sequence.[22] Characterization is therefore also sequential.

Fourth, the increase in frequency or the *repetitions* is important because the reader's perception may be influenced by the number of times that a specific expression is referenced in the narrative. If the narrator decides to repeat a very specific expression about a character, that expression takes on a narrative importance. Repetitions provide stability to the story by contributing to characterization.[23] The repetition of characteristic terms or expressions gives to the text a distinctive physiognomy,[24] and creates a *Leitmotiv* in the narrative; a leading-expression, a structural reminder guiding the reader's movement through Luke-Acts. The repetition is a means of emphasis which enables the reader to arrive at the correct interpretation of the events narrated, thus serving the education of the reader in what is central to understanding the story[25] as a necessary aspect of effective communication.[26]

Repetitions always suggest similarity in expressions and events that are nevertheless different. The technique of *reprise* appears in the details of the narrative, terms and expressions.[27] It is not exactly the same as a repetition because elements already introduced are

---

[22] If the order of the narrative is important, the *position* of a passage within the whole macro-narrative is important too. The importance of the order underlines specific *positions*. This is the reason why, in Ch.V, I pay special attention not only to the order, but also to the specific *position* within the Lukan narrative, to the beginnings and ends of each part, and to highlighted moments of the whole narrative that have special importance.

[23] If a person does something once, we may take note but reserve conclusions about the person. If the person does it twice or more, we conclude that it is characteristic of this person (see TANNEHILL, "The Gospel", 124).

[24] For example, Vanhoye uses this literary device of repetition to clarify the structure of the epistle to the Hebrews (VANHOYE, *Traduction structurée*, 3).

[25] BURNETT, "Prolegomenon", 93-94, speaks of *education of the reader* by redundancy.

[26] The length of Luke-Acts could cause the reader to forget what has already been told. Repetition combats this tendency.

[27] This Lukan technique is named "reprise, re-acceptance, or re-adoption" by COLERIDGE, *The Birth*, 223. When a repetition refers to terms with a slightly different meaning it is called *reprise*. When a repetition refers to a character it is called *parallelism*. And when the parallelism highlights the difference is called *syncrisis*.

treated in a slightly different way and thus the sense of repetition is undermined.[28] This slight contrast with an earlier trait of the same character is another technique of characterization which progressively increases and specifies the knowledge of the character.[29] Exploring these differences contributes to the significance of the story.

The fifth criterion is the presence of *reliable characters* who give information about the character's traits as interpretive statements. Sometimes an author presents characters as very reliable in their judgments and perceptive in their statements. These characters are likely to become spokespersons for the author in characterizing other characters and interpreting events of the story. We must consider what reliable characters within the story say about different traits of other characters.

The sixth criterion is the geographical *location* where the different passages take place. The connection between geography and storytelling in secular literature has been studied by Beck.[30] Writers artfully make use of geographical location to affect their readers, predominantly in shaping the meaning of a story through the role geography can play in the development of the plot and characterization. The Bible may not be a geography book, but it is a book filled with geography. In addition, biblical writers add theologically meaningful geographical locations to the plot, such as the

---

[28] Lk 2:40 and 2:52 are an example of the Lukan technique of reprise. The two growth-reports are similar but not identical. The addition of "to human beings" (v. 52) gives the sense of Jesus as one who has entered the public arena and who is becoming increasingly the object of human attention. It makes sense after the first words of Jesus (v. 49) and before the beginning of his public life.

[29] Repetition in written communication is never the return of the same. The repetition with its play of similarity and dissimilarity allows the text to signify continuity and displacement, change and identity (MARGUERAT, "Saul's Conversion (Acts 9,22,26)", 131-133).

[30] In BECK, *God as Storyteller*, 106-110, the chapter entitle "Narrative Geography defined," Beck proposes a method for narrative-geographical analysis with three consecutive steps: identify the formal references to geography, show how they increase our understanding, and integrate the geography into the narrative analysis. See as well the chapter entitled "The Storyteller and Narrative Geography," in BECK, *Translators as Storytellers*, 166-172.

Temple in Jerusalem. Because some biblical storytellers exploit geography and location to achieve strategic literary and theological ends, geographical location plays a key role in biblical studies. The temporal and spatial coordinates of events may be significant for how readers understand what is reported in a narrative.[31] Throughout the Lukan work, the geographical placements have been evaluated as being very important.[32] As Darr affirms: "The characters of Luke-Acts are delineated to a certain degree by the geographical and cultural settings within which the reader encounters them. In other words, such settings furnish valuable clues as to how the reader should assess the significance of characters."[33]

The seventh criterion is the presence of *scriptural quotations*, especially when they are highlighted by the *introductory formula* quotation.[34] In fact, all of the *scriptural quotations*[35] are explicit commentary added by the narrator to instill his interpretation of the passage and its characters, which are presented in line with the OT background. The scriptural quotation contributes towards constructing the meaning. The narrator finds God's purpose revealed in Scripture remark-

---

[31] Readers may respond differently to the story if an event occurs on a mountain (Lk 9:28-36) in a boat (Lk 5:3-11), in private (Lk 6:12) among a crowd (Lk 6:17-18), or on a Sabbath (Lk 6:1-5).

[32] On the importance of geography in Luke 1–2 see GROS LOUIS, "Different Ways", 34-48.

[33] DARR, *Herod the Fox*, 70.

[34] According to Fox, the lack of the *introductory formula quotation* implies that there is no direct scriptural quotation (FOX, "Identification", 427). The author underlines the importance of the quotation through an introductory formula in order that the reader can know the importance of the passage. MALLEN, *Reading and Transformation*, 24, agrees with Fox distinguishing between *explicit quotation*, a verbal repetition of a known antecedent text whose presence is usually indicated by some type of introductory formula, and *verbal allusion*, an informal reference to an earlier text that repeats a distinctive word or phrase but without using an introductory formula.

[35] Concerning the study of quotations, a key problem is the definition of the term *scriptural quotation*. Complete agreement as to what constitutes an OT quotation is very difficult to find. BERNARDELLI, *Intertestualità*, 27-37, considers two conditions to delineate a direct scriptural quotation: the introductory formula and the close wording link to an OT sentence. I will use Bernardelli's conditions to affirm the existence of a direct scriptural quotation. For further studies on scriptural quotations see JUNG, *The Original Language*, 62-67.

ably useful to underline the importance of the passage and explain its meaning. These are principally taken from certain key texts of the Septuagint.[36]

I believe that the episode of the Presentation is narratively highlighted by these seven features. It starts as a resolution plot, but it becomes a *revelation plot* of Jesus. This revelation plot clearly increases the knowledge that the reader has of Jesus. It presents a very important trait of Jesus, his *commission statement* in which the program of action by Jesus is introduced. Jesus' commission is to become the instrument for universal salvation of God, to bring the light of revelation for the Gentiles and the glory for Israel, to be destined for the fall and for the rise of many, to be a sign that is contradicted, and to reveal the secret thoughts of many. The Presentation passage appears in a special *position* at the beginning of Luke-Acts, and, with the other passage which takes place in the Jerusalem Temple (2:40-52), at the end of the infancy narrative. The Presentation in the Temple is a *repetition* of important features of Jesus that had been already introduced in the precedent passages, as Messiah (Χριστός),[37] holy,[38] light,[39] peace,[40] salvation,[41] glory,[42] and the fulfillment of Jewish expectations. In addition, as we shall see in the following chapter, many references to this passage are developed throughout Luke-Acts. All of this information is related by a reliable speaking character, Simeon, and supported by another reliable character, Anna. The presence of the Holy Spirit in Simeon before he speaks and the characterization of Anna as a prophetess authorize them as *reliable characters*. The fact that two different reliable characters, a male and a female, agree in their witness to Jesus, highlights the importance of Jesus' characterization. The Presentation takes place in a very important *location*, the Temple of Jerusalem; in fact it is the first time that Jesus enters into the Temple.

---

[36] On the appeal to Scripture in the NT see BELLI, *et al.*, *Vetus in Novo*, 25-67.

[37] See 2:11; 2:26.

[38] See 1:35; 2:23.

[39] See 1:78.79; 2:32.

[40] See 1:79; 2:14; 2:29.

[41] See 1:47.69.71.74.77; 2:11; 2:30. We could include here the reference to the naming of Jesus, which means "God saves" (1:31; 2:20).

[42] See 2:9.14; 2:32.

Finally, it presents the first *scriptural quotations* of Luke-Acts and many scriptural allusions; in addition, the direct quotations are solemnly introduced by the expressions "As it is written (γέγραπται) in the Law" (2:23) and "as it is said (εἰρημένον) in the Law" (2:24).

1. Characterization of Jesus in Luke 1-2

In order to better explain my analysis, I will study the whole narrative sequence of Luke 1–2 in the following order. I begin by analyzing the general structure and *plot* of the whole sequence. Then, I analyze the kind of plot that the single passages develop, how it contributes to the general plot, whether or not it can be understood as a *commission statement*, and whose is that commission. As I study the different passages in *order* according to the general structure, I will highlight the new expressions concerning Jesus and their *repetitions* trying to show how the characterization of Jesus is progressively developed for the reader. After having studied the expressions about Jesus, I pay attention to who has said them and whether or not he is a *reliable character*. Finally, I take notice to the *location* where the different passages take place and the presence of direct *scriptural quotation* in the passages.

1.1 General Structure of Luke 1-2: the Breakdown of the John-Jesus Parallelism

The delimitation of the Lukan infancy narrative as an independent sequence is accepted by the majority of the scholars.[43] As we have seen in Ch. I, the presence of the same set of characters,

---

[43] For example, FITZMYER, *Luke I-IX*, 310-311; BOVON, *Lukas* I, 45. Brown, Muñoz Iglesias, and Ortensio da Spinetoli, studying the Lukan infancy narrative, treat 1:5–2:52 as a unit separate from 3:1 (BROWN, *Birth*, 240; MUÑOZ IGLESIAS, *Los Evangelios de la Infancia* I, 6-7; ORTENSIO DA SPINETOLI, *Introduzione*, 11). Luke 1–2 has been proposed as an independent source and unity by BOISMARD, *L'évangile de l'enfance*; MUÑOZ IGLESIAS, *Los Evangelios de la Infancia* I, 315-318; BURROWS, "The Gospel of the Infancy", 34-57; WINTER, "Some Observations", 111-121; DÍEZ MERINO, "Trasfondo semítico", 70; PÉREZ RODRÍGUEZ, *La infancia de Jesús*, 55-57.

topics, and several hymns throughout Luke 1–2,[44] its uniform style with a clear OT background,[45] the kind of literary forms throughout Luke 1–2 which are very different from the forms found in Luke 3–24,[46] the literary genre of Luke 1–2 as an infancy narrative,[47] and the likely late addition of Luke 1–2,[48] delimit these chapters as a self-contained unit within the larger narrative. In addition, Lk 2:52 is understood as a conclusion to Jesus' birth and childhood, and as an introduction to the Gospel narrative presenting Jesus manifesting his wisdom. I claim that all of these findings render impossible the suggestion that one should regard Luke 1:5–3:38,[49] or 1:5–4:15,[50] or 1:5–4:30,[51] or even 1:5–4:44,[52] as the first sequence of the Lukan Gospel. That would be to neglect the solemn formal beginning and abrupt shift of 3:1-2,[53] the strong separation between Luke 2 and Luke 3, and the unity of Luke 1:5–2:52. As Fitzmyer says: "Luke 3 is so closely related to the beginning of the Gospel tradition, as known from Mark and seen in the Matthean Gospel right after its infancy narrative, that one has to resist any attempt to associate chapter 3 closely with the two foregoing chapters, which constitute the infancy narrative."[54]

Seven passages have been accepted by the majority of the scholars as structuring the final redaction of Luke 1–2: (1) Announcement of John's birth (1:5-25); (2) Annunciation of Jesus' birth (1:26-38); (3) Meeting between the two expecting mothers (1:39-56); (4) Birth-Circumcision-Naming of John the Baptist (1:57-79); (5) Birth-Circumcision-Naming of Jesus (2:1-21); (6) Jesus' presentation in the Temple (2:22-39); and (7) Jesus' find-

[44] See § I.1.2.1.
[45] See § I.1.3.2.
[46] See § I.1.3.1.
[47] See § I.1.3.3.
[48] See § I.1.4.2.c.
[49] So DAVIES, "The Lucan Prologue", 78-85.
[50] So KÜMMEL, *Einleitung*, 95; SCHMID, *Das Evangelium nach Lukas*, 33.
[51] So MORGENTHALER, *Geschichtsschreibung* I, 155.
[52] So Ó FEARGHAIL, *Introduction to Luke-Acts*, 9-38.
[53] See § I.1.4.2.b.
[54] FITZMYER, *Luke I-IX*, 312.

ing in the Temple (2:40-52).[55] Except with regard to some transitional verses such as 2:21 and 2:40, there is general consensus among the scholars about the delimitation of these seven passages.[56] The closest parallelism is between the two announcements (1 and 2), and both birth-circumcision-namings (4 and 5).[57] These parallelisms are also generally accepted by scholars.[58]

---

[55] See BROWN, *Birth*, 250. According to Burrows, this division has been made according to form, but it gives a division also according to meaning (BURROWS, "The Gospel of the Infancy", 5). Other narrative criteria, such as chronological references, changes of characters and places also delimit these seven passages. In fact, each one of these seven episodes exhibits a very similar scheme with an introduction (temporal and spatial coordinates), a main action (dialogue or canticle), and a conclusion (departure).

[56] According to Funk, Lk 2:21 and 2:40 do not vary the structure from seven passages, and do not prevent correct interpretation of the whole infancy narrative: "If interpretation depends upon segmentation, then the interpreter's task in the infancy narrative, especially its last three episodes, is very daunting indeed" (FUNK, *The Poetics of Biblical Narrative*, 85).

[57] The parallelism is maintained outside of the infancy narrative, only at the beginning of Luke 3 with John's and Jesus' first preaching (Lk 3:1-18; 4:16-30), but no longer after Luke 4.

[58] Scholars affirm these parallelisms generally following BENOÎT, "L'enfance de Jean-Baptiste", 169-194, and BENOÎT, "Les récits évangéliques", 63-94. However, there are other parallelisms proposed by some scholars. GEORGE, "Le parallèle", 146-148, also suggests the parallelism of *prophetic oracles* (*Benedictus*: 1:67-79; and *Nunc Dimittis*: 2:29-32). However, he himself recognizes the weakness of this parallelism: the *Benedictus* is Jewish in its form, language, and thought; in addition, it comes from a pre-existent source. The *Nunc Dimittis* does not, and its content and thought are focused on Jesus. The chronological and spatial contexts are different, as well: the *Benedictus* takes place immediately after John's circumcision, in the very same place, being part of the same passage, while the *Nunc Dimittis* takes place 32 days after Jesus' circumcision, in another location, the Temple, and with new characters, Simeon and Anna. In addition, George proposes the parallelism of the expressions σωτηρία (1:71.77; 2:30), λύτρωσις (1:68; 2:38), and εἰρήνη (1:79; 2:29). However, in both prophetic canticles these expressions refer to Jesus, and not to John the Baptist in the *Benedictus* and Jesus in the *Nunc Dimittis*. Furthermore, if the *Bendictus* and the *Nunc Dimittis* were parallel, what would we do with Simeon's prophecy and the account of Anna? Lastly, the scene of Zechariah is introduced by means of the conjunction καί maintaining the relationship with the previous scene; on the contrary, Simeon's scene is introduced by a temporal subordinate phrase which makes a separation with the former pericope. The information about John's (1:80) and

When parallelism is found in adjacent episodes, the term *diptych* is often used. As the passages of both announcements (1 and 2) and both birth-circumcision-namings are adjacent (4 and 5), they are called diptychs. For several scholars these two diptychs make up the structure of Luke 1–2, a structure divided in two parts composed of two diptychs.[59] According to these scholars, the last two passages (6 and 7) are part of the second side of the second diptych after Jesus' birth. All the different structures that divide Luke 1–2 into two parts have the same difficulties. First, the sequence recounting the birth of Jesus (Luke 2) encompasses approximately as much space in the narrative as all the other three sections combined: announcement of John, Annunciation of Jesus, and birth of John (Luke 1). Second, proposing such a parallel as that of John's birth (Lk 1:57-80) and Jesus' birth (Luke 2) makes the mistake of comparing the accounts of Jesus in the Temple (Lk 2:22-52) with the lack of any account of John in the Temple.

There are no narrative parallels in the John the Baptist story for the last two episodes, Jesus' Presentation in the Temple (6) and Jesus' finding in the Temple (7), and so these episodes cause difficulty for those who hold for only two diptychs. The last two passages break the narrative parallelism between John the Baptist

---

Jesus' *growing up* (2:40; 2:52) has been proposed as parallel also by LAURENTIN, *Structure*, 27-32. Nevertheless, Galbiati rejects the importance of this parallelism. He differentiates between *passage* and simple *information*. The information about John's and Jesus' growing is a simple piece of information consisting of one verse (1:80; 2:40; 2:52). According to Galbiati, the important parallelism, the narrative parallelism, happens between passages, and not between simple information (GALBIATI, "La circoncisione", 37-45). In addition, there are two depictions of Jesus' growing up (Lk 2:40.52), while there is only one about John's (Lk 1:80). I believe that the structural parallelism obtains only until Jesus' birth-circumcision-naming (Lk 2:21).

[59] LAURENTIN, *Structure*, 28-31, proposes a division between the sections before the births (1:5-56) and after the births (1:57–2:52). Each one of these two parts adds a complementary episode: the visitation, before the births (1:42-56), and the passages of Jesus in the Temple, after the births (2:22-52). Similar structures are suggested by BOYCE, "For You Today a Savior", 375, MALICK, "Literary Approach", 104-105, Ó FEARGHAIL, *Introduction to Luke-Acts*, 12-18), and KLUTZ, "The Value", 83, who speaks of *anticipations* (1:5-56), and *fulfillments* (1:57–2:52).

and Jesus in favor of Jesus who is the only one who has two passages in the Temple.[60]

In addition, the last passages are directly connected: both passages take place in the Temple of Jerusalem; both passages begin with the expression "going up" to Jerusalem (2:22; 2:42); in both passages Joseph and Mary are referred to as the "parents of Jesus" (2:27; 2:41.43); in both passages Joseph is called the "father of Jesus" (2:33; 2:48); both passages finish with the expression "coming back to Nazareth" (2:39; 2:51) and a statement about "Jesus' growth" (2:40.52).[61] These unifying bonds in the two episodes are the reasons why many other scholars propose a third diptych. These agree that the structure of Luke 1–2 is divided into three diptychs, into three different parts.[62]

This third part that breaks the parallelism between John and Jesus is underlined by the structure of Luke 1–2 because it has no parallel. Yet it is not only the structure that underlines these last two passages. As proved by Laurentin and other scholars after him, the content of the entire Lukan narrative also underlines them.[63] The presence of Jesus in the Temple is understood as the fulfillment of the

[60] As we will see in n. 72, the superiority of Jesus over John is present already in the content of both diptychs of John and Jesus. However, with these last two passages of Jesus in the Temple, without any parallel in John, Jesus' superiority over John is reflected in the structure itself.

[61] See FREED, *The Stories of Jesus' Birth*, 144-148.

[62] BURROWS, "The Gospel of the Infancy", 4-6, proposes: (1) diptych of announcements (to Zechariah and to Mary, including the visitation); (2) diptych of nativities (of John and of Jesus); and (3) diptych of Temple mysteries (presentation and finding). A similar structure is suggested by DRURY, *Tradition and Design*, 64, STRAMARE, *Vangelo*, 316, PÉREZ RODRÍGUEZ, *La infancia de Jesús*, 57, and PERROT, *L'enfance de Jésus*, 38. On the contrary, DAVIS, "The Literary Structure", 215-229, structures Luke 1–2 in three different parts and in very different way. He claims that Luke 1–2 is structured around the three visits of the angel of the Lord: (1) the visit to Zechariah (1:5-25); (2) the visit to Mary (1:26-38); and (3) the visit to the shepherds (2:1-20). Davis' proposal has not been accepted by the scholars.

[63] On a presentation on Laurentin's work, assessing his discoveries of the OT background of Luke 1–2, especially in connection with the entrance of Jesus in the Temple, but criticizing the lack of distinction he makes between tradition and redaction, see BOVON, *Vingt-cinq ans*, 172-175.

coming of the Lord to his Temple (Ml 3:1-24; Dn 9:24). On the one hand, speaking geographically, the tradition of Ml 3:1 could be used by Luke to describe the entrance of Jesus into the Temple, "I shall send my messenger to clear a way before me. And suddenly the Lord whom you seek will come to his Temple." In fact, the sequence of Luke 1–2 evoques the prophecy of Ml 3:1 with the entrance of the Lord into the Temple at the messianic age. First Jesus is proclaimed as "Christ, the Lord" (Lk 2:11) and shortly thereafter Jesus is made to come into the Temple (Lk 2:22).[64] In other words, the narration is geographically oriented towards Jerusalem. Jesus' narration is an irresistible ascent from Nazareth towards Jerusalem in four different stages: the first two to the hill country of Judah (visitation and birth); the last two to the Temple of Jerusalem (Presentation and finding). On the other hand, chronologically, the narration is also orientated towards the Presentation of Jesus. The prophecy of the 70 weeks of Dn 9:24 is fulfilled in the chronological succession of the Lukan infancy narrative: from the announcement to Zechariah until the Presentation of Jesus, exactly 490 days, or 70 weeks, pass.[65] Thus,

---

[64] Laurentin and other scholars suggest that the words of the angel to Zechariah (Lk 1:17: "With the spirit and power of Elijah, he will go before him to reconcile fathers to their children") recall Ml 3:23-24 ("I shall send you the prophet Elijah [...] He will reconcile parents to their children and children to their parents"). They claim that the coming of Jesus into the Temple inaugurates the eschatological dwelling of the Lord in the Temple that was promised by the prophet. (LAURENTIN, *Les Évangiles de l'enfance*, 82-85; STRAMARE, "Compiuti i giorni", 199-205; STRAMARE, "Significato esegetico e teologico", 40-41). BROWN, *Birth*, 444-446, also defends the importance of this tradition.

[65] LAURENTIN, *Structure*, 43-63, follows an intuition of BURROWS, "The Gospel of the Infancy", 41, in considering Dn 9:24 and the prophecy of the 70 weeks. After these 70 weeks "the transgression will stop and sin will end, guilt will be expiated, everlasting justice will be introduced" (Dn 9:24). Thus: six months (Lk 1:26.36) of Elizabeth's pregnancy equals 180 days; nine months of Mary's pregnancy equals 270 (Lk 2:6); and the forty days of the purification adds a final 40. Laurentin affirms that the name of Gabriel at the beginning of Luke's Gospel shows us that it refers to the prophecy of Daniel. Indeed, the name of the angel Gabriel only appears in Dn 8:16; 9:21. In addition, the muteness imposed on Zechariah resembles the account in Dn 10:15 because the awesome vision leaves Daniel unable to speak. The chronological connection between the Daniel tradition and the passage of the Presentation in the Temple is examined by STRAMARE, "Significato esegetico e teologico", 41-45, and PÉREZ RODRÍGUEZ, *La infancia de*

Laurentin maintains that there is an interaction in our pericope between the story of Jesus and the prophecies in Ml 3:1-24 and Dn 9:24 to underline the presence of Jesus in the Temple. According to Laurentin, these last two pericopes, without any parallel in John's narration, constitute a double conclusion of the Lukan infancy narrative.[66] Jesus in the Temple, according to Fitzmyer, following the Lukan motif of moving Jesus toward Jerusalem and its Temple, constitutes the arrival point of Luke 1–2.[67]

Recognizing that none of the analyses of the structure has been able to avoid a certain amount of subjectivism and that no one is entirely convincing,[68] I believe that the structure generally accepted by scholars, and more suitable to the text, is the structure made up of three different diptychs: the diptych of the annunciations, the diptych of the birth-circumcision-namings, and the diptych of Jesus in the Temple. The first two diptychs, being composed in one part of John and in another of Jesus, are linked by the meeting between the mothers. The passage of the visitation is like a pivot-pin between both diptychs which parallel John and Jesus. The structure stresses the last diptych that breaks the parallelism between John the Baptist and Jesus.

Jesús, 61, as well. However, BROWN, *Birth*, 446, n. 6, is dubious of the attempt to force Luke's chronological indications into a sum of 490 days.

[66] LAURENTIN, *Les Évangiles de l'enfance*, 39-40, DEL AGUA PÉREZ, "Los evangelios de la infancia", 383, and ARANDA, "Los evangelios de la infancia", 811, follow Laurentin. According to BERLINGIERI, *Il lieto annuncio*, 94-97, the Presentation in the Temple is a conclusive climax of Luke 1–2; and the twelve-year-old Jesus in the Temple would be a second conclusive climax.

[67] See FITZMYER, *Luke I-IX*, 314. And Schürmann defines these last episodes as the "powerful ending of all the prelude Luke 1–2" (SCHÜRMANN, *Das Lukasevangelium* I, 133).

[68] Brown suggests that the difficulties regarding the structure of Luke 1–2 stems from not recognizing that there were two stages of Lukan composition, namely, a basic narrative constructed by Luke, and later additions by Luke. According to BROWN, *Birth*, 250 -251, this is why the hymns are structurally awkward, unbalancing the neat pattern of diptychs, and the episodes in which they are placed are not parallel, the visitation and John's birth-circumcision-naming.

Announcement of John	1:5-25
Announcement of Jesus	1:26-38

The meeting between the two mothers	1:39-56

Birth-circumcision-naming of John	1:57-80
Birth-circumcision-naming of Jesus	2:1-21

Presentation of *Jesus in the Temple*	2:22-39
Finding of *Jesus in the Temple*	2:40-52

1.2 The Unified Plot of the Sequence Luke 1–2

The categories of *unified plot* and *episodic plot* are often used to explain sequence-narratives, or macro-narratives.[69] In a unified plot, all the parts and different micro-narratives are relevant to the whole narrative and have a bearing on the outcome of the events recounted. Every part presupposes what precedes and prepares for what follows. The plot of the sequence-narrative or macro-narrative overhangs and encompasses the plots of the micro-narratives which it contains. On the contrary, in an episodic plot the order of parts can be changed, the reader can skip a part without harm; every part is a unit in itself and does not require the clear and complete knowledge of the former episodes to be understood. I contend that Luke 1–2 develops a *unified plot*. The plot is made up of linked elements which emphasize the unity of the plot. The narrator links the different elements of the narration by means of (1) structure, (2) different passages, (3) characters, and (4) times.

First (1), the *parallel structure* of the sequence Luke 1–2 unifies the plot through the similarities and differences in the parallelism between John and Jesus, which the preceding tradition already associated together (see Mk 1:1-8). Parallelism is treated as a linguistic tool well known in the Hellenistic culture of the world at that

[69] See MARGUERAT – BOURQUIN, *Récits bibliques*, 71-72 [55-56]; SKA, *Our Fathers*, 17-19.

time.[70] The parallelism underlines the similarities between John the Baptist and Jesus: they both come to fulfill the same divine design which starts with their announcements, births, circumcisions and namings. Yet the parallelism emphasizes the differences between John and Jesus and the superiority of Jesus over John, especially through the structure[71] and the expressions used.[72] The similarities of the comparison come from the Hebrew tradition,[73] while the similarities and differences come from a Hellenistic tradition. George claims that the Hellenistic parallelisms are antithetic: they underline the antitheses or

[70] See, for example, *The Parallel lives* by Plutarch. CLARK, *Parallel Lives*, 81-113, speaks about the techniques of comparisons in Greek literature and in Luke 1–2.

[71] The last diptych of Luke 1–2 concerns only Jesus. John is announced in the Temple (1:9), but he never appears there, while Jesus is presented (2:23) and stays in the Temple for three days (2:46).

[72] [1] John is a great prophet before the Lord (1:15), the prophet of the Most High (1:76), while Jesus is the Great, the Son of the Most High (1:32); [2] John is born from a sterile mother (1:18), while Jesus is born from a virgin (1:34-35); [3] John is filled with the Holy Spirit even in his mother's womb (1:15), while Jesus' conception involves a creative act of God through the Holy Spirit (1:35); [4] John is the forerunner of the Messiah (Lk 1:17.76), while Jesus is the Messiah (2:11); [5] John will be called prophet before the Lord (1:16-17), while Jesus will be called the Lord, the Savior (2:11); [6] John does not speak, while Jesus proclaims his divine filiation (2:49); [7] John will make ready for the Lord a prepared people (1:17), while Jesus will actually rule over the house of Israel and possess a kingdom without end (1:33); [8] John's parents are "upright in God's sight" (1:6), while Mary is the "favored one" (1:28); [9] John's father queries the angel and is struck dumb (1:19-22), while Jesus' mother queries the angel and is reassured (1:34-38); [10] John's birth is not introduced by any historical and political information, while Jesus' birth is solemnly introduced (2:1-2); [11] After John's birth there are no more angelic announcements, while after Jesus' birth a multitude of angels of heaven announces the importance of Jesus (2:13-14); and [12] John's mother is not praised, while Jesus' mother is praised by John's mother (1:42a). Finally, outside of the infancy narrative, John himself breaks down the parallelism affirming that Jesus is more powerful than him and that he is not fit to undo the strap of Jesus' sandals (3:16).

[73] According to GEORGE, "Le parallèle", 147.171, the OT uses parallelism to underline the similarities of the characters: Moses and Joshua; Moses and Elijah; Elijah and Elisha. They are all like the John-Jesus parallelism because they are implicit and show the similarities between the two. PERROT, *L'enfance de Jésus*, 37, reminds us that in the first century in Palestine the rabbis were remembered by pairs, as Hillel and Shammai, underlining their similarities. DÍEZ MACHO, *La historicidad*, 15-19, affirms that parallelism, underlining the similarities, is a feature of the *midrash*.

differences.[74] In addition, Shuler has underlined the importance of differences in the parallelisms used in Greek rhetorical compositions. For Shuler, the reader in the Greco-Roman milieu of comparison was accustomed to contrasting images.[75] And Aletti affirms that "the syncrisis serves not only to underline the similarities, but it serves to underline the differences."[76] The originality of Luke is to have developed a Hebrew parallelism into a Greek syncrisis.[77]

The continuous comparison between John and Jesus clearly integrates the different passages of Luke 1–2 and develops a unified plot. In addition, the contrast between two different characters is a technique of characterization. The characterization stands out more clearly if it is contrasted with an alternative, for example, John and Jesus. The syncrisis between John and Jesus not only unifies the plot of the infancy narrative, but even helps to characterize Jesus. For example, the superiority of Jesus is the primary result underlined by the differences between John and Jesus, but not the only one. The references to John the Baptist in Luke 1–2 point to a ministry within the Jewish nation. John is to turn the sons of Israel to the Lord their God, and thus to make ready for the Lord Jesus a people prepared. His commission is for Israel (Lk 1:17b.77).[78] In comparison, Jesus' characterization is more universalistic (2:31.32).[79]

---

[74] See GEORGE, "Le parallèle", 147-171.

[75] SHULER, "Rhetorical Character", 178-180, gives numerous examples from ARISTOTLE, *Rhet.*, 1.9.20-25 (1366b), and especially from *Parallel Lives* by PLUTARCH, where many comparisons are made through similarities and differences, especially through the contrasts.

[76] ALETTI, "Le Christ raconté", 37. Syncrisis consists in putting the activity of two characters in parallel distinguishing them or clarifying the continuity from one to the other.

[77] According to MARGUERAT – BOURQUIN, *Récits bibliques*, 161, Luke is the champion of syncrisis in the NT (Lk 5:18-25; 8:49-56; Acts 9:36-43; 20:7-12). Luke is faithful to the Hebrew tradition while making an effort to reformulate his message for a new audience. A Jewish-Christian or a Gentile-Christian could understand it. TROMPF, *Historical Recurrence*, 116-178, believes that Luke-Acts reflects patterns of recurrence from both Hebrew and Greco-Roman traditions.

[78] Outside of the infancy narrative, the ministry described in Lk 3:2b-20 corresponds to this limitation in the region of the Jordan River. And Acts 13:24 affirms that "John proclaimed a baptism of repentance for the whole people of Israel." The geographical isolation of John's ministry in the area of the Jordan from that of Jesus in Galilee, Judea and Jerusalem, highlights this contrast.

[79] The only universal dimension of John's ministry is the commentary that the nar-

Another structural element which unifies the plot of Luke 1–2 is the *scheme announcement-fulfillment-praise*. Farris highlighted the importance of the scheme announcement-fulfillment-praise in the hymns of Luke 1–2, and the relationship of these hymns with their close context. The hymns always accomplish the third step of this scheme with a proclamation that serves as the unifying theme of the infancy narrative. In the three examples below the narrative follows the same pattern: there is an announcement to someone, this divine promise is effectively fulfilled, and the character reacts in praise.[80]

Character	Announcement	Fulfillment	Praise
Zechariah	Pregnancy of his wife	His son's birth	*Benedictus*
Mary	Her pregnancy	John (unborn) greets Jesus (unborn)	*Magnificat*
Simeon	His vision of the Messiah	His vision of Jesus	*Nunc Dimittis*

Secondly (2), the seven *passages* accepted by the majority of the scholars, especially the diptychs, are directly linked. The diptych of the two announcements of births is unified by the same form of announcement, the same messenger, the angel Gabriel (1:19.26), and the reference to Elizabeth in the Annunciation to Mary. Elizabeth's pregnancy helps Mary to say yes to her own pregnancy (1:34-38). The first two diptychs, the announcements and the births, are linked by the meeting between both mothers (Lk 1:39-56), which interweaves both diptychs. The meeting between Elizabeth and Mary unifies the announcement with the births through the presence of the children in their mother's wombs and because it is the only passage which concerns both families at the same time. The dip-

rator gives, outside of Luke 1–2, quoting Is 40:3-5: "All humanity will see the salvation of God" (Lk 3:6).

[80] See FARRIS, *Hymns*, 100-101.152-153. SIFFER, "Les hymnes de Lc 1–2", 299-302, follows Farris and even claims that this scheme is developed in the whole Luke-Acts, especially in some speeches of Acts (pp. 302-308).

tych of the announcements is in connection with the diptych of the births not only because the latter is the consequence of the former, but also because the namings which follow John's and Jesus' birth (1:60.63; 2:21) are foretold in the announcements (1:13; 1:31). The diptych of the two birth-circumcision-namings is unified by the same form and logical development of events. After the diptych of John's and Jesus' birth-circumcision-naming, there follow the passages concerning the infant Jesus in the Temple. All of the passages are linked by logical ordering.

Thirdly (3), the *characters* also are directly connected. John and Jesus are related through family connections, their mothers being cousins (1:36). The main characters are presented in order through the different passages of the sequence. First are introduced Zechariah and Elizabeth (1:5), John's parents (1:13), then Joseph and Mary (1:27), Jesus' parents (1:31) and, finally, the connection between them (1:36). The very same order is maintained through the diptych of births-circumcision-naming. After Jesus' birth, John's parents do not appear any more. The presence of the Holy Spirit throughout the infancy narrative likewise unifies the passages of the sequence. The Holy Spirit is present in the announcement of John's birth (1:15), the announcement of Jesus' birth (1:35), the meeting between Elizabeth and Mary (1:41), the birth-circumcision-naming of John (1:67), and the presentation of Jesus in the Temple (2:25.26).[81] The presence of angels, Gabriel (1:19.26), an anonymous angel (2:9.10), and a multitude of angels (2:13.15) also unifies the sequence.[82] Instead of isolated units, the reader finds that the characters are profoundly related in the different passages. Jesus in particular, who remains until the end of the infancy narrative, creates and unifies the plot of the entire sequence.[83]

Fourth (4), there is a *chronological link* between the different passages, established by numerous time markers scattered throughout

[81] The Holy Spirit appears in the rest of Luke's Gospel only in Lk 3:16.22; 4:1; 10:21; 11:13; 12:10.12.

[82] After these occurrences an angel appears in Luke's Gospel only in 22:43; 24:23.

[83] Chatman claims that Jesus' character makes the plot (CHATMAN, *Story and Discourse*, 22).

the Lukan infancy narrative. The diptych of the announcements is linked by a chronological reference. The Annunciation to Mary starts with the expression "in the sixth month" from the conception of John (1:26), the previous passage. A few days after the conception of Jesus, in the following passage, Mary goes into the hill country to a town in Judah to meet Elizabeth (1:39) and stays with her some three months (1:56).[84] Both references, "in the sixth month," and "Mary stayed with her some three months" add nine months. This means that Mary probably stayed with Elizabeth until John's birth and circumcision; Luke chronologically finishes a topic before starting the following one. Both parts of the diptych of John's and Jesus' birth-circumcision-naming are introduced by the same chronological expressions. Their births happen "when the time came for her to have her child, and she gave birth to a son" (1:57; 2:6-7). And both circumcision-namings happen "when the eighth day came and the child was to be circumcised, they gave him the name" (1:59; 2:21). Both passages of the diptych of the events of Jesus in the Temple are introduced by a chronological expression which refers to the previous pericope (2:22.42). Finally, the different chronological expressions throughout the infancy narrative are often related to each other (1:26.39.59; 2:21.22.42) and help to characterize Jesus throughout his progressive growth. It is a *unified plot of life by time* in which life is marked by chronological succession.[85] In fact, the whole infancy narrative is marked by time information of the life of Jesus and John.

The fact that the Lukan infancy narrative is a unified plot implies that the different passages are relevant to the whole narrative and gradually advance the plot. As every part presupposes what precedes there is a gradual presentation of the information about Jesus, and the highpoint should therefore be found at the end of Luke 1–2.

---

[84] The angel announces what Elizabeth's self-concealment has until then kept hidden (1:24), prompting Mary's journey.

[85] CULPEPPER, *Anatomy of the Fourth Gospel*, 103, who uses this concept of *unified plot of life by time* to define the plot of the Gospel of John, opposing it to the *plot of life by values*.

1.3 The Different Passages in the Unified Plot of Luke 1–2

After having analyzed the general structure and unified plot of the sequence Luke 1–2, we can study the narrative features of the different pericopes and how they contribute to the general plot. I will analyze these features in the generally accepted seven passages of the Lukan infancy narrative, except the Presentation in the Temple (2:22-39) which has been analyzed at length in Ch. III.

1.3.1 The Plots and Commission Statements throughout Luke 1–2

In § 1.2 we described the plot of the sequence Luke 1–2 as a *unified plot*. Now we have to analyze the kind of plot of the different passages which make up the sequence. Thus, we will be able to better know the importance and role of each pericope throughout the whole sequence in characterizing Jesus, and to recognize the presence of commission statements in each passage which disclose the program of action by a particular character, and provide keys to the general plot of the sequence.

The plot of the passage of the *announcement of John* is a *revelation plot*. There is no acceptance by Zechariah, there is no climactic point. There is no resolution because it seems that there is no possibility of not conceiving John. In addition, there are other typical features of a revelation plot. There is a vision (1:11), an audition (1:13-17), dialogues (1:18.19), and different expressions which reveal the identity of John (1:14-17) by a showing scene. From v. 14 the passage is focused on John and his initial *commission statement*: "he will bring back many of the Israelites to the Lord their God [...] He will reconcile fathers to their children and the disobedient to the wisdom of the upright, preparing for the Lord a people fit for him" (1:16-17).[86] There is an increasing knowledge of John's conception and his future life (1:18).

The plot of the pericope of the *Annunciation of Jesus* is a *resolution plot*: Will Mary say yes to the announcement of the angel? Will she accept to conceive and bear a son? The entire passage is directed toward the answer of Mary. The perplexity of Mary is refuted by the

[86] All of the verbs which refer to John's actions are in the future (1:14.15.16.17).

words of the angel:"Do not be afraid" (1:29-30). The tension of the plot increases with the question of Mary:"But how can this come about, since I have no knowledge of man?" (1:34). Mary's question is answered through the power of the Holy Spirit (1:35) and the example of her relative Elizabeth "for nothing is impossible to God" (1:36-37). Everything in the text aims at convincing Mary to answer yes. The climax of progressive tension arrives with the resolution of the plot and turning point of the narrative which happens right at the end of the pericope: the answer of Mary in the last verse of the passage, "let it happen to me as you have said" (1:38). Afterwards the angel can leave her.[87]

Despite the expressions concerning Jesus (1:32-33.35b), the annunciation is a *commission statement*, not of Jesus, but of Mary. In fact, Jesus' characterization is focused on *who* Jesus is, and not on *what* he will do.[88] The presence in Mary of God's favor (1:30) is mentioned so that she might accept her commission statement: "You are to conceive in your womb and bear a son" (1:31).[89] The resolution of the plot depends on her acceptance of her commission statement as mother of Jesus. This is the reason why Mary (1:34) and the reader ask, "How can this come about?"

The plot of the pericope of the *meeting between Elizabeth and Mary* is a *revelation plot*. There is no turning point, nor resolution at all. As soon as Elizabeth heard Mary's greeting, "the child leapt in her womb and Elizabeth was filled with the Holy Spirit" (1:41) to speak what her son could only express by leaping. The words of Elizabeth are answered by the words of Mary. The presence of

---

[87] The angel has been sent (1:26), enters and greets (1:28), delievers his message (1:30-33.35-38), receives her response (1:38a), and departs (1:38b). The announcements of John and Jesus have the same form. However, narratively, the presence of Mary's answer, the turning point of the narration, makes of the Annunciation a resolution plot.

[88] The only expression about *what* Jesus will do is that he will reign over the house of Jacob for ever (v. 33).

[89] Certainly Jesus is also described. Mary will bear a son who will be great and the Son of the Most High (1:32). However, the emphasis falls on the fact that Mary is to conceive in her womb and bear a son (1:31: ἰδοὺ συλλήμψῃ ἐν γαστρὶ καὶ τέξῃ υἱόν). This is what the emphatic interjection ἰδού underlines. The following verses explain who will be that son that Mary is to conceive in her womb (1:32-33).

dialogues (1:42-45) and monologues (1:46-55) is a distinctive feature of a revelation plot. In addition, the predominance of the actors (Elizabeth and Mary) over the actions, they only meet and speak to each other,[90] emphasizes the precedence of the plot of revelation over the plot of resolution. Yet who is revealed? Throughout the *Magnificat* there is no direct reference to Jesus.[91] When Elizabeth says to Mary that she is happy because she has believed that the promise made to her by God would be fulfilled (1:45), Mary answers by proclaiming the greatness of God (1:46) and the reasons she has to proclaim it. Mary's hymn shows the mercy of God regarding Mary and Israel, being simply focused on God's action in Mary and Israel. The subject of all of the phrases is always God. "He has looked" upon the humiliation of his servant (1:48), "he has done" great things for Mary (1:49), "he has used" the power of his arm, "he has routed" the arrogant of heart (1:51), "he has pulled" down princes from their thrones and "raised" high the lowly (1:52), "he has filled" the starving with good things and "sent" the rich away empty (1:53), and "he has come" to the help of Israel (1:54).[92] The *Magnificat* is a revelation of God's mercy and action. The passage develops a revelation plot in which the knowledge of God's action is increased. And there is no *commission statement*, either of Mary, or of Jesus, or of God.[93]

The plot of the episode of the *birth-circumcision-naming of John* is also a *revelation plot*. Again, the absence of any transforming action which resolves the plot,[94] the presence of a long monologue

---

[90] On the importance of the *meeting* between Elizabeth and Mary in the passage of the visitation see CHAPPUIS-JUILLARD, *Le temps des rencontres*, 57-60.

[91] Certainly Elizabeth's words are focussed on Mary and her fruit, who are blessed by her (1:42). However, the extension of these expressions addressed to Mary and Jesus, one verse, is not comparable with Mary's words in the *Magnificat* (1:46-55).

[92] The only time in which God is not the subject, the subject is God's mercy: "His faithful love extends age after age" (1:50).

[93] The reasons expressed by Mary cannot be a commission statement of God because all of the divine actions have already been accomplished, and are expressed in the aorist (1:46-55).

[94] The only resolution is Zechariah's loss of speech (1:22). However, precisely this resolution provokes the revelation plot through Zechariah's monologue (1:67-79).

and the predominance of the actors over the actions emphasize the existence of a revelation plot. Yet who is revealed in this plot? All the people throughout the hill-country of Judea were astonished because of the extraordinary birth of John and his surprising name (1:63). "What will this child turn out to be?" they wondered (1:66). The canticle of Zechariah responds to this question by describing the figure of John the Baptist and his role in the history of salvation. The emphatic meaning of the expression καὶ σὺ δέ, παιδίον (1:76) underlines the central role of John in the *Benedictus*. The passage is a revelation plot, but it reveals the personage of John the Baptist.[95]

The revelation plot of the character of John the Baptist introduces some kind of *commission statement*, but it is of John's vocation. He shall be a prophet of the Most High, will go before the Lord to prepare a way for him, will give his people knowledge of salvation through the forgiveness of their sins (1:76-77).[96]

The plot of the pericope of *Jesus' birth-circumcision-naming* is a *revelation plot*. The description of the reason for the journey (2:1-5), the actions after Mary's giving birth (2:7), the vision of the angel of the Lord (2:9) and of a great throng of the hosts of heaven (2:13), and the presence of monologues (2:10-12.14.15) underline the *showing scene*, which is a typically distinctive feature of a revelation plot. The reader, almost present in the scene as an eyewitness, learns what is being revealed in front of him. And who is revealed in this showing? The long introduction begins by presenting Jesus through his ancestry (2:1-5), and both announcements of the angels present Jesus to the shepherds. The passage is continually marked by expressions which refer to the things that are being heard and seen concerning Jesus (2: 10.13.15.17.18.20). Finally, everybody, even Mary, is astonished by what they hear about Jesus (2:19). Although it is a revelation plot

---

[95] The references to Jesus are indirect and in connection with the relationship between John and Jesus. Zechariah recognizes that the role of the infant John is conditional upon Jesus' role.

[96] This commission statement, expressed in the future, coincides with the words that the angel said about John before his birth (1:15-17) and with the presentation of John's public life (3:3-6).

of Jesus, his presentation is not very extensive. The reader learns *who* Jesus is, the Savior, the Messiah Lord (2:11), but nothing is said about *what* he will fulfill;[97] it is not a *commission statement*.

I argue that the passage of the *finding of Jesus in the Temple* (2:40-52) has two different plots. There is an overlapping of plots because the end of the *resolution plot* becomes the beginning of the more important plot, the *revelation plot*. First, the narrator tells how Joseph and Mary lose Jesus because he remains in Jerusalem (2:43). From this verse onwards, the question for the readers is: "Why has Jesus stayed in Jerusalem?" For three days they have been looking for him. The worry of Joseph and Mary becomes the reader's question: "Are they going to find Jesus?" The turning point happens when they find him among the teachers, in the Temple, listening, asking, and responding. Jesus is presented as a wise teacher whose knowledge surprises the teachers of the Temple and even Mary, who asks: "Why have you done this to us?" This question allows to develop the revelation plot: Jesus has to stay with the things of his Father. Jesus is presented in the Temple by the narrator as a wise teacher among the teachers, and by Jesus himself as the Son of God.

Although we find a revelation of Jesus, we cannot speak about a *commission statement* of Jesus. Jesus is presented through his identity as God's Son and wise young man, but nothing is said about his mission. The reader learns about *who* Jesus is, but not about *what* he will do.

Throughout the Lukan infancy narrative, the kind of plot of the passages concerning Jesus undergoes a progressive evolution. The first pericope, the Annunciation, develops a plot of resolution in which Mary's acceptance to bear a son is the turning point. After her acceptance, the rest of the pericopes concerning Jesus, his birth-circumcision-naming, his Presentation in the Temple, and his finding in the Temple, develop a *revelation plot* of

---

[97] It is striking that while in the passage of John's birth-circumcision-naming we find his commission statement, there is no such statement in the pericope of Jesus' birth-circumcision-naming. His commission statement appears in the Presentation in the Temple (2:30-32.34-35).

Jesus.[98] The character of Jesus is increasingly developed through these revelation plots. However, the Presentation in the Temple includes the only *commission statement* of Jesus throughout Luke 1–2. As a unified revelation plot, which is more interested in knowledge than in action, the knowledge is focused on *who* Jesus is. Only in the Presentation in the Temple is the plot focused not only on who Jesus is but also on *what* he will do.

1.3.2 Jesus' Characterization throughout Luke 1–2

The unified plot develops a gradual presentation of Jesus in which considerable information about the identity of Jesus is given to the reader: he is descended from David (1:32-33), Son of God (1:35), Savior (2:11), etc. The different pericopes of the unified plot progressively build this revelation of the main character. This is the reason why I will pay attention to the order in which Jesus' traits are given to the reader. Looking for the degree of progressive characterization, I will pay attention to the *reprises* of traits of Jesus, which display the characterization of Jesus in its full range.[99]

In the first passage, the *announcement of John's birth* (1:5-25), there is no reference to Jesus. The first references to Jesus happen in the *Annunciation of his birth*. The expressions that refer to Jesus' identity can be put in the following five groups according to their topic: his name (1:31: "you must name him Jesus," Ἰησοῦς);[100] his greatness

---

[98] The last two passages start with a resolution plot which introduces a revelation plot.

[99] It is not my aim to study the whole meaning of the different passages since that would take us too far from my goal. I will limit my focus to the number and quality of the different expressions which refer to Jesus in the different pericopes. A dissertation of a whole narrative study of Luke 1–2, COLERIDGE, *The Birth*, has been already published, which studies two different dimensions of the whole sequence: the divine initiative through his visitation and the human response to the divine initiative. As I am studying the Presentation of Jesus, I will focus only on the characterization of Jesus and will not enter into the human response through faith.

[100] While Matthew explains the reason for Jesus' name, "because he is the one who is to save his people" (Mt 1:21), Luke makes no such reference. However, Jesus' name speaks of his condition as Savior because heaven-given names usually have etymological significance. According to BURNETT, "Characterization", 17-18, the proper noun, especially in classical texts like the Gospels, becomes the crucial factor

(1:32: "he will be great," μέγας);[101] his divine filiation (1:32: "he will be called the Son of the Most High," υἱὸς ὑψίστου;[102] and 1:35: "the Son of God," υἱὸς θεοῦ);[103] his Davidic royalty (1:32-33: "He will reign over the house of Jacob forever, and of his kingdom there will be no end," βασιλεία);[104] and his holiness (1:35: "he will be holy," ἅγιος).[105]

In the passage of the *meeting between Elizabeth and Mary*, Jesus is presented by Elizabeth as the "blessed fruit of Mary's womb" (1:42: εὐλογημένος) and as Elizabeth's Lord (1:43, Mary is "the

---

in the construction of a character. To come on stage nameless is to be declared faceless and to bear a name is to assume an identity, to become a singular existent with a future in the story in connection with its name. Bovon says: "in the subtext of Luke's composition, one does sense a reverence for this name, as in the hymn of Ph 2:10" (BOVON, *Lukas* I, 74 [51]).

[101] LAURENTIN, *Structure*, 36, calls attention to the absolute use of μέγας, and to the fact that in the LXX the absolute is an attribute of *Yhwh* himself (Ps 48:2; 86:10; 135:5; 145:3) whereas the adjective is qualified when it is used of human beings (2 S 19:33; Si 48:22).

[102] The expression "he will be called" expresses what one is, so that it means no less than "he will be." Interchangeability of the two phrases is seen by comparing Mt 5:9, "they will be called sons of God," and its parallel in Lk 6:35, "you will be sons of the Most High." We can say the same of the expression "will be called Son of God" (1:35) (see BROWN, *Birth*, 289). In the NT the name "Most High" for God is encountered most frequently in Luke (1:32.35.76; 6:35; 8:28; Acts 7:48; 16:17). Outside of the Lukan work it only appears in Mk 5:7, and Heb 7:1. On this title as the preeminence of the divine Father of Jesus see BERTRAM, "ὕψιστος", 618-619.

[103] "The sense of υἱὸς θεοῦ is no different from that of υἱὸς ὑψίστου" says NOLLAND, *Luke 1-9:20*, 55. Luke uses a significant word: διό. The Spirit will come upon Jesus; *therefore* he will be Son of God by his being, for he was, unlike anyone else, conceived through the power of the Holy Spirit. Jesus is called the Son of God in a different sense than Israel, ancient kings, or prophets.

[104] Luke closely links his being "Son of the Most High" with his role as eternal king in the restoration of the house of David (1:32). STANTON, "Messianism and Christology", 87, after comparing Lk 1:32-33, 2 S 7:9-16 and *4Q174*, affirms that "there is nothing distinctively Christian in vv. 32-33 of Luke, except that the expected Davidic Messiah has been identified with Jesus."

[105] As the Holy Spirit will come upon his mother (1:35), so he will be holy. While ἅγιος could mean "set apart" or "consacreted," the context favors the meaning of "holy" just as God's spirit is "holy."

mother of my Lord," κύριος).[106] However, throughout the entire canticle of Mary there is no direct reference to Jesus.[107] In addition, Mary's canticle is clearly directed to God's action in herself and in Israel. On the one hand, the canticle of Mary blesses the greatness of the Lord "because he has looked upon the humiliation of his servant. Yes, from now onwards all generations will call me blessed" (1:48).[108] On the other hand, God has remembered his mercy to Israel (1:54) "according to the promise he made to our ancestors, to Abraham and to his descendants forever" (1:55). Implicitly, the fulfillment of the promises made by God to Israel is affirmed.

There are two clear references to Jesus throughout the passage of *John's birth-circumcision-naming* in the statements, "He has established for us a saving power (κέρας σωτηρίας) in the House of his servant David" (1:69), and "the rising sun (ἀνατολή) has come from on high to visit us" (1:78).[109] The first one recalls the Davidic Messiah-king expected by Israel.[110] In the second, the

---

[106] Here κύριος, "Lord," for the first time refers unmistakably to Jesus. The preceding occurrences always referred to God (1:6.9.11.25.28.32.38).

[107] The affirmation "He has used the power of his arm" (1:51) could be a remote reference to Jesus, but it could likewise refer to God.

[108] The expression "all generations will call me blessed," according to O'Toole, could include all Christians, Jews or Gentiles (O'TOOLE, *Unity*, 100). It could be a first universalistic reference. However, it is a very implicit one and it refers to Mary and not to Jesus.

[109] The noun ἀνατολή could refer to John or to Jesus (ἐπισκέψεται ἡμᾶς ἀνατολὴ ἐξ ὕψους). The argument by Bovon is clear. He says: "For Luke and, I believe, for the earlier version, ἀνατολή is the subject of ἐπισκέψεται and is not identical with the Baptist. Otherwise it is incomprehensible whose way John could be preparing" (BOVON, *Lukas* I, 109 [76]).

[110] The noun κέρας, "horn," is a symbol of strength. In addition, the verb ἐγείρω is used of God's providential summoning into existence anointed instruments of salvation for his people (see Acts 13:22; Jg 2:16.18; 3:9.15). "Horn of salvation," says FITZMYER, *Luke I-IX*, 383, "must be understood here as a title for an agent of God's salvation in David's house, as a messianic title." And STRAUSS, *Davidic Messiah*, 101, claims that "Luke continues to define the role of the coming Davidic king in language reminiscent of the national deliverance of the OT and Judaism." The Greek expression of κέρας σωτηρίας fits the Jewish expectation of a triumphant Messiah king from the house of David (see 1 S 2:10; 2 S 22:3 = Ps 18:3; Ps 132:17; Ezk 29:21).

noun ἀνατολή refers to the Messiah described as the "rising sun" which brings light to Israel.[111] Therefore, Jesus is described as a "rising sun" which will give "light" and guide the way of "peace" (1:79). These clear references to Jesus describe his status as Davidic Messiah to Israel through different metaphors: "saving power" and "rising sun."

There are two other expressions, ὕψιστος and κύριος, which may refer to Jesus. Zechariah says of his son that he will be called "prophet of the Most High (ὕψιστος), for you will go before the Lord (κύριος) to prepare a way for him" (1:76b). The expressions "Most High" and "Lord" can refer either to God or to Jesus. John could be a prophet of God or a prophet of Jesus. As the title "Most High" has been identified always with God (1:32.35), there is no reason in the infancy narrative up to that point to think that Jesus was meant by "Most High."[112] However, the title κύριος has been referred to God (1:6.9.11.25.28.32.38.45.46.58.66.68) and to Jesus (1:43). The parallelism of the expression προπορεύσῃ γὰρ ἐνώπιον κυρίου (1:76) with προελεύσεται ἐνώπιον αὐτοῦ (1:17)[113] leaves a doubt about the assignation of κύριος in Lk 1:76

[111] The word ἀνατολή occurs three times in the LXX as the translation of Hebrew צמח, "sprout, shoot, scion," a word that designates a Davidic Messiah (Jr 23:5; Zc 3:8; 6:12). Zechariah is referring to Jesus as the Messiah, as the "rising sun from on high" in the concluding verses of the *Benedictus*. The noun ἀνατολή is followed by the expression ἐξ ὕψους. The Messiah does not come from down below, from the earth, as any other person might, but from on high, from heaven. In fact, the expression ἐξ ὕψους appears again in Lk 24:49, meaning "from on high," "from heaven." Jesus will be among human beings but he comes from heaven (1:35). In addition, the verb ἐπισκέπτομαι, "to visit" is often used to refer to the coming of the Messiah (see Lk 1:68; 7:16; 19:44).

[112] Bovon claims that "ὕψιστος alludes to God, but is not simply equivalent with him. In contrast to a visitor 'from earth,' it refers to a visitor 'from heaven' (1:35)" (BOVON, *Lukas* I, 109 [76]). In other words, the Greek expression προφήτης ὑψίστου can also mean "a prophet from Most High (God)", "sent from the Most High," "sent from Heaven." The rest of the occurrences of ὕψιστος throughout Luke-Acts never refer to Jesus and always to this heavenly or divine provenience (Lk 1:76; 2:14; 6:35; 8:28; 19:38; Acts 7:48; 16:17).

[113] The grammatical subject of both phrases is John. Both verbs, προπορεύομαι and προέρχομαι, are verbs of the same semantic field, verbs of "movement ahead of" (LOUW – NIDA, *Greek-English*, § 15.16 and 15.143). The forward movement implied

to Jesus since the pronoun αὐτοῦ refers to its antecedent, κύριος ὁ θεός (1:16), which clearly explains that κύριος refers to θεός.

In any case, the description of Jesus is neither very clear nor extensive.[114] It is clear that God will act for the people of Israel with a nationalistic perspective. Zechariah blesses "the God of Israel, for he has visited and redeemed his people, (...) he has established for us a saving power in the House of his servant David, just as he proclaimed, by the mouth of his holy prophets" (1:68-70).[115] Just as Mary affirmed the fulfillment of Jewish hopes and promises that God made to their ancestors (1:55), Zechariah also affirms their fulfillment (1:68-73).

In the passage of *Jesus' birth-circumcision-naming*, the angel returns to the titles of Savior (2:11: σωτήρ)[116] and Messiah, Lord (2:11: χριστὸς κύριος) in reference to Jesus.[117] The implicit presentation of Jesus as Savior, through his name (1:31) and the expression "saving power" (1:69), is now made explicit through the

---

is expressed by the same expression: ἐνώπιον + gen (αὐτοῦ/κυρίου). In addition the antecedent of the pronoun αὐτοῦ is κύριος, which makes this the same expression as the other part of the parallelism: ἐνώπιον κυρίου.

[114] Jesus as "saving power" (1:69) and "rising sun" (1:78). The others are unlikely.

[115] O'Toole thinks that the affirmation "to give light to those who live in darkness and the shadow dark as death" (1:79a) has a universalistic meaning embracing both Jews and Gentiles (O'TOOLE, *Unity*, 100). However, this expression is explained by the following part of the same verse, "to guide our feet into the way of peace" (1:79b), whose pronoun "our" speaks of Israel. Throughout the *Benedictus* there are many first person plural pronouns (1:69.71-2x-.72.73-2x-.75.78-2x-). They all refer to the people of Israel understood as a community. In addition, there are many clearly Jewish expressions: "our ancestors" and "his holy covenant" (1:72); "the oath he swore to our father Abraham" (1:73), and "his people (λαός)" (1:77).

[116] The only time that σωτήρ had appeared in Luke 1–2 it referred to God, who is Mary's God and Savior (1:47). However, after 2:11 σωτήρ always refers to Jesus (Acts 5:31; 13:23).

[117] The juxtaposition of the two epithets, Messiah and Lord (also in Acts 2:36), seems to have as its purpose the explanation of the Jewish term "Messiah" for a Gentile audience: Messiah implies kingship. In addition, both concepts are explained by the title "Savior." Thus, the Gentile audience could understand the Jewish title of Messiah through other more common expressions, king and Savior (see STANTON, "Messianism and Christology", 89-90). It is striking that the angel uses the present tense: ἐστίν. The baby Jesus is already "Savior," "Messiah," and "Lord."

words of the angel. The implicit presentation of Jesus as Messiah in the *Benedictus* (1:68.69.78) is now made explicit. And Jesus, who had been presented as Elizabeth's Lord (1:43) is presented now as Lord, and not only of Elizabeth. Luke sets all three titles in a Davidic context: "Today in the town of David a Savior has been born to you; he is Christ the Lord."[118] What the angel Gabriel said about Jesus receiving the throne of his ancestor David (1:32) is confirmed now by Jesus' place of birth.[119]

The angel, with the great throng of the hosts of heaven, praises God, saying δόξα ἐν ὑψίστοις θεῷ καὶ ἐπὶ γῆς εἰρήνη ἐν ἀνθρώποις εὐδοκίας (2:14). The presence of Jesus is described as bringing "Glory to God in the highest heaven and peace on earth." Jesus' guidance through the way of peace for the people of Israel (1:79) is transformed now into "peace on earth." This last expression seems to first speak of a universal rule of Jesus. Nevertheless, it is only a vague reference. First, the angel introduces a "joy to be shared by the whole people" (2:10). The Greek expression is ἔσται παντὶ τῷ λαῷ. As we have seen above, the noun λαός in the singular, refers to Israel,[120] especially when preceded by the definite article through the expression πᾶς ὁ λαός.[121] That means that the joy brought by Jesus' presence will be for Israel.[122] Second, the emphatic repetition of the

---

[118] The location in the city of David underscores the Messianic dimension of the Savior. The expression "the Messiah Lord" highlights this Messianic dimension even more.

[119] The birth "in the city of David" represents the fulfillment of the prophet's promise to Israel through David's royal house (see Mi 5:2). "In the narrative of the birth of Jesus," says COLLINS – COLLINS, *King and Messiah*, 146, "Jesus' Davidic descent is emphasized."

[120] See § III.3.2.2.a, especially p. 178.

[121] See Lk 2:10; 7:29; 8:47; 9:13; 18:43; 20:45; 21:38; 24:19; Acts 3:9.11; 4:10; 5:34; 10:41; 13:24, which refer to the people of Israel or to the people present in the scene, which is always the people of Israel. In addition the expression ἅπας ὁ λαός is found in Lk 3:21; 19:48; 20:6; Acts 5:20, and always refers to the people of Israel. Both expressions are Lukan expressions with this meaning because they are found in the rest of the NT only in Mt 27:25; Jn 8:2; Rm 15:9; and Heb 9:19.

[122] I disagree with MULLOOR, "From East and West", 177-179, who contends that the "joy shared by the whole people" (2:10) parallels the expression "a census should be made of the whole inhabited world" (2:1) and should be understood in a universal

pronoun in the second person plural "for you," εὐαγγελίζομαι ὑμῖν (v. 10) and ἐτέχθη ὑμῖν (2:11), underlines the restricted designation of the people as those of Judea. Third, the whole expression says: ἐπὶ γῆς εἰρήνη ἐν ἀνθρώποις εὐδοκίας. It means that the peace is not for the whole earth, an expression which is in parallel with "in the highest heaven,"[123] but for those he favors, the chosen people, Israel.[124] Fourth, there are two references to Bethlehem in the passage. The first one links Bethlehem with David's town and Joseph with David's house (2:4).[125] The second one links the birth in the town of David with the birth of the Savior, the Messiah of the Lord (2:11). The repeated connection between Jesus, the place of his birth (the town of David), and his ancestry from King David's house present

---

sense. I believe that the Greek expressions are very different, and that παντὶ τῷ λαῷ and πᾶσαν τὴν οἰκουμένην should not be understood as synonymous. In addition, as we have just said, throughout Luke-Acts, the noun λαός has a nationalist meaning in connection with Israel and never refers to the "whole inhabited world."

[123] The *Gloria* is a hymn divided into two different parts. The expression "Glory in the highest heaven" is in contrast to the expression "on earth peace." They make a chiastic parallelism: (A) Glory, (B) heaven, (B') earth, (A') peace. God and human beings have a symmetric position at the end of each part. Then, as Jesus enters Jerusalem, the crowd of disciples will proclaim "in heaven peace and glory in the highest." Lk 19:38 refers both "glory" and "peace" to heaven.

[124] After a careful study of the textual variants and the expression ἐν ἀνθρώποις εὐδοκίας, Fitzmyer claims that the angel's song dealt neither with the "good will" of human beings toward one another, nor with the "good will" of human beings who receive peace. Rather, it was to be understood of God's "good pleasure," as "concrete people whom God has favored" with his grace or predilection (FITZMYER, *Luke I-IX*, 410-412). Moreover, Dodd has exhaustively analyzed the term εὐδοκία in the NT and concludes that it refers to a divine act of will, an option or decision of predilection (DODD, "New Testament", 104-110). Furthermore, Nolland uses different Qumran texts, which are parallel to the Lukan expression, to affirm that "the Lukan text reflects a semi-technical Semitic expression referring to God's people and having overtones of election" (NOLLAND, *Luke 1-9:20*, 109). Finally, Schürmann contends that εὐδοκία refers to the "chosen ones," those among the people of God who have been elected. God is showing favor to a chosen group, to part of his people (SCHÜRMANN, *Das Lukasevangelium* I, 114-115).

[125] Bethlehem was the home of David and the place of his anointing (Jg 17:7-9; 19:1-2; Rt 1:1-2; 1 Samuel 16; 17:12.58).

Jesus as a Davidic Messiah, King and Savior of Israel. These recurrences circumscribe the pericope to Israel.[126]

It is in the passage of the *Finding of twelve-year-old Jesus in the Temple* that Jesus pronounces his first words in the Lukan Gospel.[127] In this way Jesus presents one feature of himself, asking: οὐκ ᾔδειτε ὅτι ἐν τοῖς τοῦ πατρός μου δεῖ εἶναί με; (2:49). Being in the Temple, he says that he has to be ἐν τοῖς τοῦ πατρός μου. This synthetic and ambiguous phrase is difficult to interpret.[128] Regardless of the interpretation selected, perhaps it is deliberately ambivalent; Jesus is speaking to Joseph and Mary as the plural references of Lk 2:48b.49 testify. Since Jesus uses the second person plural, he also speaks to Joseph. Hence, he is speaking of another Father whose affairs are in connection with where Jesus is, the Temple.[129] In other words, he has God as Father, and

---

[126] The transitional verse of Jesus' circumcision-naming (2:21) says only two things about Jesus. His parents gave him the name the angel had given him before his conception, Jesus (1:31). And his parents fulfilled the Law of the circumcision, and thus, they introduced him to the Jewish traditions.

[127] This is a textual indicator that direct readers in the continuing construction of Jesus' character.

[128] It can be interpreted in three similar, but different, ways, depending on how the definite article τοῖς is interpreted. First, the definite article τοῖς is understood as neuter, in a locative sense. A number of instances have been found in biblical and extrabiblical Greek texts of the neuter plural of the definite article followed by a genitive in the sense of "the house of" (Gn 41:51; Est 7:9; Job 18:19; JOSEPHUS, *C. Ap.*, 1.18; *The Jewish Antiquities*, 16,10,1; OxyP 3,523:3). It refers to his Father's house, to the Temple. Second, the definite article τοῖς is understood as neuter, but now in a wider sense. Jesus has to stay among the things of his Father, in his Father's affairs; it would be a similar expression of τὰ τοῦ θεοῦ (Lk 20:25; Mt 16:23; Mk 8:33). Third, the definite article τοῖς is interpreted as masculine, referring to those people belonging to his Father (see Rm 16:10.11). I prefer the second interpretation. The first one, "the Temple, the house of my Father" is odd because after having just said it, Jesus leaves the Temple and retires to Nazareth (2:51). Location is not decisive. The third one, "among those people belonging to Jesus' Father," is strange because there is no reason why Mary and Joseph are not among them. I believe that Jesus has to stay with his Father's affairs, according to his Father's will. Jesus always has to act as Son of God and therefore in obedience to the will of his Father.

[129] According to De Jonge the word order of the expression "your father and I"

his relationship with God is superior to the mere human family. Jesus does not refer to himself explicitly as "Son of God." He leaves to others the task of naming him Son of God as foretold by the angel Gabriel (1:32.35).[130] However, Jesus is implicitly referring to God as his heavenly Father.

The reader is also informed of the growth of Jesus in wisdom, stature, and God's favor.[131] Lk 2:40.52 are two evaluative narrative comments by the narrator about Jesus, which form the *inclusio* of the episode. This *inclusio* highlights the growth of Jesus, especially in wisdom, which is testified by those who heard him in the Temple, the teachers, who were astounded at his intelligence and his replies (2:47).

The characterization of Jesus throughout Luke 1–2 should be considered as a continuum through several traits and reprises. This progressive presentation of Jesus has different degrees of characterization. The traits and reprises achieve a clear climax in the Presentation of Jesus in the Temple.[132] There, important traits of Jesus, already presented, are reprised, sometimes with new force. Lk 2:22-39 de-

---

(2:48b) is unusual. In Greek, if ἐγώ is linked with another word to form a composite subject, usually by καί, then normally ἐγώ comes first. This is true of the NT Greek also (Jn 8:16; 10:30; 1Co 9:6; 15:11). This striking Greek word order stresses the words "your father" in reference to Joseph in order to prepare for what Jesus will say in v. 49 in reference to God. Joseph's paternity is emphasized in v. 48 in order to prepare for its transcendence in v. 49 (DE JONGE, "Sonship", 330-331).

[130] This is an example of what ALETTI, *L'art*, 42.203, names the *indirect Christology*, in which the narrator has Jesus point the way but leaves it to the characters and readers to follow.

[131] According to LEE, *Luke's Stories*, 215, these comments can logically only be made by God, and so although the narrator writes the comments, they are focalized from God's perspective. Once again the narrator is omniscient, almost in the place of God. Throughout Luke 1–2 the narrator often appears as omniscient, knowing the feelings of Zechariah, Elizabeth, Mary, the shepherds, and Simeon, trying to provide the maximum information about Jesus to the reader.

[132] The only topics about Jesus that are presented in the rest of the infancy narrative and do not appear in the Presentation in the Temple are: the divine filiation of Jesus (1:32.35; 2:49), his title of "Lord" (1:43; 2:11), and his progressive growing up (2:40.52) to his greatness (1:32; 1:42). For further studies on this comparison see BOCK, *Luke* I, 244-245.

scribes how God, according to his plan and promise,[133] is saving his people Israel.[134] This new force is clear in the three hymns that the narrator introduces in Luke 1–2. In the *Magnificat* Mary celebrates the God who has shown himself as a Savior; in the *Benedictus* Zechariah celebrates John as the one who will prepare for the climactic saving act; and in the *Nunc Dimittis* Simeon celebrates Jesus as the embodiment of God's salvation.[135] From hymn to hymn the focus shifts from God's salvation through its preparation in John to its fulfillment in Jesus.[136] Thus the attention is progressively focused on Jesus as the instrument for God's salvation. In Lk 2:22-39 this salvation is clearly found in Jesus,[137] who is presented as Messiah (Χριστός),[138] Holy,[139] light,[140] peace,[141] glory,[142] and the fulfillment of

---

[133] This fulfillment is expressed by the prophets and the Law (1:41.45.53-55.67; 2:22.27.39).

[134] Salvation is arguably the most prominent theme echoed in Luke 1–2, indicated by the high concentration of salvation terms. God will redeem Israel (1:68; 2:38), which is variously expressed as salvation from enemies (1:69-71.74a), covenant and spiritual renewal (1:72.74b-75), release of sins (1:77), light dawning in the darkness (1:78-79), social reversal (1:46-55) and consolation (2:25).

[135] Ortensio da Spinetoli affirms that "Simeon in the Temple completes the manifestation of Jesus by means of the *Nunc Dimittis*, which is a conclusion of the information given in the *Magnificat* and *Benedictus*" (ORTENSIO DA SPINETOLI, *Introduzione*, 110).

[136] COLERIDGE, *The Birth*, 228, contends that God is the protagonist of Luke 1 and Jesus of Luke 2. Luke made the decision to begin with God rather than with Jesus. God is named as Θεός thirteen times in Luke 1 and seven times in Luke 2; and as Κύριος sixteen times in Luke 1 and nine times in Luke 2. Throughout Luke 1–2 Theology becomes Christology. In addition, Luke is the only synoptic evangelist who begins with God. Matthew begins with "Jesus Christ, son of David, son of Abraham" (Mt 1:1). Mark begins with "Jesus Christ, the son of God" (Mk 1:1).

[137] So Lk 1:47.69.71.74.77; 2:11; 2:30. We could include here the reference to Jesus' name (1:31; 2:20), and the expressions "consolation of Israel" (2:25) and "redemption of Jerusalem" (2:38). Being other ways of expressing the salvation, they are of lesser importance.

[138] So Lk 2:11; 2:26.

[139] So Lk 1:35; 2:23.

[140] So Lk 1:78.79; 2:32.

[141] So Lk 1:79; 2:14; 2:29.

[142] So Lk 2:9.14; 2:32.

Jewish expectations.[143] There, new important traits, such as universal salvation and the rejection by some and the acceptance by others, are first introduced.

1.3.3 Reliable Characters throughout Luke 1–2

Although the narrator appears as one who enjoys omniscience, his role is discrete and he prefers that the characters speak for themselves throughout the Lukan infancy narrative, especially in the key moments for the revelation and interpretation of Jesus.[144] But who are these characters who speak and develop the plot throughout the Lukan infancy narrative? Are they reliable witnesses to Jesus? Are any of them narratively highlighted by the narrator?

In *John's announcement* the angel Gabriel introduces John's birth. The angel is presented as a *reliable character* because he serves in the presence of God, has been sent by God (1:19), and what he says is fulfilled, including, initially, his prophecy that Zechariah is going to be dumb (1:20.21). The angel says that Elizabeth is going to be pregnant (1:13) and she is pregnant as predicted (1:24). Fulfillment reveals both the reliability of the celestial messenger and of the heavenly promise.

All of the *Annunciation*'s information about Jesus is said by "the angel Gabriel who was sent by God" (1:26). Thus the angel Gabriel is again a *reliable character* who can speak in the name of God. In addition, what he says is fulfilled again. The angel Gabriel says that

---

[143] Lk 2:22-39 implicitly affirms that Jesus fulfills the Jewish expectations, especially the Law and prophecies. What Mary spoke in the hill-country of Judea about the promise made to the Jewish ancestors (1:55), and Zechariah repeated, likewise in the hill-country of Judea (1:70-73), is now corroborated in the Temple of Jerusalem by Simeon and Anna linking Jesus to the fulfillment of Jewish expectations. All the expectations of the Law and the prophecies are fulfilled in Jesus in the Temple of Jerusalem (2:22.25-26.38.39). This perspective in the Lukan infancy narrative is present also in the infancy narrative according to Matthew. The different quotations of the OT expectations fulfilled in Jesus structure the whole Matthean infancy narrative (Mt 1:23; 2:6; 2:15; 2:18; 2:23).

[144] On the omniscience of the narrator throughout Luke 1–2 see COLERIDGE, *The Birth*, 214-216.

Mary is going to be pregnant (1:31) and that Elizabeth is already pregnant. And in fact, they both are pregnant as predicted (1:42-44).

The information about Jesus in the passage of the *meeting between the two expecting mothers* is given by Elizabeth. She had already been presented as a *reliable character* when the narrator affirmed of her and her husband that "they both were upright in the sight of God and impeccably carried out all the commandments and observances of the Lord" (1:6). In addition, Elizabeth, before speaking about Jesus, is "filled with the Holy Spirit" (1:41). Her witness to Jesus can be accepted as reliable.

In the passage of *John's birth-circumcision-naming*, before proclaiming the *Benedictus* the narrator affirms that Zechariah was filled with the Holy Spirit and spoke that prophecy (1:67). In addition, Zechariah had already been presented, like Elizabeth, as a faithful Jew (1:6). Zechariah, a prophet directly inspired by the Holy Spirit and a faithful Jew, is a *reliable character*.

All of the information about Jesus during the passage of his *birth* is said by the anonymous angel. He is an angel of the Lord and brings the Glory of the Lord (2:9). He is presented as a spokesperson of the Lord, as a *reliable character*.[145]

In the passage of the *finding of Jesus in the Temple*, Jesus himself is the *reliable character*, who, through his first words, affirms that God is his Father. Jesus appears as interpreter of himself. In earlier episodes, other characters have interpreted Jesus' identity. For the first time in the narrative, Jesus speaks as a free agent;[146] there is no hint of either angels or the Holy Spirit. Jesus becomes prime mover in the narrative, now fully qualified to play his unique role

[145] The little information in the transitional verse of Jesus' circumcision-naming (2:21) is directly given by the narrator. It is one of the few times in which the narrator prefers to speak.

[146] In fact, in v. 52, after Jesus' words, the narrator names Jesus absolutely for the first time in the infancy narrative (Ἰησοῦς). Earlier Jesus has been named by the narrator "a baby" (2:16: βρέφος), "this child" (2:17: τὸ παιδίον τοῦτο), "the child Jesus" (2:27: τὸ παιδίον Ἰησοῦς), "the child" (2:40: τὸ παιδίον), "the boy Jesus" (2:43: Ἰησοῦς ὁ παῖς), and "child" (2:48: τέκνον). Now as he becomes for the first time an independent agent with emotions and opinions, he becomes simply "Jesus."

in the Gospel narrative. Now the narrator passes the word to Jesus, with whom it will remain through the whole narrative.

Most of the characters throughout Luke 1–2 are associated in the narrative with God,[147] and so what they say is authoritative and reliable. They all reveal, through divine inspiration, the divine action in Jesus.[148] They all are reliable characters who invite the reader to trust them and their witness to Jesus. However, I believe that there is a progression in the different *human reliable characters* who gradually introduce Jesus throughout the Lukan infancy narrative.[149] They all are reliable characters but their reliability is in increasing progression until Simeon, Anna, and, finally, Jesus.[150]

The narrator significantly limits the understanding that the human characters other than Simeon and Anna possess of the divine plan, especially Zechariah, Mary, and Elizabeth, and thus limits their ability to speak about Jesus. In the face of the angelic revelations there is great fear (Zechariah, 1:12-13; Mary, 1:30; shepherds, 2:9-10; the Judean residents, 1:65) or "consternation/surprise" (Zechariah, 1:12; Mary, 1:29), that requires a storing of these things in the heart (Mary, 2:19; 2:51; Elizabeth goes into "retreat," 1:24; the Judean residents, 1:66). Zechariah is struck dumb by Gabriel for "unbelief" (1:20), while Mary wonders (2:33.48.50). In contrast, Simeon and Anna are not so described. Simeon reveals to Mary what her child will be in God's plan of

[147] The angel Gabriel "serves in the presence of God" (1:19). Elizabeth speaks of Jesus as "my Lord" when "filled with the Holy Spirit" (1:41). Zechariah speaks of salvation when "filled with the Holy Spirit" (1:67). The angel who speaks to the shepherds is an "angel of the Lord" (2:9); Simeon, who recognizes Jesus as the Lord's Messiah, is "guided by the Spirit" (2:26). Anna, who speaks of Jesus as the redemption of Jerusalem, is a prophetess who "never left the Temple but worshipped there with fasting and prayer day and night" (2:37).

[148] According to GUEURET, *L'engendrement*, 136-145, the characters of Luke's infancy narrative present Jesus because they "know and can decode" his presence.

[149] See GERBER, *"Il vous est né un Sauveur"*, 81-92, who analyzes the different christological affirmations of Luke 1–2 depending the speaker in each case.

[150] Other voices, both human and heavenly, resound throughout Luke 1–2, but in the end, Jesus' voice alone sounds as prime interpreter (see COLERIDGE, *The Birth*, 230.232).

salvation and even what her own role will be (2:34-35). Anna confirms Simeon's revelation to those like Mary, Elizabeth and Zechariah who are looking forward to the redemption of Jerusalem (2:38).[151] Moreover, the Presentation in the Temple is testified by two different witnesses with a concordant testimony, a male and a female. In the other passages preceding the Presentation Jesus is introduced by only one character (the angel: 1:26-38; Elizabeth: 1:39-45; Zechariah: 1:57-79; and the angel: 2:1-20). The presence of two different reliable characters who give concordant testimony to Jesus has its own narrative importance.

1.3.4 Locations throughout Luke 1–2

The location where the seven episodes of the Lukan infancy narrative take place has a narrative importance because of their changes between public and private stage or sacred and secular sphere. The narrator quickly moves between worlds, between public and private, between sacred and secular, in order to stage their meeting.[152]

The beginning of John's itinerary, the *announcement of his birth*, takes place in the Temple of Jerusalem, exactly in its ναός, the inner and most sacred part, the sanctuary (1:9). Through this passage there are two different paradoxes. First, it takes place at the heart of Judaism, the Temple of Jerusalem, but without any clear link to the cultic action. Second, it allows Luke to situate the event in the midst of the people with a public dimension (1:10: πᾶν τὸ πλῆθος ἦν τοῦ λαοῦ; see 1:21.22) and yet at the same time to have it hidden in the sanctuary with only Zechariah and the angel, to bring to light the private dimension.[153]

[151] See MOESSNER, "Ironic Fulfillment", 40-41.

[152] COLERIDGE, *The Birth*, 224-225, claims that we have a switch from one world to another, in a way that not only highlights the diversity and comprehensiveness of the divine action, but also stages a meeting of worlds made possible only by the divine action. Although I use these categories, religious and profane, public and private, I believe that there is a graduation in these categories. For example, I believe that all Judea, not only the Temple, is more "sacred" than Galilee. However, these categories help to better understand Jesus' characterization.

[153] I borrow this double paradox from COLERIDGE, *The Birth*, 33.

The first references to Jesus, during the *Annunciation* episode, take place in a town in Galilee called Nazareth (1:26). The stage is not religious and it is a marginal place. In addition, only two characters act, the angel Gabriel and Mary (1:26-27), and in a private meeting with no public dimension.

From Nazareth, Mary goes up into the hill-country, to a Judean town (1:39), to Zechariah's house (1:40). In fact, after the announcement of John's birth, Zechariah returned home (1:23) to meet there his wife who conceived. The *meeting between the expecting mothers*, Elizabeth and Mary, and their children, John and Jesus, takes place in another profane and private place.

There is geographical continuity between the last episode, the meeting between the mothers, and the last passage about John the Baptist, his *birth-naming-circumcision*. The narrator does not change the geographical location and says that "the affair was talked about throughout the hill-country of Judaea" (1:65). The presence of neighbors (1:58.65: περίοικοι) suggests that the birth-circumcision-naming took place at their house or very close to it. While the meeting between Mary and Elizabeth happens in a private context, the presence of the crowd, relatives, neighbors, and all those who listen to it in the hill-country of Judea, gives a public dimension to this passage.[154] However, the last reference to John in this passage, and in the whole Lukan infancy narrative, affirms that John "lived in the desert until the day he appeared openly to Israel" (1:80). His infancy and childhood should be lived in the desert until his public life started in Lk 3:1-18.[155]

The passage concerning *Jesus' birth* takes place in the city of David, called Bethlehem, located in Judea. It is not a sacred setting, but the explicit mention of Bethlehem, the city of David, because Joseph was of David's House and line (2:4), situates the passage in a Davidic-Messianic context. After Jesus' birth, which happens in a private sphere, the presence of hosts of angels and the announce-

[154] See COLERIDGE, *The Birth*, 125.

[155] In fact, when John starts his public life, the narrator affirms that the word of God came to him when he was in the desert (3:2). In addition, even the scriptural quotation refers to John as "a voice of one that cries in the desert" (3:4).

ment to the shepherds (2:13-15) begin to give to Jesus a public dimension.[156]

The setting of the pericope of the *finding of the twelve-year-old Jesus in the Temple*, as with the previous episode (2:22-39), is the Temple of Jerusalem. However, Jesus' first presence in the Temple is the Presentation in the Temple, which is the coming into the Temple from Nazareth to Jerusalem through the hill-country of Judea. The Temple of Jerusalem and, more precisely, its ἱερόν, or general location (2:27.37.46), places the passages in a sacred and very important context. The words of Simeon and, especially, the fact that Anna "spoke of the child to all who looked forward to the redemption of Jerusalem" (2:38) keeps the public dimension of the character of Jesus. The presence of relatives, acquaintances (2:44), teachers and everybody who heard him (2:46-47) also gives a public dimension to the passage of the finding of Jesus in the Temple.

The geographical itineraries of John and Jesus throughout the infancy narrative are very different. On the one hand, the birth of John is announced right in the sanctuary of the Temple of Jerusalem (1:9: ναός). From that sacred sphere the following scenes concerning John, his leaping in his mother's womb and his birth-circumcision-naming, take place in a secular context, the hill-town of Judea where his parents live, and in their own house. The geographical itinerary of Jesus is very different. The announcement of his birth takes place in a profane ambient, a town in Galilee called Nazareth, perhaps her house (1:26).[157] This profane sphere is maintained in the meeting of the mothers in Elizabeth's house. From that secular context the setting progressively increases in sacredness. Jesus' birth, and probably his circumcision and naming, take place in Bethlehem, the town of David. It is in Judea, closer to

[156] We do not know where the circumcision and naming of Jesus took place (2:21). The connection with Jesus' birth and the fact that the circumcision was usually performed by the parents and never in the Temple (see § III.1.1.2), seem to indicate that it did not take place in the Temple of Jerusalem (2:22) and perhaps took place in Bethlehem.

[157] The angel went "to a town in Galilee called Nazareth" (1:26). However, the expression εἰσελθὼν πρὸς αὐτήν (1:28) could mean that the angel entered into her house.

Jerusalem, and it is in connection with the religious expectations of the Davidic Messiah. The following passage concerning Jesus is his Presentation in the Temple. Jesus' itinerary throughout his infancy is from Nazareth to Judea, the hill-country first and then Bethlehem, and from Judea to the Temple of Jerusalem: from a profane sphere to a sacred one. There is a clear geographical progression throughout the infancy narrative of Jesus which finishes with his first physical presence in the Temple.[158]

On the other hand, John's itinerary starts and finishes between the private and public sphere. While the announcement of his birth takes place in private between the angel Gabriel and Zechariah, the fact of the announcement is known by all the multitude of the people, with public consequences. And while John's birth takes place in a private context, it immediately becomes public knowledge to his relatives and neighbors in the whole hill-country of Judea. However, John's infancy narrative finishes by affirming that he lived in the desert (1:80). On the contrary, Jesus' infancy narrative passes from the private sphere to the public sphere, which again achieves its high point with the presence of Jesus in the Temple. The Annunciation of Jesus' birth takes place in total privacy between the angel Gabriel and Mary. That privacy is maintained in the meeting between the expecting mothers and in Jesus' birth. From the appearance to the shepherds the passages present an increasing public dimension which finishes with the public presence of Jesus in the Temple.[159] The Presentation passage appears as the arrival point of the geographical progression towards sacredness and publicity.

---

[158] See n. 64 on Laurentin's theory about the geographical progression and its OT background.

[159] The information about Jesus' growing up says nothing about living in the desert. However, the information of Jesus going back to Nazareth (2:52), where Jesus' public life begins (4:16), introduces a quiet and private location at the end of his infancy narrative and the beginning of his public life.

1.3.5 Scriptural Quotations in Luke 1–2

In the passage of *John's announcement* there are some implicit scriptural allusions, especially in the characterization of Zechariah and Elizabeth and in what the angel Gabriel says about John. Throughout the Annunciation of Jesus there is an allusion to the OT (Gn 18:14; Jr 32:27) in Lk 1:37: "for nothing is impossible to God." However, it cannot be considered a quotation and it has no introductory formula. In the passage of the *meeting between the two mothers*, although there are many allusions to scriptural passages, especially in the *Magnificat*, there is no scriptural quotation. In the passage of the *birth-circumcision-naming of John*, throughout the *Benedictus* there are many implicit allusions to the OT, but there is no scriptural quotation. In the passage of the *birth-circumcision-naming of Jesus*, the only implicit allusion is found in the *Gloria* of the angel (2:14). Finally, neither do we find any scriptural quotation in the passage of *the twelve-year-old Jesus*.

Thus, the only *scriptural quotation* throughout the whole Lukan infancy narrative is found in the passage of the Presentation in the Temple. The narrator highlights this passage through two different direct scriptural references (2:23-24). In particular, the first one characterizes Jesus as Holy for the Lord, as consecrated to the Lord (2:23). And both are introduced by the *introductory formula* quotation, which also locates the quotation in "the Law of the Lord" (2:23.24).[160]

---

[160] As we have seen in § III.3.1, the quotations come from Ex 13:2.11; Lv 5:7; 12:2-4.8, all passages from the "Law of the Lord," the Torah. Moreover, the verbs of both introductory formulae are expressed in the perfect aspect, which emphasizes the present status of the past action: it emphasizes that the legal authority still remains and commands (see Lk 19:46; Acts 23:5; Mt 4:4.7.10; 21:13; Jn 8:17).

2. Conclusion

The sequence of the Lukan infancy narrative develops a unified plot in which the different passages repeat and progressively add features of the identity of Jesus revealing Jesus' identity and mission.[161] This sequence is unified by an elaborate pattern of reprise of Jesus' features with an increasing disclosure of Jesus. Only by studying the whole infancy narrative do we realize the depth of Jesus' mystery, and the importance of the single passages that make up Luke 1–2.

Throughout the Lukan infancy narrative there is an upward movement of the knowledge of Jesus, which constantly progresses until its climactic point in the presence of the child Jesus in the Temple.[162]

On the one hand, the passage of the Presentation in the Temple repeats many of the basic themes of the entire infancy narrative and so emphasizes its content. For example, it picks up ways of characterization of Jesus as the Messiah who fulfills the Law, prophecies, and Jewish expectations;[163] Salvation[164] is found in

---

[161] "When one considers the infancy narrative as a whole," says FITZMYER, *Luke I-IX*, 446, "one sees that its main purpose is not merely to establish a relationship between John and Jesus or to identify the latter as a Palestinian Jew born in Bethlehem and raised in Nazareth, but much more to make christological affirmations about him from the beginning of his earthly existence." Neither is its main purpose to write a prologue according to the biographies of his time. As Aletti contends, Luke began with a revealed Christology which grows by increments, a progressive specification which builds a portal as a model for the rest of the literary work (ALETTI, *Le Jésus de Luc*, 74).

[162] The last two scenes, taking place in the Temple, are the climax of the narration. Nevertheless, since the account of the 12-year-old Jesus in the Temple speaks only of the growth of Jesus and his divine filiation, and there is no scriptural quotation, nor commission statement, the characterization of Jesus in the Presentation in the Temple receives the greater emphasis from a narrative point of view. On other reasons for this greater emphasis see GALBIATI, "La presentazione", 28.

[163] The fulfillment of this project is expressed by the prophets and the Law (see 1:41.45.53-55.67; 2:22.27.39).

[164] So Lk 1:47.69.71.74.77; 2:11; 2:30. We could also include here 2:20.25.38.

Jesus, who is presented as Messiah (Χριστός),[165] Holy,[166] light,[167] peace,[168] and glory.[169]

On the other hand, the Presentation in the Temple is not a mere repetition of the main topics but rather a development of them. The Presentation in the Temple explicitly adds three important distinctive features, three new perspectives to Jesus' characterization in the previous passages.

First of all, God's work of salvation in Jesus must embrace not only Israel, but the Gentiles as well. Up to the Presentation in the Temple, statements about Jesus had been cast in terms that could easily be understood exclusively in the context of Israel. The *Magnificat* was focused first in God's action in Mary (1:47-49) and then in Israel (1:54-55). The *Benedictus* was focused on God's action in Israel.[170] However, the *Nunc Dimittis* is explicitly focused on God's action through Jesus for all the peoples, the Gentiles as well as Israel. For example, while the *Benedictus* announced the *light in Israel* (1:78-79), the *Nunc Dimittis* presents a *light for the Gentiles* (2:32); and while the canticle of Zechariah says that the God of Israel had visited his people to redeem them (1:68), the canticle of Simeon says that God has prepared his salvation for all the peoples (2:31).[171] The progression from the *Magnificat* (Mary-Israel) to the *Benedictus*, and from the *Benedictus* (Israel) to the *Nunc Dimittis* (all the peoples), shows how God's action is being manifested over a

[165] So Lk 2:11; 2:26.

[166] So Lk 1:35; 2:23.

[167] So Lk 1:78.79; 2:32.

[168] So Lk 1:79; 2:14; 2:29.

[169] So Lk 2:9.14; 2:32.

[170] The *Gloria* implicitly starts a universalism with the expression "on earth peace for those he favors" (2:14). However, as we have seen on paragraph § 1.3.2, pp. 243-244, it is just a vague reference.

[171] Salvation is always rooted in Israel's past, but the salvation which Simeon holds in his arms is both a light for the Gentiles and the glory of Israel. On this topic see FARRIS, *Hymns*, 150, and PLYMALE, "The Prayer of Simeon", 33-34.

broader spectrum.[172] Simeon's canticle advances beyond the other presentations of Jesus and sharply opens the horizon of hope.[173] Jesus, the regal, Davidic, messianic Savior has come to redeem more than the nation of Israel; he has come for the world. The *Nunc Dimittis* has just announced a prospect which the preceding canticles and the narrative heretofore have not affirmed: the salvation of the Gentiles as part of the destiny of Israel.[174]

This universalism is highlighted even more by the fact that the universal Jesus of Simeon's hymn stands in marked contrast to the exclusively nationalistic image of John the Baptist in the Lukan infancy narrative.[175] John is a contrast-figure who highlights the universalism of the *Nunc Dimittis* even more.

Secondly, the prophecy of Simeon reveals that the story will be full of conflict and tension. Readers can already anticipate that the story will concern God's comprehensive saving purpose encountering human resistance as Jesus is contradicted by many. For the first time in the narrative, opposition and conflict are associated with the coming of Jesus.[176] This is a major development for the

---

[172] N. LOHFINK, "Das Alte Testament", 218-223, contends that in the OT the hymns, for example Exodus 15; 1 Samuel 2; Jonah 2; Judges 5, were purposefully inserted in the narrative and that sometimes they were linked, for example psalms of the Psalter. According to him these two typical OT literary techniques of "embedding of psalms in narratives" and "linking of psalms in the Psalter" will help us to understand what the hymns in Luke's infancy narrative express. I think that there is a progression in the universal vision of God's project throughout the different hymns of the infancy narrative. A similar progression is defended by ALETTI, "Passages néotestamentaires en prose rythmée", 255. On the progression from God's salvation (*Magnificat*) through its preparation in John (*Benedictus*) to its fulfillment in Jesus (*Nunc Dimittis*) see the conclusion of § 1.3.2, p. 247.

[173] O'TOOLE, *Unity*, 100, who defended some kind of incipient universalism in the *Magnificat* and *Benedictus*, accepts the possibility of rejection of that universalism, but not the rejection of the universalism in the *Nunc dimittis*: "Even if someone is inclined to reject any universality in Lk 1:48 and Lk 1:79, there is no way one can dissent from the universality in the *Nunc dimittis.*"

[174] The "light of revelation for the Gentiles" is the "glory for Israel" (2:32).

[175] See n. 78 and its paragraph, which makes explicit this difference between John and Jesus.

[176] This heralds a sudden change in tone. Up to this point, all responses to the

readers. The Presentation bestows a singular light on the figure of the child Jesus, already considered with regard to the Paschal events since Lk 2:22-39 presents Jesus as the glory of Israel, but also as the suffering Messiah. In other words, Simeon speaks about Jesus' glory through the experience of pain, as well as about the mystery of passion and glory. Also, the presence of Jesus will bring division in Israel because some, rejecting Jesus, will fall, and others, accepting Jesus, will rise.[177]

And thirdly, while the other passages concerning Jesus take place in Nazareth, the hill-country of Judea, or Bethlehem, the Presentation takes place in the Temple of Jerusalem, where the fulfillment of the Law and prophecies, and the presentation of the Messiah acquire special importance.[178] In Lk 2:22-39 Jesus is in the Temple for the first time making this presentation a unique characterization of Jesus. It is important to note that the presence in the Temple has a public dimension.[179]

Messiah's birth have been positive ones of joy, rejoicing, with a generally triumphal note. Simeon's prophecy contrasts with the royal language of Gabriel's oracle (1:30-35), Elizabeth's words (1:42-43), Zechariah's *Benedictus* (1:68-75), and the angel's announcement (2:11-14). However, Lk 2:22-39 introduces not only the *heilgeschichte*, but also the *unheilgeschichte*.

[177] It is similar to the change that God brings as announced in the *Magnificat*, pulling down princes from their thrones and raising high the lowly (1:52), filling the starving with good things, but sending the rich away empty (1:53). However, while the *Magnificat* speaks of a change from rich to poor and *vice versa*, the *Nunc Dimittis* speaks of a general division regardless of social status.

[178] As we have seen in § 1.3.4, I contend that there exists a geographical progression in the revelation of Jesus throughout Luke 1–2. There is a progressive increasing closeness to Jerusalem and its Temple, and its public dimension increases as well.

[179] These new perspectives in the Lukan infancy narrative are present also in the infancy narrative according to Matthew. The visit of the wise men (Mt 2:1-12), the persecution of Jesus by Herod, and the consequent escape to Egypt (Mt 2:13-18) respectively introduce the universalism and rejection of the figure of Jesus. However, the implicit universalism of the passage of the wise men is mitigated by what is told about Jesus, "he will shepherd my people (λαός) Israel" (Mt 2:6). Moreover, in the Matthean infancy narrative Jesus does not appear in the Temple.

I assert that this increasing characterization of Jesus is narratively underlined in the Presentation in the Temple because of the following reasons:[180]

(1) It picks up many of the main features of Jesus presented in the other pericopes reaffirming what had already been taught about Jesus.

(2) At the same time, it adds three new important features of Jesus clarifying the rule of the Messiah. It explicitly affirms his universalism; it first prophesizes his rejection which will divide the people of God; and it presents Jesus in the Temple of Jerusalem for the first time.

(3) It is the only passage with a *commission statement* of Jesus; it presents not only *who* Jesus is, but also *what* he will do. It presents the identity of Jesus, who is the "Messiah of the Lord," and the "Holy one for the Lord;" and it presents the mission of Jesus, his program for action: he brings about universal salvation. Bringing this salvation, he will be rejected by many in Israel (2:34). This mission will also be to reveal the secret thoughts of many through the fall of many in Israel

(4) It is the only characterization of Jesus which is testified by two different witnesses with independent and concordant testimonies, one male and one female, who are presented as two *reliable characters*.

(5) The narrator limits the understanding that the human characters other than Simeon and Anna possess of the divine plan, especially Zechariah, Elizabeth and Mary, and thus limits their ability to present Jesus.

---

[180] There are two other passages which also present a large number of features of Jesus: the announcement of his birth and the canticle of Zechariah. Neither of them has as many features of Jesus as the Presentation. In addition, the announcement of Jesus' birth is a resolution plot, and while Zechariah's canticle is a revelation plot, it is a revelation of John and not of Jesus. They do not present any direct scriptural quotation, and they both have commission statements, but the former of Mary and the latter of John the Baptist.

(6) Jesus is physically present in the Temple and Luke makes the most of it. The physical presence of Jesus and the pious custom of the presentation of the child (παρίστημι: v. 22) highlight the importance of the public event.

And (7) it is the only passage with an explicit *scriptural quotation*, which, characterizes Jesus as a "Holy one for the Lord" (2:23).

I find that the Presentation in the Temple joins and complements many other presentations to make up a gradual unfolding presentation of Jesus that is found in these opening chapters of Luke's Gospel. These first chapters of Luke truly present Jesus. Lk 2:22-39 is, however, the broadest and most complete characterization of Jesus. The Presentation in the Temple is a concise and condensed presentation of Jesus in the general overture, the more general presentation of Jesus in Luke 1–2. This passage provides a unique and thought provoking insight into the depiction of Jesus.

In Table I, the features of the characterization of Jesus in these different passages throughout the Lukan infancy narrative are compared with the features of the characterization of Jesus in the Presentation in the Temple. The features that appear in bold are the features of the Presentation in the Temple which do not appear in the rest of Luke 1–2, or the features of the rest of the Lukan infancy narrative which do not appear in Lk 2:22-39. The implicit christological affirmations of each passage are noted in brackets. The different narrative criteria to discern the importance of each passage are also compared.

TABLE I: Comparison Table between Lk 2:22-39 and Luke 1–2 (On the explanation of the table see the previous page)

	Announcement of John Lk 1:5-25	Announcement of Jesus Lk 1:26-38	Visitation and Mary's Canticle Lk 1:39-56	Birth, Naming, and Circumcision of John Lk 1:59-79	Birth, Naming, and Circumcision of Jesus Lk 2:1-21	Presentation of Jesus Lk 2:22-39	Twelve-year-old Jesus Lk 2:40-52
Kind of Plot	Revel. (John)	Resolution	Revelation (God)	Revelation (John)	Revelation (Jesus)	Res.-Rev. (Jesus)	Res.-Rev. (Jesus)
Commiss. Stat.	Of John	Of Mary		Of John		Of Jesus	
References to Jesus				(Fulfilling the Law)	(Fulfilling the Law)	Fulfilling the Law	
		Holy				Holy	
			Israel's Fulfillment	(Fulfill. the Proph.)	(Fulfill. the Proph.)	(Fulfill. the Proph.)	
			Elizabeth's **Lord**	(Messiah)	Messiah, **Lord**	Messiah of the Lord	
		(Davidic King)		(Davidic King)	(Davidic King)	(Davidic King)	
				Peace (on Israel)	Peace (on Israel)	Peace (of Simeon)	
		(Jesus' Name)		Saving power	Savior (Jesus' Name)	God's Salvation	
						In the Sight of the Peoples	
				Light in Israel		Light **for the Gentiles**	
					Glory to God	Glory for Israel	
						Fall and Rise	
						Sign Contradicted	
		Great	**Blessed Fruit**				**Growing up**
		God's (Most High) Son					**(Son of God)**
Reliable Char.	Angel Gabriel	Angel Gabriel	Elizabeth (Holy Sp.)	Zechariah (Holy Sp.)	Angel	Simeon (Holy Sp.) & Anna	Jesus
Location	Temple	Nazareth	Hill in Judea	Hill in Judea	Bethlehem	**Temple**	Temple
Scriptural Quo.						Lk 2:23.24	

Appendix: Four Other Possible Presentations

We can ask ourselves whether there is another presentation of Jesus after Luke 1–2.[181] Is there another pericope which presents Jesus to the reader in a better and broader sense than the Presentation in the Temple? I attest that we only find confirmations of the characterization of Jesus as it has already been depicted in Luke 1–2, specifically in Lk 2:22-39. In proving this, I will study, the episodes immediately before the beginning of Jesus' public life and the first passage of his public life (Luke 3:1–4:30) using the same narrative criteria as explained at the beginning of Ch. IV. The preaching of John the Baptist about Jesus (3:1-18), the baptism of Jesus (3:21-22), the temptations in the desert (4:1-13), and the first preaching of Jesus (4:16-30)[182] all speak about Jesus and can be understood as other important presentations of Jesus.[183] As Luke 3–4 is not a sequence as is Luke 1–2, I will study each passage separately.[184] Finally, I will draw some conclusions.

---

[181] The presentation of the main character of the literary work should be in the beginning and, according to the literary manners of the time, before the protagonist's public life.

[182] I limit my study to these passages because I believe that after Jesus' preaching at Nazareth there are no more pericopes in the beginning of the Lukan work which present Jesus. The preaching at Nazareth is the beginning of the public life, where Jesus has already been presented as the main character of the Lukan work. A bit later in the macro-narrative, there are two other important characterizations of Jesus: Peter's declaration about Jesus (9:18-21) and the transfiguration (9:28-36). The former presents Jesus as the "Christ of the God" (9:20: χριστὸς τοῦ θεοῦ); we had found a similar expression in the passage of the Presentation in the Temple (2:26: χριστὸς κυρίου). The latter presents Jesus in sparkling white clothing as God's "Son, the Chosen One" (9:35); we had found expressions with similar meaning in 1:32.35; 2:49; and 3:22. Luke, after having reprised these characterizations of Jesus, beginns the travel narrative to Jerusalem (9:51).

[183] I only omit two passages: the imprisonment of John the Baptist (3:19-20) and the genealogy of Jesus (3:23-38), whose main content regarding Jesus is his human condition and his divine filiation, which is implicitly affirmed (3:23.38).

[184] I do not maintain the unity of Luke 3–4 because it is not a unified plot. The only possible parallelism would be traced by the first preaching of John (3:1-18) and Jesus (4:16-30). However, the pericopes of Baptism, genealogy, and temptations concern only Jesus. And after the first preaching of Jesus, all the passages belong to the

1. The First Preaching of John (Lk 3:1-18)

The plot of this passage is a *revelation plot.* There is no turning-point. The narrator simply describes the episode through a clear *showing* description which is made up of the reference to the historical, political and religious context (3:1-3),[185] the direct scriptural citation of the prophet Isaiah (3:4b-6), the dialogues of John with several people (3:7-14), and the final preaching of John (3:16-17). The character revealed by the plot is John the Baptist. The solemn introduction underlines the importance of John because in that historical situation the word of God came to John (3:2b). The comment of the narrator and the direct scriptural reference introduce the ministry of John. Finally, his preaching also presents his character (3:7-9). The last verses of his preaching, however, refer to Jesus, while continuing to present John: John's preaching explains that he himself is not the Messiah (3:16-17). Finally, this revelation plot of John gives his *commission statement*: his calling to repentance, his baptizing and his preparatory function to Jesus' ministry (3:4-14).

In the end of his preaching, John the Baptist speaks about Jesus (3:16-17). John recognizes that Jesus will baptize with the Holy Spirit and fire, and that Jesus will judge, dividing the wheat and the chaff. The parallelism between John and Jesus is broken by John himself: "someone is coming, who is more powerful than me and I am not fit to undo the strap of his sandals" (3:16). In addition, if Jesus will baptize with the Holy Spirit, that means that Jesus will possess the Holy Spirit. John is presented as a *reliable character* who can speak about Jesus because the word of God came to him (3:2) and because the whole area of the Jordan river accepted his preaching and was expectant (3:15).

---

public life of Jesus. In addition, there is no chronological sequence; for example, the imprisonment of John precedes Jesus' baptism by John.

[185] This solemn introduction to the passage is only in Luke's gospel. The parallel account according to Matthew (Mt 3:1-12), or Mark (Mk 1:1-8) does not describe this introduction.

The passage takes place in the Jordan area (v. 3), a *profane location*. This passage has a clear public dimension and the narrator highlights the presence of many people (3:7.10.15.18). Narratively, the passage is highlighted by the presence of a *scriptural quotation* which has an introductory formula which even mentions the book from which the quotation is cited, the prophet Isaiah (3:4a).

2. The Baptism of Jesus (Lk 3:21-22)

If I had to catalog the type of plot of these two verses, I would define it as a *revelation plot*. There is no turning point. The vision of heaven opened, the Holy Spirit descending like a dove, and a voice from heaven speaking about Jesus define a *showing scene*. The heavenly vision and voice reveal the direct relation of Jesus with the divinity. However, there is *no commission statement* which might introduce his mission.

The baptism of Jesus presents two features of Jesus. First, Jesus, who had been called Holy (1:35; 2:23) because the Holy Spirit would come upon his mother (1:35), now receives the Holy Spirit (3:22).[186] Secondly, a voice comes from heaven and says: "You are my Son" (3:22). The divine filiation expressed by the angel (1:32.35) and affirmed by Jesus himself (2:49) is now reaffirmed by the voice from heaven.[187] The presence of the Holy Spirit descending on Jesus like a dove and the voice, which comes, unmediated, from heaven, become a *reliable character*, who declares the divine filiation of Jesus.

John was baptizing in the Jordan area (3:3). As the narrator does not say anything else, it is logical that Jesus was baptized in

---

[186] Whereas Mk 1:10 mentions simply "the Spirit," Luke has added the adjective τὸ ἅγιος, "Holy." Jesus, the "Holy one" (2:32) receives the "Holy Spirit." By contrast, Mt 3:16 has "God's Spirit."

[187] In view of 1:31-32 and 2:49, the readers are not learning something completely new. What is new is only that Jesus knows the affective aspect of this filiation. Jesus hears the voice himself: "You are my Son, the Beloved; with you I am well pleased" (3:22). Bovon says: "The affective aspect ("Beloved," ὁ ἀγαπητός) accompanies the legal aspect ("my Son," ὁ υἱός μου), and surpasses it at the end ("with you I am well pleased," ἐν σοὶ εὐδόκησα)" (BOVON, *Lukas* I, 181 [129-130]).

the Jordan River. In addition, right after Jesus' genealogy, the subsequent episode, the narrator says that Jesus "left the Jordan" area where he was (4:1). The presence of "all the people" (3:21) and the public manifestation of the dove and voice coming from heaven contribute to presenting the pericope as a public revelation plot.[188] The words that come from heaven are an implicit and controversial quotation. Actually, there are two different variants depending on two different OT texts.[189] However, there is no introductory formula *nor scriptural quotations*.

3. The Temptation of Jesus (Lk 4:1-13)

This passage develops a *resolution plot*. The action and movements of both characters, the devil and Jesus, underline the resolution plot. First, Jesus goes into the desert (4:1). Then, the devil leads Jesus to a height (4:5). Finally, the devil leads Jesus to Jerusalem and sets him on the parapet of the Temple (4:9). The repeated temptations and movements, up to three times, increase the tension of the plot. After each temptation the reader asks: Will Jesus give in to temptation? Will he pass the test? The climax appears with the resolution of the plot, in the third and final temptation. "Having exhausted every way of putting him to the test, the devil left him" (4:13). The resolution of the plot, with the victory of Jesus, ends the passage.[190] There is *no commission statement* because there is no word

[188] The voice which addresses its words to Jesus: "You are my Son" (Lk 3:22) is not enough to limit the manifestation to Jesus exclusively. It could be addressed to Jesus but heard by all the people around him. In addition, while Mark and Matthew explicitly say that Jesus saw the Holy Spirit descending like a dove (Mt 3:16; Mk 1:10), Luke affirms it without any restriction, that everybody saw the dove and heard the voice from heaven.

[189] The first variant says: "You are my Son, the Beloved; with you I am well pleased." It is very well attested but it could be a harmonization of Mk 1:10 and Mt 3:16. It depends on Is 41:8; 42:1 and puts Jesus in connection with the servant of *Yhwh*. The second variant says: "You are my Son; today have I fathered you." It is attested only in D. It depends on Ps 2:7 and puts in connection Jesus with the king-Messiah. On this textual criticism discussion see FITZMYER, *Luke I-IX*, 355-358.

[190] The French semioticians call this resolution plot, "performance de qualification." On this concept see PANIER, *La tentation de Jésus au désert*, 58-71.

about Jesus' mission. All that is said about Jesus concerns his identity, *who* he is.

The Lukan redaction presents three different temptations.[191] In the last, the devil tests Jesus by telling him that if he is the Son of God, he can throw himself down from the parapet of the Temple (4:9). When Jesus has been tempted he answers him, saying: "Scripture says: 'Do not put the Lord your God to the test'" (4:12).[192] It is an implied rebuke, that the devil should not have tempted Jesus to begin with, for in effect he was trying to put the Lord God to the test. Jesus is presented by the devil as a possible "Son of God" and is presented by Jesus himself in the place of God, the Lord. The title of κύριος had been already assigned to Jesus by Elizabeth (1:43) and the angel (2:11). Now Jesus assigns that title and the title of God (θεός) to himself. Jesus is a *reliable character*, "filled with the Holy Spirit" (4:1), who reprises a dimension of his identity, that he is the Lord, explaining it through the new title of *God*.

This passage begins with the affirmation, "Jesus left the Jordan and was led by the Spirit into the desert" (4:1) where the devil tested Jesus for 40 days (4:2). The pericope takes place in the desert, in a secular and private context. This passage is narratively underlined by the presence of several *scriptural references*. Either the devil (4:10-11) or Jesus use quotations of the OT for arguing. Jesus' answer to the three temptations is introduced by an introductory formula quotation,[193] which underlines the importance of the Scriptures (4:4.8.12).

---

[191] Bovon thinks that Jesus, in the three temptations, is respectively tempted as prophet, king, and priest (BOVON, *Lukas* I, 201). NOLLAND, *Luke 1-9:20*, 180-182, however, suggests that in the first temptation Jesus was tempted as second Adam (hunger); in the second one as true Israel (worship); and in the third one as God's Son (spectacular miracle).

[192] Jesus answers citing Dt 6:16 where Israel's temptation consisted of their tempting God by demanding water from him. Jesus' answer parallels the subject who is being tempted: as Israel tempted God, the Evil one tempts Jesus, who is his Lord and God (4:12).

[193] The first two times Jesus uses the expression "it is written" (4:4.8: γέγραπται), which is the formula that the devil also uses in the third temptation (4:10). Only the third time Jesus says "it is said" (εἴρηται) (4:12). "As if the devil's use has contaminated the form 'it is written,'" says NOLLAND, *Luke 1-9:20*, 181, "now Jesus says 'it is said.'"

4. The First Preaching of Jesus (Lk 4:16-30)

The plot of the account is a *revelation plot*. Jesus stands up to read (4:16) and "all eyes in the synagogue were fixed on him" (4:20), awaiting his words. In this moment, the narrative seems to pause; time stops. Everyone watches Jesus. Jesus reveals himself affirming the fulfillment of the prophecy of Isaiah in himself. The response to this first revelation is admiration; they are astonished (4:22). After Jesus' words the assembly keeps asking who this is, surely this is Joseph's son? (4:22), which gives the reason why Jesus continues to reveal himself, this time through the examples of the prophets Elijah and Elisha. The use of a strong OT typology, through a direct quotation (4:18-19) and a clear allusion to Elijah and Elisha (4:25-27), to reveal different shades of Jesus' identity is indicative of a plot of revelation. This revelation of Jesus becomes his *commission statement*. The quotation from Is 61:1-2 becomes the description of Jesus' mission: he is been anointed to bring the good news to the afflicted, to proclaim liberty to captives, to let the oppressed go free, and to proclaim a year of favor (4:18-19).

Jesus affirms that "this text is being fulfilled today" (4:21: πεπλήρωται). Thus, Jesus presents himself as the fulfillment of the prophecy. As the Holy Spirit was upon him in his baptism (3:22), now Jesus affirms that the Spirit of the Lord is on him. Jesus was previously presented as the anointed, the Messiah (2:11.26), and now Jesus himself confirms it.

Jesus also presents himself through the example of two figures of the OT. What Jesus says about himself as prophet is now compared to the experience of two great prophets of Israel: Elijah and Elisha. He is like Elijah who helped the widow at Zarephath, a town in Sidonia (4:26). He is like Elisha who cured Naaman the Syrian (4:27); Jesus presents his universal mission. Thus, the explicit universalism affirmed by Simeon (2:31-32) is now implicitly affirmed by Jesus himself.

The assembly reacts to Jesus' implication that his activity would have results among those who are not his townspeople and that they are like the persecutors of prophets of old (4:24), trying to throw Jesus off the cliff (4:29). Thus, the rejection of Jesus affirmed by Simeon (2:34-35) is first put into action by a scene.[194]

This passage takes place in the synagogue of Nazareth (4:16), in a public context. Being a religious *location*, it is not, however, the Temple of Jerusalem. Finally, in this passage we find a clear *scriptural reference*: the prophecy of Isaiah.

5. Conclusion of Appendix

The brief study of four passages right after the infancy narrative shows that the first preaching of John takes up again one feature of Jesus, "he is more powerful than me" (3:16), and adds two new ones, Jesus baptizing with the Holy Spirit and being capable of judging, dividing the wheat from the chaff. However, it develops a revelation plot of John with his commission statement.

The baptism reprises his divine filiation (1:32.35; 2:49) and adds the presence of the Holy Spirit in him (3:22). The temptation of Jesus repeats the title of Jesus, "Lord" (1:43; 2:11), and adds a new one: "God" (4:12).[195] Both passages, the baptism and the temptation of Jesus add these dimensions of Jesus' identity, but they do not say anything about Jesus' mission and *what* he will do.

The first preaching of Jesus presents many features of him and bears great similarity to the Presentation in the Temple. In fact, there are many similar features between Lk 2:22-39 and Lk 4:16-30: they both present Jesus as the Messiah (2:26; 4:18); they both relate the fulfillment of the Jewish expectations through Jesus' presence (2:25-27.38; 4:21); they both express through different images the salvation offered by Jesus (2:29-32; 4:18-19); they both affirm that

---

[194] In fact, the examples of Elijah and Elisha also help to present Jesus as a figure rejected by their people because of the rejection of these two prophets (1 Kings 19; 2 K 6:31-32).

[195] The themes concerning Jesus that are presented in Luke 3–4 and do not appear in the Presentation in the Temple are the presence of the Holy Spirit upon Jesus (3:22), his divine filiation as the "Beloved" (3:22), and his title of "God" (4:12).

Jesus' offer will have universal dimensions (2:31-32a; 4:25-27); they both present the rejection by part of Israel of that offer of salvation (2:34; 4:28-29); the main characters in both are reliable characters; their main plot is a revelation of Jesus; they both can be considered as commission statements of Jesus; and they both contain direct scriptural quotations.

Nevertheless, I believe it is a repetition of what has already been affirmed by Simeon. What has been prophesied by Simeon is told by Luke in a narrative account. The prophecy becomes narration. The order of the narration is important: the Presentation in the Temple (2:22-39) appears two chapters before the first preaching of Jesus (4:16-30). The former takes place in the Temple of Jerusalem, and the latter takes place in the synagogue of Nazareth. In addition, the explicit universalism of the Presentation in the Temple (2:31-32) becomes an implicit universalism in the first preaching of Jesus (the examples of the prophets Elijah and Elisha).

I maintain my claim that throughout Luke 3–4 we mainly discover confirmations of the characterization of Jesus as it was presented by means of Luke 1–2, and there is no single passage which presents Jesus in as broad and thorough a way as Lk 2:22-39.

In Table II, the features of the characterization of Jesus in these different passages throughout Luke 3–4 are compared with the features of the characterization of Jesus in the Presentation in the Temple. The features that appear in bold are in the Presentation in the Temple and do not appear in the passages of Luke 3–4, or they are in the passages of Luke 3–4 and do not appear in Lk 2:22-39. The implicit christological affirmations of each passage are noted in brackets. The different narrative criteria to discern the importance of each passage are also compared.

TABLE II: Comparison Table between Lk 2:22-39 and Luke 3–4 (On the meaning of the table see the previous page)

	Presentation of Jesus Lk 2:22-39	First preaching of John Lk 3:1-18	Baptism of Jesus Lk 3:21-22	Temptation of Jesus Lk 4:1-13	First preaching of Jesus Lk 4:16-30
Kind of Plot	Resolution-Revelation	Revelation (John)	Revelation (Jesus)	Resolution	Revelation (Jesus)
Commission Statement	Of Jesus	Of John			Of Jesus
References to Jesus	**Fulfilling Law** Holy Fulfillment of the Prophecy Messiah of the Lord (Davidic King) **Peace (of Simeon)** God's salvation In the Sight of the Peoples Light for the Gentiles **Glory for Israel** Fall and Rise Sign Contradicted	(Holy **Spirit**) (Judgement)	Holy **Spirit** **Son of God, the Beloved**	**Lord** **God**	**Spirit of the Lord (prophet)** Fulfillment of the Prophecy Messiah (Davidic King) Liberation-Remission (Universalism, Elijah and Elisha) Sight to the blind Jesus' Rejection
Reliable Character	Simeon (Holy Spirit) and Anna	John (God's Word)	Voice from Heaven	Jesus	Jesus
Location	Temple of Jerusalem	Jordan River	Jordan River	Desert (Temple)	Synagogue of Nazareth
Scriptural Quotation	Lk 2:23.24	Lk 3:4b-6		Lk 4:4.8.10-12	Lk 4:18-19

CHAPTER V

THE NARRATIVE FUNCTION OF LK 2:22-39 IN LUKE-ACTS

Compared to modern narrative, the synoptic Gospels seem very episodic, consisting of short scenes with few connecting plot threads. Nevertheless, a close reading of a Gospel as a unitary narrative can help us to understand the functions of the parts within the whole.[1] The significance of Lk 2:22-39 grows as we are able to relate it to more and more of the Lukan narrative showing the contribution of this single scene to the author's literary and theological project as a whole.[2] This is the reason why, in Ch. IV, I studied the connection of the Presentation in the Temple with its immediate context, the sequence of the Lukan infancy narrative. There I could underline the novel feature of the passage. The conclusions of that chapter highlighted Jesus' first entrance into the Temple, which becomes a privileged place of revelation of his universal salvation, and the divided response that he will provoke by Israel's acceptance and rejection of him. I will now study the connection of these differentiated features of the pericope with the macro-narrative.

---

[1] Acts is also very episodic. Nor does Acts have one single human protagonist. Yet even a narrative that focuses on a number of characters may merit being read as a unified narrative.

[2] I will read Lk 2:22-39 as a part of the unity of Luke-Acts, seeking to enrich our understanding of it. To overlook Acts is to ignore something essential for the understanding of the Gospel in general, and of the Presentation in particular. I am concerned with the meanings which emerge when we note how one part interacts with a related part. Themes are developed, dropped, and then presented again. Characters and actions may echo characters and actions in another part of the story providing internal commentary on the story, clarifying meanings and suggesting additional nuances.

I contend that these distinctive features provide an important *musical key* through which the mission of Jesus and the first Christians can be interpreted more clearly.[3] Luke uses the narrative technique of *parallelism* to characterize in a similar way the main characters of his literary work, Jesus, his disciples, and Paul.[4] The features of these presentations mirror the distinctive features of Jesus' presentation and recur throughout the narrative,[5] especially at the beginning and end of the public life of each character, and, thus, Luke shows *how* the Presentation is eventually fulfilled.[6] As the fig-

---

[3] They are like the musical key at the beginning of a piece of music. A musical key fixes a tonality for the whole piece, allowing a correct interpretation of the different staves. They are the key signature within the overture, Luke 1–2, for the whole composition.

[4] Jesus is clearly the main character of the Lukan Gospel. His disciples Peter, John, Stephen, Philip, etc., mainly represented by Peter as their public "voice," become the collective main character in the first part of Acts. Finally, the main character of the second half of Acts is Paul. Apart from the three accounts of Paul's presentation (see § 3.1), out of around 1,000 verses of Acts, Paul is in the foreground in more than 600 verses, mainly in the second half, while Peter appears in 250 verses, especially at the beginning of Acts. To understand Paul's and Peter's mission is to understand the meaning that Luke tries to give to Acts. As MARGUERAT, "Metteur en scène des personnages", 282-294, has proved, Luke takes special care as he artfully characterizes the different protagonists who develop his literary plot. On character building in Mark's Gospel, including a very useful appendix on the characterization of Jesus in NT accounts, see ALETTI, "La construction du personnage Jésus", 19-42; see as well DARR, *On Character Building*.

[5] I will use the narrative terms of *review* and *preview*. *Review* is the repetition of some topic which has already been introduced. This Chapter studies how the distinctive features of the Presentation are reviewed throughout Luke-Acts, although I will avoid continually repeating that the different passages are *reviews* of Lk 2:22-39. Even a prolepsis such as Lk 2:22-39 can be reviewed until its full realization. Preview is a previous introduction of some topic which has not yet been fulfilled. On these narrative terms see TANNEHILL, *Narrative Unity* I, 22.

[6] The prolepsis created by Luke in Lk 2:22-39 advances not only the mystery of Jesus, *who* he is, but also his mission, *what* he will do, and it replaces the kind of suspense deriving from the question "What will happen?" with another kind of suspense, revolving around the question about the manner in which Jesus' mystery and mission are gradually fulfilled throughout the macro-narrative: "*How* is it going to happen?" *How* will God carry out his promises and *how* will human beings react to that divine action? This progressive revelation of the *how* provides the dynamic of the reading process: the created suspense ensures that the reader continues to read.

ure below shows, Lk 2:22-39 enables the reader to understand more clearly and profoundly the importance of other main characters of Luke-Acts, and the literary design of the whole macro-narrative.

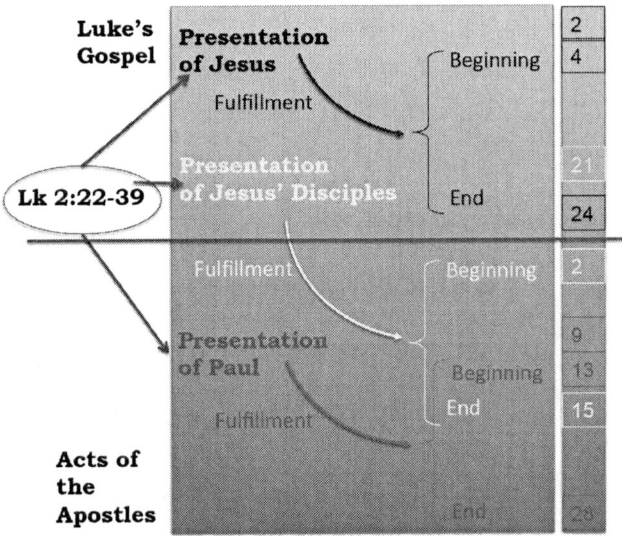

I will prove this through selected passages. Some of them present for the first time the main characters before their public lives; others fulfill in different ways those presentations in their public lives. How should these *selected* passages be chosen? I will focus on how a story is told, calling attention to the voice telling the story, the voice of the narrator through which the strategies and the shape of the narrative are presented. I will use the narrative criteria proposed in the previous chapter to discern the key texts not only about Jesus, but also about other main characters.[7] I will study the

[7] The Luke-Acts narrator seldom speaks in the first person. There are only a few exceptions: the prologue (Lk 1:1-4), in which the narrator speaks in the first person singular, and the "we passages" (Acts 16:10-17; 20:5-15; 21:1-18; 27:1–28:16). He chooses to efface himself in order to focus attention on his story. With the narrative criteria of Ch. IV, pp. 214-218, I will try to discern key texts for the narrator. The only criterion that I now will not use is the *kind of plot*. It was useful to recognize the dif-

commission which precedes the public life of each character and how it is fulfilled in their public lives, especially at the beginning and end. I will also consider the narratives which occur between the beginning and end of the public life of each character, in order to properly understand Luke's structure.[8] In these key passages I will study the distinctive features of the Presentation passage.[9]

1. Jesus in the Temple

1.1 Presentation/Commission by Simeon through the Holy Spirit

The narrator underlines the narrative importance of the Presentation in the Temple. The presentation account provides very important traits of Jesus, including his *commission statement*. It appears in a special *position* at the beginning of Luke-Acts, and, with the other passage which takes place in the Jerusalem Temple (2:40-52), at the end of the infancy narrative, as its climax. Furthermore, all of the data about Jesus is told by a *reliable character*, Simeon, and supported by another reliable character, Anna. Finally, it presents the first *scriptural quotations* of Luke-Acts and many scriptural allusions.

The *location* of this narrative, the Temple of Jerusalem (2:22. 25.27.37.38) is very important;[10] in fact it is the first time that Jesus

ferent characterizations of Jesus, but now I will study expressions and motifs of Lk 2:22-39 that are developed in Luke-Acts. They are present in many different passages whose plots would be too long to analyze.

[8] On the one hand, § 1.2.2, 2.2.2, and 3.2.2 try to show the concordance between the *inclusio* at the beginning and end of the sections dealing with each character and the narrative in the middle; on the other hand, they try to show the geographical architecture of the narrative. As Luke carefully interweaves his characters throughout his narrative, especially in Acts, these paragraphs focus on the respective character and not on a rigid delimitation. In addition, these paragraphs cover a longer narrative.

[9] I realize that I am mixing two different methodologies. I focus on aspects of the narrative level to discern the key passages of different characters, and on the linguistic level of verbal and nonverbal repetition to check the distinctive features of Lk 2:22-39. However, I think that it is a good way of studying a concrete passage with its specific expressions in connection with a long macro-narrative such as Luke-Acts.

[10] BACHMANN, *Jerusalem und der Tempel*, 132-170, provides evidence for the recip-

enters into the Temple. The route followed by the events narrated in the passages referring to Jesus in Luke 1–2 goes from Nazareth (1:26-38), passing by Judea (the hill country: 1:39-56; and Bethlehem: 2:1-21), and ending in the Temple (2:22-50). The Temple is the most fitting site for divine revelation (2:29-35; see as well 1:11-20; 2:49), also with the presence of the Holy Spirit (2:25-27). This revelation includes what is said about Jesus (2:38; see as well 2:46-47).[11]

On the other hand, the revelation of Jesus in the Temple picks up ways of characterization of Jesus presented by the previous passages, and explicitly adds two important new perspectives: the divine universal offer of salvation[12] and the human divided response in the acceptance by some and the rejection by others in Israel.[13]

---

rocal relationship between the Temple and the city. It is a question of two realities which are mutually defined. The Temple is the space which specifies the more generic dimension of the city of Jerusalem. Consequently, I will consider the terms *Temple* and *Jerusalem* to be very close, as Luke also does (Lk 21:6-24; 24:52-53; Acts 5:25-28; 24:11-12). On this close relation between the Temple and Jerusalem also see HARTMAN, "Ἱεροσόλυμα, Ἰερουσαλήμ", 436.

[11] Another feature is that the Temple is a special place for the prayer of the people (1:10); Simeon (2:28) and Anna (2:37) pray and praise in the Temple.

[12] I will study the term that Luke uses, σωτήριον (Lk 2:30), a rare word in the NT with only four occurrences (3x in Luke). The terms of universalism, λαός (in the plural, v. 31, and in the singular, Lk 2:32b) and ἔθνη (especially in the plural, Lk 2:32a), will guide my study. The term λαός is one of the favorite terms of Luke. It appears 84 times in Luke-Acts: 36 times in Luke's Gospel (3x in Mark's, 14x in Matthew's, and 3x in John's) and 48 times in Acts. The term ἔθνος is common in the Lukan literature as well. In his Gospel he uses it as the other Evangelist (Matthew, 13x; Mark 5x; Luke, 10x; John, 5x), but he uses it more often in Acts (43x). I will not enter into ethnic-racial dimensions in connection with λαός and ἔθνος. On this topic see BUELL, *Why this New Race*, 164-183, and HAYS, *From Every People and Nation*, 157-179. Because of Lk 2:32a: φῶς εἰς ἀποκάλυψιν ἐθνῶν, I will also study the connections between φῶς and ἔθνη.

[13] My study on rejection will be guided by the terms ἀντιλεγόμενον (Lk 2:34c: σημεῖον ἀντιλεγόμενον) and διαλογισμός (Lk 2:35b: ὅπως ἂν ἀποκαλυφθῶσιν ἐκ πολλῶν καρδιῶν διαλογισμοί). The verb ἀντιλέγω is a favorite of Luke. There are eleven occurrences in the NT, seven of them in the Lukan writings and none of them in the other synoptic Gospels (Lk 2:34; 20:27; 21:15; Acts 4:14; 13:45; 28:19.22; Jn 19:12; Rm 10:21; Tt 1:9; 2:9). The noun διαλογισμός is a favorite of Luke as well. It only appears eight times in the synoptic Gospels; six of them in Luke (Lk 2:35; 5:22; 6:8; 9:46.47; 24:38; Mt 15:19; Mk 7:21), and only six more times in the rest of

1.2 Fulfillment in His Public Life

1.2.1 At the Beginning: Jesus in Nazareth

The special *position* in which Luke places Jesus' first preaching (4:16-30), right at the beginning of Jesus' public life, highlights the narrative importance of the passage as a programmatic one.[14] The narrator also underlines this passage through its long *OT quotation* (4:16-17) and OT background of the prophets Elijah and Elisha (4:25-27). In fact, it is a direct quotation introduced by the expression "it is written" (γεγραμμένον) and by the liturgical assembly in which Jesus "opens the scroll of the prophet Isaiah" (4:17). Finally, Jesus is a *reliable character*, because the Spirit of the Lord is on him and has anointed him (4:18).[15]

Right after Jesus' birth, Simeon presents Jesus through distinctive features, and right at the beginning of Jesus' public life those features are confirmed. Paradoxically a prophetic passage (4:16-30) is also a first fulfillment of a previous one (2:22-39), which is reviewed by this prophetic episode.

---

the NT. As Simeon speaks about the fall and rise of "many in Israel," in trying to characterize this acceptance and rejection, I will also study the terms πίπτω, Ἰσραήλ, and Ἰουδαῖος, as expressions referring to the Jewish people and their fall. I am aware of the different nuances that each Greek term brings with it. The study of the specificity of each term would be overwhelming and would detract from the study of the topic and its general meaning in Luke-Acts.

[14] The reasons why commentators, for example TANNEHILL, "Luke 4:16-30", 21-27, use the term *programmatic* to describe the passage are the following two. First, while the three synoptic Gospels narrate this preaching in the synagogue of Nazareth, only Luke brings it forward and places it at the beginning of Jesus' public life (Mt 13:53-58; Mk 6:1-6). The fact that later Lk 8:4–9:16 follow Mk 4:1–6:45 and omit Mk 6:1-6 implies that Luke considers Lk 4:16-30 the same episode as Mk 6:1-6. Second, Luke considers Lk 4:16-30 the same episode as Mk 6:1-6 because when he follows Mk 4:1–6:45, he omits Mk 6:1-6; and as Jesus outlines his mission, this passage sets out the program for Jesus in the Gospel as well as anticipating central themes in Acts.

[15] For a long bibliography of this passage see SCHRECK, "Nazareth Pericope", 399-403.

a) Incipient Universalism

The scriptural quotation from Isaiah highlights the salvation offered by Jesus, (4:18-19). This salvation is offered to different groups of people, the afflicted, captives, the blind, the oppressed, and it is explained by the universalistic examples of those who bring salvation to non-Jews, even to enemies as Phoenicia and Syria, (4:25-27; see 1 K 17:9; 2 K 5:14), Elijah, sent to a widow in Sidon, and Elisha, cleansing the leper, Naaman the Syrian.[16] These references are still more striking because universalism is not very prominent in the common biblical portrayal of Elijah and Elisha.[17] The Lukan Jesus, however, isolated the passages in which they performed signs to those outside of Israel. The reference to these prophets, narrative prototypes of Jesus, who benefit Jews and also Gentiles, stands for the universal dimension of Jesus; the reference to Pagans indicates a major group toward which the mission is moving.[18]

---

[16] FALCETTA, *The Call of Nazareth*, 76-82, remarks that the presentation of Jesus through the quotation of Isaiah and the examples of Elijah and Elisha are a specific Lukan characterization of the universalism of Jesus because they appear only in the Lukan account.

[17] The cycle of Elijah (1 Kings 17–2 Kings 1) and the cycle of Elisha (2 Kings 2–13) present numerous wars against the non-Jews. In addition, in Elijah's triumph over the prophets of Baal on Mount Carmel, Elijah slaughtered the prophets of Baal (1 K 18:40).

[18] Elijah and Elisha are scriptural models for Jesus' healing ministry, including with foreigners: a foreign officer's servant in 7:1-10, parallels Elisha's healing of Naaman, Aram's king's servant, referred to in Lk 4:27; and Jesus' raising of the widow's son in 7:11-17, found only in Luke, recalls Elijah's raising of a widow's son in Sidon, referred to in Lk 4:25-26. In fact, SIKER, "First to the Gentiles", 86-90, contends that this parallelism develops the prophecy-fulfillment motif; the prophecy of Lk 4:25-27, is fulfilled in Lk 7:1-17. Furthermore, KIDDLE, "The Admission of the Gentiles", 165, and LANE, *Gentile Mission*, 44-45, connect not only Luke 4 and Luke 7, but also Acts 10 through the character of the centurion Cornelius, a foreign officer. For other accounts of Jesus' ministry to outsiders in Luke's Gospel, see the great crowd of people from Tyre and Sidon (Lk 6:17-19, which is in Mk 3:7-8, but not in Matthew); Jesus' words that foretell a future of mercy and grace for pagan cities (Lk 10:13-14); the possessed man in the healing of the Gerasene demoniac (Lk 8:26-39), where the presence of a herd of pigs and swineherds, and the fact that the event takes place in the Decapolis, suggest a Gentile district (Lk 8:32-34); note also the preaching about the sign of Jonah (Lk 11:29-32), in which non-Jews are portrayed as more receptive of Jesus than Jews (see O'TOOLE, *Unity*, 101; MBILIZI, *D'Israël aux nations*, 14).

b) Incipient Division in Israel

While Jesus' speech at Nazareth (4:16-22) actualizes the hope of Simeon's first speech, the synagogue's response (4:23-30) dramatically confirms the warning contained in Simeon's second speech. As Simeon foresaw Jesus dividing many in Israel through their fall and rise (2:34), this division also appears in the synagogue in Nazareth when Jesus experiences acceptance and rejection.[19] Thus, from the beginning Luke puts into action the rejection foretold by Simeon. What has been prophesied by Simeon is told by Luke in a dramatic fashion through a narrative account. The rejection's prophecy becomes narration.[20]

Right after the universalistic examples (4:25.27), the acceptance of the synagogue drastically turned into rejection (4:28-29).[21] The attempt of the angry Nazarenes to kill Jesus fails, for Jesus simply passes through their midst and goes on his way (4:30). This mysterious event may convey the impression that a power is at work which will not be blocked by human resistance until the last attempt to kill Jesus, that time in Jerusalem. In their almost successful attempt to kill Jesus, Luke provides a narrative preview of the passion.[22] Fitzmyer says: "The rejection story symbolizes the opposition that his ministry will evoke among his own. The rejection

---

[19] There is a chronological difference between Simeon's prophecy and the passage in Nazareth. While Simeon foresees division in Israel, simultaneous acceptance by some and rejection by others, the event in Nazareth describes a chronological succession: Jesus is first accepted and then rejected.

[20] There are three rejections which all occur on the narrative threshold of three geographical areas in Luke's Gospel: the rejection in Nazareth (4:28-29) before Jesus' preaching in Galilee (4:16–9:50); the rejection in Samaria (9:53) before Jesus' journey to Jerusalem (9:51–19:44); and the rejection in Jerusalem (19:47), before Jesus' preaching in Jerusalem (19:45–21:38).

[21] When the people in the synagogue heard the universalistic example of Elijah, they were enraged (4:28). HILL, "Rejection", 161-180, emphasizes the coherence of the Lukan composition: by proclaiming the year of the Lord's favor, Jesus evokes an approving amazement from the crowd; but by specifying that it will realize itself outside of Israel, he arouses angry rejection. Luke suggests that rejection within Israel will be linked to the bestowal of gifts upon Gentiles.

[22] Lk 4:29 describes the geographical situation which does not correspond to the real Nazareth. Perhaps Luke is trying to link Nazareth and Jerusalem, the first and the

of him by the people of his hometown is a miniature of the rejection of him by the people of his own *patria* in the larger sense."[23] Nazareth, the first to accept and reject Jesus, is an image of the whole of Israel. In Jesus' rejection by his persecutors, Luke anticipates the problem of the entire composition.[24]

1.2.2 Travel Narrative to Jerusalem

a) To the Temple of Jerusalem

Luke reflects the very same geographical orientation in Jesus' infancy narrative and Jesus' public life. As the account about Jesus in his infancy started in Galilee and, through Judea, arrived at the Temple of Jerusalem, so the account about Jesus' public life starts in Galilee and the region of Galilee (Nazareth: 4:16–9:50), and goes through Judea (9:51–19:44) to the Temple of Jerusalem (19:45–24:53).[25]

From the beginning of the travel narrative, the narrator affirms that "Jesus set his face to go to Jerusalem" (9:51), thereby orienting the entire travel narrative towards Jerusalem. The section is characterized by redactional additions that refer to the journey.[26] These

---

last attempt to kill Jesus; both narratives happen outside the city and on a hill (4:29; 23:26.33). On this parallelism see BOVON, *Lukas* I, 216, who cites SAMAIN, "Le discours-programme", 37.

[23] FITZMYER, *Luke I-IX*, 529.

[24] For example, the statement that "they threw him out (ἐκβάλλω) of the town" (Lk 4:29) foreshadows later situations. Anticipating his own death, Jesus tells of the tenant's treatment of the beloved son of the vineyard owner: "they threw him out (ἐκβάλλω) of the vineyard and killed him" (Lk 20:15). The report of Stephen's death is similar: "they threw him out (ἐκβάλλω) of the city and stoned him" (Acts 7:58). Paul and Barnabas are thrown out (ἐκβάλλω) of the territory of Pisidia (Acts 13:50). Finally, Paul is thrown out of the city of Lystra and stoned (Acts 14:19). On parallelisms of this passage see BONZ, *The Past as Legacy*, 123, and TANNEHILL, *Narrative Unity* I, 72.

[25] I realize that this geographical description is very broad and sometimes imprecise. However, I believe that the general geographical description of the infancy narrative is developed throughout the rest of the Lukan Gospel.

[26] Luke repeats expressions like "to go to Jerusalem," "to make the journey to Jerusalem" or "to go up to Jerusalem" (9:51.53; 13:22.33; 17:11; 18:31).

redactional references increase toward the end of the journey.[27] The verb ἐγγίζω, on the other hand, repeated successively in 19:29.37.41, evidences the imminence of the entrance into the city. However, the text of Luke does not affirm explicitly that Jesus enters Jerusalem. Instead, Luke underscores Jesus' entrance into the Temple, the place where the journey of Jesus ends. The entrance into the sanctuary becomes the culminating moment of the travel narrative.[28] This structure, particular to Luke, shows the importance that the geographical progression plays in the Gospel of Luke, in its infancy narrative and in the rest of the Gospel.

b) Incipient Universalism

Throughout the travel narrative, there are several previews of the universal mission by the Lukan Jesus.[29] I will not try to prove this historical universal mission by Jesus or his followers,[30] but Luke's particular vision of that topic and how he transmits it to the implied reader. The Lukan Jesus, who had been foreseen by Simeon as "light of revelation for the Gentiles," prepares the development of the universal mission in Acts. The commandment that the risen Christ gives at the end of the Gospel has already been implicitly announced in different ways throughout Luke's Gospel.

---

[27] In 19:1, Jesus passes to Jericho; in 19:11 he is next to Jerusalem; in 19:28 he goes up to the city; in 19:29 he is on the way to Bethphage and to Bethany through the Mount of Olives; in 19:37 he is already prepared to go down the mountain to the city, which he is able to view in 19:41. The details of these movements lead little by little to the arrival of Jesus in Jerusalem.

[28] This detail of Luke's account is more important when we realize that the other synoptics, which do not repeatedly underscore Jesus' journey to Jerusalem, do always mention his entrance into the city (Mt 21:10; Mk 11:11). Luke's redaction presents, therefore, in this point, its own specificity. The Lukan Jesus goes directly from the Mount of Olives (19:37) to the Temple (19:45).

[29] Travels of the Lukan Jesus outside Jewish confines are not narrated; there is no equivalent to those in North-East Galilee in Mt 15:21-39 and Mk 7:24-8:10.

[30] On whether or not the Gentile mission historically originated with Jesus in some way or other, see SCHNABEL, "Mission to the Gentiles", 37-58; and WILSON, *The Gentiles*, 255-267. On the delay of the Parousia in connection with the historical mission to the Gentiles see GRÄSSER, *Das Problem der Parusieverzögerung*, 209-215.

One of these previews is the parable of the light in a house.[31] There, Jesus may be implicitly presented by Luke as light for the Gentiles: "No one lights a lamp and puts it in some hidden place; they put it on the lamp-stand so that people may see the light when they come in" (11:33). It is interesting to compare the reason given by Luke for putting the lamp on the lamp-stand in comparison to the reasons given by the parallel versions of Mark and Matthew. In Mk 4:21 the reason is not given. In Mt 5:15 the reason is so the lamp gives light to all those in the house. In Lk 11:33, however, the lamp is put on the stand due to a different reason: ἵνα οἱ εἰσπορευόμενοι τὸ φῶς βλέπωσιν.[32] In addition, neither Mark nor Matthew mention the word light (φῶς) in the logion.[33]

Also among this preview are the three parables about the kingdom of God in connection with Gentiles.[34] The parable of the mustard seed is introduced by Jesus' question, What is the kingdom of God like? It appears in the three synoptic Gospels (Mt 13:31-32; Mk 4:30-32; Lk 13:18-19), and in the *Gos. Thom.* § 20.[35] Jesus com-

---

[31] On the universal dimension of this parable see LANE, *Gentile Mission*, 132-138.

[32] The participle εἰσπορευόμενοι can reasonably be taken as a secondary meaning to allude to those who are invited in to see the light, the Gentiles. Luke uses the verb εἰσπορεύομαι elsewhere in a figurative sense for entering the kingdom (18:24). Furthermore, in Acts 14:27 Luke describes the Gentiles entering the Church as coming through a door of faith. The *Gos. Thom.* § 33 affirms that that person puts the lamp on the stand so that everyone who comes in and goes out will see its light. This seems an unreasonable addition since when leaving, light in the house is no longer needed, and may have been inserted because of the proclamation directed towards outsiders.

[33] Not just once, but twice Luke has made this addition to the logion (8:16; 11:33). Because of its immediate context, namely the explanation of the parable of the Sower (8:11-15), Lk 8:16 seems to refer to God's word. The immediate context of Lk 11:33 is Jesus' words about himself as being a sign greater than Jonah and Solomon (11:29-32). When Luke repeats 8:16 later in 11:33, he obviously intends it to have a different nuance. Lk 11:33 is centered more on Jesus.

[34] Other previews are the mission of the 70 (72), which I will study in § 2.1.1, Jesus' ministry *for everyone,* poor people, women, sinners, and Samaritans, highlighting the socially and ethnically inclusive salvation already presented by Luke in Jesus' public life, or even the Lukan redaction of the genealogy of Jesus, which traces Jesus back to Adam, linking Jesus to all of humanity (3:28).

[35] For the *Gospel of Thomas* I use the bilingual edition in Coptic and Greek by U.-K. Plisch.

pares the kingdom of God to a tree where the birds of the air shelter in its branches. The reference to all the birds of heaven, which Luke shares with the other versions, is understood as meaning the nations of the world (see Ezk 17:22-23; Dn 4:11). A comparison of the Lukan version with the other versions reveals the peculiar importance of this parable. In all the other versions the mustard seed is the smallest of all the seeds, but when it has grown it becomes the largest of trees. Luke omits all reference to the size of the seed. Instead there is mention of the seed growing and becoming a tree. This Lukan version can be better understood in conjunction with the growth of the Church in Acts. Despite Jewish opposition, imprisonment of the disciples, and all kinds of difficulties, the Church grew to include not only Jews but also Gentiles; [36] all sorts of birds of the air made nests in its branches.[37]

The grown mustard tree welcoming all kinds of birds is closely connected with Jesus' subsequent saying about the kingdom. This is the parable of the narrow door, which appears in Lk 13:22-30 and in Mt 7:13-27 with variations. Luke, compared to Matthew, has toned down the emphasis on exclusion from the kingdom[38] and has emphasized the origin of those that are to be included: "people from east and west, from north and south, will come in" (13:29). It can be understood as a reference to the future inclusion of the Gentiles, who will come from all over the world in Acts.

The parable of the great banquet also speaks about the kingdom and has the same content (14:15-24). Relating how those who had been invited to the banquet gave excuses in order not to attend

---

[36] In Acts there are ten summaries of Church growth: 2:41.47; 4:4; 5:14; 6:7; 11:21.24; 14:1; 17:4; 18:8. The first five are to be seen in connection with the acceptance of the good news by Jews, while the latter five are to be viewed with regard to the inclusion of Gentiles in the Church.

[37] LANE, *Gentile Mission*, 138-143, argues that this was no accident, but was Luke's intention.

[38] For example, we can compare Lk 13:27 ("I do not know where you come from") with Mt 7:23 ("I have never known you"). This reduction of the parameters of exclusion from the kingdom is even clearer in the parable of the great banquet. There Luke omits Mt 22:7, when the king sent his troops and destroyed those men who rejected his invitation, which is peculiar to Matthew.

(14:18-20), the parable reveals how salvation has been opened up to all. This parable also occurs in Mt 22:2-10 with many variations, and in the *Gos. Thom.* § 64.[39] While the versions in Matthew and the *Gospel of Thomas* have only one stage in the process of the opening of the banquet (Mt 22:9-10), there are two stages in the Lukan process. The first command of the master of the banquet is to "go out quickly into the streets and alleys of the town" (14:21). Jesus says that invitations should be extended in the town, the Jewish society, to the outcasts, the marginalized.[40] It is an articulation of the inclusion of all kinds of citizens, all kinds of Jews. The second command, which is peculiar to Luke, seems not to refer to the town, but to the open roads and the hedgerows outside the city (14:23).[41] It is the expression of perfect universality because the invitation is addressed to those outside Jewish society.[42] According to Jeremias and other scholars, the first invitation to come into the banquet was for the tax collectors, sinners, and outcasts of Israel, and the second one for the Gentiles.[43]

---

[39] Although there is no total consensus, the parallel version of the *Gos. Thom.* § 64 is generally considered to be the closest to the words of Jesus (PERRIN, *Rediscovering*, 113). The version in the *Gospel of Thomas* has less allegory, and presents a fourth guest.

[40] According to LANE, *Gentile Mission*, 144-149, the former, the streets, would have been the normal place of communication with the elite, while the latter, the alleys, often little more than open sewers so narrow that a donkey could not travel through them, were areas where the lower strata of society lived. So the servant is asked to exceed the normal means of communication with the lesser members of Jewish society.

[41] Instead of this second command, Mt 22:11-14 affirms that when the king noticed one man who was not wearing a wedding garment, he ordered that the man be bound hand and foot and thrown into the darkness outside, because few are chosen. Luke again reduces this exclusion.

[42] According to LANE, *Gentile Mission*, 144-149, this area was inhabited by those who were not allowed to live within the city because they were impure pagans.

[43] JEREMIAS, *Die Gleichnisse Jesu*, 61-63, believes that the parable is a missionary command in that all are compelled to enter. KILGALLEN, *Twenty Parables*, 88, suggests that both invitations express with biblical style the idea of going everywhere and with all kinds of people. With differing nuances, the following scholars agree with Jeremias: DODD, *The Parables of the Kingdom*, 122; EVANS – GASQUE, *Luke*, 227; and GALBIATI, "Gli invitati al convito", 133-134. On the other hand, when Jesus calls the first disciples, only in Luke are there two boats (Lk 5:1-11; dif. Mt 4:18-22 and Mk 1:16-20). Bovon suggests that these two boats could refer to both types of Christian fishing, among Jews and among Gentiles (BOVON, *Lukas* I, 235).

These three parables about the kingdom constitute a lengthy central section in which the theme of universality, even in the entrance into the kingdom of God, is strikingly previewed.[44]

c) Incipient Division in Israel

As Simeon had foretold (2:34), the presence of Jesus creates division in Israel because, generally speaking, the people of Israel accept him and the authorities of Israel reject him.[45] On the one hand, during the journey to Jerusalem the people accompany Jesus (12:1; 14:25; 18:36; 19:3), wondering because of his miracles (11:14; 13:17), and bringing infants to him (18:15). Arriving in Jerusalem, Jesus is welcomed by the crowd as a king who comes in the name of the Lord (19:37-38).[46]

On the other hand, the clash between the authorities and Jesus is expressed in the controversies with the lawyers (10:25); a Phar-

---

[44] Their *position* (Lk 13:18–14:24) is not only at the center of Luke's Gospel, but it is even at the center of its travel narrative and Jesus' teaching throughout it (Luke 9:52–19:44). Ó FEARGHAIL, *Introduction to Luke-Acts*, 84, maintains that both volumes have a central unit on universalism (Lk 13:18–14:24; Acts 15:1-35).

[45] In the section Lk 12:51–13:9, Jesus presents himself as a cause of division. It starts with a feature that is not frequent in the synoptic Gospels, Jesus speaking in the first person singular about himself: "Do you suppose that I am here to bring peace on earth? No, I tell you, but rather division" (12:51). The call to interpret the time, to repent or perish, and the parable of the barren fig tree underline the need for an immediate decision. Because of his presence among human beings, every single person has to choose. This is the reason for the emphatic ἀπὸ τοῦ νῦν, "from now on" (12:52). For a broader study of these verses see GEORGE, "La venue de Jésus", 62-71.

[46] This acceptance by the general people of Israel was already manifest in Jesus' ministry in Galilee. The same proponents (μαθητής, ὄχλος) encountered in the earlier Galilean section are found in the journey to Jerusalem, and in similar measure. The crowd at Capernaum was impressed by his teaching (4:32), and the people came to him from all over the place to listen to his word (4:40; 5:1.17; 6:18-19; 8:4.40; 9:37). A big crowd accompanied him (7:11), exclaiming that he was the great prophet who had appeared among them (7:16), and following him even to the desert (9:11). The acceptance of Jesus by the crowd is attested to by the multitudinous congregation of people at his speeches (6:20-49; 9:10-17, up to 5,000 men), and Lk 6:17 speaks of a large gathering of his disciples. From among these disciples, Jesus chose his apostles (6:13), who leave everything to follow him (5:11).

isee criticizes the absence of ablutions (11:38) and Scribes and Pharisees who try to catch him in something he might say (11:53-54; 14:1).[47] This rejection progressively increases throughout the narrative particularly after Jesus' denunciation of Pharisees, lawyers and Scribes (11:37-53; 16:14-15), the different healings in Sabbath (6:6-11; 13:10-17; 14:1-6), and Jesus' stay among sinners (15:1). Jesus' words show it when he first says: "Anyone who is not against you is for you" (9:50), but a bit later, within a bigger controversy, he says: "Anyone who is not with me is against me" (11:23).

1.2.3. At the End: Jesus in Jerusalem

The long sequence after the end of the travel narrative brings the Lukan Gospel to an end with the presence of Jesus in Jerusalem. Through its *position*, right at the end of the Gospel, and its *location*, in the city of Jerusalem, the narrator underlines its importance. Furthermore, for more than two chapters (19:45–21:38) Jesus teaches, as a *reliable character*, in the Temple, where the Gospel finishes (24:53).

a) Presentation of Jesus in the Temple

The main feature of the relationship between Jesus and the Temple at his presentation during his infancy, the Temple as his place of revelation, is repeated during his use of the Temple in his public life.[48] In Luke, the Temple is the only place in which the activity of

---

[47] Even before the travel narrative the authorities already rejected Jesus (Φαρισαῖος, γραμματεύς, νομικός). The scribes and the Pharisees begin to think (διαλογίζομαι): "Who is this man, talking blasphemy?" (5:21-22). Jesus knows the negative thoughts (διαλογισμός) of the scribes and Pharisees judging him (6:8). Finally, the first announcement of the Passion underlines this rejection of Jesus by the authorities: "by the elders and chief priests and scribes" (9:22). The division between the people who accept and the authorities who reject also appears in John's baptism when the people are baptized but the authorities refused to be baptized (7:29-30).

[48] When Jesus enters the Temple, he himself highlights another Temple characteristic. Citing the oracle of Is 56:7, Jesus considers the Temple to be the house of God, a house of prayer (Lk 19:46).

Jesus in Jerusalem is developed. In fact Lk 19:45–21:38 is delimited at the beginning and at the end by two Lukan narrative summaries of Jesus' ministry in the Temple, which form a clear *inclusio*:

19:47-48	ἦν διδάσκων τὸ καθ' ἡμέραν ἐν τῷ ἱερῷ	ὁ λαὸς γὰρ ἅπας (...) αὐτοῦ ἀκούων
21:37-38	ἦν δὲ τὰς ἡμέρας ἐν τῷ ἱερῷ διδάσκων	πᾶς ὁ λαὸς (...) ἀκούειν αὐτοῦ

In Luke, Jesus remains in the Temple and teaches continually in it.[49] The Temple becomes the place in which the people are able to listen to the prophetic proclamation and teaching activity of Jesus (19:45-47; 20:1; 21:1-4.5-7). The people of Israel may effectively and continually be reached by Jesus in the Temple (19:48; 20:9.45; 21:37; 22:53). The Temple as a place of revelation is fully realized because Jesus reveals himself, reaching all of the Jewish people through his teaching.

b) Division in Israel

Simeon's prophecy about the division in Israel foretells that Israel is about to form two different factions: those who accept Jesus and those who reject Jesus. This prophecy is clearly fulfilled where it was foretold, i.e. in Jerusalem (2:34).[50] There, there is a general acceptance by the simple people of Israel, as Simeon and Anna welcomed Jesus, and there is a general rejection by the authorities of Israel.[51] Luke carefully distinguishes between the response of the

---

[49] Luke eliminates the changes in places and times, nights in Bethany and days in Jerusalem that are mentioned in the other synoptics (Mt 21:23; Mk 11:11.15.19.27).

[50] The division in Israel previewed during Jesus' ministry in Galilee and his travel narrative (see § 1.2.1.b and 1.2.2.c) reaches its climax in Jerusalem.

[51] Luke is the only synoptic Evangelist who employs the noun "authorities" in the passion narrative (23:35; 24:20). He uses ἄρχοντες to speak in a generic way about the Jewish leaders. When I speak of *authorities* I use this very same Lukan generic meaning which principally includes chief priests, scribes, and elders, but it also includes the whole Sanhedrin, Sadducees, etc.

inhabitants of Jerusalem, that of the common people, and that of their authorities.

The people of Israel accept Jesus during his last days in Jerusalem.[52] Jesus teaches the entire people (20:1.9.26.45; 21:38), who hang on Jesus' every word (19:48); from early morning they throng to him in the Temple to listen to him (21:38, only in Luke); the authorities do not lay hands on Jesus because they are afraid of the people who accept him (19:47-48; 20:19; 22:2).[53] Going to the crucifixion, large numbers of people follow him, and women too, who mourn and lament for him (23:27, only in Luke). At the crucifixion the people stay there watching; as for the leaders, they jeer at him (23:35, only in Luke).[54] After Jesus' death all the crowds go home beating their breasts (23:48, only in Luke).[55]

The people (λαός) appear to reject Jesus only once (23:13),[56] and it is a controversial verse; it is part of the trial before Pilate, in which

---

[52] On the role of the people in Luke's passion narrative see TIEDE, *Prophecy*, 103-118.

[53] The disciples and the people are a type of "barrier" protecting Jesus from the opposition. On the contrary, in Mark and Matthew Jesus faces his passion alone.

[54] The punctuation and the adversative δέ are important in perceiving the different reactions of the people, who passively watch, and of the leaders, actively jeering at Jesus: καὶ εἱστήκει ὁ λαὸς θεωρῶν. ἐξεμυκτήριζον δὲ καὶ οἱ ἄρχοντες. In addition, the Lukan verse is very different from the parallels which record that, "The passers-by jeered at him; they shook their heads" (Mt 27:39; Mk 15:29). On this verse see LAGRANGE, *Évangile selon Saint Luc*, 588; GOULDER, *Luke* II, 76

[55] This beating their breasts by the crowds could be understood as a recognition of their own passivity, simply seeing the unjust murder. The accusation against the people of Jerusalem of responsibility for Jesus' death in Acts (3:13-15) and the call to repentance (2:38; 3:19.26; 5:31) are like a *recognition scene*, in which persons who have acted blindly against their own interest through their passivity or actions (Acts 3:17) may at a later time discover the truth. Aristotle wrote of the importance of *recognitions* (ἀναγνωρίσεις) in tragic plots. Aristotle also notes the role of *ignorance* in those recognition scenes (ARISTOTLE, *Poet.*, 1450a; 1453b-1454a).

[56] The crowd (ὄχλος) seems to reject Jesus only twice and both occurrences refer to the Jewish authorities and not to the Jewish people. First, ὄχλος appears in the arrest scene (22:47), but the identity of those who arrive to arrest Jesus is disclosed gradually: Judas (22:47), the chief priests (22:52a), the leaders of the guard of the Temple (22:52b), and the elders (22:52c). Second, in the first appearance before Pilate, he speaks to the chief priests and the crowd (23:4: ὄχλος). However, this crowd are those who rose from the assembly and brought Jesus before Pilate (23:1); and that assembly was made up of the elders of the people, the chief priests and scribes (22:66).

he summoned the "chief priests and the leading men and the people."[57] The preceding context shows how the Sanhedrin, not the people, accuse Jesus (23:1-2). In addition, the presence of the whole people of Israel is strange in a trial before Pilate; in the subsequent verse (23:14) Pilate affirms that "you brought this man before me as that one who turns away the people" (ἀποστρέφοντα τὸν λαόν). It is strange that the people accuse Jesus of turning away the very same people. In fact, some manuscripts present the "chief priests and the leading men *of* the people (τοῦ λαοῦ)" as we find in Lk 19:47; Acts 4:8; 23:5.[58] This single and controversial occurrence is not comparable to the many occurrences in which the people accept Jesus in Jerusalem (Lk 21:38; 23:27.35.48, only in Luke).[59]

At the same moment in which Jesus is generally accepted by the common people, he is in conflict with their authorities. Jesus' warnings and admonitions to the authorities (20:9-18; 21:5-36) are juxtaposed with repeated references to the people's favorable response (20:26; 21:37-38). The verses Lk 19:47-48 are a good example.[60]

---

[57] All of the subsequent main verbs refer to this group of people and are expressed in an implicit plural. As one man, "they" howled (23:18), shouted back (23:21), and kept on shouting at the top of their voices (23:23). However, their identity is only explicitly expressed in Lk 23:13.

[58] See 16, 348, 1216, several Old Latin Versions, Latin Vulgate Version, Syriac Peshitta Version, and the Coptic Bohairic Version as referred to in THE AMERICAN AND BRITISH COMMITTEES OF THE INTERNATIONAL GREEK NEW TESTAMENT PROJECT, *The Gospel According to St. Luke* II, 208. Certainly, the external attestation of this variant is scarce, and it could be a posterior correction of scribes who wanted to make this verse agree with the whole Lukan passion narrative, where the leaders of the people reject Jesus, but not the people of Israel. The presence of this variant further underlines the difficulty of this verse.

[59] On the contrary, the people repeatedly reject and insult Jesus in Mark and Matthew (Mt 27:20-26.39-40; Mk 15:11-15.29-30). In Mark and Matthew all the Jews, both leaders and the people, are united in the hostility against Jesus. Only in Matthew and Mark do the people of Israel take an active part in Jesus' trial (Mt 27:17-20; Mk 15:8-10), and in Matthew the people recognize their guilt in Jesus' death: "Let his blood be on us and on our children!" (Mt 27:25).

[60] "The chief priests and the scribes, in company with the leading citizens, tried to do away with him, but they could not find a way to carry this out because the whole people hung on his words."

Each section of Jesus' stay in Jerusalem, his teaching in the Temple (19:45–21), and his passion (22–23), begins with a notice about the conspiracy against Jesus by the Jewish authorities, chief priests, scribes, and leaders of the people (19:47b-48; 22:1-2). In fact, the conflict is the most important motif, which also serves as the primary force driving the narrative plot forward. The Jewish authorities who reject Jesus are in the foreground during these chapters, and their rejection turns into persecution[61] and the persecution terminates in his arrest (22:52). The Jewish authorities preside over the Sanhedrin (22:66-67), take Jesus to accuse him before Pilate (23:2.4.13.14) and also appear as his accusers before Herod (23:10). They are again present calling for Jesus' execution when Pilate gives sentence (23:13). Finally, in Lk 24:20 the disciples of Emaus accuse the Jewish authorities of handing Jesus over to be sentenced to death and be crucified. Among these Jewish authorities are the chief priests and the scribes (19:47; 20:19; 22:2; 23:10), the elders (20:1; 22:52),[62] the chiefs of the people (19:47; 23:13.35; 24:20),[63] the soldiers (22:4.52), Pilate (23:2-7), and Herod (23:8-12).[64]

---

[61] The chief priests, the scribes, and the elders are suspicious of Jesus' authority (20:1-2). The Sadducees reject (v. 27: ἀντιλέγω, dif. Mk 12:18 and Mt 22:23) Jesus' doctrine on resurrection (20:27-39). And Judas makes a pact with the chief priests to betray him (22:4).

[62] García Pérez interprets the "many" of Simeon's prophecy (Lk 2:34) as a translation mistake. Appealing to Si 8:2, he argues that the original Semitic expression was misunderstood. "Many" mistakenly replaces the original "elders," those who have the power to govern. According to García, the prophecy of Simeon refers to the Passion in which the elders reject and condemn Jesus (see GARCÍA PÉREZ – HERRANZ MARCO, *La infancia de Jesús*, 92-93).

[63] However, even within the Jewish Council there is a person who accepts Jesus, Joseph of Arimathaea, "a member of the Council, a good and upright man" (23:50). He had not consented to what the others members of the Council had planned and carried out, and he put the body of Jesus in a tomb.

[64] Unlike Mt 27:62 and Jn 18:3, where the Pharisees arrest Jesus and accuse him before Pilate, the Pharisees do not appear in the Lukan passion narrative. Their last appearance is in Lk 19:39 when they call Jesus "master." Luke has already prepared this positive presentation of the Pharisees by showing them inviting Jesus to their houses (7:37; 14:1) and advising him of Herod's anger against him (13:31). However, the scribes were mainly Pharisees, and the scribes did reject Jesus (19:47; 20:19-20; 22:2; 23:10).

What reason can be given for this deadly opposition by the Jewish authorities to Jesus? They see Jesus' ministry as a direct threat to their own positions of leadership and to the institutions that perpetuate the contemporary religious order. They see Jesus as opposing God, as they understand God to be, and that is why they must resist Jesus with agressive persistence. They see all of this because of Jesus' preaching in the Temple, which appears to be the final cause of the Jewish leader's rejection. First, Jesus is acclaimed as a "king" by the people (19:38) and takes possession of the newly "cleansed" Temple (19:47).[65] This makes the Jewish leaders suspicious and jealous, and most especially of Jesus' authority with the people (20:1-2). Second, after Jesus' teaching of his parable of the wicked tenants, the scribes and the chief priests realize that the parable was aimed at them (20:19); this parable says that the tenants thought (διαλογίζομαι) of killing the heir of the vineyard. This is the reason why the scribes and chief priests test him, trying to put him under the authority of the procurator (20:20) to kill him. And third, when Jesus foretells the destruction of the Temple he announces the coming of the Son of man, his own coming, in a cloud with power and great glory (21:27); it is a self-description as one who will be glorified as judge of the world after his suffering.

The identity of those who reject Jesus is highlighted not only by what Luke narrates, but also by what he does not say. Luke omits the scene in which the Roman soldiers mock Jesus (Mk 15:16-20) and moves directly from "he delivered Jesus to *their* will" (Lk 23:25) to "and as *they* led him away" (Lk 23:26), which refer to the authorities of Israel. They are those who reject and persecute Jesus in Jerusalem, and not the pagans.[66]

---

[65] Jesus entered into the Temple driving out those who were busy trading and accusing them: "you have turned the house of prayer into a bandits' den" (19:46). Moreover, Jesus warns the people against the authorities' behavior affirming "beware of the scribes" (20:46).

[66] In addition, two accredited and formal witnesses, the governor Pilate (23:4.13.15.22) and the king Herod (23:11.15), proclaim Jesus' innocence several times. Even the narrator affirms Pilate's desire to set Jesus free (23:20). Furthermore, the centurion gives praise to God and proclaims after Jesus' death that he was an upright man (23:47). The only passage in which soldiers jeered at Jesus, offering him vinegar, is Lk 23:36, which follows

2. Christians in Jerusalem

2.1 Presentation/Commission by Jesus

Jesus' commission of his disciples is developed in two different stages. The first one, during the travel narrative, implicitly previews the disciples' universalism and rejection. The second one embraces the passion and resurrection narrative: right before his passion Jesus foretells his disciples' rejection, and immediately following his resurrection Jesus entrusts the universal mission to his disciples.

2.1.1 An Incipient Commission: The Mission of the 70 (72)

I find a preview of the Jesus' commission of his disciples in the mission of the 70 (72). There an implicit universalism and division appears, in connection with Jesus' disciples. The mission of the 70 (72) is a *commission statement* of the disciples,[67] and it is spoken by a *reliable character*, Jesus. The *position* of the mission of the 70 (72) is underlined by the fact that it occurs right at the beginning of the travel narrative to Jerusalem. Going to Jerusalem, the Lukan Jesus already thinks of the universal mission of his disciples and of their rejection.

The mission of the 70 (72) is peculiar to Luke (10:1-20).[68] It appears that Lk 10:1-12, the sending of the 70 (72), while adding new features, repeats several affirmations of Lk 9:1-6, the sending of the twelve.[69] Luke is the only Gospel with a mission "dou-

Mk 15:36. In the other passage in which "soldiers" guarded Jesus mocking and beating him (22:63-65), these "soldiers" are guards of the Sanhedrin (23:66).

[67] The commission is underlined by the numerous verbs expressed in imperatives (Lk 10:2.3.4.7.8.9) and in the future tense (Lk 10:6.13).

[68] Luke has redacted it with the material that he had from the sending of the twelve in Mark (Lk 10:4 parallels Mk 6:8-9), Q, (Lk 10:1-12 is paralleled by Mt 9:37-38 and Mt 10:7-16, while Lk 10:13-15 is paralleled by Mt 11:20-24, and Lk 10:16 is paralleled by Mt 10:40), and has added his own material and understanding (Lk 10:17-20 is without any parallel).

[69] For example, Lk 10:4 repeats Lk 9:3-5. In addition, there are similarities in form

blet," and Luke usually avoids doublets in his Gospel.[70] I will focus on the material peculiar to Luke in an attempt to discover his purpose in narrating this new mission. I claim that more universalistic features emerge in the mission of the 70 (72), and it is meant by Luke as a preview of the future Gentile mission. [71]

Of special interest is the number 70 (72), only found in Lk 10:1. Why would Luke have chosen that number? It might have been a round number,[72] but it could also have been a symbolic number with a particular significance for him. Just as the twelve obviously called to mind the twelve tribes of Israel,[73] there are good reasons to suggest that the number 70 (72) was meant by Luke to represent the number of the peoples on the earth suggested by Gn 10:32. Genesis 10 is often referred to as the *table of nations* because it records the genealogy of the 70 (72) nations of the post-diluvian world, who descended from Noah and his three sons. From these, the nations spread abroad on the earth and repopulated the world after the universal flood. Some Lukan manuscripts follow the MT of Gn 10:2-31, which lists the 70 offspring of the sons of Noah.[74] Other manuscripts follow the LXX, where the descendents of

(structure of sending and return: 9:1-6.10; 10:1-16.17-20), and in content (kingdom: 9:2; 10:9b.11; healing: 9:2; 10:9a; subjection of demons: 9:1; 10:17; no provisions: 9:3; 10:4; and divided response: 9:5;10:10.16). Luke himself links both missions, affirming that the Lord appointed 70 (72) "others" (ἕτερος: 10:1) thus implicitly referring to the other twelve chosen first.

[70] For instance, the duplication of the feeding miracle (Mk 6:32-44 and 8:1-9; Mt 14:13-21 and 15:32-38) is avoided by Luke (only Lk 9:10-17).

[71] Luke has rewritten the history of salvation shaping his Gospel in such a way so as to make his task of describing the mission to the Gentiles in Acts easier. It seems that the Gospel lays the groundwork for Acts, and it does so consciously.

[72] So GELDENHUYS, *Commentary on the Gospel of Luke*, 299.

[73] Lk 22:30 promises that the twelve apostles will sit in judgment on the twelve tribes of Israel. This link is confirmed by the fact that Jesus selected twelve apostles (Lk 6:13), and, since Judas died as a traitor, he should be replaced by another to complete the number twelve (Acts 1:15-26). On the number of twelve apostles and its connection with the twelve tribes see MEIER, "Restoration of Israel", 365-404, and BAUCKHAM, "Restoration", 469-477.

[74] These main manuscripts are the following: ℵ A C L f^1 and f^{13}. 1 En. 89:14.18-20.59 portrays the people of Israel as twelve sheep forced to live precariously in the

Shem, Ham, and Japheth number 72.[75] This textual problem of whether the number is 70 or 72 only serves to strengthen the connection with the tradition of the number of nations in Genesis 10. From a very early point, the scribes connected the mission of the 72 with the number of nations which repopulated the world after the universal flood. The mission of the 72 might be seen as anticipating the Gentile mission in Acts,[76] where the twelve remained attached to Jerusalem while many others left to spread the good news of Jesus even to many other nations.[77]

---

midst of 70 wolves (cf. Lk 10:3). The number of examples of 70 in the OT is overwhelming. There are always 70 souls in the house of Jacob, 70 elders, sons, priests (Ex 24:1), and 70 years mentioned in chronological references to important events. These examples and Nb 11:16-17 could also serve as a background with the same meaning of the number 70.

[75] The main manuscripts are the following: 𝔓[75] B D, along with Old Latin and Syriac versions. In 3 En. 17:8; 18:2; 30:2 the number of princes and languages in the world is 72, but these sporadic instances are not to be compared in significance with the tradition involving 70. As METZGER, *A Textual Commentary,* 126, affirms, "in order to represent the balance of external evidence and the indecisiveness of internal considerations, a majority of the committee decided to include the word [δύο] in the text, but to enclose it within square brackets to indicate a certain doubt that it has a right to stand there." For a fuller discussion of the external and internal evidence, see the Chapter entitled, "Seventy or Seventy-two Disciples?" in METZGER, *Historical and Literary Studies*, 67-76, who concludes that the problem cannot be decided by the conventional logic of textual criticism. The popularity of the number 70 in the Hebrew tradition, the relative obscurity of 72, and the use of the number 72 in the Septuagint argue in favor of 72 as the more original reading, subsequently "normalized" to 70 by copyists at a very early stage in the manuscript tradition. This is the reason why I prefer the 72.

[76] As BÉCHARD, *Paul Outside the Walls*, 228, has proved, many of the same motifs used to define the missionary experiences of the 72 disciples in Luke 10 are later repeated in the missionary episodes in Acts: work of healing and proclaiming God's reign (Lk 10:9; Acts 8:12; 19:8; 20:25; 28:23.31); the possibility of acceptance or rejection (Lk 10:8-12; Acts 13:51; 18:6); the subjection of demons in Jesus' name (Lk 10:17; Acts 3:6; 4:10.30; 16:18; 19:13); authority over Satan (Lk 10:18-19; Acts 13:10; 26:18); and promise that nothing will harm the witnesses (Lk 10:19; Acts 5:17-26; 12:6-11; 14:19-20; 16:25-40; 27:9-44). Likewise the joy (χαρά) attributed to the 72 disciples upon their return from the successful mission often characterizes the missionaries in Acts (Lk 10:17-18; Acts 8:8; 12:14; 13:48.52; 15:3).

[77] Who were these 72 that appear with such importance in Luke's Gospel? It is striking that the name *Acts of the Apostles* is not entirely justified, because it only gives

The mission of the 72 presents Jesus' mandate of going to houses and staying in the same house (Lk 10:5-7; Mt 10:11-13). Only Luke narrates Jesus' command of "taking what food and drink they have to offer" (Lk 10:7), and even repeats this command (Lk 10:8). Luke does not say overtly that Jesus commanded to break the Jewish dietary laws, but the commands of Lk 10:7-8 are strange if the 72 were to minister only to Jews.[78] The Lukan Jesus commands the 72 to eat and drink what is set before them and to stay in the houses, anticipating the dismantling of Jewish-Gentile social barriers in Acts 10–11, when Peter saw all kinds of animals and was ordered to eat (Acts 10:11-13) and Peter stayed in the house of the Pagan Cornelius (Acts 10:24-28).[79]

Finally, Luke does not present Mt 10:5b-6, which limits the missionary effort to Israel, without evangelizing Samaria or the nations: "Do not make your way to Gentile territory, and do not enter any

---

detailed knowledge of Peter and Paul, and the latter is not one of the original twelve. In fact, Luke is reluctant to ascribe to Paul the title "apostle" (out of the 26 occurrences of the term "apostle," only twice it refers to Paul and Barnabas), and he does not fit the stated requirements to become an apostle (Acts 1:21-22). Except concerning Peter, the only information that we learn from Acts about the apostles is that James, John's brother, was executed by the sword (Acts 12:2), and John is Peter's shadowy figure (Acts 3:1.3.4.11; 4:13.19; 8:14). The other nine are mere names (Acts 1:13). The twelve do not get nearly as much attention as could be anticipated. On the contrary, an extensive set of characters, who are not in the list of the apostles, appears. For example, Stephen, in Acts 6:8–7:60; Philip, in Acts 8:6-40; some Jerusalemites, in Acts 11:19-24; Paul and his helpers, Barnabas, Jude and Silas, Timothy, and Apollos, in Acts 15:22-40; 16:1-29; 17:4-15; 18:5.24; 19:1.22; Sopater, Aristarchus, Secundus, Gaius, and Tychicus and Trophimus, in Acts 20:4.

[78] Actually, it seems that the ministry of the 72 missionaries takes place in Samaria. Jesus sent them out ahead of him, to all the towns and places he himself would be visiting (10:1), and he was walking through Samaria (9:52.56). On the religious status of Samaria see § 2.2.2, especially pp. 315-316.

[79] Other passages of Acts that insist on the absence of any dietary law are Acts 15:19-21 with the Council at Jerusalem and its letter to the Gentile believers (Acts 15:23-29). While Acts 10 annuls the distinction between clean and unclean animals, Acts 15 progresses to dietary freedom and deals with the ways in which animals are killed and prepared for eating. In harmony with the command of staying in whatever house invites the missionaries is Acts 16:15, where Lydia said to the missionaries: "If you judge me a true believer in the Lord, come and stay with us."

Samaritan town; go instead to the lost sheep of the House of Israel."[80] The restrictions on the mission are absent in Luke, even in the first mission of the twelve. There are no restrictions, implying a universal mission.[81]

The mission of the 72 does not only preview the universal mission of Jesus' disciples, but it also previews the division that they will provoke. As Jesus divided *Israel* between those who received him and those who did not, in the same way his disciples will divide *all the towns* where they go (10:8-11).[82] And those who reject Jesus' disciples are actually rejecting Jesus and *vice versa* (10:16).[83]

2.1.2 Commission by Jesus before His Passion: Rejection by Everyone

This prediction from Jesus of his disciples' rejection takes place in a special *location*, the Temple. The narrator highlights its importance through its *position* (Lk 21:12-17), right at the end of

[80] Perhaps Luke did not know of Mt 10:5-6. However, Luke does not present Mk 7:24-30 either, even though Matthew does (Mt 15:21-28), when Jesus says to the Syrophoenician woman, "It is not fair to take the children's food and throw it to little dogs" (v. 26). Although this passage is located in a pagan region, Tyre, Luke could have omitted the whole incident, which is dominated by the Jewish disparagement of the Gentiles from the lips of the Markan Jesus.

[81] A last universalistic feature is that during the mission of the 72, Luke presents the woes to Chorazin, Bethsaida, and Capernaum (10:13-15). In fact, Matthew refers to them in a very different context (Mt 11:20-24). They are relevant because the Jewish cities, Chorazin and Bethsaida, are compared with pagan cities, Tyre and Sidon. Despite Jesus' ministry in Capernaum, the inhabitants are chided for their lack of repentance. Capernaum will be thrown into Hades, the opposite of heaven. By inserting the rebukes to Jewish cities and the good disposition of pagan cities into the mission of the 72, Luke underlines the universal mission and its acceptance by pagans.

[82] In fact, in the town where the disciples are not received, they should wipe off the very dust of that town that clings to their feet, and leave it. In Acts, when the Christians are thrown out of a city, they shake off the dust from their feet or shake out their garments and go to another city (Acts 13:51; 18:6). In doing this, they are following the instructions Jesus gave to the 72 in Lk 10:11.

[83] The repetition of the verb ἀθετέω (4x in Lk 10:16) highlights not only the importance of rejection, but also the parallelism between Jesus' rejection and his disciples' rejection.

Jesus' teaching in the eschatological speech, and through its *reliable character*, Jesus. In addition, the way in which the disciples will be received is presented in a *commission statement*.[84]

As Simeon foretold Jesus' rejection at the beginning of Luke's Gospel, Jesus foresees his disciple's rejection at the end of Luke's Gospel. Right before his passion, in Lk 21:12-17, he says to them:

> You will be seized (ἐπιβαλοῦσιν ἐφ' ὑμᾶς τὰς χεῖρας αὐτῶν) and persecuted (διώξουσιν); you will be handed (παραδιδόντες) over to the synagogues and to imprisonment, and brought (ἀπαγομένους) before kings and governors for the sake of my name and that will be your opportunity to bear witness. [...] I myself shall give you an eloquence and a wisdom that none of your opponents (οἱ ἀντικείμενοι ὑμῖν) will be able to resist (ἀντιστῆναι) or contradict (ἀντειπεῖν). You will be betrayed (παραδοθήσεσθε) even by parents and brothers, relations and friends; and some of you will be put to death (θανατώσουσιν). You will be hated by everyone on account of my name.[85]

There are three similarities between both texts. First, according to Simeon, Jesus will be a sign of contradiction: οὗτος κεῖται (...) εἰς σημεῖον ἀντιλεγόμενον (2:34c). According to Jesus, his disciples will be rejected (21:15: ἅπαντες οἱ ἀντικείμενοι ὑμῖν).[86]

Second, as Jesus was going to be a "sign of contradiction," his disciples are going to be contradicted for the sake of Jesus' person, for the sake of his name (Lk 21:12.17). In fact, the rejection of Jesus' disciples was due to the proclamation of Jesus' name

---

[84] Jesus commands his disciples to be his witness (21:13). In fact the whole speech is addressed to the future through many of its verbs in the future tense (21:12.13. 15.16.17).

[85] For a broader study of these verses in connection with their historical context see DEHANDSCHUTTER, "La persécution des chrétiens", 541-545.

[86] The verb ἀντίκειμαι is made up of the prefix ἀντι- and κεῖμαι, which is the verb used in Simeon's prophecy. The rejection expressed by the verb ἀντίκειμαι is repeated by the verbs ἀντιλέγω and ἀνθίστημι, which present the same prefix ἀντι-. However, those who will reject them (ἀντίκειμαι), although they will want to resist (ἀνθίστημι) and contradict (ἀντιλέγω), will not be able to do so because Jesus will give the Christians eloquence and a wisdom (21:15). Those who reject Stephen cannot resist against him either (Acts 6:10: ἀνθίστημι; cf. Lk 12:11-12).

(Acts 5:40-41; 9:16; 15:26; 21:13). In Jesus' disciples Jesus is still rejected. When Paul is persecuting Jesus' disciples, Jesus himself says to Paul: "Saul, Saul, why are you persecuting me?" Paul asks: "Who are you?" And the answer repeats: "I am Jesus, whom you are persecuting" (Acts 9:4-5; 22:7-8; 26:14-15).[87] And though these words were spoken only once, Luke repeats them three times. The persecution of the Christians was in truth the persecution of Jesus himself.

And third, as the cause of both rejections is the same, Jesus' prophecy about his disciples' rejection is linked to his own rejection.[88] In fact, the very same verbs of Jesus' prophecy are developed in the rejection of Jesus and his disciples.[89] Jesus' rejection is the archetype of his disciples' rejection, and Simeon's prophecy is fulfilled first in Jesus, as the prototype, and then in his disciples.[90] This terminology reflects the description of the persecution throughout Luke-Acts.[91]

The first one, ἐπιβάλλω τὰς χεῖρας ἐπί (Lk 21:12), "lay hands on," refers to Jesus (Lk 20:19), and to his followers: Peter and John (Acts 4:3), the apostles (Acts 5:18), James and other Christians (Acts 12:1), and Paul (Acts 21:27; 28:17). The second verb, διώκω (Lk 21:12), "persecute," describes how Jesus (Lc 11:49), and Christians (Acts 22:4; 26:11) have been persecuted.

---

[87] We find a similar affirmation after the persecution of Peter. The Christians lifted up their voice to God, saying: "Kings on earth take up position, princes plot together against the Lord and his Anointed, [...] against your holy servant Jesus whom you anointed" (Acts 4:26-28). Again Luke decides to repeat that the persecution against the Christians is, in fact, persecution against Jesus.

[88] The link between both rejections is highlighted by the fact that the Lukan Jesus foretells his disciples' rejection immediately before his ultimate rejection, his passion and crucifixion.

[89] As Simeon's prediction about Jesus is fulfilled in Luke's Gospel, Jesus' prediction about his disciples at the end of Luke's Gospel is explicitly fulfilled in Acts.

[90] The rejection already foretold, first by Simeon and then by Jesus, has an apologetic function, trying to avoid the scandal of leaders' persecution (Jesus, Peter, Paul, etc.). It gives comfort for the reader in the persecution.

[91] For a thorough study of these verbs in Luke-Acts see ZMIJEWSKI, *Die Eschatologiereden des Lukas-Evangeliums*, 129-140.

The third one, παραδίδωμι (Lk 21:12.16), "hand over," refers to Jesus (Lk 20:20; 22:4.6.21-22.48; 23:25; 24:7.20; cf. Lk 9:44; 18:32; Acts 3:13); Christian men and women (Acts 8:3; 22:4); Peter (Acts 12:4); and Paul (Acts 21:11; 27:1; 28:17).

The fourth one is ἀπάγω/ἄγω (Lk 21:12), "lead," used in a context of rejection. It is referred to Jesus (Lk 4:29; 22:54.66; 23:1). In fact, Philip explains that the Isaianic quotation "as a lamb led to the slaughter" (Acts 8:32) refers to Jesus. And it also refers to the apostles (Acts 5:21.26.27), Stephen (Acts 6:12), Peter (Acts 12:4), Christians (Acts 9:2.21; 22:5), Gaius and Aristarchus (Acts 19:37), and Paul (Acts 18:12; 21:34; 23:10.31). Finally, Paul especially fulfills Jesus' predictions that Christians will be led before kings (βασιλεύς) and governors (ἡγεμών) in Lk 21:12. The governor Festus has Paul led before him (Acts 25:6-12) and, later, before King Agrippa II (Acts 25:13-27; 26:1-32).[92]

The fifth verb, θανατόω, (Lk 21:16), "kill," is a *hapax* in Luke-Acts. However, Luke employs other synonymous verbs such as ἀναιρέω "to do away with," or ἀποκτείνω "to kill." Those that are "done away with" are Jesus (Lk 22:2; 23:32; Acts 2:23; 10:39; 13:28), the apostles (Acts 5:33), Paul (Acts 9:23.24.29; 23:15.21.27; 25:3), James, the brother of John (Acts 12:2), Stephen (Acts 22:20), and the Christians (Acts 26:10). Similar is Luke's use of ἀποκτείνω, because different opponents want to kill Jesus (Lk 18:33; 20:14-15; Acts 3:15; cf. Lk 9:22; 13:31.34), and Paul (Acts 21:31; 23:12.14; 27:42).

Jesus' prophecy is a much more extensive and concrete description than Simeon's prophecy. For example, it makes more precise the identity of those who are going to reject Jesus and his disciples. While Jesus was going to be rejected just by "many in Israel" (Lk 2:34), his disciples are going to be hated "by everybody" (Lk 21:17: ὑπὸ πάντων), by parents and brothers, relations and friends (Lk 21:16). It seems that Jesus' disciples' are going to be rejected not only by Israel, but universally rejected.[93]

[92] Earlier Jesus had already been led before a governor (Pilate: Lk 23:1-7) and before a King (Herod: Lk 23:8-12).

[93] Another difference is the final parenetic verse: "Your perseverance will win you your lives" (v. 19). Jesus encourages his disciples in view of their being rejected.

2.1.3 Commission by Jesus after His Resurrection: Universalism

The *position*, being the last of words of Jesus before his ascension, underlines the narrative importance of the passage (Lk 24:44-49). At this key transition point in the narrative,[94] Jesus summarizes his role as Messiah and speaks to his disciples for the last time. It is highlighted as well by the *repetition* of similar affirmations in two different passages, at the end of Luke's Gospel (Lk 24:44-49) and at the beginning of Acts (Acts 1:8). It is obvious that the risen Jesus speaks with authority, as a *reliable character*, in Luke-Acts. When Jesus is vindicated by God through resurrection, he commissions his disciples as witnesses through a *commission statement*, a universal mission.[95] After the death and resurrection of Jesus, Luke's narrative remains located in the surroundings of the Temple of Jerusalem,[96] where the last solemn words of Jesus are pronounced in a special *location* for Luke, Jerusalem.

As Simeon spoke about Jesus' universal mission in the Temple of Jerusalem at the beginning of the Gospel (2:32), at the end Jesus speaks about his disciples' universal mission in Jerusalem. In fact, so far the reader has found only previews of universalism;[97] the revelation to all the Nations has not yet been

---

[94] SCHUBERT, "Structure and Significance", 175, contends that Lk 24:44-49 belongs to the larger unit of 24:36-53, and that is the climax of the risen Lord's revelation to his disciples throughout Luke 24. When the disciples have finally understood and accepted the necessity of the Messiah's death and resurrection, Jesus can go on to instruct them about their universal mission

[95] Although the future tense does not appear in the commission of Luke 24, the future projection is present in the necessity of preaching to all nations (24:47), and in the imperative of v. 49. In addition, the thrust of the account of Acts 1 is forward looking, as it is indicated by the number of verbs in the future tense (1:8: λήμψεσθε and ἔσεσθε; 1:5: βαπτισθήσεσθε; 1:11: ἐλεύσεται).

[96] After the resurrection, it is reported only in Luke that the disciples remain in Jerusalem. In the other two synoptic Gospels, the angel who appears at the empty sepulchre orders the disciples to go to Galilee (Mk 16:7; Mt 28:7). In the Gospel of Luke, the angel says nothing of the disciples going to Galilee (Lk 24:7). On the contrary the risen Jesus orders them to remain in Jerusalem (Lk 24:49). Therefore, only Luke restricts the apparitions of the risen Jesus to Judaea.

[97] Jesus has spoken some words with an implicit universalism (see § 1.2.1.a and 1.2.2.b).

fulfilled. A small number of Gentiles have been released from sickness or demons, but the nations have not yet seen the light of God's salvation. The narrative tension caused by this unrealized promise is resolved by Jesus commissioning his disciples to carry on his mission. This is why the risen Jesus, before his ascension, entrusts a universal commission to the apostles and those who were with them (24:33).

a) From the Temple...

Just as the infancy narrative begins and ends in the Temple, the whole of the Gospel of Luke also begins and ends in the Temple.[98] The minor *inclusio* (Lk 1:9; 2:46) anticipates the major *inclusio* (Lk 1:9; 24:53).

Jesus' mandate of remaining in Jerusalem is found in both Lk 24:49 and in Acts 1:4. In this way Luke not only closes the Gospel, but he also unifies the two parts of his work. Thus Luke creates both an skilful *inclusio* to conclude the third Gospel and an effective bridge to the beginning of Acts. Jerusalem becomes the focus that unites the Gospel of Luke with Acts. I suggest the following concentric structure:[99]

---

[98] The Gospel opens with the offering of incense to God in the Temple (1:8) and closes with the praise of God in the Temple (24:53). In addition, the Gospel starts with a priest, Zechariah, who neither blesses nor speaks (1:22), and finishes with Jesus, who both speaks and blesses (24:46-49.50). On this priestly connection between Zechariah and Jesus see GRAPPE, "De Zacharie à Jésus ressuscité", 298-303. HUTCHEON, "God is With us", 20, asserts: "The Gospel opens with the sequence 'Temple,' 'descent' (of Gabriel to Zechariah and Mary), and 'blessing' (Zechariah's *Benedictus* at Lk 1:67), and closes in reverse order with 'blessing,' 'ascent,' and 'Temple.'"

[99] On these concentric structures, which although are part of the signifier, hold the narrative, and also its signified, see n. 32 in Ch. III.

"Preaching from Jerusalem to all the nations:"[100]	24:47
"You are witnesses:"	24:48
"Sending of the Spirit (promise of the Father):"	24:49a
"Remaining in the city:"	24:49b
Ascension of Jesus:	24:50-51
Praise in the Temple:	**24:52-53**
Ascension of Jesus:[101]	1:2
"Remaining in Jerusalem:"	1:4a
"Sending of the Holy Spirit (promise of the Father):"	1:4b.8a
"You will be witnesses:"	1:8b
"Preaching from Jerusalem through the limits of the land:"	1:8c

The concentric structure at the end of the third Gospel and the beginning of the Acts shows the direct relationship between both books of the NT: the story of Jesus and the story of his witnesses.[102] Luke carefully avoids a big division between the two parts of his one narrative.[103] The fact that the disciples remained

---

[100] The quotation marks highlight Jesus' words.

[101] While in Lk 24:50-51 the ascension of Jesus is narrated, it is only referenced in Acts 1:2. On the difference between both ascension stories see BOVON, "The Lukan Ascension Stories", 583. The first is connected to the Jewish tradition about the priestly responsibilities of blessing the people of God (Si 50:1-21; 2 Kings 2; 2 Baruch), and the second one resembles more the Greco-Roman tradition about the end of Romulus and Heracles.

[102] The relationship between the end of the third Gospel and the beginning of Acts is not limited exclusively to the concentric structure described above. The end of Luke's Gospel speaks of the persecution that the Jewish authorities undertake against Jesus, as the beginning of Acts describes the persecution of the Jewish authorities against the first Christians (4:1; 5:24). The Temple serves as a place of refuge for Jesus in the third Gospel (19:48; 22:2.6) and for his disciples in Acts (4:21; 5:26). For other lexical repetitions such as the "two men in brilliant clothes" (Lk 24:4; Acts 1:10), or the question of the heavenly characters regarding the reason for the human witnesses' behavior (Lk 24:5; Acts 1:11), see PUIG I TÀRRECH, "La finale de Luc", 222-224.

[103] The recommended procedure for this is the *interweaving of extremities*. The end of the first part previews the beginning of the second part, while the beginning of the second part reviews what is been told at the end of the first part (LUCIEN, *Hist. Conscr.*, 55.64; DUPONT, "La question du plan des Actes", 28-36). KRÄNKL, *Jesus der Knecht Gottes*, 166, holds that the ascension at the same time ends the Gospel of Luke, and serves as a solemn beginning of Acts. The same happens at the end of 2 Chronicles and the beginning of Ezra: they both narrate Cyrus' edict.

in the Temple, praising God, is the center of this concentric structure, and it clearly underlines its importance.

b) ... To the Gentiles

If we pay closer attention to these words of the risen Jesus, we find an important repetition of the topic of universalism.

Lk 24:47a:	καὶ [...] εἰς **πάντα τὰ ἔθνη.**
Lk 24:47b:	ἀρξάμενοι ἀπὸ **Ἰερουσαλήμ**
Lk 24:48:	ὑμεῖς **μάρτυρες** τούτων.
[...]	
Acts 1:8a:	ἔσεσθέ μου **μάρτυρες**
Acts 1:8b:	ἔν τε **Ἰερουσαλήμ** [...]
Acts 1:8c:	καὶ ἕως **ἐσχάτου τῆς γῆς.**

In the inner part of this parallel structure (Lk 24:48; Acts 1:8a), Jesus' words underline the importance of witness. The first Christians receive the mission of being witnesses, in charge of the diffusion of Jesus' name (Acts 5:27.32; 22:1.15; 26:1.16).[104]

This spreading of the good news should start at Jerusalem (Lk 24:47b; Acts 1:8b). In this city, which is the center of the history of salvation, the activity of universal proclamation begins. Jerusalem is indeed the place in which the message of salvation is proclaimed for the first time by the witnesses of the risen Lord and the center and point of departure for the mission to the entire world.[105] There is only one mission, which is a universal one, although the point of departure is Jerusalem.[106]

---

[104] The commission before Jesus' passion presented his disciples as his witnesses through the term μαρτύριον (Lk 21:13), and their rejection will be for the sake of Jesus' name.

[105] Rasco, *La teologia de Lucas*, 122, contends that Luke urged his readers to remember that the city is not the goal and boundary of the evangelizing activity of the apostles.

[106] It would be possible to understand the expression ἀρξάμενοι ἀπὸ Ἰερουσαλήμ as a first stage of the mission, the preaching first to Jews (Acts 3:26; 13:46; 18:6; 28:28); the mission would then have two stages, first a mission among Jews, and then a mission among pagans. Following Betori, "Luke 24:47", 107-112, I argue that the expression ἀρξάμενοι ἀπὸ Ἰερουσαλήμ is to be understood rather in an inclusive sense: "beginning in Jerusalem" (see Acts 1:8b). At Jerusalem a universal mission be-

The last parallelism of this structure is made up of the expressions εἰς πάντα τὰ ἔθνη/ἕως ἐσχάτου τῆς γῆς (Lk 24:47a; Acts 1:8c). The expression ἕως ἐσχάτου τῆς γῆς appears in Acts 13:47 as well.[107]

Acts 13:47b	τέθεικά	σε	εἰς φῶς	ἐθνῶν
Acts 13:47c	τοῦ εἶναί	σε	εἰς σωτηρίαν	ἕως ἐσχάτου τῆς γῆς

This verse manifests the parallelism between σωτηρία and φῶς; salvation is expressed by the symbol of light.[108] And it parallels ἔθνη and ἕως ἐσχάτου τῆς γῆς, which become two synonymous expressions. The expression ἕως ἐσχάτου τῆς γῆς does not have a merely geographical meaning, but means universalism without limits.[109] Luke changes the terms but retains the same meaning.[110]

---

gins that, starting in Jerusalem, starts with Jews, but it is already a universal mission. The mission which is said to begin in Jerusalem (Lk 24:47b) is the action mentioned in v. 47a, namely, the preaching of conversion to all nations, and not some other preaching. In Lukan literature the verb ἄρχομαι, in the middle-passive voice, never expresses an action different from that of the verb with which it is linked. This is evident from the mainly pleonastic use of the phrase "begin to" (Lk 3:8; 4:21; 5:21; Acts 1:1; 2:4; 11:4.15). In addition, the expression ἄρχομαι ἀπό never separates two different actions; rather, it serves to emphasize the initial moment of the one action (Lk 23:5; 24:27.47; Acts 1:22; 8:35; 10.37). For example, right before our passage, in Lk 24:27 the action in question is the interpretation of all the Scriptures in relation to Jesus. Moses, the Law, and the prophets are simply parts of these Scriptures. There is no initial period during which the Gospel is offered to the Jews alone, followed by a second period of turning to the Gentiles.

[107] This expression, attested in Dt 33:11; Ps 46:10; 48:11; 72:8; Pr 17:24; Jb 28:24; Mi 5:3; Zc 9:10; Is 46:9; 48:10; 62:11, is studied in VAN UNNIK, "Der Ausdruck", 386-401.

[108] On this parallelism see § 3.2.1.b, where Acts 13:47 is studied at greater depth.

[109] MOORE, "To the End", 399, affirms: "To the end of the earth is not limited to only one aspect of the expansion (geography) but rather carries ethnic significance as well. Geographically the phrase denotes the end of the world in a general sense. In its ethnic significance it denotes the movement of the gospel into the Gentile world." Similar opinions are held by DUPONT, "La conclusion", 403-404, and MARTINI – VENTURINI, *Atti degli Apostoli*, 38.

[110] In addition, both expressions are presented by the narrator as a correction of previous nationalistic affirmations by disciples of Jesus. The disciples of Emmaus

This link highlights the connection between Jesus' commission statement and the disciples' commission statement. The disciples' commission resembles Simeon's words about Jesus because they both speak about the mission to the Gentiles (Lk 2:32a; 24:47a: ἔθνη). In Lk 24:47a (εἰς πάντα τὰ ἔθνη) and Acts 1:8c (ἕως ἐσχάτου τῆς γῆς) we find the parallelism which appears in Acts 13:47, which directly cites Is 49:6. The Isaianic text, a common external material, links both verses, Lk 24:47 and Acts 1:8b, to Lk 2:32, which also depends on Is 49:6. Thus, Lk 2:32 is linked with Lk 24:47 and Acts 1:8b, thanks to the triangulation with Is 49:6.[111]

The end of Luke's Gospel provides the basis for the missionary nature of the Christian faith; because of Jesus' command, his followers should preach the Gospel to the Gentiles. In speaking of the future, Jesus is giving a commission which will guide their actions, not only to his contemporary followers, but even to later Christians.[112] The beginning of Acts is more precise than the end of the Gospel. It constitutes an "announcement of the subject," a brief formula which presents the theme to be discussed.[113] It has a programmatic function because the four places mentioned in Acts 1:8, "Jerusalem," "throughout Judaea," "Samaria," and the "earth's remotest end" will be important hinges for the narrative of the diffusion of God's

---

hoped that Jesus would be the one to set Israel free (Lk 24:21). Jesus qualifies the affirmation, entrusting to his disciples the liberation not just of Israel, but of all the nations (Lk 24:47). At the beginning of Acts, the disciples ask Jesus whether the time has come for him (Jesus) to restore the kingdom to Israel (Acts 1:6). Jesus corrects this question, entrusting a universal mission to them, not only in Jerusalem, but throughout Judaea and Samaria to the earth's remotest end (note the conjunction ἀλλά in Acts 1:8).

[111] Lk 2:32a, φῶς εἰς ἀποκάλυψιν ἐθνῶν, and Lk 24:47, εἰς πάντα τὰ ἔθνη, depend on Is 49:6, εἰς φῶς ἐθνῶν. And Acts 1:8, ἕως ἐσχάτου τῆς γῆς, depends on Is 49:6, ἕως ἐσχάτου τῆς γῆς. On the dependence of these Lukan texts on Is 49:6 see PAO, *Acts*, 97.

[112] The end of Luke's Gospel is open to the future because it invites the reader to perform what has been commanded to the disciples. The readers become witnesses of the offer of salvation to all nations (DUPONT, "L'Apôtre comme intermédiaire", 132; TANNEHILL, *Narrative Unity* I, 294).

[113] I borrow this expression from Vanhoye who uses this literary device to make known the structure of the epistle to the Hebrews (VANHOYE, *Traduction structurée*, 3 [3]).

word.[114] Acts 1–8:4 describes the events in Jerusalem; the spread of the Gospel in Judaea and Samaria is narrated in Acts 8:5-40; Acts 9 and the following chapters describe the spread of the Gospel to the ends of the earth. Acts 1:8 synthesizes the movement from the particular boundaries to beyond the boundaries; in short, it moves towards universalism in its perfect expression.

This initiative by the risen Jesus, who entrusts the universal preaching to the disciples, appears in Matthew's Gospel as well (Mt 28:19-20).[115] However, while Matthew does not say anything of its realization, Luke extensively describes the deeds of that universal preaching in Acts. According to Luke, the realization of the mission to preach is important enough to be narrated in great detail.[116]

2.2 Fulfillment in the Public Lives of Jesus' Disciples

2.2.1 At the Beginning: Christians in Jerusalem

The *position* of the beginning of Acts highlights its narrative importance. The primitive Church is led by the figure of Peter who often prays, cures, speaks and teaches as a public voice of the first disciples. Peter appears as a *reliable character*, delivering his first speech after receiving the Holy Spirit. Finally, the long *direct quotation* highlights even more his first speech (Acts 2:17-21), which takes place in Jerusalem, a special *location* for Luke.

---

[114] According to BENÉITEZ, "Un capítulo de narrativa bíblica", 329-382, Acts 1:1-12 presents the starting point and impulse that puts in motion the entire narrative structure of Acts, which is made up of sequences of event-speech-response.

[115] It appears as well in Mk 16:15 and Mark affirms its fulfillment in one verse: "They, going out, preached everywhere" (Mk 16:20). However, these verses of Mark's Gospel are part of the end of Pseudo-Mark, Mk 16:9-20, which was not written by Mark.

[116] BALCH, "ἀκριβῶς ... γράψαι (Luke 1:3)", 229-239, studies what historians meant when they claimed to write ἀκριβῶς, and he translates it as "fully" (Lk 1:3: ἔδοξε κἀμοὶ παρηκολουθηκότι ἄνωθεν πᾶσιν ἀκριβῶς καθεξῆς σοι γράψαι). According to him, ἀκριβῶς is governed by the infinitive γράψαι, not by the particle παρηκολουθηκότι. Luke is not claiming "to have followed accurately," but "to write a full narrative," which includes the universal mission developed in Acts.

a) Presentation of the Infant Church in the Temple

Betori supports the idea that Acts 1:12–8:4 forms a unity because it develops, without a break, in Jerusalem.[117] No other *location* appears in this sequence with so much frequency and as well distributed as the Temple (2:42-47; 3:1-26; 5:12-16; 5:17-41; 6:13). It constitutes the center of particular interest in these first chapters.

The presence of the infant Church in the Temple mirrors the presence of Jesus in the Temple during his infancy. As Jesus placed himself in the Temple (Lk 2:22-52), the first Christians place themselves in the Temple (Acts 2:46; 3:1; 5:12).[118] I claim that the growing Church has the same relationship with the Temple at the beginning of Acts as Jesus had with the Temple in his infancy at the beginning of Luke. The Temple is still a place of revelation, also with the presence of the Spirit (4:8; 5:32),[119] because the growing Church teaches, preaches (3:12-26; 4:8-12; 5:29-33)[120] and reveals itself in the Temple (4:1; 5:12.20.25.42).[121] Moreover, the Temple is still a privileged place of proclamation of Jesus because the early

---

[117] Following BETORI, "Perseguitati", 20-41, the unity is delimited by the *inclusio* through 1:12-14 and 8:1b-4. The arguments are: the mention of the city of Jerusalem; the mention of the apostles, the women, Mary and the brothers of Jesus (Church); and the verb ὑποστρέφω εἰς Ἰερουσαλὴμ (1:12), which indicates the centripetal movement toward Jerusalem on the part of the first Christian community, while the verb διασπείρω (8:4), opposed to the verb ὑποστρέφω, which indicates the centrifugal movement leaving Jerusalem.

[118] According to TAYLOR, "The Jerusalem Temple", 464, and 473, Christian appropriation of the Temple courts as a venue for proclaiming the Gospel in the early chapters of Acts corresponds with the text in which Jesus, being in the Temple says: "I must be in my Father's house" (Lk 2:49).

[119] As the Spirit inspires Simeon (Lk 2:25-27), so also he inspires Peter (Acts 4:8; 5:32). In addition, the description of Jesus' conception through the Spirit parallels the description of the "conception" of the Church through the Spirit (δύναμις, ἐπέρχομαι ἐπί and πνεῦμα ἅγιον in Lk 1:35 and Acts 1:8).

[120] In these chapters, the location of the apostles' preaching is very frequently the Temple. Even the angel, after releasing the apostles from the jail, commands them to "stand in the Temple and tell the people the whole message about this life" (Acts 5:20).

[121] The other feature of the Temple, as a place of prayer (Lk 2:28.37-38), also appears because the first Christians often pray in the Temple (Acts 2:46; 3:1).

Church preaches Jesus: his name remains present in the Temple through the primitive Church's preaching (2:36; 3:13-16; 4:10-12; 5:30-32); through the memory of his words (6:13-14); and through miracles performed in his name (3:6; 4:30).[122] The reason for the conflicts is that the authorities require the Christians to reject the name of Jesus (4:17-21; 5:28.40), but the apostles claim the authority to instruct the people in Jesus' name.[123]

b) Incipient Universalism in Peter's First Speech

Peter's first long speech, after Pentecost, presents a preview of the universal offer of salvation achieved by Jesus. Although the speech is addressed to Jews staying in Jerusalem, Peter's words, the audience of his speech, and those who received the Holy Spirit, bear witness to this message addressed to Jews but possessing universal connotations. First, Peter takes advantage of the universalism of the passage Jl 3:1-5a, which Peter, with a slightly adapted quotation, cites at the beginning of his discourse (2:17-21)[124] and again in his final exhortation (2:38-39).[125] Peter affirms that God will

---

[122] Later, Jesus himself even appears in the Temple (Acts 22:17-21).

[123] The frequent references to the *name* of Jesus are especially characteristic of this unity of Acts. They begin with the reference to invoking the "name of the Lord" in 2:21, followed by the reference to being baptized "in the name of Jesus Christ" in 2:38. And the name of Jesus Christ is presented as the effective power behind the healing of the lame man (3:6.16; 4:7.10.12). Later the first Christians are called "those who invoke the name of the Lord" (9:14.21; 22:16).

[124] If Luke cites Jl 3:3-4 in Acts 2:19-20, it is not because of the apocalyptic description of the Day of the Lord that it contains (Joel). The description of the sun that becomes darkness and the moon that is transformed into blood seems ill-placed since nothing of this sort happens at the Pentecost event (Acts 2:20). It is in order to arrive at verse 5a of Joel, in which universal salvation is mentioned: "Then everyone who calls on the name of the Lord shall be saved" (Acts 2:21= Jl 3:5a).

[125] According to DUPONT, "L'utilisation", 299, Acts 2:38-39 is a further reference to the Joel passage already cited in Acts 2:17-21. Whereas in the earlier references from the prophet Luke has Peter quote from Joel 3:1-5a, in v. 39 Peter reflects on Jl 3:5 in its entirety. Dupont suggests that in place of "the ones on Mount Zion and in Jerusalem" Luke has substituted "you and your children and all those who are far off," increasing the universal meaning of the affirmation.

pour out his Spirit on "all humanity" (2:17),[126] that salvation "is for you and your children, and for all those who are far away,[127] for all those whom the Lord our God is calling to himself" (2:39), and that that salvation will affect the whole world, described as "the sky above and the earth below" (2:19). The result is a salvation not only for a particular people, but extended to "all who call on the name of the Lord" (2:21).

Second, the audience is in fact made up of Jews staying in Jerusalem,[128] but the Lukan description is "devout men coming from every nation (ἔθνη) under heaven" (2:5). Luke indicates the wide range of origins of the hearers, even listing the places from which these people came (2:9-11). According to Béchard, the list of nations in Acts 2:9-11 is an *update*[129] of the *table of nations* tradition

---

[126] This "all humanity" is specified by means of sons, daughters, young people, old people, slaves, men, and women (2:17-18). The narrative traces the partial fulfillment of this universalistic promise as Samaritans (8:15-17) and Gentiles (10:44-46) receive the Spirit.

[127] In Acts 22:21, Paul relates a vision in which Jesus ordered him: "I am sending you out to the gentiles far away (μακράν)." Ep 2:13-17 repeatedly identifies "those who are far off" (μακράν) with Gentiles, while "those who are near" are understood to be Jews. Moreover, in the OT, Gentiles are called those that they are "far away" (μακράν: Zc 6:15; Is 49:1; 57:19).

[128] In the description which Acts gives of the life of the Christian community in Jerusalem, there is no trace of preaching addressed to pagans. Luke is an historian and, as such, cannot allow himself to distort reality and offer a reconstruction of events that lacks all probability, simply in order to promote a theological vision (see BETORI, "Luke 24:47", 114-118).

[129] Although Luke makes no explicit references to the names and motifs found in Genesis 10, several allusions, both direct and indirect, to the biblical traditions about Noah strongly suggest that Luke was familiar with Gn 10:2-32 writing Acts 2:9-11. Luke's catalogue of nations includes representatives of each of the family groups descended from Noah's three sons. Of the sixteen peoples and places named in Acts 2:9-11, nine are also found in Josephus' updated version of Gn 10:2-32 (JOSEPHUS, *The Jewish Antiquities*, 1,6,1-4). And frequent allusions to the central motifs of Genesis 10 found in other OT books suggest its wide acceptance as an authoritative description of the nations of the world: 1 Chronicles 1:1–2:2; Ezekiel 38–39; Is 66:18-20; Daniel 11 (see BÉCHARD, *Paul Outside the Walls*, 209-224; and PARSONS, "The Place of Jerusalem", 163).

found in Gn 10:2-32.[130] Luke, listing the nations of Acts 2:9-11, seems desirous of showing a universal representation of Jews from throughout the world, evoking a complete universality that includes the Gentiles.

Finally, those who received the Holy Spirit, the apostles, begin to speak in other languages (2:6). The action of the Holy Spirit does not make the audience understand the language of the apostles, but makes the apostles speak in the native languages of all the members of the audience. Pentecost is a multiplication of the languages that the first Christians speak in order to reach all peoples. This fact characterizes the universalism that embraces all the cultures expressed by those languages.

c) Division in Israel

At the beginning of Acts, Jesus' disciples, being rejected due to Jesus' name, fulfill Jesus' prophecy of their rejection (Lk 21:12-17). This also establishes a link with Lk 2:34c. As at the end of the third Gospel, where Jesus was mainly accepted by the people of Israel and rejected by their authorities,[131] so at the beginning of Acts his disciples are rejected by the authorities and accepted by the people of Israel.[132] Simeon's prophecy of the division in Israel is fulfilled (Lk 2:34b).

---

[130] BÉCHARD, *Paul Outside the Walls*, 172, contends that Luke's imaginative map of the world reflects a convergence of the Jewish literary tradition alongside the work of Hellenistic geographers. Many of these Hellenistic authors accepted as authoritative the testimony of Homer in his detailed *Catalogue of Ships* in *Iliad* 2.1-877. For a possible connection between Luke's list and the catalogue of conquered peoples in Virgil's *Aeneid* see BONZ, *The Past as Legacy*, 104-110.

[131] On the echoes of Luke's passion narrative in the first chapters of Acts see TANNEHILL, "Acts 3-5", 208-214.

[132] This split between the people and their religious leaders is clearly put forward in the passage of the healing of the crippled beggar. The healing causes "all the people" to gather (3:11), which becomes the occasion for Peter's teaching them. This speech in turn provokes the Temple authorities to arrest Peter and John (4:1-3).

The rejection by Jewish authorities of the Gospel continues at the beginning of Acts.[133] On the one hand, we find analepsis of the past authorities' rejection of Jesus during his passion.[134] On the other hand, there are many repetitions of the present authorities' rejection of Jesus' disciples. For example, the Temple authorities try to contradict (ἀντιλέγω) Peter and John (4:14).[135]

On the contrary, the first speeches of Peter (2:14-36; 3:12-26) have a powerful effect and many among the people of Jerusalem respond (2:38-41; 4:4). There is an initially favorable response from the people (3:9-12; 4:21; 5:16.26), and the believers have the favor of the entire people who praise them (2:47; 4:33; 5:13). The Temple authorities, who in 4:1-3 oppose the apostles, are unable to act effectively because the apostles enjoy the people's support (4:21; 5:26).[136] And the account of the conversions reveals a clear progression: 3,000 Jews are converted (2:41); then 5,000 (4:4); still more are added than before

---

[133] Those that thought that they had rid Israel of Jesus now have to reject his disciples: chief priests (4:1.6.23; 5:17.21.24.27), elders (4:5.23), scribes (4:5), leaders of the people (4:5), the Sanhedrin (5:21.27), soldiers (4:1; 5:24.26), and Sadducees who reject the resurrection (4:1-2; 5:17; 23:6-8; 24:21). The Sadducees had already shown their opposition to this teaching when they confronted Jesus over this question (Lk 20:27). However, now that the Christians preach Jesus' resurrection, their rejection is even stronger (see MOESSNER, "The Christ Must Suffer", 228). I claim that after the first rejection by the Jewish authorities, Jesus' resurrection advances the plot as a new oportunity for the authorities, and also for the Jewish people. Now, again, they can accept Jesus or reject him through his disciples (see Acts 3:19).

[134] Peter's speech in the Temple (3:13-15) and both of his speeches before the Sanhedrin (4:10; 5:30), refering to the details of Jesus' trial and the Jewish authorities' rejection, are *analepsis*.

[135] However, not all of the authorities rejected Jesus' disciples. A single possible acceptance of Jesus within the Sanhedrin is the Pharisee Gamaliel with his persuasive argument (5:34-39). Accepting the two possibilities of the origin of Christianity, being "from humans" or "from God," Gamaliel suggests that Christianity really is from God. He also recognizes that Jesus' followers are different from the followers of Theudas and Judas the Galilean, who disappeared with the death of their leader. Gamaliel's warning to "take care [...] what you are about to do" and to beware of becoming "fighters against God" emphasizes the significance of the decision about to be made by the Sanhedrin. In addition, the narrator affirms once that "many priests accepted the faith" (6:7).

[136] This situation mirrors the passion story, where the people support Jesus, preventing the authorities from taking action against him (Lk 20:19; 22:2, but also Lk 19:47.48; 20:26; 21:38).

(5:14); the number is increased enormously (6:1.7).[137] The beginning of Acts tells of its greatest triumphs in Jerusalem.[138]

As Jesus' rejection became persecution against him, his disciples' rejection becomes a persecution which,[139] albeit progressively, involves the people of Israel who, step by step, join their authorities in persecuting the Christians. Stephen's stoning is the climax of this progression.

There is a repetitive pattern of arrests, interrogations, and releases in Acts 4–5, which narrate two incidents involving the apostles' conflicts before the Sanhedrin (4:1-22; 5:17-42). A third conflict is Stephen's trial. The conflict develops in three stages which are dramatized through a face-to-face confrontation between the Jewish authorities and Jesus' witnesses, with speeches in direct discourse. This pattern has a reinforcing function, reminding readers of the authorities' rejection.[140]

These three incidents present an evolving conflict that moves towards a crisis. The opposition to the apostles' message gradually builds to the point of drastic action: from no punishment at all (4:21) to lashes (5:40), and from lashes to stoning (7:59). The action contemplated in Acts 5:33, the attempt to kill Peter and John, is carried out against the new witness, Stephen; the narrative goes from the desire to murder (5:33) to real murder (7:60).[141]

---

[137] Later the Jewish-Christians of Jerusalem inform Paul that there are tens of thousands of believing Jews in Jerusalem (21:20). Without the assumption of a single Jewish convert in Jerusalem after 6:7, the myriads in 21:20 only summarize conversions accomplished before Acts 6:7.

[138] Luke carefully distributes these remarks throughout his account with the purpose of showing the general acceptance of Christian faith by the Jewish people in Jerusalem.

[139] For example, Peter's trial parallels Jesus' trial. The arrest is during night, while the trial before the Sanhedrin is during day (Lk 22:66; Acts 4:3-5); there is a question about the authority (Lk 20:2; Acts 4:7), which is answered through Ps 118:22 (Lk 20:17; Acts 4:11); and the trial is used to bear witness to Jesus' identity (Lk 22:66-70; Acts 4:8-12).

[140] See TANNEHILL, "Acts 3-5", 199; and TANNEHILL, "Peter's Mission Speeches", 173-179.

[141] The continuity between the actions is also made clear by the use of the same verb of strong emotion: διεπρίοντο. It means "they were infuriated," and it appears in the NT only in Acts 5:33; 7:54, always in this same form. In the former text this leads to the desire to "do away with" (5:33: ἀναιρέω) the apostles. In the latter it leads to the actual "doing away with" Stephen (8:1: ἀναίρεσις).

In addition, the people, initially a fertile field for the Christian mission, are easily swayed by false charges. The turning point comes when the authorities are finally able to arouse the people by false charges against Stephen (6:11-13). The role of the people in Stephen's death is clear in the stoning: they make a concerted rush at him (7:57). Furthermore, the "engine" which moves the action of Stephen's arrest and trial are not the Jewish authorities, but certain *people* from Cyrene and Alexandria who were members of the synagogue and others from Cilicia and Asia (6:9).[142] The mass of people, who had originally been favorable to the apostles, now align themselves with their leaders against Stephen.

Finally, the term λαός is especially frequent at the beginning of Acts and plays a role in a significant development, expressing the acceptance by the general Jewish people at the beginning of Acts.[143] Following Stephen's event the Jews (Ἰουδαῖοι) appear frequently as a threatening opposition group, which represents a significant shift in the way in which the people (λαός) were presented. The martyrdom of Stephen marks the change from a generally positive to a negative Jewish response. The Jewish people, who are presented as supporters of the Christian mission at the beginning of Acts, will act primarily as opponents following the death of Stephen.

[142] The parallels between Stephen and Jesus are many. Stephen's arrest (Acts 6:12) and the Jewish trial before the Sanhedrin (Acts 6:11.14) are crafted as a reflection of Jesus' arrest (Lk 22:47) and his Jewish trial before the Sanhedrin (Lk 22:66-71). His death (Acts 7:59-60) is depicted by Luke in an evocatively similar fashion to Jesus' death (Lk 23:34.46, only in Luke). However, there are two main differences: Stephen does not have a Roman trial, and the crowd arresting and taking part in killing Stephen does not parallel Jesus' death. Both differences highlight the participation of the people in Stephen's death.

[143] More than one half (24/47) of its occurrences throughout Acts appear in the first seven chapters, the first quarter of the macro-narrative of Acts (7/28). After Stephen's speech (7:34) its occurrences clearly decrease, and there are no further Jewish conversions in Jerusalem.

2.2.2 Dispersion Narrative: A Progressive Universalism

After the stoning of Stephen, the first Christians scatter and go from place to place preaching the Good News (8:1). There is a progressive process of inclusion of Gentiles, made up of different stages: first, the Samaritan Pentecost (8:4-25); second, the Ethiopian eunuch (8:26-40); and third, the Gentile Pentecost (10:1-48). Each of these stages is granted by divine approval; God is the *reliable character* who guarantees these stages.

First, Philip goes to a Samaritan town and proclaims Christ to them (8:4-5). Because of the success of Philip's mission at Samaria,[144] Peter and John go down there and pray for them to receive the Holy Spirit (8:14-17). This Samaritan Pentecost is striking because the Samaritans were historically linked to Jews, but they cannot be strictly considered Jews; they were a schism from Judaism,[145] they were in mid-position between the Jews and

[144] Nowhere does Luke report greater triumphs for the Gospel than in Samaria. The reports about mass conversions among Jews in Jerusalem (2:41; 4:4; 5:14; 6:1.7) are always associated with the rejection of the Gospel by the authorities of Israel. In Samaria it is different. Here the masses unanimously accept the Gospel (8:6). Although Simon Magus has deceived the entire population (8:9-11), this entire population is baptized by Philip, Simon Magus included (8:12.13).

[145] I believe that Luke does not consider Samaritans as one hundred percent Jews, but as a separate group of people, not only with geographical differences, but also with ethnic and religious differences. The Samaritans did not receive Jesus because he was making for Jerusalem, and the Samaritans used to worship in the temple on Mount Gerizim (only in Lk 9:51-53) using only the Samaritan Pentateuch. The parable of the Good Samaritan underlines the difference between the Jews, the priest and the Levite, and the Samaritan (only in Lk 10:29-37). In the account of the ten lepers, all the stress is on the fact that the only grateful one was a Samaritan, with the obvious implication that the rest were Jews. In fact, the Samaritan is named by Jesus as "this foreigner" (ὁ ἀλλογενὴς οὗτος: only in Lk 17:18). Outside of Luke, in Mt 10:5-6 it is obvious that the Samaritans are not Jews, for there the "house of Israel" is contrasted with the Samaritans who are paralleled to the Gentiles. John's Gospel relates the story of the Samaritan woman where the obvious point is that the Samaritans are not Jews, with the Jewish disdain for the Samaritans (Jn 4:9; 4:22; see as well 8:48). Josephus also reports the mutual hostility between Jews and Samaritans (JOSEPHUS, *The Jewish Antiquities,* 20,6,1).

the Gentiles.[146] The many miracles performed by Philip in Samaria (8:6.7.13) and the reception of the Holy Spirit (8:15-17) guarantee the divine approval of the mission in Samaria.

Another stage in the inclusion of Gentiles is the baptism of the Ethiopian eunuch (8:26-40),[147] whose religious status is imprecise. He could be classified as a Jew because he had been on pilgrimage to Jerusalem (8:27: προσκυνήσων εἰς Ἰερουσαλήμ) and, coming back, he was reading the prophet Isaiah (8:28). However, he could also be classified as Gentile, because he was an Ethiopian, a eunuch,[148] and an officer at the court of the kandake, or queen of Ethiopia (8:27).[149] The divine approval of his evangelization is clear because the angel of the Lord (8:26) and the Holy Spirit (8:29) guide Philip to the Ethiopian.[150]

The last stage in the inclusion of the Gentiles is Peter's meeting with Cornelius and the Gentile Pentecost that happened at Cornelius' house (Acts 10).[151] Cornelius' Latin name and his pro-

---

[146] See KIDDLE, "The Admission of the Gentiles", 165-166, who is followed by MENOUD, "Le plan des Actes", 46. "From a Jewish point of view," says Samkutty, "the identity of the Samaritans is ambiguous and ambivalent, and the legitimacy of Samaritans is in question" (SAMKUTTY, *The Samaritan Mission in Acts*, 85). Though their Jewishness is obvious at certain levels, they were often treated as a rival sect outside Judaism (See BARRETT, *Acts of the Apostles*, 402; and FITZMYER, *The Acts of the Apostles*, 400).

[147] According to MARGUERAT, "Metteur en scène des personnages", 292, Ethiopia was considered in the first century as the extremity of the Roman Empire; the Ethiopian Eunuch represents men coming from the antipodes, thus embodying the Lukan universalism.

[148] Dt 23:2 says: "A man whose testicles have been crushed or whose male member has been cut off must not be admitted to the assembly of *Yhwh*."

[149] According to HAENCHEN, *Die Apostelgeschichte*, 303-304, Luke's vagueness in identifying the Ethiopian is intentional.

[150] Apparently this progressive inclusion is interrupted by the official presentation of Paul with the first account of his vocation (9:1-19). Paul will, however, become the main character of the mission to the pagans from Acts 13. After Paul's vocation, he preaches in Damascus and goes to Jerusalem (9:20-30). Afterwards, Luke presents Peter preaching and healing in Lydda and Joppa where the first meeting with the emissaries of Cornelius happens (9:31-43).

[151] RACINE, "L'hybridité des personnages", 563, emphasizes that Peter crosses the border of division with the pagans. His coming into Cornelius' house is framed in slow motion through the verb εἰσελθεῖν used over 3 verses, Acts 10:25-27.

fession as a centurion of the Italica cohort present him as a pagan (10:1). In fact, both Peter and the Jewish-Christians of Jerusalem consider him to be a pagan (10:28-29; 11:3). But although Cornelius is a pagan, he is characterized by Luke in a specific way, as a devout *God-fearer* (10:2). He does not fit into the normal definition of a pagan.[152] The repeated visions, the presence of the angel of God (10:3-7), the trance with heaven thrown open and the voice coming from it (10:10-15), the voice of the Spirit (10:19), and the coming down of the Holy Spirit (10:44) guarantee the divine approval of the evangelization of Cornelius and his household.

Luke has progressively presented different characters in an increasing degree of paganism to destroy the binary and opposed categories of Jews and pagans.[153] Samaritans who had been Jews but are now an excision of Judaism, the Ethiopian eunuch with his imprecise religious status, and Cornelius with his paganism but closeness to Judaism, present to the reader examples of progressively more pagan people that become Christians. I agree with Racine, who suggests that this progression is a narrative strategy that tries to shade in the distinctive lines between Jews and Gentiles.[154] The divine approval helps the reader to respond just as Peter's audience did in Jerusalem:[155] "This account satisfied them, and they gave glory to

---

[152] COOK, "The Mission to the Jews", 120, claims that the God-fearers serve a transitional function from the Jews to the pagans. This is why their placement is only in the middle chapters of Acts (10:2.22; 13:16.26). JERVELL, "Jews and Godfearers", 11-20, thinks that the first preaching was addressed to Jews and God-fearers. TYSON, "Jews and Judaism", 32-33, even believes that Luke-Acts may be approached as an evangelistic text addressed to God-fearers. Ravens and Franklin opine that Luke himself was a God-fearer who was a follower of Paul and who interpreted Paul for a later age (RAVENS, *Restoration of Israel*, 253-254; FRANKLIN, *Interpreter of Paul*, 378-379).

[153] The rabbi Cohen has proved how we can speak about progressive degrees of Judaism as well. Both concepts, increasing degrees of paganism and of Judaism, are connected. COHEN, *The Beginnings of Jewishness*, 341, says, "the degree of social interaction between Jews and non-Jews was sufficiently great that it was not always easy to tell who was a Jew and who was not."

[154] RACINE, "L'hybridité des personnages", 559.

[155] An increasing manifestation of the divine approval could also be argued. The

God: 'God has clearly granted to the Gentiles too the repentance that leads to life'" (11:18).

2.2.3 At the End: the Council at Jerusalem

The narrator underlines the episode of Acts 15:5-21 through its *position*, in the middle of Acts, its *location* in the assembly of Jerusalem, and its *reliable characters,* the Church, the apostles and elders (15:2.4), with a concluding speech by Peter first, and then by James. It is underlined as well by a *biblical quotation* in Acts 15:16-17.

a) Division among Jewish-Christians and Gentile-Christians

In Acts 15 the reader finds the solemn and definitive solution to universalism. The preaching throughout Samaria, the conversion of the Ethiopian Eunuch and the centurion Cornelius, lead up to the council at Jerusalem with its letter to the Gentile believers, the official answer to the question of the Gentiles' entry into Christianity.

The council at Jerusalem shows the internal consequences of this universalism, and is the answer to the question about salvation according to the Mosaic law: "Unless you have yourselves circumcised in the tradition of Moses you cannot be saved" (15:1). The Pharisees who had become believers insisted that Gentiles should be circumcised and keep the Law of Moses (15:5).[156] The Jewish-Christians tried to impose Jewish customs to some from Antioch who were probably Gentile-Christians. In Jerusalem, Paul faces the same Jewish-Christian rejection as Peter did in Acts 11:2-3, when the circumcised believers protested to him because he had been visiting the uncircumcised and eating with them.[157]

---

three steps are guaranteed by the Holy Spirit (8:15-17; 8:29; 10:12.44). However, while the Samaritans' Pentecost is guaranteed by miracles (8:6.7.13), the Eunuch's baptism by the angel of the Lord (8:26), and the pagan Pentecost of Cornelius is guaranteed by miracles such as visions, with heaven thrown open (10:3-7.10-15), the heavenly voice, even the Spirit (10:13.15.19), and the angel of the Lord (10:3).

[156] The issue is broader than the question of circumcision (15:1.5) and includes keeping the dietary law (15:20.29) and the visits to pagan houses (11:3).

[157] This conflict lasts until Paul returns to Jerusalem for the last time. He is informed of certain feelings harbored by the Jewish-Christians, who have been told that

b) The Universalism of Peter's Speech in Acts 15

Peter responds to this internal division between Jewish-Christians and Gentile-Christians by affirming salvation in Jesus and not in the Mosaic Law, and claiming a universal offer of salvation (15:11).

Peter appeals to his meeting with the pagan Cornelius recognizing what the Jews in Jerusalem already know about his meeting (15:7). In fact, after his meeting with Cornelius, Peter went to Jerusalem to justify his conduct (11:1-18). Now, again in Jerusalem, he appeals to the Cornelius incident so that it functions as a proof (15:7-9) in the account of the council at Jerusalem.[158]

The last speech of Peter (15:7-11) is clear in its universalism not only because of its connection with the Cornelius' event, but also because Peter affirms that God chose him to teach the good news to the Gentiles, and thus they become believers. God showed his approval of them (Gentiles) by giving the Holy Spirit to them just as he had to "us" (Jews), and God made no distinction between "them" and "us" (15:7b-9a). God is the reliable character who guarantees it.

---

he tells the Jews not to circumcise their children or observe the customs (21:20-21; cf. 6:1; 11:2-3). These texts show some kind of division among the Christian community (see TYSON, "Jewish Rejection in Acts", 133-137).

[158] The links include implicit indications that one event (Acts 10) causes another to happen (Acts 11) and Acts 10–11 is the proof used for the resolution of the assembly in Acts 15. Powell contends that these *causal and proof links* should be studied in narrative analysis. "In making sense of a narrative," he says, "readers are especially attentive to links that are established between the events that are related" (POWELL, "Narrative Criticism", 245). These are the main links between both events: (1) The solution to the question of circumcision of the Gentiles comes from the fact that the Holy Spirit came upon the Gentiles even without their being circumcised (Acts 15:8; 10:44-45; 11:15). (2) In the council at Jerusalem, Peter affirms that in the meeting with Cornelius he saw that God made no distinction between "them" (the Gentiles) and "us" (the Jews), since he purified their hearts by faith (Acts 15:9; 10:28.34-35.43). It is the same thing that Peter says at the end of his self-justification at Jerusalem: "God was giving them (the Gentiles) the identical gift he gave to us (the Jews) believing in the Lord" (Acts 11:17). And (3) Luke has constructed the story by repeating a number of times the vision of Cornelius (Acts 10:3-6.30-33; and referred to in 10:22; 11:13-14; 15:14), that of Peter (Acts 10:11-15.16.28; 11:4-9; and referred in 15:9), and the coming of the Holy Spirit (Acts 10:44-48; 11:15-17; and referred in 15:8). On a structural study of these causal links see BARTHES, "Structural Analysis", 130-136.

c) James' Speech: The Gentiles' Inclusion from ἔθνη to λαοί

Simeon said that Jesus is the salvation "made ready in the sight of the peoples (λαοί), light of revelation for the Gentiles (ἔθνη) and glory for your people (λαός) Israel" (Lk 2:31-32). Jesus has been prepared as the salvation of peoples (λαοί), in which the plural use of λαοί embraces Jews and Gentiles (ἔθνη); λαός (Israel) becomes λαοί (Israel plus Gentiles) including the Gentiles (ἔθνη).[159] In the council of Jerusalem, James, assigning the term λαός to the ἔθνη, amplifies again the concept of λαός which embraces again not only Israel, but also the Gentiles (Acts 15:14).

Generally speaking, Luke reserves the plural ἔθνη to speak of the Gentiles and the singular λαός to speak of Israel, as *technical terms*.[160] However, Acts 15:14 is a clear case in which Luke assigns λαός, God's people, to the ἔθνη, the Gentiles.[161]

Dupont, Kruijf, and Dahl contend that there are four different OT passages connected with Acts 15:14: the closest one is Dt 14:2; the expression is slightly different in Dt 7:6; and there are two identical passages, Ex 19:5 and 23:22.[162] The modifications of detail in Acts express the biblical formulation with a meaning that does not correspond to the primitive OT pattern.[163] The formulation of Acts 15:14 expresses

---

[159] See Ó FEARGHAIL, *Introduction to Luke-Acts*, 142.

[160] This clear distinction comes from the LXX, in which the term ἔθνη usually translates the Hebrew term גוי, while the term λαός is the Greek translation of עם. On these terms with their profane and religious meanings, in which λαός-עם refers to being part of the Jews and ἔθνος-גוי refers to opposing to the Jews see WALTER, "ἔθνος", 928; BERTRAM – SCHMITZ, "ἔθνος, ἐθνικός", 361; FRANKEMÖLLE, "λαός", 839-846; STRATHMANN – MEYER, "λαός", 32-34.

[161] Acts 18:10 is the unique case in which Luke assigns λαός to the Christians.

[162] See DUPONT, "ΛΑΟΣ 'ΕΞ 'ΕΘΝΩΝ", 47-50; DUPONT, "Un peuple", 221-235. DE KRUIJF, "Das Volk Gottes im NT", 127, adds a fifth text, Zc 2:15. DAHL, "A People for his Name", 323, adds three more texts as OT background of Acts 15:14: Ezk 36:24; 36:28; 37:23. The number of similar texts of the OT indicates that Acts 15:14 is modeled upon a general pattern rather than upon any individual passage. "The whole speech from v. 14 through v. 18 is a composition of Luke based upon the Greek Bible" says DAHL, "A People for his Name", 320.

[163] The main modifications are that the election of the Israelite chosen people (ἐκλέγομαι, προαιρέομαι, and περιούσιος) is not present in Acts, and that in Acts those

not the election of Israel as God's people, as the old biblical pattern holds, but the entrance of the Gentiles into the *people of God*. Acts 15:14 affirms that God (ὁ θεός) took (λαμβάνω) from the Gentiles (ἐξ ἐθνῶν) a people (λαός) for his name; the Gentiles (ἔθνη) are now part of God's people (λαός).[164] The terms λαός and ἔθνη, which designated mutually opposed and exclusive entities, are now compatible.[165]

The passage contributes not only the incorporation of the Gentiles into God's people, but the way in which they will enter, simply as Gentiles and without circumcision and obedience to the Law (15:5.19.20).[166] Once universal salvation in Christ has been confirmed by the council's letter (15:20.29; 21:25), the mes-

---

that are being elected are not only the people of Israel, but also those from the Gentiles (ἐξ ἐθνῶν: origin or proceeding).

164 We find an opposite example in Peter's speech in Solomon's portico. Peter affirms that whoever refuses to listen to that prophet (Jesus) shall be "cut off from the people" (ἐξολεθρευθήσεται ἐκ τοῦ λαοῦ: Acts 3:23). In other words, those among the Jews who do not listen to Jesus will not be part of the λαός anymore, and all the nations of the earth will be blessed through this prophet (Acts 3:25). In addition, both verses have a strong OT background influenced by Gn 12:3; 22:18; Lv 23:29. The OT is used by Luke not only to affirm that the Gentiles are part of God's people, but also to suggest that some Jews, those who reject Jesus, can be excluded from God's people. Both cases show that the continuous history of God's salvation includes a new stage in which the inclusion of Gentiles as part of God's people and the exclusion of some Jews from God's people are contemplated. Both depend on Jesus' acceptance by some Gentiles, and on his rejection by some Jews.

165 Furthermore, Luke inserts a literal quotation from the Greek text of Am 9:11-12 with a small nuance of Jr 12:15, which says as well that "all the nations [...] will look for the Lord" (Acts 15:16-17), highlighting the universalism of the passage even more. In fact, Acts 3:25 also added this universalism affirming: "all the nations of the earth will be blessed."

166 If it was clear from the beginning in the preaching to the Jews that the Gentiles should also share in the salvation of Israel, how is this passage to be understood? Why was the progressive emphasis on paganism, from the Samaritans to Cornelius and the council at Jerusalem, necessary? The problem is not the Gentiles' sharing in salvation, but in what way they should receive salvation. These passages explain the way in which they are saved, simply as Gentiles. The Cornelius event and the council at Jerusalem show not only the *what*, but also the *how* (see JERVELL, "The Divided People", 64).

sage spreads rapidly to the Gentiles. According to the author of Acts, it is Peter, not Paul, who initiates the mission to the Gentiles (10:1–11:18), which will then be carried out especially by Paul, as we will see in the following paragraph.

3. Paul in the Diaspora

3.1 Presentation/Commission by Jesus

There is a triple presentation of Paul (Acts 9:3-19; 22:6-21; 26:12-18).[167] He becomes the leading character in the second half of Acts, with nearly equal space devoted to his mission journeys (Acts 13–20) and his imprisonment (Acts 21–28). The three accounts of the single event signal that the event on the road to Damascus is important for Luke.[168] This narrative *repetition* is a technique to which Luke rarely resorts; if he uses it, he especially wants to impress something upon the reader.[169]

---

[167] Source criticism coped with the excess of narrative by appealing to a multiplicity of documents (BOTTINO, "La missione", 340-345). Lohfink has drawn attention to Luke's own literary creativity and, thus, commentators most commonly identify a traditional narrative behind Acts 9, of which the narrator then gives two redactional variants in Acts 22 and 26 (LOHFINK, "Eine alttestamentliche Darstellungsform", 252).

[168] It is a *repetitive account* in which the narrator relates several times something that has happened once, and thus he underscores that unique event (see ALETTI, *et al.*, *Vocabulaire raisonné*, 79). The *duration* of the three passages, the connection of the extension of a passage in narrative time with the duration of the story time, is considerable as well.

[169] As we saw in n. 70, the Gospel of Luke avoids literary doublets. The question of doublets receives a different treatment depending on whether one deals with the Gospel or with the book of Acts because there are other cases of repetitions in the book of Acts: the Ascension account is related in two variant forms (Lk 24:50-51 and Acts 1:9-11); the events surrounding the meeting between Peter and Cornelius are related as many as four times between Acts 10 and 11, and yet again at the Jerusalem assembly (Acts 15:7-11). The apostolic decree, promulgated by this same assembly (15:20) regulating the communion among Christians, is duplicated in Acts 15:29 and in Acts 21:25. It is notworthy that all of these repetitions are linked to universalism.

There is no unanimity in the description of Paul's call. The same story is told, often with identical wording and with a typical form of "epiphany account," but certain details are omitted, changed or added. The first account is the only one told by the narrator. This is the presentation of Paul to the community, while the other two are told by Paul in the first person in two different apologies.[170] The second account, before Jews, the people of Israel, reveals Paul's uninterrupted faithfulness to Jewish tradition and justifies Paul's mission as a fulfillment of his Jewishness (22:1.3.5); even Ananias is presented as a devout and observant Jew who cures Paul, transmits to him his divine commission, and encourages him to be baptized in Jesus' name (22:12-16). It is an apologetic speech of Paul's Jewishness. The third account, before pagans, including king Agrippa, underlines the power of the Risen one to whom one cannot show disobedience.[171] Despite the differences among the three accounts, they present the very same Pauline *commission statement* made by a very *reliable character*, the risen Christ: "I am Jesus whom you are persecuting" (Acts 9:5; 22:8; 26:15).[172]

---

[170] In the former, the omniscient narrator, knowing the light and voice from heaven (9:3-7) and Ananias' vision (9:10-16), underlines the veracity and objectivity of Saul's conversion into Paul. The prior references to Saul manifest a growing menace: 7:58 presents Saul minding the clothing of the witnesses who stone Stephen; 8:1 underlines that Saul approved of Stephen's killing; 8:3 describes how Saul himself began doing great harm to the Church; and 9:1 affirms that Saul was still making threats to slaughter the Lord's disciples. However, by divine intervention Paul is converted into a universal missionary. This conversion is guaranteed by the omniscient narrator, who serves here as a literary mediation for the precedence of God's intervention. Coming towards the end of the Acts narrative, Paul's speeches also provide a retrospective summary of Paul's mission.

[171] FLICHY, "Histoire racontée", 389, claims that the function of each account within the plot of the book of Acts is different because they are adapted to suit the needs of the situation. For the difference between the three accounts see LOHFINK, *Paulus vor Damaskus*, 11-27.

[172] The commission statement is underlined by the fact that the three accounts present many imperatives (9:6; 22:16.18.21; 26:16) and future tenses (9:15; 22:14-15; 26:16-17).

3.1.1 Universalism

The three accounts present the mission entrusted to Paul in the context of both light (φῶς) from heaven (9:3; 22:6; 26:13) and universalism.[173] In the first one, speaking about Paul, Jesus says to Ananias: "this man is my chosen instrument to bring my name before Gentiles (ἔθνη)" (9:15). In the second one, Ananias says to Paul himself: "you are to be his witness before all humanity (πρὸς πάντας ἀνθρώπους)" (22:15).[174] In the third one, Jesus says directly to Paul: "I send you to the people (λαός) and to the Gentiles (ἔθνη)" (26:17). On each of the three occasions, the universal mission is the central part of Paul's commission.

A discrete progression of the speakers and hearers appears in the three accounts. In the first one the mediation of Ananias clearly appears (9:10-19); in the second, his presence is reduced (22:12-16); in the third, he disappears completely. The suppression factor applies to the role of Ananias. Only in the last narrative does Jesus entrust his commission statement directly to Paul (26:16-18).

Acts	Speaker	Hearer	Content
9:3-18	Jesus	Ananias	Instrument to bring my name before Gentiles
22:6-21	Ananias	Paul	You are to be his witness before all humanity
26:12-23	Jesus	Paul	I send you to the people and to the Gentiles

I find this universal commission in the other commission statements of the other protagonists. Jesus has been "made ready in the

[173] Paul, who was first surrounded by a light from heaven for his salvation, later became the light for the Gentiles' salvation (13:47; 26:18).

[174] This expression reaches its full meaning when the Lord tells Paul: "Go! I am sending you out to the Gentiles (ἔθνη) far away" (Acts 22:21). Only the second account presents this revelation directly by the Lord in the Temple, while the words of Ananias are uttered in Damascus.

sight of the peoples, light of the revelation for the Gentiles" (Lk 2:31) and the disciples should "preach to all nations" (Lk 24:47). In this way Luke links the three commission statements of his main characters.[175] The accounts of Paul's vocation therefore strengthen the observation that his ministry fulfills the same divine plan given to Jesus and the disciples.[176]

3.1.2 Rejection

Paul learned directly from the risen Christ how his witness would be often rejected. His three accounts of his vocation underline how Jesus himself has foreseen Paul's suffering rejection: "I myself will show him how much he must suffer for my name" (9:16); "they (Jews in Israel) will not accept the testimony you are giving about me" (22:18); and "I shall rescue you from the people and from the Gentiles" (26:17: ἐκ τοῦ λαοῦ καὶ ἐκ τῶν ἐθνῶν).[177]

This vehement opposition is linked to Simeon's second speech. However, while Simeon foretold that Israel would be divided because of the rejection by many in Israel (Lk 2:34), the risen Jesus gradually increases the prophesied rejection of Paul. The first account simply speaks of Paul's sufferings (9:16); the second one presents the rejection by the Jews (22:18); and the third one affirms the persecution by Israel and the Gentiles (26:17). As the

---

[175] I believe that all of these commissions depend on Is 52:10, ἐνώπιον πάντων τῶν ἐθνῶν, which links them to each other. The third account presents an echo of Is 49:6 which links this text (26:17) with earlier references to Is 49:6, which also make up the other commission statement of the main characters of Luke-Acts: Jesus (Lk 2:32), and his disciples (Lk 24:47; Acts 1:8).

[176] In addition, as in the commission statement of the disciples the risen Jesus presented them as his witnesses (μάρτυς: Lk 24:48; Acts 1:8), now Paul is presented by the risen Jesus as his witness (μάρτυς: Acts 22:15; 26:16). Jesus in Lk 21:13 presents his disciples bearing witness (μαρτύριον), and Acts 9:15 affirms that Paul is Jesus' chosen instrument to bring his name to everyone. See the discussion in CLARK, *Parallel Lives*, 337-338.

[177] All these rejections led Paul to formulate the cry: "We must (δεῖ) experience many hardships before we enter the kingdom of God" (Acts 14:22). It recalls the δεῖ which forms an essential part of the passion predictions of Jesus about himself (Lk 9:22.44; 13:13; see as well 24:7.26.44.46).

prophecy of the disciples' rejection opened the rejection to everybody (Lk 21:17), Paul's rejection will be by Jews and Gentiles.

3.2 Fulfillment in Paul's Public Life

3.2.1 At the Beginning: Paul in Antioch of Pisidia

Paul, after his presentation to the community in Acts 9:3-19, is a *reliable character* who speaks through two *biblical quotations*, one in Acts 13:41, and the other in Acts 13:47. These words are highlighted by the narrator by means of their *position*. Up to Acts 13, Paul has developed his mission among Jewish synagogues (9:20-22) or the Christian community (11:26) with short references to his preaching. However, Acts 13:16-47 presents the first long speech of Paul at the beginning of Paul's mission narrative.[178]

a) Rejection by Jews

This speech is a prototype of Paul's rejected mission, which introduces the subsequent rejections and persecutions that Paul will suffer.[179] After the account of the journey to Antioch of Pisidia (13:13-14), Paul enters into the synagogue on the Sabbath and addresses his preaching to the Jewish people (13:16-41).[180] The first reaction is acceptance of the Christian message, and they ask

[178] The Pauline speeches are the following passages: in the synagogue of Antioch, which represents the Pauline preaching to the Jews (13:16-47); in Athens, which represents his preaching to the pagans (17:22-30); in Miletus, dedicated to those who will lead the communities founded by Paul, especially the elders of Ephesus (20:18-35). And there are three Pauline apologies: before the people of Jerusalem (22:1-21), before the governor Felix (24:10-21), and before the king Agrippa (26:2-23). Other smaller speeches are found in Acts 14:15-17; 26:25-27; 27:21-26; 28:17-29; and 28:25-28.

[179] Jewish resistance in city after city conveys a general impression of the way things are going. Other travels which follow this pattern are: Iconium in 14:1-28; Thessalonica in 17:1-15; Corinth in 18:1-11; Ephesus in 19:8-10; and Rome in 28:17-28.

[180] When Paul leaves Judea, he and his companions regularly begin their mission in a Jewish synagogue (9:20; 13:5.14; 17:10; 17:17; 18:19). In fact, Acts 14:1 says that they went to the synagogue according to their custom, as usual (see as well 17:2; 19:8).

Paul to speak the following Saturday (13:42-43). However, the Jews, filled with jealousy because of the Christian success, contradict (ἀντιλέγω) what Paul was saying the following Saturday using blasphemies (13:44-45).[181] Paul, seeing the Jewish rejection, affirms his turning to the Gentiles in a moment of intense drama (13:46).[182] Finally, the disciples are persecuted until they are expelled from the territory (13:50-52).[183] We may appropriately speak of a literary *pattern* or *type-scene* in Acts that, with some variation, includes the following elements: (1) preaching in a synagogue; (2) divided response by the acceptance of the Christian message by some Jews and opposition from other Jews; (3) persecution by those who reject Christianity; and (4) change of lo-

[181] Other examples of this rejection are found in 14:5.6.19.20.22; 16:20-21; 17:5-9.13.14; 18:12-17; 19:9.29.34.40; 20:3.19.25; 28:22. Resistance is openly expressed and involves personal attacks that would make continued preaching in the synagogue difficult. It is what Luke names a "plot of the Jews" (ἐπιβουλὴ τῶν Ἰουδαίων: 9:24; 20:3.19; 23:30).

[182] On two more occasions, Paul announces that he is turning to the Gentiles (Corinth, 18:6; Rome, 28:28; cf. 19:9). However, even after saying that he will turn to the Gentiles, he keeps addressing the Jews. After the way to the Gentiles is opened, the preaching and success among the Jews continues. Paul never definitely ignores Israel or the Jews, and always begins his preaching in the different synagogues, as we saw in n. 180. Dupont claims that this turning to the Gentiles reflects the historical level, and not the ontological level, the divine intention (DUPONT, "La portée christologique", 37; DUPONT, "Le salut des Gentils", 393-398). The evangelization of the Gentiles is not the result of fortuitous circumstances, such as the rejection by the Jews, or an afterthought or a second choice; it is rooted in God's will. It is not true that only when the Jews have rejected the gospel is the way opened to Gentiles; it is more correct to say that only when part of the Jews have accepted the Gospel can the way to Gentiles be opened because Gentiles are called to salvation through the faithful behaviour of some of the Jews. The divine plan of salvation includes, from the beginning, both Jews and Gentiles. This was announced by Simeon, an inspired prophet (Lk 2:30-32), and what Simeon says is fulfilled throughout Luke-Acts. This will of God can be known in Luke-Acts by humans through the prophecies of the Scriptures, visions, the Holy Spirit, and miracles (O'TOOLE, "Reflections", 532).

[183] In almost every city the preaching finishes with the expulsion of Jesus' disciples from the synagogue or the city: Damascus (9:20-25), Pathos (13:6-12), Iconium (14:2.5.19), Thessalonica (17:5-9.13-14), Corinth (18:6-7), and Ephesus (19:8-9).

cation, which sometimes involves turning to Gentiles. The paradigm of this pattern is Antioch in Acts 13. Luke freely uses this pattern with variations, while clearly following it.[184]

As with Jesus (Lk 4:22) and Peter (Acts 2:37-41), the initial response of the Jews is positive (Acts 13:42). Acceptance quickly turns to rejection (Acts 13:44-45) speaking against Paul (ἀντιλέγω and βλασφημέω) as they did with Jesus (Lk 4:28-29)[185] and Peter (Acts 5:17). In each case Luke recounts the speech containing a quotation from Scripture that interprets his mission, and the divided response. All the preaching by Jesus, Peter, and Paul fulfill Simeon's prophecy about the division caused by the rejection by part of Israel (Lk 2:34).

b) Paul as Jesus: God's Salvation and Light for the Gentiles

This speech, Acts 13, is a prototype of the Pauline universal mission as well. In fact, its *location*, Antioch of Pisidia, also with Antioch, is a paradigmatic town of the preaching to the Gentiles and that preaching is the ultimate reason for the council of Jerusalem (Acts 14:26).[186] The arrival point of the episode in Antioch is the quotation of Acts 13:47, signaling the transference of Jesus' mission to Paul and Barn-

---

[184] The first to underline this pattern of rejection in the Diaspora was ZUMSTEIN, "L'apôtre", 380-386, who even put it in connection with another pattern of rejection in Jerusalem. Ska affirms that "type-scenes contain a given set of repeated elements or details, not all of which are always present, not always in the same order, but enough of which are present to make the scene a recognizable one" (SKA, *Our Fathers*, 36). This literary *pattern* which often appears in Acts shows the importance of the division and universalism foretold by Simeon in Acts. While at the beginning some of the Jews usually accept the Christian preaching, eventually the majority of the Jews reject it. This rejection forces the disciples to go to another city, thus dispersing the Gospel.

[185] This parallels the function of the Nazareth synagogue sermon (Lk 4:16-30), since both serve to introduce the content of the preaching of a main character in the setting of a synagogue. The term ἐκβάλλω, to expel, is used in both situations, Jesus' first speech (Lk 4:29), and Paul's (Acts 13:50).

[186] On the preaching to pure Gentiles in Antioch see MENA SALAS, "Misión cristiana", 163-199, and MENA SALAS, *También a los Griegos*, 77-157, who analyzes the conditions that make possible the conversion of the first Gentiles to the Christian faith: the continuity between the missionary and the convert in their social, cultural, and religious ideas.

abas, who will fulfill it in Jesus' name. In the *Nunc Dimittis* Jesus is presented by Simeon as God's salvation (σωτήριον), and in apposition to this expression, as "light of the revelation for the Gentiles" (v. 32a: φῶς εἰς ἀποκάλυψιν ἐθνῶν). This apposition equates *light* with a *salvation* that includes Gentiles.[187] We find a very similar expression in Acts 13:47, where these words are applied not to Jesus, but to Paul and Barnabas.[188] The continuity between the ministries of Jesus and that of the apostles is thus symbolized by the chiastic repetition of this phrase applied to different characters.

Lk 2:30:	εἶδον οἱ ὀφθαλμοί μου τὸ **σωτήριόν** σου, [...]
Lk 2:32:	**φῶς** εἰς ἀποκάλυψιν **ἐθνῶν**
Acts 13:47b:	τέθεικά σε εἰς **φῶς ἐθνῶν**
Acts 13:47c:	τοῦ εἶναί σε εἰς **σωτηρίαν** ἕως ἐσχάτου τῆς γῆς

Both passages, Lk 2:30-32 and Acts 13:47, repeat the very same words: σωτήριον/σωτηρία, which is expressed as a light which comes even to the Gentiles (φῶς ἐθνῶν). What was said about Jesus by Simeon, that he was going to be an instrument for God's salvation, illuminating with his light all of the Gentiles,[189] is now said about Paul and Barnabas.[190] Both affirmations are very similar.[191]

---

[187] The image of *light* equating with *salvation* was already present in the *Benedictus*, but only in connection with Israel, not with the Gentiles (Lk 1:78-79).

[188] GRELOT, "Actes, XIII, 47", 368-372, contends that the phrase of Acts refers to the glorified Christ. However, the plural pronoun ἡμῖν of Acts 13:47 can refer only to Paul and Barnabas (13:46). The singular pronoun σέ comes from the quotation from Is 49:6, but is applied to the plural ἡμῖν.

[189] On Jesus illuminating the Gentiles see § 1.2.1.a, especially n. 18, and § 1.2.2.b.

[190] Although the statement attributed to "the Lord" in Acts 13:47 could be said by God or by the risen Jesus, it seems more likely that a christological reference is intended. In Lk 24:47 and Acts 9:5; 22:8; 26:15 the risen Christ is the one who utters similar words. Although it is unclear whether the expression "Lord" refers to God or to the risen Jesus, the title ὁ κύριος, with the definite article, has divine connotations; Paul is bringing God's salvation.

[191] The universalism of Paul and Barnabas is underlined by the expression "so that my salvation may reach the remotest parts of the earth" (Acts 13:47c), and the fact that "it made the Gentiles very happy to hear this and they gave thanks to the Lord for his message" (Acts 13:48-49).

Paul and Barnabas' witness will have an important role in fulfilling the prophetic words of Simeon because the risen Christ will be "light for the Gentiles" only through the witness of the first Christians (Acts 1:8), who also become "light for the Gentiles."[192]

In addition, Acts 13:46-47 is linked to Paul's commission, especially its third account. In his speech to king Agrippa, Paul gave a "definition" of his preaching and again claimed that he had been appointed by the Lord to the people (λαός) and Gentiles (ἔθνη), to open their eyes that they may turn from darkness to light (φῶς) (Acts 26:17-18). And Acts 26:23 says again that the risen Christ "was to proclaim a light (φῶς) for our people (λαός) and for the Gentiles (ἔθνη)." Again, Jesus' and Paul's universal mission are described through the image of "light."[193]

3.2.2 Travel Narrative to Jerusalem and Rome

a) A Geographical Universalism

I claim that the geographical disposition of Luke-Acts is used by Luke to express the universalism brought by the Christ event. Paul's travel narrative states the fulfillment of the risen Jesus' universal mandate, of his own vocation, and of the *Nunc Dimittis* by Simeon.[194] I affirm it because of three major reasons: the parallelism between Jesus' and Paul's travels to Jerusalem; the centripetal movement of Luke's Gospel which becomes a centrifugal

---

[192] In the Gospel of John, Jesus himself says: "I am the light of the world" (Jn 8:12; 9:5) and in Matthew's Gospel he says to his disciples: "You are the light of the world" (Mt 5:14). Both affirmations are present in Luke-Acts.

[193] We find, therefore, four equations between light and Gentiles, the first (Lk 2:32a) and the last one (Acts 26:23) referring to Jesus, and both in the middle referring to Paul (Acts 13:47; 26:18). I believe that this equation depends on the prophecy of Dt-Is (Is 49:6; see Is 42:16; 51:4). On the turning from darkness to light of Gentiles in Dt-Is see VLKOVÁ, *Cambiare*, 107-124; 148-162.

[194] The universalism previewed during Jesus' ministry (see § 1.2.1.a and 1.2.2.b), entrusted by Jesus to his disciples (see § 2.1.3.b), previewed in Peter's first speech (see § 2.2.1.b), introduced in the dispersion narrative (see § 2.2.2) and affirmed at the council in Jerusalem (see § 2.2.3.b and 2.2.3.c) reaches its climactic point with Paul's mission.

one in Acts; and the progressive decrease of the Temple and increase of the private household throughout Luke-Acts.

First, just as we found Jesus' journey to Jerusalem in the third Gospel,[195] we find Paul's journey to Jerusalem in the book of the Acts (19:21–21:16). Luke parallels Jesus and Paul travelling to Jerusalem with several similarities and differences. I suggest that Luke wanted to compare Paul travelling to Jerusalem and later to Rome, to Jesus' journey, because both fulfill the divine plan. That is to say, it is the divine plan that Jesus go to Jerusalem, and subsequently that Paul exceeds the boundaries of Jerusalem going to Rome. This divine plan downplays the importance of the Temple of Jerusalem and, by divine intervention, opens the doors of Christianity to universalism. The goal is no longer that of Jerusalem and the Temple.

If we want to know the particular position of Luke with respect to Paul's journey, we have to compare this journey with other narratives of the same voyages. The narratives that we possess are found in the letters written by Paul himself.[196]

On one hand, Paul reveals in his letters that what is called the *third missionary journey* (from Ephesus, passing through Macedonia, then arriving at Corinth) is due to the problems in the churches and included an effort to promote a monetary collection. On the other hand, before leaving Ephesus, according to the First Letter to the Corinthians, Paul had not yet decided to go to Jerusalem or to send delegates from each individual Church to carry the collection (1 Co 16:3-4), while in Romans Paul has undertaken to go to Jerusalem (Rm 15:25). In the Pauline corpus, if Paul goes to Jerusalem, his purpose clearly would be to bring the collection.[197]

---

[195] As we saw in § 1.2.2.a, especially p. 281, Jesus' travel narrative to Jerusalem mirrored Jesus' entering into the Temple in the infancy narrative.

[196] On the routes of Paul's journeys in the Pauline letters, comparing them to those of the so-called missionary journeys of Paul in Acts, see the stimulating articles by CAMPBELL, "Paul's 'Missionary Journeys'", 80-87, and PEREIRA, "Pablo, como Jesús", 37–45, which I follow.

[197] Paul initiates the collection not only as a gesture of generosity (2 Co 8:9; 9:6-15) and equality (2 Co 8:13-14), but also as a sign of *communion* (κοινωνία, Rm 15:25-27; 2 Co 8:4; 9:13).

Luke, on the contrary, presents a Paul that has already firmly decided to go to Jerusalem and to Rome (Acts 19:21). The Paul of Acts departs from Ephesus, travels through Greece and, having decided to go to Rome, passes through Jerusalem, which is not a small detour. Luke mentioned neither the attention to the churches nor the monetary collection as motives of his journey.[198] What is the reason for this difference? I suggest that the main reason is that Luke wants to present Paul traveling to Jerusalem as Jesus did, and later to Rome, in order to fulfill the divine plan, as Jesus did.

In Paul's travel to Jerusalem, there are several texts that remember sayings and events of Jesus. At the beginning of both jourmeys (Acts 19:21-39; Lk 9:51-56), the verbs "to accomplish" (συμπληρόω/πληρόω)[199] and "to go to Jerusalem" (τοῦ πορεύεσθαι εἰς Ἰερουσαλήμ) appear. It is necessary to travel to accomplish God's will.[200] Furthermore, both texts mention the name of two collaborators and the hostility that they receive. James and John witnessed the hostility in Samaria, just as Timothy and Erastus witness the hostility in Ephesus.[201]

---

[198] The silence regarding the collection in Acts 19:21–21:16 cannot be justified by saying that Luke did not know about it, because it is alluded to in Acts 24:17 (see as well Acts 11:29-30).

[199] On the analogy between Lk 9:51 and Acts 19:21 see RADL, *Paulus und Jesus*, 103-126.

[200] On one side, Jesus decides to set off on his journey because the days of his "ascent" (the same root of the ascension, ἀνάλημψις: Acts 1:2; 1:11.22) were fulfilled; that is, the days of his "ascent" to the Father, of being taken up to his Father. Likewise, Paul decides to initiate his travel because "it is necessary" (δεῖ), a verb that, in Luke's work, evokes the plan of God (Lk 2:49; 4:43; 9:22; 11:42; 12:12; 13:33; 15:32; 17:25; 18:1; 19:5; 21:9; 22:7.37; 24:7.26.44; Acts 1:16.21; 3:21; 4:12; 5:29; 9:6.16; 14:22; 16:30; 17:3; 19:36; 20:35; 23:11; 24:19; 25:10.24; 26:9; 27:24.26). By another, Luke presents both decisions with two very elaborate formulas: literally, Jesus "set his face" in order to go to Jerusalem and Paul "proposed in spirit" to go to Jerusalem.

[201] In addition, both Jesus and Paul go to Jerusalem to suffer, to be condemned and to die (Lk 9:51-56; Acts 19:21-22.23-39).

Acts 19:21-22.23-39	Lk 9:51-56
After these things had been *accomplished*, Paul proposed in Spirit to **go to Jerusalem.** "Afterwards, I must (δεῖ) visit Rome."	When the days were *accomplished* for him to be taken up, he set his face to **go to Jerusalem**.
Sending of *two collaborators, Timothy and Erastus,* and **hostility** in Ephesus.	Sending of messengers, intervention of *two, James and John,* and **hostility** in Samaria.

However, the existing parallels do not stop at the beginning of both travels. On the one hand, Paul's journey to Jerusalem is presented in two stages: Macedonia and Achaia (Acts 19:21). Both of these stages parallel the two regions that Jesus has to cover in his journey to Jerusalem: Galilee and Samaria (Lk 17:11). These four regions are always introduced by the verb διέρχομαι. On the other hand, the account of Miletus opens three predictions of tribulations and hostilities that Paul will face in Jerusalem (Acts 20:22.23.36-38; 21:4-6; 21:10-14). These three announcements parallel the three announcements of the passion of Jesus (Lk 9:22; 9:43b-45; 18:31-34),[202] and they respond to a common pattern.[203]

[202] I consider here only these three announcements. I reject Lk 13:31-33 because it is a further reference to the passion of Jesus. I realize that the first two predictions take place before the travel narrative, but they are located in its immediate context, previewing the suffering Messiah presented in the travel narrative. In fact, they frame Jesus' transfiguration (Lk 9:28-36) in which Jesus speaks about his departure that he was to accomplish in Jerusalem; they are preparatory scenes which set the stage for Jesus to travel to Jerusalem.

[203] We find more parallels between Jesus and Paul in Jerusalem. As the climax of Jesus' rejection took place at Jerusalem, the climax of the rejection of Paul likewise takes place at Jerusalem. Jesus and Paul have an initially positive reception (Lk 19:37-38; Acts 21:17-20) entering the Temple with positive motivations (Lk 19:45-48; Acts 21:26); they both are seized by hostile mobs (Lk 22:47-54; Acts 21:30) and slapped by assistants of the high priest (Lk 22:63-64; Acts 23:2); the final words of the community in the process of accepting their destiny in the image of Christ, "the Lord's will be done" (Acts 21:14), are a parallel of "Father [...] not my will but yours be done" (Lk 22:42), pronounced in

The narrative technique of syncrisis is elegantly employed by Luke. The parallels between Jesus and Paul happen in a natural manner, without being rigid. The author shows sufficient common elements in order to evoke the memory of past history and sufficient diverse elements that respect the originality of the new events.

However, the syncrisis underlines the differences, and the parallelism is broken for good reason. Paul, by divine imperative, goes also to Rome (Acts 19:21).[204] The Lukan narrative shows on numerous occasions and in distinct modes that Paul ought to steer himself toward the pagans and go to Rome in order to preach to the Gentiles. The risen Jesus himself says to Paul in the Temple that he has to go away from Jerusalem, "Go, for I will send you far away to the Gentiles" (22:21). After his trial before the Sanhedrin, the Lord appears to Paul and says to him that he must (δεῖ) bear witness also (καί) in Rome (23:11). And finally, among storms and shipwreck, an angel says to him that he must stand before the emperor (27:24).[205] It is the divine plan that Paul exceeds the boundaries of Jerusalem and arrives in the capital of the Empire.

Gethsemane; both are judged by the Sanhedrin (Lk 22:66-71; Acts 22:30–23:11) and the Roman authorities try to acquit both (Lk 23:13-35; Acts 23:29); both appear in four trials: Jesus before the Sanhedrin (Lk 22:54-71), before the Roman procurator Pilate (Lk 23:1-5); before the Jewish client king Herod (Lk 23:8-12), and before Pilate and the Jewish leaders (Lk 23:13-25); Paul before the Sanhedrin (Acts 22:30–23:10), before the Roman governor Felix (Acts 24:1-26), before Felix' successor Festus (Acts 25:6-12), and before the Jewish client king Agrippa (Acts 26:1-32); and they both are rejected by the Jewish leaders but regarded favorably by a Roman centurion (Lk 23:47; Acts 27:3.43).

[204] PUIG I TÀRRECH, "Les voyages à Jérusalem", 493-505, parallels Jesus' travel to Jerusalem, in his earthly travel, and then, after his resurrection, to heaven, while Paul's travel to Jerusalem, and then to Rome. However, all of the texts which refer to Paul's travel to Rome do not appear in Jesus "travelling" to heaven. Moreover, the duration of Paul's journey to Rome (Acts 23–28) is not comparable with the duration of Jesus' ascension to heaven (Lk 24:50-51). Furthermore, at the outset of Jesus' ascension, there is only an implicit reference through the name ἀνάλημψις (Lk 9:51), which indirectly refers to Jesus' heavenward journey. On the contrary, Paul's travel to Jerusalem and then to Rome is explicitly referred in Acts 19:21. That is why I prefer to maintain the ending of the parallelism.

[205] As Peter receives the celestial command of sacrificing and eating and not con-

Second, this same conclusion may be achieved through the geographical orientation of both parts of the Lukan work. While the third Gospel starts and ends in the Temple of Jerusalem, Acts starts from Jerusalem but does not end in Jerusalem; instead, Acts ends in Rome (28:16-31).[206] The centripetal force that drags Luke's entire Gospel to Jerusalem becomes a centrifugal force that, starting from Jerusalem, arrives at the confines of the land represented by the capital of the Empire. Not only do we find this centripetal movement at the end of the third Gospel (εἰς Ἰερουσαλήμ: Lk 24:52) and centrifugal one at the beginning of Acts (ἐξ Ἰερουσαλήμ: Acts 1:8), but also in the second account of the conversion of Paul (Acts 22:17-21). Paul affirms that he went to Jerusalem (εἰς Ἰερουσαλήμ: Acts 22:17) and, being in the Temple, saw the risen Jesus who said to him: "go from Jerusalem (ἔξελθε ἐξ Ἰερουσαλήμ: Acts 22:18)." As the apostles receive the mandate of the risen Jesus to set off from Jerusalem to the confines of the land (Acts 1:8), now Paul receives from the risen Jesus the mandate to leave Jerusalem.

As the figure below shows, Jesus' travel to Jerusalem in his infancy, from Nazareth through Judea to the Temple of Jerusalem, mirrors Jesus' travel to Jerualem in his public life, and his disciples' travels, especially that to Jerusalem and Rome. However, while Jesus' travels finish in Jerusalem, his disciples' travels finish in the earth's remotest end, Rome.

---

sidering anything impure (Acts 10:13; 11:7), Paul receives these celestial mandates, going to the Gentiles. Both Peter and Paul, having received a divine vision, show that God's will is the expansion of Christianity to the Gentiles. Luke shows repeatedly that it is not that Peter had decided to eat impure food and stay in the house of pagans, nor had Paul wanted to pass through the boundaries of Jerusalem by himself; in both cases God asks the apostle to do it (see BOVON, "Holy Spirit", 34-35).

[206] BALTZER, "The Meaning of the Temple", 277, and LARSSON, "Temple-Criticism", 394, have seen an *inclusio* in Acts similar to that in Luke's Gospel. For them, Acts begins in Jerusalem, the Temple-city, and it closes with a quotation from Isaiah 6:9-10, drawn from the Temple vision (Acts 28:26-27). In my opinion the reader is not able to perceive that *inclusio* because there is no direct reference to the Temple in the text.

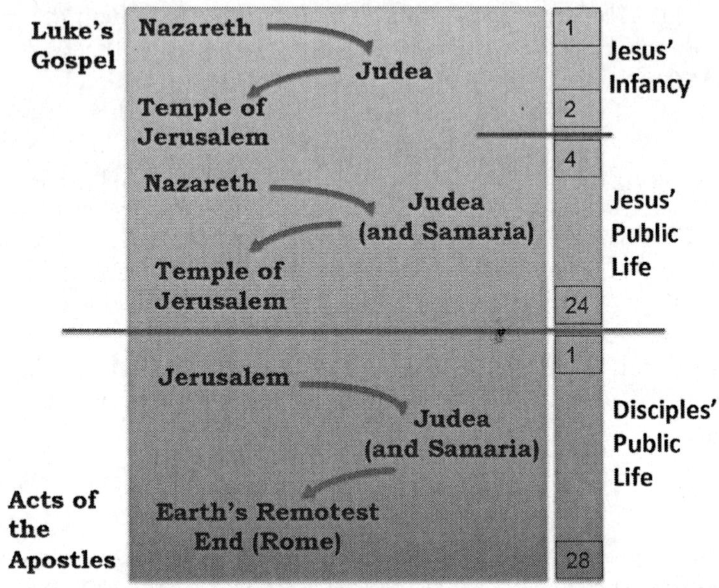

Thirdly, this geographical universalism is expressed as well by the fact that as the importance of the Temple decreases in Acts, the importance of private houses progressively increases. In the Gospel the story begins (1:5-23) and ends (24:50-53) in the *Temple*. In Acts, however, it begins (1:12-14) and ends (28:30-31) in the *house*. At the end of the third Gospel, after the ascension of Jesus, the disciples "return to Jerusalem, where they were continually in the *Temple* blessing God" (Lk 24:52-53). However, in the beginning of Acts, after the ascension of Jesus, the disciples "return to Jerusalem (…) and they went to the room upstairs where they were staying" (Acts 1:12-13), and they receive the Spirit "that filled the entire *house* where they were sitting" (Acts 2:2). In fact, as Jesus enters Jerusalem going directly to the *Temple* (Lk 19:45), Paul enters Jerusalem going directly to a *house* (Acts 21:4). After the miraculous liberation of the disciples, the angel orders them: "Go, stand in the *Temple*" (Acts 5:20). However, later, after the miraculous liberation of Peter, the angel drives him to the streets of the city (Acts 12:10) and "to the *house* of Mary" (Acts 12:12). At the beginning, the Jewish authorities head for the *Temple* in order to find the first Christians (Acts 5:26-27). But, as the narrative advances, "Saul was ravaging the Church by entering *house* after *house*" (Acts 8:3). According to Elliot, in the Lukan economy of salvation, the Temple and the household represent opposed types of social institutions, but only one of which, the household, is capable of embodying the structures, values and goals of an inclusive Gospel of universal salvation.[207] I do not believe that in Luke-Acts both institutions are opposed, but agree with this latter idea.

Furthermore, L. Michael White supports the idea that the Jewish community, after the destruction of the Temple, translated certain values of the Temple to the synagogue.[208] Something similar could be said among the Christians, translating some of the values of the Temple to the primitive Christian community or to the houses where they lived.[209] In fact, the house acquires many of the values of the Temple institution, such as a place of revelation (Acts 1:13-26; 2:42; 5:42; 9:10-19; 10:1-8.9-23; 11:4.13-14; 13:2; 18:7-11; 20:7-12.20; 28:30-31; even with the presence of the Spirit: Acts 2:1-4; 9:17; 10:44).[210] However, the institution of the household adds new features which exceed the Temple: it is a place to receive Baptism (10:48; 16:15), to receive the Spirit (2:2-4; 10:44) and to break bread (2:46; 20:7 like the Last Supper, also celebrated in a house, Lk 22:10-20). The Temple symbolism has been broadened to embrace the institution of the household.

---

[207] ELLIOTT, "Household and Meals Versus Temple", 107. See as well ELLIOTT, "Temple Versus Household", 88-120, especially 115-118.

[208] WHITE, *From Jesus*, 90-92. BILLERBECK, "Ein Synagogengottesdienst", 143-161, and MENES, "Temple und Synagoge", 268-276, hold that the architecture and the liturgical movement in the synagogue took over several elements of the Temple cult.

[209] Luke, calling the Temple *house* (οἶκος: Lk 6:4; 11:51; 13:35; 19:46; Acts 7:47; 7:49), helps the reader to make the transition from the Temple of Jerusalem to the households. In this way, the reader can easily see that the functions of the Temple have been assumed by the household (see BACHELARD – JOLAS, *The Poetics of Space*).

[210] The house also becomes a place of prayer (Acts 10:30; 12:12; 16:15; 16:31; 18:8).

b) The Increased General Rejection by the Jews ('Ἰουδαῖοι)

As the Jewish leaders reject Jesus and his disciples, so now the leaders reject Paul. The chief priests (23:2.14; 24:1; 25:1.15; 26:10-12), the elders (23:14; 24:1; 25:15), the scribes, Sanhedrin (22:5), and leaders of the people (25:2) are good examples of this. However, the prominence of the authorities decreases throughout Acts, because many of the people of Israel join their leaders in rejecting Paul.

In fact, Paul's preaching in the synagogues of the Diaspora only yields individual acceptance by Jews, such as the leader of the synagogue, Crispus (Acts 18:8)[211] and limited and imprecise conversions.[212] The different ways in which Luke uses the singular 'Ἰουδαῖος and the plural 'Ἰουδαῖοι shows the significant difference between the conversion of individual Jews and the rejection by Jews as a whole. 'Ἰουδαῖος appears only ten times throughout Luke-Acts, always in the Diaspora in Acts. Luke usually uses the term *Jew* in the singular to designate a specific person, without any pejorative value. Actually, of the ten occurrences, nine are positive, in connection with the Christian faith, and only one is negative, rejecting Paul.[213] There are individual conversions of Jews who represent, as Simeon and Anna, the acceptance of Christianity by individual Jews.

---

[211] Other individual conversions are Lydia (16:14) and Jason (17:5).

[212] Some Jews of Damascus (9:20), of Antioch (13:43), of Iconium (14:1.4, made up of both Jews and Greeks), of Lystra (16:1), of Beroea (17:12), and of Ephesus (19:1-7) convert. Others show their acceptance of Christianity by trying to convince Paul to stay with them longer (18:20), or invoking the name of Jesus over demons (19:13-17).

[213] Timothy, who became an associate and disciple of Paul, is identified as the son of a Jewish woman (16:1); Aquila, who accepts Paul at his house and becomes an associate of Paul (18:2); Apollos, who had been given instruction in the Way of the Lord and preached with great spiritual fervor (18:24-25); Sceva, a Jewish chief priest, who pronounce the name of the Lord Jesus over people possessed (19:14); Alexander, who apparently would have been a defender of Paul in Ephesus, if he had been allowed to speak (19:33); Drusilla, the wife of Felix, a Jewish woman who heard Paul on the subject of faith in Christ Jesus (24:24); finally, Peter and Paul are each presented as a *Jew* who has accepted the Christian faith (10:28; 21:39; 22:3). The only negative example is 13:6-12, where a Jewish magician and false prophet called Bar-Jesus tries to prevent the proconsul's conversion to the Christian faith.

The Jews (ʼΙουδαῖοι), however, come to the foreground of the scenes of the rejection of Paul, whose persecution is led by the people of Israel in general.[214] Jews, and not only their authorities, work out a plot to kill Paul (Acts 9:23). Although it is not said who these Jews are, it seems to be inconceivable that every Jew was concerned with Paul. It is more likely that, by Acts 9:23, the word *Jews* has become a word by which Luke indicates those Jews who rejected Jesus and his disciples.

The use of ʼΙουδαῖοι is very particular in Luke-Acts. The plural Ιουδαῖοι appears 74 times in Luke-Acts: only five times in Luke's Gospel,[215] only three times before Acts 9:23,[216] and the remaining 66 occurrences from Acts 9:22 to the end of Acts. Although ʼΙουδαῖοι is frequently used in a neutral sense, to describe Jewish customs, Jewish synagogues, or Jewish people, the characteristic and most striking uses are those that speak collectively of Jews as opponents. They are a threatening group, filled with jealousy against Paul (13:45); they incite others (13:50); as the mission of Paul develops, the Jews are persistent persecutors, even following Paul from city to city until they stone Paul (14:19); they instigate a virulent attack against Christian preachers (17:5); they come from Thessalonica to Beroea to make trouble and stir up the people against Paul (17:13); they attack Paul in Corinth (18:12); they plot against him in Greece (20:3); they hold a secret meeting to kill Paul (23:12.21); and they contradict (ἀντιλέγω) Paul in Rome (28:19).[217]

The opposition of the ʼΙουδαῖοι against Paul reaches its zenith in his trial. There is a clear progression in the participation of the Jewish people in the different trials narrated in Luke-Acts. While the prominence of the authorities progressively decreases, the participation of the Jews (ʼΙουδαῖοι) progressively increases. In the trials of

[214] From Acts 22 to the end of the story Paul is in chains.

[215] It refers to the elders of the *Jews* (7:3) and to the king of the *Jews* (23:3.37.38.51).

[216] It is used in the Pentecost speech to refer to the whole audience (2:5.11.14).

[217] On the role of the ʼΙουδαῖοι as those who reject and persecute the Christians see KILGALLEN, "Persecution", 148-150. On the role of the Jews in Acts see WILLS, "Jews in Acts", 631-644.

Jesus, the major opposition comes from the authorities.[218] The trials of Peter take place before the religious authorities, without the presence of the people. In Jesus' and Peter's trials the authorities do not publicly attack them because they are afraid of the people, who admire them. In the trial of Stephen the authorities start the trial, turn the people against him, and the people of Jerusalem join their authorities in seizing and stoning him. And the chief opponents in Paul's trial are simply the Jews. The Jews incite riots (21:27), are persecutors because they oppose preaching that Jesus is risen (26:2.7), and accuse him before Roman authorities (22:30; 24:9; 25:7.24).[219] Paul is actually seized by the entire people, who close the gates of the Temple (21:30).[220]

When Luke speaks about Ἰουδαῖοι, he refers to those Jews who have not accepted the Gospel, even though he does not say so explicitly; the term Ἰουδαῖοι is used for non-Christian Jews, and not for Christian Jews.[221] Luke does not mean to implicate all Jews in the many times that he speaks in general about "Jews;" in fact, Luke is presenting all of his main characters as Jews. The obvious question is: if Luke did not mean all the Jews, then why did he only say so in Acts 14:2, where we find the expression "the Jews who re-

---

[218] As we have seen at the end of § 1.2.3.b, there is only one text, itself ambiguous, which links the people of Israel with their authorities (Lk 23:13).

[219] In the trial against Paul not only the authorities act, but also the *people* (21:30.36.39-40) and the *Jews* (23:12-15.20.27; 24:19.27; 25:9; 26:21; 28:19).

[220] Luke implicates the whole people in Paul's arrest, those dwelling in Jerusalem (21:30) as well as those who have arrived from Paul's mission field in the Diaspora, but not their authorities (21:27). However, in Jesus' arrest those present are Judas, the chief priests and captains of the Temple guard, and the elders (Lk 22:52); nothing is said about the people. In Peter's arrest, only the priests, the guard of the Temple, and the Sadducees act (Acts 4:1; 5:17). The people, the elder, and the scribes arrested Stephen (Acts 6:12).

[221] D. P. Béchard has demonstrated that the theological concept denoted by the term *Judaea* in Luke-Acts has been decidedly altered in light of the Christ event (BÉCHARD, "Theological Significance of Judaea", 675-691). I believe that the term Ἰουδαῖοι has been altered in the light of the general rejection of Jesus by the Jewish people. In fact, Luke uses the term Ἑβραῖος, "Hebrew," when he wants to speak about Christian Jews (Acts 6:1).

fused to believe"? Salmon believes that Luke did say it only once because it was not necessary. It would have been obvious to Paul and to his audience which Jews he meant.[222]

On the contrary, the term Ἰσραήλ is used for the repentant group of Jews, that is, Christian Jews who accept Jesus and his disciples, and not for non-Christian Jews.[223] As Ἰσραήλ accepts Jesus and his disciples, it is the believing Israel which receives the promised salvation and its own glory.[224] As Simeon prophesied glory for Israel, δόξα λαοῦ σου Ἰσραήλ (Lk 2:32b), Ἰσραήλ receives that glory by accepting Jesus. The Christian proclamation served to divide the Jewish people into two groups: the believers and the non-believers, the repentant and the obdurate. It seems that Luke prefers to use the terms Ἰσραήλ, Ἰουδαῖος, and λαός,[225] especially at the beginning of Acts, to express the ac-

---

[222] SALMON, "Insider or Outsider?", 81, claims that Luke was an *insider* who criticizes those Jews who have not accepted the fulfillment of the Jewish prophecies in Jesus. As another insider, I use the term "Jews," as Luke did, to mean those Jews who reject Christianity.

[223] See Acts 9:15; 10:36; 13:17.23.24; 28:20. O'TOOLE, "The Christian Mission", 376-379, has formulated what he names "Luke's redefinition of 'Israel.'" According to him, those who accept Jesus are the true and faithful development of Israel. Although Luke does not explicitly speak of a new Israel, he does so portray those who believe in Christ and thus redefines who belongs to Israel. To belong to Israel, one must believe in Jesus. O'Toole uses texts like Acts 3:22.23; 15:16-18, or Jesus' symbolic selection of the Twelve, as an image of the *true* Israel (Lk 22:30). In the Pauline literature, Rm 9:6, Paul affirms: "Not all born Israelites belong to Israel." RAVENS, *Restoration of Israel*, 250-251, claims that Luke's presentation of the restoration of Israel has two purposes: to convince Jewish Christians that they have made the right decision and are still members of Israel; and to show Gentile believers that they are now, through God's grace, members of Israel with the same inheritance as the Jews. On this topic see MCNICOL, "Rebuilding the House of David", 25-38; FULLER, *The Restoration of Israel*, 197-269.

[224] See DUPONT, "La conclusion des Actes", 359-404.

[225] As we have seen in § 2.2.1.c, especially p. 314, the use of the term λαός clearly decreases after Acts 7:4 with only 23 of 47 occurrences after this verse. In addition, this term presents a negative connotation of opposition against Christianity only in six occurrences (12:11; 21:28.30.36; 26:17; 28:27) and one of these is because λαός is linked to the term Ἰουδαῖοι (12:11: λαὸς τῶν Ἰουδαίων).

ceptance by part of the people of Israel,[226] and afterwards the term Ἰουδαῖοι to express the rejection by part of the Jews.[227]

3.2.3 At the End: Paul in Rome

The last passage of the book of Acts, which finishes Acts as well as the entire Lukan work, is especially important because of its *position* (28:17-31). Since the ending of a narrative helps to clarify key elements and to leave a final impression on the reader, the manner of ending is a significant decision for an author.[228] Paul is the *reliable character* who speaks through a relative lengthy *direct quotation* (28:26-27). Even more, the invocation of the authority of the Holy Spirit and the prophet Isaiah underscores the significance of the quotation (28:25). The *location* of the passage, Rome, the capital of the Empire, highlights the universal dimension of the passage.

This pericope in Rome resembles the passage in Antioch of Pisidia and so brackets the ministry of Paul by the same features. In Antioch and in Rome, Paul dedicates two different moments to the Jews (13:16b-43; 13:46b-47; and 28:17-22; 28:23-28). The first polite interchange (28:17-22) reflects similar positive responses to the message of Paul in Antioch (13:42-43).[229] The second meeting also follows a familiar pattern, this time of division and rejection

---

[226] Both terms, λαός and Ἰσραήλ, appear in the Presentation passage in connection with the Jewish acceptance of Jesus (2:31-32).

[227] I believe that the increasing use of the term Ἰουδαῖοι throughout Luke-Acts is due to the increasing rejection by part of the Jews and to the geographical situation of the Diaspora in which those who come from Judea are also called Ἰουδαῖοι.

[228] According to MARGUERAT, "The Enigma", 284, the last words of Luke possess a peculiar power not only because they are the end of the literary work, and thus the last image the reader has, but also because they mean that Acts culminates in an open end. Luke remains silent about the appeal to Caesar, which represents the avowed motive for Paul's transfer to Rome (28:19); he remains mute about the interminable wait for the apostle's trial announced throughout the book (23:11; 25:11; 26:32; 27:24); he does not speak of the outcome of the trial, whether favorable or not. These expectations of the reader finish with the last word of the narrator in the conclusive summary of Acts 28:30-31, which is truly important for Luke. The omission of Paul's fate suggests that Luke's main concern lies instead with Paul's proclamation of the gospel to all people.

[229] It is similar as well to the first response to Jesus (Lk 4:22) and to Peter (Acts 2:37-41).

(13:44-50; and 28:23-28).[230] Paul's preaching ends with a solemn warning (13:40-41; and 28:25-27); afterward, Paul announces the turn to the Gentiles (13:46-47; and 28:28).[231] These episodes effectively frame Paul's mission in chapters 13–28.[232]

a) The Inclusio *in Luke-Acts: Universal Salvation through Rejection*

Simeon says that Jesus represents τὸ σωτήριον (Lk 2:30). The substantive σωτήριον appears two further times in Luke's work. The last one is located right at the end of Acts of the Apostles (Acts 28:28). The verb ἀντιλέγω, at the end of the Lukan narrative (Acts 28:19.22) is linked to the same verb at the beginning of the Lukan Gospel (Lk 2:34).[233] The *position* of these terms form

[230] It is similar as well to the rejection of Jesus (Lk 4:23-30) and of Peter (Acts 5:17).

[231] In both passages a quotation from Isaiah occupies the center of Paul's words. On this parallelism see DUPONT, "Je t'ai établi", 343-349.

[232] In the midst of the Pauline mission, midway between Antioch and Rome, Paul preaches in Athens the message of salvation addressed to "everyone and everywhere" (Acts 17:30). The universal offer of salvation is preached, without any OT quotation in this geographical symbol of Greek culture where the Areopagus in Athens takes the place of the Sanhedrin in Jerusalem.

[233] The scarcity of the terms σωτήριον (Lk 2:30; 3:6; Acts 28:28) and ἀντιλέγω (Lk 2:34; 20:27; 21:15; Acts 4:14; 13:45; 28:19.22) throughout Luke-Acts further emphasizes this repetition in both passages. In addition, both passages speak of a division, which will be caused by Jesus (Lk 2:34b) or which Paul's preaching is causing (Acts 28:24-25). Both texts present faithful Israelites who announce universal salvation and are rejected by other Jews while remaining faithful Israelites (Lk 2:22.39; Acts 28:17.20.23). In fact, all of the main characters of Luke-Acts receive their universal but rejected mission, and progressively fulfill it, in a Jewish context. Jesus' first preaching is in the synagogue of Nazareth, on a Sabbath, and follows the liturgical reading from Isaiah (Lk 4:16). His disciples' commission takes place in Jerusalem and accords with everything written in the Law of Moses, in the Prophets and in the Psalms (Lk 24:44). The Pentecost speech and the solemn council take place in Jerusalem and before a Jewish audience (Acts 2:1). Paul's commission takes place when Saul is presented as a faithful Jew receiving from the high priest the right to arrest any follower of the Christian way (Acts 9:3); moreover, the risen Christ's appearance in the Temple links Paul's vocation to the core of his Jewish faith and piety (Acts 22:17). And his presentation in the synagogue of Antioch in Pisidia is as a faithful Jew (Acts 13:16). The compatibility between universalism and rejection with Jewishness also appears in the relationship between the mission of the twelve and the

an *inclusio* in Luke-Acts, delimiting the entire Lukan work through the terms σωτήριον and ἀντιλέγω, which become a clue to understand the whole narrative because they define the Christian mission: a salvation which implies a rejection.[234]

The term σωτήριον is always connected with a universal offer of salvation by God. The first occurrence affirms that Jesus is God's salvation, τὸ σωτήριόν σου, where the personal pronoun σοῦ refers to God because Simeon is speaking to God. God has made ready this salvation, Jesus, for the sake of the nations, a light of revelation for the Gentiles (Lk 2:30-32).[235] The last occurrence says: τοῖς ἔθνεσιν ἀπεστάλη τοῦτο τὸ σωτήριον τοῦ θεοῦ (Acts 28:28).[236] The emphatic position of the expression τοῖς ἔθνεσιν underlines the fact that even the Gentiles are the addressees of this salvation.[237] The fact that Paul "welcomed all (πάντας) who came to visit him" (Acts 28:30) highlights even more the universalism of the salvation offered.[238] These occurrences are strongly linked by close syntactic and semantic ties. In other words, Luke's work de-

mission of the 72. The twelve represent the twelve tribes of Israel, and are linked to the 72 peoples of the earth, and both groups will suffer rejection. On this relationship between both missions see BRAWLEY, *Luke-Acts and the Jews*, 137.

[234] These terms are disposed in a chiastic composition: A (σωτήριον: Lk 2:30); B (ἀντιλέγω: Lk 2:34); B' (ἀντιλέγω: Acts 28:22); A' (σωτήριον: Acts 28:28).

[235] The second occurrence is also linked to a universal offer of salvation by God (Lk 3:6). Luke follows Mk 1:2-3, but instead of limiting the quotation of Is 40:3, as Mark does, Luke carefully lengthens the prophetic text to Is 40:3-5. In this way he can close his OT quotation with an allusion to God's universal salvation: "And all flesh shall see the salvation (σωτήριον) of God" (Lk 3:6).

[236] The demonstrative pronoun τοῦτο refers to the salvation of God offered to the Jews through the presence of Jesus (Acts 28:23).

[237] BOVON, "How Well", 43-50, highlights the universalism of the pericope because of the manner in which a passage is quoted and a discrete transformation at the end of the quote.

[238] According to KILGALLEN, "Acts 28,28 - Why?", 176-187, because of this πάντας what is affirmed in the passage is a knowledge of the plan of God to offer salvation to Jews, Gentiles, and Christians. Paul's three audiences are recapitulated because the end of the book mentions all three of them (Acts 28:17.23; 28:28; 28:15), and Paul welcomes all who came to visit him (28:30).

scribes the salvation of God, and σωτήριον in Luke is a universal offer of salvation by God in Jesus.[239]

	God's Salvation	Universalism	Rejection
Luke 2	**τὸ σωτήριόν σου**	φῶς εἰς ἀποκάλυψιν **ἐθνῶν**	ἐν τῷ Ἰσραὴλ **ἀντιλεγόμενον**
Acts 28	**τὸ σωτήριον τοῦ θεοῦ**	τοῖς **ἔθνεσιν** ἀπεστάλη	πανταχοῦ **ἀντιλέγεται**

b) Rejection Everywhere: by Jews, Pagans, and Christians

However, while at the beginning of the macro-narrative the rejection was in Israel, at the end of Luke-Acts it is everywhere (πανταχοῦ: Acts 28:22).[240] Throughout the narrative the rejection

[239] Luke uses the language of *salvation* just as the other synoptic Gospels do, to speak about a profane salvation, the deliverance of one's life from a very serious danger, and with an eschatological meaning and, finally, for a salvation expressed by a bodily healing. However, there are two other meanings that are specific to Luke. On one hand, there is a communal salvation, offered to Jews (Lk 1:55.68.69; 2:10-11; Acts 2:14.22.36.39; 5:31; 13:23.26) and Gentiles (Acts 13:47; 16:17; 28:28). Only Luke speaks first of the salvation of the people of Israel, and then of the salvation of the Gentiles because only Luke, among the Gospels, underlines the universal dimensions of salvation. On the other hand, there is also an actual non-physical salvation, a non-eschatological salvation not linked to any healing (Lk 7:48-50; 8:12; 17:19; 19:7-10; 23:43; Acts 2:21.47; 11:14). Both of them are applied to Jesus in this *inclusio* by Luke. First, the salvation of the community was already predicted by Simeon in foretelling universal salvation, whether for Gentiles or for Jews (Lk 2:31-32), and it also appears in the offer of salvation to Gentiles (28:28) and in the welcome offered to all by Paul (28:30). And secondly, the actual non-physical salvation is seen by Simeon and Anna when, being with Jesus, they see salvation in that precise moment and yet are not healed from any illness (Lk 2:30.38); it appears also in Paul's offer of present salvation without any corporal healing. On the different meanings of the term *salvation* in Luke-Acts see GEORGE, "L'emploi", 309-320.

[240] This majority rejection has caused some scholars to speak about the general condemnation of the Jews and the impossibility of Jewish conversion after Paul's

increases not only because of the increasing rejection by the Jewish people, who join their leaders in rejecting Christianity,[241] but also because Luke-Acts tells of a rejection by some pagans as well, and even by some Christians.

For example, In Acts 14:5 Jews and pagans stone Paul and Barnabas. In Philippi Paul is jailed for having caused a young girl to be freed from the evil spirit which had empowered her to predict fortunes and thus for having deprived her owners of finan-

---

preaching in Rome (SANDERS, "The Salvation of the Jews", 104-107). LOHFINK, *Die Sammlung Israels*, 30-60, and BOVON, "How Well", 43-50, on the contrary, contend that there is also a reference to believing Jews because of the last verb of the citation appears in the future: ἰάσομαι αὐτούς, "I will heal them." Moreover, witnessing even to individual Jews is still possible, because Acts 28:30 affirms that Paul "welcomed all who came to visit him," even Jews (TANNEHILL, "Rejection by Jews", 83). I claim that Paul's interest in the Jews is clear throughout Luke-Acts, including at its very end. Luke devoted a great deal of attention to the salvation of the Jews. There are Jewish conversions throughout the whole composition, even at the end (Acts 28:24a), but individual conversions progressively decrease and the general rejection increases. In addition, the last rejection affirmed in Acts, rejection "everywhere" (Acts 28:22) does not refer only to Jews. For a more extensive treatment of the end of Acts see PUSKAS, *The Conclusion of Luke-Acts*, 106-114.

[241] Tannehill affirms that the end of Acts dramatizes the recurrent rejection of salvation by the Jews. According to him, since the birth narrative emphasizes the fulfillment of promises of salvation for Israel, the expectations awakened at the beginning are not fully realized. He says: "Much of Israel, in fact, rejects salvation through Jesus, creating tension between the hopes and expectations aroused at the beginning and the actual course of the narrative. This twist in the plot has a tragic effect" (TANNEHILL, "Tragic Story", 69-85). I claim that this rejection of many in Israel had been already foretold by Simeon. The reader could expect it and this expectation reduces the tragic effect. In fact, when Tannehill analyzes Lk 2:22-39, he studies terms like χριστὸς κύριος, προσδέχομαι, σωτήριον, and διαλογισμός, but he does not pay sufficient attention to the expression σημεῖον ἀντιλεγόμενον (TANNEHILL, *Narrative Unity* I, 38-44). In addition, O'Toole, using composition criticism, claims that the promises of salvation in the infancy narrative do not require that all the people of Israel have to accept this savior, but that salvation is offered to all the people of Israel (O'TOOLE, "The Christian Mission", 374-376). RÄISÄNEN, "The Redemption of Israel", 94-111, also opposes Tannehill. Finally, I believe that there is a double irony: first, Israel reaches its hope through the rejection of part of "Israel," the rejection of part of "Israel" engenders Israel's glory; and second, the Lukan characters are presented as faithful Jews, but they are rejected by part of the Jews for preaching the fulfillment of the hope and expectations of Israel (Acts 26:6-7; 28:20).

cial profit. The owners take Paul and Barnabas to the agora, before the magistrates and praetor, because Paul and Barnabas were Jews urging the people to embrace religious practices opposed to Roman law (16:16-24). After Paul's speech in the Areopagus of Athens, some of them burst out laughing when they heard of the resurrection of the dead (17:32). And the pagans of Ephesus reject Paul because they think that Christianity will replace the cult of Artemis (19:23-27).

And even among the first Christians we find rejection of Christianity. Unlike those who were selling their property and presenting all the money to the apostles (4:34-37), Ananias and Sapphira defrauded the apostles, keeping back part of the price, an action which led to their downfall (πίπτω) (5:2.10). Even among the circle of disciples of Jesus, even among his apostles who had accepted him from the beginning, there are two who reject Jesus in Jerusalem. Judas plots with the chief priests and scribes to kill Jesus (Lk 22:4.6) and betrays him with a kiss (Lk 22:48); and Peter begins rejecting Jesus to the point of affirming three times that he does not know him (Lk 22:57.58.60).

The last passage of Acts highlights the division foretold by Simeon (Lk 2:34b), division which appears throughout the entire macro-narrative. It is the last picture, and it is a picture of a people divided over the Christian mission: "some were convinced by what he (Paul) said, while the others were skeptical" (28:24). The division is indicated by the multitude of discordant speeches that the Greek word ἀσύμφωνοι expresses; they were not in "symphony," "they disagreed among themselves" (28:25). Acts 28 makes sense in the context of the whole Lukan literary work, where a general division is developed.[242] All of the groups which approach the Gospel are split when confronted with the Christian message.

---

[242] Other examples of division throughout the Pauline section are the following. In Antioch Paul's speech achieves a two-fold result: a great number of Jews and proselytes are converted (13:43) while others reject the Gospel (13:46). In Iconium the people in the city are divided by the Christian preaching (14:4). In Thessalonica (17:4-5) and Beroea (17:10-14) some Jews are converted while others begin a persecution. Paul and his companions are often met with favor and rejection at the same time (18:1-17; 19:8-10).

4. Conclusion

In the relationship of Lk 2:22-39 with Luke-Acts as a whole, we see that while many pericopes are meaningful in isolation, they receive additional meaning by being read in the context of the entire Lukan corpus. Many of the connections which I discuss had been noted before by various scholars, but when they are drawn together they become much more impressive and give a new vision of Lk 2:22-39. The Presentation in the Temple helps us to better understand the whole Lukan narrative where it can be interpreted as a real presentation of the entire macro-narrative.[243]

The distinctive features of the Presentation become important topics and are fulfilled throughout Luke-Acts.[244] In fact, Lk 2:22-39 contains a heavy concentration of prolepsis of what is to be realized in the subsequent story. Simeon is the first spokesperson of universal salvation and division, which are developed at length throughout Luke-Acts. Simeon's prophecy is always kept in the mind of the attentive readers, although direct references are not frequent.

The Presentation passage contributes to the overall interpretative framework of the narrative. Key points in the narrative, the conclusion (Acts 28:17-31) and the hinge between the two parts of the work follow the Presentation passage (Lk 24:47–Acts 1:8). Moreover, the key texts of the main characters of Luke-Acts are linked to Lk 2:22-39. The Presentation passage becomes a hermeneutical framework in which the main characters of Luke-Acts, Jesus, his disciples, and Paul, can be interpreted.[245]

---

[243] I do not say that Lk 2:22-39 illuminates the whole macro-narrative, but looking back to the infancy narrative, it seems that Simeon was closer to the mark than the other hopes expressed in the infancy narrative. It thus appears that Luke has used Simeon's speeches at several key points in the narrative to help explain the main lines of the plot and to introduce the mission of the protagonists.

[244] We find the Lukan motif of promise-fulfillment within the Lukan narrative itself.

[245] In the texts linked to Lk 2:22-39, sometimes a motive is prominent, and other times that motive is subordinate to the other motives, but all of the distinctive features of the Presentation in the Temple are present in the different protagonists, in different proportions.

I notice a *common architecture* in the characterization of the protagonists of Luke-Acts. This common design starts with the Presentation of Jesus in the Temple. All of the different main figures of Luke-Acts are also characterized by a presentation which includes a commission statement;[246] each presentation mirrors the distinctive features of the Presentation in the Temple and is fulfilled in very significant *positions* in Luke-Acts, from the very beginning of their public lives until the very end.[247] Luke often expresses the language and images of each character in a manner that echoes the language foretold by Simeon.[248] The same motives, and sometimes even the same terms, appear in the different characters.[249] These images, which recur in different texts, sometimes depend on the same OT text, which links those texts together.[250] These similar-

[246] The commission statements of the different protagonists display a consistency among themselves. The disciples' commission (Lk 21:12-17; 24:46-49; Acts 1:8) agrees with that of Jesus (Lk 2:22-39), and that of Paul (Acts 9:3-12; 22:6-21; 26:12-18) with those of Jesus and of the disciples.

[247] The beginning and end of the ministry of Jesus, his disciples, and Paul share certain features among them. At the beginning the features of their commission are previewed; at the end they are reviewed; and the middle agrees with the beginning and the end. For example, one common feature is the preaching of a sermon which summarizes the main message of the character at the beginning of their public lives (Jesus: Lk 4:16-30; Peter: Acts 2:14-36; Paul: Acts 13:16-47). A second common feature is that the main message of the character always contains a universal offer of salvation (Lk 4:25-26; Acts 2:39; Acts 13:47). A third common feature is that the response of the hearers always implies some kind of divided response (Lk 4:22.28; Acts 2:41; 5:17; Acts 13:42-45). A fourth common feature is the use of a scriptural text, not always a direct quotation, that reveals something of the character's mission (Lk 4:18-19; Acts 2:17-21; Acts 13:47). These features help the reader to understand the mission of the leading protagonists since the beginning of the narrative. A similar analysis could be made on the same features of the last speech of each character.

[248] Jesus is the archetype because this prophecy is first fulfilled in Jesus and, through the syncrisis, fulfilled later in his disciples.

[249] For example, the rejection of Jesus and his disciples is expressed throughout Luke-Acts with the same verbs that Jesus uses for his disciples' commission statement in Lk 21:12-17.

[250] These OT texts often come from Dt-Is prophecy. It is striking that the four canticles of the servant are linked with the words spoken by Simeon about Jesus. The first two canticles, speaking about universalism and presenting the servant as "light

ities indicate that Luke purposely presents other protagonists in light of Jesus' presentation.[251]

Luke's expert use of syncrisis among the different main characters points not only to the similarities, but also to the differences between them. Although Simeon presented the important features of universalism and rejection, the rest of the macro-narrative resolves the suspense of that presentation and tells *how* it is developed. There is an increasing progression in the fulfillment of the universalism and in the quantitative measure of the rejection throughout Luke-Acts.[252]

Jesus only implicitly previews *universal mission* through some parables with universalistic meaning and with some ministry to non-Jews, including performing some miracles among them. At the end of the earthly life of Jesus his universal commission has not yet been fulfilled. Jesus' death appears to thwart God's universal plan. This narrative tension caused by the unrealized promise is resolved by the resurrection of Jesus and his subsequent commissioning of the disciples as witnesses, moving the program into another phase. This is the reason why the risen Christ clearly commits his disciples to this universalism in Jesus' name. Luke "repeats" these words at the end of his Gospel and at the beginning of Acts. As Simeon foretold the universal mission at the beginning of Luke, Jesus commands it for his disciples at the beginning of Acts. The different stages of the spread

---

for the Gentiles" (Is 42:6; 49:6), are linked with Simeon's first speech, the *Nunc Dimittis*; and the last two canticles, presenting the suffering servant who is rejected (Is 50:6; 53:4-7), are linked with Simeon's second speech, his prophecy.

[251] As Jesus' disciples are presented as a collective character in light of Jesus' presentation through the Dt-Is prophecy, Jesus first, and then his disciples, respectively fulfill the individual and collective aspects of the servant of *Yhwh* bringing a universal salvation which involves a suffering rejection. The collective dimension, often in connection with Israel (see Is 41:8.9; 43:10; 441:1.2.21; 45:4; 48:20), is fulfilled by the disciples; and the individual dimension, which cannot be linked to Israel because it presents some kind of mission in Israel (see Is 42:1; 49:5.6.7; 50:10; 52:13; 53:11), is fulfilled by Jesus. On these individual and collective aspects of the suffering servant see VAN DER PLOEG, *Les chants du serviteur*, 106-160, and NORTH, *The Suffering Servant*, 6-103.

[252] The different main characters crystallize a theological motif of the entire plot: the universal divine salvation through human rejection. The different characters sucessively anticipate and confirm this plot.

of the Gospel as commanded by the risen Christ at the beginning of Acts sketches the plot of Acts: Jerusalem, throughout Judaea and Samaria, and to earth's remotest ends (Acts 1:8). Universalism spreads progressively and broadens its reach through the Samaritans, the Ethiopian Eunuch, the pagan God-fearer Cornelius, and the council at Jerusalem, which confirms the entrance of the Gentiles into Christianity without keeping the Mosaic Law or circumcision. However, while Peter is the first who preaches the Gospel to Gentiles, Paul really fulfills Christian universalism by going beyond the Diaspora. What Peter pioneered as a new step, Paul took up as a permanent pattern. His mission includes both Jews and Gentiles and stretches from Jerusalem to Rome. The narrative makes clear that the apostles' witness is largely confined to Jerusalem and Judea and is mostly directed to Jews, while Paul goes to the Diaspora with his itinerant ministry.[253] As the figure below shows, Paul is the witness to the Gentiles par excellence, who fulfills the universal mission.

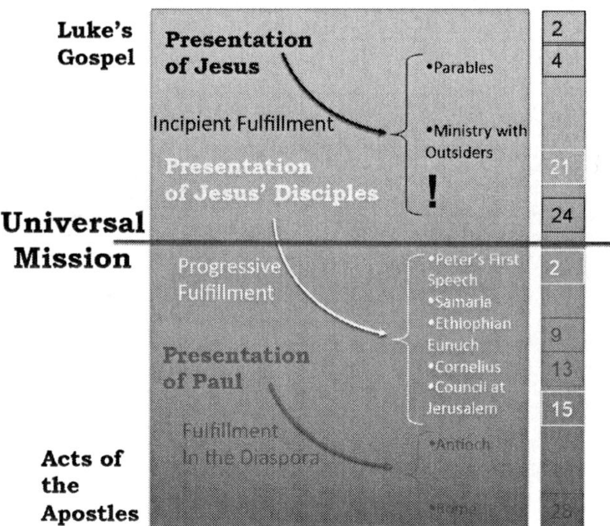

[253] In particular, to Cyprus, Antioch, and Asia Minor (Acts 13–14.16), Thessalonica and Athens (Acts 17), Corinth (Acts 18), Ephesus (Acts 19), Caesarea (Acts 24), and Rome (Acts 28).

This increasing universalism is underscored as well by the geographical structure of the Lukan composition. While the Gospel ends in the Temple, with a centripetal force, Acts begins in the Temple, but from Jerusalem goes on to the capital of the Empire, Rome, with a centrifugal force. While Jesus travels to the Temple of Jerusalem to fulfill God's will, Paul travels to Jerusalem, and from there to Rome, likewise fulfilling God's will. In fact, the presence of the Temple decreases not only quantitatively, but also qualitatively. As the commission statement of Jesus took place in the Temple, his disciples' commission statement took place in Jerusalem, and Paul's commission statement took place on the way from Jerusalem to Damascus, close to Damascus (Acts 9:3). Moreover, the houses of the first Christians progressively supplant the Temple's importance and authority throughout Luke-Acts. The household embraces the universalistic values better than the Temple.

Similiarly there is an *increasing rejection* throughout Luke-Acts, so that rejection is a quasi-constitutive feature of Luke-Acts. Simeon affirms that rejection is going to be by "many in Israel" (Lk 2:34b). Jesus is first accepted by the people of Israel and rejected only by the authorities. Even in his passion, the pagan Pilate proclaims Jesus' innocence four times (Lk 23:4.13.15.22) desiring to set Jesus free (Lk 23:20), and the centurion proclaims that Jesus was an upright man (Lk 23:47). However, the statement by Jesus commissioning his disciples foretells not only their rejection in Israel, but their rejection "by everyone" (Lk 21:17), and Paul's commission also speaks about rejection by Jews and Gentiles (Acts 26:17).[254] In fact, Jesus' disciples are initially accepted by the people of Israel as well, but the people slowly join their authorities in rejecting Christianity. Individual Jewish acceptance and corporate rejection stand side by side in Acts.[255] In fact, Luke

[254] The prophecies of the rejection by "many in Israel" (Lk 2:34), by "everyone" (Lk 21:12), and by "Gentiles" (Acts 26:17) parallel the three prophecies of Jesus' rejection in the travel to Jerusalem: by the "Jewish authorities" (Lk 9:22), by "human beings" (Lk 9:44), and by "Gentiles" (Lk 18:31).

[255] One example is found right at the end of Acts where 28:24 expresses the individual Jewish acceptance, while 28:25-28 designates the corporate Jewish rejection.

mainly uses Ἰουδαῖος to speak about the acceptance by individual Jews, and Ἰουδαῖοι to speak about the corporate rejection by Jews. The progressive participation of the people of Israel in the different trials against Jesus and his disciples highlights this progressive rejection by the Jewish people. In fact, Luke, who reserves the nouns λαός for the acceptance by some Jews, and Ἰουδαῖοι for the rejection by the Jews more generally, progressively decreases the use of the former term and increases the use of the latter, especially after the stoning of Stephen. But not only the people of Israel join their authorities in rejecting Christians; but so do some pagans, and even some Christians. The prediction by Jesus about the rejection by everyone is fulfilled. As the figure below shows, Paul's last passage focuses even more on this increasing rejection asserting the Christians' rejection "everywhere" (Acts 28:22).

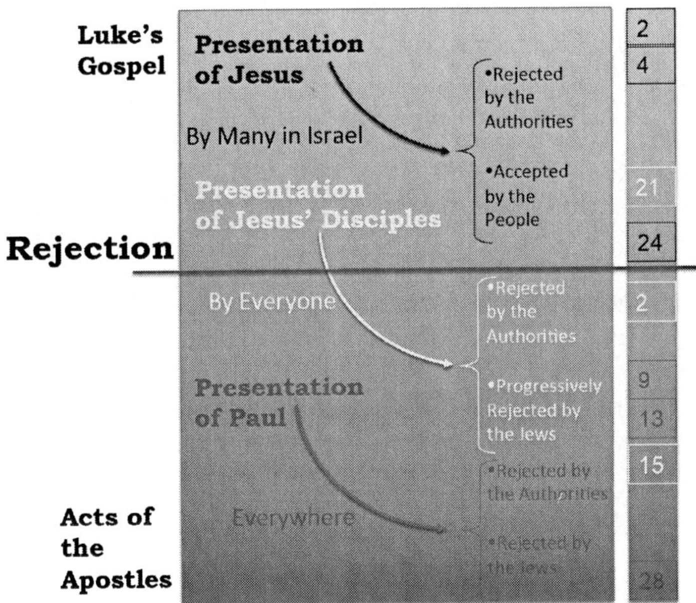

The increasing rejection implies that the division happens everywhere. In all of the religious groups there is both acceptance and rejection. Firstly among the people of Israel because there is division even among Jewish authorities. Not all of the authorities rejected Christianity; instead, some Pharisees seem to accept Jesus, inviting Jesus to their houses (Lk 7:36; 11:37) and advising him of Herod's anger against him (Lk 13:31), and they also seem to defend Paul: "we find nothing wrong in this man" (Acts 23:9). Moreover, there are exceptions in a few members of the Sanhedrin who accept Jesus and his followers: Joseph of Arimathaea (Lk 23:50) and Gamaliel (Acts 5:34). There is division among the pagans as well. There are Gentiles who immediately accept the Christian preaching, such as Cornelius, and pagans who clearly reject it, like those in the Areopagus who burst out laughing upon hearing the preaching on the resurrection of the dead (Acts 17:32). There is division even among the followers of Jesus. Not all of them accepted Jesus and his disciples all the time; actually, Judas (Lk 22:3) and Peter (Lk 22:57) rejected Jesus during his Passion,[256] and Ananias and Sapphira rejected his disciples (Acts 5:1). Furthermore, the council at Jerusalem reflects a division between Jewish-Christians and Gentile-Christians (Acts 15:2).

The division in Luke-Acts is not between Jews, Gentiles, and Christians, but between *obdurate* Jews, pagans, and Christians and *repentant* Israel, Gentiles, and Christians; between those who reject Jesus and those who accept Jesus. When a group is approached with the Gospel, some believe and some disbelieve. This same phenomenon is present among the Jews, the Gentiles, and the Christians. The proportion of rejection and acceptance differs,[257] but all of the groups are divided when confronted with the Christian message.

---

[256] Under Satan's influence Judas, the follower, turned into a traitor and entered into an agreement with Jesus' enemies without any repentance. Peter is different thanks to Jesus' intercession in order that he can strength the brethren (Lk 22:32) and because of Peter's bitter weeping as an expression of remorse for his denial (Lk 22:62). Both these make possible Peter's second conversion and prepare Peter for the prominent leadership role in Acts. This is the reason why Peter should not be substituted by another apostle, while Judas should (Acts 1:15-26).

[257] Talbert contends that Luke makes much of the Jewish rejection and little of the pagan disbelief because it is part of the status reversal theme (TALBERT, "Once Again", 197-109).

Lk 2:22-39 has a *narrative importance* because it discloses the narrator's clues that help to differentiate the two parts of the macro-narrative, and at the same time, it holds the whole story together, confirming Luke and Acts as one work. On the one hand, it is the presentation of Jesus, which concerns the Gospel of Luke. The separation between Luke and Acts is justified by the distinction between the main characters, Jesus and his disciples, including Paul.

On the other hand, the Presentation in the Temple is a key passage from which to contemplate the *narrative coherence of Luke-Acts* for the following reasons.[258] First, the structure just proposed perfectly interweaves the successive protagonists of Luke-Acts. Luke keeps the unity of the plot of the macro-narrative through the continuous overlapping of the main characters, which unify the single literary work.[259] Before the public life of Jesus has been completed, Luke introduces the following main character, Jesus' disciples, through their commission before and after Jesus' passion.[260] Before the public life of Jesus' disciples, especially of Peter, has been completed, Luke introduces the following protagonist, Paul, through the first account of his vocation (Acts 9:3-19), which is Paul's presentation to the community and to the reader. In fact, right in the middle of the step towards universalism made by the Samaritan Pentecost, the Ethiopian Eunuch and Cornelius' event, Luke introduces Paul, the witness to the Gentiles par excellence.

---

[258] This is meant to manifest a unified divine plan which is seen in the different presentations of the main characters of Luke-Acts. The Scriptures show how the mission of the main human characters fits within God's wider plan. Hence the actions of the chief human characters in the narrative are explained and legitimized through reference to God's purposes as revealed in Scripture. It is the one God who is coherently directing the story through different characters.

[259] I agree with KRÄNKL, *Jesus der Knecht Gottes*, 88-97, who claims that Luke likes transitions, such as John the Baptist as the last prophet and first Christian; John serves simultaneously as conclusion and introduction. The same happens with Lk 2:52, which is at the same time the conclusion to the infancy narrative and the introduction to the public life narrative. I add this new example of Luke's sensitivity for continuity.

[260] This commission takes place at the end of Luke's Gospel, but it is fulfilled throughout Acts.

Second, Jesus' *geographical itinerary* in his infancy displays a progression going from Nazareth in Galilee, through Judea, Bethlehem, to the Temple of Jerusalem. Luke maintains this progressive itinerary in Jesus' public life, which begins in Nazareth around Galilee, and moves through Samaria and Judea to the Temple of Jerusalem. In addition, as Jesus' journey to Jerusalem structures the central part of the Gospel, Paul's travels, specifically to Jerusalem and Rome, structure the central part of Acts. Moreover, the Presentation in the Temple forms an *inclusio* which surrounds the Lukan infancy narrative and Gospel with the Temple of Jerusalem, which in turn serves to link the end of the Gospel to the beginning of Acts, which also takes place in Jerusalem. The Temple of Jerusalem is the center of a concentric structure, which interweaves the end of the first part of the Lukan work with the beginning of the second part. Finally, the presence of Jesus in the Temple at the beginning of the Gospel parallels the presence of his disciples in the Temple at the beginning of Acts.

And third, I find an *inclusio* of the entire literary work between the Presentation of Jesus at the beginning of Luke and the last scene of Paul at the end of Acts. The ending of the narrative in Acts 28 is a resumption of the themes first introduced in Simeon's oracles. Both passages embrace the whole macro-narrative with the same terms and topics. Both passages speak about a σωτήριον, which is God's salvation (Lk 2:30; Acts 28:28);[261] both passages speak of contradiction, ἀντιλέγω, which Jesus will suffer or which the Christians are suffering (Lk 2:34; Acts 28:22). This *inclusio* also shows a narrative surprise of Simeon's prophecy; speaking primarily about Jesus, it is developed through Jesus' disciples too.

[261] As Jesus' name means *Yhwh* saves, God's salvation (Mt 1:21), this means that the whole macro-narrative is embraced by the name of Jesus, by his person.

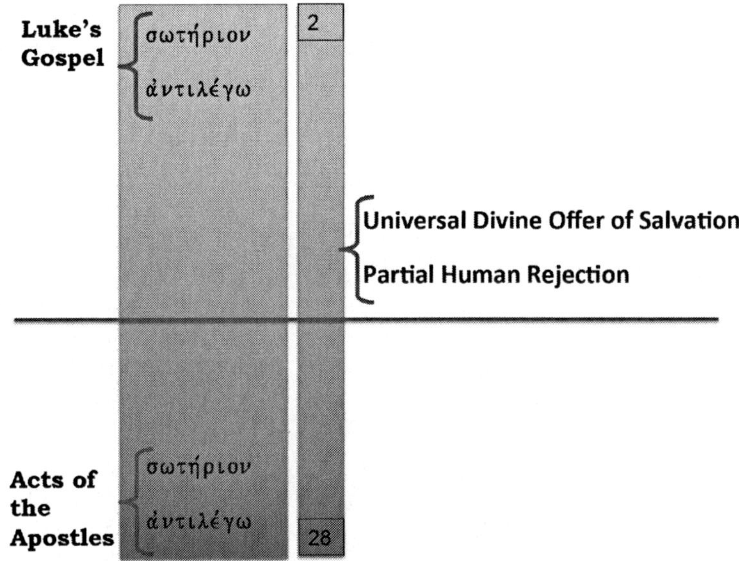

In fact, Lk 2:22-39 has a *theological importance* because it discloses the narrator's insights with regard to Jesus and his disciples. Luke presents and develops his characters, Jesus, his disciples, and Paul, in a very similar way. Their commission statements and fates are placed in parallel by Luke. There is a unity between the teacher and his disciples. Simeon's prophecy has important Christological insights, and even ecclesiological insights because it unifies the characters of Jesus and his followers. The presentation of Jesus is reoriented by the surprise of becoming also the presentation of his disciples. Just as Jesus is presented in the Temple at the beginning of Luke's Gospel, so too are Jesus' disciples depicted in the Temple at the beginning of Acts. As the Temple becomes a place of revelation of Jesus through Simeon's speeches and through Jesus' own teaching in the Temple in his public life, so too are Jesus' disciples presented in the Temple through their preaching (Acts 3).[262] Jesus' commission statement implies a universal salvation, whereas his disciples' commission statement implies a universal mission. Where Jesus is seen as the "light of revelation for the Gentiles" (Lk 2:32), so too are Paul and Barnabas seen as the "light for the Gentiles", so that God's salvation may reach the remotest parts of the earth (Acts 13:47).[263] The disciples' mission is always to become witnesses to Jesus (disciples in Lk 21:13; 24:48; Acts 1:8; and Paul in Acts 9:15; 22:15; 26:16) with a common rejection of Jesus and of his disciples (Lk 10:16; 21:12.17). As Simeon foretells Jesus' rejection at the beginning of the Gospel (Lk 2:34), so Jesus foretells his disciples' rejection at the end of the Gospel (Lk 21:12-19). In fact, all of the verbs used by Jesus in his prophecy about the rejection of his disciples are later developed by Luke either in the rejection of Jesus, or in the rejection of his disciples. As Jesus is not only rejected, but even persecuted and judged, his disciples, especially Peter, John, Stephen, and Paul, are not only rejected, but also persecuted and judged. Jesus and his disciples both provoke division through their acceptance and rejection.

The presentation of Jesus is used by Luke also to present of the first Christians; Simeon's prophecy is primarily developed in Jesus (Luke's Gospel), but also in his disciples (Acts). These statements verify that Lk 2:22-39 is not a foreign body tacked on at the beginning of the Gospel. Lk 2:22-39 makes sense within the entire narrative because it is a credible presentation of the whole literary work, both Luke and Acts.

---

[262] As the Temple was a place of prayer during Jesus' life, so the Temple is a place of prayer for Jesus' disciples.

[263] As Jesus brings an actual non-physical salvation to Simeon and many others (the anonymous woman, Lk 7:50; the Samaritan Leper, Lk 17:19; Zacchaeus, Lk 19:9; or the good thief, Lk 23:43), so the first Christians bring an actual non-physical salvation to many others (the Ethiopian Eunuch, Acts 8:16-18; Cornelius, Acts 10:44-47; or Paul's jailer, Acts 16:31).

FINAL CONCLUSIONS AND FURTHER IMPLICATIONS

1. Final Conclusions

This research studies the narrative function of Lk 2:22-39 in Luke-Acts, a text which presents important features that might at first view seem unconnected, but in fact, these features have a distinct purpose. All of these features prove that Lk 2:22-39 is indeed a real and important presentation, intradiegetically to God in the Temple, but also, extradiegetically, to the reader in the literary work. The fact that it is a narrative presentation is demonstrated by (1) its *position* in the Lukan narrative as a whole, (2) the *plot* and structure of the passage, (3) its *position* in the Lukan infancy narrative, (4) its *broad content* containing repeated and novel features, and (5) the *development of its distinctive features* throughout the entire macro-narrative. The novel features are like a *musical key* by which we are able to interpret not only the overture of Luke 1–2 but, especially, the whole composition of Luke-Acts.

(1) Being part of the infancy narrative, Luke situates the presentation of Jesus right at the beginning of his literary work. The beginning has a particular role in any process, including in literary texts; it is an *indication* of what the literary work will be about, and possesses a *primary effect* which suggests that that material placed early in the narrative will take on special importance as its introduction. In addition, redaction criticism has suggested that it is very likely that Luke composed Luke 1–2 when he had already written the rest of his Gospel and the Acts of the Apostles. This is why it is likely that the Lukan infancy narrative was composed with the benefit of the hindsight of the rest of the Lukan literature, being a real overture through which to start to listen

the chords that will be heard again and again in the coming narratives of the whole composition.

In fact, the infancy narratives are a broad *topos* with similar motifs in Greco-Roman and Jewish literature. Luke, using this common topos, makes the most of its features and inserts the contents into a form that was familiar to Jewish and pagan readers, in an attempt to appeal to a broader audience and to universalize his writing. The form of this topos is very similar in the different traditions: the hero's family lineage, signs of his future greatness, and examples of the child's education as part of his pre-public career. The most important of these similarities is the proleptic purpose of the infancy narrative. Being at the beginning of the literary work, as a clear introduction, an infancy narrative usually serves to foretell things that will be later developed, in order that the reader can better understand the accounts that will be narrated later. Moreover, intradiegetically, the characters of the infancy narratives engender trust in this presentation and, thus, extradiegetically, persuade the reader to trust the account and to keep reading with that important information in mind.

The Lukan infancy narrative follows the Jewish tradition more closely in two important aspects. In one aspect it presents the protagonist primarily through long direct speeches which lend a great importance and vivacity, allowing the information given to stay effortlessly in the memory of the reader. Then it presents many prophecies which are more concrete than the pagan generalizations about portents and dreams. The concrete titles and expressions referring to Jesus in these prophecies help to better present him throughout Luke 1–2. Lk 2:22-39 directly emphasizes these distinctive features. Jesus is presented in the Temple, the best place to present the main character in infancy narratives, and he is presented through two speaking characters and through two direct speeches about him. Jesus is presented in great detail precisely through these speeches. One of the speeches is a prophecy, with many concrete expressions referring to him. However, while the infancy narratives usually foretell the future greatness of the main character, the Presentation in the Temple speaks both about Jesus' future greatness (God's salvation, light of revelation for the Gentiles and glory for Israel: 2:30.32) and about his future tribulation (the child is destined to be a sign that will be contradicted: 2:34). It is distinctive of Jesus' characterization that both positive and negative dimensions are foretold; Jesus' paradoxical mystery is presented. Luke uses the infancy narrative in his own way, using his own original contents while displaying his attempt to describe the uniqueness of the child Jesus, all the time respecting the common form.

(2) Luke introduces two *resolution plots* concerning the Jewish customs of purification and redemption, and concerning Jewish expectations of the Messiah; they are respectively resolved by Mary and Joseph's obedience to the Law, and Simeon and Anna's obedience to the Spirit. The resolution of these plots introduces the plot which Luke further develops, a *revelation plot* of Jesus, which functions to present Jesus. That means that obedience to the Law and to the Spirit leads to a true recognition of Jesus, the Messiah of the Lord (2:33). The entire passage revolves around what is said of Jesus, who is consequently the focus of the passage. In fact, the structural center of the pericope is the admiration expressed of the things said about Jesus (2:33). All of the different characters of the pericope react to Jesus and speak about him: through deeds and words they present Jesus. The message of the presentation is the focal point of Lk 2:22-39, having greater importance than the concepts of purification and redemption.

(3) The Presentation in the Temple is a very important part of the Lukan infancy narrative. Luke 1–2 is a *unified plot* which progressively reveals Jesus' identity. However, there is an upward dynamic in the reader's knowledge of Jesus, which constantly progresses until its climactic point in the Temple. In fact, the evangelist brings attention to Jesus' first appearances in the Temple in the structure of Luke 1–2 because the parallelism between John and Jesus is broken by Jesus' presence in the Temple. In addition, it is the only passage of Luke 1–2 which has a *scriptural quotation* and presents Jesus through two different *reliable characters*, both of whom have a good understanding of Jesus. Moreover, these reliable characters are the only ones who speak about Jesus' *commission statement*, his program for action in accordance with God's plan.

(4) Lk 2:22-39 is the broadest and most complete characterization of Jesus and its mission in the first chapters of Luke's Gospel. The passage speaks of Jesus' identity, *who* he is: He is the "Holy" one (2:23b), the "Messiah of the Lord" (2:26b); and about Jesus' mission, *what* he will perform: he will bring about universal salvation, which will embrace not only Israel, but the Gentiles as well (2:31-32). In doing so, he will be rejected by many in Israel (2:34). Jesus' story will be full of conflict and tension. The Presentation passage picks up many of the main features of Jesus contained in the previous episodes and adds important features that are not present in the other pericopes. It repeats ways of characterization of Jesus as salvation, Messiah, Holy, light, peace, and glory. However, the pericope clearly adds three distinctive features: the first presence of Jesus in the Temple, a privileged place of revelation, the universal offer of salvation in Jesus, and the division in Israel because many in Israel will accept Jesus and many will reject him.

(5) Features of this passage which are distinct from other infancy narratives and from the rest of the Lukan infancy narrative are very well developed throughout Luke-Acts.[1] When we consider the presentation passage not in isolation but in relation to subsequent actions, we realize its narrative importance. The significance of these verses grows as we are able to relate them to more and more of the entire Lukan macro-narrative. It was expected that Lk 2:22-39, being part of the infancy narrative, would have a proleptic function, and would thus be developed by the rest of the entire Lukan macro-narrative. Indeed, the whole narrative testifies to this proleptic function, developing especially the distinctive fea-

---

[1] It is striking that the distinctive features of Lk 2:22-39 in comparison with other infancy narratives, and in comparison with other passages of the first chapters of Luke, are consistently developed in the rest of the Lukan work: a concrete characterization of Jesus by Simeon's speeches and prophecies, which introduce the universal offer of salvation brought by Jesus and his paradoxical characterization, with both positive and negative dimensions, through his acceptance and rejection by many. This fact further highlights the Lukan authorship of the passage and his good sense of composition, by putting the pericope in connection with his entire literary work.

tures of the Presentation passage, which guide the reader in understanding the story. Lk 2:22-39 presents important motifs that are reviewed throughout Luke-Acts. This gives it a key function in the narrative. The episode of the Presentation is a concise presentation of Jesus within the general presentation of Jesus; its novel features are a musical key in the more general overture of Luke 1–2.

As Simeon and Anna proclaim the fulfillment of previous prophecies, the reader will be able to proclaim the fulfillment of Simeon's prophecies. In fact, the Holy Spirit had revealed to Simeon that he would not see death until he had seen the Messiah of the Lord (2:26) and this prophecy is fulfilled when Simeon, embracing Jesus, affirms: "Now, Master, according to your word, you let your servant go in peace" (2:29). Anna also spoke of Jesus to all who looked forward to the redemption of Jerusalem because she saw fulfilled in Jesus the prophecies about the redemption of Jerusalem in the OT (2:38).[2] The fulfillment of these promises and prophecies of the past helps to increase the reader's confidence that the subsequent prophecies will prove to be true throughout Luke-Acts.[3] The fulfillment of predictions provides an interpretive framework to emphasize the trustworthiness of

---

[2] Luke 1–2 is replete with fulfilled promises and prophecies. Some of these prophecies refer to external predictions, foretold outside of Luke's work, which are recognized as fulfilled by the Lukan characters, especially Mary and Zechariah (1:55.70.72.73). However, other prophecies are internal, foretold and fulfilled within the very same Lukan narrative. Zechariah receives the promise of his wife's pregnancy (1:13) and some time later his wife Elizabeth conceives (1:24). Mary receives the promise of conceiving in her womb and bearing a son (1:31) and Elizabeth's son recognizes the presence of Mary's son (1:41-44). As Lk 1:45 affirms, the promise made by the Lord is fulfilled. The promise of finding a baby wrapped in swaddling clothes and lying in a manger (2:12) is immediately fulfilled (2:16). In fact, Simeon and Anna bear witness to the fulfillment of these two types of prophecies: Simeon within the Lukan narrative and Anna outside the Lukan narrative.

[3] Luke's interest in showing that Jesus and the earliest Christians fulfilled OT prophecy has been studied at length by Lukan scholars. Yet less attention has been paid to the predictions made in the narrative itself, including that of Simeon. Even less attention has been paid to the relationship between the fulfillment of OT external prophecy and the fulfillment of these internal narrative predictions (see FREIN, "Narrative Predictions", 26).

Simeon's prophecy, which should be fulfilled in the macro-narrative.[4] Equally, the fulfillment of Simeon's prophecies throughout Luke-Acts proves that Simeon's words about Jesus were, in fact, presenting Jesus to the reader.

Simeon's characterization of Jesus, particularly in his commission statement with its universal salvation and divided response, are fulfilled not only in Jesus, but, surprisingly, also in his disciples who are the other main characters of Luke-Acts. I state that there is a common architecture in the characterization of the protagonists of the entire macro-narrative. All of the different protagonists, Jesus, his disciples, and Paul, are characterized by a presentation which includes a commission statement; each presentation mirrors the distinctive features of Jesus' presentation and is fulfilled throughout the public life of the character, from the very beginning until its end. The presentation of Jesus is reoriented by the surprise of becoming the presentation of his disciples as well.

However, this common design, a progressive accumulation with increasingly specific features, is developed by Luke with some nuances. At the end of the literary work the reader knows more than at the beginning; the reader knows the *how* of the real fulfillment of the distinctive features of Lk 2:22-39. The narrative suspense of *how* what has been foretold will be fulfilled is resolved throughout the macro-narrative. There is a progressive evolution in the fulfillment of the universalism of the prophecy and in the quantitative measure of the rejection of Jesus and his disciples throughout Luke-Acts.

On the one hand, there is a progressive fulfillment of the *Nunc Dimittis'* universal offer of salvation, not only to Jews but also to Gentiles. Jesus only implicitly previews a universal salvation through some parables with implicit universalistic meaning and some ministry to outsiders, even performing some healing miracles among them.

---

[4] Jesus is at the same time the end point of the prophecies (analepsis), and the departure point of the new predictions (prolepsis). In fact, the fulfillment in Jesus of the prophecies and the internal predictions at the end of Luke's Gospel is not the end of the Lukan composition, but a springboard to the reading throughout Acts of the Apostles of the fulfillment of the new predictions, not only in Jesus, but also in his disciples.

However, at the end of Jesus' public life his universal commission has not yet been fulfilled. This narrative tension is resolved after Jesus' resurrection, when he commands his disciples to fulfill this universal mission, which also advances the plot. After this latter commission Jesus' disciples are his witnesses empowered by his Spirit and charged with the fulfillment of his mission in his name. Jesus is salvation in the sight of the peoples and the light of revelation for the Gentiles because everyone who calls on his name will be saved (see Acts 2:21). Universalism progressively spreads in Jesus' name through a preview in Peter's first speech, the Samaritans' conversion, the Ethiopian Eunuch's baptism, the Gentile God-fearer Cornelius' conversion and that of his family, and the council at Jerusalem, which confirms the entrance of Gentiles into Christianity without the necessity of observing the Mosaic Law. After this solemn entrance of Gentiles, Paul ultimately fulfills the universal character of Christianity by going to the Diaspora and coming to Rome.[5]

On the other hand, the people who reject Jesus and his disciples increase in number throughout Luke-Acts. Simeon's prophecy affirms the divided response to Jesus by "many in Israel" (Lk 2:34), and, in fact, generally speaking, the people of Israel accept Jesus while their authorities reject him. Yet, Jesus foretells the rejection of his disciples not only by many in Israel, but "by everyone" (Lk 21:17), and in fact, overall, the people of Israel initially accept Christianity but slowly join their authorities in rejecting Jesus' disciples. Paul's last passage highlights this increasing rejection even more so by asserting the Christian message's rejection "everywhere" (Acts 28:22). Acts shows that Jesus' disciples are rejected by everyone and everywhere because they are increasingly rejected by the people of Israel and their authorities, and also by some pagans, and even by a few Christians. The division in Israel prophesied by Simeon is developed by Luke in a division among Jews, pagans, and Christians, a division be-

[5] This increasing fulfillment of universalism is also underscored by the geographical structure of the Lukan macro-narrative: as Jesus travels to Jerusalem where Luke's Gospel ends, Paul travels to Jerusalem and Rome, where Acts ends; and the household, throughout Luke-Acts, progressively increases its importance, while the Temple's importance decreases.

tween those who reject Christianity and those who accept Christianity. All of the groups split in two when confronted with the Christian message.

2. Further Implications

The fact that Lk 2:22-39 is a narrative presentation sheds more light on two broader and more theological topics in Lukan studies, which are illuminated and opened to further research by this study: the narrative coherence of Luke-Acts and the unity between Jesus and his disciples. As Lk 2:22-39 does not introduce only Luke's Gospel but also the Acts of the Apostles, and as it does not present only Jesus but also his disciples, the Presentation in the Temple is a key passage from which to contemplate both topics.

First, the Presentation passage holds the two parts of the single Lukan literary work together because the syncrisis between Jesus and his disciples determines the structure of Luke-Acts.[6] There are three features which guarantee the unity of Luke-Acts. First, the proposed structure, made up by presentation and fulfillment in the public life of each character of Luke-Acts, especially at the beginning and end of the accounts of each one, perfectly interweaves the successive protagonists of Luke-Acts and, thus, Luke maintains the unity of the plot of the macro-narrative. Second, Jesus' journey to Jerusalem in his infancy mirrors Jesus' journey to Jerusalem in his public life, which structures the central part of the Gospel, just as Paul's travels, especially that to Jerusalem and Rome, structure the central part of Acts. Moreover, the Temple of Jerusalem is the center of a concentric structure which interweaves the end of Luke's Gospel with the beginning of Acts. And third, the *inclusio* of the terms σωτήριον and ἀντιλέγω embraces the whole literary work between the Presentation of Jesus at the

[6] At the same time, it differentiates the two parts of the macro-narrative because it speaks about Jesus, whose presentation is developed throughout Luke's Gospel. The different protagonists, viewed through Lk 2:22-39, help to differentiate Luke's Gospel from Acts of the Apostles.

beginning of Luke (Lk 2:30.34) and the last scene of Paul at the end of Acts (Acts 28:22.28). These terms are actualized by faithful Israelites who preach a universal salvation and cause a division through their rejection or acceptance.

This narrative coherence of Luke-Acts shows the one plan of God which could be summarized as a universal offer of salvation which involves human rejection. There is a unique divine plan which is expressed by God himself in the different commissions of the protagonists of Luke-Acts. In fact, Simeon foretells Jesus' mission through the Holy Spirit, as Jesus himself foretells his disciples rejection (Lk 21:12-19). Eventually, the risen Jesus commits the universal misson to his disciples (Lk 24:47-48; Acts 1:8), and, later, to Paul (Acts 9:15; 22:15.21; 26:17-18).[7] This divine plan is fulfilled through human freedom, through some who accept it, and others who reject it. In the human plot the divine plot is developed. The human stories tell the divine Story.

Second, Luke is a theologian and Jesus' presentation of Luke-Acts is determined by its theological project. The Presentation passage has both christological and ecclesiological implications: the universal offer of salvation which implies a rejection affects not only Jesus, but also his followers. The commission statements and fates of Jesus and his disciples, including Paul, are placed in parallel by Luke. There is a clear continuity between the teacher and his disciples which is seen in recurring motifs: the Temple, which is a privileged place of revelation for the infant Jesus and the infant Church; salvation, which is offered by Jesus and his disciples in Jesus' name; the light of revelation for the Gentiles, which is personified in Jesus and in his disciples, especially Paul and Barnabas; a division of those who accept and those who reject, which is caused by Jesus and his disciples; and the persecution and different trials suffered by Jesus, Peter, John, Stephen, and Paul, all clearly parallel Jesus to his followers. Simlarly, Simeon's and Anna's pres-

[7] The Spirit-inspired prophetic figures of Simeon, the risen Jesus, Peter (Acts 2:17.21), James (Acts 15:14-17), and Paul (Acts 13:47; 28:23-28) speak with one voice: God fulfills his purpose for Israel by bringing his salvation to all peoples and this universal salvation will involve the rejection by some.

entation is fulfilled not only in Jesus, but also in his disciples. The first Christians are presented by Luke in Acts according to the presentation of Jesus made in Luke's Gospel. This is the main novelty introduced by this passage, and by the Lukan infancy narrative more generally, in comparison with other presentations in other Greco-Roman and Jewish infancy narratives: Luke sees a strong relationship between Jesus and his disciples. In fact, the disciples' commissions are always presented as becoming Jesus' witnesses (Lk 21:13; 24:48; Acts 1:8; 9:15; 22:15; 26:16).

I am brought to the conclusion that, for Luke, every Christian directly depends on Christ, the Messiah, and this dependency configures the Christian. Jesus' commission statement implies a universal salvation, whereas his disciples' commission statement implies a universal mission. The soteriological function of Jesus is to bring the universal salvation offered by his unique person, the chosen agent of God's redemptive purpose. He alone is the Holy One, the awaited Messiah who fulfills the prophecies. However, this universal salvation implies the universal mission of Jesus' disciples, who are his witnesses, bearing witness to the Savior and acting in his name.[8] This missionary function of the disciples sometimes involves their rejection, as the soteriological function of Jesus sometimes involved his rejection. This configuration of the Christian with Christ, the disciple with the Master, in Luke-Acts has a pragmatic function. As the reader is presented as *Theophilus*, friend of God, a believer who has already received the Christian teaching (Lk 1:3-4), every reader, another disciple, is invited to configure himself with Jesus' disciples in Luke-Acts and, ultimately, through them with Jesus Christ. Following this dynamic, even we, Christians of the twenty first century, are called to witness to Jesus' universal offered of salvation, even if this mission will at times involve rejection.

---

[8] On Jesus' ministry in the Gospel anticipating the apostles' activity in the Acts, and the parallels and differences between the missions of Jesus and his disciples, see LANE, *Gentile Mission*.

WORKS CITED

Primary Sources

1 (Ethiopic Apocalypse of) Enoch, in CHARLESWORTH, J. H. (ed.), *The Old Testament Pseudepigrapha.* I. Apocalyptic Literature and Testaments (Garden City, NY 1983), 13-89.

2 (Syriac Apocalypse of) Baruch, in CHARLESWORTH, J. H. (ed.), *The Old Testament Pseudepigrapha.* I. Apocalyptic Literature and Testaments (Garden City, NY 1983), 621-652.

3 (Hebrew apocalypse of) Enoch, in CHARLESWORTH, J. H. (ed.), *The Old Testament Pseudepigrapha.* I. Apocalyptic Literature and Testaments (Garden City, NY 1983), 255-315.

3 Maccabees, in CHARLESWORTH, J. H. (ed.), *The Old Testament Pseudepigrapha.* II. Expansions of the "Old Testament" and Legends, Wisdom and Philosophical Literature, Prayers, Psalms, and Odes, Fragments of Lost Judeo-Hellenistic Works (Garden City, NY 1983), 517-529.

4Q174 (ed. J. M. ALLEGRO) (DJD 5; Oxford 1968).

11Q13 (ed. F. GARCÍA MARTÍNEZ – E. J. C. TIGCHLAAR – A. S. WOUDE) (DJD 23; Oxford 1998).

AMBROSE, *Expositio Evangelii secundum Lucam* (ed. G. TISSOT) (SC 45; Paris [2]1971).

ARISTOTLE, *Ars rhetorica* (ed. W. D. ROSS) (SCBO; Oxonii 1959).

————, *De arte poetica liber* (ed. K. RUDOLFUS) (SCBO; Oxonii 1968).

BEDE, *In Lucae evangelium expositio* (ed. D. HURST) (CCh.SL 120; Turnholti 1960), 5-425.

————, *Homilies on the Gospels* (ed. L. T. MARTIN – D. HURST) (CistSS 110; Kalamazoo, MI 1991).

Catenae Graecorum Patrum in Novum Testamentum. II. In Evangelia S. Lucae et S. Joannis (ed. J. A. CRAMER) (Oxonii 1844).

DIOGENES LAERTIUS, *Vitae Philosphorum* (ed. R. D. HICKS) (LCL; London – Cambridge, MA 1958) I.

EPHRAEM, *Commentaire de l'Évangile concordant ou Diatessaron* (ed. L. LELOIR) (SC 121; Paris 1966).

Evangelium infantiae salvatoris arabicum, in SANTOS OTERO, A., *Los Evangelios Apócrifos.* Colección de textos griegos y latinos, versión crítica, estudios introductorios y comentarios (BAC 148; Madrid [9]1996), 303-332.

Evangelium Nicodemi, in SCHNEEMELCHER, W., *Neutestamentliche Apokryphen in deutscher Übersetzung.* I Evangelien (Berlin [5]1987), 395-424.

Evangelium Pseudo-Matthaei, in SANTOS OTERO, A., *Los Evangelios Apócrifos.* Colección de textos griegos y latinos, versión crítica, estudios introductorios y comentarios (BAC 148; Madrid [9]1996), 173-236.

Evangelium Pseudo-Thomae de infantia Salvatoris, in SANTOS OTERO, A., *Los Evangelios Apócrifos.* Colección de textos griegos y latinos, versión crítica, estudios introductorios y comentarios (BAC 148; Madrid [9]1996), 279-300.

The Fourth Book of Ezra, in CHARLESWORTH, J. H. (ed.), *The Old Testament Pseudepigrapha.* I. Apocalyptic Literature and Testaments (Garden City, NY 1983), 525-559.

FRONTO, *Epistulae* (ed. C. R. HAINES) (LCL; London – Cambridge, MA 1982, 1963) I-II.

The Gospel According to St. Luke. Edited by the American and British Committees of the International Greek New Testament Project. Part I: Chapters 1-12. Part II: Chapters 13-24 (The New Testament in Greek 3; Oxford 1984, 1987).

The Gospel of Thomas (ed. U.-K. PLISCH) (Stuttgart 2008).

The Greek New Testament (ed. K. ALAND – M. BLACK – C. M. MARTINI – B. METZGER – A. WIKGREN) (Stuttgart [4]2000).

HOMER, *Illiad.* I. Libros i-xii. (ed. D. B. MONRO – T. W. ALLEN) (SCBO; Oxonii [3]1969).

JOSEPHUS, *Antiquitates Judaicae.* IV: Books i-iv. V: Books v-viii (ed. J. THACKERAY – R. MARCUS) (LCL; London – Cambridge, MA 1930, 1935).

————, *Contra Apionem* (ed. E. CAPPS – T. E. PAGE – W. H. D. ROUSE) (LCL; London – New York 1926) I.

————, *Vita* (ed. E. CAPPS – T. E. PAGE – W. H. D. ROUSE) (LCL; London – New York 1926) I.

————, *The New Complete Works of Josephus* (ed. W. WISHTON – P. L. MAIER) (Grand Rapids, MI 1999).

Jubilees, in CHARLESWORTH, J. H. (ed.), *The Old Testament Pseudepigrapha.* II. Expansions of the "Old Testament" and Legends, Wisdom and Philosophical Literature, Prayers, Psalms, and Odes, Fragments of Lost Judeo-Hellenistic Works (Garden City, NY 1983), 52-142.

Leben und Taten Alexanders von Makedonien. Der griechische Alexanderroman nach der Handschrift L (ed. H. VAN THIEL) (Texte zur Forschung 13; Darmstadt 1974).

The Life of Adam and Eve, in CHARLESWORTH, J. H. (ed.), *The Old Testament Pseudepigrapha*. II. Expansions of the "Old Testament" and Legends, Wisdom and Philosophical Literature, Prayers, Psalms, and Odes, Fragments of Lost Judeo-Hellenistic Works (Garden City, NY 1983), 258-295.

The Lives of the Prophets, in CHARLESWORTH, J. H. (ed.), *The Old Testament Pseudepigrapha*. II. Expansions of the "Old Testament" and Legends, Wisdom and Philosophical Literature, Prayers, Psalms, and Odes, Fragments of Lost Judeo-Hellenistic Works (Garden City, NY 1983), 385-399.

LUCIEN, *Historia conscribenda*, in ROSS, W. D. (ed.), *Luciani opera*. III Libelli 44-68 (SCBO; Oxonii 1980), 287-319.

LYDUS, *De magistratibus populi romani* (ed. R. WUENSCH) (BSGRT; Teubneri 1903).

New Testament Greek Manuscripts. Variant Readings Arranged in Horizontal Lines Against Codex Vaticanus: Luke (ed. R. J. SWANSON) (Sheffield 1995).

Novum Testamentum Graece (ed. E. & E. NESTLE – B. & K. ALAND – J. KARAVIDOPOULOS – C. M. MARTINI – B. M. METZGER) (Stuttgart [27]2004).

ORIGÈN, *Homélies sur s. Luc*. Texte latin et fragments grecs (ed. H. CROUZEL – F. FOURNIER – P. PÉRICHON) (SC 87; Paris 1962).

The Oxyrhynchus Papyri. L. Numeros 3,522-3,600 (ed. B. P. GRENFELL – A. S. HUNT) (Egypt Exploration Society; Oxford 1983).

PHILO, *De vita Moysis* (ed. F. H. COLSON) (LCL; London – Cambridge, MA 1950) VI.

PLATO, *Respublica* (ed. S. R. SLINGS) (SCBO; Oxonii 2003).

PLINY THE YOUNGER, *Epistulae* (ed. B. RADICE) (Baltimore 1963).

PLUTARCH, *Plutarchi vitae parallelae* (ed. G. P. GOOLD – E. H. WARMINGTON) (LCL; London – Cambridge, MA 1968-1986) I-XI.

————, *Vidas paralelas* (ed. A. PÉREZ JIMÉNEZ) (Biblioteca clásica Gredos 77; Madrid 1985).

Protoevangelium Iacobi, in SANTOS OTERO, A., *Los Evangelios Apócrifos*. Colección de textos griegos y latinos, versión crítica, estudios introductorios y comentarios (BAC 148; Madrid [9]1996), 130-170.

Protoevangelium Iacobi, in STRYCKER, E. D., *La forme la plus ancienne du Protévangile de Jacques* (Subsidia hagiographica 33; Bruxelles 1961).

PSEUDO-CALLISTHENES, *Alexander Romance* in HANSEN, W. F. (ed.), *Anthology of Ancient Greek Popular Literature* (Bloomington 1998), 168-248.

————, *Alexander Romance* in REARDON, B. P. (ed.), *Collected Ancient Greek Novels* (Berkeley 1989), 654-735.

PSEUDO-PHILO, *Liber antiquitatum biblicarum* (ed. D. HARRINGTON – J. CAZEAUX) (SC 229; Paris 1976) I.

QUINTUS CURTIUS, *Historiae Alexandri Magni Macedonis* (ed. E. H. WARMINGTON) (LCL; London – Cambridge, MA 1971) I.

————, *The History of Alexander* (ed. J. YARDLEY – W. HECKEL) (Penguin Classics; Harmondsworth – New York 1984).

Septuaginta. I. Leges et historiae. II. Libri poetici et prophetici (ed. A. RAHLFS) (Stuttgart [9]1984).

The Scripture Documents. An Anthology of Official Catholic Teachings (ed. D. P. BÉCHARD) (Collegeville, MN 2002).

SPARTIANUS, *Vita Hadriani* (ed. J. CENTERWALL) (Whitefish, MT 2008).

SUETONIUS, *Lives of the Caesars* (ed. J. HENDERSON) (LCL; London – Cambridge, MA 2001) I-II.

————, *Lives of Illustrious Men* (ed. J. HENDERSON) (LCL; London – Cambridge, MA 2001) II.

————, *Vida de los doce Césares* (ed. M. BASSOLS DE CLIMENT) (Colección hispánica de autores griegos y latinos; Barcelona 1964).

TERTULLIAN, *Contre Marcion IV* (ed. R. BRAUN – C. MORESCHINI) (SC 456; Paris 2001).

Text und Textwert der griechischen Handschriften des Neuen Testaments. IV. Die Synoptischen Evangelien. 3. Das Lukasevangelium (ed. K. & B. ALAND – K. WACHTEL) (ANTT 28; Berlin – New York 2003).

VIRGIL, *Aeneid* (ed. R. A. B. MYNORS) (SCBO; Oxonii 1972).

Secondary Sources

ABEL, F. M., *Grammaire du grec biblique* (Paris 1927).

ABRAMS, M. H., *A Glossary of Literary Terms* (Orlando, FL [5]1988).

DEL AGUA PÉREZ, A., *El método midrásico y la exégesis del Nuevo Testamento* (Biblioteca Midrásica 4; Valencia 1985).

————, "El papel de la 'escuela midrásica' en la configuración del Nuevo Testamento", *EE* 60 (1985) 333-349.

————, "Aproximación al relato de los evangelios desde el midrás/derás", *EstB* 45 (1987) 257-284.

DEL AGUA PÉREZ, A., "Los evangelios de la infancia: ¿Verdad histórica o verdad teológica?", *RF* 230 (1991) 381-399.

ALETTI, J.-N., *L'art de raconter Jésus Christ.* L'écriture narrative de l'évangile de Luc (Paris 1989).

————, "Le Christ raconté. Les Evangiles comme littérature?", *Bible et littérature: l'homme et Dieu mis en intrigue* (ed. F. MIES – J.-N. ALETTI – M. GILBERT – J.-P. SONNET) (Le livre et le rouleau 6; Bruxelles – Namur 1999) 29-53.

————, "La construction du personnage Jésus dans les récits évangéliques: Le cas de Marc", *Analyse narrative et Bible.* Deuxième Colloque internationale du RRENAB, Louvain-la-Neuve, avril 2004 (ed. C. FOCANT – A. WÉNIN) (BEThL 191; Leuven – Paris – Dudley, MA 2005) 19-42.

————, "Les passages néotestamentaires en prose rythmée. Propositions sur leurs fonctions multiples", *Les hymnes du Nouveau Testament et leurs fonctions* (ed. D. GERBER – P. KEITH) (LeDiv 225; Paris 2009) 239-263.

————, *Le Jésus de Luc* (Jésus et JésusChrist 98; Paris 2010).

ALETTI, J.-N. – GILBERT, M. – SKA, J. L. – DE VULPILLIÈRES, S., *Vocabulaire raisonné de l'exégèse biblique.* Les mots, les approches, les auteurs (Outils bibliques; Paris 2005).

ALTER, R., *The Art of Biblical Narrative* (New York 1981).

ANDREWS, E. A. – FREUND, W. – LEWIS, C. T. – SHORT, C., *A Latin Dictionary.* Founded on Andrews' Edition of Freund's Latin Dictionary (Oxford 1991).

ARANDA, G., "Los evangelios de la infancia de Jesús", *ScrTh* 10 (1978) 793-848.

AUNE, D. E., *The New Testament in its Literary Environment* (LEC 8; Philadelphia, PA 1987).

AYTOUN, R. A., "The Ten Lucan Hymns of the Nativity in Their Original Language", *JThS* 18 (1917) 274-288.

BACH, A., "Signs of the Flesh: Observations on Characterization in the Bible", *Semeia* 63 (1993) 61-79.

BACHELARD, G. – JOLAS, M., *The Poetics of Space* (Boston 1994).

BACHMANN, M., *Jerusalem und der Tempel.* Die geographisch-theologischen Elemente in der lukanischen Sicht des jüdischen Kultzentrums (BWANT 109; Stuttgart 1980).

BAILEY, J. A., *The Traditions Common to the Gospels of Luke and John* (NT.S 7; Leiden 1963).

BALCH, D. L., "ἀκριβῶς ... γράψαι (Luke 1:3)", *Jesus and the Heritage of Israel.* Luke's Narrative Claim Upon Israel's Legacy (ed. D.P. MOESSNER) (LIntI 1; Harrisburg, PA 1999) 229-250.
BALLHORN, E., "Simeon: Der Jesaja des Neuen Testaments (Lk 2,21-40)", *Propheten* (Stuttgart 2003) 70-79.
BALTZER, K., "The Meaning of the Temple in the Lukan Writings", *HThR* 58 (1965) 263-277.
BAR-EFRAT, S., *Narrative Art in the Bible* (BiLiSe 17; Sheffield 1989).
BARR, D. – WENTLING, J., "The Conventions of Classical Biography and the Genre of Luke-Acts: A Preliminary Study", *Luke-Acts, New Perspectives from the Society of Biblical Literature Seminar* (ed. C.H. TALBERT) (New York 1984) 63-88.
BARRETT, C. K., *A Critical and Exegetical Commentary on the Acts of the Apostles* (ICC; Edinburgh 1994) I.
BARTHES, R., "The Structural Analysis of a Narrative from Acts X-XI", *Structuralism and Biblical Hermeneutics.* A Collection of Essays (ed. A.M. JOHNSON) (PThMS 22; Pittsburgh, PA 1979) 109-143.
BAUCKHAM, R., "The Restoration of Israel in Luke-Acts", *Restoration.* Old Testament, Jewish, and Christian Perspectives (ed. J.M. SCOTT) (JSJ.S 72; Leiden 2001) 435-487.
BAUER, W., *A Greek-English Lexicon of the New Testament and Other Early Christian Literature* (Chicago, IL 1957).
BAZYLIŃSKI, S., *A Guide to Biblical Research* (SubBi 36; Rome 2009).
BEARD, M. – NORTH, J. A., *Pagan Priests.* Religion and Power in the Ancient World (Ithaca, NY 1990).
BÉCHARD, D. P., "The Theological Significance of Judaea in Luke-Acts", *Unity of Luke-Acts* (ed. J. VERHEYDEN) (Louvain 1999) 675-691.
————, *Paul Outside the Walls.* A Study of Luke's Socio-Geographical Universalism in Acts 14:8-20 (AnBib 143; Roma 2000).
BECK, J. A., *Translators as Storytellers.* A Study in Septuagint Translation Technique (StudBL 25; New York 2000).
————, *God as Storyteller.* Seeking Meaning in Biblical Narrative (St. Louis, MO 2008).
BELLI, F. – CARBAJOSA, I. – JÓDAR, C. – SÁNCHEZ, L., *Vetus in Novo.* El recurso a la Escritura en el Nuevo Testamento (Madrid 2006).
BENÉITEZ, M., "Un capítulo de narrativa bíblica. Los 'encargos' de Hch 1,1-12", *MiscCom* 43 (1985) 329-382.
BENOÎT, P., "L'enfance de Jean-Baptiste selon Luc I", *NTS* 3 (1957) 169-194.
————, "'Et toi-même, un glaive te transpercera l'âme!' (Luc 2,35)", *CBQ* 25 (1963) 251-261.

BENOÎT, P., "'Non erat eis locus in diversorio' (Lc 2,7)", *Mélanges bibliques en hommage au R. P. Béda Rigaux* (ed. A.L. DESCAMPS – A. HALLEUX) (Gembloux 1970) 173-186.

———, "Quirinius", *SDB* IX, 693-720.

———, "Les récits évangéliques de l'enfance de Jésus", *Exégèse et théologie* (ed. P. BENOÎT) (Paris 1982) IV, 63-94.

BERENGUER AMENÓS, J., *Gramática griega* (Barcelona [34]1994).

BERGER, K., "Das Canticum Simeonis (Lk 2,29-32)", *NT* 27 (1985) 27-39.

BERLIN, A., *Poetics and Interpretation of Biblical Narrative* (BiLiSe 9; Sheffield 1983).

BERLINGIERI, G., *Il lieto annuncio della nascita e del concepimento del precursore di Gesù (Lc 1,5-23.24-25) nel quadro dell'opera lucana.* Uno studio tradizionale e redazionale (AnGr 258; Roma 1991).

BERNARDELLI, A., *Intertestualità* (Biblioteca 23; Firenze – Milano 2000).

BERTRAM, G., "ὕψιστος", *ThWNT* VIII, 613-619.

BERTRAM, G. – SCHMITZ, K. L., "ἔθνος, ἐθνικός", *ThWNT* II, 361-370.

BETORI, G., "Perseguitati a causa del Nome. Strutture dei racconti di persecuzione in Atti 1,12-8,4", *Bib.* 97 (1981) 20-41.

———, "Luke 24:47: Jerusalem and the Beginning of the Preaching to the Pagans in the Acts of the Apostles", *Luke and Acts* (ed. G. O'COLLINS – G. MARCONI) (New York 1993) 103-120.

BILLERBECK, P., "Ein Synagogengottesdienst in Jesu Tagen", *ZNW* 55 (1964) 143-161.

BLACK, M., *An Aramaic Approach to the Gospels and Acts* (Oxford [3]1967).

BLASS, F. W. – DEBRUNNER, A. – REHKOPF, F., *Grammatik des neutestamentlichen Griechisch* (Göttingen [14]1975).

BLOCH, R., "Écriture et tradition dans le Judaïsme. Aperçus sur l'origine du Midrash", *CSio* 8 (1954) 9-34.

BOBZIEN, S., *Determinism and Freedom in Stoic Philosophy* (Oxford 1998).

BOCK, D. L., *Proclamation from Prophecy and Pattern.* Lucan Old Testament Christology (JSNT.S 12; Sheffield 1987).

———, *Luke* (BECNT 3; Grand Rapids, MI 1994) I.

———, *Luke* (The NIV Application Commentary; Grand Rapids, MI 1996).

BOISMARD, M.-É., *En quête du Proto-Luc* (EtB.NS 37; Paris 1997).

———, *L'évangile de l'enfance (Luc 1–2) selon le proto-Luc* (EtB.NS 35; Paris 1997).

BONZ, M. P., *The Past as Legacy.* Luke-Acts and Ancient Epic (Minneapolis, MN 2000).

BORG, M. J. – CROSSAN, J. D., *The First Christmas.* What the Gospels Really Teach About Jesus's Birth (New York 2007).

BORGEN, P., *Philo of Alexandria an Exegete for his Time* (NT.S 86; Leiden – New York 1997).

BOTTINO, A., "La missione 'fino all'estremità della terra' e i suoi protagonisti negli Atti degli apostoli", *San Luca Evangelista Testimone della Fede che unisce.* Atti del congresso internazionale; Padova, 16-21 Ottobre 2000 (ed. G. LEONARDI – F. G. B. TROLESE) (FRSEP 28; Padova 2002) I, 335-350.

BOURNEUF, R. – QUELLET, R., *L'univers du roman* (Littératures modernes 2; Paris [2]1975).

BOURQUIN, Y., "Vers une nouvelle approche de la focalisation", *Analyse narrative et Bible.* Deuxième Colloque internationale du RRENAB, Louvain-la-Neuve, avril 2004 (ed. C. FOCANT – A. WÉNIN) (BEThL 191; Leuven – Paris – Dudley, MA 2005) 497-506.

BOVON, F., *Luc le théologien.* Vingt-cinq ans de recherches (1950-1975) (MoBi; Genève [2]1988).

————, *Das Evangelium nach Lukas* (EKK 3; Zürich 1989) I; Engl. Trans. *Luke* I. A Commentary on the Gospel of Luke 1:1–9:50 (Hermeneia; Minneapolis, MN 2002).

————, "The Holy Spirit, the Church and Human Relationships According to Acts 20:36-21:16", *New Testament Traditions and Apocryphal Narratives* (ed. F. BOVON) (PTMS 36; Allison Park, PA 1995) 27-42.

————, "'How Well the Holy Spirit Spoke Through the Prophet Isaiah to Your Ancestors!' (Acts 28:25)", *New Testament Traditions and Apocryphal Narratives* (ed. F. BOVON) (PTMS 36; Allison Park, PA 1995) 43-50.

————, "The Child and the Beast. Fighting Violence in Ancient Christianity", *HDB* 27/4 (1998) 16-21.

————, "Names and Numbers in Early Christianity", *NTS* 47 (2001) 267-288.

————, "The Christians Who Dream: The Authority of Dreams in the First Centuries of Christianity", *Studies in Early Christianity* (ed. F. BOVON) (Grand Rapids, MI 2005) 144-162.

————, *Luc le théologien* (MoBi 5; Genève [3]2006).

————, "The Lukan Ascension Stories", *KNTS* 17 (2010) 563-595.

BOXALL, I., "Christ in the Gospels", *PrPe* 17 (2003) 455-459.

BOYCE, J. L., "For You Today a Savior: The Lukan Infancy Narrative", *WaW* 27 (2007) 371-380.

BRAWLEY, R. L., *Luke-Acts and the Jews*. Conflict, Apology, and Conciliation (SBL.MS 33; Atlanta, GA 1987).

BRENNER, A., "Female Social Behaviour: Two Descriptive Patterns Within the 'Birth of the Hero' Paradigm", *VT* 36 (1986) 257-273.

BROWN, R. E., "The Presentation of Jesus (Luke 2:22-40)", *Worship* 51 (1977) 2-11.

————, "Luke's Method in the Annunciation Narrative of Chapter One", *Perspectives on Luke-Acts* (ed. C.H. TALBERT) (Danville 1978) 126-138.

————, "Gospel Infancy Narrative Research from 1976 to 1986: Part II (Luke)", *CBQ* 48 (1986) 660-680.

————, *A Coming Christ in Advent*. Essays on the Gospel Narratives; Preparing for the Birth of Jesus Matthew 1 and Luke 1 (Collegeville, MN 1988).

————, *The Birth of the Messiah*. A Commentary on the Infancy Narratives in the Gospels of Matthew and Luke (New York [2]1993).

BROWN, W. J., *The Gospel of the Infancy* (London 1923).

BUELL, D. K., *Why this New Race*. Ethnic Reasoning in Early Christianity (New York 2005).

BULTMANN, R., *Die Geschichte der synoptischen Tradition* (FRLANT 29; Göttingen [7]1967).

BURNETT, F. W., "Prolegomenon to Reading Matthew's Eschatological Discourse: Redundancy and the Education of the Reader in Matthew", *Semeia* 31 (1985) 91-109.

————, "Characterization and Reader Construction of Characters in the Gospel", *Semeia* 63 (1993) 3-28.

BURRIDGE, R. A., *What Are the Gospels?* A Comparison with Graeco-Roman Biography (The Biblical Resource Series; Grand Rapids, MI [2]2004).

BURROWS, E., "The Gospel of the Infancy: the Form of Luke Chapters 1 and 2", *The Gospel of the Infancy and Other Biblical Essays* (ed. E.F. SUTCLIFFE) (BellS 6; London 1940) 1-58.

BUSSE, U., "Das 'Evangelium' des Lukas. Die Funktion der Vorgeschichte im lukanischen Doppelwerk", *Der Treue Gottes trauen*. Beiträge zum Werk des Lukas: für Gerhard Schneider (ed. G. SCHNEIDER – C. BUSSMANN – W. RADL) (Freiburg 1991) 161-177.

CADBURY, H. J., *The Making of Luke-Acts* (New York 1927).

CAMPBELL, T. H., "Paul's 'Missionary Journeys' as Reflected in his Letters", *JBL* 74 (1955) 80-87.

CAVALLETTI, S., "Il metodo derashico nei racconti lucani dell'infanzia", *RSB* 4/2 (1990) 5-12.

CERQUIGLINI, B., *Eloge de la variante*. Histoire critique de la philologie (Des travaux; Paris 1989).

CHAPPUIS-JUILLARD, I., *Le temps des rencontres*. Quand Marie visite Elisabeth (Luc 1) (Aubonne 1991).

CHATMAN, S. B., *Story and Discourse*. Narrative Structure in Fiction and Film (Ithaca, NY [4]1988).

CLARK, A. C., *Parallel Lives*. The Relation of Paul to the Apostles in the Lucan Perspective (Paternoster Biblical and Theological Monographs; Carlisle 2001).

CLINES, D. J. A., *The Esther Scroll*. The Story of the Story (JSOT.S 30; Sheffield 1984).

COHEN, S. J. D., *The Beginnings of Jewishness*. Boundaries, Varieties, Uncertainties (Hellenistic Culture and Society 31; Berkeley 1999).

COLERIDGE, M. B., *The Birth of the Lukan Narrative*. Narrative as Christology in Luke 1-2 (JSNT.S 88; Sheffield 1993).

COLLINS, A.Y. & J. J., *King and Messiah as Son of God*. Divine, Human, and Angelic Messianic Figures in Biblical and Related Literature (Grand Rapids, MI 2008).

CONYBEARE, F. C., "Ein Zeugnis Ephräms über das Fehlen von c. 1 und 2 im Texte des Lucas", *ZNW* 3 (1902) 192-197.

CONZELMANN, H., *Die Mitte der Zeit*. Studien zur Theologie des Lukas (Beiträge zur historischen Theologie 17; Tübingen [4]1962).

COOK, M. J., "The Mission to the Jews in Acts: Unraveling Luke's Myth of the 'Myriads'", *Luke-Acts and the Jewish People*. Eight Critical Perspectives (ed. J.B. TYSON) (Minneapolis, MN 1988) 102-123.

CORSATO, C., *La Expositio euangelii secundum Lucam di sant'Ambrogio: ermeneutica, simbologia, fonti* (Diss. Institutum Patristicum Augustinianum; Roma 1993).

CRADDOCK, F. B., *Luke* (Int.BCTP; Louisville, KY 1990).

CREED, J. M., *The Gospel According to St. Luke* (London 1930).

CRESPO, E., *Sintaxis del Griego Clásico* (Madrid 2003).

CROSS, F. M., *The Ancient Library of Qumran and Modern Biblical Studies*. The Ancient Library (The Haskell Lectures; Garden City, NY 1961).

————, *The Ancient Library of Qumran* (BiSe 30; Sheffield [3]1995).

CULLMANN, O., "Infancy Gospels", *New Testament Apocrypha* (ed. E. HENNECKE – W. SCHNEEMELCHER) (Philadelphia, PA 1963) I, 363-417.

CULPEPPER, R. A., *Anatomy of the Fourth Gospel*. A Study in Literary Design (F&F.NT; Philadelphia, PA 1983).

CULTER, A., "Does the Simeon of Luke 2 Refer to Simeon the Son of Hillel?", *JBR* 34 (1966) 29-35.

CUNNINGHAM, P. J., "A Tale of Two Creches", *BiTod* 37 (1999) 378-381.

D'AGOSTINO, M., *L'annuncio come rappresentazione*. Strategie drammaturgiche in Luca 1-2 (Assisi 2009).

DAHL, N. A., "'A People for his Name' (Acts XV.14)", *NTS* 4 (1958) 319-327.

DANIÉLOU, J., *Les Évangiles de l'enfance* (Paris 1967).

DANKER, F. W., "St. Luke for a New Millennium: The Middle and the End Are in the Beginning", *CThMi* 28 (2001) 5-16.

DARR, J. A., *On Character Building*. The Reader and the Rhetoric of Characterization in Luke-Acts (LitCBI; Louisville, KY 1992).

——————, "Narrator as Character: Mapping a Reader-Oriented Approach to Narration in Luke-Acts", *Semeia* 63 (1993) 43-60.

——————, *Herod the Fox*. Audience Criticism and Lukan Characterization (JSNT.S 163; Sheffield 1998).

DAVIES, J. H., "The Lucan Prologue (1-3): An Attempt at Objective Redaction Criticism", *Studia Evangelica Vol. VI*. Papers Presented to the Fourth International Congress on New Testament Studies Held at Oxford, 1969 (ed. E.A. LIVINGSTONE) (TU 112; Berlin 1973) 78-85.

DAVIS, C. T., "The Literary Structure of Lk 1-2", *Art and Meaning*. Rhetoric in Biblical Literature (ed. D.J.A. CLINES – D.M. GUNN – A.J. HAUSER) (JSOT.S 19; Sheffield 1982) 215-229.

DAWSEY, J. M., *The Lukan Voice*. Confusion and Irony in the Gospel of Luke (Macon, GA 1986).

——————, "The Literary Unity of Luke-Acts: Questions of Style-A task for Literary Critics", *NTS* 35 (1989) 48-66.

DE JONG, I., "Homer and Narratology", *A New Companion to Homer* (ed. I. MORRIS – B.B. POWELL) (Suplementum 163; Leiden – New York 1997) 305-325.

DE JONGE, H. J., "Sonship, Wisdom, Infancy: Luke II.41-51a", *NTS* 24 (1977-1978) 317-354.

DEHANDSCHUTTER, B., "La persécution des chrétiens dans les Actes des Apôtres", *Les Actes des Apôtres*. Traditions, rédaction, théologie (ed. J. KREMER) (BEThL 48; Gembloux – Leuven 1979) 541-546.

DENAUX, A., "The Theme of Divine Visits and Human (In)hospitality in Luke-Acts. Its Old Testament and Greco-Roman Antecedents", *The Unity of Luke-Acts* (ed. J. VERHEYDEN) (Leuven 1999) 255-280.

DERRETT, J. D. M., "Further Light on the Narratives of the Nativity", *NT* 17 (1975) 81-108.

DERRETT, J. D. M., "'Ἀντιλεγόμενον, ῥομφαία, διαλογισμοί (Lk 2:34-35): The Hidden Context", *FilNT* 6 (1993) 207-218.
DIBELIUS, M., *Die urchristliche Überlieferung von Johannes dem Täufer* (FRLANT 15; Göttingen 1911).
————, *Die Formgeschichte des Evangeliums* (Tübingen [6]1971).
DÍEZ MACHO, A., "Derás y exégesis del Nuevo Testamento", *Sef.* 35 (1975) 37-89.
————, *La historicidad de los Evangelios de la Infancia.* El entorno de Jesús (Valencia 1977).
DÍEZ MERINO, L., "Trasfondo semítico de Lucas 1-2", *EstB* 50 (1992) 35-72.
————, "La transfixión de María en el templo de Jerusalén (Lc 2,35) y en el Calvario (Jn 19,25-27)", *EstMar* 70 (2004) 39-69.
DILLON, R. J., "Simeon as a Lucan Spokesman (Lk 2,29-35)", *"Il Verbo di Dio è vivo".* Studi sul Nuovo Testamento in onore del cardinale Albert Vanhoye, S.I (ed. J.E. AGUILAR CHIU – F. MANZI – A. VANHOYE – C. ZESATI ESTRADA – F. URSO) (AnBib 165; Roma 2007) 189-217.
DODD, C. H., *The Parables of the Kingdom* (London 1936).
————, "New Testament Translation Problems II", *BiTr* 28 (1977) 104-110.
DORNISCH, L., *A Woman Reads the Gospel of Luke* (Collegeville, MN 1996).
————, "A Woman Reads the Gospel of Luke: Introduction and Luke 1: the Infancy Narratives", *BR* 42 (1997) 7-22.
DRURY, J., *Tradition and Design in Luke's Gospel.* A Study in Early Christian Historiography (London 1976).
DUFFY, J., "Playing at Ritual: Variations on a Theme in Byzantine Religious Tales", *Greek Ritual Poetics* (ed. D. YATROMANOLAKIS – P. ROILOS) (Hellenic Studies 3; London – Cambridge, MA 2004) 199-209.
DUPONT, J., "L'utilisation apologétique de l'Ancien Testament dans les discours des Actes", *EThL* 29 (1953) 289-327.
————, "ΛΑΟΣ 'ΕΞ 'ΕΘΝΩΝ (Act. XV,14)", *NTS* 3 (1956-1957) 47-50.
————, "La conclusion de l'Évangile et l'introduction des Actes", *Études sur les Actes des Apôtres* (ed. J. DUPONT) (LeDiv 45; Paris 1967) 401-404.
————, "Le salut des Gentils et la signification théologique du Livre des Actes", *Études sur les actes des Apôtres* (ed. J. DUPONT) (LeDiv 45; Paris 1967) 393-419.

DUPONT, J., "La conclusion des Actes et son rapport à l'ensemble de l'ouvrage de Luc", *Les Actes des Apôtres*. Traditions, rédaction, théologie (ed. J. KREMER) (BEThL 48; Gembloux – Leuven 1979) 359-404.

———, "Je t'ai établi lumière des nations (Ac 13,14.43-52)", *Nouvelles études sur les Actes des Apôtres* (ed. J. DUPONT) (LeDiv 118; Paris 1984) 343-349.

———, "L'Apôtre comme intermédiaire du salut dans les Actes des Apôtres", *Nouvelles études sur les Actes des Apôtres* (ed. J. DUPONT) (LeDiv 118; Paris 1984) 112-132.

———, "La portée christologique de l'évangélisation des nations d'après Luc 24,47", *Nouvelles études sur les Actes des Apôtres* (ed. J. DUPONT) (LeDiv 118; Paris 1984) 37-57.

———, "La question du plan des Actes des Apôtres à la lumière d'un texte de Lucien de Samosate", *Nouvelles études sur les Actes des Apôtres* (ed. J. DUPONT) (LeDiv 118; Paris 1984) 28-36.

———, "Un peuple d'entre des nations (Actes 15,14)", *NTS* 31 (1985) 221-235.

ELLIOTT, JAMES K., "Jerusalem in Acts and the Gospels", *NTS* 23 (1976-1977) 462-469.

———, "Anna's Age (Luke 2:36-37)", *NT* 30 (1988) 100-102.

ELLIOTT, JOHN H., "Household and Meals Versus Temple Purity Replication Patterns in Luke-Acts", *BTB* 21 (1991) 102-108.

———, "Temple Versus Household in Luke-Acts: a Contrast in Social Institutions", *HTS* 47 (1991) 88-120.

ELTROP, B., "Simeon und Hanna. Lk 2,22-40: Dezember - Weihnachten", *Entdecken: Lese- und Arbeitsbuch zur Bibel*. Zwölfmal Bibel (ed. F.-J. ORTKEMPER) (Stuttgart 2002) 132-140.

EPP, E. J., "The Multivalence of the Term 'Original Text' in New Testament Textual Criticism", *HThR* 92 (1999) 245-281.

———, "It's All about Variants: A Variant-Conscious Approach to New Testament Criticism", *HThR* 100 (2007) 275-308.

ERDMANN, G., *Die Vorgeschichten des Lukas- und Matthäus-Evangeliums und Vergils vierte Ekloge* (Göttingen 1932).

ESTRADA, N., "Praise for Promises Fulfilled: a Study on the Significance of the Anna the Prophetess Pericope", *AJPS* 2/1 (1999) 5-18.

EVANS, CHRISTOPHER F., *Saint Luke* (TPI New Testament Commentaries; London 1990).

EVANS, CRAIG A. – GASQUE, W.W., *Luke* (NIBC 3; Peabody, MA 1990).

FACQ, F., *Les enfants et l'enfance dans le monde gréco-romain à travers l'oeuvre de Plutarque* (Diss. Lille III-Charles de Gaulle; Paris 2000).

FALCETTA, A., *The Call of Nazareth.* Form and Exegesis of Luke 4:16-30 (CRB 53; Paris 2003).

FARRIS, S. C., *The Hymns of Luke's Infancy Narratives.* Their Origin, Meaning and Significance (JSNT.S 9; Sheffield 1985).

FEUILLET, A., "L'épreuve prédite à Marie par le vieillard Siméon (Lc 2,35a)", *A la rencontre de Dieu.* Mémorial Albert Gelin (BFCTL 8; Le Puy 1961) 243-263.

FIGUERAS, P., "Syméon et Anne ou le témoignage de la loi et des prophètes", *NT* 20 (1978) 84-99.

FITZMYER, J. A., *The Gospel According to Luke I-IX.* Introduction, Translation, and Notes (AncB 28; Garden City, NY 1981) I.

————, *The Acts of the Apostles* (AncB 31; New York 1998).

FLANAGAN, N. M., "The Position of Women in the Writings of St. Luke", *Mar.* 40 (1978) 288-304.

FLENDER, H., *Heil und Geschichte in der Theologie des Lukas* (München [2]1968).

FLICHY, O., "Histoire racontée, parole rapportée: les trois récits de la conversion de Paul", *La Bible en récits: L'exégèse biblique à l'heure du lecteur.* Colloque international d'analyse narrative des textes de la Bible, Lausanne (mars 2002) (ed. D. MARGUERAT) (MoBi 48; Genève 2003) 386-394.

————, "Quand le récit se fait poésie: les hymnes de Luc 1-2", *Analyse narrative et Bible.* Deuxième Colloque internationale du RRENAB, Louvain-la-Neuve, avril 2004 (ed. C. FOCANT – A. WÉNIN) (BEThL 191; Leuven – Paris – Dudley, MA 2005) 389-406.

FOWLER, R. M., "Characterizing Character in Biblical Narrative", *Semeia* 63 (1993) 97-104.

FOX, M. V., "The Identification of Quotations in Biblical Literature", *ZAW* 92 (1980) 416-431.

FRANKEMÖLLE, H., "λαός", *EWNT* 2, 837-848.

FRANKLIN, E., *Luke.* Interpreter of Paul, Critic of Matthew (JSNT.S 92; Sheffield 1994).

FREED, E. D., *The Stories of Jesus' Birth.* A Critical Introduction (BiSe 72; Sheffield 2001).

FREI, H. W., *The Identity of Jesus Christ.* The Hermeneutical Bases of Dogmatic Theology (Philadelphia, PA 1975).

FREIN, B. C., "Narrative Predictions, Old Testament Prophecies and Luke's Sense of Fulfillment", *NTS* 40 (1994) 22-37.

FULLER, M. E., *The Restoration of Israel.* Israel's Re-gathering and the Fate of the Nations in Early Jewish Literature and Luke-Acts (BZNW 138; Berlin – New York 2006).

FUNK, R.W., *The Poetics of Biblical Narrative*. Poetics (F&F.LF; Sonoma, CA 1988).

GALBIATI, E., "La presentazione al Tempio (Lc 2,22-40)", *BeO* 6 (1964) 28-37.

————, "Gli invitati al convito", *BeO* 7 (1965) 129-135.

————, "La circoncisione di Gesù (Lc 2,21)", *BeO* 8 (1966) 37-45.

GANE, R. E., "The Function of the Nazirite's Concluding Purification Offering", *Perspectives on Purity and Purification in the Bible* (ed. B.J. SCHWARTZ) (Library of Hebrew Bible/Old Testament Studies 474; New York 2008) 9-17.

GARCÍA PÉREZ, J. M. – HERRANZ MARCO, M., *La infancia de Jesús según Lucas* (SSNT 6; Madrid 2000).

GARCÍA VIEYRA, A., "Purificación de María y Oblación del Señor en el Templo", *ETF* 5 (1963) 7-36.

GELDENHUYS, N., *Commentary on the Gospel of Luke* (NIC; Grand Rapids, MI 1954).

GENETTE, G., *Figures III* (Poétique; Paris 1966).

GEORGE, A., "La présentation de Jésus au temple", *De Noël à l'Epiphanie* (ASeign 11; Paris 1970) 29-39.

————, "Le parallèle entre Jean-Baptiste et Jésus en Luc 1-2", *Mélanges bibliques en hommage au R. P. Béda Rigaux* (ed. A.L. DESCAMPS – A. HALLEUX) (Gembloux 1970) 147-171.

————, "La venue de Jésus, cause de division entre les hommes", *Vingtième dimanche ordinaire* (ASeign 51; Paris 1972) 62-71.

————, "L'emploi chez Luc du vocabulaire du salut", *NTS* 23 (1976-1977) 308-320.

————, *Études sur l'oeuvre de Luc* (SBi; Paris 1978).

GEORGI, D., "The Records of Jesus in the Light of Ancient Accounts of Revered Men", *Book of Seminar Papers* (ed. L.C. MCGAUGHY) (Los Angeles, CA 1972) II, 527-542.

GERBER, D., "Le Magnificat, Le Benedictus, Le Gloria et Le Nunc Dimittis: Quatre hymnes en réseau pour une introduction en surplomb à Luc-Actes", *La Bible en récits: L'exégèse biblique à l'heure du lecteur*. Colloque international d'analyse narrative des textes de la Bible, Lausanne (mars 2002) (ed. D. MARGUERAT) (MoBi 48; Genève 2003) 353-367.

————, *"Il vous est né un Sauveur"*. La construction du sens sotériologique de la venue de Jésus en Luc-Actes (MoBi 58; Genève 2008).

GERBER, D., "'Ton salut que tu as préparé'. Les diverses fonctions du cantique de Syméon en Luc-Actes", *Les hymnes du Nouveau Testament et leurs fonctions* (ed. D. GERBER – P. KEITH) (LeDiv 225; Paris 2009) 83-98.

GERTNER, M., "Midrashim in the New Testament", *JSSt* 7 (1962) 267-292.

GEYSER, A. S., "The Youth of John the Baptist", *NT* 1 (1956) 70-75.

GILL, C., "The Character-Personality Distinction", *Characterization and Individuality in Greek Literature* (ed. C.B.R. PELLING) (Oxford – New York 1990) 1-31.

GOODENOUGH, E. R., *An Introduction to Philo Judaeus* (Brown Classics in Judaica; Lanham, MD ²1986).

GOULDER, M. D., *Luke*. A New Paradigm (JSNT.S 20; Sheffield 1989) I-II.

GRAPPE, C., "De Zacharie à Jésus ressuscité, la construction de la figure du prêtre de part et d'autre de l'Évangile selon Luc et au début des Actes", *Analyse narrative et Bible*. Deuxième Colloque internationale du RRENAB, Louvain-la-Neuve, avril 2004 (ed. C. FOCANT – A. WÉNIN) (BEThL 191; Leuven – Paris – Dudley, MA 2005) 297-308.

GRÄSSER, E., *Das Problem der Parusieverzögerung in den synoptischen Evangelien und in der Apostelgeschichte* (BZNW 22; Berlin 1957).

GREEN, J. B., "The Problem of a Beginning: Israel's Scriptures in Luke 1-2", *BBR?* 4 (1994) 61-86.

GREIMAS, A. J., *Sémantique structurale* (Paris 1966).

GRELOT, P., "Note sur Actes, XIII, 47", *RB* 88 (1981) 368-372.

—————, "Le Cantique de Siméon (Luc II, 29-32)", *RB* 93 (1986) 481-509.

GROS LOUIS, K. R., "The Jesus Birth Stories", *Literary Interpretations of Biblical Narratives* (ed. K.R. GROS LOUIS – J.S. ACKERMAN) (Nashville, TN 1982) II, 273-284.

—————, "Different Ways of Looking at the Birth of Jesus", *BiRe* 1 (1985) 33-40.

GROSSO, F., "L'epigrafe di Ippona e la vita di Suetonio con i Fasti dei pontefici di Vulcano a Ostia", *RAL* 14 (1959) 263-296.

GRYGLEWICZ, F., "Die Herkunft der Hymnen des Kindheitsevangeliums des Lucas", *NTS* 21 (1975) 265-273.

GUEURET, A., "Luc I-II. Analyse sémiotique", *SémBib* 25 (1982) 35-42.

—————, *L'engendrement d'un récit*. L'Evangile de l'enfance selon Saint Luc (LeDiv 113; Paris 1983).

GUNKEL, H., *Genesis* (Göttingen ⁹1977).

HAENCHEN, E., *Die Apostelgeschichte* (Göttingen ¹⁶1977).

HAMILTON, J. R., *Alexander the Great* (London 1973).
HANFORD, W. R., "Deutero-Isaiah and Luke-Acts: Straightforward Universalism?", *CQR* 168 (1967) 141-152.
HANSEN, H. – QUINN, G. M., *Greek.* An Intensive Course (New York [2]1992).
HARNACK, A., "Das Magnificat der Elisabeth (Lk 1,46-55) nebst einigen Bemerkungen zu Lk I und II", *SKAW* 27 (1900) 538-556.
HARRINGTON, D. J., "The Original Language of Pseudo-Philo's Liber Antiquitatum Biblicarum", *HThR* 63 (1970) 503-514.
————, "The Biblical Text of Pseudo-Philo's Liber Antiquitatum Biblicarum", *CBQ* 33 (1971) 1-17.
————, "Birth Narratives in Pseudo-Philo's Biblical Antiquities and the Gospels", *To Touch the Text* (ed. M.P. HORGAN – P.J. KOBELSKI) (New York 1989) 316-324.
HARTMAN, L., "Ἱεροσόλυμα, Ἰερουσαλήμ", *EWNT* II, 432-439.
HARVEY, W., *Character and the Novel* (Ithaca, NY 1966).
HATCH, W. H. P., "The Text of Luke II, 22", *HThR* 14 (1921) 377-381.
HAYS, J. D., *From Every People and Nation.* A Biblical Theology of Race (NSBTh 14; Downers Grove, IL 2003).
HEAD, P., "Acts and the Problems of Its Texts", *The Book of Acts in Its Ancient Literary Setting* (ed. B.W. WINTER – A.D. CLARKE) (Gran Rapids, MI 1993) 415-444.
HENK, J., "Sonship, Wisdom, Infancy: Luke 2:41-51a", *NTS* 24 (1978) 317-354.
HERRANZ, A. A., "Presentación de Jesús en el Templo (Lc 2,22-39)", *CB* 6 (1949) 35-42.
HILL, D., "The Rejection of Jesus at Nazareth (Luke IV 16-30)", *NT* 13 (1971) 161-180.
HILLMANN, J., "Die Kindheitsgeschichte Jesu nach Lukas kritisch Untersucht", *JPTh* 17 (1890) 192-261.
HILTON, M. – MARSHALL, G., *The Gospels and Rabbinic Judaism.* A Study Guide (Hoboken, NJ 1988).
HOMEYER, H., "Zu den Anfängen der griechischen Biographie", *Ph.* 106 (1962) 75-85.
HOOKER, M. D., *Beginnings: Keys that Open the Gospels.* The 1996 Diocese of British Columbia John Albert Hall Lectures at the Centre for Studies in Religion and Society in the University of Victoria (London 1997).
HORSLEY, R. A., *The Liberation of Christmas.* The Infancy Narratives in Social Context (New York 1989).

HUTCHEON, C. R., "'God Is with Us': The Temple in Luke-Acts", *SVTQ* 44 (2000) 3-33.

IRIGOIN, J., "La composition rythmique des cantiques de Luc", *RB* 98 (1991) 5-50.

JAEGER, W., *Paideia.* The Ideals of Greek Culture (New York 1939) I.

JEREMIAS, J., *Die Gleichnisse Jesu* (Göttingen [6]1962).

————, "Miszelle: Ierousalem/Ierosolyma", *ZNW* 65 (1974) 273-276.

JERVELL, J., "The Divided People of God. The Restoration of Israel and Salvation for the Gentiles", *Luke and the People of God.* A New Look at Luke-Acts (ed. J. JERVELL) (Minneapolis, MN 1972) 41-74.

————, "The Church of Jews and Godfearers", *Luke-Acts and the Jewish People.* Eight Critical Perspectives (ed. J.B. TYSON) (Minneapolis, MN 1988) 11-20.

JOHN, D., "How Old Was Anna?", *BiTr* 26 (1975) 247.

JONES, C. P., *Plutarch and Rome* (Oxford 1972).

JONES, G. C., "'Flat' and 'Round' Characters, the Example of Stendhal", *Australian Journal of French Studies* 20 (1983) 115-129.

JOÜON, P., "Notes philologiques sur les Evangiles. Lc 2,31", *RSR* 18 (1928) 352.

JUNG, C.-W., *The Original Language of the Lukan Infancy Narrative* (JSNT.S 267; London 2004).

KATTENBUSCH, F., *Gibt es buddhistische Einflüsse in den kanonischen Evangelien?* (ThStKr 2; Gotha 1916).

KELLERMANN, U., "Jesus - das Licht der Völker: Lk 2,25-33 und die Christologie im Gespräch mit Israel", *KuI* 7 (1992) 10-25.

KERMODE, F., *The Genesis of Secrecy.* On the Interpretation of Narrative (The Charles Eliot Norton Lectures; Cambridge, MA 1980).

KIDDLE, M., "The Admission of the Gentiles in St. Luke's Gospel and Acts", *JThS* 34 (1935) 160-173.

KILGALLEN, J., "Persecution in the Acts of the Apostles", *Luke and Acts* (ed. G. O'COLLINS – G. MARCONI) (New York 1993) 143-160.

————, "Jesus, Savior, the Glory of Your People Israel", *Bib.* 75 (1994) 305-328.

————, *Twenty Parables of Jesus in the Gospel of Luke* (SubBi 32; Roma 2008).

————, "Acts 28,28 - Why?", *Bib.* 90 (2009) 176-187.

————, *A Wealth of Revelation.* The Four Evangelists' Introductions to Their Gospels (SubBi 34; Roma 2009).

KILPATRICK, G. D., "Laos (*sic*) at Luke 2:31 and Acts 4:25, 27", *JThS* 16 (1965) 127.

KINGSBURY, J. D., *Matthew as Story* (Philadelphia, PA [2]1988).

KLAWANS, J., *Purity, Sacrifice, and the Temple.* Symbolism and Supersessionism in the Study of Ancient Judaism (New York 2006).

KLOSTERMANN, E. – GRESSMANN, H., *Die Synoptiker Evangelien* (HKNT; Tübingen 1919).

KLUTZ, T. E., "The Value of Being Virginal: Mary and Anna in the Lukan Infancy Prologue", *The Birth of Jesus.* Biblical and Theological Reflections (ed. G.J. BROOKE) (Edinburgh 2000) 70-86.

KNOX, J., *Marcion and the New Testament.* An Essay in the Early History of the Canon (Chicago, IL 1942).

KOEHNE, M., "Jesus the Torah. An Exegesis of the Presentation (Luke 2:22-35)", *ScrB* 35 (2005) 5-17.

KOET, B. J., "Holy Place and Hannah's Prayer: A Comparison of LAB 50-51 and Luke 2:22-39 à Propos 1 Samuel 1-2", *Dreams and Scripture in Luke-Acts.* Collected Essays (ed. B. J. KOET) (CBET 42; Leuven 2006) 123-144.

KORZENIEWSKI, D., *Die Zeit des Quintus Curtius Rufus* (Köln 1959).

KRÄNKL, E., *Jesus der Knecht Gottes.* Die heilsgeschichtliche Stellung Jesu in den Reden der Apostelgeschichte (BU 8; Regensburg 1972).

KRÜCKEMEIER, N., "Der zwölfjährige Jesus im Tempel (Lk 2.40-52) und die biographische Literatur der hellenistischen Antike", *NTS* 50 (2004) 307-319.

DE KRUIJF, T. C., "Das Volk Gottes im NT", *Theologische Berichte III.* Judentum und Kirche: Volk Gottes (ed. J. PFAMMATER – F. FURGER) (Einsiedeln 1974) 119-133.

KUHN, K. A., "Beginning the Witness: the αὐτόπται καὶ ὑπηρέται of Luke's Infancy Narrative", *NTS* 49 (2003) 237-255.

KÜMMEL, W. G., *Einleitung in das neue Testament* (Heidelberg [21]1983).

KURZ, W. S., "Hellenistic Rhetoric in Christological Proof of Luke-Acts", *CBQ* 42 (1980) 171-195.

————, "Narrative Approaches to Luke-Acts", *Bib.* 68 (1987) 195-220.

————, *Reading Luke-Acts.* Dynamics of Biblical Narrative (Louisville, KY 1993).

LAGRANGE, M.-J., "La présentation de Jésus au Temple", *VS* 26 (1931) 129-135.

————, *Évangile selon Saint Luc* (EtB; Paris [7]1948).

LANE, T. J., *Luke and the Gentile Mission.* Gospel Anticipates Acts (EHS.T 571; Frankfurt am Main 1996).

LARSSON, E., "Temple-Criticism and the Jewish Heritage: Some Reflexions on Acts 6-7", *NTS* 39 (1993) 379-395.

LAURENTIN, R., *Structure et théologie de Luc I-II* (EtB; Paris 1957).

———, *Les Évangiles de l'enfance du Christ.* Vérité de Noël au-delà des mythes: exégèse et sémiotique, historicité et théologie (Paris 1982).

———, "Vérité des evangiles de l'enfance", *NRTh* 105 (1983) 691-710.

———, *Les Évangiles de Noël* (Paris 1985).

LAURINI, H. C., "Esquema exegético-litúrgico de Lc 1–2", *RCB* 85-86 (1998) 127-144.

LEE, D., *Luke's Stories of Jesus.* Theological Reading of Gospel Narrative and the Legacy of Hans Frei (JSNT.S 185; Sheffield 1999).

LEFEBVRE, P., "Anne de la tribu d'Asher: Le bonheur d'une femme (Lc 2,36-38)", *SémBib* 91 (1998) 3-32.

LEFKOWITZ, M. R., *The Lives of the Greek Poets* (Classical Life and Letters; London 1981).

LEGRAND, L., "L'Arrière-Plan Néo-Testamentaire de Lc I,35", *RB* 70 (1963) 161-192.

———, *L'Annonce à Marie (Lc 1,26-38).* Une apocalypse aux origines de l'Évangile (LeDiv 106; Paris 1981).

LEJEUNE, P., *Le pacte autobiographique* (Paris 1975).

LÉTOURNEAU, P., "Commencer un Évangile: Luc", *La Bible en récits: L'exégèse biblique à l'heure du lecteur.* Colloque international d'analyse narrative des textes de la Bible, Lausanne (mars 2002) (ed. D. MARGUERAT) (MoBi 48; Genève 2003) 326-339.

LIEBESCHUETZ, J., *Continuity and Change in Roman Religion* (Oxford – New York 1979).

LOHFINK, G., "Eine alttestamentliche Darstellungsform für Gotteserscheinungen in Damaskusberichten (Apg 9; 22; 26)", *BZ* 9 (1965) 246-257.

———, *Paulus vor Damaskus.* Arbeitsweisen der neueren Bibelwissenschaft dargestellt an den Texten Apg 9,1-19; 22,3-21; 26, 9-18 (Stuttgart 1965).

———, *Die Sammlung Israels.* Eine Untersuchung zur lukanischen Ekklesiologie (StANT 39; München 1975).

LOHFINK, N., "Psalmen im Neuen Testament: Die Lieder in der Kindheitsgeschichte bei Lukas", *Neue Wege der Psalmenforschung* (ed. K.D. SEYBOLD – E. ZENGER) (Freiburg 1994) 105-125.

LOHFINK, N., "Das Alte Testament und der christliche Tageslauf. Die Lieder in der Kindheitsgeschichte bei Lukas", *Im Schatten deiner Flügel.* Grosse Bibeltexte neu erschlossen (ed. N. LOHFINK) (Freiburg 1999) 218-236.

LÓPEZ MAULEÓN, J. M., "τὸ πνεῦμα (τὸ) ἅγιον en san Lucas", *Mayéutica* 31 (2005) 273-370.

LOUW, J. P. – NIDA, E. A., *Greek-English Lexicon of the New Testament.* Based on Semantic Domains (New York [2]1989).

LUZ, U., *Matthew 1-7.* A Commentary (Edinburgh 1990).

MCGAUGHY, L. C., "Infancy Narratives and Hellenistic Lives. Luke 1-2", *Forum* 2 (1999) 25-39.

MCHUGH, J., *The Mother of Jesus in the New Testament* (London 1975).

MCNICOL, A. J., "Rebuilding the House of David: The Function of the Benedictus in Luke-Acts", *RestQ* 40 (1998) 25-38.

MCQUEEN, E. I., "Quintus Curtius Rufus", *Latin Biography* (ed. T.A. DOREY – E. JENKINSON) (London, 1967) 17-43.

MAGGIONI, B., "The Ordinary Made Extraordinary: The Hidden Life of Jesus Through the Lens of the Lucan Infancy Narratives", *Com(US)* 31 (2004) 8-15.

MAGRIS, A., *L'idea di destino nel pensiero antico.* Da Platone a S. Agostino (Università degli studi di Trieste, Facoltà di Magistero 15; Udine 1985) II.

————, "Stoicism", *EncRel* XIII, 8740-8744.

MALBON, E. S., *Mark's Jesus.* Characterization as Narrative Christology (Waco, TX 2009).

MALICK, D. E., "A Literary Approach to the Birth Narratives in Luke 1-2", *Integrity of Heart, Skillfulness of Hands.* Biblical and Leadership Studies in Honor of Donald K. Campbell (ed. C.H. DYER – R.B. ZUCK) (Grand Rapids, MI 1994) 93-107.

MALLEN, P., *The Reading and Transformation of Isaiah in Luke-Acts* (LNTS 367; London – New York 2008).

MANICARDI, E., "Redazione e tradizione in Lc 1-2", *RSB* 4/2 (1992) 13-53.

————, "Il racconto lucano dell'infanzia di Gesù e la cristologia", *Rivista di Teologia dell'Evangelizzazione* 4 (2000) 7-28.

MANNS, F., *Le Midrash: approche et commentaire de l'Écriture* (SBFA 56; Jerusalem 2001).

MARCONI, G., "Il bambino da vedere: l'estetica lucana nel Cantico di Simeone e dintorni", *Gr.* 72 (1991) 629-654.

MAREC, E. – PFLAHM, H. G., *Nouvelle inscription sur la carrière de Suétone l'historien* (CRAI; [*s. l.*] 1952).

MARGUERAT, D., "Saul's Conversion (Acts 9,22,26) and the Multiplication of Narrative in Acts", *Luke's Literary Achievement*. Collected Essays (ed. C.M. TUCKETT) (JSNT.S 116; Sheffield 1995) 127-155.

————, "The Enigma of the Silent Closing of Acts (28:16-31)", *Jesus and the Heritage of Israel*. Luke's Narrative Claim Upon Israel's Legacy (ed. D.P. MOESSNER) (LIntI 1; Harrisburg, PA 1999) 284-304.

————, "Luc, metteur en scène des personnages", *Analyse narrative et Bible*. Deuxième Colloque internationale du RRENAB, Louvain-la-Neuve, avril 2004 (ed. C. FOCANT – A. WÉNIN) (BEThL 191; Leuven – Paris – Dudley, MA 2005) 281-295.

MARGUERAT, D. – BOURQUIN, Y., *Pour lire les récits bibliques*. Initiation à l'analyse narrative (Paris – Genève – Montréal 1998); Engl. Transl. *How to Read Bible Stories*. An Introduction to Narrative Criticism (London 1999).

MARSHALL, I. H., *The Gospel of Luke*. A Commentary on the Greek Text (NIGTC; Exeter 1978).

————, "'Israel' and the Story of Salvation: One Theme in Two Parts", *Jesus and the Heritage of Israel*. Luke's Narrative Claim upon Israel's Legacy (ed. D.P. MOESSNER) (LIntI 1; Harrisburg, PA 1999) 340-357.

MARTINI, C. M. – VENTURINI, N., *Atti degli Apostoli* (Venezia 1965).

MARTINS TERRA, J. E., "O Evangelho da infância (Lc 1–2) à luz do AT", *RCB* 85-86 (1998) 41-59.

MASINI, M., "I 'Vangeli dell'Infanzia' di Gesù: Traguardi e prospettive", *Mar.* 54 (1992) 451-460.

MATHER, P. B., "The Search for the Living Text of the Lukan Infancy Narrative", *Living Text* (ed. D.E. GROH – R. JEWETT) (Lanham, MD 1985) 123-140.

MBILIZI, É. L., *D'Israël aux nations*. L'horizon de la rencontre avec le Sauveur dans l'oeuvre de Luc (Frankfurt am Main 2006).

MEIER, J. P., *A Marginal Jew*. Rethinking the Historical Jesus (AncBRL; New York 1991).

————, "Jesus, the Twelve, and the Restoration of Israel", *Restoration*. Old Testament, Jewish, and Christian Perspectives (ed. J.M. SCOTT) (JSJ.S 72; Leiden 2001) 365-404.

MENA SALAS, E., "Condiciones para una misión cristiana a los gentiles en el entorno sirio. El ejemplo de Antioquía", *EstB* 64 (2006) 163-199.

MENA SALAS, E., *"También a los Griegos" (Hch 11,20): factores del inicio de la misión a los gentiles en Antioquía de Siria* (Plenitudo temporis 9; Salamanca 2007).

MENES, A., "Temple und Synagoge", *ZAW* 50 (1932) 268-276.

MENOUD, P. H., "Le plan des Actes des Apôtres", *NTS* 1 (1954) 44-51.

METZGER, B., *Historical and Literary Studies, Pagan, Jewish, and Christian* (Leiden 1968).

————, *A Textual Commentary on the Greek New Testament* (New York [2]2001).

MEYER, E., *Ursprung und Anfänge des Christentums* (Stuttgart 1983).

MEYNET, R., "Dieu donne son Nom à Jésus. Analyse rhétorique de Lc 1, 26-56 et de 1Sam 2, 1-10", *Bib.* 66 (1985) 39-72.

————, *L'Évangile de Luc* (Rhétorique sémitique 1; Paris 2005).

MEYNET, R. – MOUNIN, G., *Quelle est donc cette parole?* Lecture "rhétorique" de l'Évangile de Luc (1-9, 22-24) (LeDiv 99-99B; Paris 1979).

MINEAR, P. S., "Luke's Use of the Birth Stories", *Studies in Luke-Acts* (ed. L.E. KECK – J.L. MARTYN – P. SCHUBERT) (Nashville, TN – Ithaca, NY 1966) 111-130.

MIYOSHI, M., "Jesu Darstellung oder Reinigung im Tempel unter Berücksichtigung von 'Nunc Dimittis' Lk 2,22-38", *AJBI* 4 (1978) 85-115.

MOESSNER, D. P., "'The Christ Must Suffer': New Light on the Jesus-Peter, Stephen, Paul Parallels in Luke-Acts", *NT* 28 (1986) 220-256.

————, "The Ironic Fulfillment of Israel's Glory", *Luke-Acts and the Jewish People: Eight Critical Perspectives* (ed. J.B. TYSON) (Minneapolis, MN 1988) 35-50.

MOLONEY, F. J., *Beginning the Good News.* A Narrative Approach (Collegeville, MN 1995).

MOMIGLIANO, A., *The Development of Greek Biography* (Cambridge, MA 1993).

MONTES PERAL, L. Á., "A la búsqueda de identidades: Santiago el Zebedeo, Santiago el de Alfeo, Santiago de Nazaret", *EstB* 67 (2009) 111-160.

MOORE, T. S., "'To the End of the Earth': The Geographical and Ethnic Universalism of Acts 1:8 in Light of Isaianic Influence on Luke", *JETS* 40 (1997) 389-399.

MORALES GÓMEZ, G., "Jerusalén-Jerosólima en el vocabulario y la geografía", *Revista catalana de teología* 7 (1982) 131-186.

MORGENTHALER, R., *Die lukanische Geschichtsschreibung als Zeugnis.* Gestalt und Gehalt der Kunst des Lukas (AThANT 14; Zürich 1949) I.

MORGENTHALER, R., *Statistik des neutestamentlichen Wortschatzes* (Zürich 1958).
MOUNT, W., "Jesus in Luke 1-2: Some Aspects of Luke's Editorial Work", *PerkJ* 26 (1972) 41-46.
MÜLLER, F. M., *The Dhammapada, a Collection of Verses*. Being One of the Canonical Books of the Buddhists (SBE 10; Delhi 1968).
MULLOOR, A., "'From East and West, from North and South.' Lukan View of Universalism", *Jeev* 30 (2000) 177-189.
MUÑOZ IGLESIAS, S., "Midrás y Evangelios de la Infancia", *EE* 47 (1972) 331-359.
———, "Derás y Nuevo Testamento", *EstB* 46 (1988) 303-314.
———, *Los Evangelios de la Infancia*. I: Los Cánticos del Evangelio de la Infancia según San Lucas. II: Los anuncios angélicos previos en el Evangelio lucano de la infancia. III: Nacimiento e infancia de Juan y de Jesús en Lucas 1-2 (BAC 508, 479, 488; Madrid 1987, [2]1990).
MUÑOZ LEÓN, D., *Derás: los caminos y sentidos de la palabra divina en la Escritura*. Primera serie: Derás targúmico y Derás neotestamentario (Bibliotheca Hispana Biblica 12; Madrid 1987).
———, "La distinción entre acontecimiento-base y artificio literario en los relatos derásicos. Una discusión con el Prof Muñoz Iglesias en su obra 'Los Evangelios de la Infancia'", *EstB* 50 (1992) 123-148.
NEIRYNCK, F., *L'Evangile de Noël*. Selon S. Luc (Paris 1960).
NICCACCI, A., "Dall'aoristo all'imperfetto o dal primo piano allo sfondo. Un paragone tra sintassi greca e sintassi ebraica", *LASBF* 42 (1992) 85-108.
NOCK, A. D., *Conversion*. The Old and the New in Religion from Alexander the Great to Augustine of Hippo (Brown Classics in Judaica; Lanham, MD 1988).
NOLLAND, J., *Luke 1-9:20* (WBC 35A; Dallas, TX 1989).
NORTH, C. R., *The Suffering Servant in Deutero-Isaiah*. An Historical and Critical Study (London 1948).
Ó FEARGHAIL, F., *The Introduction to Luke-Acts*. A Study of the Role of Lk 1,1-4,44 in the Composition of Luke's Two-Volume Work (AnBib 126; Roma 1991).
OCKENGA, H. J., "Simeon and the Child Jesus", *ChrTo* 15 (1970) 4-6.
O'DAY, G. R., "Singing Woman's Song: A Hermeneutic of Liberation", *CThMi* 12 (1985) 203-210.
OGG, G., "The Quirinius Question Today", *ET* 79 (1968) 231-236.

OLIVER, H. H., "The Lucan Birth Stories and the Purpose of Luke-Acts", *NTS* 10 (1964) 202-226.

OMANSON, R. L. – METZGER, B. M., *A Textual Guide to the Greek New Testament*. An Adaptation of Bruce M. Metzger's Textual Commentary for the Needs of Translators (Stuttgart 2006).

ORSATTI, M., "Storicità e Vangeli dell'infanzia", *RThL* 9 (2004) 603-622.

ORTENSIO DA SPINETOLI, *Introduzione ai Vangeli dell'infanzia* (MVI 4; Brescia 1967).

————, "I problemi di Matteo 1-2 e Luca 1-2. Orientamenti e proposte", *RSB* 4/1 (1992) 7-44.

OSBORNE, T. P., "Les 'hymnes' du récit de l'enfance de l'évangile de Luc. Première partie: cinq thèses sur la fonction des hymnes de Lc 1-2", *Les hymnes du Nouveau Testament et leurs fonctions* (ed. D. GERBER – P. KEITH) (LeDiv 225; Paris 2009) 281-294.

————, "'Récitez entre vous des psaumes, des hymnes et des cantiques inspirés' (Ep5,19). Un état de la question sur l'étude des 'hymnes'", *Les hymnes du Nouveau Testament et leurs fonctions* (ed. D. GERBER – P. KEITH) (LeDiv 225; Paris 2009) 239-263.

OSWALT, J. N., *The Book of Isaiah*. Chapters 40-66 (NICOT; Grand Rapids 1998).

O'TOOLE, R. F., *The Unity of Luke's Theology*. Analysis of Luke-Acts (Good News Studies 9; Wilmington, DE 1984).

————, "Reflections on Luke's Treatment of Jews in Luke-Acts", *Bib.* 74 (1993) 529-555.

————, "How Does Luke Portray Jesus as Servant of YHWH?", *Bib.* 81 (2000) 328-346.

————, "The Christian Mission and the Jews at the End of Acts of the Apostles", *Biblical Exegesis in Progress*. Old and New Testament Essays (ed. J.-N. ALETTI – J.L. SKA) (AnBib 176; Roma 2009) 371-396.

PANIER, L., *Récit et commentaires de la tentation de Jésus au désert*. Approche sémiotique du discours interprétatif (Thèses Cerf; Paris 1984).

————, *La naissance du Fils de Dieu*. Sémiotique et théologie discursive: lecture de Luc 1-2 (CFi 164; Paris 1991).

PAO, D. W., *Acts and the Isaianic New Exodus* (WUNT 130; Tübingen 2000).

PARSONS, M. C., "The Place of Jerusalem on the Lukan Landscape: an Exercise in Symbolic Cartography", *Literary Studies in Luke-Acts*. Essays in Honor of Joseph B. Tyson (ed. R.P. THOMPSON – T.E. PHILLIPS) (Macon, GA 1998) 155-171.

PARSONS, M. C. – PERVO, R. I., *Rethinking the Unity of Luke and Acts* (Minneapolis, MN 1993).

PELLING, C. B. R., "Childhood and Personality in Greek Biography", *Characterization and Individuality in Greek Literature* (ed. C.B.R. PELLING) (Oxford – New York 1990) 213-244.

PEREIRA, Á., "Pablo, como Jesús, camino de Jerusalén", *ResBib* 60 (2008) 37-45.

PÉREZ RODRÍGUEZ, G., *La infancia de Jesús (Mt 1-2; Lc 1-2)* (Teología en diálogo 4; Salamanca 1990).

PERRIN, N., *Rediscovering the Teaching of Jesus* (London 1967).

PERROT, C., "Les récits d'enfance dans la haggada antérieure au IIe sicle de notre Áre", *RSR* 55 (1967) 481-518.

———, *Les récits de l'enfance de Jésus: Matthieu 1-2; Luc 1-2* (CEv 18; Paris 1976).

PERRY, M., "Literary Dynamics: How the Order of a Text Creates its Meanings", *PoeT* 1 (1979) 35-63; 311-361.

PETZKE, G., "διαλογισμός", *EWNT* I, 740-741.

PFISTER, F., *Der Alexanderroman mit einer Auswahl aus den verwandten Texten* (Meisenheim am Glan 1978).

PLUMMER, A., *A Critical and Exegetical Commentary on the Gospel According to St. Luke* (ICC; Edinburgh 1908).

PLYMALE, S. F., "The Prayer of Simeon (Luke 2:29-32)", *Lord's Prayer and Other Prayer Texts from the Greco-Roman Era* (ed. J.H. CHARLESWORTH – M. HARDING – M.C. KILEY) (Valley Forge, PA 1994) 28-38.

DE LA POTTERIE, I., "Les deux noms de Jérusalem dans l'évangile de Luc", *RSR* 69 (1981) 57-70.

POWELL, M. A., *What is Narrative Criticism?* (GBS.NTS; Minneapolis, MN 1990).

———, *The Bible and Modern Literary Criticism.* A Critical Assessment and Annotated Bibliography (BIRS 22; New York 1992).

———, "Narrative Criticism", *Hearing the New Testament.* Strategies for Interpretation (ed. J.B. GREEN) (Grand Rapids, MI 1995) 239-255.

POWER, E., "In festo Purificationis", *VD* 5 (1925) 34-41.

PREMA, S., "A Christmas Meditation: the Shepherds and the Widow", *ITS* 40 (2003) 451-463.

PUIG I TÀRRECH, A., "Les voyages à Jérusalem (Lc 9,51; Ac 19,21)", *The Unity of Luke-Acts* (ed. J. VERHEYDEN) (Leuven 1999) 493-506.

PUIG I TÀRRECH, A., "La finale de Luc: Une synthèse ouverte", *Analyse narrative et Bible*. Deuxième Colloque internationale du RRENAB, Louvain-la-Neuve, avril 2004 (ed. C. FOCANT – A. WÉNIN) (BEThL 191; Leuven – Paris – Dudley, MA 2005) 223-239.

PUSKAS, C. B., *The Conclusion of Luke-Acts*. The Significance of Acts 28:16-31 (Eugene, OR 2009).

QUARLES, C. L., "The Protevangelium of James as an Alleged Parallel to Creative Historiography in the Synoptic Birth Narratives", *BBR?* 8 (1998) 139-149.

RABATEL, A., *La construction textuelle du point de vue* (Sciences des discours; Lausanne – Paris 1998).

RACINE, J.-R., "L'hybridité des personnages: Une stratégie d'inclusion des gentils dans les Actes des Apôtres", *Analyse narrative et Bible*. Deuxième Colloque internationale du RRENAB, Louvain-la-Neuve, avril 2004 (ed. C. FOCANT – A. WÉNIN) (BEThL 191; Leuven – Paris – Dudley, MA 2005) 559-566.

RADL, W., *Paulus und Jesus im lukanischen Doppelwerk*. Untersuchungen zu Parallelmotiven im Lukasevangelium und in der Apostelgeschichte (EHS.T 49; Bern 1975).

————, *Der Ursprung Jesu*. Traditionsgeschichtliche Untersuchungen zu Lukas 1-2 (Herders biblische Studien 7; Freiburg 1996).

————, "Die Beziehungen der Vorgeschichte zur Apostelgeschichte: Dargestellt an Lk 2:22-39", *Unity of Luke-Acts* (ed. J. VERHEYDEN) (BEThL 142; Louvain 1999) 297-312.

RÄISÄNEN, H., "The Redemption of Israel: A Salvation-Historical Problem in Luke-Acts", *Luke-Acts*. Scandinavian Perspectives (ed. P. LUOMANEN) (SESJ 54; Helsinki – Göttingen 1991) 94-111.

RASCO, E., *La teología de Lucas: origen, desarrollo, orientaciones* (AnGr 201; Roma 1976).

RAVENS, D., *Luke and the Restoration of Israel* (JSNT.S 119; Sheffield 1995).

REICKE, B. I., "Jesus, Simeon, and Anna (Luke 2:21-40)", *Saved by Hope: Essays in Honor of Richard C. Oudersluys* (ed. R.C. OUDERSLUYS – J.I. COOK) (Grand Rapids, MI 1978) 96-108.

REICKE, B. I. – BERTRAM, G., "παρίστημι, παριστάνω", *ThWNT* V, 835-840.

RESENHÖFFT, W., *Die Apostelgeschichte in Wortlaut ihrer beiden Urquellen*. Rekonstruktion des Büchleins von der Geburt Johannes des Täufers, Lk 1-2 (Frankfurt – Bern 1974).

RHOADS, D. M., *Mark as Story*. An Introduction to the Narrative of a Gospel (Minneapolis, MN [2]1999).

RICŒUR, P., *Temps et récit* (L'ordre philosophique; Paris 1983).

———, "Interpretative Narrative", *The Book and the Text.* The Bible and Literary Theory (ed. R.M. SCHWARTZ) (Cambridge, MA 1990) 236-257.

RIESNER, R., "Jame's Speech (Acts 15:13-21), Simeon's hymn (Luke 2:29-32) and Luke's Sources", *Jesus of Nazareth: Lord and Christ.* Essays on the Historical Jesus and New Testament Christology (ed. J.B. GREEN – M. TURNER) (Grand Rapids, MI 1994) 263-278.

RIVES, J. B., *Religion in the Roman Empire* (Blackwell Ancient Religions; Malden, MA 2007).

RODGER, L., "The Infancy Stories of Matthew and Luke: An Examination of the Child as a Theological Metaphor", *HBT* 19 (1997) 58-81.

ROGERS, C. L., JR. & C. L., III – RIENECKER, F., *The New Linguistic and Exegetical Key to the Greek New Testament* (Grand Rapids, MI 1998).

ROSSÉ, G., "Approcci esegetici al testo della presentazione (Lc 2,22-40)", *Theotokos* 6 (1998) 17-30.

ROUILLER, G., "*Il vous est né un Sauveur*". Une naissance annoncée et célébrée Luc 1-2 et Matthieu 2 (Cahiers de l'ABC 5; Fribourg 1996).

RUDDICK, C.T., "Birth Narratives in Genesis and Luke", *NT* 12 (1970) 343-348.

RYAN, J. M., "Luke's Infancy Narrative", *BiTod* 35 (1997) 340-344.

SALAZAR, A. M., "Questions About St Luke's Sources", *NT* 2 (1958) 316-317.

SALMON, M., "Insider or Outsider? Luke's Relationship with Judaism", *Luke-Acts and the Jewish People.* Eight Critical Perspectives (ed. J.B. TYSON) (Minneapolis, MN 1988) 76-82.

SAMAIN, E., "Le discours-programme de Jésus à la synagogue de Nazareth, Lc 4, 16-30", *CBFV* 10 (1971) 25-43.

SAMKUTTY, V. J., *The Samaritan Mission in Acts* (LNTS 328; London – New York 2006).

SÁNCHEZ MIELGO, G., "Los Evangelios de la infancia: ¿Historia, relato, teología?", *Communio* 34 (2001) 103-180.

SAND, A., "παρίστημι, παριστάνω", *EWNT* III, 96-98.

SANDERS, JACK T., "The Salvation of the Jews in Luke-Acts", *Luke-Acts, New Perspectives from the Society of Biblical Literature Seminar* (ed. C.H. TALBERT) (New York 1984) 104-128.

SCHABERG, J., *The Illegitimacy of Jesus.* A Feminist Theological Interpretation of the Infancy Narratives (Sheffield 1995).

SCHILLE, G., *Frühchristliche Hymnen* (Berlin 1965).
SCHMID, J., *Das Evangelium nach Lukas* (RNT 3; Regensburg [4]1960).
SCHNABEL, E. J., "Jesus and the Beginnings of the Mission to the Gentiles", *Jesus of Nazareth: Lord and Christ.* Essays on the Historical Jesus and New Testament Christology (ed. J.B. GREEN – M. TURNER) (Grand Rapids, MI 1994) 37-58.
SCHNACKENBURG, R., *Das Johannesevangelium* (HThK 4; Freiburg – Basel – Wien 1965) I.
SCHNEIDER, G., *Das Evangelium nach Lukas* (ÖTBK 3; Gütersloh 1977) I.
SCHRECK, C. J., "The Nazareth Pericope: Luke 4:16-30 in Recent Study", *L'Évangile de Luc - The Gospel of Luke* (ed. F. NEIRYNCK) (BEThL 32; Leuven 1989) 399-471.
SCHRENK, G., "διαλογισμός", *ThWNT* II, 96-98.
SCHUBERT, P., "The Structure and Significance of Luke 24", *Neutestamentliche Studien für Rudolf Bultmann.* Zu seinem 70. Geburtstag am 20. August 1954 (ed. W. ELTESTER – A.N. WILDER) (BZNW 21; Berlin 1954) 165-186.
SCHÜRER, E. – VERMÉS, G. – MILLAR, F., *The History of the Jewish People in the Age of Jesus Christ (175 B.C.-A.D. 135)* (Edinburgh 1973).
SCHÜRMANN, H., "Aufbau, Eigenart und Geschichtswert der Vorgeschichte von Lukas 1-2", *BiKi* 21 (1966) 106-111.
————, *Traditionsgeschichtliche Untersuchungen zu den synoptischen Evangelien* (KBANT; Düsseldorf 1968).
————, *Das Lukasevangelium.* Kommentar zu Kap. 1,1-9,50 (HThK 3; Freiburg 1969) I.
————, *Ursprung und Gestalt.* Erörterungen und Besinnungen zum Neuen Testament (KBANT; Düsseldorf 1970).
SCHÜSSLER FIORENZA, E., *In Memory of Her.* A Feminist Theological Reconstruction of Christian Origins (New York 1983).
SCHWEIZER, E., "Zum Aufbau von Lukas 1 und 2", *Intergerini Parietis Septum (Eph 2:14)* (ed. D.Y. HADIDIAN) (Pittsburgh, PA 1981) 309-335.
SCHWERTNER, S., *Internationales Abkürzungsverzeichnis für Theologie und Grenzgebiete.* Zeitschriften, Serien, Lexika, Quellenwerke mit bibliographischen Angaben (Berlin – New York [2]1992).
SCOTT, B. B., "The Birth of the Reader", *Semeia* 52 (1990) 83-102.
SECCOMBE, D., "Luke and Isaiah", *NTS* 27 (1981) 252-259.
SEDLEY, D., "Stoicism", *Routledge Encyclopedia of Philosophy* (ed. E. CRAIG) (London – New York 1998) IX, 141-161.
SEGALIA, G., "L'Ombra della Croce nel Vangelo dell'Infanzia", *PSV* 9 (1964) 39-45.

SERRA, A. M., "'E anche a te una spada trapasserà l'anima': Luca 2,35a alla luce dell'antica tradizione giudaico-cristiana", *Mar.* 64 (2002) 51-111.

———, "'Maria conservava tutte queste cose' (Lc 2,19: cfr. 2,51b). La madre di Gesù, fonte di informazione per l'evangelo dell'infanzia? Scrittura e Tradizione a confronto", *San Luca Evangelista Testimone della Fede che unisce.* Atti del congresso internazionale; Padova, 16-21 Ottobre 2000 (ed. G. LEONARDI – F.G.B. TROLESE) (FRSEP 28; Padova 2002) 423-438.

SHULER, P. L., "The Rhetorical Character of Luke 1-2", *Literary Studies in Luke-Acts* (ed. R.P. THOMPSON – T.E. PHILLIPS) (Macon, GA 1998) 173-189.

SIFFER, N., "Les 'hymnes' du récit de l'enfance de l'évangile de Luc. Seconde partie: les hymnes de Lc 1–2 et l'accomplissement du dessein salvifique de Dieu", *Les hymnes du Nouveau Testament et leurs fonctions* (ed. D. GERBER – P. KEITH) (LeDiv 225; Paris 2009) 295-308.

SIKER, J. S., "'First to the Gentiles': A Literary Analysis of Luke 4:16-30", *JBL* 111 (1992) 73-90.

SILBERMAN, L. H., "A Model for the Lukan Infancy Narratives", *JBL* 113 (1994) 491-493.

SIMÓN MUÑOZ, A., "Cristo, luz de los gentiles: puntualizaciones sobre Lc 2:32", *EstB* 46 (1988) 27-44.

———, "La 'permanencia' de Israel: Una nueva lectura de Lc 2,34a", *EstB* 50 (1992) 191-223.

———, *El Mesías y la hija de Sión.* Teología de la redención en Lc 2,29-35 (SSNT 3; Madrid 1994).

SKA, J. L., *"Our Fathers Have Told Us".* Introduction to the Analysis of Hebrew Narratives (SubBi 13; Roma 2000).

SMYTH, H. W. – MESSING, G. M., *Greek Grammar* (Cambridge, MA 1956).

SOARDS, M. L., "Luke 2:22-40", *Interp.* 44 (1990) 400-405.

SPANNEUT, M., *Permanence du Stoïcisme.* De Zénon à Malraux (Gembloux 1973).

SPITTA, F., "Das Magnificat ein Psalm der Maria und nicht der Elisabeth", *Theologische Abhandlungen: eine Festgabe zum 17. Mai 1902 für Heinrich Julius Holtzmann* (ed. W. NOWACK – H.J. HOLTZMANN) (Tübingen 1902) 63-94.

———, "Die chronologischen Notizen und die Hymnen in Lk I und II", *ZNW* 7 (1906) 281-317.

STANTON, G., "Messianism and Christology: Mark, Matthew, Luke and Acts", *Redemption and Resistance.* The Messianic Hopes of Jews and Christians in Antiquity (ed. W. HORBURY – M.N.A. BOCKMUEHL – J.C. PAGET) (London – New York 2007) 78-96.

STEIDLE, W., *Sueton und die antike Biographie* (Zet. 1; München ²1963).

STERLING, G. E., *Historiography and Self-definition: Josephus, Luke-Acts, and Apologetic Historiography* (NT.S 64; Leiden 1992).

STERNBERG, M., *The Poetics of Biblical Narrative.* Ideological Literature and the Drama of Reading (Indiana Literary Biblical Series; Bloomington 1985).

STOCK, K., "Maria nel Tempio (Lc 2,22-52)", *PSV* 6 (1982) 114-125.

STRAMARE, T., "La presentazione di Gesù al Tempio (Lc 2,22-40). Significato esegetico e teologico", *CJos* 29 (1981) 37-61.

————, "Compiuti i giorni della loro purificazione (Lc 2,22). Gli avvenimenti del Nuovo Testamento conclusivi di un disegno", *BeO* 24 (1982) 199-205.

————, *Vangelo dei misteri della vita nascosta di Gesù.* Matteo e Luca 1-2 (BeO.S; Bornato in Franciacorta 1998).

STRATHMANN, H. – MEYER, R., "λαός", *ThWNT* IV, 28-57.

STRAUSS, M. L., *The Davidic Messiah in Luke-Acts.* The Promise and its Fulfillment in Lukan Christology (JSNT.S 110; Sheffield 1995).

STRICKERT, F. M., "The Presentation of Jesus: The Gospel of Inclusion: Luke 2:22-40", *CThMi* 22 (1995) 33-37.

SYLVA, D. D., "Jerousalem and Hierosoluma in Luke-Acts", *ZNW* 74 (1983) 207-221.

TALBERT, C. H., *Literary Patterns, Theological Themes, and the Genre of Luke-Acts* (SBL.MS 20; Missoula, MT 1974).

————, "Prophecies of Future Greatness: the Contribution of Greco-Roman Biographies to an Understanding of Luke 1:5-4:15", *Divine Helmsman* (ed. J.L. CRENSHAW – S. SANDMEL) (New York 1980) 129-141.

————, "Once Again: the Gentile Mission in Luke-Acts", *Der Treue Gottes trauen: Beiträge zum Werk des Lukas (für Gerhard Schneider)* (ed. C. BUSSMANN – W. RADL) (Freiburg 1991) 99-109.

————, "Jesus' Birth in Luke and the Nature of Religious Language", *Reading Luke-Acts in its Mediterranean Milieu* (ed. C.H. TALBERT) (NT.S 107; Leiden 2003) 79-90.

TANNEHILL, R., "Israel in Luke-Acts: a Tragic Story", *JBL* 104 (1985) 69-85.

————, *The Narrative Unity of Luke-Acts* (Philadelphia, PA 1986) I.

TANNEHILL, R., "Rejection by Jews and Turning to Gentiles: The Pattern of Paul's Mission in Acts", *Luke-Acts and the Jewish People*. Eight Critical Perspectives (ed. J.B. TYSON) (Minneapolis, MN 1988) 83-101.

————, "The Story of Israel within the Lukan Narrative", *Jesus and the Heritage of Israel*. Luke's Narrative Claim upon Israel's Legacy (ed. D.P. MOESSNER) (LIntI 1; Harrisburg, PA 1999) 325-339.

————, "The Composition of Acts 3-5: Narrative Development and Echo Effect", *The Shape of Luke's Story*. Essays on Luke-Acts (ed. R. TANNEHILL) (Eugene, OR 2005) 185-219.

————, "The Functions of Peter's Mission Speeches in the Narrative of Acts", *The Shape of Luke's Story*. Essays on Luke-Acts (ed. R. TANNEHILL) (Eugene, OR 2005) 169-184.

————, "The Mission of Jesus According to Luke 4:16-30", *The Shape of Luke's Story*. Essays on Luke-Acts (ed. R. TANNEHILL) (Eugene, OR 2005) 3-30.

————, "The Story of Zacchaeus as Rhetoric", *The Shape of Luke's Story*. Essays on Luke-Acts (ed. R.C. TANNEHILL) (Eugene, OR 2005) 73-83.

————, "The Gospel and Narrative Literature", *The Shape of the Gospel*. New Testament essays (ed. R.C. TANNEHILL) (Eugene, OR 2007) 99-126.

TATUM, W. B., "Epoch of Israel: Luke 1-2 and the Theological Plan of Luke-Acts", *NTS* 13 (1967) 184-195.

TAYLOR, N., "The Jerusalem Temple in Luke-Acts", *HTS* 60 (2004) 459-485.

TESTA, E., *Maria Terra Vergine* (SBF.CMa 31; Gerusalemme 1985).

THOMAS, C., "The Infancy Narrative in Luke's gospel", *BiTod* 41 (2003) 295-301.

THURSTON, B. B., "Who was Anna?: Luke 2:36-38", *PRSt* 28 (2001) 47-55.

TIEDE, D. L., *Prophecy and History in Luke-Acts* (Philadelphia, PA 1980).

————, *Luke* (ACNT; Minneapolis, MN 1988).

TROIANI, L., "La genèse historique des antiquités juives", *Josephus and Jewish History in Flavian Rome and Beyond* (ed. J. SIEVERS – G. LEMBI) (JSJ.S 104; Boston 2005) 21-28.

TROMPF, G.W., *The Idea of Historical Recurrence in Western Thought*. From Antiquity to the Reformation (Berkeley – Los Angeles – London 1979).

TURNER, N., "Relation of Luke 1 and 2 to Hebraic Sources and to the Rest of Luke-Acts", *NTS* 2 (1955) 100-109.

TYSON, J. B., "The Problem of Jewish Rejection in Acts", *Luke-Acts and the Jewish People*. Eight Critical Perspectives (ed. J.B. TYSON) (Minneapolis, MN 1988) 124-137.

———, "The Birth Narratives and the Beginning of Luke's Gospel", *Semeia* (1990) 103-120.

———, "Jews and Judaism in Luke-Acts: Reading As a God-fearer", *NTS* 41 (1995) 19-38.

VAN UNNIK, W. C., "Der Ausdruck ἕως ἐσχάτου τῆς γῆς (Apg. 1.8) und sein alttestamentlicher Hintergrund", *Sparsa collecta*. Evangelia, Paulina, Acta (ed. W.C. VAN UNNIK) (NT.S 29; Leiden 1973) I, 386-401.

UNSNER, H., "Geburt und Kindheit Christi", *ZNW* 4 (1903) 1-21.

USPENSKI, B. A., *A Poetics of Composition*. The Structure of the Artistic Text and Typology of a Compositional Form (Berkeley – Los Angeles – London 1973).

VACCARI, A., "ΕΔΗΣΑΝ ΑΥΤΟ ΟΘΟΝΙΟΙΣ (Joh. 19,40)", *Miscellanea biblica B. Ubach* (ed. R.M. DÍAZ CARBONELL) (SDM 1; Montisserrati 1953) 375-386.

VALENTINI, A., "I cantici in Lc 1–2", *RSB* 4/2 (1992) 81-108.

———, "'Καταρισμοῦ αὐτῶν' e 'ῥομφαία' (Lc 2,22.35). Due cruces interpretum", *"Il Verbo di Dio è vivo"*. Studi sul Nuovo Testamento in onore del cardinale Albert Vanhoye, S.I (ed. J.E. AGUILAR CHIU – F. MANZI – A. VANHOYE – C. ZESATI ESTRADA – F. URSO) (AnBib 165; Roma 2007) 169-187.

VAN BIEMA, D., "Behind the First Noel", *Time* 13 (2004) 48-54.

VAN DER PLOEG, J. S., *Les chants du serviteur de Jahvé: dans la seconde partie du livre d'Isaïe (chap. 40-55)* (Paris 1936).

VANHOYE, A., *Traduction structurée de l'Épître aux Hébreux* (Rome 1963); Engl. Transl. *A Structured Translation of the Epistle to the Hebrews* (Rome 1964).

VARELA, A. T., "Lk 2,36-37. Is Anna's Age What is Really in Focus?", *BiTr* 27 (1976) 446.

DE VAUX, R., *Les institutions de L'Ancien Testament*. Le nomadisme et ses survivances. Institutions familiales. Institutions civiles (Paris 1958) I; Engl. Transl. *Ancient Israel*. Volume 1. Social Institutions (New York – Toronto 1965).

VISSER, N., "Hier is meer dan Jozua. Over de opdracht van Jezus in de tempel en zijn ontmoeting met Simeon en Hanna", *BenT* 47 (1986) 139-154.

VLKOVÁ, G. I., *Cambiare la luce in tenebre e le tenebre in luce.* Uno studio tematico dell'alternarsi tra la luce e le tenebre nel libro di Isaia (TGr.T 107; Roma 2004).

VOGELS, H. J., "Die 'Eltern' Jesu (Textkritisches zu Lk 2,23ff)", *BZ* 11 (1913) 33-43.

VÖLTER, D., *Die evangelischen Erzählungen von der Geburt und Kindheit Jesu.* Kritisch Untersucht (Strassburg 1911).

WALLACE, D. B., *Greek Grammar Beyond the Basics.* An Exegetical Syntax of the New Testament (Grand Rapids, MI 1996).

WALLACE-HADRILL, A., *Suetonius.* The Scholar and his Caesars (New Haven, CT 1984).

WALTER, N., "ἔθνος", *EWNT* I, 924-929.

WARDMAN, A., *Plutarch's Lives* (Berkeley 1974).

WASSERBERG, G., *Aus Israels Mitte - Heil für die Welt* (BZNW 92; Berlin – New York 1998).

WEITZMAN, S., *Song and Story in Biblical Narrative.* The History of a Literary Convention in Ancient Israel (ISBL; Bloomington – Indianapolis 1997).

WELLHAUSEN, J., *Das Evangelium Lucae* (Berlin 1904).

WHITE, L. M., *From Jesus to Christianity* (San Francisco 2004).

WILCOX, M., *The Semitisms of Acts* (Oxford 1965).

WILKINSON, J. R., *A Johannine Document in the First Chapters of St. Luke's Gospel* (London 1902).

WILLS, L. M., "The Depiction of the Jews in Acts", *JBL* 110 (1991) 631-654.

WILSON, S. G., *The Gentiles and the Gentile Mission in Luke-Acts* (MSSNTS 23; Cambridge, MA 1973).

WINANDY, J., "La prophétie du Syméon (Lc II,34-35)", *RB* 72 (1965) 321-351.

WINTER, P., "Some Observations on the Language in the Birth and Infancy Stories of the Third Gospel", *NTS* 1 (1954) 111-121.

————, "Ὅτι Recitativum in Luke 1:25,61, 2:23.", *HThR* 48 (1955) 213-216.

WITHERINGTON, B., "Mary, Simeon or Anna. Who First Recognized Jesus as Messiah?", *BiRe* 21 (2005) 12.14.51.

WOLTER, M., "Israel Zukunft und die Parusieverzögerung bei Lukas", *Eschatologie und Schöpfung: Festschrift für Erich Grässer zum siebzigsten Geburtstag* (ed. E. GRÄSSER – M. EVANG – H. MERKLEIN – M. WOLTER) (BZNW 89; Berlin – New York 1997) 405-426.

WRIGHT, A. G., "The Literary Genre Midrash", *CBQ* 28 (1966) 103-138, 417-457.

YAMASAKI, G., *Watching a Biblical Narrative*. Point of View in Biblical Exegesis (London 2007).

DE YOUNG, J. C., *Jerusalem in the New Testament: the Significance of the City in the History of Redemption and in Eschatology* (Diss. Kok University; Kampen 1960).

YULE, G., *Pragmatics* (Oxford Introductions to Language Study; Oxford 1996).

ZELLER, E., "Die älteste Überlieferung über die Schriften des Lukas", *ThJb* 7 (1948) 528-572.

ZERWICK, M., *Analysis philologica Novi Testamenti graeci* (Romae [3]1966).

———, *Graecitas biblica*. Novi Testamenti exemplis illustratur (Romae [5]1966).

ZIMMERMANN, H., *Neutestamentliche Methodenlehre*. Darstellung der historisch-kritischen Methode (Stuttgart 1967).

ZIPPERT, C., "Des alten Simeon Lobgesang", *Quat.* 65 (2001) 34-37.

ZMIJEWSKI, J., *Die Eschatologiereden des Lukas-Evangeliums*. Eine traditions- und redaktionsgeschichtliche Untersuchung zu Lk 21,5-36 und Lk 17,20-37 (BBB 40; Bonn 1972).

ZUMSTEIN, J., "L'apôtre comme martyr dans les Actes de Luc", *RThPh* 112 (1980) 371-390.

INDICES

I. INDICES OF ANCIENT LITERARY SOURCES

a. Index of Classical Texts

Aristotle

Ars rhetorica
3.14.5-6 65 n. 143
1.9.20-25 72 n.180, 229 n. 75
59.33 126 n. 156

De arte poetica liber
1450a 289 n. 55
1453b-1454a 289 n. 55

Diogenes Laertius

Vitae Philosophorum
3,2 89 n. 4

Fronto

Ad Verum
14 97 n. 31

Ad Amicos
1,13 97 n. 31

Homer

Illiad
2.1-877 311 n. 130

Lucien

Historia conscribenda
55.64 303 n. 103

Lydus

The magistratibus populi romani
2,6 97 n. 31
2,7 98 n. 34
2,7-8 98 n. 35

Plato

Respublica
2.377b 65 n. 142

Pliny the Younger

Epistulae
1.18 97 n. 33
1.24 97 n. 33
3.8 97 n. 33
5.10 97 n. 33
9.34 97 n. 33
10.94-95 97 n. 33

Plutarch

Plutarchi vitae parallelae

Theseus
3,1-2 102 n. 52, 134 n. 178
4 101 n. 48
7,2-4 101 n. 46

Romulus
2,3-6 128 n. 162
2,4 100 n. 44
9,1 128 n. 162

Plutarchi vitae parallelae

Numa
3,4-5 128 n. 162
3,7 101 n. 48
5,1-7,1 128 n. 162

Themistocles
1,1-4 102 n. 52, 134 n. 178
2,1-3 101 n. 48, 103 n. 60, 104 n. 67, 127 n. 159

Lucullus
1,1 102 n. 52, 134 n. 178
1,2-5 105 n. 72

Pericles
4-6 101 n. 48
6,1-3 125 n. 152

Fabius Maximus
1,4-6 102 n. 51, 135 n. 181

Crassus
1,1-2,2 106 n. 78

Alcibiades
1,1-3 102 n. 52, 134 n. 178
1,3-5 102 n. 51
1,4-5 135 n. 181
2,1-3 125 n. 158

Coriolanus
1,1-2 102 n. 52, 134 n. 178
1,1-3 102 n. 52
2,1-2 102 n. 51, 135 n. 181

Sulla
2,1 102 n. 51, 135 n. 181

Pompey
2,1-3 101 n. 51, 135 n. 181

Brutus
1-2 102 n. 52, 134 n. 178

Demosthenes
4,1-3 102 n. 52, 134 n. 178
4,1-5 101 n. 48
5,1-4 128 n. 162
5,5-6 101 n. 48

Cicero
2,1 101 n. 46, 105 n. 72
2,2-3 101 n. 48, 108 n. 85
2,4-5 128 n. 162
3-4 101 n. 48

Alexander
1,1 93 n. 20
1,2 93 n. 18
2,3-5 100 n. 44, 103 n. 63
2,6 100 n. 44
3,5 100 n. 45
3,5-6 99 n. 41, 101 n. 46, 125 n. 151
3,7-9 128 n. 162
3,9 101 n. 46
4,1-7 135 n. 181
4,2 102 n. 51
4,8-11 128 n. 161
5,7-8 101 n. 48
6,2-8 128 n. 160
7,1 101 n. 48
8,1 101 n. 48, 108 n. 84, 128 n. 161

Cato
1,1-3 102 n. 52, 134 n. 178
1,2 99 n. 41, 105 n. 72
1,2-3 101 n. 46
1,3-5 102 n. 51, 135 n. 181
2,1-4 101 n. 47

Plutarchi vitae parallelae

Demetrius
2,2 102 n. 51, 135 n. 181

Antony
1,1-2 102 n. 52, 134 n. 178

Pyrrhus
1 102 n. 52, 134 n. 178
3,4 102 n. 51, 135 n. 181

Caius Marius
2,1 102 n. 51, 135 n. 181
3,1 102 n. 52, 128 n. 162, 134 n. 178

Agis
4,1-2 127 n. 158
7,2-4.19-20 127 n. 158
14,3-4 127 n. 158

Philopoemen
2,1-6 102 n. 51, 135 n. 181

Artaxerxes
1,1-4 102 n. 52, 134 n. 178

Pseudo-Callisthenes

Alexander
1,1-3 102 n. 52
1,1-25 95
1,4 99 n. 39
1,7-11 100 n. 44
1,8 128 n. 162
1,12 101 n. 46, 103 nn. 61, 63, 104 n. 67, 105 n. 74
1,12.16.17 105 n. 73, 137 n. 192
1,13 101 n. 48, 128 n. 161
1,13-14 128 n. 160
1,14 99 n. 41, 101 n. 47
1,16 99 n. 42, 101 n. 48, 104 n. 60
1,17 99 n. 41, 103 n. 54, 128 n. 160
1,18 103 n. 59
1,18-19 107 n. 79, 128 n. 160, 137 n. 191

Quintus Curtius

Alexander
1:1-11 95
1,4,1 100 n. 44, 102 n. 52
1,5,2 108 n. 84
4 99 n. 41
4,1 101 n. 48, 103 n. 62
4,4,21 95 n. 25
5,7 99 n. 42, 101 n. 48, 104 n. 67, 105 n. 74, 128 n. 161, 137 n. 192
10,9,3-6 95 n. 25
11,1 99 n. 41, 101 n. 48

Spartianus

Vita Hadriani
11,3 97 n. 31

Suetonius

De Vita Caesarum

Augustus
1-4 102 n. 52, 134 n. 178
5 100 n. 45
94 125 n. 153, 135 n. 182
94,1 105 n. 72
94,2 99 n. 41, 103 n. 63
94,3 105 n. 74, 137 n. 192
94,3.4 100 n. 44
94,4.8 99 n. 42
94,5-7 99 n. 41, 103 nn. 58, 65
94,6 99 n. 42, 103 n. 54

De Vita Caesarum

Tiberius
1-4 102 n. 52, 134 n. 178
14,2 99 n. 42, 100 n. 44, 103 n. 61

Caligula
7 102 n. 52, 134 n. 178
8,1 100 n. 45
19,3 97 n. 30

Claudius
2,1 100 n. 45
2,2-3,1 102 n. 49

Nero
1-5 102 n. 52, 134 n. 178
6,1 100 n. 45, 103 n. 54, 106 n. 77, 135 n. 184, 137 n. 191
6,1-2 135 n. 183, 141 nn. 211, 213
6,2 103 n. 64, 106 n. 75
7,1 101 n. 48
56 103 n. 64
57,2 97 n. 30

Galba
4 102 n. 52, 103 n. 64, 134 n. 178
4,1 100 n. 45
4,2 99 n. 42, 103 n. 64, 104 n. 67
4,2-3 103 n. 56, 104 n. 68
4,3 99 nn. 41, 42, 103 n. 65

Otho
1 102 n. 52, 134 n. 178
2,1 100 n. 45
10,1 97 n. 30

Vitellius
1-2 102 n. 52, 134 n. 178

Vespasian
2,1 100 n. 45
5,2 99 nn. 41, 42, 103 nn. 55, 57, 63, 104 n. 68

Titus
1 100 n. 45
2,1 102 n. 49
3,1 102 n. 49, 140 n. 209
5,1-2 99 n. 42

Domitian
1,1 100 n. 45
12,2 97 n. 30
14 125 n. 153, 135 n. 182
14,1 103 nn. 54, 61

Epistulae
94 97 n. 30

VIRGIL
Aeneid 311 n. 130

b. INDEX OF OLD TESTAMENT TEXTS

Genesis (Gn)
4:23–24 45 n. 65
10:2–31 294
10:2–32 310 n. 129, 311
10:32 294
12:3 321 n. 164
13:9 178 n. 96
15:2 174 n. 82
16:7–16 45 n. 64
17:15–18:15 110

Genesis (Gn)
18:14 255
18:15 110
21:1-34 40 n. 43
21:4 149 n. 5
21:22 199 n. 182
22:18 321 n. 164
25:19-28 110
25:25 130 n. 165
27–43 46
27:22.36 130 n. 16
28:12 47 n. 72
32:3 194 n. 159
32:31 194 n. 159
38:1 199 n. 182
41:51 245 n. 128

Exodus (Ex)
1 115
2:1-10 110, 115
2:6 115 n. 106
2:9 116 n. 106
2:10 129, 135 n. 184
2:11 135
3–4 45 n. 64
3:10 155
4:25 149 n. 5
13:1-2 168 n. 65
13:1-2.11-16 168 n. 61
13:2 163 n. 39, 165 n. 44, 168 n. 60
13:2.11 255 n. 160
13:2.12 156
13:2.12.15 148
13:12 163 n. 39
13:13.15 156
15 45 n. 65
15:1 36 n. 29, 258 n. 172
15:20-21 81
19:5 320
23:22 320
24:1 295 n. 74
29:36 155
33:11 194 n. 159
34:20 156
34:29 156

Leviticus (Lv)
5:7 255 n. 160
5:11 164, 169 n. 66
12 156
12:1-4 148
12:1-8 164, 169 n. 66
12:2-8 168 n. 66
12:2-4.8 255 n. 160
12:4.6 156 n. 17, 157
12:8 163 n. 39
14:32 155
15:13 155
23:29 321 n. 164

Numbers (Nb)
3:12 164
6 164 n. 41
11:16-17 295 n. 74
12:2 81
12:7-8 194 n. 159
14:18 155
18:15-16 164, 168 n. 61
20:29 174 n. 82
23–24 45 n. 65

Deuteronomy (Dt)
3:11 305 n. 107
6:16 267 n. 102
10:1.8 199 n. 182
10:8 167 n. 59
17:12 167 n. 59
18:5 167 n. 59
19:15 199
23:2 316 n. 148
32:1-43 45 n. 65
33:11 305 n. 107
33:24-25 194 n. 159
34:1-12 80 n. 219
34:10 194 n. 159

Joshua (Jos)

19:24-31	194 n. 159

Judges (Jg)

2:16.18	240 n. 110
3:9.15	240 n. 110
4:4	81
5	36 n. 29, 45 n. 65, 258 n. 172
6	45 n. 64
8–25	136 n. 187
8:8	194 n. 159
8:8.1	194 n. 159
13	45 n. 64, 110
13:2-7	116
13:3.9	121
13:6	134 n. 180
13:8-25	116
13:9	124
13:16.19	137 n. 191
13:20	124
13:22	116
13:24	135
17:7-9	244 n. 125
19:1-2	244 n. 125

Ruth (Rt)

1:1-2	244 n. 125

1 Samuel (1 S)

1–2	40 n. 43, 78, 79, 80 n. 217
1–3	45 n. 64, 46, 79 n. 216, 110, 116
1:1-2	134 n. 178
1:9	120
1:9-16	116
1:9.24	124
1:10-11	78
1:11	116
1:11.22.28	168 n. 63
1:17	116, 134 n. 180, 137 n. 191
1:19	78
1:19-28	117
1:24	78
1:24-28	79
1:28	78
2	36 n. 29, 258 n. 172
2:1-10	45 n. 65, 123
2:1-11	117
2:11	78
2:12-36	117
2:18-21	79 n. 216
2:20.21.26	79
3	117
3:3	124
3:4.8.10-14	121
3:11-13	37 n. 191
3:12-13	134 n. 191
3:19	135
16	244 n. 125
17:12.58	244 n. 125

2 Samuel (2 S)

7:9-16	239 n. 104
19:33	239 n. 101
22:2-51	45 n. 65

1 Kings (1 K)

12:25	194 n. 159
12:32	167 n. 59
14:1	199 n. 182
17–18	194 n. 159
17	279 n. 17
17:9	279
18:15	167 n. 59
18:40	279 n. 17
19	269 n. 194
19:11-12	194 n. 159

2 Kings (2 K)

1	279 n. 17
2–13	279 n. 17
2	303 n. 101
3:4	167 n. 59

2 Kings (2 K)
5:14 279
5:16 167 n. 59
6:31-32 269 n. 194
16:6 199 n. 182
18:6 199 n. 182
22:12-20 81

1 Chronicles (1 Ch)
1:1 1:1–2:2
23:28 155

Ezra (Ezr)
3:11 196 n. 171

Nehemiah (Ne)
10:33-37 168 n. 63
12:45 155

Tobit (Tb)
3:6.13 174 n. 82

Judith (Jdt)
16:23 81

Esther (Est)
7:9 245 n. 128

1 Maccabees (1 M)
1:61 149 n. 5

2 Maccabees (2 M)
7:9 174 n. 82

Job (Jb)
1:1 173 n. 78
7:21 155
18:19 245 n. 128
28:24 305 n. 128

Psalms (Ps)
2:1-2 178 n. 98
2:2 178 n. 98
2:7 266 n. 189
9:9 178 n. 98
18:3 240 n. 110
23:5 178 n. 96
46:10 305 n. 107
47:9-10 178 n. 97
48:2 239 n. 101
48:11 305 n. 107
67:3 178 n. 98
72:8 305 n. 107
77:15 178 n. 97
78:13 196 n. 171
86:10 239 n. 101
87:6 178 n. 97
88:45 156 n. 16
88:49 174 n. 82
97:6 178 n. 98
98:9 178 n. 98
99:1-2 178 n. 98
118:22 184, 313 n. 138
132:17 240 n. 110
135:5 239 n. 101
145:3 239 n. 101
148:11 178 n. 98

Proverbs (Pr)
14:9 155
17:24 305 n. 107

Eclesiasticus (Si)
8:2 291 n. 62
48:1.3.10 46 n. 70
48:22 239 n. 101
50:1-21 303 n. 101

Isaiah (Is)
1:10-11 78
2:31 81
6:9-10 335 n. 206
8 184 n. 123
8:14 184

Isaiah (Is)

8:18	184 n. 123
26:19	79 n. 215
28:16	184
38:10-70	45 n. 65
40–55	38
40:1	81
40:3	344 n. 235
40:3-5	230 n. 79, 344 n. 235
40:5	81
40:9	198 n. 180
41:8	266 n. 189
41:8.9	350 n. 251
41:27	198 n. 180
42:1	266 n. 189, 350 n. 251
42:6	81, 350 n. 250
42:16	330 n. 193
43:10	350 n. 251
44:1.2.21	350 n. 251
45:4	350 n. 251
45:25	81
49:1	310 n. 127
49:6	306, 350 n. 250
46:9	305 n. 107
46:13	81, 180
48:10	305 n. 107
48:20	350 n. 251
49:5.6.7	350 n. 251
49:6	81, 180, 325 n. 175, 330 n. 193
50:6	350 n. 250
50:10	350 n. 251
51:4	330 n. 193
52:7	198 n. 180
52:8-12	81
52:9	81, 198
52:10	325 n. 175
52:13	350 n. 251
53:4-7	350 n. 250
53:11	350 n. 251
56:7	287 n. 48
57:19	310 n. 127
60:1.19	180
61:1-2	268
62:11	305 n. 107
66:18-20	310 n. 129

Jeremiah (Jr)

12:15	321 n. 165
23:5	241 n. 111
32:27	255

Ezekiel (Ezk)

14:17	79 n. 215
17:22-23	284
29:21	240 n. 110
36:24	320 n. 162
36:28	320 n. 162
37:1-14	79 n. 215
37:23	320 n. 162
38–39	310 n. 129

Daniel (Dn)

4:8.18	172 n. 75
4:11	284
5:12	172 n. 75
6:4	172 n. 75
7–10	45 n. 64
7:9	46
8:16	225 n. 65
9:20-21	46 n. 70
9:20-26	46
9:21	225 n. 65
9:21-24	46 n. 70
9:24	225, 226
9:25	46
10:7	46
10:7.12	46 n. 70
10:15	225 n. 65
10:16-17	46 n. 70
12:6	155
12:16-17	46

Hosea (Ho)

6:2	79 n. 215

Joel (Jl)
3:1-5a 309
3:3-4 309 n. 124
3:5 309 n. 125
3:5a 309 n. 124

Amos (Am)
9:11-12 321 n. 165
9:12 190 n. 146

Jonah (Jon)
2 36 n. 29, 258 n. 172

Micah (Mi)
5:2 243 n. 119
5:3 305
6:4 81

Zechariah (Zc)
2:15 320 n. 162
3:8 241 n. 111
6:12 241 n. 111
6:15 310 n. 127
9:10 305 n. 107

Malachi (Ml)
2:6 46
3:1 46 n. 70, 225
3:1.23 46 n. 70
3:1-24 225, 226
3:1.23-24 46 n. 70
3:23 46 n. 70
3:23-24 225 n. 64

c. Index of Pseudoepigrapha

1 Enoch
89:14.18-20.59 294 n. 74

2 Baruch 113 n. 102, 303 n. 101

3 Enoch
17:8 295 n. 75
18:2 295 n. 75
30:2 295 n. 75

3 Maccabees
6:33 196 n. 171

The Fourth Book of Ezra 113 n. 102, 303 n. 103

Jubilees 90 n. 6
22:7-9 79

The Life of Adam and Eve 90 n. 6

The Lives of the Prophets 89 n. 6, 90 n. 6

d. Index of Dead Sea Scrolls

4Q174 239 n. 104
1QH 2.8-10 184 n. 123
1QM 14.10-11 184 n. 123

e. INDEX OF HELLENISTIC JEWISH TEXTS

JOSEPHUS

Antiquitates Judaicae

1,6,1-4 310 n. 129
2,9 50 n. 84, 114
2,9,2 119 n. 114, 120 n. 124, 121 n. 128, 130 n. 167, 134 n. 180, 136 n. 186, 137 n. 190
2,9,3 119 n. 115, 120 n. 120, 121 n. 126, 130 n. 166, 134 n. 180, 137 n. 190
2,9,3-4 119 n. 116, 121 n. 129
2,9,3.7 123 n. 135, 138 n. 193
2,9,4 118 n. 113, 136 n. 189
2,9,4.7 136 nn. 188, 189
2,9,5 116 n. 106
2,9,6 119 n. 117, 120 nn. 118, 119, 129 n. 165, 134 nn. 178, 179, 135 n. 181
2,9,7 122 n. 130, 123 n. 134, 131 n. 168, 138 n. 194
5,8 50 n. 84, 114
5,8,1-2 136 n. 187
5,8,2 123 n. 137, 131 n. 169, 134 n.180, 137 n. 190,
5,8,2 138 n.196
5,8,2.3 121 n. 125
5,8,3 116 n. 108, 118 n. 113
5,8,4 123 n. 136, 12 n. 145, 135 n.184, 138 n. 195
5,10 50 n. 84, 114
5,10,1 117 n. 110, 120 n. 120
5,10,1.2 121 n. 128, 12 n. 139, 136 n.186, 138 n. 197
5,10,3 135 n. 184
5,10,3-4 134 n. 180, 137 n. 190
5,10,3.4 134 n. 180
5,10,4 121 n. 127
16,10,1 245 n. 128
20,6,1 315 n. 145
20,12,1 114 n. 104

Contra Apionem

1.18 245 n. 128

Vita

1-2 114
1,1 120 n. 119
1,2 119 n. 117

PHILO

De vita Moysis

1,1-31 112
1,4 110 n. 91
1,5-7 120 n. 119, 134 n. 178
1,9 120 n. 118, 134 n. 179
1,13 115 n. 106

De vita Moysis
1,17 129 n. 165, 135 n. 184
1,21-23 119 n. 117
1,21-24 135 n. 181
6 50 n. 84

Pseudo-Philo

Liber antiquitatum biblicarum
1.2.4 134 n. 178
9,3.6 120 n. 120
9,6 136 n. 189
9,7 118 n. 112
9,7-8 129 n. 163, 134 n. 180, 137 n. 190
9,9-10 120 n. 122
9,10 119 n. 116, 12 n. 125, 129 n.164, 134 n.180, 136 n. 187, 137 n.190, 138 n. 193
9,10.16 123 n. 135, 135 n. 184
9,14-15 115 n. 106
9,15 119 n. 116, 120 n. 123
9,16 21 n.128, 122 n. 131, 129 n.165, 136 n. 186
42,1 120 n. 119, 134 n. 178, 134 n. 178
42,2 124 n. 146
42,2.5 137 n. 191
42,3 116 n. 107,
123 n. 137, 134 n. 180, 135 n. 184, 136
123 n. 187, 137 n. 190, 138 n. 196
42,3.5 121 n. 125
42,5 118 n. 112, 124 n. 147
42,6 116 n. 108
42,7 21 n. 129, 136 n. 189
42,9 118 n. 113, 124 n. 145
47,7-8 134 n. 180, 137 n. 190
49 117 n. 109, 136 n. 188
49,7 138 nn. 197, 198
49,7-8 119 n. 114, 121 n. 126
49,8 122 n. 132, 123 n. 139
50,3.7.8 120 n. 121
50,8 123 n. 139, 138 n. 197
51,1 120 n. 118, 135 n. 184
51,2 123 n. 144, 138 n. 202
51,3-4 120 n. 121, 123 n. 138
51,3-5 137 n. 191
51,3-6 134 n. 180, 137 n. 190, 139 n. 207
51,3.6.7 123 n. 141, 138 n. 199
51,6 123 nn. 142, 143, 138 nn. 200, 201
51,6.7 123 n. 138, 138 n. 197
51,7 122 n. 133,
136 n. 189, 137 n. 191
53 121 n. 127, 136 n. 186
53,5 124 n. 148

f. Index of New Testament Texts (Except Luke 1–2 and Lk 2:22-39)

Matthew (Mt)

1:1 247 n. 136
1:1-16 47 n. 74
1:2-16 30
1:20-24 139 n. 204
1:20-25 30
1:21 141 n. 212, 175, 238 n. 100, 356 n. 261
1:23 36 n. 27, 47 n. 74, 248 n. 143
1–2 30, 35 n. 24, 36 n. 27, 47 n. 74, 67 n. 151, 71
2:1-12 30 n. 3, 259 n. 179
2:6 36 n. 27, 47 n. 74, 248 n. 143, 259 n. 179
2:11 186 n. 131
2:12 139 n. 204
2:13-15 30 n. 3, 139 n. 204
2:13-18 259 n. 179
2:15 36 n. 27, 47 n. 74, 248 n. 143
2:16 30 n. 3, 186 n.131
2:16-18 30 n. 3
2:18 36 n. 27, 47 n. 74, 248 n. 143
2:19 36 n. 27
2:19-20 139 n. 204
2:19-23 30 n. 3, 31 n. 4
2:23 30 n. 3, 47 n. 74, 248 n. 143
3:1-12 264 n. 185
3:16 266 nn. 186, 188, 189
4:4.7.10 255 n. 160
4:18-22 285 n. 43
4:21 34 n. 21
5:9 239 n. 102
5:14 330 n. 192
5:15 283
7:13-27 284
7:23 284 n. 38
9:37-38 293 n. 68
10:1 190 n. 148
10:2 34 n. 21
10:5-6 297 n. 80, 315 n. 145
10:5b-6 296
10:7-16 293 n. 68
10:11-13 296
10:34 188 n. 140
10:40 293 n. 68
11:20-24 293 n. 68
11:25 199 n. 182
12:1 199 n. 182
13:15 178 n. 97
13:31-32 283
13:53-58 278 n. 14
13:55 34 n. 21
14:1 199 n. 182
14:13-21 294 n. 70
15:8 178 n. 97
15:19 191 n. 150, 277 n. 13
15:21-28 297 n. 80
15:21-39 282 n. 29
15:28 199 n. 182
15:32-38 294 n. 70
16:23 245 n. 128
17:1 34 n. 21
19:28 195 n. 164
20:28 192 n. 153
21:10 282 n. 28
21:13 255 n. 160
21:23 288 n. 49
21:42 184

Matthew (Mt)
22:2-10 285
22:7 284 n. 38
22:9-10 285
22:11-14 285 n. 40
22:23 291 n. 61
24:24 190 n. 148
25:14 186 n. 132
27:1 190 n. 148
27:17-20 290 n. 59
27:20-26.39-40 290 n. 59
27:25 243 n. 121, 290 n. 59
27:39 289 n. 54
27:56 34 n. 21
27:62 291 n. 64
28:7 301 n. 96
28:19-20 307

Mark (Mk)
1:1 59, 247 n. 136
1:1-8 59 n. 122, 227, 164 n. 185
1:10 265 n. 186, 266 nn. 188, 189
1:16-20 285 n. 43
1:44 155
3:7-8 279 n. 18
3:13-19 195 n. 164
3:18 34 n. 21
3:21 58
4:1–6:45 278 n. 14
4:21 283
4:30-32 283
5:7 239 n. 102
6:1-6 58, 278 n. 14
6:3 32, 34 n. 21
6:8-9 293 n. 68
6:32-44 294 n. 70
6:43 195 n. 164
7:21 191 n. 150, 277 n. 13
7:24-30 297 n. 80
7:24–8:10 282 n. 29
8:1-9 294 n. 70
8:20 194 n. 163
8:33 245 n. 128
10:35 34 n. 21
10:45 192 n. 153
11:11 282 n. 28
11:11.15.19.27 288 n. 49
12:18 186 n. 130, 291 n. 61
13:3 34 n. 21
13:22 190 n. 148
14:33 34 n. 21
15:8-10 290 n. 59
15:11-15.29-30 290 n. 59
15:16-20 292
15:29 289 n. 54
15:36 293 n. 66
15:40 34 n. 21
16:1 34 n. 21
16:7 301
16:9-20 60 n. 126, 307 n. 115
16:15 307 n. 115
16:20 307 n. 115

Luke (Lk)
1:1 215 n. 18
1:1-2 215 n. 19
1:1-4 22 n. 3, 29 n. 1, 59, 66 n. 146, 68 n. 160
1:2 32 n. 9, 33 n. 16
1:3 215 nn. 18, 19, 307 n. 116
1:3-4 207 n. 207, 368
1:5 29 n. 1, 231
1:5-22 44
1:5-25 23 n. 6, 39, 40, 56, 57 n. 114, 61 n. 130,

Luke (Lk)
1:5-25 141 n. 211, 165 n. 48, 221, 224 n. 62, 238, 262
1:5-56 223 n. 59
1:5-80 40, 61 n. 130
1:5–2:52 29 n. 3, 60 n. 124, 66 n. 148, 68 n. 160
1:5–3:38 221
1:5–4:15 221
1:5–4:30 221
1:5–4:44 221
1:6 228 n. 72, 249
1:6.9.11.25 240 n. 106, 241
1:7.18 194 n. 160
1:8 302 n. 98
1:9 228 n. 71, 251, 253, 302
1:10 251, 277 n. 11
1:11 46, 233
1:11-20 139 n. 205, 140, 277
1:11.26 66 n. 150
1:12 250
1:12-13 250
1:13 231, 248, 363 n. 2
1:13-17 142, 233
1:13-20 42
1:14-17 39 n. 41, 233
1:14.15.16.17 233
1:15 173 n. 76, 228 n.72, 231
1:15-17 236 n. 96
1:15.35.41.67 172 n. 75
1:15.41.67.80 66 n. 150
1:16 46, 242
1:16-17 228 n. 72, 233
1:16.77 74
1:17 46, 225 n. 64, 228 n. 72, 241
1:17.76 228 n. 72
1:17b.77 229
1:18 228 n. 72, 233
1:18.19 233
1:19 46, 166 n. 51, 167 n. 58, 248, 250 n. 147
1:19-22 228 n. 72
1:19.26 230, 231
1:20 250
1:20.21 248
1:21.22 251
1:22 302 n. 98
1:23 153, 252
1:24 248, 250, 363 n. 2
1:24.26.57 33
1:26 31 n. 4, 47 n. 72, 232, 234 n. 87, 248, 252, 253
1:26-27 181 n. 110, 252
1:26-29 46 n. 70
1:26.36 225 n. 65
1:26-38 30, 39 n. 42, 44, 46 n. 71, 61 n. 130, 139 n. 205, 140, 164 n. 42, 221, 224 n. 62, 251, 262, 277
1:26.39.59 232
1:27 41, 231
1:27.32-33.69 173 n. 80
1:28 228 n. 72, 234 n. 87, 253 n. 157
1:29 142, 250
1:29-30 234
1:30 234, 250
1:30-35 42 n. 53, 259 n. 176
1:30-37 142
1:30-38 42
1:30-33.35-38 234
1:31 72, 219 n. 41, 231, 234, 238, 242, 245 n. 126, 247 n. 137, 249,

Luke (Lk)

1:31 363 n. 2
1:31-32 265 n. 187
1:31-35 41
1:32 141, 142, 228 n. 72, 234 n. 89, 239, 243, 246 n. 132
1:32-33 234 n. 89, 238, 239
1:32-33.35b 234
1:32-35 62
1:32.35 241, 246, 263 n. 182, 265, 269
1:32.35.76 239 n. 102
1:33 142, 228 n. 72, 234 n. 88
1:34 142, 234
1:34-35 228 n. 72
1:34-38 228 n. 72, 230
1:35 141, 165 n. 44, 186 n. 132, 219 n. 38, 228 n. 72, 231, 234, 238, 239, 241 n. 111, 247 n. 139, 257 n. 166, 265, 308 n. 119
1:36 231
1:36-37 234
1:37 255
1:38 153
1:38a 234 n. 87
1:38b 234 n. 87
1:39 232, 252
1:39-45 44, 251
1:39-56 61 n. 130, 78, 221, 230, 262, 277
1:40 252
1:41 139, 173 n. 76, 186 n. 131, 231, 234, 249, 250 n. 147
1:41-44 363 n. 2
1:41.45.53-55 247 n. 133, 256 n. 163
1:42 235 n. 90, 239, 246 n. 132
1:42a 228 n. 72
1:42-43 186 n. 131, 259 n. 176
1:42-45 42, 139, 182 n. 113, 235
1:42-56 223 n. 59
1:43 142, 239, 241, 243, 246 n. 132, 267, 269
1:43-44 41
1:45 235, 363 n. 2
1:46 235
1:46-50 30 n. 3
1:46-55 36, 42, 82, 182 n. 113, 235, 247 n. 134
1:46-56 44, 142, 176 n. 88
1:47 242 n. 116
1:47-49 257
1:47.69.71.74 219 n. 41, 247 n. 137, 256 n. 164
1:48 38, 39, 240, 258 n. 173
1:49 235
1:50 180 n. 104, 235 n. 92
1:51 235, 240 n. 107
1:52 235, 259 n. 177
1:53 235, 259 n. 177
1:54 38, 235, 240
1:54-55 257
1:55 240, 242, 248 n. 143
1:55.68.69 345 n. 239
1:55.70.73 178 n. 95
1:55.70.72 363 n. 2
1:56 153, 232
1:57 232
1:57-58 39, 44

Luke (Lk)
1:57-79 221, 251
1:57-80 61 n. 130, 165 n. 48, 223
1:58.65 252
1:59 232
1:59-63 39
1:59-66 44
1:59-79 262
1:60.63 231
1:63 236
1:64-65 46
1:65 250, 252
1:66 236, 250
1:67 140, 173 n. 76,
231, 249, 250 n. 147, 302 n. 98
1:67-79 30 n. 3, 82, 139 n. 206, 222 n. 58, 235 n. 94
1:68 222 n. 58, 241 n. 111, 247 n.134, 257
1:68-70 36, 242
1:68-73 242
1:68-75 259 n. 176
1:68-79 42, 44, 142, 176 n. 88
1:68.77 38
1:68.78 67
1:68.69.78 243
1:69 141, 173 n. 80, 240, 242
1:69.71 242 n. 115
1:69-71.74a 247 n. 134
1:70-73 248 n. 143
1:71 38
1:71.77 222 n. 58
1:72 242 n. 115
1:72.73 242 n. 115
1:72.74b-75 247 n. 134
1:73 242 n. 115
1:75.78 242 n. 115
1:76 38, 46 n. 70, 228 n. 72, 236, 241
1:76b 241
1:76-77 39, 163 n. 37, 236
1:77 242 n. 115, 247 n. 134
1:78 240, 242 n. 114
1:78-79 163 n. 37, 219 n. 39, 247 nn. 134, 140, 257, 329 n. 187
1:79 38, 219 n. 40, 222 n. 58, 241, 243, 247 n. 141, 257 n. 168, 258 n. 173
1:79b 242 n. 115
1:80 38, 223 n. 58, 252, 254
2:1-2 228 n. 72
2:1-3 30, 31, 41
2:1-5 236
2:1-7 44, 142 n. 214
2:1-20 56, 57 n. 114, 149, 150, 151, 152 n. 8, 224 n. 62, 251
2:1-21 72, 221, 262, 277
2:4 41, 244, 252
2:4-5 31 n. 4
2:4-5.16.19 162
2:4.11 173 n. 80
2:5 41
2:6 33, 151, 225 n. 65
2:6-7 42 n. 53, 232
2:7 163, 236
2:8 148
2:8-20 36 n. 26, 41, 139 n. 205, 140, 142 n. 216
2:9 66 n. 130, 236, 249

Luke (Lk)

2:9.10 231, 250
2:9.14 219 n. 41, 247 n. 142, 257 n. 169
2:10 178 n. 97, 243, 244
2:10-11 182 n. 113, 345 n. 239
2:10-12 142
2:10-14 44
2:10-12.14 236
2:10.13.15 236
2:11 46, 62, 66 n. 150, 141, 173 n. 80, 192 n. 153, 219 nn. 37, 41, 225, 228 n. 72, 237, 238, 242, 244, 246 n. 132, 247 nn. 137, 138, 256 n. 164, 257 n. 165, 267, 269
2:11-14 259 n. 176
2:11.26 268
2:11.30.49 74
2:12 186 n. 129, 363 n. 2
2:13 236
2:13-14 228 n. 72
2:13.15 231
2:14 36, 42, 44, 182 n. 113, 219 n. 40, 241 n. 112, 243, 247 n. 141, 255, 257 n. 168
2:15 140, 149, 150 n. 6
2:16 249 n. 146, 363 n. 2
2:16.17.21 163 n. 36
2:16.22.27 41 n. 49
2:17 68 n. 157, 249 n. 146
2:19 236, 250
2:19.33.51 41
2:19.51b 32 n. 13
2:20 150 n. 6, 153, 186 n. 131, 247 n. 137
2:20.25.38 256 n. 164
2:21 44, 72, 83, 84, 141 n. 212, 148, 149, 150, 151, 152 n. 8, 156 n. 20, 165 n. 48, 169 n. 67, 175, 222, 223 n. 58, 231, 232, 245 n. 126, 249 n. 145
2:22.42 232
2:22-50 277
2:22-52 223, 308
2:27.37.46 253
2:27.43.52 72
2:33.48.50 250
2:40 41, 54, 140 n. 209, 152, 153. 217 n. 28, 222, 223 n. 58, 249 n. 146
2:40-41 153 n. 12
2:40-52 30 n. 3, 45, 139 n. 209, 141 n. 211, 165 n. 48, 212 n. 4, 222, 237, 262, 276
2:40.52 139, 140, 223 n. 58, 246
2:41 153
2:41-42 140
2:41-52 41, 54, 55, 72
2:41.43 224
2:41.43.46 151
2:42 30 n. 3, 151,

Luke (Lk)
2:42 153 n. 12, 224
2:43 159 n. 26, 237, 249 n. 146
2:44 253
2:46 152, 228 n. 71
2:46-47 253, 277
2:47 152, 153, 246
2:48 41 n. 49, 188 n. 140, 224, 249 n. 146
2:48b 246 n. 129
2:48b.49 245
2:48-50 41, 152
2:49 72, 141, 165 n. 44, 169 n. 64, 188 n. 140, 228 n. 72, 245, 246 n. 132, 263 n. 182, 265, 269, 277, 308 n. 118, 332 n. 200
2:51 153, 224, 245 n. 128, 250
2:52 41, 54, 140 n. 209, 217 n. 28, 221, 223 n. 58, 249 n. 146, 254 n. 139, 355 n. 259
3 58, 59, 60 n. 124, 221
3–4 263, 270
3–24 31, 35 n. 25, 52 n. 97, 56, 221
3:1 59
3:1-2 59
3:1-3 264
3:1-18 215 n. 21, 222 n. 57, 252, 262, 264, 271
3:1-20.23-25 57
3:1–4:30 263
3:2 252 n. 155, 264
3:2b 264
3:2.15-20 61 n. 128
3:2b-20 229 n. 78
3:3 265
3:3-6 236 n. 96
3:4 252 n. 155
3:4a 265
3:4b-6 271
3:4-14 264
3:4b-6 264
3:6 230 n. 79, 343 n. 233, 344 n. 235
3:7-9 264
3:7-14 264
3:7.10.15.18 265
3:8 305 n. 106
3:15 264
3:16 264, 269
3:16-17 264
3:16.22 231 n. 81
3:19-20 215 n. 21, 263 n. 183
3:21 266
3:21-22 215 n. 21, 263, 265, 271
3:22 263 n. 182, 265, 188, 268, 269
3:23 61 n. 128
3:23-38 30, 139 n. 204, 263 n. 183
3:23.38 263 n. 183
3:28 283 n. 34
4:1 231 n. 81, 266, 267, 303 n. 102
4:1-13 263, 266, 271
4:2 267
4:4.8 267 n. 193
4:4.8.10-12 271
4:4.8.12 267
4:5 266

Luke (Lk)

4:9 266
4:10 267 n. 193
4:10-11 267
4:12 267, 267 n. 193, 269
4:13 266
4:16 254 n. 159, 268, 269, 343 n. 233
4:16-17 278
4:16-22 280
4:16-30 57, 222 n. 57, 263, 268, 269, 271, 278, 328 n. 185, 349 n. 247
4:16–9:50 280 n. 20, 281
4:17 278
4:18 269
4:18-19 268, 269, 271, 279, 349 n. 247
4:20 268
4:21 192 n. 153, 268, 269, 303 n. 102, 305 n. 106
4:22 61 n. 128, 268, 328, 342 n. 229
4:22.28 349 n. 247
4:23-30 280, 343 n. 230
4:24 268
4:25-26 279 n. 18, 349 n. 247
4:25-27 268, 270, 278, 279
4:25.27 280
4:26 269
4:27 268, 279 n. 18
4:28 280 n. 21
4:28-29 270, 280, 328
4:29 190 n. 148, 269, 280 n. 22, 281 nn. 22, 24, 300, 328 n. 185
4:30 280
4:30-32 60 n. 124
4:32 286 n. 46
4:40 286 n. 46
4:43 332 n. 200
5:1-11 285 n. 43
5:1.17 286 n. 46
5:3-11 218 n. 31
5:10 34 n. 21
5:11 286 n. 46
5:18-25 229 n. 77
5:21 305 n. 106
5:21-22 287 n. 47
5:22 191 n. 150, 277 n. 13
5:24 303 n. 102
5:26 303 n. 102
5:33 61 n. 128
6:1-5 218 n. 31
6:4 337 n. 209
6:6-11 287
6:8 191 n. 150, 277 n. 13, 287 n. 47
6:12 218 n. 31
6:13 286 n. 46, 294 n. 73
6:14 34 n. 21
6:15 34 n. 21
6:17 286 n. 46
6:17-18 218 n. 31
6:17-19 279 n. 18
6:18-19 286 n. 46
6:20-49 286 n. 46
6:35 239 n. 102, 241 n. 112
6:46-49 185
7:1-10 279 n. 18
7:1-17 57, 279 n. 18
7:11 286 n. 46
7:11-17 279 n. 18
7:16 67, 241 n. 111, 286 n. 46

Luke (Lk)

7:18-33 61 n. 128
7:26-27 59
7:29 243 n. 121
7:29-30 287 n. 47
7:31-35 57
7:36 354
7:36-50 57
7:37 291 n. 64
7:48-50 345 n. 239
7:50 192 n. 153, 358 n. 263
8:1 215 n. 19
8:3 34
8:4.40 286 n. 46
8:4–9:16 278 n. 14
8:11-15 283 n. 33
8:12 345 n. 239
8:16 283 n. 33
8:19 188 n. 140
8:19-21 61 n. 128
8:26-39 279 n. 18
8:26-56 57
8:28 239 n. 102, 241 n. 112
8:32-34 279 n. 18
8:47 243 n. 121
8:49-56 229 n. 77
8:51 34 n. 17
9:1 294 n. 69
9:1-6 293
9:1-6.10 294 n. 69
9:2 294 n. 69
9:3 294 n. 69
9:3-5 293 n. 69
9:7-9.19 61 n. 128
9:10-17 286 n. 46, 294 n. 70
9:11 286 n. 46
9:13 243 n. 121
9:18-21 263 n. 182
9:20 263 n. 182
9:22 183 n. 115, 287 n. 47, 300, 332 n. 200, 333, 352 n. 254
9:22.44 325 n. 177
9:28-36 218 n. 31, 263 n. 182, 333 n. 202
9:28.54 34 n. 21
9:30 201 n. 188
9:35 263 n. 182
9:37 286 n. 46
9:43b-45 333
9:44 183 n. 115, 300, 352 n. 254
9:45 190 n. 148
9:46-47 191 n. 150, 277 n. 13
9:50 287
9:51 263 n. 182, 281, 332 n. 199, 334 n. 204
9:51-53 315 n. 145
9:51.53 281 n. 26
9:51-56 332, 333
9:51–19:44 280 n. 20, 281
9:52 190 n. 148
9:52.56 296 n. 78
9:52–19:44 286 n. 44
9:53 280 n. 20
10:1 294, 296 n. 78
10:1-12 293
10:1-20 293
10:1-16.17-20 294 n. 69
10:2.3.4.7.8.9 293 n. 67
10:3 295 n. 74
10:4 293 nn. 68, 69, 294 n. 69
10:5-7 296
10:6.13 293 n. 67
10:7 296
10:7-8 296

Luke (Lk)

10:8	296
10:8-11	297
10:8-12	295 n. 76
10:9	295 n. 76
10:9a	294 n. 69
10:9b.11	294 n. 69
10:11	297 n. 82
10:13-14	279 n. 18
10:13-15	293 n. 68, 297 n. 81
10:16	293 n. 68, 297, 358
10:17	294 n. 69, 295 n. 76
10:17-18	295 n. 76
10:17-20	293 n. 68
10:18-19	295 n. 76
10:19	295 n. 76
10:21	199 n. 182, 231 n. 81
10:21.22	181 n. 109
10:25	286
10:26	169 n. 66
10:29-37	315 n. 145
11:1	61 n. 128
11:13	231 n. 81
11:14	286
11:23	287
11:19-32	186
11:27	189
11:29-32	279 n. 18, 283 n. 33
11:33	283
11:37	354
11:37-53	287
11:38	287
11:42	332 n. 200
11:49	299
11:51	337 n. 209
11:53-54	287
12:1	286
12:2	181 n. 109
12:10.12	231 n. 81
12:11-12	298 n. 86
12:12	199 n. 182, 332 n. 200
12:36	198 n. 176
12:51	181 n. 125, 286 n. 45
12:51-53	188 n. 140
12:51–13:9	286 n. 45
12:52	175 n. 85, 286 n. 45
13:1	199 n. 182
13:1.31	199 n. 182
13:10-17	57, 287
13:13	325 n. 177
13:17	286
13:18-19	283
13:18-21	57
13:18–14:24	286 n. 44
13:22-30	284
13:22.33	281 n. 26
13:27	284 n. 38
13:29	284
13:31	291 n. 64, 354
13:31-33	183 n. 115, 333 n. 202
13:31.34	300
13:33	332 n. 200
13:34-35	185
13:35	337 n. 209
14:1	287, 291 n. 64
14:1-6	287
14:15-24	284
14:18-20	285
14:21	285
14:23	285
14:25	286
14:31	186 n. 132
15:1	287
15:2	198 n. 176
15:4-10	57

Luke (Lk)

15:32 332 n. 200
16:14-15 287
16:16 61 n. 128, 201 n. 188
16:16.17 169 n. 66
17:11 281 n. 26, 333
17:18 315 n. 145
17:19 192 n. 153, 345 n. 239, 358 n. 263
17:25 332 n. 200
17:30 181 n. 109
18:1 332 n. 200
18:1-8 57
18:15 286
18:24 283 n. 32
18:31 281 n. 26, 352 n. 254
18:31-33 183 n. 115
18:31-34 333
18:32 300
18:33 300
18:36 286
18:43 243 n. 121
19:1 282 n. 27
19:3 286
19:5 332 n. 200
19:5.9 192 n. 153
19:7-10 345 n. 239
19:9 358 n. 263
19:10 192 n. 153
19:11 282 n. 27
19:24 166 n. 51
19:28 282 n. 27
19:29 180 n. 104, 282 n. 27
19:29.37.41 282
19:37 282 nn. 27, 28
19:37-38 286, 333 n. 203
19:37-40 33 n. 17
19:38 36, 241 n. 112,
19:38 244 n. 123, 292
19:39 291 n. 64
19:41 282 n. 27
19:42 175 n. 85
19:44 67
19:45 282 n. 28, 336
19:45-48 333 n. 203
19:45–21 291
19:45–21:38 280 n. 20, 287, 288
19:45–24:53 281
19:46 255 n. 160, 287 n. 48, 337 n. 209
19:47 280 n. 20, 290, 291, 292
19:47-48 288, 289, 290, 312 n. 136
19:47b-48 291
19:48 289, 303 n. 102
20:1 288, 291
20:1-2 291 n. 61, 292
20:1.9.26.45 289
20:2 313 n. 139
20:4-6 61 n. 128
20:9.45 288
20:9-18 290
20:14-15 300
20:15 281 n. 24
20:16-18 185
20:17 313 n. 139
20:19 199 n. 182, 289, 291, 292, 299, 312 n. 136
20:19-20 291 n. 64
20:20 190 n. 148, 292, 300
20:25 245 n. 128
20:26 290, 312 n. 136
20:27 186 n. 130, 312 n. 133, 343 n. 233

Luke (Lk)

20:27-39 291 n. 61
20:45 243 n. 121
20:46 292 n. 65
21:1-4.5-7 288
21:5-36 290
21:6-24 277 n. 10
21:9 332 n. 200
21:12 299, 300, 352 n. 254
21:12.16 300
21:12-17 297, 298, 311, 349 n. 246
21:12.17 298, 358
21:12.13.15 298 n. 84
21:12-19 358, 367
21:13 298 n. 84, 304 n. 104, 325 n. 176, 358, 368
21:15 186 n. 130, 298, 343 n. 233
21:16 300
21:17 300, 326, 365
21:23 178 n. 97
21:24 184
21:27 292
21:37 288
21:37-38 288, 290
21:38 243 n. 121, 289, 290, 312 n. 136
22–23 291
22:1-2 291
22:2 289, 291, 300, 312 n. 136
22:2.6 303 n. 102
22:3 33 n. 17, 354
22:4 291 n. 61
22:4.6 347
22:4.6.21-22 300
22:4.52 291
22:7.37 332 n. 200
22:10-20 337
22:14-38 33 n. 17
22:19-20 186 n. 132, 192 n. 153
22:30 294 n. 73, 341 n. 223
22:32 354 n. 256
22:33 180 n. 105
22:39-46 108 n. 86
22:39-53a 33 n. 17
22:42 333 n. 203
22:43 231 n. 82
22:47 314 n. 142
22:47-52 205 n. 200
22:47-54 333 n. 203
22:48 347
22:52 291, 340 n. 220
22:52a 289 n. 56
22:52b 289 n. 56
22:52c 289 n. 56
22:53 288
22:53b-71 33 n. 17
22:54.66 300
22:54-71 334 n. 203
22:57 354
22:57.58.60 347
22:62 354 n. 256
22:63-64 333 n. 203
22:63-65 293 n. 66
22:66 289 n. 56, 313 n. 139
22:66-67 291
22:66-70 313 n. 139
22:66-71 314 n. 142, 334 n. 203
22:69 175 n. 85
23:1 289 n. 56
23:1-2 290
23:1-5 334 n. 203
23:1-7 300 n. 92
23:1-25 33 n. 17
23:2-7 291

Luke (Lk)
23:2.4.13 291
23:3.37.38 339 n. 215
23:4.13.15 292 n. 66, 352
23:5 305 n. 106
23:8-12 291, 300 n. 92, 334 n. 203
23:10 291
23:11.15 292 n. 66
23:13 289, 290 n. 57, 291, 340 n. 218
23:13-25 334 n. 203
23:13-35 334 n. 203
23:13.35 291
23:14 290
23:18 290 n. 57
23:20 292 n. 66, 352
23:21 290 n. 57
23:23 290 n. 57
23:25 292, 300
23:25-56 33 n. 17
23:26 292
23:26.33 281 n. 22
23:27 289
23:27.35 290
23:32 300
23:34.46 314 n. 142
23:35 288 n. 51, 289
23:36 292 n. 66
23:43 192 n. 153, 345 n. 239, 358 n. 263
23:47 169 n. 64, 292 n. 66, 334 n. 203, 352
23:48 289
23:49 34
23:50 291 n. 63, 354
23:51 198 n. 176
23:66 293 n. 66
24 31 n. 9, 301 n. 94
24:1-22 68 n. 157
24:3 68 n. 157
24:4 303 n. 102
24:5 303 n. 102
24:5.23 68 n. 157
24:7 301 n. 96
24:7.20 300
24:7.26.27 45
24:7.26.44 325 n. 177, 332 n. 200
24:9 68 n. 157
24:10 34
24:12 68 n. 157
24:13-35 202 n. 193
24:19 243 n. 121
24:20 288 n. 51, 291
24:21 192 n. 153, 306 n. 110
24:23 231 n. 82
24:26 183 n. 115
24:27 67 n. 154
24:27.42 305 n. 106
24:33 302
24:36-53 301
24:38 191 n. 150, 277 n. 13
24:44 169 n. 66, 343 n. 233
24:44-49 301
24:46-49 349 n. 246
24:46-49.50 302
24:47 301 n. 95, 303, 306, 325, 329 n. 190, 348
24:47a 304, 305, 306
24:47b 304, 305 n. 106
24:47-48 367
24:48 303, 304, 325 n. 176, 358, 368
24:49 241 n. 111, 301 nn. 95, 96, 302
24:49a 303

Luke (Lk)

24:49b	303
24:50-51	303, 334 n. 204
24:52	335
24:52-53	277 n. 10, 303, 336
24:53	287, 302

John (Jn)

1:1-3	62
1:1-18	59 n. 120, 69
1:19-34	59 n. 120
2:1-11	41 n. 52
2:6	155
3:25	155
4:9	315 n. 145
4:22	315 n. 145
6:7	190 n. 148
8:2	243 n. 121
8:12	330 n. 192
8:16	246 n. 129
8:17	255
8:48	315 n. 145
8:51	174 n. 82
9:5	330 n. 192
10:30	246 n. 129
11:37	190 n. 148
12:12-19	33 n. 17
13:1-17	33 n. 17
13:2.27	33 n. 17
18:1-12	33 n. 17
18:3	291 n. 64
18:13-28	33 n. 17
18:29–19:16	33 n. 17
19:12	186 n. 130, 277 n. 13
19:17-42	33 n. 17
19:25-27	33, 188 n. 139
21:1-2	34 n. 21

Acts

1	301 n. 95
1–2	66
1–8:4	307
1:1	22 n. 3, 139 n. 208, 305 n. 106
1:1-12	307 n. 114
1:2	303, 332 n. 200
1:3	166 n. 52, 167
1:4	302
1:4a	303
1:4b.8a	303
1:5	301 n. 95
1:5.22	61 n. 128
1:5-23	336
1:6	306 n. 110
1:8	301, 306, 307, 308 n. 119, 325 nn. 175, 176, 330, 335, 348, 349 n. 246, 351, 358, 367, 368
1:8a	304
1:8b	303, 304, 306
1:8c	303, 304, 305, 306
1:9-11	322 n. 169
1:10	166 n. 51, 303 n. 102
1:11	301 n. 95, 303 n. 102
1:11.22	332 n. 200
1:12	308 n. 117
1:12-13	336
1:12-14	308 n. 117, 336
1:12–8:4	308
1:13	34 n. 21, 296 n. 77
1:13-26	337
1:14	34, 61 n. 128
1:15-26	294 n. 73, 354 n. 256
1:16.21	332 n. 200
1:21	59 n. 122
1:21-22	58, 296 n. 77

Acts
1:22 59, 67, 305 n. 106
2:1 343 n. 233
2:1-4 337
2:2 336
2:2-4 337
2:4 305 n. 106
2:5 310
2:5.11.14 339 n. 216
2:6 311
2:9-11 310, 311
2:14-36 312, 349 n. 247
2:14.22.36 345 n. 239
2:17 66 n. 150, 310
2:17-18 310 n. 126
2:17-21 307, 309, 349 n. 247
2:17.21 367 n. 7
2:19 310
2:19-20 309 n. 124
2:20 309 n. 124
2:21 309 nn. 123, 124, 310, 365
2:21.47 345 n. 239
2:23 183 n. 115, 300
2:23-24.32 58
2:36 66 n. 150, 242 n. 117, 309
2:37-41 328, 343 n. 229
2:38 289 n. 55, 309 n. 123
2:38-39 309
2:38-41 312
2:39 310, 349 n. 247
2:41 312, 315 n. 144, 349 n. 247
2:41.47 284 n. 36
2:42 337
2:42-47 308
2:46 308, 337
2:47 312
3 358
3:1 308
3:1.3.4.11 296 n. 77
3:1-26 308
3:6 295 n. 76, 309
3:6.16 309 n. 123
3:9.11 243 n. 121
3:9-12 312
3:11 311 n. 132
3:12-26 308, 312
3:13 300
3:13-15 289 n. 55, 312 n. 134
3:13-16 309
3:14-15 58
3:15 300
3:17 289 n. 55
3:19 312 n. 133
3:19.26 289 n. 55
3:20 190 n. 145
3:21 332 n. 200
3:22.23 341 n. 223
3:23 321 n. 164
3:24 215 n. 19
3:25 321 nn. 164, 165
3:26 304 n. 106
4–5 313
4:1 308, 312 n. 133, 340 n. 220
4:1-2 312 n. 133
4:1-3 311 n. 132, 312
4:1-22 313
4:1.6.23 312 n. 133
4:3 299
4:3-5 313 n. 139
4:4 284 n. 36, 312, 315 n. 144
4:5 312 n. 133
4:5.23 312 n. 133
4:7 313 n. 139
4:7.10.12 309 n. 123
4:8 290, 308
4:8-12 308, 313 n. 139
4:10 58, 243 n. 121, 312 n. 134
4:10-12 309

Acts

4:10.26	166 n. 51	5:21.26.27	300
4:10.30	295 n. 76	5:24.26	312 n. 133
4:11	313 n. 139	5:25-28	277 n. 10
4:12	192 n. 153, 332 n. 200	5:26	312
4:13.19	296 n. 77	5:26-27	337
4:14	186 n. 130, 277 n. 13, 312, 343 n. 233	5:27.32	304
4:17-21	309	5:28.40	309
4:21	312, 313	5:29	332 n. 200
4:24	177 n. 90	5:29-33	308
4:25-27	178 n. 98	5:30	312 n. 134
4:25.27	178 n. 98	5:30-32	309
4:26	166 n. 51	5:31	242 n. 116, 289 n. 55, 345 n. 239
4:26-28	299 n. 87	5:32	308
4:27	178 n. 98	5:33	300, 313
4:30	309	5:34	243 n. 121, 354
4:33	312	5:34-39	312 n. 135
4:34-37	347	5:40	313
5:1	354	5:40-41	299
5:2.10	347	5:42	337
5:12	308	6:1	319 n. 157, 340 n. 221
5:12-16	308	6:1.7	313, 315 n. 144
5:12.20.25	308	6:7	284 n. 36, 312 n. 135, 313 n. 137
5:13	312	6:8–7:60	296 n. 77
5:14	284 n. 36, 313, 315 n. 144	6:9	314
5:16.26	312	6:10	298 n. 86
5:17	328, 340 n. 220, 343 n. 230	6:11	180 n. 104
5:17-26	295 n. 76	6:11-13	314
5:15-41	308	6:11.14	314 n. 142
5:17	312 n. 133, 349 n. 247	6:12	300, 314 n. 142, 340 n. 220
5:17.21.24	312 n. 133	6:13	308
5:17-42	313	6:13-14	309
5:18	299	7:3	339 n. 215
5:19	66 n. 150	7:4	341 n. 225
5:20	243 n. 121, 308 n. 120, 336	7:34	314 n. 143
5:21.27	312 n. 133	7:47	337 n. 209
		7:48	239 n. 102, 241 n. 112

Acts
7:49 337 n. 209
7:54 313 n. 141
7:57 314
7:58 281 n. 24, 323 n. 170
7:59 313
7:60 313
8:1 313 n. 141, 315, 323 n. 170
8:1b-4 308 n. 117
8:3 300, 323 n. 170, 337
8:4 308 n. 117
8:4-5 315
8:4-25 315
8:5-40 307
8:6 315 n. 144
8:6.7.13 316, 318 n. 155
8:6-40 296 n. 77
8:8 295 n. 76
8:9-11 315 n. 144
8:12 295 n. 76
8:12.13 315 n. 144
8:14 296 n. 77
8:14-17 315
8:15-17 310 n. 126, 316, 318 n. 155
8:16-18 358 n. 263
8:26 66 n. 150, 316, 318 n. 155
8:26-40 315, 316
8:27 316
8:28 316
8:29 318 n. 155
8:32 300
8:35 305 n. 106
9 307, 322 n. 167
9:1 323 n. 170
9:1-19 316 n. 150
9:2.21 300
9:3 324, 343 n. 233, 352
9:3-7 323 n. 170
9:3-12 349 n. 246
9:3-18 324
9:3-19 322, 326, 355
9:4-5 299
9:5 323, 329 n. 190
9:6 323 n. 172
9:6.16 332 n. 200
9:10-16 323 n. 170
9:10-19 324, 337
9:14.21 309 n. 123
9:15 323 n. 172, 324, 325, 341 n. 223, 358, 367, 368
9:16 299, 325
9:17 337
9:20 326 n. 180, 338 n. 212
9:20-22 326
9:20-25 327 n. 183
9:20-30 316 n. 150
9:22 339
9:23 339
9:23.24 300
9:24 327 n. 181
9:31-43 316 n. 150
9:32-43 57 n. 114
9:36-43 229 n. 77
9:39 166 n. 51
9:41 166 n. 52, 167
10 296 n. 79, 316, 319 n. 158, 322 n. 169
10–11 61 n. 130, 296, 319 n. 158
10:1 317
10:1-8 61 n. 130
10:1-8.9-23 337
10:1-48 315
10:1–11:18 322
10:2 317

Acts

10:2.22 317 n. 152
10:3 66 n. 150, 318 n. 155
10:3-6.30-33 319 n. 158
10:3-7 317
10:3-7.10-15 318 n. 155
10:9-23 61 n. 130
10:10-15 317
10:11-13 296
10:11-15.16 319 n. 158
10:12.44 318 n. 155
10:13 335 n. 205, 335 n. 205
10:13.15.19 318 n. 155
10:19 317
10:22 319 n. 158
10:24-28 296
10:24-43 61 n. 130
10:28 338 n. 213
10:28-29 317
10:28.34-35 319 n. 158
10:30 337 n. 210
10:36 341 n. 223
10:36-41 61 n. 126
10:37 59, 61 n. 128, 67, 305 n. 106
10:37-43 58
10:38 59 n. 122
10:39 300
10:39-40 58
10:41 243 n. 121
10:44 317, 337
10:44-45 319 n. 158
10:44-46 310 n. 126
10:44-47 358 n. 263
10:44-48 319 n. 158
10:44–11:18 61 n. 130
10:48 337
11 319 n. 158, 322 n. 169
11:1-18 319
11:2-3 318, 319 n. 157
11:3 317, 318 n. 156
11:4 215 n. 19
11:4-9 319 n. 158
11:4.13-14 337
11:4.15 305 n. 106
11:7 335 n. 205
11:13-14 319 n. 158
11:14 345 n. 239
11:15 319 n. 158
11:15-17 319 n. 158
11:16 61 n. 128
11:17 319 n. 158
11:18 318
11:19-24 296 n. 77
11:26 326
11:29-30 332 n. 198
12:1 199 n. 182, 299
12:2 34 n. 21, 296 n. 77, 300
12:4 300
12:6-11 295 n. 76
12:7 66 n. 150
12:10 336
12:11 178 n. 97, 341 n. 225
12:12 336, 337 n. 210
12:14 295 n. 76
12:17 34 n. 21
12:20 34
13 326, 328
13–14.16 351 n. 253
13–20 322
13–28 343
13:1 34
13:2 337
13:5.14 326 n. 180
13:6-12 327 n. 183, 338 n. 213
13:10 295 n. 76
13:13-14 326
13:15 201 n. 188

Acts

13:16 343 n. 233
13:16.26 317 n. 152
13:16-41 326
13:16-47 326, 349 n. 247
13:16b-41 178 n. 95
13:16b-43 342
13:17 178 n. 97
13:17.23 178 n. 95
13:17.23.24 341 n. 223
13:22 240 n. 110
13:23 192 n. 153, 242 n. 116
13:23.26 345 n. 239
13:24 67, 229 n. 78, 243 n. 121
13:24-25 59, 61 n. 128
13:25 59 n. 122
13:28 300
13:40-41 343
13:41 326
13:42 328
13:42-43 327, 342
13:42-45 349 n. 247
13:43 338 n. 212, 347 n. 242
13:44-45 327, 328
13:44-50 343
13:45 186 n. 130, 277 n. 13, 339, 343 n. 233
13:46 304 n. 106, 327, 329 n. 188, 347 n. 242
13:46-47 330, 343
13:46b-47 342
13:47 305, 306, 324 n. 173, 326, 328, 329, 330 n. 193, 345 n. 239, 349 n. 247, 358, 367 n. 7
13:47b 305, 329
13:47c 305, 329
13:48-49 329 n. 191
13:48.52 295 n. 76
13:50 281 n. 24, 328 n. 185, 339
13:50-52 327
13:51 295 n. 76, 297 n. 82
14:1 326 n. 180
14:1.4 338 n. 212
14:1-28 326 n. 179
14:2 340
14:2.5.19 327 n. 183
14:4 347 n. 242
14:5 346
14:5.6.19.20 327 n. 181
14:15-17 326 n. 178
14:19 281 n. 24, 339
14:19-20 295 n. 76
14:21 180 n. 104
14:22 325 n. 177, 332 n. 200
14:26 328
14:27 283 n. 32
15 296 n. 79, 319
15:1 318
15:1.5 318 n. 156
15:1-35 286 n. 44
15:2 354
15:2.4 318
15:3 295 n. 76
15:5 318
15:5.19.20 321
15:5-21 318
15:7 319
15:7-9 319
15:7b-9a 319
15:7-11 319. 322
15:8 319 n. 158
15:9 319 n. 158
15:11 192 n. 153, 319
15:13 34 n. 21
15:13-21 171 n. 71

Acts

15:14 319 n. 158, 320, 321
15:14-17 367 n. 7
15:16-17 318, 321 n. 165
15:16-18 341 n. 223
15:17 190 n. 145
15:18 320 n. 162
15:19-21 296 n. 79
15:20 322 n. 169
15:20.29 318 n. 156, 321
15:22-40 296 n. 77
15:23-29 296 n. 79
15:26 299
15:29 322 n. 169
15:30 180 n. 104
16:1 180 n. 105, 338 nn. 212, 213
16:1-29 296 n. 77
16:10-17 275
16:14 338 n. 211
16:15 296 n. 79, 337
16:16-24 347
16:17 239 n. 102, 241 n. 112, 345 n. 239
16:18 199 n. 182, 295 n. 76
16:20-21 327 n. 181
16:25-40 295 n. 76
16:30 332 n. 200
16:31 192 n. 153, 337 n. 210, 358 n. 263
17 351 n. 253
17:1-15 326 n. 179
17:2 326 n. 180
17:3 332 n. 200
17:4-5 347 n. 242
17:4-15 296 n. 77
17:5 338 n. 211, 339
17:5-9.13-14 327 nn. 181, 183
17:10 326 n. 180
17:10-14 347 n. 242
17:12 338 n. 212
17:13 339
17:17 326 n. 180
17:18 108 n. 86
17:22 169 n. 64
17:22-30 326 n. 178
17:22-34 108 n. 86
17:30 343 n. 232
17:32 347, 354
18 351 n. 253
18:1-11 326 n. 179
18:1-17 347 n. 242
18:2 338 n. 213
18:5.24 296 n. 77
18:6 295 n. 76, 297 n. 82, 304 n. 106, 327 n. 182
18:6-7 327 n. 183
18:7-11 337
18:8 337 n. 210, 338
18:12 300, 339
18:12-17 327 n. 181
18:19 326 n. 180
18:20 338 n. 212
18:23 215 n. 19
18:24-25 338 n. 213
18:25 61 n. 128
19 351 n. 253
19:1-7 338 n. 212
19:1.22 296 n. 77
19:3-4 61 n. 128
19:8 295 n. 76, 326 n. 180
19:8-9 327 n. 183
19:8-10 326 n. 179, 347 n. 242
19:9 327 n. 182
19:9.29.34 327 n. 181
19:13 295 n. 76
19:13-17 338 n. 212
19:14 338 n. 213

Acts

19:21 332, 333, 334
19:21-39 332
19:21–21:16 331, 332 n. 198
19:21-22.23-39 332 n. 201, 333
19:23 199 n. 182
19:23-27 347
19:33 338 n. 213
19:36 332 n. 200
19:37 300
20:3 339
20:3.19 327 n. 181
20:3.19.25 327 n. 181
20:4 296 n. 77
20:5-15 275
20:7 337
20:7-12 229 n. 77
20:7–12.20 337
20:18-35 326 n. 178
20:22.23 333
20:25 295 n. 76
20:28 192 n. 153
20:35 332 n. 200
21–28 322
21:1-18 275
21:2.3 186 n. 132
21:4 336
21:4-6 333
21:10-14 333
21:11 300
21:13 299
21:14 333 n. 203
21:17-20 333 n. 203
21:18 34 n. 21
21:20 313 n. 137
21:20-21 319 n. 157
21:25 321, 322 n. 169
21:26 333 n. 203
21:27 299, 340
21:28.30.36 341 n. 225
21:30 333 n. 203, 340
21:30.36.39-40 340 n. 219
21:31 300
21:34 300
21:39 338 n. 213
22 322 n. 167
22:1.3.5 323
22:1.15 304
22:1-21 326 n. 178
22:3 338 n. 213
22:4 180 n. 104, 299, 300
22:5 300, 338
22:6 324
22:6-21 322, 324, 349 n. 246
22:7-8 299
22:8 323, 329 n. 190
22:12-16 323, 324
22:13 199 n. 182
22:14-15 323 n. 172
22:15 324, 325 n. 176, 358, 368
22:15.21 367
22:16 309 n. 123
22:16.18.21 323 n. 172
22:17 335, 343 n. 233
22:17-21 309 n. 122, 335
22:18 325, 335
22:20 300
22:21 310 n. 127, 324 n. 174, 334
22:30–23:10 334 n. 203
22:30–23:11 334 n. 203
22:30 340
23–28 334 n. 204
23:1 300
23:2 333 n. 203
23:2.4 166 n. 51
23:2.14 338
23:5 255 n. 160, 290
23:6-8 312 n. 133
23:9 354
23:10.31 300
23:11 332 n. 200, 334, 342 n. 228

Acts

23:12.14 300
23:12.21 339
23:12-15.20.27 340 n. 219
23:14 338
23:15.21.27 300
23:21 198 n. 176
23:24 166 n. 52, 167 n. 54
23:24.33 166 n. 52
23:29 334 n. 203
23:30 327 n. 181
23:33 167
24 351 n. 253
24:1 338
24:1-26 334 n. 203
24:9 340
24:11-12 277 n. 10
24:13 166 n. 51
24:14 201 n. 188
24:15 198 n. 176
24:17 332 n. 198
24:19 332 n. 200
24:19.27 340 n. 219
24:21 312 n. 133
24:24 338 n. 213
24:50-53 336
25:1.15 338
25:2 338
25:3 300
25:6-12 300, 334 n. 203
25:7.24 340
25:9 340 n. 219
25:10.24 332 n. 200
25:11 342 n. 228
25:13-27 300
25:15 338
26 322 n. 167
26:1.16 304
26:1-32 300, 334 n. 203
26:2.7 340
26:2-23 326 n. 178
26:6-7 346 n. 241
26:9 332 n. 200
26:10 300
26:10-12 338
26:11 299
26:12-18 322, 349 n. 246
26:12-23 324
26:13 324
26:14-15 299
26:15 323, 329 n. 190
26:16 323 n. 172, 325 n. 176, 358, 368
26:16-17 323 n. 172
26:16-18 324
26:17 186 n. 132, 324, 325, 341 n. 225, 352
26:17-18 330, 367
26:18 163 n. 37, 324 n. 173, 330 n. 193
26:21 340 n. 219
26:22 201 n. 188
26:23 330
26:25-27 326 n. 178
26:32 342 n. 228
27:1–28:16 275
27:1 300
27:3.43 334 n. 203
27:4 167
27:9-44 295 n. 76
27:13 166 n. 51
27:20-44 169 n. 64
27:21-26 326 n. 178
27:23 66 n. 150
27:24 166 n. 52, 334, 342 n. 228
27:24.26 332 n. 200
27:42 300
28 345, 347, 351 n. 253
28:15 344 n. 238
28:16-31 335
28:17 299, 300
28:17-22 342

Acts
28:17.23 344 n. 238
28:17.20.23 343 n. 233
28:17-28 326 n. 179
28:17-29 326 n. 178
28:17-31 342, 348
28:19 339, 340 n. 219, 342 n. 228
28:19.22 186 n. 130, 277 n. 13, 343
28:20 341 n. 223, 346 n. 241
28:22 327 n. 181, 344 n. 234, 345, 346 n. 240, 353, 356, 365
28:22.28 367
28:23 201 n. 188, 344 n. 236
28:23-28 342, 343, 367 n. 7
28:23.31 295 n. 76
28:24 347, 352 n. 255
28:24a 346 n. 240
28:24-25 343 n. 233
28:25 342, 347
28:25-27 343
28:25-28 326 n. 178, 352 n. 255
28:26.27 178 n. 97, 335, 342
28:27 341 n. 225
28:28 304 n. 106, 327 n. 182, 343, 344, 345 n. 239, 356
28:30 344, 345 n. 239, 346 n. 240
28:30-31 336, 337, 342 n. 228

Romans (Rm)
1:1 58 n. 119
1:3 58 n. 119
1:3-4 58
1:21 191 n. 150
2:16 58 n. 119
6:13.19 167 n. 59
9–11 186 n. 128
9:30-32 184
10:21 186 n. 130, 277 n. 13
12:1 167 n. 59
14:1 191 n. 150
15:9 243 n. 121
15:11 178 n. 98
15:16 58 n. 119
15:25 331
15:25-27 331 n. 197
16:10.11 245 n. 128

1 Corinthians (1 Co)
3:20 191 n. 150
5:2 190 n. 148
9:6 246 n. 129
9:24 190 n. 148
14:21 178 n. 97
15:3-4 58
15:7 34 n. 21
15:11 246 n. 129
16:3-4 331

2 Corinthians (2 Co)
1:17 190 n. 148
8:4 331 n. 197
8:9 331 n. 197
8:13-14 331 n. 197
9:6-15 331 n. 197
9:13 331 n. 197

Galatians (Ga)
1:19 34 n. 21
2:9.12 34 n. 21

Galatians (Ga)
4:4 58 n. 119
5:17 190 n. 148

Ephesians (Ep)
2:13-17 310 n. 127

Philippians (Ph)
2:10 239 n. 100
2:14 191 n. 150

1 Thessalonians (1 Th)
1:9-10 58
5:4 190 n. 148

1 Timothy (1 Tm)
2:8 191 n. 150

2 Timothy (2 Tm)
2:15 167 n. 59

Titus (Tt)
1:9 186 n. 130, 277 n. 13
2:9 277 n. 13

Hebrews (Heb)
1:3 156
4:12 187 n. 138, 188 n. 138
7:1 239 n. 102
9:19 243 n. 121
11:15 174 n. 82
12:3 187 n. 133

James (Jm)
2:4 191 n. 150

1 Peter (1 P)
2:8 184

2 Peter (2 P)
1:9 156

1 John (1 Jn)
1:9 190 n. 148

Revelation (Rv)
1:4 194 n. 163
1:16 188 n. 138
2:16 188 n. 138
2:20 193
6:10 176 n. 90
5 194 n. 163
5–8 194 n. 163
7:9 178 n. 98
8–11 194 n. 163
9:20 190 n. 148
10:11 178 n. 98
11:9 178 n. 98
13:13.15 190 n. 148
15–17 194 n. 163
17:15 178 n. 98
19:15-21 188 n. 138
21:3 178 n. 98
22:14 190 n. 148

g. Index of Early Christian Apocryphal Texts

Evangelium infantiae salvatoris arabicum 63 n. 135

Evangelium Nicodemi 171 n. 71

Evangelium Pseudo-Matthaei
1–5 136 n. 185
14 136 n. 185
18,1-2 136 n. 185
23 136 n. 185

Evangelium Pseudo-Thomae de infantia Salvatoris 63 n. 135
2,2-5 136 n. 185
9,1-3 136 n. 185
17,1-2 136 n. 185
18,1-2 136 n. 185

The Gospel of Thomas

	285, 285 n. 39
20	283
33	283 n. 32
64	285

Protoevangelium Iacobi

	34, 63 n. 135
1–16	136 n. 185
4,1–9,3	136 n. 185
6,2	168 n. 63
16,1-3	136 n. 185
24,4	171 n. 71

h. Index of Early Christian Texts

Ambrose

Expositio Evangelii secundum Lucam
2,62 195 n. 165

Bede

In Lucae evangelium expositio
2,38 195 n. 165

Ephraem

Commentaire de l'Evangile concordant ou Diatessaron 60 n. 124

Origen

Homélies sur s. Luc
14.2-5 155 n. 15
14.5-10 157 n. 21

Tertullian

Contre Marcion IV
7,1 60 n. 124

II. INDEX OF MODERN AUTHORS

Abel, F. M., 190 n. 149
Abrams, M. H., 161 n. 32
del Agua Pérez, A., 48 n. 68, 49 n. 80, 81 n. 225, 226 n. 66
Aletti, J.-N., 25 n. 16, 28 n. 21, 37 n. 30, 63 n. 136, 105 n. 70, 161 n. 32, 198 n. 178, 229, 246 n. 130, 256 n. 161, 258 n. 172, 274 n. 4, 322 n. 168
Alter, R., 24 n. 10
Andrews, E. A., 106 n. 76
Aranda, G., 226 n. 66
Aune, D. E., 52 n. 94
Aytoun, R. A., 36 n. 26
Bach, A., 212 n. 3
Bachelard, G., 337 n. 209
Bachmann, M., 170 n. 69, 276 n. 10
Bailey, J. A., 33 n. 17
Balch, D. L., 307 n. 116
Ballhorn, E., 81 n. 227
Baltzer, K., 335 n. 206
Bar-Efrat, S., 24 n. 10, 206 n. 204
Barr, D., 52 n. 94, 92 n. 17, 131 n. 170
Barrett, C. K., 316 n. 146
Barthes, R., 319 n. 158
Bauckham, R., 294 n. 73
Bauer, W., 185 n. 125
Bazyliński, S., 20 n. 2
Beard, M., 103 n. 64

Béchard, D. P., 23 n. 7, 24 n. 12, 295 n. 76, 310 n. 129, 311 n. 130, 340 n. 221
Beck, J. A., 217 n. 30
Belli, F., 219 n. 36
Benéitez, M., 307 n. 114
Benoît, P., 31 nn. 4, 5, 38, 39 n. 37, 40 n. 46, 56 n. 112, 187 n. 135, 22 n. 58
Berenguer Amenós, J., 190 n. 146
Berger, K., 79 n. 212
Berlin, A., 213 n. 7
Berlingieri, G., 23 n. 6, 40 n. 47, 52 n. 97, 55 n. 107, 57 n. 117, 226 n. 66
Bernardelli, A., 218 n. 35
Bertram, G., 166 n. 49, 167 nn. 58, 59, 239 n. 102, 320 n. 160
Betori, G., 187 n. 134, 304 n. 106, 308 n. 117, 310 n. 128
Billerbeck, P., 337 n. 208
Black, M., 184 n. 119
Blass, F. W., 173 n. 80, 190 n. 145, 199 n. 181
Bloch, R., 48 n. 78
Bobzien, S., 109 n. 90, 125 n. 150
Bock, D. L., 156 n. 21, 157 n. 21, 170 n. 68, 184 n. 123, 246 n. 132
Boismard, M.-É., 42 n. 54, 220 n. 43
Bonz, M. P., 87 n. 1, 281 n. 24, 311 n. 130
Borg, M. J., 67 n. 151, 70 n. 175
Borgen, P., 112 n. 96
Bottino, A., 170 n. 69, 322 n. 167
Bourneuf, R., 214 n. 15
Bourquin, Y., 24 n. 10, 25 n. 17, 28 n. 21, 69 n. 167, 126 n. 154, 148 n. 2, 169 n. 64, 171 n. 72, 193 n. 156, 202 n. 192, 206 n. 203, 227 n. 69, 229 n. 77
Bovon, F., 34, 35 n. 23, 40 n. 44, 49 n. 82, 51 n. 92, 59 n. 123, 61 n. 130, 76 n. 201, 78 nn. 209, 210, 79 n. 215, 99 n. 40, 108 n. 82, 132 n. 172, 184 n. 123, 194 nn. 162, 163, 220 n. 43, 224 n. 63, 239 n. 101, 240 n. 109, 241 n. 112, 266 n. 187, 267 n. 191, 281 n. 22, 285 n. 43, 303 n. 101, 335 n. 205, 344 n. 237, 346 n. 240
Boxall, I., 62 n. 132, 70 n. 172
Boyce, J. L., 22 n. 5, 23, 223 n. 59
Brawley, R. L., 344 n. 233
Brenner, A., 50 n. 89, 90 n. 10
Brown, R. E., 31 n. 4, 32 n. 14, 33 n. 18, 34 n. 22, 37 n. 30, 39 nn. 39, 42, 40 nn. 42, 45, 41 n. 52, 43 nn. 59, 60, 49 n. 81, 50, 51 n. 90, 54 nn. 102, 104, 105, 55, 58 n. 119, 59 n. 121, 60, 61 nn. 126, 129, 66 nn. 148, 149, 150, 70 n. 176, 73 n. 186, 80 n. 217, 81 n. 225, 152 n. 9, 172 n. 75, 188, 220 n. 43, 222 n. 55, 225 n. 64, 226 nn. 65, 68, 239 n. 102
Brown, W. J., 33, 34 n. 20
Buell, D. K., 277 n. 12
Bultmann, R., 39 n. 41, 40 n. 47, 41 n. 50, 44 n. 62, 48 n. 76, 75 n. 194, 77, 78 n. 207, 168 n. 61
Burnett, F. W., 213 nn. 9, 11, 214 n. 11, 216 n. 25, 238 n. 100
Burridge, R. A., 51 n. 94, 87 n. 3, 92 n. 16, 93 n. 18
Burrows, E., 33 n. 16, 42 n. 55, 46 n. 68, 51 n. 92, 79 n. 216, 220 n. 43, 222 n. 55, 224 n. 62, 225 n. 65
Busse, U., 61 n. 130, 67 n. 154, 68 n. 163, 70 n. 174
Cadbury, H. J., 22 n. 3
Campbell, T. H., 331 n. 196
Cavalletti, S., 49 n. 79, 67, 68 n. 157, 131 n. 169
Cerquiglini, B., 155 n. 14
Chappuis-Juillard, I., 235 n. 90
Chatman, S. B., 133 n. 175, 202 n. 5, 231 n. 83
Clark, A. C., 228 n. 70, 325 n. 176

Clines, D. J. A., 126 n. 154
Cohen, S. J. D., 317 n. 153
Coleridge, M. B., 42 n. 53, 63 n. 136, 67 n. 155, 68 n. 160, 71 n. 178, 83 n. 233, 84, 133 n. 175, 213 n. 10, 216 n. 27, 238 n. 99, 247 n. 136, 248 n. 144, 250 n. 150, 251 nn. 152, 153, 252 n. 154,
Collins, A.Y. & J. J., 243 n. 119
Conybeare, F. C., 60 n. 124
Conzelmann, H., 56 n. 110, 64, 65 n. 141, 69
Cook, M. J., 317 n. 152
Corsato, C., 195 n. 165
Craddock, F. B., 180 n. 106
Creed, J. M., 179 n. 102, 180
Crespo, E., 166 n. 53
Cross, F. M., 113 n. 99, 155 n. 14
Cullmann, O., 34 n. 21, 61 n. 127, 63 n. 135
Culpepper, R. A., 63 n. 136, 206 n. 204, 232 n. 85
Culter, A., 171 n. 71
Cunningham, P. J., 31 n. 4
D'Agostino, M., 69 n. 171
Dahl, N. A., 320 n. 162
Daniélou, J., 32 n. 12, 76 n. 196, 79 n. 214
Danker, F. W., 65 n. 145, 177 n. 94
Darr, J. A., 25 n. 17, 212 n. 2, 213 n. 6, 214 n. 11, 218 n. 33, 274 n. 4
Davies, J. H., 221 n. 49
Davis, C. T., 224 n. 62
Dawsey, J. M., 25 n. 17, 64 n. 140
De Jong, I., 28 n. 21, 104 n. 66
De Jonge, H. J., 245 n. 129, 246 n. 129
Dehandschutter, B., 298 n. 85
Denaux, A., 144 n. 218
Derrett, J. D. M., 31 n. 7, 191 n. 151
Dibelius, M., 39 n. 40, 44 n. 62, 48 n. 76, 77 n. 206, 78 n. 207, 168 n. 61
Díez Macho, A., 48 n. 78, 228 n. 73
Díez Merino, L., 42 n. 55, 187 n. 136, 220 n. 43
Dillon, R. J., 174 n. 84
Dodd, C. H., 244 n. 124, 285 n. 43
Dornisch, L., 34 n. 19, 74 n. 190
Drury, J., 47 n. 73, 65 n. 145, 144 n. 218, 224 n. 62
Duffy, J., 136 n. 185
Dupont, J., 303 n. 103, 305 n. 109, 306 n. 112, 309 n. 125, 320 n. 162, 327 n. 182, 341 n. 224, 343 n. 231
Elliott, James K., 81 n. 222, 170 n. 69, 195 n. 165
Elliott, John H., 337 n. 207
Eltrop, B., 195 n. 166
Epp, E. J., 154 n. 14, 155 n. 14
Erdmann, G., 82 n. 230
Estrada, N., 176 n. 88
Evans, Christopher F., 75 n. 192, 180 n. 106
Evans, Craig A., 285 n. 43
Facq, F., 96 n. 28, 107 n. 81
Falcetta, A., 279 n. 16
Farris, S. C., 230 n. 80, 257 n. 151
Feuillet, A., 185 n. 126, 188
Figueras, P., 80 n. 219, 81 n. 223, 194 n. 159, 202 n. 190
Fitzmyer, J. A., 37 n. 30, 39 n. 38, 40 n. 44, 45 n. 64, 46 n. 70, 49 n. 83, 51 n. 93, 52 n. 98, 54 n. 104, 55 n. 107, 58 n. 119, 59 n. 122, 60, 61 n. 126, 62 n. 133, 70 nn. 174, 175, 77 n. 205, 188, 198 n. 175, 220 n. 43, 221 n. 54, 226 n. 67, 240 n. 110, 244 n. 124, 256 n. 161, 266 n. 189, 280, 281 n. 23, 316 n. 146
Flanagan, N. M., 57 n. 114
Flender, H., 57 n. 114
Flichy, O., 64 n. 138, 323 n. 171
Fowler, R. M., 212 n. 3
Fox, M.V., 218 n. 34
Frankemölle, H., 320 n. 160

Franklin, E., 317 n. 152
Freed, E. D., 37 n. 30, 55 n. 107, 140 n. 209, 224 n. 61
Frei, H. W., 25 n. 16
Frein, B. C., 363 n. 3
Fuller, M. E., 341 n. 223
Funk, R. W., 222 n. 56
Galbiati, E., 152 n. 9, 223 n. 58, 256 n. 162, 285 n. 43
Gane, R. E., 149 n. 4
García Pérez, J. M., 291 n. 62
García Vieyra, A., 165 n. 45
Geldenhuys, N., 294 n. 72
Genette, G., 207 n. 206, 215 n. 17
George, A., 38 nn. 34, 36, 76 nn. 198, 200, 81 n. 225, 222 n. 58, 228 n. 73, 229 n. 74, 286 n. 45, 345 n. 239
Georgi, D., 110 n. 92
Gerber, D., 62 n. 134, 67 n. 156, 178 n. 95, 250 n. 149
Gertner, M., 48 n. 78
Geyser, A. S., 75 n. 193
Gill, C., 107 n. 80
Goodenough, E. R., 109 n. 87, 112 n. 96
Goulder, M. D., 35 n. 24, 289 n. 54
Grappe, C., 302 n. 98
Grässer, E., 282 n. 30
Green, J. B., 47 n. 73
Greimas, A. J., 73 n. 184
Grelot, P., 39 n. 39, 54 n. 106, 55, 76 n. 199, 168 n. 61, 329 n. 188
Gros Louis, K. R., 63 n. 136, 71 n. 177, 218 n. 32,
Grosso, F., 97 n. 32
Gryglewicz, F., 36 n. 26, 37, 38 n. 32
Gueuret, A., 63 n. 136, 73 n. 187, 84 n. 237, 250 n. 148
Gunkel, H., 44 n. 62
Haenchen, E., 64 n. 139, 316 n. 149
Hamilton, J. R., 94 n. 22
Hanford, W. R., 81 n. 226, 179 n. 101
Hansen, H., 190 n. 146
Harnack, A., 37 n. 31
Harrington, D. J., 49 n. 81, 112 n. 98, 113 nn. 99, 101
Hartman, L., 277 n. 10
Harvey, W., 213 n. 8
Hatch, W. H. P., 158 n. 24
Hays, J. D., 277 n. 12
Head, P., 24 n. 9
Henk, J., 139 n. 209
Herranz, A. A., 152 n. 10, 165 n. 47
Hill, D., 280 n. 21
Hillmann, J., 55 n. 108
Hilton, M., 110 n. 92
Homeyer, H., 92 n. 14
Hooker, M. D., 61 n. 130, 65, 66 nn. 146, 147, 67 n. 152, 69 n. 166
Horsley, R. A., 74 n. 189
Hutcheon, C. R., 302 n. 98
Irigoin, J., 177 n. 93
Jaeger, W., 107 n. 81
Jeremias, J., 170 n. 69, 285 n. 43,
Jervell, J., 317 n. 152, 321 n. 166
John, D., 194 n. 161
Jones, C. P., 96 n. 26
Jones, G. C., 213 n. 8
Joüon, P., 178 n. 96
Jung, C.-W., 218 n. 35
Kattenbusch, F., 78 n. 207
Kellermann, U., 76 n. 197, 152 n. 9, 173 n. 77, 174 n. 82
Kermode, F., 63 n. 136
Kiddle, M., 279 n. 18, 316 n. 146
Kilgallen, J., 65, 66 n. 146, 80 n. 218, 180 n. 106, 285 n. 43, 339 n. 217, 344 n. 238
Kilpatrick, G. D., 178 n. 98
Kingsbury, J. D., 63 n. 136
Klawans, J., 149 n. 4
Klostermann, E., 48 n. 76
Klutz, T. E., 223 n. 59
Knox, J., 60 n. 124

Koehne, M., 172 n. 74
Koet, B. J., 123 n. 144
Korzeniewski, D., 95 n. 23
Kränkl, E., 303 n. 103, 355 n. 259
Krückemeier, N., 139 n. 209
de Kruijf, T. C., 320 n. 162
Kuhn, K. A., 31 n. 9, 32 n. 9
Kümmel, W. G., 221 n. 50
Kurz, W. S., 63 n. 136, 72, 73 n. 183
Lagrange, M.-J., 152 n. 10, 289 n. 54
Lane, T. J., 68 n. 159, 69 n. 166, 279 n. 18, 283 n. 31, 284 n. 37, 285 nn. 40, 42, 368 n. 8
Larsson, E., 335 n. 206
Laurentin, R., 32 n. 11, 44, 45 nn. 63, 66, 46 n. 69, 48 n. 78, 73 n. 187, 78 n. 211, 79 n. 213, 168 n. 61, 184 n. 124, 197 n. 173, 223 nn. 58, 59, 224, 225 nn. 64, 65, 226 n. 66, 239 n. 101
Laurini, H. C., 46 n. 69
Lee, D., 212 n. 4, 246 n. 131
Lefebvre, P., 196 n. 169
Lefkowitz, M. R., 128 n. 162
Legrand, L., 46 n. 71, 57 n. 118, 58 n. 119
Lejeune, P., 87 n. 2
Létourneau, P., 66 n. 146
Liebeschuetz, J., 104 n. 69
Lohfink, G., 322 n. 167, 323 n. 171, 346 n. 240
Lohfink, N., 36 n. 29, 38, 258 n. 172
López Mauléon, J. M., 70 n. 175
Louw, J. P., 153 n. 11, 197 n. 174, 198 n. 180, 241 n. 113
Luz, U., 139 n. 204
McGaughy, L. C., 90 n. 9, 108 n. 83, 132 n. 172
McHugh, J., 33 n. 15
McNicol, A. J., 341 n. 223
McQueen, E. I., 95 n. 23
Maggioni, B., 168 n. 62
Magris, A., 109 n. 88, 109 n. 89
Malbon, E. S., 212 n. 4
Malick, D. E., 223 n. 59
Mallen, P., 218 n. 34
Manicardi, E., 40 n. 48, 41 n. 51, 76, 77 n. 202, 80 n. 217
Manns, F., 48 n. 78
Marconi, G., 174 n. 81
Marec, E., 97 n. 32
Marguerat, D., 24 n. 10, 25 n. 17, 28 n. 21, 69 n. 167, 126 n. 154, 148 n. 2, 168 n. 64, 171 n. 72, 193 n. 156, 202 n. 192, 217 n. 29, 227 n. 69, 229 n. 77, 274 n. 4, 316 n. 147, 342 n. 228
Marshall, I. H., 22 n. 3, 110 n. 92, 160 n. 31, 168 n. 63
Martini, C. M., 305 n. 109
Martins Terra, J. E., 47 n. 73
Masini, M., 45 n. 64
Mather, P. B., 56 n. 110, 57 n. 116
Mbilizi, É. L., 279 n. 18
Meier, J. P., 32 n. 14, 294 n. 73
Mena Salas, E., 328 n. 186
Menes, A., 337 n. 208
Menoud, P. H., 316 n. 146
Metzger, B., 155 n. 14, 159 nn. 27, 29, 295 n. 75
Meyer, E., 143 n. 217
Meynet, R., 72 nn. 181, 182, 83 n. 235, 84
Minear, P. S., 56 nn. 112, 113, 61 n. 130, 69 n. 165, 77 n. 202
Miyoshi, M., 77 n. 203, 164 n. 41
Moessner, D. P., 251 n. 151, 312 n. 133
Moloney, F. J., 65, 66 n. 146, 72 n. 179, 86 n. 240
Momigliano, A., 50 n. 86, 90 n. 7, 91 n. 12, 92, 126 n. 155
Montes Peral, L. Á., 34 n. 21
Moore, T. S., 305 n. 109
Morales Gómez, G., 170 n. 69
Morgenthaler, R., 56 nn. 111, 113, 221 n. 51

Mount, W., 57 n. 118
Müller, F. M., 88 n. 4
Mulloor, A., 243 n. 122
Muñoz Iglesias, S., 36 nn. 26, 28, 29, 38 n. 35, 42 n. 55, 45 n. 67, 48 n. 78, 53 n. 99, 75 n. 193, 80 n. 217, 81 n. 228, 168 n. 62, 220 n. 43
Muñoz León, D., 49 nn. 79, 80
Neirynck, F., 46 n. 71, 53, 54 n. 101
Niccacci, A., 171 n. 70
Nock, A. D., 144 n. 218
Nolland, J., 75, 76 n. 195, 79 n. 217, 80 nn. 217, 220, 81 n. 224, 82 nn. 229, 231, 180 n. 106, 239 n. 103, 244 n. 124, 267 n. 191, 268 n. 193
North, C. R., 350 n. 251
Ó Fearghail, F., 52 n. 94, 144 n. 218, 221 n. 52, 223 n. 59, 286 n. 44, 320 n. 159
Ockenga, H. J., 185 n. 126
O'Day, G. R., 74 n. 190
Ogg, G., 31 n. 5
Oliver, H. H., 68 n. 161
Omanson, R. L., 159 n. 29
Orsatti, M., 31 n. 4, 47 n. 74
Ortensio da Spinetoli, 41 n. 49, 45 n. 64, 47, 48 n. 75, 220 n. 43, 247 n. 135
Osborne, T. P., 36 n. 26, 37 n. 30
O'Toole, R. F., 242 n. 115, 341 n. 223
Panier, L., 73 n. 187, 267 n. 190
Pao, D. W., 306 n. 111
Parsons, M. C., 22 n. 3, 310 n. 129
Pelling, C. B. R., 105 n. 71, 131, 132 n. 171
Pereira, Á., 331 n. 196
Pérez Rodríguez, G., 42 n. 55, 220 n. 43, 224 n. 62, 225 n. 65
Perrin, N., 285 n. 39
Perrot, C., 105 n. 70, 224 n. 62, 228 n. 73
Perry, M., 65 n. 144
Petzke, G., 191 n. 150
Pfister, F., 94 n. 21
Plummer, A., 32 n. 10, 55, 56 n. 109
Plymale, S. F., 173 n. 78, 257 n. 171
de la Potterie, I., 170 n. 69
Powell, M. A., 24 n. 10, 63 n. 136, 87 n. 2, 196 n. 170, 215 n. 21, 319 n. 158
Power, E., 165 n. 46
Prema, S., 73, 74 n. 188
Puig i Tàrrech, A., 303 n. 102, 334 n. 204
Puskas, C. B., 346 n. 240
Quarles, C. L., 35 n. 23
Rabatel, A., 206 n. 203
Racine, J.-R., 316 n. 151, 317 n. 154
Radl, W., 43 n. 60, 66 n. 148, 191 n. 153, 332 n. 199
Räisänen, H., 346 n. 241
Rasco, E., 304 n. 105
Ravens, D., 317 n. 152, 341 n. 223
Reicke, B. I., 81 n. 224, 152 n. 9, 166 n. 49, 167 nn. 58, 59, 171 n. 71, 195 n. 165,
Resenhöfft, W., 61 n. 130
Rhoads, D. M., 63 n. 136
Ricœur, P., 214 n. 15, 215 n. 20
Riesner, R., 171 n. 71
Rives, J. B., 103 n. 64
Rodger, L., 69 n. 169
Rogers, C. L., 196 n. 171
Rossé, G., 39 n. 39, 77 n. 204, 82 n. 232, 152 n. 9
Rouiller, G., 43 n. 60
Ruddick, C. T., 46 n. 72, 47
Ryan, J. M., 63 n. 136, 70 n. 175
Salazar, A. M., 43 n. 58
Salmon, M., 341 n. 222
Samain, E., 281 n. 22
Samkutty, V. J., 316 n. 146
Sánchez Mielgo, G., 33 n. 15, 54 n. 103, 69 n. 168
Sand, A., 166 n. 50
Sanders, Jack T., 346 n. 240
Schaberg, J., 35 n. 23

Schille, G., 36 n. 26
Schmid, J., 221 n. 50
Schnabel, E. J., 282 n. 30
Schnackenburg, R., 33 n. 17
Schneider, G., 48 n. 77
Schreck, C. J., 278 n. 15
Schrenk, G., 191 n. 150
Schubert, P., 67 n. 153, 301 n. 94
Schürer, E., 31 n. 5
Schürmann, H., 52 n. 96, 70 n. 173, 75 n. 192, 78 n. 208, 187 n. 134, 226 n. 67, 244 n. 124
Schüssler Fiorenza, E., 74 n. 190
Schweizer, E., 53 n. 100, 185 n. 128
Schwertner, S., 20 n. 1
Scott, B. B., 69 n. 165
Sedley, D., 109 n. 90
Segalia, G., 158 n. 68
Serra, A. M., 32 n. 13, 184 n. 124
Shuler, P. L., 35 n. 24, 50 n. 88, 68 n. 158, 72 n. 180, 229 n. 75
Siffer, N., 230 n. 80
Siker, J. S., 279 n. 18
Silberman, L. H., 40 n. 43, 51 n. 93
Simón Muñoz, A., 85 n. 238, 185 n. 128, 186 n. 128
Ska, J. L., 25 n. 17, 28 n. 21, 130 n. 165, 147 n. 1, 202 n. 192, 213 n. 8, 227 n. 69, 328 n. 184
Smyth, H. W., 190 n. 146
Soards, M. L., 152 n. 9
Spanneut, M., 108 n. 86
Spitta, F., 39 n. 37
Stanton, G., 239 n. 104, 242 n. 117
Steidle, W., 97 n. 29
Sterling, G. E., 52 n. 94, 143 n. 217
Sternberg, M., 24 n. 10
Stock, K., 191 n. 153
Stramare, T., 152 n. 9, 224 n. 62, 225 nn. 64, 65
Strathmann, H., 320 n. 160
Strauss, M. L., 173 n. 80, 240 n. 110
Strickert, F. M., 152 n. 9, 200 n. 183
Sylva, D. D., 170 n. 69
Talbert, C. H., 51 n. 91, 135 n. 185, 143 n. 217, 354 n. 257
Tannehill, R., 25 n. 15, 26 n. 18, 63 n. 136, 64 n. 140, 81 n. 225, 214 n. 16, 216 n. 23, 274 n. 5, 278 n. 14, 281 n. 24, 306 n. 112, 311 n. 131, 313 n. 140, 346 nn. 240, 241
Tatum, W. B., 68 n. 164, 201 n. 189
Taylor, N., 308 n. 118
Testa, E., 73 n. 185
Thomas, C., 68 n. 162
Thurston, B. B., 194 n. 159
Tiede, D. L., 70 n. 175, 289 n. 52
Troiani, L., 114 n. 103
Trompf, G. W., 229 n. 77
Turner, N., 43 n. 58
Tyson, J. B., 69 n. 170, 317 n. 152, 319 n. 157
van Unnik, W. C., 305 n. 107
Unsner, H., 55 n. 108
Uspenski, B. A., 206 n. 203
Vaccari, A., 158 n. 23
Valentini, A., 45 n. 65, 54 n. 106, 81 n. 225, 188 n. 141
Van Biema, D., 143 n. 217
Van der Ploeg, J. S., 350 n. 251
Vanhoye, A., 216 n. 24, 306 n. 113
Varela, A. T., 195 n. 165
de Vaux, R., 149 n. 5
Visser, N., 80, 81 n. 221
Vlková, G. I., 330 n. 193
Vogels, H. J., 159 n. 25
Völter, D., 40 n. 42, 75 n. 193
Wallace, D. B., 193 n. 157, 195 n. 168
Wallace-Hadrill, A., 97 n. 29
Walter, N., 320 n. 160
Wardman, A., 96 n. 26, 107 n. 80
Wasserberg, G., 179 n. 98

Weitzman, S., 36 n. 29
Wellhausen, J., 48 n. 78, 49 n. 80, 55 n. 108
White, L. M., 337 n. 208
Wilcox, M., 176 n. 90
Wilkinson, J. R., 40 n. 42, 75 n. 193
Wills, L. M., 339 n. 217
Wilson, S. G., 282 n. 30
Winandy, J., 79 n. 215
Winter, P., 42 n. 55, 163 n. 38, 220 n. 43
Witherington, B., 175 n. 86
Wolter, M., 184 n. 122
Wright, A. G., 49 n. 81
Yamasaki, G., 206 n. 203
de Young, J. C., 170 n. 69
Yule, G., 166 n. 53
Zeller, E., 60 n. 124
Zerwick, M., 186 n. 132, 198 n. 177
Zimmermann, H., 44 n. 61
Zippert, C., 178 n. 95
Zmijewski, J., 299 n. 91
Zumstein, J., 328 n. 184

Finito di stampare nel mese di giugno 2016
presso Mediagraf Spa - Noventa Padovana (PD)